MICROSOFT® CERTIFIED APPLICATION DEVELOPER
& MICROSOFT® CERTIFIED SOLUTION DEVELOPER

MCAD/MCSD Visual Basic® .NET™ Web Applications Study Guide

(Exam 70-305)

MW00908745

Wayne Cassidy is President and owner of a small consulting firm that specializes in the design and development of scientific and statistical software. To keep himself sane and sociable he also teaches computer programming and software design in the corporate arena and develops courseware for this purpose. Wayne's areas of expertise include Object-Oriented Analysis and Design, C/C++, CORBA, Visual C++ with MFC, COM/DCOM/COM+, Visual Basic, Java, Web application development, and he has a special interest in cross-platform computing. He presently resides in Ottawa, Ontario, Canada, with his wife, Heidi, and their cat Max. Wayne graduated with high honors from Carleton University with a BSc in Neuroscience, concentrating in Molecular Neurobiology.

David Shapton, MCSD, MCT, and CTT+, is Vice President of SciStat, Inc., a software development and a training company in Ottawa, Ontario. Although first introduced to computer programming in the mid-1970s, he didn't make it his career until 1984. Since then he has been involved in many aspects of the business, including application development, project management, training, and writing. David lives in Kanata, Ontario, with his wife, Shauna, and their three children, Krista, Olivia, and Mitchell.

About LearnKey

LearnKey provides self-paced learning content and multimedia delivery solutions to enhance personal skills and business productivity. LearnKey claims the largest library of rich streaming media training content that engages learners in dynamic media-rich instruction complete with video clips, audio, full motion graphics, and animated illustrations. LearnKey can be found at www.LearnKey.com.

MCAD/MCSD Visual Basic® .NET™ Web Applications Study Guide

(Exam 70-305)

Wayne Cassidy
David Shapton

McGraw-Hill Osborne

New York   Chicago   San Francisco   Lisbon   London   Madrid
Mexico City   Milan   New Delhi   San Juan   Seoul   Singapore   Sydney   Toronto

The **McGraw·Hill** Companies

McGraw-Hill/Osborne
2600 Tenth Street
Berkeley, California 94710
U.S.A.

To arrange bulk purchase discounts for sales promotions, premiums, or fund-raisers, please contact **McGraw-Hill**/Osborne at the above address. For information on translations or book distributors outside the U.S.A., please see the International Contact Information page immediately following the index of this book.

MCAD/MCSD Visual Basic® .NET™ Web Applications Study Guide (Exam 70-305)

1234567890 CUS CUS 0198765432

Book p/n 0-07-212578-0 and CD p/n 0-07-212579-9
parts of
ISBN 0-07-212580-2

Publisher	**Acquisitions Coordinator**	**Indexer**
Brandon A. Nordin	Jessica Wilson	Jack Lewis
Vice President &	**Technical Editor**	**Computer Designers**
Associate Publisher	Matthew MacDonald	Carie Abrew, Elizabeth Jang
Scott Rogers		
	Copy Editor	**Illustrators**
Senior Acquisitions Editor	Rachel Lopez	Lyssa Wald, Michael Mueller
Nancy Maragioglio		
	Proofreader	**Series Design**
Project Editor	Mike McGee	Roberta Steele
Jennifer Malnick		

This book was published with Corel VENTURA™ Publisher.

To my wife and best friend, Heidi.—Wayne

To Shauna, my wife, for her love, encouragement, and understanding.—David

ACKNOWLEDGMENTS

This book would never have been completed without the understanding and support of many individuals. I would like to thank my partner and co-author Dave for the many hours we have spent on the phone helping each other make concrete thoughts out of what was often incoherent ramblings.

I would like to thank my parents, Pat, Mike, Linda, and Lanny (all four of them), for being the supportive parents that they are. To my sister, Ilona, her husband, Norm, and my two lovely nieces, Cassidy and Virginia, I would like to say thank you and I am sorry your uncle was not around as much as he would have liked to be. I would also like to thank my closest friends John, Jimmy, Shell, Christine, and the newest and youngest addition to the group, Madeline Mae, for still calling me friend after months of neglect.

I would like to extend my deepest thanks to the California girl, Jennifer Malnick (who made me laugh), and Jessica Wilson from McGraw-Hill/Osborne for their help in turning my thoughts into something comprehensible. I would especially like to thank Nancy Maragioglio for her guidance and her special ability to keep me moving forward in the kindest of ways. For this you will have my undying gratitude.

Finally, I would like to thank my wife and soul mate, Heidi, whose patience and understanding were invaluable during the writing of this book; and to our cat Max, who is furry.

—*Wayne*

Thanks are due to the following people for their support on this project:

The whole team at McGraw-Hill/Osborne, with special thanks to Nancy Maragioglio and Jennifer Malnick for their hard work, understanding, and for nagging with a sense of humor.

To Krista, Olivia, and Mitchell for understanding and putting up with the disruption caused by Dad's work; and to my wife, Shauna, for making sure they understood.

—*David*

CONTENTS AT A GLANCE

CONTENTS

Part II

Create and Manage Components and .NET Assemblies . . . 145

PREFACE

This book was written to assist you in preparing for and passing the Developing and Implementing Web Applications with Microsoft Visual Basic .NET and Microsoft Visual Studio .NET Exam 70-305. The text and exercises were created to help familiarize you with the topics you will be tested on during the actual exam.

In This Book

While this book is designed to be a focused exam preparation tool, you will also find discussions of the theory and methodologies behind working with the .NET Framework. The hands-on exercises were designed to give you additional experience with the .NET Framework while reinforcing the understanding of the concepts.

In Every Chapter

The Study Guide series contains a number of chapter elements that were designed to help you identify important items, reinforce key points, and offer expert tips for taking the exam. Each chapter contains the following:

- **Certification Objectives**   Each chapter begins with a listing of the exam objectives that will be covered in the chapter.

- **Exam Watches**   These are tips from our expert authors designed to help you focus your studies on areas that will be important for the exam.

- **Practice Exercises**   Hands-on experience is a key factor to success on exam day, and these practice exercises are designed to help you reinforce your skills. It's important that you work through these exercises rather than simply read them, so that you increase your exposure and familiarity to the .NET Framework.

- **On the Jobs**   Designed to let you benefit from our authors' experience, this element provides insights into the practical application of the theories presented in the text.

■ **Scenario and Solutions**   This element provides you with common situations you may encounter on the job, and provides you with quick solutions.

SCENARIO & SOLUTION

How do I validate a field value based on the value on another field?	Use the CompareValidator control. Set the ControlToCompare to the field value you are checking and the Operator to specify the condition.
How do I pop up a message box to notify the user that there are input errors?	Use a ValidationSummary control and set the ShowMessageBox property to true.
How do I test for a required input and a range check on a field?	Use both a RequiredFieldValidator and a RangeValidator control for the field.

■ **The Certification Summary**   This is a general review of the material that was presented in the chapter. The summary provides a quick-review option prior to taking the exam.

 ■ **The Two-Minute Drill**   At the end of every chapter you will find a listing of the key objective points from the chapter. These are great as a final review study tool.

 ■ **The Self Test**   Our self-assessment section presents questions similar to those you'll find on the actual exam, and is designed to help you identify those areas in which you may need additional study. Complete answers with explanations are located at the end of each chapter.

■ **Lab Questions**   Lab questions are designed to give you practice in evaluating a scenario and developing the appropriate solution. You'll find these throughout the text.

On the CD-ROM

This book includes a CD-ROM with simulation assessment and training software. Be sure to look through the software—there is more than one hour of interactive instructional video training, hundreds of practice test questions found only using the CD-ROM, and CertCam audio-visual demonstrations of exercises from the book. For more information about the CD-ROM, please see Appendix A.

INTRODUCTION

Welcome to *MCAD/MCSD Visual Basic .NET Web Application Study Guide (Exam 70-305)*. The authors have written this book to help you prepare for the **Developing and Implementing Web Applications with Microsoft Visual Basic .NET and Microsoft Visual Studio .NET** certification exam. Whether you're preparing for your MCSD, or getting started with your MCAD, this book will guide you through the key points of each of the exam objectives.

MCAD vs. MCSD

How do you know whether to pursue MCAD (Microsoft Certified Application Developer) or MCSD (Microsoft Certified Solution Developer)? Consider your career plan—while the MCAD is a less comprehensive certification than the MCSD, it may reflect your actual interests and skills better than the MCSD. You may decide to start with the MCAD, then add exams until reaching the MCSD level as your career changes.

According to Microsoft, candidates for the MCAD certification credential are professionals who use Microsoft technologies to develop and maintain department-level applications, components, Web or desktop clients, back-end data services, or work in teams developing enterprise applications.

Comparatively, candidates for the MCSD certification are lead developers who design and develop leading-edge enterprise solutions with Microsoft development tools, technologies, platforms, and the Microsoft .NET Framework.

MCSD certification encompasses the skill set of the MCAD certification, and MCAD can be considered an interim step toward MCSD certification.

MCSD Certification Requirements

Achieving the MCSD certification requires passing four core exams and one elective exam. The core exams are listed next.

MCSD Core Exams
Solution Architecture Exam (Required) Exam 70-300: Analyzing Requirements and Defining .NET Solution Architectures
Web Application Development Exams (One Required) Exam 70-305: Developing and Implementing Web Applications with Microsoft Visual Basic .NET and Microsoft Visual Studio .NET **OR** Exam 70-315: Developing and Implementing Web Applications with Microsoft Visual C# .NET and Microsoft Visual Studio .NET
Windows Application Development Exams (One Required) Exam 70-306: Developing and Implementing Windows-based Applications with Microsoft Visual Basic .NET and Microsoft Visual Studio .NET **OR** 70-316: Developing and Implementing Windows-based Applications with Microsoft Visual C# .NET and Microsoft Visual Studio .NET
Web Services and Server Components Exams (One Required) Exam 70-310: Developing XML Web Services and Server Components with Microsoft Visual Basic .NET and the Microsoft .NET Framework **OR** Exam 70-320: Developing XML Web Services and Server Components with Microsoft Visual C# and the Microsoft .NET Framework

In addition to the core exams, you must pass one of the following elective exams:

- **Exam 70-229** Designing and Implementing Databases with Microsoft SQL Server 2000, Enterprise Edition
- **Exam 70-230** Designing and Implementing Solutions with Microsoft BizTalk Server 2000, Enterprise Edition
- **Exam 70-234** Designing and Implementing Solutions with Microsoft Commerce Server 2000

MCAD Certification Requirements

Microsoft's MCAD only requires three core exams and one elective, and permits the use of some exams as either core or elective credit.

Web Application Development Exams (One Required) Exam 70-305: Developing and Implementing Web Applications with Microsoft Visual Basic .NET and Microsoft Visual Studio .NET **OR** Exam 70-315: Developing and Implementing Web Applications with Microsoft Visual C# .NET and Microsoft Visual Studio .NET
Windows Application Development Exams (One Required) Exam 70-306: Developing and Implementing Windows-based Applications with Microsoft Visual Basic .NET and Microsoft Visual Studio .NET **OR** 70-316: Developing and Implementing Windows-based Applications with Microsoft Visual C# .NET and Microsoft Visual Studio .NET
Web Services and Server Components Exams (One Required) Exam 70-310: Developing XML Web Services and Server Components with Microsoft Visual Basic .NET and the Microsoft .NET Framework **OR** Exam 70-320: Developing XML Web Services and Server Components with Microsoft Visual C# and the Microsoft .NET Framework

In addition to the core exams, you must pass one of the following elective exams:

- **Exam 70-229** Designing and Implementing Databases with Microsoft SQL Server 2000, Enterprise Edition
- **Exam 70-234** Designing and Implementing Solutions with Microsoft Commerce Server 2000

Furthermore, the following may be used for elective credit if they have not been used toward core exam credit:

Exams 70-305,70-306, 70-310, 70-315, 70-316, 70-320

exam
ⓦatch

For the latest information on available exams, visit www.microsoft.com. Exams are subject to change without notice, so be sure to check this site frequently as you prepare for your exam.

Exam Credit

When you pass Exam 70-305, you immediately achieve the status of Microsoft Certified Professional (MCP), and earn credit toward either the MCAD for .Microsoft .NET or MCSD for Microsoft .NET certification:

- **Core credit** toward MCSD (Microsoft Certified Solution Developer) certification
- **Core or Elective credit** toward MCAD (Microsoft Certified Application Developer) certification

Skills Being Measured

You can view the complete set of skills being measured at the MCSD Web site at www.microsoft.com/traincert/mcp/mcsd/requirements.asp. The following is a quick summary of what you'll be faced with on the exam, according to Microsoft:

Create User Services

- Create ASP.NET Pages.
- Add and set directives on ASP.NET pages.
- Separate user interface resources from business logic.
- Add Web server controls, HTML server controls, user controls, and HTML code to ASP.NET pages.
- Set properties on controls.
- Load controls dynamically.
- Apply templates.
- Set styles on ASP.NET pages by using cascading style sheets.
- Instantiate and invoke an ActiveX control.
- Implement navigation for the user interface.
- Manage the view state.
- Manage data during postback events.
- Use session state to manage data across pages.
- Validate user input.
- Validate nonLatin user input.

- Implement error handling in the user interface.
- Configure custom error pages.
- Implement Global.asax, application, page-level, and page event error handling.
- Implement online user assistance.
- Incorporate existing code into ASP.NET pages.
- Display and update data.
- Transform and filter data.
- Bind data to the user interface.
- Use controls to display data.
- Instantiate and invoke a Web service or component.
- Instantiate and invoke a Web service.
- Instantiate and invoke a COM or COM+ component.
- Instantiate and invoke a .NET component.
- Call native functions by using platform invoke.
- Implement globalization.
- Implement localizability for the user interface.
- Convert existing encodings.
- Implement right-to-left and left-to-right mirroring.
- Prepare culture-specific formatting.
- Handle events.
- Create event handlers.
- Raise events.
- Implement accessibility features.
- Use and edit intrinsic objects. Intrinsic objects include response, request, session, server, and application.

Create and Manage Components and .NET Assemblies

- Create and modify a .NET assembly.
- Create and implement satellite assemblies.
- Create resource-only assemblies.
- Create Web custom controls and Web user controls.

Consume and Manipulate Data

- Access and manipulate data from a Microsoft SQL Server database by creating and using ad hoc queries and stored procedures.
- Access and manipulate data from a data store. Data stores include relational databases, XML documents, and flat files. Methods include XML techniques and ADO.NET.
- Handle data errors.

Test and Debug

- Create a unit test plan.
- Implement tracing.
- Add trace listeners and trace switches to an application.
- Display trace output.
- Debug, rework, and resolve defects in code.
- Configure the debugging environment.
- Create and apply debugging code to components, pages, and applications.
- Provide multicultural test data to components, pages, and applications.
- Execute tests.
- Resolve errors and rework code.

Deploy a Windows-Based Application

- Plan the deployment of a Windows-based application.
- Plan a deployment that uses removable media.
- Plan a Web-based deployment.
- Plan the deployment of an application to a Web garden, a Web farm, or a cluster.
- Create a setup program that installs a Web application and allows for the application to be uninstalled.
- Deploy a Web application.
- Add assemblies to the Global Assembly Cache.

Maintain and Support a Web Application

- Optimize the performance of a Web application.
- Diagnose and resolve errors and issues.

Configure and Secure a Web Application

- Configure a Web application.
- Modify the Web.config file.
- Modify the Machine.config file.
- Add and modify application settings.
- Configure security for a Web application.
- Select and configure authentication type. Authentication types include Windows Authentication, None, Forms-based, Microsoft Passport, Internet Information Services (IIS) authentication, and custom authentication.
- Configure authorization. Authorization methods include file-based methods and URL-based methods.
- Configure role-based authorization.
- Implement impersonation.
- Configure and implement caching. Caching types include output, fragment, and data.
- Use a cache object.
- Use cache directives.
- Configure and implement session state in various topologies such as a Web garden and a Web farm.
- Use session state within a process.
- Use session state with session state service.
- Use session state with Microsoft SQL Server.
- Install and configure server services.
- Install and configure a Web server.
- Install and configure Microsoft FrontPage Server extensions.

Performance-Based vs. Knowledge-Based Questions

The exam questions fall into two broad categories: knowledge-based and performance-based. Knowledge-based questions are designed to test your knowledge of specific facts. Performance-based questions are designed to measure your ability to perform on the job by presenting examples of situations and scenarios a developer might encounter in the real world.

Finally, be aware that your exam may consist of several different types of items, as summarized here:

■ **Free Response items** Traditional multiple-choice items, designed to test your basic knowledge of facts.

■ **Case Study-based items** Designed to simulate which situations developers actually encounter on the job, these questions test your ability to analyze information and make decisions.

You can, and should, get some practice with different types of questions prior to taking the exam. Sample questions are available for download from the Exam and Testing Procedures' Web page at www.microsoft.com/traincert/mcpexams/faq/procedures.asp.

Study Strategies

Exam 70-305 will test your overall understanding of Visual Basic .NET in a Web environment. Experience is the best teacher, so be sure to work through the exercises and labs as you read through the text.

Take the self tests at the ends of the chapters and immediately review any material that you have difficulty with. Continue to review the material as you progress through the book.

Use the test engine on the CD-ROM. This engine was developed to help give you the experience of facing a certification challenge in a setting similar to the actual testing scenario. Being familiar with the process will let you focus on the exam rather than the environment.

Signing Up

To schedule your exam, call any Sylvan Prometrics or VUE center. Online registration is also available through the Register for an Exam Web page at www.microsoft.com/traincert/mcpexams/register. This site gives you information about the registration process and locations of testing centers near you.

MCAD/MCSD
MICROSOFT® CERTIFIED APPLICATION DEVELOPER
& MICROSOFT® CERTIFIED SOLUTION DEVELOPER

Part I

Create User Services

CHAPTERS

1

Create ASP.NET Pages: Build the Interface

CERTIFICATION OBJECTIVES

A SP.NET is a new Microsoft web development technology that is based on the .NET platform, which provides many advantages over traditional ASP Web development tools by including multiple language support, compiled code, full object orientation, server controls, and Web services. It also provides improved security and scalability, cookie-less sessions, and much easier configuration and deployment.

In this chapter, we will discuss building an ASP.NET page interface using Microsoft Visual Basic .NET. We will examine the .NET Framework architecture and the ASP.NET execution model, and learn to set ASP.NET directives. We then will progress to adding Web server controls, HTML server controls, user controls, and HTML code to ASP.NET pages. Finally, we will separate interface elements from business logic, which will give us a much cleaner programming model and make debugging easier.

CERTIFICATION OBJECTIVE 1.01

Add and Set Directives on ASP.NET Pages

Traditional ASP developers are familiar with the *directives* used in ASP pages that set the codepage, scripting language, and so forth. Directives are instructions for the compiler (or in the case of ASP, the interpreter). Because ASP.NET is a more complex environment than classic ASP, it has more complex directives. In addition to Pages (Web Forms), ASP.NET includes directives in User Controls to set the OutputCache and to Register Namespaces. To understand the use of Directives, it is important that we first understand the .NET Framework and the ASP.NET execution model.

The .NET Framework

ASP.NET applications use a completely different architecture from that of traditional ASP development. The .NET Framework supplies the .NET application development platform that enables the development of cross-platform applications in multiple languages. This ensures compatibility, stability, and security and includes the following components:

- Common Language Runtime
- Base class library

- Data
- Web Forms and Web services
- Win Forms

To understand how the .NET Framework processes and executes code, we will discuss the functions of the Common Language Runtime (CLR), and the .NET Framework base class library.

The Common Language Runtime (CLR)

The Common Language Runtime is responsible for code execution and management within the .NET Framework. The term *managed code* refers to code written in a compiler that targets the CLR. Microsoft's Visual Basic .NET, Visual C ++, C#, JScript, and third-party compilers such as PERL or COBOL produce managed code.

Traditional language source code is directly compiled into native code specific to the processor and operating system on which the application will be running. It includes the type libraries or Interface Definition Language (IDL) to reference types required by the application. The result is source code that must be compiled separately for the specific computer architecture on which the application will be executed. With the .NET Framework and CLR, the source code is first compiled into a platform-independent intermediate language, which includes the data usually contained in type libraries and IDLs, and then into native code for the specific machine it will be running on.

Microsoft Intermediate Language (MSIL)   Managed code is first translated by the CLR into Microsoft Intermediate Language (MSIL), which is a set of instructions that can easily be further compiled to native code specific to the CPU. The compiler also produces metadata, which includes information about the types and members required to execute the code at run time. The MSIL and metadata are contained in a *portable executable* (PE) file, which defines the code in a Multilanguage and multiplatform fashion. Using metadata eliminates the need to store application information in the registry (as this is supplied with the PE) and greatly simplifies installation and deployment.

When the program is executed, the CLR compiles the MSIL into native code using a *Just-in-Time compiler (JITc)* specific to the CPU. This enables the CLR to compile the application into any architecture it supports. The JITc verifies that the code is *type safe,* which means it accesses only memory locations that are authorized, thereby preventing memory leaks, corruption, and potential crashes.

Application Domains and Assemblies Operating systems traditionally use processes to isolate applications. Each process runs one application and manages the resources required. Process boundaries isolate applications from each other so that a failure in one process will not interfere with other processes. The .NET Framework uses something called *application domains,* which are smaller units of processing. Because the JITc verifies that the code is type safe, the CLR requires fewer resources to monitor the processes, which results in a more efficient and robust process model. It is possible for an application to consist of multiple application domains—each with separate isolation boundaries—which results in improved fault tolerance.

Assemblies, which run inside application domains, are collections of resources that form a unit of logical functionality—as such, they are the basic building blocks of the .NET Framework. Assemblies can contain ASP.NET pages, VB.NET source files, images, PE files, and so forth. They can be compared to dynamic linked libraries in the traditional Windows environment, but provide much greater control over security, versioning, and activation scoping.

The CLR can execute only code contained in an assembly; therefore, even ASP.NET pages are contained in assemblies, which are dynamically created as the page is requested. Unlike DLLs, you can run multiple versions of assemblies at the same time, which enables side-by-side execution. We will discuss assemblies in more detail in Chapter 4.

The .NET Framework Class Library

The .NET Framework class library is a collection of reusable classes that integrate with the CLR. The classes are organized into *namespaces* and provide functionality that can be used from any language that produces managed code. Each namespace is a hierarchical collection of classes with related functionality. For example, the System.Data namespace contains classes for ADO.NET and the System.Web.UI.WebControls contains classes for creating Web Server Controls on an ASP.NET page.

Each ASP.NET page in an ASP.NET application actually is an object derived from the System.UI.Web.Page class. ASP.NET generates a new class for each page based on the System.UI.Web.Page but extended with the controls, code, and static HTML built into the page by the developer, thus extending the page class functionality. Each ASP.NET page automatically imports certain namespaces that are required for the page class. Other namespaces must be imported as needed. For example, the System.Data namespace supplies ADO.NET classes to access databases. If the page uses ADO.NET, it must import the System.Data namespace. This process is similar to referencing a type library in Visual Basic 6 programming.

e x a m
ⓦ a t c h   *Microsoft tends to concentrate exam questions on new technology features.*
Make sure you understand the .NET Framework and ASP.NET execution model.

The ASP.NET Execution Model

Now that we have some understanding of the .NET Framework, let's look at the ASP.NET execution model to understand how ASP.NET pages are processed on the server. ASP.NET pages are identified with an .aspx extension on the Web server. When the client's browser makes the request for the page, the *Parser* reads and interprets the contents of the page. It then passes the page to the *Compiler*, which translates the page into the intermediate language.

The .NET Framework provides a machine-wide code cache called the *Assembly Cache*, which holds the precompiled (Intermediate Language) code versions of the page. The CLR compiles to native code and places some items in *Memory* where they are available for retrieval without requiring reconstruction. The entire page, including all objects and data, is placed in the *Output Cache* where it remains for subsequent requests from the client.

This model has many advantages over the classic ASP model. A classic ASP file is either interpreted VBScript or JScript. Each time a client requests a page, the .asp script is parsed and interpreted, and the result is returned to the client browser. Because ASP.NET pages are compiled on the first request, subsequent requests can be handled directly from the Output Cache, greatly improving performance.

o n   t h e
ⓙ o b   *It is not necessary to convert existing classic ASP pages into ASP.NET pages
to include them in a Web application. ASP pages can coexist in the same
application but ASP.NET will not compile or execute them. It might be
advantageous from a performance perspective to convert them; however,
depending upon their function, it might not be worth the effort.*

ASP.NET Directives

Now that we have had a quick overview of the .NET Framework and execution model, we can reasonably discuss directives in ASP.NET pages. Directives are instructions for specific conditions that must be set before or during the compilation of the source code. Directives are placed in code render blocks (with <% …%> tags) at the top of the page. ASP.NET provides directives for pages, user controls, importing namespaces, and the OutputCache.

exam
ⓦatch

Make sure you are familiar with all the directives, but pay particular attention to the more common directives; especially for the page and OutputCache.

@ Page Directives

ASP.NET page directives are identified with an @ Page followed by the specific directive(s), as shown here:

%@ Page attribute="value" [attribute="value"...] %>

The common @ Page attributes are presented in Table 1-1. For a full list, refer to the .NET Framework SDK documentation.

In classic ASP development, an important directive is to set the @ LANGUAGE attribute. Without this, the source code could be interpreted as VBScript when it actually is JScript, and therefore fail. As we have already discovered, ASP.NET source

TABLE 1-1	Attributes	Description
Common @ Page Directives	Culture	Indicates the culture setting for the page.
	Debug	Indicates whether the page should be compiled with debug symbols.
	Description	Provides a text description of the page, which is ignored by the ASP.NET Parser.
	EnableSessionState	Defines session-state requirements for the page. Options are true or false; the default is true.
	EnableViewState	Indicates whether view state is maintained across page requests. The default is true.
	ErrorPage	Specifies a target URL to which to redirect if unhandled page exceptions occur.
	Explicit	Specifies that the page should be compiled with the Visual Basic Option Explicit mode. The default is false.
	Inherits	Specifies a code-behind class for the page to inherit. Can be any class derived from the Page class.
	Language	Specifies the compiler language for all inline code rendering (<% %>) and code declaration blocks within the page.
	Trace	Indicates whether tracing is enabled. The default is false.
	TraceMode	Indicates whether trace messages should be displayed when tracing is enabled. Values are SortByTime and SortByCategory. The default is SortByTime.

code can be written in a number of languages that target the CLR; therefore, the language must be specified so the appropriate compiler is used. The following sets the language to Visual Basic .NET for the page:

```
<% @ Page Language="VB" %>
```

Only one @ Page directive can be included for each .aspx file. If there is more than one page attribute to be set, each is separated by a space. The following directive sets the language to VB and specifies that all variables must be explicitly declared:

```
<% @ Page Language="VB" Explicit="True" %>
```

Notice that the @ Page directive is used to specify the Option Explicit option. In VB6 or VBScript, this was handled with a separate Option Explicit statement at the top of the code.

@ Control Directives

@ Control directives are defined in user controls, which are covered in detail in Chapter 5. For example:

```
<%@ Control attribute="value" [attribute="value"...] %>
```

Except for tracing, user control directives support all the same attributes as the @ Page directive.

The @ Import Namespace Directive

Another important directive is to register a namespace required by the code to implement specific classes from the base class library. ASP.NET pages automatically import the following set of default namespaces required for page development:

- System
- System.Collections
- System.IO
- System.Web
- System.Web.UI
- System.Web.UI.HtmlControls
- System.Web.UI.WebControls

To register other namespaces use the @ Import namespace directive. The following imports the System.Data namespace, for access to ADO.NET:

```
<% @ Import NameSpace="System.Data" %>
```

For a complete list of the .NET Framework namespaces, refer to the .NET Framework SDK documentation.

The @ OutputCache Directive

In ASP.NET, you can control the output and data caching to reflect the specific requirements of the page. For example, you might want a page's output to expire immediately; thus, for each request, the code is re-executed. On the other hand you may set a specific cache time duration (in seconds) to specify the amount of time the page should be cached before it expires. Cached pages will result in the same output as previous requests until the cache expires. For example, the following code sets the output cache duration parameter to 30 seconds:

```
<% @ OutputCache Duration="30" Location="Any"%>
```

If this page contained any server-side code to display the time, each subsequent request for the page would display the same time until the page expired (30 seconds), at which point the page would be executed again and would reflect the time of execution again for another 30 seconds.

The second parameter for the OutputCache is the location, which specifies where the output is to be cached. The valid values for the location parameter are shown as follows:

Value	Description
Any	The default. Any of the following.
Client	Output cache on the browser client.
Downstream	On a server downstream from the server that processed the request. Used for proxy servers.
None	No output caching enabled for the page.
Server	Output cache on the Web server processing the request.

Caching is discussed further in Chapter 11.

Let's create an ASP.NET project in Visual Studio and view the structure of a Web Form.

EXERCISE 1-1

Create an ASP.NET Project in Visual Studio .NET

In this exercise, we will start a Web application in Visual Studio .NET, and view the default .aspx file including the @ Page directives and Web Form HTML.

1. From the Start menu, open Visual Studio .NET.

2. On the Start page, choose New Project and then ASP.NET Web Application.

3. Accept the default application name and click OK.

4. Click the HTML designer button on the bottom left. Your screen should look like Figure 1-1.

FIGURE 1-1   Default HTML for WebForm1.aspxr

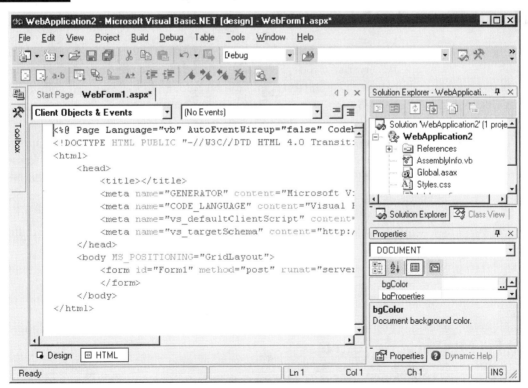

5. Read through the HTML. Notice the @ Page directive. What directives have been set by ASP.NET?

6. Notice that the <HTML>, <HEAD>, <BODY>, and <FORM> tags have been inserted for you. The <BODY> tag contains a positioning attribute and the <FORM> is set to `runat="server"`.

7. Choose File | Save All to save the project.

CERTIFICATION OBJECTIVE 1.02

Add HTML Server, Web Server, User Controls, and HTML Code to ASP.NET Pages

ASP.NET pages are also known as Web Forms. A Web Form consists of server controls and server-side code. Server controls are objects with methods, properties, and events that run on the server and can be accessed from server-side code placed in <script> sections on the page. This approach creates a programming environment remarkably similar to event-driven languages such as Microsoft Visual Basic.

Server controls automatically render client-specific HTML to the client browser, eliminating the need to query the client browser type and conditionally return client-specific HTML, based upon the browser capabilities. This feature of ASP.NET eliminates the need to create separate pages for different browser types or versions. The server controls now will automatically generate the appropriate code specific to the client's requirements. An added advantage to server controls is their capability to automatically maintain state between trips to the server (as long as they are placed within the <form> tags). This eliminates the need to repopulate the control values in the response to the client. These features of ASP.NET create a much cleaner programming model than classic ASP.

Add HTML Server Controls

HTML Server Controls are objects created on the server that correspond to HTML elements. They look the same as standard HTML elements, except they have a `runat="server"` attribute added to the element tag. HTML controls return the HTML control element on the Web page to the client browser and create an instance of the control object on the server. The server control object supports methods, properties, and events that can be accessed from server code. When the page is run, the control automatically generates the HTML output based on the client browser's capabilities.

For example, you can create a text box server control with the following element tag:

```
<input type="text" id="CourseName" runat="server" />
```

The `runat="server"` identifies this as a server control; the *id* attribute allows the developer to write code to the control's events, change property values, or execute methods. For example, to change the text in the control, you can use the following code:

```
CourseName.Value = "Introduction to VB6"
```

Add Web Server Controls

Web server controls are similar to HTML controls except they are not restricted to HTML elements. Some Web controls, such as the textbox and label controls, perform the same function as the HTML server controls; however, there are other, more complex controls such as calendars, datagrids, and validation controls that provide for a much richer user interface design. Web controls are subdivided into four subsets:

- **Intrinsic controls** These map to HTML elements such as asp:TextBox and asp:Button.

- **Validation controls** These provide automatic server and client-side input validation.

- **Rich controls** These provide richer interface functionality such as the Calendar control and AdRotator.

- **List-bound controls** Includes controls such as DataGrid and DataList.

exam
ⓦatch

Exam 70-305 will expect you to be familiar with each of the intrinsic Web server controls and their common properties.

Web server controls are provided by the System.Web.UI.WebControls namespace that is automatically included in ASP.NET pages. They are placed on the page using a namespace tag with an asp: prefix and must include the `runat="server"` attribute. The following tag creates a textbox Web server control:

```
<asp:TextBox id="StudentName" runat="server"></asp:TextBox>
```

In Visual Studio .NET, the Web controls are available in the toolbox under the WebForms tab (you must be in design mode to access this). The controls can be dragged onto the page, and positioned and resized dynamically.

Add User Controls

User controls are custom-built controls that consist of reusable interface elements. Building user controls will be covered in detail in Chapter 5. To be used in a page, they first must be registered with the @ Register directive. The syntax is as follows:

<% Register TagPrefix= *"Prefix"* TagName= *"ControlName"* src= *"filepath"* NameSpace= *"name"* %>

A user control TagPrefix can be anything you decide, as long as it refers to the group to which the control belongs (all Web controls are grouped into the asp— TagPrefix, for example). The TagName is the control name, src is the pathname to the control, and the NameSpace is an optional attribute that refers to a namespace associated with the TagPrefix.

User controls are saved as *.ascx* files. If we had a custom user control named *LogOn.ascx*, it would be registered with the following code:

```
<% Register TagPrefix="CUSTCONTROL" TagName="Logon"
src="LogOn.ascx" %>
```

The scr attribute is the file pathname. It must reside in the Web application or /bin directory, or be given a full pathname. Add it to the Web Form using the following tag:

```
<form runat="server">
    <CUSTCONTROL:LogOn id="ctlLogOn" runat="server"
    /CUSTCONTOL:Logon>
</form>
```

Set Properties on Controls

Control properties can be set both at design time and dynamically from code. At design time, the property values can be included in the HTML tag either by manually inserting the property value, or by using the Properties window in Visual Studio.NET. Using the Properties window is much easier and less prone to error. To set properties from the Properties window, click the control in design view (or within the tag itself in HTML view) and change the value of the appropriate property in the Properties window, as in Figure 1-2. When you press the ENTER key or click off the property, the value will be updated in the HTML tag.

To set a property within the HTML, add the *PropertyName="Value"* within the tag itself. The following sets an intrinsic label control to display the text "Hello World" in italics:

```
<asp:Label runat="server" id="lblMessage" Text="Hello World"
Font-Italic="true"></asp:Label>
```

FIGURE 1-2   Changing properties in Visual Studio.NET

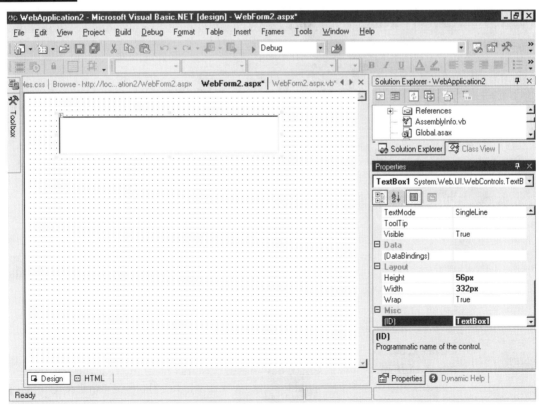

FROM THE CLASSROOM

Upgrade Web Applications from ASP to ASP.NET

Existing ASP Web applications can certainly benefit from an upgrade to ASP.NET, especially if they are in need of extensive maintenance. Converting ASPs to ASP.NET generally requires a bit more work than just adding an *x* to the file extension, but the time and effort expended in the conversion process is likely to be worthwhile.

A Web application does not have to be based on one technology or the other; it can be a mixture of ASP, COM, ASP.NET and .NET Framework components. Depending on the application, it might be reasonable to take a step-by-step approach to the conversion, using ASP.NET for new pages and gradually

upgrading existing ASP to ASP.NET pages in response to maintenance and performance issues. However, this approach can introduce its own problems, such as the inability to share Application and Session State between the ASP and ASP.NET pages.

ASP.NET offers many advantages over traditional ASP, including increased performance, greater scalability, improved security, and easy configuration and deployment. Any or all of these features might play a part in your decision to upgrade the Web application—in whole or in part—to ASP.NET.

—David Shapton, MCSD, MCT, CTT+

To change the value of a property from code, use the control id to refer to the control, a period, and the property name = value. The following code will change the text property on our label control to "Goodbye":

```
LblMessage.Text = "Goodbye"
```

Setting or changing control properties at run time is an important feature of an application. Although we haven't yet discussed adding code to Web Forms, having control properties change in response to events or conditions at run time is an important feature of interface implementation.

Load Controls Dynamically

In most instances, the interface design will be static, meaning that the controls added to the Web Form at design time will provide all the functionality required for the interface. However, in some instances, the number of controls required might not be known until run time. It would be unreasonable to create the interface with the maximum possible number of expected controls if only some of them will be actively used in most instances.

Controls must exist within a container, which can be either the page itself or a container control such as a panel. The following code dynamically adds a new label to the page from the Page_Load event. It creates a new instance of a label control, adds it to the controls collection of the page (the container), and sets its id and text properties.

```
sub Page_Load(obj as Object, e as Eventargs)
dim objLabel as new label
page.controls.add(objLabel)
objlabel.id="lblOne"
objlabel.text="One"
End Sub
```

This code can be placed in a variable loop in any code block and will dynamically create a variable number of controls required by the application interface at run time.

EXERCISE 1-2

Add Server Controls

In this exercise, we will add HTML elements, HTML server controls, and Web server controls to the page. Then we'll view the HMTL returned to the browser.

1. Open the project saved from Exercise 1-1 and view the Web Form in design view.

2. Click the HTML tab on the ToolBox and drag a label onto the form.

3. Put a text field beside it.

4. Switch to HTML and view the HTML code. Notice the text field is an <INPUT> HTML element with its style set to text, and that it is placed between the <FORM></FORM> tags.

5. Add a Submit button under the text field and view the HTML.

6. Right-click the page and choose View in Browser. Save the file if prompted to do so. Notice that unlike Visual Interdev, Visual Studio .NET allows you to view .aspx files from within the interface. Your page should look like this:

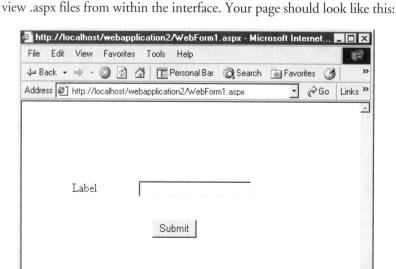

7. Type your name in the text field and click the Submit button. The content of the text is cleared.

8. Open the page in your browser. The URL should be *HTTP://localhost/WebApplication1/WebForm1.aspx* unless you have a different Web application name.

9. Click View | Source from the browser menu. Notice that the Web Form server control has returned HTML to the browser that includes an action attribute set to the Web Form and a hidden field called "_VIEWSTATE".

10. Return to the HTML in Visual Studio and add the `runat="server"` attribute to both the text field and the Submit button. Refresh the page in the browser and enter text, then click the Submit button. The text did not clear this time because the HTML elements are now HTML server controls

and the Web Form is preserving the state of the controls between posts on the hidden field.

11. Switch back to design view and click the Web Forms tab on the Toolbox. Add a Label and a DropDownList to the form. These are intrinsic Web server controls.

12. Change the text of the labels to read "Name" and "Employment Status." Click the list box to make sure it has focus and from the Properties window click the Items property. Click the ellipsis button and then the Add button. Add "Full Time," "Part Time," "Self Employed," and "Unemployed" in the text properties and click OK.

13. Save the Web Form and view it in the browser. It should look like Figure 1-3. Enter your name and employment status, and click Submit. Notice that the state is maintained. Switch to the HTML in Visual Studio and look at the tags for the Web server controls you added.

FIGURE 1-3   A Web Form with Employment Status

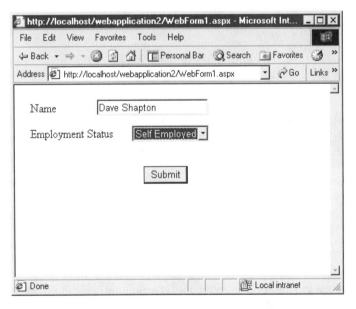

Instantiate and Invoke an ActiveX Control

ActiveX controls, like all other COM components, are older technology and not part of the .NET Framework model. Components in the .Net Framework contain the metadata that provides a description of the component to the CLR. COM components (including ActiveX controls and COM code components) require their type libraries, CLSIDs, and other information to be entered into the Windows Registry. COM objects are *unmanaged code,* which means the CLR cannot identify their types and so forth; therefore, it cannot manage them.

ASP.NET still supports these objects; however, they should be replaced with managed components. ActiveX controls can be instantiated and invoked in the HTML code with an <OBJECT> tag. The control must be installed and registered on the client machine. The <OBJECT> tag can include a CODEBASE attribute that provides the path and filenames required to install the object on the client. The following example is the <OBJECT> tag for the progress bar control. Notice that it contains the class identifier (CLSID) and property settings.

```
<OBJECT id=ProgressBar1 style="LEFT: 0px; TOP: 0px"
Classid="clsid:0713E8D2-850A-101B-AFC0-4210102A8DA7"
BorderStyle="0" Appearance="1" Enabled="1" Min="0" Max="100">
</OBJECT>
```

Now that we know something about Web Form controls, let's go over some scenario questions and their answers.

SCENARIO & SOLUTION

I already have a Web page interface in HTML. How can I easily change this to server controls?	Add the runat="server" attribute in the beginning HTML element tag.
I want my server-side code to return HTML specific to the browser. How do I do this?	Use Web server controls instead of HTML elements.
How do I get a Label to display different text as a message at run time?	Set the text property for the control in server-side code.
The number of items I need to display changes for each use of the page. How do I handle this?	Dynamically load the required number of controls from the server code.

Add HTML code

Coding in ASP.NET has more in common with coding in event-driven languages such as Visual Basic than with classic ASP scripting. The Web server controls are objects on the server that can be manipulated by server-side code and return the browser-appropriate HTML to the client. Therefore it is not recommended to use <% %> tags to produce inline code, as this inserts the results of the code execution directly into the HTML response based on its position within the HTML code. This mixes the server code with the HTML code, making if difficult to manage.

HTML code and server code should be separated to provide a cleaner programming model. HTML code can be manually added to the page via the HTML view, or by adding HTML or Web controls from the Design view by dragging them from the Toolbox. It is preferable to use Web controls, as they provide a more consistent object model than their HTML counterparts, including the use of common properties.

Handle Events

ASP.NET code is placed in <SCRIPT> sections on the page. Both the language attribute and `runat="server"` attributes must be set in the opening script tag, as shown here:

```
<SCRIPT LANGUAGE="VB" runat="server">
```

It is important to specify the `runat ="server"` attribute; otherwise, the code will be returned as text to the browser. Omitting the language attribute might not cause any great grief, as the default language is Visual Basic—unless of course you have set the @ Page language directive to something else and used VB code in the script block!

Functions and subprocedures are declared within <script> tags. They all can be contained within one script block or separated into sections:

```
<SCRIPT LANGUAGE="VB" runat="server" >
    Sub ProcessData
        'code to process data
    End Sub
</SCRIPT>
```

Script sections can be placed anywhere on the page but it's a good idea to separate them from the interface elements, as it makes it easier to read and debug your code. ASP.NET has a method to completely separate the code from the interface using *code-behind pages,* which we will discuss later, in the section "Create and Use Code-Behind Pages."

ASP.NET will use any language that targets the MSIL (managed code). When using the VB language in ASP.NET, remember that you are using VB.NET—not VBScript or Visual Basic 6. There have been many changes to the VB language syntax for .NET. These changes were required so that VB can produce Managed Code that can use the .NET Framework classes. Some of the major differences in VB.NET from previous versions are as follows:

- **Variables** There is no longer a Variant data type; you must declare the type of variable when you declare it. Also, it now is possible to initialize the variable in the declaration line, as in `Dim intCount as Integer = 1`.

- **Procedure parameters** All parameters passed to procedures, whether functions or subprocedures, must be enclosed in parentheses. They also are passed by value unless *ByRef* is specified in the parameter list. This is the opposite of earlier versions.

- **Object variables** There is no more *Set* and *Let.* Object variables are assigned just as any other type. VB.NET does not support the concept of default properties and methods, which means all object references must be fully qualified.

- **Structured error handling** Error handling is now handled using *Try…Catch…Finally,* which allows nesting of exception handling and the capability to respond with cleanup code for both error and non-error conditions.

Remember that Exam 70-305 tests the development of Web applications with Visual Basic.NET. You will not have to explicitly write code in the exam, but many of the questions will contain VB.NET code as answers. Be sure of your VB.NET coding skills before taking the exam.

ASP.NET server controls have properties, methods, and events that can be accessed from code running on the server. We have seen how to access properties from code; now let's see how to create event handlers for these controls.

Create Event Handlers

ASP.NET has a specific syntax to create event handlers for server controls. You first must assign a method name to the name of the event in the tag for the control. This tag for the intrinsic button control has a method of "button1_click" assigned to the OnClick event, as shown here:

```
<asp:Button id="Button1" runat="server" Text="Button"
OnClick="button1_click"></asp:Button>
```

It obviously is important to know the supported events for each control. This is made easier with the intrinsic controls, as they have standard common events that apply to most of the controls. Intrinsic controls do not have the same number of events you might find in a typical event-driven environment. Although the controls and code are on the Web server, the events are being triggered on the client browser; each event would generally require a round trip to the server.

Therefore, the supported events are limited to actions such as a click or change—not to mouse or keyboard events, for example, which would generate an unacceptable number of round trips. In fact, only click events cause the form to be submitted to the server; change events are placed in a queue and processed after a click event has posted the form to the server. Check the .NET Framework SDK documentation for the control events if you are unsure.

The second step is to create an event handling subprocedure in the page code. The event handlers take two arguments: the sender of the event as type object and the event arguments as type EventArgs. The EventArgs generally are empty, but some controls have a specific type depending upon the event raised, so again be careful to check the documentation. The following code defines the button_click sub procedure for the button OnClick method:

```
<script runat="server">
Sub Button1_Click(ByVal sender As Object, ByVal e As System.EventArgs)
Label1.Text="You clicked on button1"
End Sub
</script>
```

When the user clicks the button, the subprocedure Button_Click is executed, changing the text of Label1 to "You clicked on button1."

Visual Studio .NET simplifies the creation of event handlers by using a similar method to that used in Visual Basic. If you double-click the control in design view, it will create the event handler and open the HTML code window so you can add the implementation code directly into the subprocedure. It does this by wiring up the events in code-behind pages, which are separate classes that derive from the System.Web.UI.Page class; the .aspx class then derives from that class.

The end result is that you have a method of separating the user interface elements from the code. Visual Studio .NET does this automatically by creating a code-behind form for each .aspx file (a class file with the same name as the .aspx but with a .vb extension) and setting the appropriate @ Page directives. We will discuss code-behind forms in detail in the section "Separate User Interface Resources from Business Logic," later in this chapter.

ASP.NET pages have a set series of events that occur each time a page is viewed:

- Page_Init is responsible for initialization; therefore, it can be used to initialize variables.

- Page_Load occurs every time a page is loaded. Server control properties can be set in the page load event.

- Change events on the form controls, triggered by user input in the form controls.

- Click event on a form control, which results in the posting of the form.

- The Page_Unload event occurs when the user moves to another page. It can be used to do the usual housekeeping tasks such as closing connections, files, and so on.

Apply Templates

Templates allow you to customize and manipulate the layout of a particular control using HTML elements, controls, and embedded server controls. Three of the ASP.NET server controls—the Repeater, DataList, and DataGrid—are called list controls because they automatically display data in a list. These controls act as containers for other controls or HTML elements. To control the display of data in these controls, you use templates, which allow you to control the different layout portions of the control such as headers and footers, row items, alternating items, and so forth. Each of the three controls supports different templates, which are defined in Table 1-2.

All three of these controls require a data source to render the data, which will be covered in detail in Chapters 6 and 7. The DataGrid control is also used in those chapters. Templates are also discussed in Chapter 5.

To demonstrate templates, we will use the Repeater control, create the required templates, and programmatically create a DataView and a table and add data to it from an array.

TABLE 1-2	Templates and Controls	
Template	**Description**	**Control**
ItemTemplate	Produces one row of output for each row in the data source.	Repeater, DataList, and DataGrid
AlternatingItemTemplate	Produces one row of output for every alternating row in the data source.	Repeater and DataList
SelectedItemTemplate	Contains elements and controls that are rendered only when an item is selected in the control.	DataList
EditItemTemplate	Contains elements and controls that are rendered when an item is in Edit mode.	DataList and DataGrid
HeaderTemplate	Contains elements and controls that are rendered before all the data rows have been rendered.	Repeater, DataList, and DataGrid
FooterTemplate	Contains elements and controls that are rendered after all the data rows have been rendered.	Repeater, DataList, and DataGrid
SeparatorTemplate	Contains elements that are rendered between each row.	Repeater and DataList
PagerTemplate	Contains elements and controls that are rendered while paging the information.	DataGrid

EXERCISE 1-3

Apply Templates to the Repeater Control

In this exercise, we will use templates in a Repeater control to display some simple course data.

1. Open the Web application from the previous exercise and add a new Web Form called "Courses.aspx."

2. From Design view, add a Repeater control to the page.

3. Double-click the page to open the code-behind page, then add the following code to the Page_Load event:

```
Dim DataTable1 As DataTable
Dim DataRow1 As DataRow
Dim strCourse(3) As String
Dim iCount As Integer
```

```
strCourse(0) = "Introduction to XML"
strCourse(1) = "Basic ASP.NET"
strCourse(2) = "Programming XML"

'create a DataTable
DataTable1 = New DataTable()
DataTable1.Columns.Add(New DataColumn("Course", GetType(String)))

'Create rows and put in sample data
For iCount = 0 To 2
    DataRow1 = DataTable1.NewRow()
    DataRow1(0) = strCourse(iCount)
    DataTable1.Rows.Add(DataRow1)
Next

Repeater1.DataSource = New DataView(DataTable1)
Repeater1.DataBind()
```

This code programmatically creates a DataView and a table with a Course field and loads three data items into the table from an array. It then sets the DataSource of the control to the DataView's table (DataTable1) and calls the repeater control's DataBind method to bind the data to the control.

4. Switch to HTML view for the page and add the following code to the top of the page to import the System.Data namespace:

```
<%@ Import Namespace="System.Data" %>
```

5. Add the following code to the HTML for the Repeater control:

```
<asp:repeater id="Repeater1" runat="server">
<ItemTemplate>
    <tr>
      <td>
          <%# DataBinder.Eval(Container.DataItem, "Course") %>
      </td>
    </tr>
</ItemTemplate>
</asp:repeater>
```

The Repeater control requires an ItemTemplate at a minimum. This code binds the item to the Course field in the data source.

6. Save the files, build the solution, and test it in the browser. You will notice that the items are displayed across one line in the browser. This is because the Repeater control does not have any layout of its own.

7. Insert the following code to add a separator template:

```
<SeparatorTemplate> <br> </SeparatorTemplate>
```

8. Save and view the page. You will now have the items displayed in separate rows.

9. Add the following code before the <ItemTemplate> tag to create a table heading and set a border on the table:

```
<HeaderTemplate>
   <table border="1">
      <tr>
         <td><b>Courses</b>
      </tr>
</HeaderTemplate>
```

10. Add the following code to create alternating rows with a light blue background:

```
<AlternatingItemTemplate>
   <tr>
      <td bgcolor="lightblue">
         <%# DataBinder.Eval(Container.DataItem, "Course") %>
      </td>
   </tr>
</AlternatingItemTemplate>
```

11. Save and view the page in the browser. The data is now displayed in a table with a heading and alternating rows displayed in light blue.

Set Styles on ASP.NET Pages by Using Cascading Style Sheets

Cascading style sheets (CSS) contain style definitions that are applied to elements in HTML documents. Styles define how elements are displayed on the page and are used to override the default style properties in HTML tags. Styles can be placed inline within the HTML element, specified in a style block in the HEAD section of the page, or linked to an external CSS style sheet.

Inline Styles

CSS style rules have two parts, a selector and a declaration. The selector is the element such as <H1> or <BODY>. The declaration consists of a property and value combination such as color and red. For example, the following code sets an inline style for the <DIV> element changing the background color to blue:

```
<DIV STYLE="BACKGROUND-COLOR: blue">
```

This example will set the style for this individual element and will override any previous styles defined for <DIV> elements on the page.

Style Blocks

To specify styles for all elements of a specific type on the page, you can use style blocks. For example, the following code would be placed within the <HEAD> </HEAD> tags and will set all occurrences of H2s to be red and centered on the page:

```
<STYLE>H2 { COLOR: red; TEXT-ALIGN: center }</STYLE>
```

Styles for multiple elements can be included in the style block and those styles will be uniformly applied to all elements on the page. For example, the following style block sets the styles for all H1, H2, and H3 elements on the page:

```
<STYLE>
  H1 {COLOR: blue;TEXT-ALIGN: left}
  H2 {COLOR: red; TEXT-ALIGN: center}
  H3 {COLOR: Green TEXT-ALIGN: right}
</STYLE>
```

External CSS Style Sheets

To apply common styles to all pages, you can link the page to a CSS style sheet document, which is just a text file saved with a .css extension that contains the style rules in the same format used in style blocks. Each Web application you build in Visual Studio .NET automatically includes a default style sheet called styles.css. You can link to this (or any other) external style sheet by placing a <LINK> tag within the <HEAD> tag of the page. The following code links the page to the styles.css style sheet provided by the Visual Studio Web application:

```
<LINK REL=stylesheet Type="text/css" HREF="styles.css">
```

Once the link is established on the page, all elements will be formatted with the styles defined in the linked style sheet.

Visual Studio provides an easy-to-use style editor to modify and add styles to an external style sheet. You can use this to modify or add style rules using dialog boxes. To access the styles double-click the styles.css file in the Project Explorer.

CSS Style Rule Precedence

CSS styles cascade (hence the name Cascading Style Sheets) in the sense that higher-level rules apply unless a lower-level rule exists to contradict it. For example, a style in an external linked CSS file will apply to all elements unless it is contradicted by a rule in a style block on the page. Similarly, inline styles will override any styles specified in either style blocks or an external CSS file. This means that you can use external styles to define your style elements for an application and modify each element either individually or at the page level when required.

Any rules that are not contradicted at a lower level of style are still enforced. For example, a <H1> element is automatically defined in a larger font and bolded. If you change its color to red and make it italic in the external linked CSS file, that does not affect the size and bold attributes. If you then change the color to blue in a style block on the page, the element will still be large, bold, and italic but its color will now be blue.

CERTIFICATION OBJECTIVE 1.03

Implement Navigation for the User Interface

Because of the request/response nature of web development, managing state on the interface has always been more complex than in non–web-based applications. When a user fills in a form and submits it to the Web server, the server-side code validates and processes the data. If the form has to be re-sent to the user because of missing or incorrect information, it is necessary to repopulate the control values with the posted data. ASP.NET will automatically handle the view state of forms.

Manage the View State

ASP.NET Web Forms without an action attribute will automatically post back to themselves. Visual Studio .NET creates a default form for each .aspx file with the following tags:

```
<form id="form1" method="post" runat="server" >
</form>
```

If you run this page in the browser and choose View | Source, you see the following HTML:

```
<form name="Form1" method="post" action="WebForm1.aspx" id="Form1">
<input type="hidden" name="__VIEWSTATE" value="dDwtMjUzMTQ3NzY1Ozs+" />
```

Notice that the HTML response to the client browser has included an action attribute set to the .aspx file. This is done automatically as long as an action attribute is not set in our form tag to identify another page the form is to be posted to. The second line of HTML has defined a hidden control called _VIEWSTATE and set its value to a string of interesting characters. This control contains the state of the form (encrypted) so the values do not disappear when posted back to the user.

As you can see, managing the view state in ASP.NET is remarkably simple. Everything is taken care of by the server side form control; however, you will need to manage the default behavior of the control when posting back to the client.

Manage Data During Postback Events

Managing the viewstate automatically is very helpful but it can cause problems by replacing user-entered values with default values on postback. In some situations, you might be populating controls on the form with default values in the Page_Load event. The following code defaults the Country text to Canada in the Page_Load:

```
Sub Page_Load(s as Object, e As EventArgs)
    txtCountry.Text = "Canada"
End Sub
```

However, there is a problem with this example. Because the Page_Load event runs every time the page is loaded, it will overwrite the user's entries with the default values on every load. When the user enters another value and submits the form, the postback will reset the value to Canada. To avoid this situation, you must code a conditional check on the *IsPostBack* property of the page object in the Page_Load event. If the page is being posted back, do not initialize the control values and overwrite the data.

In the following Page_Load event code, the txtCountry textbox control defaults to Canada but only on the first page load:

```
Sub Page_Load(s as Object, e As EventArgs)
    If Not Page.IsPostBack Then
        txtCountry.Text = "Canada"
    End If
End Sub
```

The first line of code checks to see if it is a postback to the Web Form (triggered by clicking the form). If not, it sets the txtcountry to Canada. Otherwise, it drops out of the If statement and does nothing.

EXERCISE 1-4

Manage ViewState with IsPostBack

In this exercise, we will add a control to our Web application, and initialize a default value and manage it with the IsPostBack property.

1. Open your Web application from Exercise 1-2 in Visual Studio.

2. Delete everything in the @ Page directive except the language attribute. This will remove the attributes to set the code-behind page.

3. Add a label and a textbox intrinsic control to the page and change the ID property of the textbox to *txtCitizenShip*.

4. View the HTML on the page, right-click the bottom of the file, and choose Insert Script Block and Server. This will insert a server-side script block. This can be done anywhere in the file, but it's better to separate it from the interface elements.

5. Add the following code to create the Page_Load event handler:
   ```
   Sub Page_Load(s As Object, e As EventArgs)
       txtCitizenship.text = "U.S."
   End Sub
   ```

6. Save and open the page in the browser. The result should be similar to this:

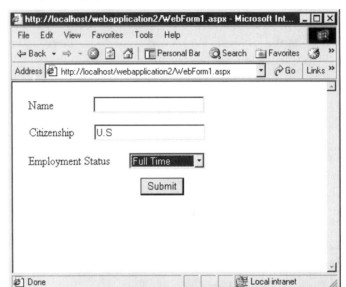

7. Change the Citizenship to "Canada" (or anything else you want). Click the Submit button. The Citizenship viewstate is not maintained and resets to "U.S."

8. Modify the code to use the IsPostBack property of the page:

```
Sub Page_Load(s As Object, e As EventArgs)
    If Not Page.IsPostBack Then
        txtCitizenship.text = "U.S."
    End If
End Sub
```

9. Save the file and test it in the browser. The first load will default the citizenship to U.S., but the viewstate will be maintained after you submit it.

Using Session State to Manage Data Across Pages

In a Web application, it often is necessary to save data from one page to be referenced on another. For example, a logon page might supply the user's name, which also might be required on other pages. The problem is that variables on Web pages are local to the page and cannot be referenced from another page. ASP solved this problem by providing a Global.asa file with Application and Session objects, and session and application variables that are available to all pages—either for each specific user session or globally to all sessions for the lifetime of the application. ASP.NET has retained the same approach, except now the file is the Global.asax.

Session Variables

To maintain data from page to page during the user's session, you can assign the data value to a session variable. For example, to maintain the user name from the logon page, you create a session variable in the page and assign the user name to it. A logical place to do this is in the code for the Click event handler of the Submit button. The following code creates a session variable called "UserName" and sets it to the value of the UserName textbox:

```
Session("UserName") = txtUserName.Text
```

This stores the value of the txtUserName textbox in the session variable UserName. This variable now is available from any other page for that user session. You could display the user's name in a label by writing the following code in the Page_Load event of another Web Form:

```
lblUserName.Text = Session("UserName")
```

The Session Object

The Session object is created when a user first accesses a page in the Web application. Each session is given a unique Session ID, which is stored on the client as a cookie. As the user navigates to other pages in the Web application, ASP.NET reads the cookie from the user, thereby tracking the user and managing session variables.

By default, a session will remain active for 20 minutes if there is no activity from the user. Depending upon the nature of the application, the timeout might need to be changed. The following example changes the timeout value to 15 minutes:

```
Session.TimeOut = 15
```

Because each session object is taking up resources on the Web server, 20 might be too long a time period. Remember that each session is active on the server even if the user has left the site. Setting the timeout for too short a period might cause problems, so be careful how you handle timeouts.

For instance, an e-commerce application in which the user is placing items in a shopping cart might need a longer timeout to ensure the user does not lose the contents of the cart while browsing the contents of the page; a secure site might want to abandon the session earlier. For example, online banking sites generally will abandon a session after four or five minutes of inactivity, requiring you to log back on if you wish to continue.

The session can be explicitly abandoned from code by using the following:

```
Session.Abandon
```

This usually is in response to a LogOut from the user interface.

A standard problem with sessions has been their reliance on cookies. Users can set their browser security to refuse cookies and therefore negate the Session ID. ASP.NET is designed to automatically handle this situation. Before sending a page to the client, ASP.NET adds an encoded Session ID to all hyperlinks on the page. When a user clicks the hyperlink, the encoded Session ID is passed to the page in the request. The page reads the value, un-encodes the ID, and uses it to identify the session.

Although implementing ASP.NET session state is similar to ASP, it provides much improved management capabilities, including the capability to store the session variables on another server. Configuring Session State is discussed in Chapter 11.

However, sometimes there are problems with managing state, as outlined in the following:

SCENARIO & SOLUTION

Why is my ViewState is not being maintained?	Make sure both the Web Form and the HTML controls have the "runat="server"" in the opening tag.
The values of fields I've entered are being replaced with default values on postback. What is the cause of this?	Check the code of the Page_Load that initializes the control values to make sure it tests the IsPostBack property. Otherwise, it will populate the controls with the default values.
I'm setting a session variable to the value of a control in the Page_Unload event, but it isn't getting initialized. Why is this?	If it is set to the value of a control, it should be done in a click event on the form. Setting the value in the Page_Unload event will not work because by the time the event fires, the controls no longer exist.

Separate User Interface Resources from Business Logic

Classic ASP pages contain a mix of HTML and server-side script, often with inline scripting inserted into the flow of the response to the browser. Except for the use of *Server-Side Includes* (separate files containing HTML) and scripts that are inserted into the ASP page, there is no way to separate the code from the interface content. Even in Includes, the code is modularized only to the extent that it doesn't require duplicating in each page, as it still is inserted into the flow of the HTML on the page and actually can make the code more difficult to read and debug.

ASP.NET has been built to fully enable the separation of code and interface content by using code-behind pages, user controls, and *components*. In this section, we will discuss code-behind pages; user controls and components will be addressed in Chapter 3.

Create and Use Code-Behind Pages

ASP.NET promotes the separation of code and interface elements through the use of script blocks and a more event-driven interface style than ASP. It also provides a method of completely separating the logic of the page in a code-behind page, which, as mentioned earlier, is a class file written in any of the supported .NET Framework languages (managed code). The code-behind page contains the logic to support the user interface, such as event handlers and other script blocks.

The ASP.NET page can be developed as a user interface file that contains server controls, HTML elements, and @ Page directives. The two files are linked to each other by setting an *Inherits* and *Src* attribute in the @ Page directive. Inherits specifies the class file to inherit from; Src, the path to the file. When the ASP.NET page is created, it inherits from the code-behind page specified in the directive; in turn, that inherits from the System.Web.UI.Page class. The ASP.NET page now includes the classes from the code-behind page.

on the
ὀ o b

You can use code-behind pages to allow people on a development team to develop in the language of each individual's choice, building the code in isolation from other team members. This enables one team member to create the interface while another is building the business logic without directly impacting one another.

The code-behind class file can contain one or more classes; each class can contain any number of public variables, functions, and subprocedures. They must be public so that the ASP.NET page can invoke them. Because a class file does not automatically import any namespaces, at a minimum it must import the System and System.Web namespaces from the .NET Framework. The structure of the class file is as follows:

```
Imports System
Imports System.Web
'Imports any other namespaces that are required for the logic

Public Class 'Classname
Inherits System.Web.UI.Page 'Required to integrate with the ASP.NET Page
'Public variable as variable_type
'Public Function FunctionName(parameters) As return_type
'function code
'End Function

End Class
```

Visual Studio .NET automatically creates a code-behind class for each ASP.NET page. It also sets the @ Page directives in the page and wires the class to handle event procedures in the Web Form. All the developer has to do is build the interface in the ASP.NET page, double-click the controls to open the class file, and write code to the events. The next exercise steps us through this process.

EXERCISE 1-5

Using Visual Studio to Implement Code-Behind Pages

This exercise uses Visual Studio to create and use a code-behind page for our Web Form:

1. Open the ASP.NET project in Visual Studio and add a new Web Form.

2. Navigate to the WebForm1.aspx file (click the WebForm1.aspx tab in the code window) and view the HTML.

3. Assign a method of Submit_Click to the OnClick event in the Submit button tag.

   ```
   <asp:Button id="Button1" runat="server" Text="Submit"
   OnClick="Submit_click"></asp:Button>
   ```

4. Create a Submit_Click subprocedure in the script block on the page, and add the code to create a session variable called "Name" and a redirect to WebForm2.aspx as shown here:

```
Sub Submit_Click (s as Object, e as EventArgs)
    Session("Name") = txtName.value
    'Note: Use the value property if the textbox is an
    'HTML server control or the text property if it's a
    'Web control.
    Response.Redirect ("WebForm2.aspx")
End Sub
```

5. Switch to WebForm2.aspx in design view (this is the new ASP.NET page we added).

6. Add a label Web control to the form and change its ID property to **lblGreeting**.

7. Double-click anywhere on the form. This opens the code-behind page for the Web Form (WebForm2.aspx.vb). Find the Page_Load event and add the following code to initialize the label from the session variable:

```
lblGreeting.Text = "Hello " & Session("Name")
```

8. Save all files and then build and browse from the File menu (or press CTRL-F8). The code-behind pages must be compiled into an assembly so you can build the project.

9. Enter your name in the Name textbox and click the Submit button. The page should redirect to WebForm2 and display "Hello *YourName*" in the label.

CERTIFICATION SUMMARY

In this chapter, we discussed building ASP.NET interfaces using Microsoft Visual Basic .NET. We first examined the .NET Framework architecture and how the Common Runtime Library manages code. We then explored the ASP.NET execution model to understand how ASP.NET processes Web pages. Additionally, we discovered the importance and use of directives, and how they relate to the .NET Framework and ASP.NET.

We then began building the interface by defining the nature and use of Web and HTML server controls, user controls, and HTML code in ASP.NET pages. We looked at how to write event code for the controls and how to implement navigation for the interface by managing view state, using the postback capability of Web Forms, managing the postback events, and using session state to handle data across pages. Finally, we separated interface elements from business logic on the pages by implementing code-behind pages.

✓ TWO-MINUTE DRILL

Add and Set Directives on ASP.NET Pages

❑ The .NET Framework enables the development of cross-platform applications in multiple languages, ensuring compatibility, stability, and security.

❑ The two main components of the .NET Framework are the Common Language Runtime (CLR), and the .NET Framework base class library.

❑ The Common Language Runtime is responsible for code execution and management within the .NET Framework.

❑ The .NET Framework class library is a collection of reusable classes that integrate with the CLR.

❑ Directives are instructions for specific conditions that must be set before or during the compilation of the source code.

Add HTML Server, Web Server, User Controls, and HTML Code to ASP.NET Pages

❑ Server controls are objects with methods, properties, and events that run on the server and can be accessed from server-side code placed in <script> sections on the page.

❑ Server controls automatically render client-specific HTML to the client browser, eliminating the need to query the client browser type and conditionally return client-specific HTML dependant upon the browser capabilities.

❑ ASP.NET code should be placed in <script> sections and must have both the language attribute and `runat="server"` set in the opening script tag.

❑ ASP.NET requires server controls event handlers to be assigned as a method name in the tag for the control.

❑ ASP.NET Web Forms without an action attribute will automatically post back to themselves.

Implement Navigation for the User Interface

❏ Each server control on a Web Form defines a hidden control called _VIEWSTATE that maintains the state of the call in a postback.

❏ To maintain data from page to page during the user's session, you can assign the data value to a session variable.

Separate User Interface Resources from Business Logic

❏ ASP.NET has been built to fully enable the separation of code and interface content by using code-behind pages.

SELF TEST

The following self test questions will help you measure your understanding of the material presented in this chapter. Read all the choices carefully as there might be more than one correct answer. Choose all correct answers for each question.

Add and Set Directives on ASP.NET Pages

1. The Common Language Runtime (CLR) supplies what functionality in the .NET Framework?

   A. The base classes

   B. Registration of COM components

   C. Management of code

   D. Web Forms

2. You want to ensure your Web Form will recognize only variables that have been declared. How do you do this?

   A. Put "Option Explicit" on the first line of code.

   B. You don't have to do anything as this is the default behavior in ASP.NET.

   C. Include in the @ Page directive: "Explicit=True".

   D. This feature is not available in ASP.NET.

3. What is the purpose of the Just-in-Time compiler (JITc)?

   A. Compiles the MSIL into native code specific to the computer on which it's being executed.

   B. Produces a portable executable file.

   C. Interprets the code on a line-by-line basis as needed.

   D. Produces the metadata.

4. Which Microsoft compilers are available that can produce managed code?

   A. JScript

   B. Visual Basic

   C. VBScript

   D. C#

5. What is the purpose of the Output cache?

   A. Holds the MSIL and metadata for the page, which are compiled to native code and executed when the user requests the page.

   B. Holds the page and data for subsequent requests from the user.

   C. Holds the assembly for the Web Form.

   D. Holds the page source code, which is compiled when requested by a client.

6. Which of the following statements is *incorrect* about assemblies?

   A. ASP.NET pages are contained in a dynamically created assembly.

   B. Assemblies can contain compiled code, PE files, and ASP.NET pages.

   C. Code must be contained in an assembly to be executed by the CLR.

   D. Only one version of an assembly can run at a time.

Add HTML Server, Web Server, User Controls, and HTML Code to ASP.NET Pages

7. ASP.NET pages are derived from what class?

   A. System.Data

   B. System

   C. System.UI.Web.Page

   D. System.Web

8. You are testing a Web Form built using HTML controls in Visual Studio .NET. When you fill in the fields and click the Submit button, the form is posted back but the contents of the controls clear. How would you fix this problem?

   A. Read the values of the form controls in the server code and post them back to the control values on the form.

   B. Initialize the values of the controls in the Page_Load event.

   C. Change the HTML controls to server controls by adding the `runat="server"` attribute to each control.

   D. Create hidden fields on the form and save the value of the controls to the hidden fields.

9. A Web Form contains a Web control with an ID of *lblCaption* and the following code. An error occurs when running the Web Form. What is the cause of the error?

    ```
    Dim objLabel as Label
    Set objLabel = lblCaption
    lblCaption.Text = "Welcome"
    ```

    A. *Label* is not a valid object.
    B. *Text* is not a valid property.
    C. *Set* is not a valid keyword.
    D. *Dim* is not a valid keyword.

10. Which is not a default namespace of a Web Form?

    A. System
    B. System.IO
    C. System.Collections
    D. System.Data

11. Which of the following statements is true of ActiveX controls in ASP.NET?

    A. They are not supported.
    B. They are supported.
    C. They are managed by the CLR.
    D. They are not managed by the CLR.

12. What is the order of events in the Page event life cycle?

    A. Page_Load, Page_Init, Change, Click, Page_Unload
    B. Page_Load, Page_Init, Click, Change, Page_Unload
    C. Page_Init, Page_Load, Click, Change, Page_Unload
    D. Page_Init, Page_Load, Change, Click, Page_Unload

13. You are designing a Web page that will need to display a variable number of items based on run-time conditions. What is the best approach to use when building the page?

    A. Create the expected maximum number of controls and use only those that will be required.
    B. Create the page with a set number of controls and resend the page with additional data.

    C. Use Web server controls and dynamically add the required controls at run time from the server code.

    D. Use inline coding on the server to dynamically add HTML <input> elements.

14. You are developing a Web page in Visual Studio .NET. When you attempt to add a Web control to the page, the Toolbox does not display the Web Forms tab. Why is this?

    A. You need to set your toolbox options from the Tools | Options menu.

    B. The toolbox properties need to be set to define the Web Form tab.

    C. You are in HTML view.

    D. The toolbox does not have a Web Forms tab.

15. Many of the Web pages you develop need to display the same interface elements. What is the best way of handling this situation in ASP.NET?

    A. Copy and paste the HTML and code into each page.

    B. Create an ActiveX control and use it in each page.

    C. Use a Server-Side Include.

    D. Create an ASP.NET user control and add it to each page.

16. You add a user control to a Web Form using the following code:

```
<MyControls:TestControl id="TestControl1" runat="server"
```

To use the control in the page, it must be registered. Which of the following would do this correctly, assuming the preceding code is correct?

    A.
```
<%@ Register TagPrefix="MyControls" TagName="TestControl"
Src="TestControl.ascx" %>
```

    B.
```
<%@ Register TagPrefix="TestControl" TagName=" MyControls"
Src="TestControl.ascx" %>
```

    C.
```
<%@ Register TagPrefix="MyControls" TagName="TestControl"
Src="TestControl.aspx" %>
```

    D.
```
<%@ Register TagPrefix="MyControls" TagName="TestControl" %>
```

Implement Navigation for the User Interface

17. You are building a secure Web application. Users must log on and, when validated, have access to sensitive, real-time financial data. Which approach to the session state and OutputCache should you use?

    A. None. Leave the session state timeout and OutputCache duration to their defaults.

    B. Increase the session timeout but leave the OutputCache duration at the default.

    C. Decrease the session timeout and set the OutputCache to expire immediately.

    D. Increase the session timeout and OutputCache duration.

18. You want to avoid having to code your page to return HTML that is specific to the user's browser capabilities. How should you do this?

    A. Use only HTML element tags.

    B. Use only HTML controls.

    C. Use only Web server controls.

    D. Use only HTML server controls.

Separate User Interface Resources from Business Logic

19. You are coding a class file to serve as a code-behind page. What must you include in the class file? (Choose all that apply.)

    A. Import the System and System.Web namespaces.

    B. Reference the Web Form.

    C. Inherit the System.Web.UI.Page class.

    D. Create private procedures as a method of the class.

20. When you test a Web Form with a code-behind page, you receive a parser error stating that the code-behind page is not a valid type. What would be the most likely cause of this error?

    A. The code-behind and Imports attributes are not set properly in the @ Page directive of the Web Form.

    B. The code-behind page does not import the System.Web.UI.Page namespace.

    C. The project was not built so the class is not compiled.

    D. The @ Page directives are not correct in the class file.

LAB QUESTION

You have decided to upgrade an existing ASP Web application to ASP.NET. The server-side script in the ASP pages is VBScript. There are some custom ActiveX controls on the pages and some pages use an ActiveX calendar control. The pages support multiple browser types and versions by redirecting to browser-specific pages.

Outline the changes that will be required to convert the .asp pages to .aspx. Explain changes that could be made but are not required.

SELF TEST ANSWERS

Add and Set Directives on ASP.NET Pages

1. ☑ C. The CLR handles code management.
   ☒ A is incorrect as the base classes are provided by the .NET Framework, B is wrong because COM components are unmanaged code and not handled by the CLR, and D is wrong because Web Forms are a base class.

2. ☑ C. In ASP.NET, this is done in the page directive.
   ☒ A is wrong as it is the ASP VBScript method. B is incorrect as Option Explicit defaults to false if not specified in the machine.config file or in the page directive. D is incorrect as the feature is available.

3. ☑ A. The JITc compiles MSIL and metadata into native code.
   ☒ B and D are incorrect. This is handled by the CLR prior to the JITc.
   C is incorrect.

4. ☑ A, B, and D. JScript, VB, and C# compilers are available for .NET.
   ☒ C. VBScript is not supported in ASP.NET.

5. ☑ B is correct. The OutputCache holds the compiled page for subsequent user requests.
   ☒ A is wrong as the MSIL and metadata are compiled by the JITc before being placed in the OutputCache. C is incorrect because this is done in the Gobal Assembly Cache, and D is just plain wrong.

6. ☑ D is the correct answer. One of the features of assemblies is that more than one version can run at a time.
   ☒ A, B, and C are all true about assemblies.

Add HTML Server, Web Server, User Controls, and HTML Code to ASP.NET Pages

7. ☑ C. System.UI.Web.Page is the base class for ASP.NET pages.
   ☒ A, B, and D are base classes for other objects.

8. ☑ C. By changing the HTML controls to server controls, the viewstate is maintained by the Web Form.
   ☒ A and D are redundant, and B would populate only the values on the first load.

9. ☑   C. Set is not valid in VB.NET.
    ☒   A, B, and D are valid.

10. ☑   D is correct because System.Data is used for ADO.NET and must be explicitly imported.

11. ☑   B and D are correct. ActiveX controls are supported by ASP.NET but are unmanaged code.
    ☒   A and C are incorrect.

12. ☑   D is correct. The page is initialized and then loaded. If any control Change events occur, they are stored until a control Click event occurs.
    ☒   A, B, and C are in the wrong order.

13. ☑   C is the best approach in ASP.NET. It is more manageable than the other choices.
    ☒   A, B, and D are all methods that could be used but are much more inefficient. A is ugly, B is annoying to the user, and D will result in browser-specific HTML and server code interspersed with HTML code.

14. ☑   C. You cannot add Web server controls from the HTML view. You need to switch to Design view in order to do this.
    ☒   A is incorrect. There are no settings for the toolbox. B is wrong as there are no toolbox properties. D is incorrect.

15. ☑   D is the best choice. This creates a component that is managed by the CLR.
    ☒   A, B, and C are all options but do take advantage of the ASP.NET environment.

16. ☑   A is correct. The TagPrefix is the namespace, in this case "MyControls," the TagName is the control name, which is "TestControl," and the Src is the control filename.

Implement Navigation for the User Interface

17. ☑   C is the best answer for this situation. By decreasing the session.timeout, you are saving resources on the server if the user abandons the session without logging out, and ensuring security in that if the user leaves the computer with the application still logged on, it will timeout quickly. By setting the OutputCache to expire immediately, you make sure that the user is getting real-time data.

18. ☑   C is correct. Web server controls will return browser-specific HTML.
    ☒   A, B, and C are wrong because they will return standard HTML.

Separate User Interface Resources from Business Logic

19. ☑ A and C are correct. You must import the system and system Web namespaces, and inherit the system.Web.UI.Page.

    ☒ B is incorrect. You do not reference the Web from a class file. D is wrong because procedures need to be public in the class.

20. ☑ C is correct. If the project is not built, the class file is not compiled into the assembly and will result in this error.

    ☒ A is incorrect because even if the Web form @ Page directives are not set, the Class file would still be valid. B is wrong because again the file would be valid, and D is wrong because there are no @ Page directives in a class file.

LAB ANSWER

The first required step is to change the file extensions of the ASP pages to .aspx. This will be identified as an ASP.NET page and will be handled by the .NET Framework.

Next, you will need to modify the directives on each page. Remove any Option Explicit statements on the page and add an @ Page directive to set the language to VB, and Explicit to true. Add any other directives that might be required. Remove the ASP directives.

Modify the syntax of the VBScript to conform to VB.NET syntax. This will require converting all error handling to the Try...Catch...Finally method. You will need to add parentheses around arguments in calls to subprocedures and functions (such as Response.Write) and fully qualify object property names in the code (no more default properties). Delete the Set from all object variable assignments.

Although these are basic steps, you still might get errors when testing the pages. If you are using any COM components that are apartment threaded (such as ADODB recordsets), you will also need to set the aspcomp attribute to true in the @ Page directive.

Other considerations could be to convert all HTML elements to HTML server controls or replace them with Web server intrinsic controls, replace any ActiveX controls with equivalent rich Web server controls (the Calendar controls, for example), and build ASP.NET custom controls to replace ActiveX custom controls. Using Web server controls would allow you to remove the browser specific code from the pages as the control will return browser-specific HTML.

MCAD/MCSD

MICROSOFT® CERTIFIED APPLICATION DEVELOPER
& MICROSOFT® CERTIFIED SOLUTION DEVELOPER

2

Create ASP.NET Pages: Enable the Interface

CERTIFICATION OBJECTIVES

C hapter 2 explores those features within ASP.NET that enable the developer to create a robust user interface. We will begin by discussing input validation and how the new Input Validation controls work in ASP.NET. Once validation is implemented, we will add error handling to the interface using exception handling, and error events on the pages and in the Global.asax. Additionally, we will learn how to incorporate online user assistance; then we'll discuss the various ways of incorporating existing code into our Web pages.

CERTIFICATION OBJECTIVE 2.01

Validate User Input

Validating user input is a requirement for any user interface, regardless of whether it is Web based. Due to the disconnected nature of the Web, input validation has been somewhat more limited than in standard Windows programming.

The Web user interface is running on the client browser with no direct connection to the server; therefore, when a user enters data into a form, it is much more efficient if the input validation can be done on the client side. If the input validation must be done on the server, the contents of the form controls first must be submitted to the server, then validated, and the response returned to the browser. This results in a request/response round trip, which increases traffic and degrades performance.

Client-side validation certainly is preferred, but the implementation can become complex, as the developer has to provide the client-side code supported by each user's browser. As different browser types and versions support different languages (or none at all) the developer must either choose the lowest common denominator or build pages that respond to each browser's capability.

For example, later versions of Microsoft's Internet Explorer browser support Jscript, VBScript, and DHTML; Netscape supports client-side JavaScript and DHTML, but not in the same way as IE—and even that depends on the specific version of Netscape being used. Some earlier browsers do not support any client-side scripting at all; therefore, all validation must be handled on the server. Most input validation on Web pages falls into specific types:

- **Required fields** The field has to contain a value.
- **Range checks** The field value must fall within a specific range.

■ **Comparison checks**   A field value must be identical to another field.

■ **Pattern checking**   The field value must conform to a specific pattern of characters such as a social security number or postal code.

Handling these validation checks generally requires quite a lot of coding, so ASP.NET provides a set of components that will handle the majority of validation requirements for most Web pages.

Using Input Validation Controls

As we have already seen, ASP.NET has addressed the browser capability issue by providing Web server controls that automatically return browser-specific HTML. To simplify the validation job, it also provides validation server controls, which offer a standard programming model for the developer, and automatically respond to the browser with browser-specific HTML and client-side code, if supported. If the browser does not support client-side validation, it is automatically performed on the server.

Table 2-1 lists the Input Validation controls provided by ASP.NET. These controls greatly simplify the validation process for the developer. Each control performs one specific type of validation, so you will often need to use two or more controls to validate one field. For example, a field might be required, but in addition, the input value must fall within a certain range, match a particular pattern, or compare in some way to another field's value.

TABLE 2-1   Types of Input Validation Controls

Control	Description
RequiredFieldValidator	Checks that the user has entered a value into a control.
RegularExpressionValidator	Checks user input against a pattern defined by a regular expression. This enables checking for an expected or required series of characters such as postal codes, telephone numbers, and so forth.
CompareValidator	Compares an input control to another input control or a fixed value. It can be used to verify a password, for example, or typed date and number comparisons.
RangeValidator	Checks that the input is between two fixed values or between the values of other input controls.
CustomValidator	Allows the programmer to write code to take part in the validation.

The controls other than the RequiredFieldValidator do not validate a blank field, so be sure to use the RequiredFieldValidator on all required fields in addition to any other validation controls that might be required. If this is not done, the field will validate successfully with a blank value.

Add Input Validation Controls to a Page

The standard HTML syntax for adding validation controls to a page is as follows:

```
<asp:validator_control id="validator_control_id" runat="server"
ControlToValidate="control_id"
ErrorMessage"error_message_text"
display="static/dynamic/none"
</asp:validator_control>
```

The following properties are common to all input validation controls:

- ControlToValidate property is the ID of the control to be validated.

- ErrorMessage is the error message string that will be displayed if the input is invalid.

- Display determines whether the validation control will take up a fixed space on the page even if no error message is displayed, or dynamically move other controls when a message is displayed.

In addition, each type of validation control has properties specific to its function.

RequiredFieldValidator Control   The RequiredFieldValidator control ensures that a field has a value. It requires only the ControlToValidate and errorMessage properties to accomplish this. The following code uses a RequiredFieldValidator to ensure the password is entered:

```
<asp:TextBox id="txtPassword" runat="server"
TextMode="Password"></asp:TextBox>
<asp:RequiredFieldValidator id="PasswordRequiredFieldValidator"
runat="server"
ErrorMessage="Password is required"
ControlToValidate="txtPassword">
</asp:RequiredFieldValidator>
```

RangeValidator Control   The RangeValidator ensures that the field value falls within a specified range. In addition to the common validation properties, it requires three additional properties: MinimumValue, MaximumValue, and Type. The following example tests the range of the txtLoanAmount and checks that it is between $5,000 and $50,000:

```
<asp:TextBox id="txtLoanAmount" runat="server"></asp:TextBox>
<asp:RangeValidator id="LoanRangeValidator"
 runat="server"
 ErrorMessage="Loan amount must be between $5,000 and $50,000"
 ControlToValidate="txtLoanAmount"
 MaximumValue="50000"
 MinimumValue="5000"
 Type="Currency">
</asp:RangeValidator>
```

CompareValidator Control   The CompareValidator tests the value of one control against another or tests a control value against a specific value. To test a value, you set the ValueToCompare and Type properties; to test a control value, you set the ControlToCompare property. In either case you must set the Operator property to define the operation. The Operator property defaults to *Equal*. The next example validates that txtIncome is over $15,000:

```
<asp:TextBox id="txtIncome" runat="server"></asp:TextBox>
<asp:CompareValidator id="IncomeCompareValidator" runat="server"
 ErrorMessage="Income must be greater than $15,000"
 ControlToValidate="txtIncome"
 Type="Double"
 ValueToCompare="15000"
 Operator="GreaterThanEqual">
</asp:CompareValidator>
```

RegularExpressionValidator Control   The RegularExpressionValidator control checks that a control value matches a specific pattern. It requires the ValidationExpession property to be set using a regular expression. The following code checks for a valid Canadian Social Insurance Number (SIN):

```
<asp:textbox id="txtSIN" runat="server"></asp:textbox>
<asp:RegularExpressionValidator
id="SINRegularExpressionValidator"
 runat="server"
```

```
ErrorMessage="Not a Valid Social Insurance Number"
ControlToValidate="txtSIN"
ValidationExpression="\d{3}-\d{3}-\d{3}">
</asp:RegularExpressionValidator>
```

A *regular expression* is a string of symbols that represents a pattern of characters. In case you are not familiar with regular expressions, Visual Studio supplies you with a limited list of standard expressions in the ValidationExpression property in the properties window for ZIP codes, European Postal Codes and phone numbers, U.S. Social Security Numbers and phone numbers, and so forth. Table 2-2 lists the basic characters used in regular expressions. Check under "Regular Expression Syntax" in the Visual Studio.NET help for a full description of the characters.

exam
Ⓦatch
Be sure to be familiar with the specific properties for each of the validation controls—for example, which properties are required to compare values from one control to another. Be prepared to identify the correct property settings in a code listing for each specific validation type.

| TABLE 2-2 | Common Characters Used in Regular Expressions |

Character	Definition
a	Literal value. Must use the letter *a* in lower case. Any letter that is not preceded by a backslash (\) or part of a range is a requirement for that literal value.
1	Literal value. Must use the number 1. Any number that is not preceded by a backslash (\) or part of a range is a requirement for that literal value.
?	0 or 1 item.
*	0 to N items.
+	1 to N items (at least 1).
[0-n]	Integer value range from 0 to n.
{n}	Length must be *n* characters.
|	Separates multiple valid patterns.
\	The following character is a command character.
\w	Must have a character.
\d	Must have a digit.
\.	Must have a period.

CustomValidator Control   The standard validation controls can handle most validation needs; however, custom validation is still necessary. For example, some values such as credit card numbers, driver license numbers, and so forth can be validated by applying an algorithm that verifies their authenticity. When a CustomValidator control is used, the code always runs on the server; therefore, it is not returned in client-side script that the user can view. The CustomValidator control is similar to the other validation controls, except the programmer must write an event handler for OnServerValidate to handle the validation. The following code validates that a password is between six and ten characters:

```
<form id="Form1" method="post" runat="server">
<asp:TextBox id="txtPassword" runat="server"
 TextMode="Password"></asp:TextBox>
<asp:CustomValidator id="CustomValidator1" runat="server"
 ErrorMessage="Password must be 6 to 10 characters"
 ControlToValidate="txtPassword"

OnServerValidate="ValidatePasswordLength"></asp:CustomValidator>
</form>
<script runat="server">
     Sub ValidatePasswordLength(ByVal source As System.Object, _
     & ByVal args As_
System.Web.UI.WebControls.ServerValidateEventArgs)
          If Len(args.Value) <= 6 Or Len(args.Value) > 10 Then
               args.IsValid = False
          Else
               args.IsValid = True
          End If
     End Sub
</script>
```

Now that we've looked at each of the validation controls; let's build a simple Web input form in Visual Studio and add the required validation using the validation controls.

on the **!** job

Be careful to test the validation controls in various browsers. Although they will return browser-specific content that will function, the rendering of the controls in some browsers can result in overlapping and misplaced controls on the interface. Be especially careful when using the grid layout in Visual Studio if the target browsers include those other than Internet Explorer.

┌───┐
│ 🔲 WebForm1 - Microsoft Internet Explorer   _ □ ✕   │
│ File   Edit   View   Favorites   Tools   Help   │
│ ⬅ Back ▾ ⇨ ▾ ⊗ ⌕ ⌂ │ ⬚Search ⬚Favorites ⬚Media ⬚ ⬚▾ ⬚ » │
│ Address 🔲 http://localhost/Chapter2/Excercise1.aspx ▾ ⬚ Go │ Links » │
│   │
│   FirstName   [   ]   │
│   │
│   LastName   [   ]   │
│   │
│   Email   [   ]   │
│   │
│   Phone Number   [   ]   │
│   │
│   Age   [   ]   │
│   │
│   UserName   [   ]   │
│   │
│   Password   [   ]   │
│   Confirm Password   [   ]   │
│   │
│   [Submit   ]   │
│   │
│ 🔲 Done   🔲 Local intranet   │
└───┘

Add Validation Controls

This exercise will demonstrate the use of validation controls on a simple Web Form that could be used to gather new account information from a user.

1. Open a new project in Visual Studio named "Chapter 2" with a Web Form called "Exercise1.aspx." Using the Web server controls, build the form to resemble Figure 2-1. Name each of the text boxes to describe the content, such as **txtFirstName**, **txtLastName**, and so forth.

2. For our purposes, the name fields, username, and password information are required. E-mail, phone number, and age are optional. For each

required field add a RequiredFieldValidator control beside the field. Set the controlToValidate and errorMessage properties appropriately for each validation control; for example, the first validation control should set controlToValidate to "txtFirstName" and the errorMessage to "First Name" as a required field.

3. Save and test the page. If you click the Submit button without entering a value in any of the required fields, the errorMessage will display in the RequiredFieldValidator control for that field.

4. The password and confirm password fields must be identical. To validate this, add a CompareValidator control below txtConfirmPassword. Set the ControlToValidate property to "txtConfirmPassword" and ControlToCompare to "txtPassword." Add an errorMessage to the control. Notice that, by default, the Type property is set to "String" and Operator to "Equal."

5. Save and test the page again. This time enter different values in the Password and Confirm Password fields, and notice the result.

6. Although age is not a required field, if it is entered, it must be greater than 0. Add another CompareValidator beside the age field. Set the errorMessage property to display "Age must be greater than zero." Set the ControlToValidate to txtAge, the ValueToCompare to 0, and the Operator to "Greater Than." This control now will compare the value of txtAge to 0 and display the error message if it's less than 1.

7. The final two fields, e-mail and phone number, are not required, but if entered, should conform to a specific pattern. We will use the RegularExpressionValidator control to test their validity and, to keep it simple for the exercise, validate the phone numbers for North American format. Add two RegularExpressionValidator controls beside each of the input controls. Change the errorMessage and ControlToValidate properties to match the field that is being validated. Click the ellipsis button for the ValidationExpression property and choose "Internet e-mail Address" for the e-mail and "U.S. Phone Number" for the phone number.

8. Save and test the page. Each field should be validated properly. Your results should be similar to this:

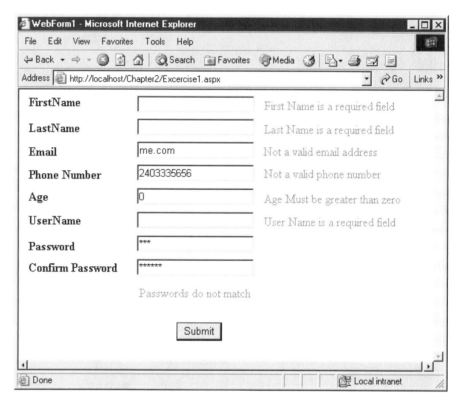

9. View the source HTML from the browser. Notice the client-side code that has been generated by the controls (assuming you are using a browser that supports it).

Adding validation controls is a relatively simple task in Visual Studio, and there are controls that can handle most of your validation needs. Remember that multiple validations on the same controls will require multiple validation controls.

Validate the Page

Before executing server-side logic, it is necessary to ensure that all controls on the page are validated, even if the client browser supports client-side validation. There are basically two reasons for this; the most obvious is that you might need to compare input to stored values such as passwords or values in a database and only the server-side code can access these values. The second reason is that the user could bypass the input validation on the client side and return nonvalidated values—or worse yet, include values as code that could access or damage data on the server.

Server-side Validation

Client-side validation controls run on the browser if the browser supports client-side scripting. All input validation controls are repeated on the server even if they are run on the browser. This avoids the situation where users might try to bypass the client-side validation and input invalid values. If a user changes or disables the client script that validates the input, they are then able to input values that are not valid. It might be possible for the user to then submit code in the control value that could access data on the server or cause some other damage. To further prevent this possibility, do not rely on client-side validation alone. Use the Page.IsValid property before continuing with any logic that requires validation to ensure that the validation is correct.

Validation controls can be used exclusively on the server side by setting the *EnableClientScript* property of the validation control to false. This will force the validation to be handled only on the server while still enjoying the ease and functionality of the validation controls. This approach is necessary when the validation requires a comparison with stored values such as passwords or specific lookups in a database.

The Page.IsValid Property

The simplest way to determine that all validations are successfully completed is to test the Page.IsValid property. This can be handled in the button click event handler for the form. If it is true, the code can proceed with the business logic, as shown here:

```
Sub submit(s As Object, e As EventArgs)
    If Page.IsValid = True then
        'Continue with the logic
    End If
End Sub
```

If the page is not valid, you could redirect to an error page, Response.Write an error string back to the client, or simply refuse the field values and post the form back to the user.

The Validation Summary Control

Each of the validation controls on the page will display a message when an error is input. Depending on the number of validations and the layout of the page, sometimes it is more efficient to contain all these errors in one area; for example, at the top or bottom of the page. The Validation Summary control will display all ErrorMessage properties from the validation controls in a list at the location of the summary control; the individual validation controls will not display their ErrorMessages.

To display a message in each validation control, set the text property of each control. The text property will be displayed at the validation control location, replacing the ErrorMessage. For example, setting the text property to "*" for a control will display the * in the validation control itself while the control's ErrorMessage will be displayed in the Summary controls list.

on the
()ob

The Validation Summary control does not have a display property that can be set to dynamic. Depending on the number of potential errors that could occur on the page, the list could be quite long. If the control is placed at the top of the page, you must ensure there is enough room to display the full list without overlapping other controls. This means it will require a fairly large blank area at the top of the form to accommodate the control; therefore, for aesthetic reasons, it probably would be better to place it at the bottom of the page.

EXERCISE 2-2

CertCam 2-02

Using the Validation Summary Control

This exercise will use the Validation Summary control to display the ErrorMessage properties from all validation controls on the page. Your result should be similar to Figure 2-2.

1. Open the project from the previous exercise and add a Validation Summary control on the right side of the page.

2. Set the HeaderText property to "The following errors occurred:", and ensure that ShowSummary is set to True, and DisplayMode is set to BulletList.

3. Save and test the page. Notice that the summary control displays the error messages from the validation controls, but each control still displays its own message.

4. Change the Display property of all the validation controls to None. Test the page.

5. Add an "*" to the text property of all the validation controls; test the page again.

6. Set the ShowMessageBox property on the ValidationSummary control to True and test the page again.

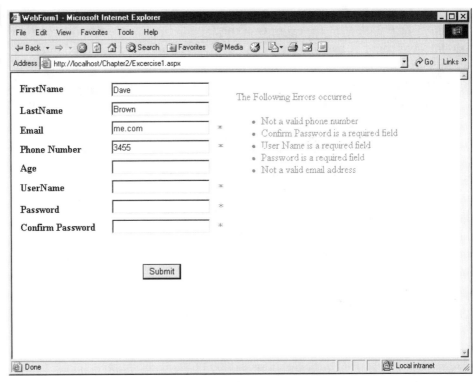

FIGURE 2-2

The ValidationSummary control error messages

FROM THE CLASSROOM

Why Input Validation Controls?

In recent years, there has been an explosion of activity from governments, banks, and other organizations to implement services on the Web. You can submit applications online for loans, credit cards, fishing licenses, and all manner of services. However, one of the main issues for these types of Web applications is input validation. Most fields on the form need to be validated in some manner; and if support by the browser, the majority of the validations could be handled on the client without requiring any interaction with the server until the form is posted.

Think of any application form you fill out—on or off the Web. How many fields are mandatory? How many fields are mandatory dependent on values in other fields? For example, if you check the employed field, you will need to enter employment information, if you check the married field, the spouse's information is required, and so forth. How many fields are required to be of a certain pattern, such as Social Security numbers,

telephone numbers, and so forth? If you have done this on the Web, how many times has the page taken time to submit your form to the server and then returned with a list of input errors for you to correct?

The best user experience happens when the validation is done on the browser and feedback is immediate; if you TAB away from a required field, you are immediately warned, if you enter an invalid number, the control will not accept it. Implementing this kind of functionality requires writing code to determine whether or how the browser supports that functionality and then returning the appropriate client-side code for the user's browser type (JavaScript, DHTML, and so forth) to do the job. If it is not supported by the browser, it all must be handled on the server.

ASP.NET validation controls greatly simplify this process, providing a browser-independent implementation of validation logic for Web Forms.

—David Shapton, MCSD, MCT, CTT+

SCENARIO & SOLUTION

How do I test for a required input and a range check on a field?	Use both a RequiredFieldValidator and a RangeValidator control for the field.
How do I validate a field value based on the value on another field?	Use the CompareValidator control. Set the ControlToCompare to the field value you are checking and the Operator to specify the condition.
None of the validation controls fit the type of validation I need to do. How do I handle this?	Use the CustomValidator control and code the logic for your validation in an event handler triggered by the OnServerValidate event.
How do I pop up a message box to notify the user that there are input errors?	Use a ValidationSummary control and set the ShowMessageBox property to true.

CERTIFICATION OBJECTIVE 2.02

Implement Error Handling in the User Interface

Error handling in a Web application generally serves two purposes: to catch bugs in the application code and handle exceptions (errors) that might occur at run time. With proper design and input validation checking, most potential errors should be avoided and any bugs in the code should be addressed in the testing phase.

However, errors can occur at run time even with well-designed and bug-free code. As an example, server-side code accessing a database will throw an exception if a connection to the data server cannot be established for any reason. If an exception is not explicitly handled in code, ASP.NET will force the application to terminate and display an error page. Unfortunately, although this error page might be of great use to the developer, it's likely to be confusing to the user.

To implement error handling in our application, we need to understand how to use *structured exception handling* to respond to errors as they occur, configure custom error pages that are friendly to the user, and use the error events at the page and application level.

Structured Exception Handling

ASP developers will be familiar with the *Error* object and the *On Error Resume Next* syntax. The process is relatively simple but laborious, requiring the code to check whether an error occurred at every step. If this is not done for each line of code that could result in an error, you run the risk that the error will be ignored and the code will continue executing. For example,

```
<%
On Error Resume Next 'Sets the error trapping to ignore any errors and
                     'Continues with execution.
Object1.BadMethod     'An error will occur on this line
If Error.Number <> 0 Then
   Response.Write ("An error occurred")
   Response.End       'Checks to see if an error occurred and sends a
                       response
                      'to the user notifying them of the problem
End If
Object2.BadMethod     'Causes another error which should be checked.
%>                     'As we don't check for the error the code continues
                       'to execute and the error is ignored.
```

In ASP.NET, all languages used follow the CLR specification and all use structured exception handling. Structured exception handling forces the programmer to deal with exceptions as they occur using *try-catch-finally* blocks, which results in more robust error trapping. This approach to error handling places the code into a try block, followed by a catch block that will contain additional code to manage any errors that may occur. The finally block consists of code that will execute after the try block is finished regardless of whether any errors occurred. The following is the VB.NET method using try-catch-finally blocks to handle exceptions:

```
<Script runat="server"

Public sub Page_Load (s as object, e as EventArgs)
    Try
         'Code that could cause an error
    Catch
         'Code to manage the error
    Finally
         'Code that will run after the Try block is finished
         'regardless of whether an error occurred
    End Try
End Sub
```

Using try-catch-finally blocks provides management of the error in the Catch block, which allows a method of potentially handling the error. Exceptions are grouped hierarchically starting with the System.Exception base class. There are more than sixty derived classes beneath System.systemexception. Each class includes exceptions of a specific type, such as System.ArithmeticException, System.Data.DataException, and so forth.

As you move down the hierarchy, the exceptions become more specific—for example, System.ArithmeticException includes System.DivideByZeroException, System.NotFiniteNumberException, and System.OverFlowException. To identify a specific exception, you code the catch block to catch only that exception. To test for multiple exceptions, you must include multiple catch blocks. For example:

```
Catch objEx as ArithmeticException
```

This code will catch an arithmetic exception of any of the three subclasses. To specifically catch and respond to each one, you would have to code the following:

```
Catch objEx as DivideByZeroException
    Response.Write("Divide by Zero error")
Catch objEx as OverFlowException
    Response.Write("OverFlow")
Catch objEx as NotFiniteNumber
    Response.Write("Not a finite number")
```

When catching exceptions, it is important to order the catch statements from the most specific to least specific. In the preceding example, if the catch for the ArithmeticException is coded first, it would always catch that and never drop down to the specific exception such as the DivideByZeroException. Code the catch block to handle each specific exception you want to deal with and then follow with a catch to get anything else that might occur.

exam

ⓦatch

Expect multiple questions about either exceptions or exception handling. Be familiar with the more common exceptions, which are more likely to be handled, such as System.Data.DataExceptions

The exception class provides the following objects that can be used to evaluate and manage the specific exception that was thrown:

Object	Description
InnerException	Gets the Exception instance that caused the current exception.
Message	Gets a message that describes the current exception.
Source	Gets or sets the name of the application, or the object that causes the error.
StackTrace	Gets a string representation of the frames on the call stack at the time the current exception was thrown.
TargetSite	Gets the method that throws the current exception.

Wrapping all your code in try-catch-finally blocks is a lot of work to handle all possible exceptions that could occur. It makes sense to do this around the code that is attempting a specific function, such as establishing a connection to a data server, as you could expect an error to occur if the connection is not successful and possibly recover from it.

However, exceptions caused by abnormal situations, such as a server crash, can be totally unexpected. It would be unreasonable to have to write exception blocks around all code to handle such an occurrence, or for every eventuality that might occur. For this reason, ASP.NET enables us to handle errors in events that will be fired at the page, or the application level if an unhandled exception occurs. These include the Page_Error event in the .aspx file and the Application_Error event in the Global.asax file.

Implement Global.asax, Application, Page-level, and Page Event Error Handling

The Page_Error Event

The Page_Error event can be used to respond to unhandled exceptions (those not in try-catch-finally blocks) that occur at the page level. This feature allows the programmer to respond to any errors that occur on the page from one block of event code, which can either display specific information about the error or redirect to a user-friendly error page.

EXERCISE 2-3

Using the Page_Error Event

In this exercise, we will cause an error by throwing an exception in the Page_Load event and code the Page_Error event to handle the error, first by responding with specific information and then by redirecting to a specific error page.

1. Add a new Web form to the Chapter 2 project.

2. Remove all the @Page directives except for *Language="vb"*, as we will not be using a code-behind page.

3. Add a Page_Load event with the following code to throw an exception:

```
Public sub Page_Load (s as object,e as EventArgs)
    Throw New System.Exception("An error has occurred")
End Sub
```

This forces an error of our making to test the error handling.

4. Save and view the page in the browser. The result will be a detailed error page with a description, exception details, source code for the error, the source file name and line number of the error, and a stack trace. The resulting error page should be like this:

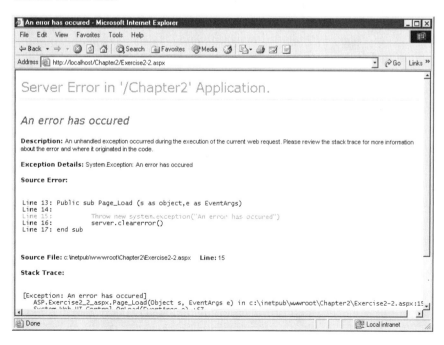

5. If you have the capability, view the page from a client browser on another machine. The remote error page (viewed from a client browser; not on the Web server) contains different information and should look like the following illustration. The content of this page is dependent on the settings in Web.Config, which we will reconfigure later to present different information.

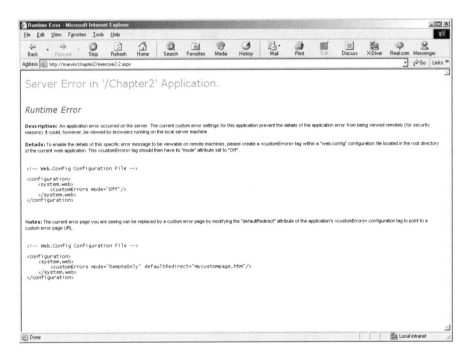

6. Now that we've generated a page error, we can code the Page_Error event to respond to the error. Create a Page_Error event and add the following code:

```
Public Sub Page_Error(s as Object,e as EventArgs)
    Dim objError as Exception objError = Server.GetLastError
    Response.Write("Error in " & Request.Url.ToString() & _
            "<br>" & objError.Message.ToString()" & _
            " & objError.StackTrace())
    Server.ClearError
End Sub
```

The first line of the code declares objError and initializes it to the error. A response then is returned to the browser containing the page that caused the error, the error message, and a stack trace. The Server.ClearError clears the error and prevents it from cascading on to the Application_Error event in the Global.asax.

7. Save and test the page. The result is a custom response that overrides the default error page from ASP.NET and displays the URL, error message, and stack trace.

8. From the menu, choose Project | Add HTML Page... and name it **Error.htm**. Add the following HTML to the page (the body tags should already be in the file):

```
<body>
<h1>An error has occurred</h1>
</body>
```

9. Comment out or delete all the code in the Page_Error event and add this:

```
Response.Redirect("Error.htm")
```

Save and test the page. The error page should be displayed.

Error messages to users should be kept as simple as possible. It's great to have detailed information for debugging purposes but a user will generally get confused or annoyed when presented with source code, stack traces, and so forth. The last step of the exercise presents a simple error page that communicates to the user that an error has occurred without overloading him or her with information.

The Application_Error Event

The Application_Error event allows the developer to trap errors that occur in the application. The Application_Error event is an event of the *Global.asax* file. Due to its applicationwide scope (hence the name "Global"), it can record error information in the Windows event log or send an e-mail to notify an administrator of a critical exception in the application. In addition, the user can be notified of the error either by redirecting to an error page or by using *Response.Write* to respond with the exception information directly to the browser.

The Gobal.asax file is created automatically in the ASP.NET project when using Visual Studio.NET. The file contains a public class called "Global" that inherits the System.Web.HttpApplication namespace. The Global.asax imports both the SystemWeb and SystemWeb.SessionState namespaces. The Global class implements the following application-level events:

- **Application_Start**   Fires when the application is started (when the first request is received from the first user after the application is deployed). This can be used to initialize values in application variables, such as a hit counter that was saved before the Web application was shut down.

- **Session_Start**   Occurs when each session starts. This can be used to initialize session variables.

- **Application_Begin request**   Fires at the beginning of each request.

- **Application_Authenticate request**   Fires when attempting to authenticate the user.

- **Application_Error**   Fires when an unhandled exception occurs in the application.

- **Application_End**   Fires when the application is shut down. This can be used to persistently store application variable values to a file or database; for example, a hit counter value to be stored when the application is shut down and retrieved when the application is started again.

Write Errors to the Windows Event Log   We use the Application_Error event of the Global.asax to handle application-level errors and write the details out to the Windows Event Log. To write to the event log, we need to import the System.Diagnostics namespace. This namespace includes classes that allow you to interact with system processes, event logs, and performance counters. In this case, we will need only the classes for event logs.

The next table enumerates the basic classes required to manipulate the event log. See the .NET SDK documentation for a full listing of all classes in the System.Diagnostics namespace.

Class	Description
EntryWrittenEventArgs	Provides data for the EntryWritten event.
EventLog	Provides the Windows event logs object.
EventLogEntry	Defines a single record in the event log.
EventLogEntryCollection	Defines size and enumerators for a collection of EventLogEntry instances.
EventLogInstaller	Enables the user to install and configure a specific event log that the application can read from or write to. This class is called by the installation utility—for example, InstallUtil.exe—when installing an event log.

The Global.asax file is a class; therefore, you will need to build the project after each change in the code.

EXERCISE 2-4

Using the Application_Error Event to Write to the Windows Event Log

In this exercise, we will trap errors in the Application_Error event in the Global.asax, and write error information to the Application log.

1. Comment out the previous code in the Page_Error event on the page from the previous exercise.

2. Open the Glogal.asax file in Visual Studio and view code for the page. Add the following statement to the top of the file before the class definition:

```
Imports System.Diagnostics
```

This is required to use the event log.

3. Add the following code to the Application_Error event:

```
Sub Application_Error(ByVal sender As Object, ByVal e As EventArgs)
    Dim strmessage As String = Request.Path & " Error " & _
```

```
                    Server.GetLastError.ToString()
            Dim oLog As New EventLog()
            oLog.Source = "Application"
            oLog.WriteEntry(strmessage, EventLogEntryType.Error)
            Server.ClearError()
            Response.Redirect("Error.htm")
        End Sub
```

Let's take a moment to step through the code to understand what it's doing. The first line declares a message string variable, and initializes it to the page name that caused the error (Request.Path) and the error that occurred (Server.GetLastError.ToString). The second line instantiates a new EventLog object as oLog and the third line sets its source property to "Application." Line 4 calls the WriteEntry method passing strMessage and specifying that it is an entry type of error. This inserts the message into the Application event log. The last two lines clear the error and redirect the user to the error page created earlier.

4. Save the files, and build and view the page. The error.htm page will be displayed in the browser.

Open the event viewer and click the application log. The last error in the log should be the application error. Figure 2-3 shows the event viewer with the error log. Double click the error and view the details. Figure 2-4 displays the details of the error.

Send E-mail in Response to an Error   In addition to writing an entry in the application log, we can send automatic e-mails to people requiring notification of application errors. Not all errors would necessarily result in an e-mail; only those severe enough to warrant immediate notification.

E-mails can be easily handled using classes in the System.Web.Mail namespace and some simple code. You must have a valid SMTP server; either on the localhost or available from another server. If the SMTP server is on another server, you must set the *Smtp.SmtpServer* property in the code to a valid SMTP server. The following exercise will step through the process of sending e-mail in response to an exception. If you don't have an SMTP server available, you will not be able to test the result.

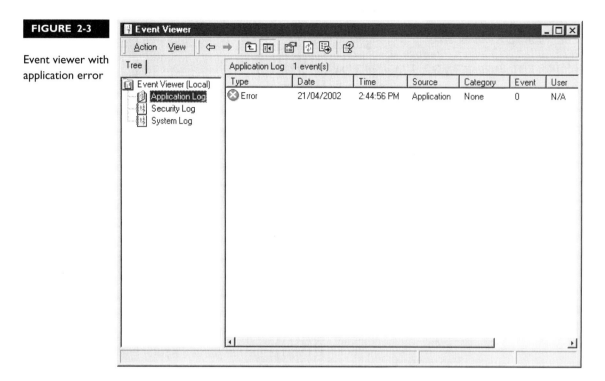

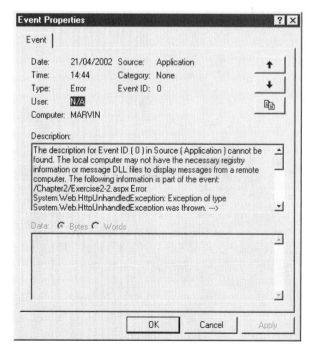

Using the Application_Error Event to Send E-Mail

We will now add e-mail support to an application. This exercise assumes you have SMTP available on localhost.

1. Add the following code to the Application_Error event in Global.asax:

```
Dim ErrMessage As New MailMessage()
ErrMessage.To = admin@mycompany.com
ErrMessage.From = "Chapter Two Error Test Application"
ErrMessage.Subject = "Critical Application Error " & _
                          Request.Path
ErrMessage.Body = Request.Path & vbCrLf & _
Server.GetLastError.ToString()
SmtpMail.Send(ErrMessage)
```

Change the errMessage.To property to your e-mail. You can obviously add any other information you might require in the body of the message.

2. Make sure that the file imports the System.Web.Mail namespace.

3. Save the file, build, and test.

Configure Custom Error Pages

We have already determined that if no exception handling is implemented, ASP.NET's default behavior is to display an error page and terminate the page. If errors are handled in Try-Catch-Finally blocks, or by using the page or application error events, we can either display our own error information or redirect to a custom error page. If a call to Server.ClearError is not made in the error code, or the error is not trapped in a Page_Error or Application_Error event, ASP.NET handles the error according to settings in the Web.config file.

The Web.config file contains the configuration information for ASP.NET resources. The file is a nested hierarchy of XML tags and subtags with attributes for the configuration settings. A sample Web.config file with default settings created by Visual Studio.NET is shown next.

```
<?xml version="1.0" encoding="utf-8" ?>
        <configuration>
        <system.web>
        <compilation defaultLanguage="vb" debug="true" />
        <customErrors mode="RemoteOnly" />
        <authentication mode="Windows" />
        <authorization>
        <allow users="*" /> <!-- Allow all users -->
        </authorization>
        <tr_'0e en_u98 ?led="false" requestLimit="10"
         pageOutput="false"
         tr_'0eMode="SortByTime" localOnly="true" />
        <sessionState mode="InProc" cookieless="false"
         timeout="20"/>
        <globalization requestEncoding="utf-8"
         responseEncoding="utf-8" />
        </system.web>
        </configuration>
```

exam
Ⓦatch

*Be sure to be familiar with all sections of Web.config before writing the exam.
This chapter deals with only the customErrors section of the Web.config file,
but other sections of the file are discussed throughout the book.*

The <customErrors> section of the file contains the attributes that establish the
behavior when errors are encountered. It has one required attribute, mode, which
can have one of three settings:

- **On**   Enables custom errors. Redirects to the custom error page if specified
  in the *defaultRedirect* attribute. Used mainly in production.

- **Off**   Disables custom errors. This allows display of detailed errors and does
  not redirect to a custom error page. Used mainly in development.

- **RemoteOnly**   Custom error specified in the *defaultRedirect* attribute is
  shown to remote clients. Users accessing the site from the local host are
  shown the exception information. This is the default and is used mainly
  for debugging.

The optional attribute defaultRedirect is available to specify a custom error page.
This can be an .aspx or .htm file. Whether it is displayed in response to an error is
dependent on the mode attribute setting.

Additional <error> child elements also can be specified within the <customErrors> element to specify a redirect for a specific HTML error. The <error> element has two optional attributes:

■ **StatusCode** Specifies the HTML status code that will trigger a redirect to the error page.

■ **Redirect** Specifies the error page to which to redirect.

The following example specifies the custom error page as Errors.htm. The mode is on; therefore, it will always use the custom error page unless the error is "HTML 404 File Not Found," in which case it will redirect to a custom FileNotFound.aspx page.

```
<customErrors defaultRedirect="Error.htm" mode="On">
    <error statusCode="404" redirect="FileNotFound.aspx" />
</customErrors>
```

The FileNotFound.aspx page could be designed to be a smart page; for example, it could notify the user of the error and display a list of valid pages as hyperlinks from which the user could choose.

on the *job* *When testing the application, it's a good idea to set the customErrors mode to remote and provide a defaultRedirect page. The details of the errors should be either written out to the Windows event log or a custom event log. This gives you an accurate record of the errors that occurred but your users don't get overwhelmed with error details.*

EXERCISE 2-6

Configure Custom Error Pages

In this exercise, we will explore the different configurations available in Web.config.

1. In Visual Studio, open the project from the previous exercise.

2. Make sure the Server.ClearError and Response.Redirect("Error.htm") lines of code in the Page_Error and Application_Error events are commented out.

3. Create a new Web form called FileNotFound.aspx and insert the following code:

```
<body>
<h1>FileNotFound in Response to HTML 404
 Statuscode</h1><br>
<%response.write(request.path)%>
</body>
```

Save the file.

4. In the Solution Explorer, double click the Web.config file, find the `<customErrors>` element in the file, and add the following:

```
<customErrors defaultRedirect="Error.htm" mode="On">
<error statusCode="404"
redirect="FileNotFound.aspx" />
</customErrors>
```

5. Save all files and build the project. Test the file by viewing the page in the browser. You should get the custom page *Error.htm*. Enter a misspelled page name in the URL; you should get the custom page FileNotFound.aspx.

6. Experiment by changing the mode attribute and testing the page from both the server and a remote client (if possible).

Now that we have covered error handling, let's look at some typical scenarios and solutions concerning errors.

SCENARIO & SOLUTION

Why is my code in the Application_Error event not executing in response to an error?	If the error that is occurring is trapped in exception handling code or in a Page_Error event that calls Server.ClearError, it will not cascade to the Application_Error event. If this is not the case, make sure you build the project before testing, as the Global.asax is a class file and must be compiled.
I am getting build errors when attempting to test Application_Event code that writes to the Windows Event Log. What should I do?	Make sure that the Global.asax imports the System.Diagnostics namespace. This is not a default in the file and must be added.
The custom error page (defaultRedirect) specified in the Web.config file `<customErrors>` section is not displaying either on the server or client. What should I do?	Set the `<customErrors mode="On">`. Make sure the O is capitalized, as it is case sensitive.

CERTIFICATION OBJECTIVE 2.03

Implement Online User Assistance

A user-friendly interface should always provide some kind of help option. A well-designed application usually will include immediate feedback features and a context-sensitive help environment that provides assistance to the user on demand. In most windows applications, this is a relatively simple process to implement.

Due to the nature of the Request/Response model Web applications cannot respond immediately with context-sensitive help. To implement more extensive online help requires adding controls such as buttons or hyperlinks to the page which, when clicked, open a help page. The cleanest method for this is to use client-side JavaScript to open a new browser window that displays the help page. When this method is used, the user can read the help while still viewing the page, then close the window and return to the main page, whereas using a standard hyperlink would replace the current page in the browser with the help page and require navigation back to that page. ASP.NET provides no way to code a pop-up window; it must be handled by client-side script.

ASP.NET's Web server controls include ToolTip properties that will automatically pop up text when the user moves the mouse over the control. This feature can provide immediate feedback or simple instructions to the user. We will implement JavaScript code to display help in a new browser window and tool tips on the Web page we completed in Exercise 2-2. This page used validation controls to validate user input and a validation summary control to display a list of error messages.

EXERCISE 2-7

Implement Online User Assistance

In this exercise, we will add online help to the input page we created in Exercise 2-2.

1. Open the page in Visual Studio and add ToolTip text to each of the input controls on the page. For example, add something short and informative such as **Re-enter the password** in the ToolTip for txtConfirmPassword.

2. Save and view the page in the browser. Move the mouse over each of the controls to see the result.

3. Add a new HTML page to the project called "Helpme.htm" and add the following to the page:

```
<h1>This is the help file for the Exercise</h1>.
```

4. Open the Web form in design view and click the validation summary control. Change the *HeaderText* property to:

```
The Following Errors occurred<br><a href="#"
onClick="helpWindow();">Click for Help</a><br>
```

This will add a link to run a JavaScript function that will open a new browser window with the Helpme.htm file displayed.

5. Add the following code to the page:

```
<script language="javascript">
<!--
function helpWindow()
{
Location_window
=Window.open("http://localhost/chapter2/helpme.htm",
"plain","width=400,height=500");
}
//-->
</script>
```

6. This JavaScript function will open a new browser window displaying the Helpme.htm file. The window is specified as plain—without menu, toolbars, or a locator. Change "localhost" to your server name if you intend to use or test this from a client machine. Save all files and test the page. View the page in the browser and click the Submit button. The validation control will display the header with the link to the help file. The result should be similar to Figure 2-5. If you click the link, the help file should be displayed in a new browser window, as shown in Figure 2-6.

FIGURE 2-5

Link to help
in Validation
Control Error
header

FIGURE 2-6

Help page
displayed from
link

Incorporate Existing Code into ASP.NET Pages

There are three ways to incorporate existing code into ASP.NET pages: code-behind pages, user and custom controls, and Server-Side Includes.

Code-behind Pages

As code-behind pages were discussed in Chapter 1, we will not go into detail again here. Although they are a method of incorporating code into a page, the code in a code-behind page contains event code, which usually is unique to that page; therefore, generally it does not lend itself to use in multiple pages. Code-behind pages therefore do not strictly apply as a method of incorporating existing code into multiple pages.

User Controls and Custom Controls

We will discuss user controls and custom controls in great detail in Chapter 5. For current purposes, we need to mention only that unlike code-behind pages, these consist of generic code, which encapsulates functionality that can be reused in multiple pages and applications. These controls are specifically for displaying user interface elements.

Server-Side Includes

Server-Side Includes are files that can be inserted into a Web Form. They can contain UI elements (controls and HTML elements), logic, text files, and HTML elements for graphics and such that are reused in multiple pages. Server-Side Includes separate the content of the included file from the page; therefore, they can be updated independently. When the content of a Server-Side Include file is modified, it will automatically apply to all pages it is included in. ASP.NET allows you to access files on the entire server, which allows great flexibility.

The syntax for Server-Side Includes is

```
<!--#include file="filename"-->
<!--#include virtual="filename"-->
```

The #include file statement defines a relative path to the file that is making the call to the Server-Side Include. The include file can be in the same physical directory of the page in which it is included or in a subdirectory below that directory, but not in a directory above the page directory. This can present a problem if the files are moved to a location beyond the page directory.

ASP.NET also allows you to define a virtual path to a virtual directory in the Web site. By using the virtual path, the include file can be accessed by multiple pages in separate Web applications without having to copy the file into each application's home directory.

EXERCISE 2-8

Using Server-Side Includes

In this exercise, we will create a very simple header file with hyperlinks to other pages in the Web application, including that header in the pages.

1. Create three new pages in your project named **Home.aspx**, **Exercise2-7.aspx**, and **Header.aspx**.

2. Replace all the code in Header.aspx with the following:

```
<html>
<body>
<a href="Home.aspx">Home</a> <a
href="Exercise2-7.aspx">Exercise 2-7</a>
</body>
</html>
```

3. Add the following code after the <body> tag in Exercise2-7.aspx:

```
<!--#include file="header.aspx"-->
<h1>Exercise 2-7</h1>
```

4. Add the following code after the <body> tag in Home.aspx:

```
<!--#include file="header.aspx"-->
<h1>Home</h1>
```

5. Save all files and view Exercise2-7.aspx. The result should look like the following:

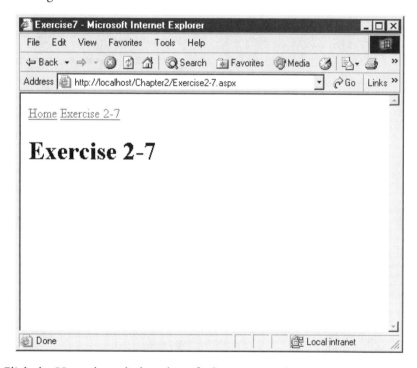

6. Click the Home hyperlink and verify that it opens the Home page. Click the Exercise2-7 link to make sure it returns to that page.

CERTIFICATION SUMMARY

This chapter covered validating user input using ASP.NET's validation controls. We explored the use of the RequiredFieldValidator, RegularExpressionValidator, CompareValidator, and RangeValidator controls to handle the common types of validation encountered on input forms. For other validation requirements, we explained the use of the CustomValidator control to implement our own validations. We discovered that the validation controls implement both server- and client-side validation, depending on browser capabilities; and that validation is always repeated on the server-side to guard against spoofing by the user. We explained page validation and the use of the Validation Summary control to centralize validation control error messages.

We explored the various methods for handling errors in the user interface by using Try-Catch-Finally code blocks, the Page and Application event handlers, and configuring custom error pages in the Web.config file. We discussed implementing online user assistance using ToolTips and help pages in the application. Finally, we used Server-side Includes to incorporate existing code into our Web pages.

TWO-MINUTE DRILL

Validate User Input

❑ ASP.NET provides validation controls that handle most validation requirements.

❑ Validation controls perform both client-side and server-side input validation.

❑ Validation controls are available to perform required field validation, input pattern matching, comparison validations, range validation, and custom validations.

❑ Each validation control can be forced to do only server-side validation by setting the EnableClientScript property to false.

❑ Validation controls always repeat the validation on the server after the form has been posted.

❑ The Validation Summary control lists all the error messages from validation controls on the page.

Implement Error Handling in the User Interface

❑ VB.NET implements structure exception handling using Try-Catch-Finally blocks.

❑ Exceptions are grouped hierarchically starting with the System.Exception base class.

❑ The Page_Error event can be used to respond to exceptions that occur at the page level.

Implement Online User Assistance

❑ The Global.asax Application_Error event can be used to trap errors at the application level, and write the error information into the event log or send e-mail with the error specifics.

❑ The Web.config file contains the configuration information for ASP.NET resources and includes a customErrors section that can specify a custom error page.

❑ The child element <errors> within <customErrors> can specify a custom page for each HTML error.

Incorporate Existing Code into ASP.NET Pages

❏ ASP.NET Web controls have a ToolTip property for displaying simple pop-up text.

❏ Existing code can be incorporated into ASP.NET pages using code-behind pages, user controls, and Server-Side Includes.

SELF TEST

The following self-test questions will help you measure your understanding of the material presented in this chapter. Read all the choices carefully—there might be more than one correct answer. Choose all correct answers for each question.

Validate User Input

1. What effect does the statement Server.ClearError have when included in the Page_Error event?

   A. Nothing; the error is cleared after the error event has handled it with or without this statement.

   B. Clears the error so it does not cascade to the Application_Error event and get handled again by that code.

   C. Clears the error so that any new error occurring will take precedence.

   D. Clears the error so that a Try-Catch-Finally exception handler won't respond to it.

2. Which property values are required on the RangeValidator control in addition to the ErrorMessage?

   A. MaximumValue, MinimumValue, ControlToValidate

   B. MaximumValue, MinimumValue, Type

   C. MinimumValue, MaximumValue

   D. MaximumValue, MinimumValue, ControlToValidate, Type

3. By default, where do validation controls perform the validation?

   A. Client side or server side but not both.

   B. Always on the browser.

   C. Both client and server side.

   D. Only on the server.

4. An input field on a form is both a required field and also needs to match another field. How would you accomplish this?

   A. Use a CompareValidator control to compare the control values.

   B. Use the Validation Summary control.

    C. Use a RequiredFieldValidator control.

    D. Use both a RequiredFieldValidator and a CompareValidator to validate the field.

5. The CompareValidator control is used for what types of validation? (Choose all that apply.)

    A. To compare the contents of an input control to a specific value.

    B. To compare the contents of an input control to another field.

    C. To compare the contents of an input control to a pattern of characters.

    D. To compare the contents of an input control to a range of values.

6. Which validation control would you use to validate a telephone number?

    A. CompareValidator

    B. RangeValidator

    C. RegularExpressionValidator

    D. CustomValidator

7. You are using a ValidationSummary control and want each of the validation controls on the form to individually display a message when an input error occurs. How can you do this?

    A. Set the ShowErrorMessage property to true on each of the controls.

    B. Do nothing; this is the default.

    C. Set the Text property on each validation control to the message you want to display.

    D. Set the ShowErrorMessages property to False on the ValidationSummary control.

8. How do you set a CompareValidator control to validate that an input control value is more than 0?

    A. Set ControlToValidate to the input control, ValueToCompare to 0, Operator to GreaterThan, and ErrorMessage to the error text.

    B. Set ControlToCompare to the input control, ValueToCompare to 0, Operator to GreaterThan, and ErrorMessage to the error text.

    C. Set ControlToCompare to the input control, ValueToCompare to 0, Operator to GreaterThanEqual, and ErrorMessage to the error text.

    D. Set ControlToValidate to the input control, ValueToCompare to 0, Operator to GreaterThanEqual, and ErrorMessage to the error text.

Implement Error Handling in the User Interface

9. What effect does the statement Server.ClearError have when included in the Page_Error event?

   A. Nothing; the error is cleared after the error event has handled it with or without this statement.

   B. Clears the error so it does not cascade to the Application_Error event and get handled again by that code.

   C. Clears the error so that any new error occurring will take precedence.

   D. Clears the error so that a Try-Catch-Finally exception handler won't respond to it.

10. You are testing your application after some maintenance and want to display custom error pages to clients that are using the application, and detailed error pages to anyone testing from the Web server. How do you configure the <customErrors> in Web.config to do this?

    A. Set the defaultRedirect to the custom error page and the mode to On.

    B. Set the mode to RemoteOnly.

    C. Set the mode to Off.

    D. Set the mode to RemoteOnly and the defaultRedirect to the custom error page.

11. How do you specify a custom error page in response to HTML errors?

    A. Code the Application_Error event to display a custom page when the HTML error occurs.

    B. Use a Catch block to trap the error in the Page_Load event and redirect to a custom error page.

    C. Add an <error> subtag in the <customErrors> section of the Web.config file for each HTML error. Set the statusCode attribute to the error number and the redirect to the custom error page.

    D. Redirect to the custom error page from the Page_Error event.

12. Which namespace is required to send e-mail from the Application_Error event?

    A. System.Web.Mail

    B. System.Data

    C. System.Diagnostics

    D. System.Web

13. What is the default behavior if an error occurs and no exception handling is implemented in the application?

A. The error is ignored and the code execution continues.

B. The error is ignored and the code execution terminates.

C. A default error page is displayed and the code execution continues.

D. A default error page is displayed and the code execution terminates.

Implement Online User Assistance

14. Which namespace is required to write error information to the event log?

A. System.Exception

B. System.Data

C. System.Diagnostics

D. System.Web

15. You want to pop up a message box in response to input errors when using validation controls. How do you do this?

A. Write client-side script to display the message box.

B. Use a ValidationSummaryControl and set the ShowMessageBox property to True.

C. Set each individual validation control's ShowMessageBox property to True.

D. You cannot do this.

16. How do you pop up feedback when a user moves the mouse over a Web control?

A. Code the MouseMove event to display the text.

B. Set the ToolTip property to the text you want displayed.

C. Set the Text property to the text you want displayed.

D. Set the Value property to the text you want displayed.

Incorporate Existing Code into ASP.NET Pages

17. What methods are available to incorporate existing code in ASP.NET pages? (Choose all that apply.)

A. Server-Side Includes

B. User controls

C. Custom controls

D. Code-behind pages

18. Which of the following is true of Server-Side Includes?

    A. They can contain a combination of code and HTML.

    B. They must be re-included in all pages if they are modified in any way.

    C. They can contain only HTML.

    D. They cannot contain server-side code or controls.

19. What is the difference between a code-behind page and a Server-Side Include?

    A. A Server-Side include requires compiling; a code-behind page does not.

    B. A code-behind can contain only HTML, whereas the Server-Side Include can contain only server side code.

    C. A code-behind can only contain UI logic, whereas the Server-Side Include can contain only HTML.

    D. A code-behind page is a class that contains logic; the Server-Side Include is another file that can be inserted into other pages.

20. You want to include a file in a Web Form that is used in another Web application. It exists in a directory in the other Web site's application root directory on the same server. Which statement would do this?

    A. <!--#include filename="*filename*"-->

    B. <!--#include file="*filename*"-->

    C. <!--#include virtualpath="*filename*"-->

    D. <!--#include virtual="*filename*"-->

LAB QUESTION

You are building a Web application in ASP.NET that includes login forms and a sign-up form, which gather information to create an account for the user and insert the data into a database. Explain the error checking that should be included in the application.

SELF TEST ANSWERS

Validate User Input

1. ☑ C. Setting EnableClientScript to false will force the validation to be done on the server.
   ☒ A would work, but requires coding; B does not use controls and everything is handled on the server; D does not use client-side validation.

2. ☑ D. You require minimum and maximum data types, and the control to validate.
   ☒ A, B, and C are all incorrect.

3. ☑ C. The validation is done client side if supported and repeated server side.
   ☒ A is wrong because it occurs both places. B is wrong because it does it both places and some browsers do not support client-side validation. D is incorrect because you have to explicitly set the controls to validate only on the server.

4. ☑ D. Both controls are needed to handle each validation function.
   ☒ A, B, and C are all incorrect.

5. ☑ A and B are correct.
   ☒ C is incorrect; to validate a pattern of characters, use the RegularExpressionValidator control. D is incorrect; to validate a range, use the RangeValidator.

6. ☑ C. The RegularExpressionValidator matches input value against patterns of characters.
   ☒ A will only compare a value, B will check that a value falls within a range, and D is used to create custom validations not covered by the other validation controls.

7. ☑ C. Validation controls will not display error messages individually if there is a ValidationSummary control on the form, but they will display the text property.
   ☒ A does not exist. B is wrong—it is not the default. D does not exist.

8. ☑ A is correct.
   ☒ B is wrong because it uses ControlToCompare instead of ControlToValidate. C has the same mistake and will include 0, as it uses GreaterThanEqual. D is wrong as it also uses GreaterThanEqual.

Implement Error Handling in the User Interface

9. ☑   B. It clears the error.
   ☒   A is wrong; the error is not cleared automatically. C is wrong because a new error occurring will not have any bearing on whether the previous error was cleared. D is wrong because it wouldn't have reached the error event if handled by an exception handler.

10. ☑   D is correct. Setting mode to RemoteOnly and defaultReDirect to the custom error page will mean remote users get the custom error. Testers from localhost will get the full ASP.NET error page.
    ☒   A is incorrect as it will set the custom error page for everyone. B is wrong as it does not specify the custom error page. C will give everyone the default ASP.NET error pages.

11. ☑   C is correct.
    ☒   HTML errors are application in scope, so B and D would never occur.

12. ☑   A. The System.Web.Mail namespace must be imported into the Global.asax file to support e-mail.
    ☒   B, C, and D are not required for e-mail implementation.

13. ☑   D is correct. A default error page will be displayed, dependent on the Web.config <customErrors> settings, and the code execution will terminate.
    ☒   A, B, and C are all wrong.

Implement Online User Assistance

14. ☑   C. System.Diagnostics supplies the classes for the logs.
    ☒   A, B, and D are all incorrect.

15. ☑   B. The validationSummary control will automatically display a message box with the error messages from the validation controls if you set the ShowMessageBox property to True.
    ☒   A is wrong as you can use the ShowMessageBox property on the controls. C doesn't exist. D is wrong because you can do this.

16. ☑   B is correct. The ToolTip property will automatically display on the browser when the user points to the control.
    ☒   A is wrong, as there is no MouseMove event on Web controls—although this could be done with Dynamic HTML. C and D are wrong, as this will display the text in the control, depending upon the type of control.

Incorporate Existing Code into ASP.NET Pages

17. ☑ A, B, C, and D are all correct.

18. ☑ A is true.
☒ B, C, and D are all incorrect.

19. ☑ D is correct.
☒ A is incorrect. Server-Side Includes do not require compilation before inserting them in the page. B is wrong as the code-behind page can contain code. C is incorrect as the Server-Side Include can contain anything including HTML, text, server-side code, and so forth.

20. ☑ D is the correct syntax to include a file in a virtual directory.
☒ A and C are incorrect as neither filename nor virtualpath are syntactically correct. B is incorrect as it would require the file to be either in the same directory or a subdirectory of the page it's included in.

LAB ANSWER

All input controls should be validated. Required fields must contain values, range checks should be done, and phone numbers and e-mail addresses should be tested for validity. Passwords should be tested for a minimum or maximum number of characters (two to ten characters, for example). Input validation should be handled on the client to reduce round trips to the server, and error messages should be concise and informative. A summary of all input errors should be displayed.

Server-side validation should be checked to make sure the user has not spoofed the input and that the control values do not contain any harmful contents before inserting into or updating the database.

Exception handling should be implemented around code that establishes the database connection and when sending commands to the database (Update or Insert). If problems occur, a catch block should address them and notify the user that the data could not be stored at that time.

Page- and application-level error trapping should be enabled to handle any unexpected exceptions. The user should be notified in a friendly way with custom error pages and the application exception details should be logged for follow-up.

MCAD/MCSD

MICROSOFT® CERTIFIED APPLICATION DEVELOPER
& MICROSOFT® CERTIFIED SOLUTION DEVELOPER

3

Create ASP.NET Pages: Extend the Interface

This chapter builds on the interface development covered in the first two chapters, extending the functionality of the Web application by using components, implementing globalization, and using intrinsic objects. We will begin by exploring various component technologies including COM, Web Services, .NET Components, and function APIs (Application Programming Interfaces). We will learn how to globalize the application by localizing the Web pages to culture-specific formatting, building resource files to implement multilanguage support, and converting application encoding. We also will learn to handle right-to-left text flow. Finally, we will cover ASP.NET's intrinsic objects and look at their common uses.

CERTIFICATION OBJECTIVE 3.01

Instantiate and Invoke Web Services or Components

Three-tier (and multitier) application development logically separates the interface, business logic, and data into separate tiers. Separating the tiers has a number of advantages in simplifying the design, implementation, deployment, and maintenance of an application. In traditional three-tier windows development, the business logic is written in Visual Basic 6, Visual C++, or J++ and compiled as COM code components. These components are installed and registered on the server, then instantiated and used by the interface as needed. The interface could be a Visual Basic or Visual C++ application, an application developed in Microsoft Office, or a Web application using classic ASP. The benefits of this architecture are many and include

- **Component re-use**   Granular components can be developed and tested to provide functionality that can be re-used in multiple applications.

- **Isolation of the business logic from the interface**   The same logic can be used by different user interfaces. For example, a Web interface developed in ASP can access and use the same logic components as a Win32 interface written in Visual Basic. The application therefore can be easily designed to provide an internal application interface for employees from workstations, and a Web interface for clients or customers accessing from the Internet.

■ **Easier maintenance**   When logic is encapsulated within discrete components, maintenance is simplified, because only the code in the individual components needs modification and recompiling.

■ **Increased scalability**   When the application is separated into logical tiers, the components of the application can be deployed to multiple servers, thereby distributing the load.

Microsoft Transaction Server (MTS) and COM+ provide the infrastructure for managing the components, and in addition, add capabilities such as role-based security, resource pooling (such as data connection and thread pooling), fault isolation, asynchronous execution, and transaction management.

ASP.NET includes support for COM components and calling native API functions such as the Win32 API. In addition, it can use .NET components and XML Web services.

Instantiate and Invoke a Web Service

One of the major problems for developers is integration. Applications developed on different platforms, in different languages, using differing object models, and separated by distance do not easily lend themselves to integration. ASP.NET has addressed this problem by using XML Web services, which provide a model for integrating local and distant services using XML and the Internet. We will begin the discussion by defining Web services and building a simple example. Once this is complete, we will see how to instantiate and invoke Web services from our Web forms.

exam
ⓦatch

At the time of writing, the Preparation Guide for Exam 70-305 did not list an exam objective for developing XML Web services (just consuming them) as there will be a separate exam for developing Web services. However, be aware that the exam probably will include questions that require knowledge in this area.

What Are Web Services?

A Web service basically is a black box that provides functionality that can be accessed over the Internet. It provides a programmatic interface that describes the services provided but does not have a user interface. Web services can be written in any .NET programming language and communicate using Hypertext Transfer Protocol (HTTP), Extensible Markup Language (XML), and Simple Object Access Protocol (SOAP). Any Web server that supports these standards can support Web services.

When a Web service receives a request from an application, it creates a new object, which is destroyed after that object is returned; for this reason, there is no state maintained in the service. Each request and response to the service is unique and can additionally be separated into a request/response to start the service, and a second request/response to receive the results. In this way, asynchronous communication is enabled, allowing the application using the service to continue processing while waiting for a response.

Create a Web Service

To learn how to instantiate and invoke a Web service, it would make sense to create one ourselves. We will use Visual Studio .NET to do this using the ASP.NET Web service template. This will create all the required files, folders, and a Web service page for us, including a default Web method we can modify for our own uses.

EXERCISE 3-1

Build an XML Web Service

In this exercise, we will use Visual Studio to build a simple Web service that will return the current interest rates on different types of loans.

1. Open Visual Studio .NET and create a new ASP.NET Web service project called "Interest Rates."

2. Open the Service1.asmx page and view the code. This is the implementation logic for the Web service in a code-behind page. Uncomment the HelloWorld Web method, and save and build the project.

3. Open your browser and navigate to http://localhost/InterestRates/Service1.asmx. The result should be the same as the following image. Notice the information on the default namespace at Tempuri.org. Click the Hello World link and then click the Invoke button. You will get a returned XML document with the results of the HelloWorld Web method.

4. Add another Web service to the project from File | Add New Item and call it "BankingService.asmx."

5. Now we will implement a Web method of a BankingService class called "ReturnRate" that accepts a LoanType as string and returns the current interest rate for that loan type. Replace the HelloWorld Web method with the following code:

```vb
<WebService(Namespace:="http://microsoft.com/webservices/",
            Description:="Banking Service Class")> _
Public Class BankingService
    Inherits System.Web.Services.WebService

    <WebMethod(Description:=" Returns current interest rates for specific loan
                types ")>
Public Function ReturnRate(ByVal LoanType As String) As Double
    Dim dblBaseRate As Double
        dblBaseRate = 0.0375
        Select Case LoanType
            Case "Used Car"
                Return dblBaseRate + 0.035
            Case "New Car"
                Return dblBaseRate + 0.03
            Case "Personal Loan"
                Return dblBaseRate + 0.045
```

```
         End Select
End Function
End Class
```

The Web service imports the System.Web.Services namespace to supply
the methods and property classes for the XML Web services. The first line
of the preceding code specifies the XML namespace. An XML namespace is
not a .NET namespace but a method to associate a URI with each tag set
in the XML document. This avoids having ambiguous elements in the XML
document by prefixing them with a specific namespace.

The XML namespace defines the tag within that namespace and differentiates
it from any tags of the same name used within a different namespace application.
This line has been changed to a Microsoft URI, which will remove the message
information we had with the Tempuri.org namespace. It also adds a description
of the Web service. The rest of the code implements a BankingService class
with the method ReturnRate, which uses a select case statement to calculate
the current rate. Notice the description for the Web method.

6. Save and rebuild the project. Open the InterestRates.asmx file in the browser.
   The result is shown here:

7. Click Return Rate. Your page should be the same as this:

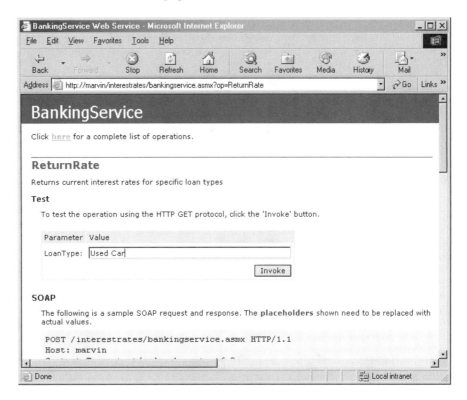

8. Enter **Used Car** and click invoke. The resulting XML should be the same as this:

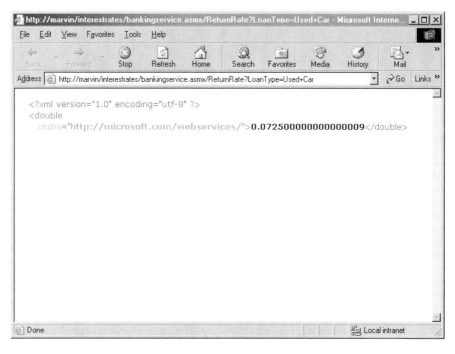

Let's take a look at the files resulting from the exercise to make sure we thoroughly understand the process. First of all, the InterestRates.asmx file is created with the following code:

```
<%@ WebService Language="vb" Codebehind="BankingService.asmx.vb"
Class="InterestRates.BankingService" %>
```

The @WebService directive defines the file as a Web service (as opposed to a user control or Web Form). The language is set to Visual Basic and the code-behind page is defined. The class attribute specifies the base class that supports the Web service.

Using Web Services

Accessing a Web service through HTTP from a browser is useful only to test the Web service or find out the Web methods supported by the service. To build Web applications that integrate with Web services, a Web Form must be built that references the Web service and communicates with it using SOAP over HTTP.

Discover Web Services　To use a Web service other than your own, you need to know how to access it and what functionality it provides. To find XML Web services, you can use one of the discovery services that publish descriptions and locations for Web services in a *Universal Description, Discovery, and Integration (UDDI)* Web site. Two sites available for this purpose are

- http://www.uddi.org
- http://uddi/microsoft.com

These sites allow you to search for XML Web services that meet your needs by providing the location of discovery documents and service descriptions.

Discovery files are made available to users to determine what services are offered. You can access the discovery file to find the Web service URL and a Web Services Description Language (WSDL) document URL, which can be used to build a proxy object in your Web Form to bind to the Web service. Discovery files are XML files that include links to resources that enable programmatic discovery of Web services. There are two types of discovery files: static (.disco) and dynamic (.vsdisco). Static discovery files are automatically generated when the service is accessed using ?DISCO in the query string. The following is the static BankingService.disco file generated by the BankingService.asmx file we created in the last exercise:

```
<?xml version="1.0" encoding="utf-8"?>
<discovery xmlns:xsd=http://www.w3.org/2001/XMLSchema
  xmlns:xsi=http://www.w3.org/2001/XMLSchema-instance
  xmlns="http://schemas.xmlsoap.org/disco/">
  <contractRef ref=http://localhost/interestrates/bankingservice.asmx?wsdl
   docRef=http://localhost/interestrates/bankingservice.asmx
   xmlns="http://schemas.xmlsoap.org/disco/scl/" />
```

```
<soap address=http://localhost/interestrates/bankingservice.asmx
 xmlns:q1=http://microsoft.com/webservices/
 binding="q1:BankingServiceSoap"
 xmlns="http://schemas.xmlsoap.org/disco/soap/" />
</discovery>
```

Visual Studio automatically generates dynamic discovery files during development of a Web service. You should use dynamic discovery files only on the development Web server. It includes root nodes called <dynamicDiscovery> and <exclude> nodes that specify which paths should not be searched in the discovery process. The following is the BankingService.vbdisco file:

```
<?xml version="1.0" encoding="utf-8" ?>
<dynamicDiscovery xmlns="urn:schemas-dynamicdiscovery:disco.2000-03-17">
    <exclude path="_vti_cnf" />
    <exclude path="_vti_pvt" />
    <exclude path="_vti_log" />
    <exclude path="_vti_script" />
    <exclude path="_vti_txt" />
    <exclude path="Web References" />
</dynamicDiscovery>
```

Using a Proxy to Access XML Web Services   To make use of a Web service, it must be called programmatically from a Web Form. To call a Web service from a Web Form, you first must reference the Web service from within the Web application and create a proxy class. The proxy has the same methods as the Web service class but contains marshaling and transport logic, not implementation logic. The proxy object allows the client to access the Web service as if it were a COM object. Visual Studio .NET automatically creates a proxy when you add a Web reference to your project. The process occurs in the following steps:

1. The client sends a URL request from the browser to the Web Form in the application that requires a call to the Web service.

2. The Web Form instantiates the proxy, which calls the Web service using SOAP.

3. The Web service responds using SOAP.

4. The Web Form uses the response.

As mentioned earlier, the Simple Object Access Protocol (SOAP) is a lightweight XML protocol for exchanging structured information on the Web. The SOAP envelope basically is just XML using a standardized type representation. The SOAP protocol defines a simple standard messaging framework that can travel over standard transport protocols. This generally is HTTP, but it could be any method of transporting the SOAP envelope including FTP, SMTP, or removable media such as a floppy disk.

Both the request and response to the Web service are defined in a SOAP envelope. The following SOAP request and response envelopes are used for a call to the ReturnRate Web method of our BankingService.asmx. First the request:

```
<?xml version="1.0" encoding="utf-8"?>
<soap:Envelope xmlns:xsi=http://www.w3.org/2001/XMLSchema-instance
 xmlns:xsd=http://www.w3.org/2001/XMLSchema
 xmlns:soap="http://schemas.xmlsoap.org/soap/envelope/">
    <soap:Body>
        <ReturnRate xmlns="http://microsoft.com/webservices/">
          <LoanType>string</LoanType>
        </ReturnRate>
    </soap:Body>
</soap:Envelope>
```

The string within the <LoanType> tags would be the actual request argument as a string type, such as "Used Car." In the response, the return value is found within the <ReturnRateResult> tags as a double type:

```
<?xml version="1.0" encoding="utf-8"?>
<soap:Envelope xmlns:xsi=http://www.w3.org/2001/XMLSchema-instance
xmlns:xsd=http://www.w3.org/2001/XMLSchema
xmlns:soap="http://schemas.xmlsoap.org/soap/envelope/">
  <soap:Body>
    <ReturnRateResponse xmlns="http://microsoft.com/webservices/">
        <ReturnRateResult>double</ReturnRateResult>
    </ReturnRateResponse>
  </soap:Body>
</soap:Envelope>
```

We will build a Web application using the BankingService Web service we created in the first exercise and call it from an ASP.NET Web Form called GetRates.

Using an XML Web Service from a Web Form

In this exercise, we will build a new Web application that will use the Web service we created in the last exercise.

1. Create a new Visual Studio project called "Chapter 3" with a Web Form called "GetRates.aspx."

2. Build the interface so that it looks like the following image using Web controls. Set the ID property of the drop-down list box to lstLoanType and "Used Car," "New Car," and "Personal Loan" to the Items property. Name the return label beneath the list box "lblRate."

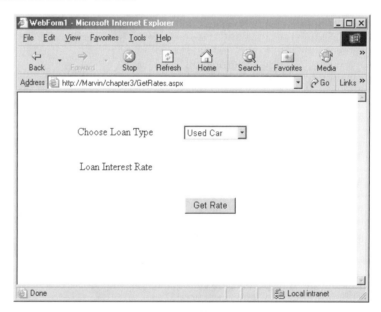

3. Choose Project | Add Web Reference from the menu, type **http://localhost/ InterestRates/BankingService.asmx** into the Address box and press ENTER. If successful, the screen should look like the following. Click the Add Reference button.

4. In the Solution Explorer, change the name of the localhost Web reference to "RatesWebRef." This will uniquely identify the Web reference for this project.

5. Double-click the Get Rate button on the page to open the code-behind page and add the following code to the button click event:

```
Private Sub Button1_Click(ByVal sender As System.Object, ByVal e As _
System.EventArgs) Handles Button1.Click
    Dim ProxyGetRate As New RatesWebRef.BankingService()
    lblRate.Text =
ProxyGetRate.ReturnRate(lstLoanType.SelectedItem.Text)
End Sub
```

This code instantiates the proxy RatesWebRate.BankingService as ProxyGetRate and calls the ReturnRate Web method, passing the item selected in the list box and returning the rate to the lblRate label.

6. Choose Build | Build Solution from the menu and test it in a browser. For each item you choose in the list box, you should get the appropriate interest rate when clicking the Get Rate button.

Handle Errors in Web Services   Errors can occur when using Web services because of three conditions: the Web service is unavailable, there is an excessively long response interval, or an error occurs internally in the Web service. You should write your code in Try-Catch-Finally blocks to catch the exceptions.

If the service is not available, you can just catch the exception and display a message to the user:

```
Try
    'Code to call the Web service
Catch err as exception
    lblmesage.text = err.message
End Try
```

In the case of a long response interval, no exception will be raised unless you specify a maximum limit to wait for the response. You can do this by setting the TimeOut property in the Web service proxy to a time in milliseconds:

*ProxyName.*Timeout = *value in millisec*

The preceding exception code will then catch the exception that will be thrown if the proxy times out.

on the
job

In some cases, the Web service might be slow to respond because of processing requirements. Rather than waiting for the response, you can call the Web service using the BeginWebMethodName and EndWebMethodName in the proxy file. You then can use a WaitHandle to wait for the response from one or many Web services, and force a time out if it takes too long. This can be very useful when your application uses multiple Web services simultaneously.

If an error occurs within the Web service so that it is unable to process the request, it probably will return an error using a SOAP exception. You can catch a SoapException error in the code and respond with an error message to the user:

```
Try
    'Code to call the Web service
Catch err as SoapException
    lblmesage.text = "An error occurred in the Web Service"
End Try
```

Instantiate and Invoke a COM or COM+ Component

COM components are used in distributed enterprise applications to encapsulate the business logic. As mentioned earlier, the user interface that implements these components can be a Web application using ASP, a Win32 client application developed in Visual Basic, Visual C++ and the like, or VBA code in a Microsoft Office application. Most COM components will work with ASP.NET, and can be instantiated and invoked in the same manner as they are handled with classic ASP, using late binding.

As an example, the following code will instantiate a COM component that has a ProgID of MyApp.Getdata in ASP.NET:

```
Dim objData as Object
objData = Server.CreateObject("MyApp.GetData")
```

The only difference between this VB.NET code in ASP.NET and classic ASP is the language syntax. VB.NET does not use the *Set* statement that was required in VBScript. Because VBScript is not compiled, it always uses *late binding*. ASP.NET can use *early binding,* which is much more efficient. Early binding requires a reference to the object's type library and an explicit declaration of the object. This enables the resolution of the object's definition at compile time rather than at run time (late binding), resulting in increased performance.

To use early binding, the COM components in the DLL files must be converted to .NET Framework assemblies. This is accomplished using the Type Library Importer (Tlbimp.exe) included with the .NET Framework SDK. This utility builds managed code wrappers around the COM components, allowing them to be early bound to managed code in ASP.NET. The assembly file built by Tlbimp.exe must be placed in the Web application's \bin directory. To simplify the use of the component, you then include a directive in the code to import the namespace:

```
<%@Import Namespace="ConvertedComDll"%>
```

If the COM component is single threaded (STA) you must include the *aspcompat=true* in the @Page directive, which forces the page to execute in single-threaded mode. All COM components developed in Visual Basic are STA and will throw an exception if the ASP compatibility attribute is not set. STA components can be used only in ASP.NET pages in the .NET Framework; they cannot be used from compiled .NET assemblies.

FROM THE CLASSROOM

Using Microsoft Transaction Server from ASP.NET

When Microsoft released Beta 1 of the .NET Framework and Visual Studio .NET, it immediately garnered a lot of attention. As corporate developers became familiar with the new technology, many were instantly interested and started plans to build future applications with this environment. One of the first questions to come up concerned the capability of the .NET Framework applications to use Microsoft Transaction Server (COM+) services.

The reason for using COM+ services in .NET applications is to take advantage of the automatic transaction processing, just-in-time activation, object pooling, queued components, and role-based security offered by the service. .NET components can be developed to interact with COM+ services by creating a class library and creating all the classes so that they inherit from the

System.EnterpriseServices.ServicedCompents class.

.NET components actually streamline the development process when compared to VB6 by inheriting the functionality of the ServicedComponents class. For example, you can set attributes that control transaction types, role-based security, and queuing. Methods now have an <AutoComplete()> attribute that will automatically perform the functions of SetComplete and SetAbort in VB6. Unlike VB6, .NET components can use something other than the Single-Threading Apartment model (STA), which means now they can take advantage of object pooling.

Overall, .NET makes it easier to implement components that use COM+ services and to add those components into existing COM and COM+ components.

—David Shapton, MCSD, MCT, CTT+

Instantiate and Invoke a .NET Component

.NET components are components developed in the .NET Framework using .NET languages. Instantiating and invoking a .NET component is no different from using a COM component except there are no worries about compatibility as the component is written in a .NET language in managed code. As long as the code is built (compiled) and placed in an assembly in the \bin directory under our application directory, the component can be instantiated and used from any Web Form in the Web application.

You can add components to the Web application in Visual Studio .NET and use them directly from the Web pages. The following exercise builds a simple .NET component we call from our Web page to calculate the monthly payment on a loan based on the loan type we choose (and the rate given to us by the Web service).

EXERCISE 3-3

Build and Invoke a .NET Component

In this exercise, we will build a .NET component to calculate the monthly payment on a loan and use this from the GetRates.aspx page we created in the last exercise.

1. Open the Chapter 3 project in Visual Studio.

2. Choose Project | Add Component… from the menu and give it the name "Payment.vb."

3. Add a public function called MonthlyPayment to the class that accepts three arguments: PrincipleAmount, InterestRate, and Term. It will calculate the monthly payment using the Pmt function, as in the following code:

```
Public Function MonthlyPayment(ByVal PAmt, ByVal Interest, ByVal Term)
    Return Pmt(Interest / 12, Term * 12, -PAmt)
End Function
```

4. Modify the GetRates.aspx page by adding text boxes to input the principal amount (txtAmount) and term (txtTerm). Add a label Web control to display the calculated monthly payment. Move the controls around so they

make some visual sense and modify the borders and colors. The end result should look something like the following:

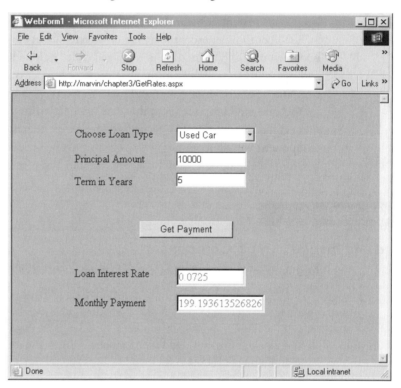

5. Add the following code to the Button1_click event on the page to instantiate the Payment component and call the MonthlyPayment method:

```
Dim objPayment As New Payment()
lblMthlyPayment.Text = objPayment.MonthlyPayment & _)
    txtAmount.Text,lblRate.Text, txtTerm.Text)
```

6. Build the project and test it in the browser.

Call Native Functions by Using Platform Invoke

Platform-specific Application Programming Interfaces (APIs), which consist of functions implemented as Dynamic Link Libraries (DLLs)—such as the Win32 API or specific product APIs—can still be useful to the developer. These native functions are not objects but libraries of unmanaged code functions. The following steps are required for calls to invoke the function:

1. Locate the DLL containing the function.

2. Load the DLL into memory.

3. Locate the address of the function in memory and push its arguments onto the stack, marshaling data as required.

4. Transfer control to the unmanaged function.

If an error occurs in the unmanaged function, Platform Invoke throws the exception to the managed caller.

In VB.NET, the process of calling native functions is similar to the procedure in previous versions of Visual Basic and requires the following steps:

- Identify the functions and DLL libraries.

- Use an existing class to hold the functions (on the Web Form) or create a class for each unmanaged function.

- Create a prototype in managed code. Import the System.Runtime.InterOpServices namespace, which provides classes to access COM objects and native APIs from .NET and then use the DECLARE statement to prototype the unmanaged function.

- Call the function as you would any managed method.

The following code example prototypes the Win32 GetFileVersionInfoSize function, which returns the size of the specified file in bytes if the file version information is available:

```
Imports System.Runtime.InteropServices
Public Class Win32
   Declare Auto Function GetFileVersionInfoSize Lib "Version.dll" _
(lptstrFilename as String, lpdwHandle as Long) As Long
End Class
```

The Declare function specifies the name of the function (GetFileVersionInfoSize) and the library (Lib and the DLL name as string) with the arguments. There are considerations concerning the data types of the arguments and versions of the functions. You will need to refer to the documentation for the specific function you are calling to determine the exact syntax requirements.

To invoke the function, you call it like any other managed method using the class (Win32) and the method (GetFileVersionInfoSize):

```
Win32. GetFileVersionInfoSize (filename, 0)
```

on the **job**

It is relatively rare to use function APIs in Web applications, as most needs are now handled by classes or COM objects. However, you might find that the only solution to, or workaround for, a specific requirement or problem is to use a function API. If this is the case, you should consider building a class file with either separate classes for each function or one class that contains a set of related functions. This approach will make it easier to manage and maintain your code.

Let's look at some scenarios and solutions concerning component use in ASP.NET.

SCENARIO & SOLUTION

I believe one of the organizations in my field has a Web service that I could use in my application. How can I find out if this exists and whether it would be useful to me?	Use one of the Universal Description, Discovery, or Integration Web sites, and search under the business name.
One of the Web services accessed in the application seems to occasionally become overloaded. When this happens, my Web page processing halts until it receives a response. Is there any way to respond to this?	Set the timeout value in the proxy to a reasonable time value to wait for a response. If the response time exceeds that value, an exception will occur, to which the Web code can catch and respond accordingly.
We have COM components written in VB6 that we have been using in ASP. When attempting to use them from ASP.NET, they cause an error. Can I use these components from ASP.NET?	Yes. Make sure that aspcompat=true attribute is set in the page directive.

CERTIFICATION OBJECTIVE 3.02

Implement Globalization

Anyone with access to the Internet can potentially use a Web application, each user using his or her own specific culture setting. Globalization is the process of developing an application that supports different cultures and languages. Support for globalization requires the capability to identify the culture of each user and respond with the appropriate language, date, and number formats that correspond to the user's cultural conventions. ASP.NET allows the developer to support multinational users by creating multiple resource files that contain culture-specific information (strings, images, and so forth) that are dynamically applied to the Web pages based upon the specific culture of each user.

Implement Localizability for the User Interface

Localizing the user interface requires the application to identify the localization setting of each user and respond with the appropriate culture and language. You can determine the language and, optionally, the location of the user by determining the settings for the user's browser using the Request.UserLanguage object; then you can set the culture information for the ASP.NET page by setting the *System.Globalization.CultureInfo* object. This object contains culture-specific settings including country, date and time formats, calendar format, and language.

The culture codes use a primary/secondary format in which the primary defines the language and the secondary is a country/region code. For example, *de* specifies a neutral setting for German while *de-AT* is the code for Austrian German, and *en-CA* is English Canadian while *fr-CA* is French Canadian. Table 3-1 displays some of the more common culture codes.

TABLE 3-1	Language	Code
	Arabic(Egypt)	ar-EG
Some Common	Chinese(Hong Kong)	zh-HK
Culture Codes	English(Australia)	en-AU
	English(Canada)	en-CA
	English(United Kingdom)	En-GB
	English(United States)	en-US
	French(France)	fr
	German(Germany)	de
	German(Austria)	de-AT
	German(Swiss)	de-CH
	Italian(Italy)	it
	Japanese	ja
	Korean	ko
	Portuguese(Portugal)	pt
	Russian	ru
	Spanish(Mexico)	es.MX
	Spanish(Spain)	sp

EXERCISE 3-4

Identify the Browser's Culture Settings

In this short exercise, we will build a Web Form that will identify the user's culture from the browser settings and display it on the page. We will add a text box and initialize it to the system date to see the date format, and then test the page by changing the language preference in the browser and testing the page.

1. Add a new Web Form to the Chapter 3 project called "Localize.aspx."

2. Add two label Web controls, one named "lblMessage" and one beneath it called "lblToday."

3. Double-click the page (in design view) to access the code-behind page and add the following code to the Page_Load event:

```
lblMessage.Text = "User Language " & Request.UserLanguages(0).ToString
lblToday.Text = Today
```

The first line will display the primary language of the user's browser using the Request.UserLanguages(0) object and convert it to string. The second line simply initializes the lblToday label to the system date.

4. Save your files, build the solution, and test it in the browser. The result should match your current browser language settings.

5. Change your browser language settings to include other languages. If you are using Microsoft Internet Explorer, go to Tools | Internet Options… and click the Languages button, then click the Add… button and choose a language from the list. Choose the language you just added from the list and click the Move Up button to make it the highest priority. This will now be UserLanguage(0) in the Request object. The Language Preference dialog box is displayed here:

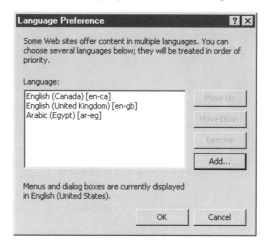

5. Refresh the page in the browser and notice that the label displays the new language setting. If you chose a language that would change the date format, you will notice that this does not change (in the label control lblToday), as at this point we are only determining the browser language settings; not setting the culture for the page.

Prepare Culture-Specific Formatting

Now that we know how to identify the user's language settings in the browser, we can set the culture on the Web server. There are two culture values on the server: Culture and UICulture. Culture determines how the culture-specific functions such as date and currency format should be displayed; UICulture is used to determine a specific lookup for resource data to load, which will contain strings and image data specific to the language.

The Culture value can be set only to specific cultures such as en-CA or en-GB; not neutral language settings such as en, which, if used, would cause problems in identifying such things as the currency symbol. The Culture and UICulture values do not have to be the same, which can be useful when the page needs to respond with the user-interface culture that matches the browser, but display currency in the culture specific to the site; for example, in an e-commerce application where the prices would be displayed as U.S. dollars regardless of the client's culture.

There are three ways to set the Culture and UICulture values:

- In the Globalization section of the web.config file, add code similar to the following:

  ```
  Culture="en-US"
  uiCulture="fr-CA"
  ```

- In the .aspx file, add the Culture and UICulture values to the @Page directive:

  ```
  <% Page UICulture="fr-CA" Culture="en-US"
  ```

- You can set them in the code by setting the CurrentCulture and CurrentUICulture properties:

  ```
  Imports System.Globalization
  Imports System.Threading

  Thread.CurrentThread.CurrentCulture = _
  CultureInfo.CreateSpecificCulture(Request.UserLanguage(0))

  Thread.CurrentThread.CurrentUICulture = New _
  CultureInfo(Request.UserLanguage(0))
  ```

This example sets both values to the culture specified in the browser. To respond to the browser's culture, the values must be set in code (web.config and @Page directives are static). You must import the System.Globalization and System.Threading namespaces to set these values, and use the CreateSpecificCulture method to set the CurrentCulture, as it must be set to a specific culture (not just a language). The culture values are set to the currently running thread.

EXERCISE 3-5

Set the Culture and UICulture Values from Code

In this exercise, we will set the Culture and UICulture values to the browser language settings.

1. Open the code-behind page Localize.aspx.vb and add code to import the System.Globalization and System.Threading namespaces.

```
Imports System.Gobalization
Imports System.Threading
```

2. Add code to the Page_Load event to set the CurrentCulture and CurrentUICulture properties to the primary browser language, and display the CurrentCulture in the lblMessage label:

```
Private Sub Page_Load(ByVal sender As System.Object, _
    ByVal e As  System.EventArgs) Handles MyBase.Load

  Thread.CurrentThread.CurrentCulture = _
   CultureInfo.CreateSpecificCulture(Request.UserLanguages(0).ToString)

  Thread.CurrentThread.CurrentUICulture = New _
   CultureInfo(Request.UserLanguages(0).ToString)

  lblToday.Text = Today

  lblMessage.Text = "Culture Info Display Name " & _
    Thread.CurrentThread.CurrentCulture.DisplayName
End Sub
```

3. Save, rebuild, and test the page by changing your language preferences in the browser. If you choose a language that changes the date format, it will now display in that format in the label control lblToday.

Resource Files

The last thing we need to do to fully localize the Web Form is produce resource files that load language-specific data into the page based on the UICulture settings. Using resource files allows us to present the page in different languages without modifying the code. The first step in using resource files is to build text files for each supported language containing name-value entries for each string required. The text files then are converted into .resources files using the Resgen.exe utility. The resources can be accessed directly using the ResourceManager from resource files or from satellite assemblies.

Create and Use .resource Files

We will build two very simple resource files for French and English, and use them in our Localization page.

1. Open a new file in NotePad and type in one line:

   `Greeting=Hello!`

2. Save the file as **data.en-US.txt** in the Web application directory (\inetpub\wwwroot\Chapter3).

3. Create another file using "Greeting=Bonjour!" as the content and name it "data.fr-CA.txt."

4. Open a command window, change the directory to \inetpub\wwwroot\Chapter3, and enter

   `Resgen data.en-US.txt data.en-US.resource.`

   You should get two lines echoed on the screen if successful:

   ```
   Read in 1 resources from 'data.en-US.txt'
   Writing resource file... Done.
   ```

   As Resgen.exe is not in the system path, you probably will have to fully qualify the file name with a path. Resgen.exe is in the \Program Files\Microsoft Visual Studio .NET\FrameworkSDK\bin directory.

5. Repeat Step 4 for the data.fr-CA.txt file.

6. Add a label Web control to the page and give it an ID of lblGreeting.

7. Open the code for the Localize Web Form and add the following:

```
Import System.Resources
```

8. Add the following code to the Page_Load event:

```
Dim objRM As ResourceManager
objRM = ResourceManager.CreateFileBasedResourceManager("data", _
Server.MapPath("."), Nothing)
lblGreeting.Text = objRM.GetString("Greeting")
objRM.ReleaseAllResources()
```

This code declares a resource manager object, and calls the CreateFileBasedResourceManager method, passing the prefix for the files ("data"), and the path to the resource files (we used Server.MapPath to return the physical directory). The last argument is an optional object to parse the resources, which we will not use. The lblGreeting.text is set using the GetString method of ResourceManager, which will automatically choose the right resource file based on the UICulture setting. The last line tidies up by releasing the resources.

9. Save, build, and test the Localize.aspx page. Change your language preference in the browser to fr-CA and watch the result. Comment out the line of code that sets the Thread.CurrentThread.CurrentUICulture, then save, rebuild, and test. Notice the error that is generated because the UICulture value is not set.

on the **Job**

Rather than coding every page in the application, it makes sense to place the localization code in the Application_BeginRequest event of the Global.asax file. The client will not likely be changing culture or language preferences during the session, and you can ensure that each user's culture is set automatically for each request to all pages.

Satellite Assemblies

We will discuss *assemblies* in detail in Chapter 4. In this section, we will access resources that have been built into *satellite assemblies*. Assemblies are the fundamental building blocks of the .NET Framework. An assembly is either an .exe or a .dll file, and a collection of types and resources for the application.

Satellite assemblies contain culture-specific resource information. As the name implies, a satellite assembly must be related to a main assembly. The satellite cannot stand alone; it requires the main assembly to serve as its anchor, as it contains information that relates to, and must be used in conjunction with, the main assembly. You can think of it as a moon that orbits a planet; there can be multiple satellite assemblies, each containing different culture resources.

ASP.NET pages are converted into assemblies dynamically; therefore, the assembly name is not known in advance. To ensure the accuracy of the hierarchical relationship between the main and satellite assemblies, the satellite assemblies must be placed in separate subdirectories from the application \bin directory. For example, an en-CA subdirectory would contain the en-CA.resources.dll and an en-GB subdirectory would contain the en-GB.resourses.dll. When the assemblies are deployed in this fashion, they are all shadow copied into the Global Assembly Cache.

The ResourceManager is used to access the strings from the satellite assemblies in the same way it's used for resource files. The main assembly for the application will be found in the \bin directory and called *applicationname*.dll. Chapter 3 main assembly is Chapter3.dll, for example. The satellite assemblies are located in separate subdirectories of the \bin directory and each contains an assembly named to the culture it represents.

To read strings from the appropriate satellite, you first must instantiate the main assembly and then instantiate a new ResourceManager object passing the name of the main assembly (basename) as the first argument and the assembly object as the second. You then can use the Getstring method to access the required string. The following code shows this using the Chapter3 example we used in the lab.

```
Dim a As Assembly = Assembly.Load("Chapter3")
Dim objRM As ResourceManager = New ResourceManager("Chapter3", a)

Thread.CurrentThread.CurrentCulture = _
CultureInfo.CreateSpecificCulture(Request.UserLanguages(0).ToString)
Thread.CurrentThread.CurrentUICulture = _
New CultureInfo(Request.UserLanguages(0).ToString)

lblGreeting.Text = objRM.GetString("Greeting")
```

exam
ⓦatch

Assemblies are an important concept in .NET. This section deals with only satellite assemblies for localization purposes; Chapter 4 discusses assemblies in detail. Be sure to have practical experience building and deploying assemblies before writing the exam.

Convert Existing Encodings

By default, Web Forms handle all string data as Unicode. You can change the encoding for data sent to the client, data sent from the client to the server, and the encoding used to interpret the data in the aspx file.

The ResponseEncoding attribute sets the encoding used to send data to the client. The CharSet attribute on the content type of the HTTP header is set automatically according to the value of the ResponseEncoding. This means the browser can determine the encoding of data sent to it.

The RequestEncoding attribute sets the encoding used to interpret data sent from the client to the server. The FileEncoding attribute identifies the encoding used for data included in the aspx file.

There are two methods to specify encoding:

■ Set the encoding in the web.config file—for example:

```
<configuration>
   <system.web>
      <globalization
            fileEncoding="utf-8"
            requestEncoding="utf-8"
            responseEncoding="utf-8"
      />
   </system.web>
</configuration>
```

■ Add the encoding values to the @Page directive:

```
<%@ Page ResponseEncoding="utf-8" RequestEncoding="utf-8"%>
```

When changing the encoding in the web.config file, you must save the file in the same encoding. You do this by using File | Advanced Save Options and choosing the encoding from the list.

Implement Right-to-Left and Left-to-Right Mirroring

Some languages require the text to flow from right to left (for example, Arabic). This can be handled using the dir (direction) attribute in either the <HTML> or <BODY> tags, which then will control the direction of the HTML elements on the page. If specified in the <BODY> tag, frames and captions will not inherit the direction. If specified in the <HTML> tag, it will enable a vertical scroll bar on the left side of the page.

To set the direction on the page, either select the document in Design view in Visual Studio and set the dir property to ltr or rtl, or modify the tags in HTML view as shown here:

```
<HTML dir="rtl">
```

or

```
<BODY dir="rtl">
```

To override the direction on any controls on the page relative to the document direction, either set the dir property on the control or set the attribute in the control tag:

```
<TABLE dir="ltr">
```

SCENARIO & SOLUTION

The main language preference of some users is not supported by resources in the application. How should I handle this?	Iterate through the UserLanguages until one matches a supported resource. If none are supported, leave the page in the culture of the server.
The culture is set in the page directive and also from code on the page. Which takes precedence?	The code takes precedence. If you set the Thread.CurrentThread.CurrentCulture in code, it will override the page directive.

CERTIFICATION OBJECTIVE 3.03

Implement Accessibility Features

Like ASP, ASP.NET includes intrinsic objects, most of which will be familiar to classic ASP developers. Interestingly, these objects are not actually limited to ASP.NET; they are part of the .NET Framework, and as such can be used by any application running under the framework. Some of the objects have properties and methods that are specific to the .NET Framework (the HttpResponse.CacheControl property, for example); therefore, they will be unfamiliar to the ASP developer. The intrinsic objects include these:

- HttpResponse
- HttpRequest
- Page
- Session
- Server
- Application

Use Intrinsic Objects

Using any object requires setting and reading properties, and executing methods. The intrinsic objects provide a great deal of functionality, some of which we have already seen. It is beyond the scope of this book to exhaustively cover all methods and properties of these objects so we will concentrate on the more common aspects of using these objects.

The *HttpResponse* Object

The *Response* object enables the server to communicate or respond to the client. When a user requests a page, an instance of the *HttpResponse* object is created. This object is referred to in code as Response, and of course, all properties and methods are then available. Table 3-2 lists some of the common *HttpResponse* properties; Table 3-3 lists the common *HttpResponse* methods. For a complete list, check the .NET Framework SDK.

TABLE 3-2   Common *HttpResponse* Properties

Property	Description
Buffer	Indicates whether to buffer output and send it after the entire response is finished processing.
BufferOutput	Indicates whether to buffer output and send it after the entire page is finished processing.
Cache	Gets the caching policy (expiration time, privacy, vary clauses) of a Web page.
Charset	Gets or sets the HTTP character set of the output stream.
ContentEncoding	Gets or sets the HTTP character set of the output stream.
ContentType	Gets or sets the HTTP MIME type of the output stream.
Cookies	Gets the response cookie collection.
Expires	Gets or sets the number of minutes before a page cached on a browser expires. If the user returns to the same page before it expires, the cached version is displayed.
ExpiresAbsolute	Gets or sets the absolute date and time at which to remove cached information from the cache.
IsClientConnected	Gets a value indicating whether the client is still connected to the server.
Output	Enables output of text to the outgoing HTTP response stream.
OutputStream	Enables binary output to the outgoing HTTP content body.
SuppressContent	Gets or sets a value indicating whether to send HTTP content to the client.

TABLE 3-3   Common *HttpResponse* Methods

Method	Description
AddHeader or AppendHeader	Adds an HTTP header to the output stream.
BinaryWrite	Writes a string of binary characters to the HTTP output stream.
Clear or ClearContent	Clears all content output from the buffer stream.
ClearHeaders	Clears all headers from the buffer stream.
End	Sends all currently buffered output to the client, stops execution of the page, and raises the Application_EndRequest event.
Flush	Sends all currently buffered output to the client.
Redirect	Redirects a client to a new URL.
Write	Writes information to an HTTP output content stream.
WriteFile	Writes the specified file directly to an HTTP content output stream.

The Response object contains the complete response from the server to the client. This includes all HTML, client-side code, postback values to form controls, and so forth. The Response properties and methods can be used to control the response; for example, if the Reponse.Buffer is set to true, all output will be buffered until the entire response is finished processing on the server. This means all server-side logic must be finished executing before anything is returned to the client.

Depending on the nature of the processing, it might be logical to send some of the completed response to the client, even if an error occurs in the processing. This can be accomplished by using the Response.Flush method, which will return all currently buffered responses, which is everything that has been processed up to that point.

Another useful method is Response.Write, which will return a string in the response based on its position on the page. This generally is used in server-side script blocks to display single strings of output to the user, but also can be placed in line using the <% %> tags. For example:

```
<% Response.Write "Today is " & Today %>
```

will insert the string "Today is" with the current date on the server into the response stream relative to its position in the HTML.

If Response.Write is used within event code for ASP.NET Web server controls, the response string will always be written at the top of the page. If other controls or HTML elements are positioned at the top of the page, the response string will appear behind them.

exam
ᗯatch

Many of the methods and properties of the intrinsic objects are the same as ASP. Some are included in ASP.NET only to provide compatibility with ASP. Be sure that you are familiar with the most commonly used members of these objects and pay particular attention to the new ASP.NET properties.

HttpRequest Object

The Request object enables client-to-server communication and represents the client requesting the page. Although there is a lot of information included in the HttpRequest, most of it is automatically handled by ASP.NET.

One of the major uses of the Request object is the transmission of data from the client to the server. Depending on the data transfer method (GET or POST), form data could be in the querystring or forms collections. As we saw in Chapter 1, ASP.NET server controls handle the submitted data without the programmer having to explicitly write code to access the data values. In fact, ASP.NET automatically handles most of the work that would require explicit coding in ASP. For example, as we saw in Chapter 1, ASP.NET Web controls will identify the user's browser from the browser property and return the appropriate response based on that browser's capabilities.

Request properties all are set on the client and their values are accessed in server-side code. We have already used the Request.UserLanguages property to identify the client's language preference to localize the page. Tables 3-4 and 3-5 list the common Request properties and methods.

TABLE 3-4 Common *HttpRequest* Properties

Property	Description
ApplicationPath	Gets the ASP.NET application's virtual application root path on the server.
Browser	Gets information about the requesting client's browser capabilities.
ClientCertificate	Gets the current request's client security certificate.
ContentLength	Specifies the length, in bytes, of content sent by the client.
Cookies	Provides the collection of cookies sent by the client.
FilePath	Gets the virtual path of the current request.
Form	Gets a collection of form variables.
Headers	Gets a collection of HTTP headers.
IsAuthenticated	Gets a value indicating whether the user has been authenticated.
IsSecureConnection	Gets a value indicating whether the HTTP connection uses secure sockets (HTTPS).
Path	Gets the virtual path of the current request.
PhysicalApplicationPath	Gets the physical file system path of the currently executing server application's root directory.
PhysicalPath	Gets the physical file system path that corresponds to the requested URL.
QueryString	Gets the collection of HTTP query string variables.
ServerVariables	Gets a collection of Web server variables.
Url	Gets Information about the URL of the current request.
UserLanguages	Gets a sorted string array of client language preferences.

TABLE 3-5	*HttpRequest* Methods

Method	Description
BinaryRead	Performs a binary read of a specified number of bytes from the current input stream.
MapPath	Maps the virtual path in the requested URL to a physical path on the server for the current request.
SaveAs	Saves an HTTP request to disk.

EXERCISE 3-7

Create and Use Cookies

In this exercise, we will use the Response.Cookies method to write cookies to the client browser and the Request.Cookies to access the values of those cookies. We then will use the Response.Write to display the cookie values on the page.

1. Add a new Web Form to the Chapter3 project called "Logon.aspx."

2. Build a simple logon form that looks like the next image. Use Web server textbox controls for the User Name and Password fields; name them "txtUserName" and "txtPassword." Add two RequiredFieldValidator controls to validate both fields.

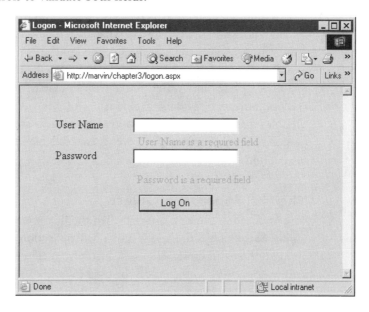

3. Name the button "btnLogon" and add the following code to its click event:

```
If Page.IsValid Then
    Response.Cookies("UserName").Value = txtUserName.Text
    Response.Redirect("GetRates.aspx", True)
End If
```

The code checks that the page is validated, and if so, creates a cookie called "UserName" and assigns the contents of the User Name field to the cookie value. It then redirects to the GetRates.aspx page.

4. Add the following code in the HTML for GetRates.aspx on the line before the <Form> tag:

```
<% Response.write ("Hello " & _
Request.cookies("UserName").value)%>
```

This is in-line code that will display "Hello" and the value of the cookie.

5. Save the files and rebuild. Open the Logon page in the browser and test it. If you enter values in the fields, it will redirect to the GetRates page, and display Hello and the user name at the top of the page.

The *Session* Object

The Session object represents each user session on the application. We discussed session objects and session state in Chapter 1. The Session object is instantiated when a user first accesses a page on the site and continues until either the session times out (a default value of 20 minutes) or is specifically abandoned. A unique SessionID identifies each session, which actually is a cookie that allows the application to keep track of individual sessions as users navigate through the site. You can create session variables that enable the application to maintain state data for each user session. Session_Start and Session_End events are available in the Global.asax file to handle session initialization and cleanup.

The *HttpApplication* Object

The Application object is created when the first user accesses the Web application. Unlike Session objects, there is only one Application object; it exists until the Web application is shut down, either explicitly from IIS or due to some disaster on the server. Application variables can be used to hold data that is required for all sessions or is needed to tabulate information over the whole application, such as a hit counter (a counter variable that keeps the total number of visitors to the site). The following Application events are available in the Global.asax file:

- **Application_Start**   Occurs when the application is started.
- **Application_BeginRequest**   Occurs at the beginning of each user request.
- **Application_AuthenticateRequest**   Occurs when attempting to authenticate the user.
- **Application_Error**   Occurs when an error occurs in the application.
- **Application_End**   Occurs when the application is shut down.

In Chapter 2, we used the Application_Error event to both write errors to the Application Event Log and to send an e-mail with the details of the error to the server administrator.

The *HttpServerUtility* Object

The server object has a number of methods that are useful for Web development. The Server.Transfer method transfers to another page. This is similar to Response.Redirect except that it doesn't involve the browser. The response object is sent to the browser, so when you use Response.Redirect it requires a round trip to the client to tell the browser where to go. Server.Transfer accomplishes the same thing without making the trip, which of course is much more efficient. Server.Execute has a similar function in that it transfers execution to another page, but in addition, it will return to the original page when it's finished.

Server.MapPath translates a virtual path to a physical path on the server. This is very useful; for instance, when you are writing files to the server, as in the following:

```
Server.MapPath("/Chapter3")
```

would translate to

```
c:\inetpub\wwwRoot\Chapter3
```

Server.ScriptTimeout sets the maximum time a script can execute before being terminated. The timeout value is set in seconds and allows the developer to limit execution time in case an endless loop or some other problem in the code would cause the script to keep executing forever.

Server.CreateObject is used to instantiate COM objects identified by a ProgID. This was discussed at the beginning of the chapter.

Server.URLEncode converts the string to URLEncoding rules, including escape characters. The syntax is Server.URLEncode(*string*). As an example, the following code:

```
Response.Write(Server.UrlEncode("http://mcgraw-hill.com"))
```

will produce the following output string:

http%3a%2f%2fmcgraw-hill.com

Server.URLEncode can be used to convert strings into the correct format to be used as URL parameters in query strings.

CERTIFICATION SUMMARY

In this chapter, we learned how to build and use Web services from our Web application, and how to discover published Web services that are available for our use on the Web. We instantiated and invoked COM components from our Web pages, built and used .Net components, and learned how to use Platform Invoke to access native functions such as the Win32 API and so forth.

We implemented globalization for the application by setting culture and language capabilities on the Web pages in response to the client's preferences, and built resource files to implement multilanguage support for the interface. Finally, we reviewed ASP.NET's intrinsic objects and looked at some of their common uses.

✓ TWO-MINUTE DRILL

Instantiate and Invoke Web Services or Components

❑ XML Web services provide a model for integrating local and distant services using XML and the Internet.

❑ We can develop XML Web services for use in our applications or make them available over the Internet for customers and other Web applications to use.

❑ To programmatically access Web services, you must create a proxy class, which communicates using SOAP.

❑ COM components can be accessed from ASP.NET in much the same way as from other environments such as ASP, but will be late bound.

❑ To take advantage of early binding, COM components must be converted to .NET Framework assemblies.

❑ .NET components can be developed in any .NET language and accessed from ASP.NET pages in a similar fashion to that of using COM.

❑ Any function-based APIs can be used from ASP.NET by using Platform Invoke.

Implement Globalization

❑ You set the culture information for the ASP.NET page by setting the System.Globalization.CultureInfo object.

❑ Culture determines how the culture-specific functions such as date and currency format should be displayed; UICulture is used to determine a specific lookup for resource data to load.

❑ Culture and UICulture can be set in the web.config file, in the @Page directive on the page, and in code using the CurrentCulture and CurrentUICulture properties of System.Threading.

❑ Resource files enable us to present the page in different languages without having to modify the code or page content.

❑ Text files containing key/value pairs are converted into .resources files using the Resgen.exe utility.

❑ The Response object enables the server to communicate with the client.

Implement Accessibility Features

❑ Request properties all are set on the client and their values are accessed in server-side code.

❑ The Session object represents each user session on the application.

SELF TEST

The following self test questions will help you measure your understanding of the material presented in this chapter. Read all the choices carefully as there might be more than one correct answer. Choose all correct answers for each question.

Instantiate and Invoke Web Services or Components

1. What is required to use a single-threaded COM component from an ASP.NET page?

   A. Instantiate and invoke the component from a compiled .NET assembly.

   B. Copy the Type Library for the component into the bin directory for the Web application.

   C. Set the *aspcompat=true* attribute in the @Page directive.

   D. Use the Tlbimp.exe utility to convert the component to multithreaded.

2. Which Web protocols can Web services use?

   A. FTP

   B. HTTP

   C. SOAP

   D. XML

3. What must you do to take advantage of early binding when using COM components from ASP.NET?

   A. Instantiate the component from a compiled .NET assembly.

   B. Convert the components to .NET Framework assemblies.

   C. Specify the GUID when using CreateObject.

   D. You can't use early binding with COM components in ASP.NET.

4. Which statements about XML Web Services are true?

   A. They support asynchronous communication.

   B. They require registering on the client computer.

   C. They are stateless.

   D. They require client-side scripting to implement.

5. What is the purpose of a proxy object in a Web Form that accesses a Web service?

   A. It creates a copy of the Web service in the Web Form.

   B. It provides marshaling and transport logic to call the Web service.

   C. It reproduces implementation code from the Web service in the proxy class.

   D. It enables asynchronous communication with multiple Web services.

6. Which statements about XML Web services are false?

   A. They can be developed in any .NET language.

   B. They are stateless.

   C. They support asynchronous communication.

   D. They can communicate using FTP.

7. Which statement is true about COM in the .NET Framework?

   A. All COM objects must be rewritten as .NET components to be used in the .NET Framework.

   B. COM components can be used only as late-bound components.

   C. COM components can be used only as early-bound components.

   D. To use early binding, COM components must be wrapped in assemblies.

8. When using Platform Invoke to call a function in a native API, which namespace is required?

   A. System.Runtime.InterOpServices

   B. System.EnterpriseServices.ServicedComponents

   C. ConvertedComDll

   D. System.Web

9. What protocol is used to communicate between a Web Form proxy and an XML Web service?

   A. HTML

   B. FTP

   C. SOAP

   D. XML

10. Which intrinsic object is used to instantiate a COM object?

    A. Page

    B. HttpServerUtility

    C. HttpResponse

    D. HttpRequest

11. What is the purpose of a Universal Description, Discovery, and Integration (UDDI) Web site?

    A. Provides documents on the standards and implementation of Web Forms.

    B. Gives information on integrating .NET applications with applications running on UNIX.

    C. Publishes descriptions and locations for XML Web services.

    D. Provides downloads of code you can use to build your own Web services.

12. How can you test a Web service and find out what methods are supported?

    A. Write a Web Form that calls the service and iterates through the methods.

    B. Access the Web service from a browser. The methods and parameters will be displayed.

    C. Ask for documentation from the provider of the Web service.

    D. Use the COM viewer to display the methods and arguments.

Implement Globalization

13. What is the purpose of Server.MapPath?

    A. Translates a physical path to a virtual path.

    B. Translates a virtual path to a physical path.

    C. Provides the Web application root directory.

    D. Sets the path to the server.

14. You are building an online auction site and want to localize the pages to respond to the user language preference using resource files, but want the currency to be displayed in U.S. dollars. How would you set the CurrentCulture and CurrentUICulture properties to accomplish this?

    A. Set CurrentCulture to Request.UserLanguage(0) and CurrentUICulture to en-US.

    B. Set both CurrentCulture and CurrentUICulture to en-US.

    C. Set CurrentCulture to en-US and CurrentUICulture to Request.UserLanguage(0).

    D. Set both CurrentCulture and CurrentUICulture to Request.UserLanguage(0).

15. Which code would mirror a page so that text flows from left to right, enables a scroll bar on the left hand side of the page, and includes all frames on the page?

    A. <BODY dir ="rtl">

    B. <BODY dir="ltr">

    C. <HTML dir="rtl">

    D. <HTML dir="ltr">

16. How do you create resource files?

    A. Use the Resource Manager to build the files and save the files in the Web root.

    B. Write the files in a text editor and save them as *filename*.resources.

    C. Create the files in a text editor and use Resgen.exe to generate the .resources files.

    D. Use Visual Studio to add the file to the Web application using the Resource File template.

17. What can a satellite assembly contain?

    A. Only culture-specific resource information

    B. Any resource information required by the Web application

    C. Type information for Web services

    D. Type information for Web Forms

18. Once implemented and deployed, resource files and satellite assemblies are used to localize the language of the client. What property identifies which file or assembly is to be used?

    A. UICulture

    B. Culture

    C. UserLanguage

    D. ResponseEncoding

19. What methods are available to specify encoding for the Web page?

    A. In the web.config file

    B. In code on the Web page

    C. In the @Page directive

    D. In a resource file or satellite assembly

Implement Accessibility Features

20. Which are valid methods to programmatically navigate the user to another page? (Choose all that apply.)

A. Server.Redirect

B. Server.Transfer

C. Server.Execute

D. Response.Redirect

LAB QUESTION

You are designing a Web site for a company that leases machinery to international clients. The site will allow clients to determine the leasing costs online. The costs are volatile, depending on changes in the interest rates of the home county of the company, and the shipping costs are dependant on the client's location. You need to design the application so that it will present the page in the language of the client (if possible) and provide an estimated cost in the customer's currency. Discuss the aspects of globalization and component use that could be used in this scenario.

SELF TEST ANSWERS

Instantiate and Invoke Web Services or Components

1. ☑ C. You need to set the aspcomt attribute to true on the Web page to force it to use a Single-Threaded Apartment model if it is to use single-threaded COM components.
   ☒ A is incorrect. B is wrong. The Type Library for a COM component is identified in the registry. D is wrong. The Tlbimp.exe utility is used to convert a COM component to a .NET Framework assembly.

2. ☑ B, C, and D. You can access a Web service using HTTP to test the service and its exposed methods, which will return an XML document with the response. The proxy communicates using SOAP.
   ☒ A is incorrect, as XML Web services do not use FTP.

3. ☑ B. To use early binding of COM components, they must be converted to assemblies.
   ☒ A means rewriting the component, which is not necessary. C is wrong, as it doesn't make any sense and D is wrong, as you can use early binding.

4. ☑ A and C.
   ☒ B and D both are incorrect.

5. ☑ B. The proxy object is called from the Web Form code and provides the logic to marshal and transport the call to the Web service.
   ☒ A, C, and D are all incorrect.

6. ☑ D is false; Web services do not use FTP.
   ☒ A, B, and C are all true statements.

7. ☑ D is the only true statement.
   ☒ A is wrong; otherwise, we wouldn't be using COM in .NET. B and C are wrong, as we can do both.

8. ☑ A is correct. You need the System.Runtime.InterOpServices.
   ☒ B, C, and D all are wrong, although System.Web is defaulted on a Web page.

9. ☑ C is correct. SOAP is used to communicate between a Web service and the proxy.
   ☒ A, B, and D are wrong.

10. ☑ B is correct. HTTPServerUtility is the server object. Server.CreateObject is used to instantiate a COM object.
☒ A, C, and D are wrong.

11. ☑ C is correct. UDDI sites publish Web service locations and descriptions.
☒ A, B, and C are all wrong.

12. ☑ B is correct. By accessing the Web service URL from a browser, you will know the Web service is active and it will present an interface describing the methods and allowing you to test them.
☒ A is wrong and would need a proxy anyway. C is wrong but you can find information from the discovery file. D is totally wrong.

Implement Globalization

13. ☑ B. MapPath converts a virtual path on the server to a physical path.
☒ A, C, and D are all incorrect.

14. ☑ C is correct. The CurrentCulture sets the culture formatting, which will display the currency as US dollars. The CurrentUICulture sets the appropriate resource file or satellite assembly to get the strings in the client's language preference
☒ A, B, and C are all incorrect.

15. ☑ C is correct.
☒ A is wrong, as it would not work on the frames. B is wrong for the same reason, plus it specifies left to right. D specifies left to right.

16. ☑ C contains the correct steps to creating resource files.
☒ A is incorrect. The ResourceManager is used to access the files at run time. B is incorrect, as the files must be generated using Resgen. D is wrong, as Visual Studio does not have this capability.

17. ☑ A is correct. Satellite assemblies can contain only resource information.
☒ B, C, and D are wrong.

18. ☑ A. UICulture identifies the resource to be used.
☒ B is wrong. Culture sets the data formatting to the culture specified. C is the Request.UserLanguage; the client identifies the language preference from the browser. D is the encoding used in data sent to the client.

19. ☑ A and C are correct.
    ☒ B is wrong. You cannot change the encoding for a page in code, as it has already loaded with the specified encoding. D is wrong; neither resource files nor satellite assemblies have anything to do with the encoding of the Web page.

Implement Accessibility Features

20. ☑ B will transfer to the specified page directly on the server. C will transfer to the page directly on the server and return when the page is processed. D will respond to the client; then the client will request the page.
    ☒ A. There is no such thing as Server.Redirect.

LAB ANSWER

First of all, from a localization point of view, the Web pages will need to respond with the client's culture. As you want to present the currency formatting, date formatting, and so forth in the local culture, you will need to set the culture to match the client's needs. You also will need to set the UICulture to the same culture and provide resource files or satellite assemblies to respond in the client's language.

The culture settings could be identified from the Request.UserLanguage of the user's browser, or you might want to consider a menu of supported languages or graphics depicting flags that would identify the cultures supported. You can set the culture based on the user choice. This approach has the advantage of presenting the languages and cultures that the application supports.

If you use the browser language preference and there truly is an international client base, you might not actually support their culture. Another problem with this approach is that the browser could be set to a neutral language setting, which will not allow you to set the culture. You also probably will have to consider the encoding of the pages and the data.

Base costs for the products will be accessed from a database. As interest rates don't change on a daily basis, they too will probably be stored in the database. Shipping charges probably are based on business logic that should be handled by a component. It will need to access the database for information on shipping methods available to the destination, routes, customs duties, and so forth.

Providing the estimated costs in local currency would be a good case for a Web service. Due to the constant fluctuation of currencies, the current rate could be accessed online from a Web service to provide an accurate cost estimate.

MCAD/MCSD
MICROSOFT® CERTIFIED APPLICATION DEVELOPER
& MICROSOFT® CERTIFIED SOLUTION DEVELOPER

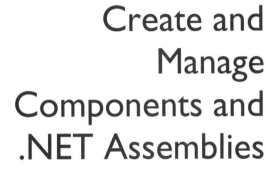

Part II

Create and Manage Components and .NET Assemblies

CHAPTERS

4

Create and Modify a .NET Assembly

CERTIFICATION OBJECTIVES

4.01	Create Resource-Only Assemblies
4.02	Create and Implement Satellite Assemblies
✓	Two-Minute Drill
Q&A	Self Test

One of the most difficult and time-consuming activities in software development is enabling applications to use varied languages (that's human languages—not computer programming languages). This gets even more complicated when you consider that many countries that share a common language will have subtle differences in the way they implement that language.

For example, in the English spoken in North America, we call the little dot at the end of a sentence a *period;* however, in the English spoken in Britain, that same little dot is called a *full stop.* I'm sure you'll agree that differences such as these create a logistical nightmare when developing applications that are expected to run in different countries; especially when supporting different languages. With the advent of the World Wide Web this has become even more important, as the goal of any decent Web application is to reach as many people as possible—and indeed the number of people who have access to the application becomes much greater.

The traditional solution to this dilemma was to create parallel applications for each language. This essentially meant that we were creating one application (or Web site) for each region in which we expected the software to be used. This meant global applications were quite expensive to create.

From early on, Microsoft has made a serious effort to help developers create global applications cheaply and easily. If you're experienced with Visual Basic 6, you'll remember the string tables, which did a lot to ease this burden. However, the features of Visual Basic .NET will make this task much easier, and should reduce the cost associated with designing and implementing global applications. In this chapter, we will use resource files and assemblies to separate the culture-specific portions of our Web application (typically user interface elements) from the portion of our Web application that is common to all cultures (the business and programming logic).

CERTIFICATION OBJECTIVE 4.01

Create Resource-Only Assemblies

The first thing we'll do is separate the culture-specific portions of our application from the business logic. The basic idea is to store all messages, captions, labels, and any pictures that might have a cultural meaning outside of our Web pages. For this example, inside of our Web pages we will use code from Chapter 3 to load all of these messages and captions just before the page is sent back to the user requesting it. As you will see, it still takes a little bit more effort to write global applications than it does to create an application specific to one language and one country; however, it won't take too much extra effort and certainly is much easier than it has been in the past.

So the question of the day is this: "Where are we going to store all of this stuff?" The answer, of course, is in a resource file. This way we can have one resource file for every culture we are supporting and simply use the appropriate resource file based on the user's regional settings. If our application supports English and French, we can create two resource files with the captions for our application (one contains the English words and one contains the French words). We then can determine the language settings of the user's browser, and return the appropriate captions and text for the appropriate language.

Global Applications

Now that we have a basic understanding of the mission at hand, we can take a look at some of the common principles of creating global applications; in Web development, global applications should be the norm—not the exception. Because the main goal of today's Web applications is to share information and services with as many people as possible, we must accept the fact that by excluding the possibility of other languages and regions, we also drastically reduce the number of people who could possibly benefit from our application. On another note, by allowing people to use their languages of choice, we make our applications much more user friendly.

Globalization

Globalizing an application consists of segregating culture-specific portions of our application from the portions of our application that are not dependent on culture. This basically entails removing from the Web page all text that the user will see or read. It also can involve removing culture-specific pictures such as flags or pictures that contain text. We then must write code within our Web pages that will load the text and graphics when the pages are rendered.

To make the development process easier, we usually identify a default culture for the application. For example, if the majority of the users of this application will be from the United States, we will make our default culture English as used in the United States. We then can put all of the text for the user interface elements in an external resource file.

Globalizing can be very hard for a developer who is new to the process. The most important thing to remember is that the Web application should not have any hard-coded text that would be displayed to the user. This process should be done from the start, as removing all of the text from a Web application is very time consuming.

on the
①ob

One of the most common mistakes developers make is forgetting to remove error messages; we often get overly obsessed with the functionality of our application and neglect exception-handling code. I have often seen English error messages in applications running under a different language. Don't forget that when you are globalizing an application, you must globalize error messages as well.

Localization

Once the application has been written and tested using our default language in a resource file, we have successfully globalized the application. Our next step is to add one resource file for each culture we plan to support. This process is known as *localizing* the application, as now we are adding information for specific locations.

The best part about this scenario is that these culture-specific resources can be added even after the application has been released. This gives us great flexibility in creating our applications and allows us to get them to market as quickly as possible, expanding as necessary. We could create a Web application for release in North America and release it immediately, thus allowing us to get it out there and possibly make money. We then can add culture-specific information for our application in the order of greatest benefit without having to redeploy the application. Although redeploying a Web-based application is much easier than redeploying a Windows-based application, avoiding any downtime whatsoever is something to be desired.

exam
ⓦatch

It is important to understand the difference between globalization and localization. Globalization is preparing your application to support multiple cultures, which in practice means separating the text and graphics for the user interface from the programming logic by using resource files. Localization is the process of creating specific resource files for specific cultures. Thus, first we globalize; then we localize.

Cultures

The next thing we'll have to look at before we are ready to start creating global applications is what defines a culture. A culture is not characterized only by the language spoken; culture involves two main concepts: language and location. Although the location is most often the country, it can also be a region within the country.

Often there are differences in the way a language is used within different regions of a country, and almost always there is a difference in the way a language is used in different countries. For this reason, Microsoft decided on a four-letter code based on the RFC 1766 standard to define a culture. The first part of the code (in lowercase letters) defines the language and is derived from ISO 639-1. The second part of the code (in uppercase) defines the country or region and is derived from ISO 3166. This gives us a format of xx-XX. As an example, for English as spoken in the United States, the code would be en-US.

There also are location-neutral codes that use only the first two letters. As an example, for English spoken anywhere, the code would be en. Some common cultures can be seen in Table 4-1; however, these represent only a small number of the possibilities and I would suggest looking in the MSDN library for the *CultureInfo* class to get a full listing.

TABLE 4-1	**Culture Name**	**Language/Country-Region**
Examples of Culture Names	En	English
	en-US	English–United States
	en-CA	English–Canada
	en-GB	English–United Kingdom
	Fr	French
	fr-CA	French–Canada
	fr-FR	French–France
	De	German
	de-DE	German–Germany
	de-CH	German–Switzerland

As you will see later in this chapter, these culture names are used by the .NET Framework to find the appropriate resource file to load for each user. The *CultureInfo* class then can be created with the right settings.

exam

ⓦatch

Take special note of the difference between a neutral culture and a specific culture. Neutral cultures will not have any slang or region-specific terms, whereas a specific culture will have common slang and region-specific terms. It also is worth mentioning that the neutral culture is the parent of all the specific cultures with the same language—for example, en is the parent of en-CA. As we will see later in this chapter, if the Framework cannot find a resource file for the user's specific culture, it will fall back to the parent culture.

Resource Files

We now can finally implement a global application. In the next section, we will look at the details of creating and using resource files. Just like everything else Microsoft has offered us, there is more than one way to skin this cat: You will note that there is more than one way to store and create your resources, and there also is more than one way to use them.

What Is a Resource File?

In short, a resource file is simply a file that stores resources. Of course, something tells me this is not a definition you would find on the exam (and if it is, you probably should look carefully at the other options). To fully define a resource file, we first need to define a *resource*. Early in this chapter, we said resources are simply the text and graphics we put in our applications. Strictly speaking, a resource is anything your application needs to function (such as memory, I/O, file handles, graphics, and so forth). You'll often hear C++ programmers talk about requesting resources from the operating system.

In our case, and for the purposes of this chapter, we are concerned only with user interface resources, which are resources used by our application to display information to the user. Therefore, the long definition is that a resource file contains the text and graphics needed by our application to properly display the user interface. In a standard Windows application, this would mean our resource file would contain anything the user can read on the forms including menu captions, button captions, labels, and any graphics displayed on the form.

On a more technical level, what we can put into a resource file are strings and *serializable objects,* which implement the *ISerializable* interface, or are marked with the *Serializable* attribute and include things such as pictures and fonts. The most common resource file you'll work with most likely will contain strings; however, the capability to add graphics to a resource file enables us to localize graphics that contain text or are location-specific pictures such as flags. Our resource files then can be either used directly from our Web application or packaged into assemblies to improve flexibility and performance.

Do not forget that fonts also can be stored in a resource file. This is especially useful for cultures that use the same basic character set but have small differences in certain letters, such as the addition of an accent.

Name Your Resource Files

Technically, you can name a resource file anything you want as long as it has the proper extension (.txt, .resX, or .resources). However, if we don't follow a standard naming convention, we cannot take advantage of the localization capabilities of the .NET Framework; therefore, in the context of this chapter, we will need to follow the standard naming convention.

The first resource file we need to worry about contains our default resources (the resource file containing the culture of the majority of our users). In the case of this file, you actually can call the resource file anything you want. When it comes time to create the resource files for each specific culture we plan to support, we must follow a more standard naming convention.

Essentially, there are three parts to the name. The first part is the filename of our default resource file without the extension. The second part is the culture names seen in Table 4-1, and the final part is the file extension. All three parts must be separated by a ".". For example, if we were to create a default resource file called Strings.txt, we would call the resource file specific to German-Switzerland, like this:

```
strings.de-CH.txt
```

Without following this naming convention, the .NET Framework has no way to figure out how to load the appropriate file for the appropriate culture. The next table is a quick reference for naming your files.

SCENARIO & SOLUTION	
What should I name a default resource file if it is for U.S. English and is a text file?	filename.txt
What should I name a culture-specific file if it is for U.S. English and is a text file?	filename.en-US.txt
What should I name a culture-specific file if it is for neutral German and is a text file?	filename.de.txt
What should I name a default resource file if it is for Canadian French and is a text file?	filename.txt
What should I name a culture-specific resource file if it is for United Kingdom English and is a text file?	filename.en-GB.txt

Types of Resource Files

In Visual Basic.NET, we can use three different types of resource files (text files, XML files, and .NET compatible resource files). We create resource files using either text files (.txt) or XML files (.resX), which then are converted or compiled to a format compatible with the.NET framework (.resources files). If you are an adventurous developer, you also can write code that creates and adds resources directly to a .resources file.

Text Files (.txt)   Text files often are used when creating resource files, as they are very easy to manipulate and can be edited with almost any ASCII text editor (such as Notepad). Text files themselves must be converted to another type of resource file before they can be used by our application (see the section ".NET-compatible Resource File" later in this chapter).

One of the down sides to using text files is that they can only store strings. Of course, if the graphics in your application are not culture specific, this is an excellent solution, as creating a resource file from a text file is extremely easy. The following is an example of a text file called strings.txt containing string resources for a login dialog box:

```
; strings.txt
; Comments are made by starting the line with a semicolon
; Notice the key = value pairs

[strings]
Login_Greeting = Please enter your username and password.
Login_btnOK = OK
Login_btnCancel = Cancel
```

You'll notice three main components in this text file; the first is the *comments.* Comments are created by preceding a line with a semicolon in the same way that a comment in Visual Basic is created by preceding a line with an apostrophe. Surely you've heard this a thousand times in every programming course you ever taken but I'm afraid I have to say it again: Comment your code! Yes, I realize this is not code; however, you should be commenting it just the same. The average application contains a ton of strings; organizing them into categories can make your life much easier in the long run. It also will save you the pain of being assaulted by your coworkers.

Next, we should notice the actual strings. You'll see that I have used the header [strings], which is optional; however, it's a good idea to let people know where your strings start. The strings themselves are entered by using a key value pair. For those of you who remember Visual Basic 6, we entered strings using a number (integer) associated with the string. This was not terribly easy to work with, as you had to remember that 172 (or whatever unique number we decided to use) represented the string for the Cancel button.

Now we can use names instead of numbers, which should make our lives much easier; this name becomes our key. A suggested naming scheme is to use the name of the page or form the user interface element is on, followed by an underscore, and the name of the user interface element (for example, Login_btnOK). Of course, you can use any naming convention you want; just make sure it's easy for others to understand.

After the equal sign is the text (or value) we wish to associate with the name. You'll notice that you do not have to place it in quotes and that spaces do not affect the system. The system will read the value up until it reaches the end of the line, which means don't try to put your string on two lines. Sound simple enough? Well it is, and it will make the process of creating different resources for different cultures very easy.

If, like me, you're someone who speaks only one language (and even that's debatable) you can still be involved in almost all aspects of developing a global application. You can create your resources using a text file full of English strings and at some point during development send a copy of this text file off for translation. Thanks to the simplicity of this format, we won't have to worry about the technical background of the translator; more important, he or she will not need to install Visual Studio .NET.

I'm sure you'll agree that with a five-minute explanation of the format of this text file, any translator would be capable of working directly with it. This also saves us the hassle of converting the translation back into the appropriate format, because it already is in the appropriate format (a text file).

XML Files (.resX)   The next file format we can work with is XML. Microsoft uses a file with the extension .resX. For those of you who are not familiar with XML, it is similar to HTML with the added bonus that you can create your own tags in order to store structured information. The following is an example of our Strings.txt file in XML format:

```
<?xml version="1.0" encoding="utf-8"?>
<root>
...
  <data name="Login_Greeting">
    <value>Please enter your username and password.</value>
  </data>
  <data name="Login_btnOK">
    <value>OK</value>
  </data>
  <data name="Login_btnCancel">
    <value>Cancel</value>
  </data>
...
</root>
```

First, you should notice that I've removed some of the XML (where you see the …). The XML removed is the schema data added by the ResGen.exe program I used to convert our strings.txt file to strings.resX (you will see how to do that soon); the schema data is not important for our discussion. However, the schema data would need to be there for this file to be useful. The important thing to notice is that the data is structured in a series of tags just like HTML.

Just like the strings.txt file we looked at previously, the strings.resX file cannot be used directly by Visual Basic .NET; it must be converted to another format. So the big question is: Why would we want to use this? The answer: Text files cannot store object data. If we want to store graphics, fonts, or any other serializable object in our resource file, we must use the XML format instead of a text file. This is also the format Visual Studio .NET uses within the development environment, and as such, probably is the format you will deal with most often.

The decision of which file format to use is quite simple. Normally, you will use the XML format through Visual Studio; however, if you will be sharing your resource file with others, it might be useful to use a text format for the sake of simplicity, especially if you do not expect them to have Visual Studio available. Also, if you wish to store graphics or any other object type data, you will have no choice but to use an XML file.

Now we come to the problem of creating the XML file. When I created the strings.resX file, I simply used the ResGen.exe tool that ships with the .NET Framework SDK to convert our strings.txt file to an XML file (strings.resX). However, this probably is not the way you would normally create an XML file. The capability to convert back and forth between text files and XML files is more for convenience and situations in which you will not be creating the resources yourself (for example, it's coming from a translator).

Although you can edit and create an XML file directly in any text editor the problem with this approach (aside from learning the XML schema for .resX files) is that the object data is stored in *binary format,* which means unless you have a computer chip in your brain, it's doubtful you'll be able to enter the object data. You probably are thinking that there must be some kind of tool that ships with Visual Studio .NET that will allow you to create and edit a .resX file—and you're right. In Visual Studio, you can click Project | Add New Item and select Assembly Resource File, which will add a .resX file to your project, as shown here:

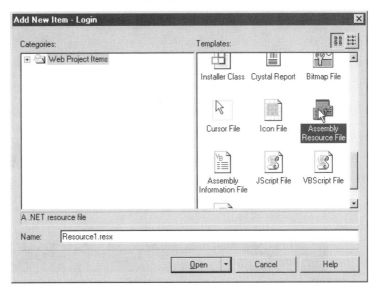

You then can edit the XML directly from the XML tab or edit your resource file in a tabular format using the Data tab.

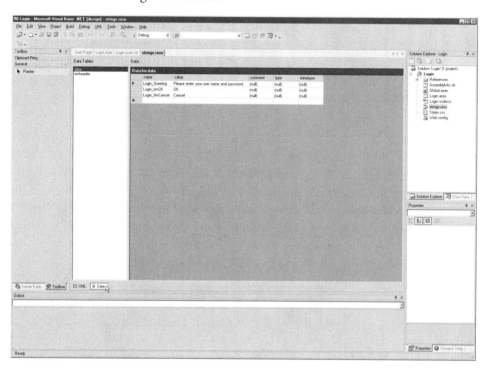

There are a few other programs that ship with Visual Studio .NET that enable us to edit and create .resX files. Probably the best one for the job actually is a sample application that ships with the .NET Framework SDK and is not part of Visual Studio .NET (although that's not really a problem because the .NET Framework SDK itself ships with Visual Studio .NET). The following table is a list of available tools that will enable you to edit and create .resX files that come with the .NET Framework SDK:

Tool	Functionality
ResGen.exe	Can create a .resources file from a text or XML file, and covert them back and forth.
ResXGen.exe	.NET Framework SDK sample program that creates a XML file from an image file.

Tool	Functionality
WinRes.exe	.NET Framework SDK program that enables you to edit XML and .resources files. You cannot add or remove a resource from the file; you can only edit it.
ResEditor.exe	.NET Framework SDK sample program that enables you to create and edit XML and .resources files (very useful).

The ResGen.exe tool's primary job is to create .resources files from .txt files and .resX files. We will discuss this tool in more depth shortly; however, as mentioned previously, this tool can create XML files from .txt files.

The ResXGen.exe tool actually is a sample application that ships with the .NET Framework SDK. It is a console utility (I hope you don't have an aversion to command-line tools) that enables us to convert an image file into a .resX file. This sample application was designed to show you how to programmatically add an image file to a .resX file; therefore, it is not very useful unless you want to quickly convert an image file to a .resX file. The program usually can be found in *C:\Program Files\ Microsoft.NET\FrameworkSDK\Samples\Tutorials\ResourcesAndLocalization\ResXGen* (depending on where you installed Visual Studio .NET) and uses the following command line syntax:

ResXGen [/i:<*inputfile*> /o:<*outputfile*> /n:<*name*>]

where *inputfile* is the name of the image file you wish to convert, *outputfile* is the name of the .resX file you wish to make, and *name* is the name you wish to refer to this image within your code.

The *Windows Resource Editor* (WinRes.exe) enables you to edit .resX and .resources files (which we will discuss shortly); however, you can change only resources that already exist within the file. You cannot add new resources to the file or delete resources that already exist. This tool was designed for resource maintenance and therefore doesn't really help us when it comes to creating new XML files.

By far the best SDK tool for creating and editing XML files is a sample program; a Windows application that enables us to add to strings, images, and other objects to an XML file. It is very simple to use and, as it is a sample project, comes with all of the source code so you can see how to create your own resource editor (which we will be discussing next). The program usually can be found in *C:\Program Files\Microsoft Visual Studio .NET\FrameworkSDK\Samples\Tutorials\ResourcesAndLocalization\ ResEditor* (depending on where you installed Visual Studio .NET) and, as it is a

Windows program, you can either double-click the icon or create a shortcut to it (you might have to build it by running build.bat). The user interface is fairly straightforward, as you can see in the following illustration:

The *ResXResourceWriter* class gives us the functionality to programmatically create and edit XML files, whereas the *ResXResourceReader* class gives us the functionality to programmatically read an XML file. These classes exist in the *System.Resources* namespace. The basic principle of creating an XML file programmatically involves these steps:

1. Instantiate a ResXResourceWriter object that creates the file.

2. Create the strings or objects if necessary.

3. Add the strings and objects to the ResXResourceWriter object.

4. Generate the file.

5. Close the file.

The following code illustrates creating a .resX file and storing a string and a bitmap in the newly created .resX file. You will need to remember to import the *System.Resources* namespace.

```
' Create a new .resX file by instantiating the ResXResourceWriter
Dim resWriter As ResXResourceWriter = New ResXResourceWriter("MyRes.resX")
```

```
' Create the string and bitmap
Dim strGreeting As String = "Hello World!"
Dim bmpCanada As Bitmap = New Bitmap("mapleleaf.bmp")

' Add the string and bitmap to the ResXResourceWriter
resWriter.AddResource("Greeting_Label", strGreeting)
resWriter.AddResource("flag", bmpCanada)

' Generate the file and close it
resWriter.Generate()
resWriter.Close()
```

When the *ResXResourceWriter* is instantiated, the file is created. You also will notice that the *AddResource* method works for both strings and bitmaps (and other objects). This might be strange to you, as in previous versions of Visual Basic *method overloading* was not allowed. Method overloading is the capability to define more than one method with the exact same name but with different arguments.

In the case of the *AddResource* method, there are three versions that can take a string, an object, or a *blob* (binary large object) as the second argument. Also, if you fail to execute the *generate* method the file will automatically be generated when the *close* method is executed. Of course, it's still a good idea to execute both methods for code clarity.

.NET-compatible Resource File (.resources)   To use a resource file in a Web application, it must be in a .NET-compatible resource file. The only file type acceptable is the .resources file. This means that in order to use a resource file, we have one of two choices: create a text file or XML file and convert it to a .resources file, or create a .resources file directly.

If we are using an XML file in Visual Studio, it will automatically be converted to a .resources file and packaged into an assembly when we build the application (click Build | Build Solution). If we have decided to create our resource files by using a text file or XML file, we can also use the ResGen.exe command line utility to convert these files to a .resources file. The ResGen.exe utility simply reads the text or XML file and uses the *ResourceWriter* class (similar to the *ResXResourceWriter* class) to create the .resources file. The following are examples of converting our strings.txt and strings.resX files to .resources files using the ResGen.exe utility:

```
ResGen strings.txt
ResGen strings.resX
```

FROM THE CLASSROOM

Binary Large Objects (Blobs)

A blob is a special way to store objects in files; it involves taking all the bits and pieces of the object (the data members) and sticking them end to end to form a continuous stream of information. This binary stream then can be stored in a file. Of course, in order to read the object from the file, we have to know where each data member starts and ends, and the order in which it was stored. For this reason, only objects that inherit the *ISerializable* interface can be stored in resource files.

The *ISerializable* interface enables us to teach the object how to write itself as a blob and re-create itself from a blob. You might be wondering what data members would be found in an image. Bitmaps, JPEGs, and other image files contain a header section with information about what kind of image it is, its size, and how it is stored; and the image data itself (as well as some more information we won't get into). The bitmap class in Visual Basic has data members that correspond to the different bits of information in a bitmap file.

If you find that an object of your own creation can be localized and you want to define how that serialization takes place, you can store it in a resource file by simply implementing the *ISerializable* interface (search the MSDN library for *ISerializable*). If you do not wish to define how serialization takes place and are willing to let the .NET framework take care of it, you can simply add the *Serializable* attribute to your class.

—*Wayne Cassidy, Bsc, MCSD, MCT*

As you can see, this is one command-line utility that is not very frightening. The utility determines whether the input file is a text file or XML file, and spits out a corresponding .resources file. Your application can use this directly or can be packaged into an *assembly*. (An assemby is compiled code or resources that can be used by the .NET Framework and is very similar to an executable file or dynamic linked library, but we will look at this later.)

Those of you with an adventurous spirit can programmatically create a .resources file using the *ResourceWriter* class the same way we used the ResXResourceWriter class to create XML files. It is so similar that you can literally take the code we saw for creating XML files programmatically and simply change all references to *ResXResourceWriter* to *ResourceWriter*. For clarity, let's look at the new code:

```
' Create a new .resX file by instantiating the ResourceWriter
Dim resWriter As ResourceWriter = New
ResourceWriter("MyRes.resources")

' Create the string and bitmap
Dim strGreeting As String = "Hello World!"
Dim bmpCanada As Bitmap = New Bitmap("mapleleaf.bmp")

' Add the string and bitmap to the ResourceWriter
resWriter.AddResource("Greeting_Label", strGreeting)
resWriter.AddResource("flag", bmpCanada)

' Generate the file and close it
resWriter.Generate()
resWriter.Close()
```

As you can see, it's almost identical to what we had before; in fact, the ResourceEditor sample application we discussed earlier simply uses the ResXResourceWriter class to write to .resX files and the ResourceWriter class to write to .resources files. To fully investigate creating your own resource editor, I strongly suggest you take a look at the sample application.

exam
ⓌaTch
Remember that a .resources file is the only type of file that can be used by our applications or packaged into an assembly. Unless you are using Visual Studio to create and build resource files, you'll have to remember to use the ResGen tool to convert them into this format before trying to package them into an assembly. This is worth mentioning, as Visual Studio typically hides this fact from us.

Converting Resource Files from One Type to Another

One of the most interesting features of the previously mentioned ResGen.exe utility is its capability to convert resource files from one type to another. It can convert text files to XML or .resources files, XML files to text files or .resources files, or .resources files back to XML files or text files. This is extremely useful when you find yourself supporting an application that was written by a disorganized development team. Often I have faced situations in which bits of source code have gone missing even though the compiled versions still exist. The capability to take a .resources file and convert it back into a XML or text file can be extremely useful.

Another common use for this capability is to create strings in a text file (which can be done very quickly) and convert them to an XML file, at which point you can add graphics to your resource file. You can convert back and forth between file types with the following command:

ResGen *<inputfile> <outputfile>*

ResGen.exe will determine the conversion based on the file extensions of *inputfile* and *outputfile*. As an example, to convert our MyStrings.resources file back to a text file, we would execute the following command:

ResGen strings.resources strings.txt

It is important to remember that text files do not support the inclusion of objects, whereas XML files and .resources files do. Therefore, if your .resources file contains any objects such as images, you will simply see the name of the image inserted into the text file instead of the binary image itself. An error also will occur; however, the process will continue, which makes this a useful way to pull strings out of a .resources file.

on the job

One way we can use the ResGen.exe tool is to convert a .resources file back into a text file. Remember that any of the comments or headers in your original text file were stripped out when you originally converted the text file into a .resources file; you should not count on the comments being there. If you create any tools to parse your resource files while they're in a text format, you should take this into consideration.

Now that we have an understanding of three resource file formats and how to convert them from one form to another, we need an easy way to decide what formats we wish to work with.

Where to Put Your Resource Files

We finally have our resources packaged into a .NET-compatible resource file (a .resources file). We can leave them the way they are (which we call *loose resources*)

SCENARIO & SOLUTION

I'm creating a small Web application that will support three different languages, all three of which I read and write fluently. How should I proceed?	Use assembly resource files from Visual studio (which are XML files). When you build your Web application, the resource files will be packaged into assemblies and placed in the proper directories for you. It will be easy to maintain them and easy to add more later if you wish.
I'm creating a large Web application that will support many languages, and the resources will have to be sent to a professional translator for translation. How should I proceed?	Create your first resource file as a text file that will contain the resources for your default language. When you need to translate them, you can simply send the text file to a translator, who can easily translate the resources within this file with very little instruction (he or she could easily be taught over the phone). When you receive them back from the translator, you can use the ResGen.exe tool to convert them to XML format (.resX file) and add them to your Visual Studio project. Visual Studio then can take care of packaging them into assemblies, which we will discuss in the next section.
I'm creating a Web application that I will be selling to my clients. I want to give them a tool that will enable them to edit their own resource files and package them into assemblies automatically. I have no way to ensure that they have access to Visual Studio; even if I did, I doubt they would know how to use it. What should I do?	Use the *ResourceWriter* and *ResourceReader* class to create a program that reads and writes .resources files. You then can run them through the assembly generation tool (shell to al.exe, write a script, and so forth.) to create the assembly and place it in the appropriate directory.
I want to remotely add resource files for specific cultures to my application but I have only telnet access to the server where my Web site resides. What should I do?	You can use any resource format that is most convenient, but you'll have to package and deploy them using the command line tools (ResGen.exe and al.exe).

or we can package them into assemblies. Packaging them into assemblies is by far the best option; this is what Visual Studio will do when you build your application.

However, it is quite possible to use the resources as they are. If we are going to use loose resources the next question is: Where do we put these files? If you do not want

Visual Studio to build your resources into assemblies, you must set the Build Action property of your resource to None.

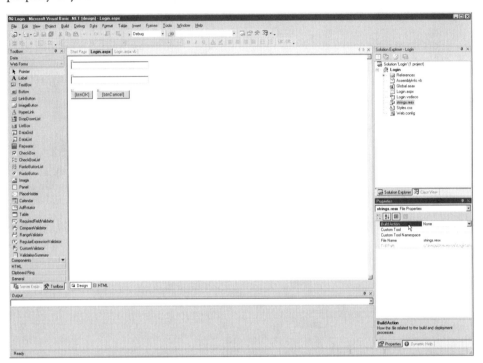

We can put the files anywhere we have access to them as long as they all are in the same directory. Putting them in the same directory allows the .NET Framework to load the appropriate resource file for the appropriate culture without the hassle of specifying where to find individual files within our Web pages. To compartmentalize our Web application, we should put all of our resource files in a subdirectory of our virtual directory called "Resources." By doing this, we are essentially further segregating our user interface resources from our application code.

Although putting all of our resource files (.resources files) into a resource directory is acceptable, it is not desirable. One problem with this approach occurs when we need to change one of the resource files while it is in use. Multiple users will be accessing the same resource files at the same time, which will not cause problems as they are simply reading these files. If we then decide to change the contents of one of our resource files, we will get a locking problem.

On a Windows system, you cannot write to a file opened by another user for reading or writing. This is to prevent file contents from changing while a user is in the middle of reading it, which obviously could cause problems. Essentially, this means we have to shut down our Web site to change the file. A solution to this problem is to package our resources into assemblies which, as mentioned previously, is what Visual Studio does when we build our application and is what we will discuss next.

e x a m
ⓦa t c h

Exam 70-305 will expect you to understand how to package resource files into assemblies. This is by far the preferred method of using resource files; therefore, you should focus on gaining some experience with this method instead of using loose resource files.

Assemblies

Assemblies are the deployment unit of the .NET Framework. In a *managed* Windows application (a .NET Framework application), an executable file is stored as an assembly when you compile it. In a Web application, the assembly is created at runtime, which means Web developers will not be as concerned with creating assemblies unless they are creating compiled components such as controls, dynamic linked libraries (DLLs), or resource-only assemblies. We can package our resource files in assemblies to prevent the previously discussed locking problems when they are updated. In this section, we will examine using assemblies for this purpose.

What Is an Assembly?

To start our discussion of assemblies, let's talk about how assemblies are used for traditional Windows applications. C++ programmers probably will recognize the file format for a Windows executable file, which is known as a *portable executable file (PE file)*. Visual Basic programmers probably will recognize these as executable files compiled to native code. PE files are Windows executable files in the traditional sense. Although not truly portable (they will not run on a UNIX system), this file format allows Windows programs to run on different versions of the Windows operating system with different underlying hardware.

Assemblies are a further advancement on this concept. An assembly basically looks like a standard EXE or DLL; however, there are some major differences, of which the most drastic is they no longer contain machine language code. The following is a list of the contents of an assembly:

- MSIL code
- Assembly metadata (the manifest)
- Type metadata
- Resources

The first in our list is our compiled code; however, instead of machine code, it is in the form of *Microsoft Intermediate Language (MSIL or IL)*. This code is compiled from your source code into machine language when the program is run by the *Just-In-Time compiler (JITc)*. In this way, .NET Assemblies are just as portable as Java class files.

Java developers will recognize that you can transfer to, and run on any machine and any platform as the exact same compiled Java class, so long as the platform has the *Java Run-Time environment* installed *(JRE or JDK)*. In the same way, a .NET assembly will run on any machine that has the .NET Framework installed. Although presently the only platforms that support the .NET Framework are versions of Windows, probably the .NET Framework soon will be ported to other platforms, making .NET assemblies just as portable as Java classes. In the context of Web development, assemblies are primarily used to deploy controls and to contain resources used for localization.

Assembly metadata is simply data about our assembly. The word *metadata* just means data about data. Web developers will already be experienced using metadata, as we often use Meta tags on our Web pages to describe the contents of the Web page for search engines and development tools. This metadata forms the *manifest* for the assembly.

Type metadata is simply data that describes the different types available in our assembly. These types most often are classes and other structured data that our assembly exposes. In the context of this chapter, this is not terribly important, as the assemblies we will create will contain only resources and not types that are defined in code.

The final elements in an assembly are resources. This is of specific interest to us because we will be packaging our resource files in assemblies, creating what are known as *resource-only assemblies,* or *satellite assemblies.* These assemblies are used to store resources, which we will use to provide localization capabilities to our Web applications.

In a Windows application, the main assembly is the executable file for the program and will contain the resources for the default culture along with the code of the application. Because an ASP.NET application is not a single executable but a collection of files in a virtual directory, we do not have a main assembly (actually it is created dynamically when the site is loaded, so we never see it). However, we can create a parallel main assembly (a DLL used to put resources and code, such as the code behind the web pages), which, if this was a Windows application, we normally would have packaged into the main assembly. This parallel main assembly is where we put the resources for default culture. If you look in the bin directory of your application's virtual directory, often you'll find a DLL with the same name as your project in it, (although not always); this is the parallel main assembly. The satellite assemblies we create are resource-only assemblies used to support specific cultures; they are stored in subdirectories of the bin directory, which we will see later. We should note that if you compile your project with Visual Studio .NET, a parallel main assembly will always be created for you and can be found in the bin directory. This is one of the major differences between compiling with Visual Studio .NET and the command-line compiler. If you use the command-line compiler, you will have to create the parallel-main assembly yourself.

Add a Resource File to an Assembly

The first thing to point out is that a resource file must be in a .NET Framework–compatible format to be added to an assembly. There's only one format acceptable: the .resources format. When using the Visual Studio Development Environment, we can use the compiler to add our resource files to our assembly simply by clicking Build | Build Solution.

This is by far the easiest way to do this; however, we also have access to a command-line utility: the *Assembly Generation Tool* (AL.exe), which is similar in function to the Visual C++ linker. This linker will allow us to add one or more resource files to an assembly. Technically, the Assembly Generation Tool is not only for resource files; it also will link any other files that can be put into an assembly. However, for the purposes of our discussion, we will only add resource files to our assemblies.

The Assembly Generation Tool is a command-line utility that has numerous switches that control its behavior (UNIX programmers are going to love this). If you are wondering why we are discussing this when Visual Studio will do it for us, it is for situations in which either Visual Studio is not present (you can install the .NET Framework without Visual Studio) or it is just more convenient. I'm sure some of you have created ASP pages in Notepad; basically this is the same thing. On that note, the following is the command line syntax for the Assembly Generation Tool:

al [*options*] [*sources*]

It actually doesn't look that bad—until you consider all the options. [Options] are the command-line switches we can use to instruct the Assembly Generation Tool on how to create our assembly, and [sources] are the files you want to link into the assembly. The following is a list of the more common linker options you'll use to create your resource assemblies:

- **/t[arget]:lib[rary]**   Create a library or DLL instead of an EXE.
- **/c[ulture]:<text>**   Supported culture (see Table 4-1 for culture names).
- **/out:<filename>**   Output file name.
- **/embed[resource]:<filename>[,<name>[,Private]]**   Embed the file as a resource in the assembly.

For example, if we had a resource file called str.fr-CA.resources we wanted to package into an assembly, we would execute the following command from the command prompt:

```
al /t:lib /out:str.Resources.Dll /c:fr-CA /embed:str.fr-CA.resources,
str.fr-CA.resources,Private
```

The keyword "Private" at the end of the command tells the assembly generation tool whether to expose our resources to other assemblies or not. We usually set this to private. You probably won't use the assembly generation tool from the command line that often; however, it is comforting to know it's there for those odd situations such as using a machine that doesn't have Visual Studio installed, or when you're using ResGen.exe to convert text files to .resources files and you're at the command line already.

Resource-Only Assemblies (Satellite Assemblies)

There are only a few important points regarding resource-only assemblies that we have not talked about already. The most important thing to say is that a *satellite assembly* is, by definition, a resource-only assembly. Our entire discussion thus far has focused on creating resource-only assemblies, which means without even knowing it we just learned how to create satellite assemblies. The best part is that the knowledge gained up to this point is equally applicable to creating global Windows-based applications, as you also will have to create satellite assemblies with these applications.

The last thing I will mention is that packaging your resources into satellite assemblies is extremely important, as it allows the .NET Framework to copy your assemblies to the *global assembly cache,* which is where all shared assemblies are stored (this process is called *shadow copying*). The .NET Framework does this because those users with open sessions on your Web site will be sharing the same resources and therefore the same assemblies. As mentioned earlier, the biggest benefit of this is that it enables us to edit our assemblies (and the resources within them) while our Web site is running without running into locking problems.

The clients of your Web site will be using the version of the assembly stored in the global assembly cache, whereas you will change the assembly stored in your virtual directory. For those of you who have some experience with creating Windows-based applications, you might be wondering whether we have to manually install our assemblies in the global assembly cache. The shadow copying process is done automatically for ASP.NET applications. In the following exercise, you will build resource files in Visual Studio and from the command line.

EXERCISE 4-1

Create Resource Files and Package Them into Assemblies

In this exercise, we first will look at using Visual Studio to create two new XML resource files and package them into assemblies. Then we will use text files as our resource files and use the command-line utilities to convert them to .NET Framework–compatible resource files, and package them into assemblies.

Create Resource Assemblies with Visual Studio:

1. Launch Visual Studio.

2. Create a new ASP.NET project called "Login" (if you're not sure how to do this, please refer back to Chapter 1).

3. Click Project | Add New Item and select Assembly Resource File from the Add New Item dialog box. Name the assembly resource file "Login.resx."

4. Click Open.

5. Add some resources to your file and click the Save button on the toolbar. The Resource Editor and your resources should look like the following illustration:

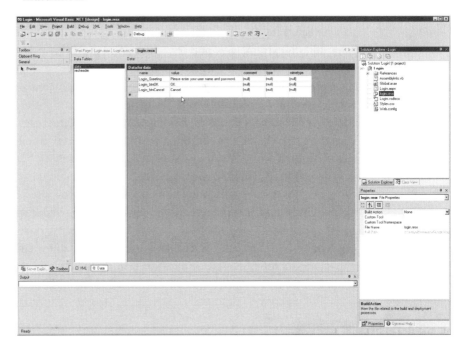

6. Create another resource file called "Login.de-DE.resx" by repeating Steps 3–5.

7. Build your project by clicking Build | Build Login.

8. Examine the bin subdirectory of the virtual directory for your new project. In most cases, it will be in C:\Inetpub\wwwroot\Login\bin, depending on your setup.

9. Notice that your default resources are in the Login.dll file in the bin directory and your German resources are in the Login.resources.dll file, which is in the de-DE subdirectory.

Create Resource Assemblies with the Command-line Utilities:

1. Launch Notepad by clicking Start | Run and typing **notepad**.

2. Enter the following resources into Notepad, remembering to comment your file and use a header called "strings":

Login_Greeting	Please enter your username and password.
Login_btnOK	OK
Login_btnCancel	Cancel

3. Save the file by clicking File | Save with the following parameters:

Filename	strings.txt
Location	c:\temp (You may have to create this directory first.)

4. Open the command prompt by clicking Start | Programs | Microsoft Visual Studio .NET | Visual Studio .NET Tools | Visual Studio .NET Command Prompt.

5. Type **cd c:\temp.**

6. Type **resgen strings.txt.**

7. Type **dir** and notice that a new file exists called "strings.resources."

8. Type **al /t:lib /out:strings.resources.dll /c:en /embed:strings.resources, str.resources,Private.**

9. Type **dir** and notice that your new resource-only assembly exists and is called strings.resources.dll.

CERTIFICATION OBJECTIVE 4.02

Create and Implement Satellite Assemblies

Now we can create resources for applications, store them in resource files, and package them into assemblies. You also have seen (in Chapter 3) how to get the information from our assemblies for use on our Web pages. We're going to take this opportunity to stand back a little bit and consider the bigger picture. The primary focus of this section will be how to set up our applications so they can properly take advantage of the resource files we create for them. We will learn how to create an application that uses multiple resource files for supporting multiple languages and cultures.

Neutral and Culture-Specific Assemblies

In our discussion on creating resource-only assemblies, we talked about identifying a default culture for your application. This default culture was essentially the most common culture used by the clients of your application. We're going to use this culture not only as a starting point for development, but as a fallback point for clients whose browsers are set to a culture we're not yet supporting.

The basic idea is that we don't want to get into a situation in which the user requests a Web page and gets an error because we're not supporting his or her culture. A better idea would be to give them the information in some language, which is better than nothing at all. This means if our default language is U.S. English and the user's browser is set to the culture we don't support, he or she will still get a response—it will just be in U.S. English. If we're lucky, the user will speak enough English to get some benefit from our page, which obviously is better than getting no benefit at all.

If you're creating your application in the Visual Studio IDE and you're using code-behind in your Web pages, you will notice that in the bin subdirectory of your virtual directory there's a DLL with the same name as your project. This is the parallel-main assembly that contains all of the compiled code-behind in your Web application and also is the assembly we will use to store our default resources.

If you are not using code-behind in your Web pages, you will have to create a parallel main assembly that contains only the resources of your default culture. Either way, this is an extremely easy thing to do from within Visual Studio. It simply involves adding an assembly resource file, which can be called anything you like (I usually call mine strings); Visual Studio will take care of the rest.

When you build your application, this resource file will be compiled into the assembly and will be the default resource for our application. At this point, it would not be unreasonable to deploy our application and allow users to start taking advantage of all the goodies we've put into it.

on the !Job

You might find that the default language for the job is not the language you speak. In this situation, simply develop your application using your own language as the default language; once complete, you can change the filenames of your resource files within Visual Studio so that your language resource file forms a satellite assembly and the real default language file forms the parallel main assembly. After rebuilding your application, the resources will be in the right spots.

Now that we have taken care of our default culture and possibly released our application, our next step is to add our localized assemblies, which will be satellite assemblies (resource-only assemblies). Now naming our assembly resource files becomes important. You should remember from the last section on creating resource-only assemblies that the name of our resource file will have to be the same name as our default resource file but with the culture name in the middle (for example, strings.fr-CA.resX). We must simply add one assembly resource file for every localized culture we plan to support.

Once we have added all of the resource files to our project, Visual Studio will create the satellite assemblies and put them in the right directories for us. If you're not using Visual Studio, you'll have to use the command-line utilities we discussed previously to do this manually.

One important point to note is that even though all of your culture-specific resource files will have slightly different names, the culture name in the middle will be different for each one. The Assembly Generation Utility strips the culture name from the filename; the result is that all of your satellite assemblies will wind up having the exact same name. The assembly file does not need the culture name as part of its final name because the manifest within the assembly contains this information. The following is a list of resource file names and associated assembly file names for some compiled resource files:

Resource File Name	Assembly File Name
strings.en.resources	strings.resources.dll
strings.en-US.resources	strings.resources.dll
strings.de-CH.resources	strings.resources.dll

As you'll see in the next section, these assemblies will go into different subdirectories of the bin directory. Remember: Don't try to create all of your assemblies in the same directory (can you say "name conflict?"). When creating satellite assemblies from the command line, it is best to create the directory structure you'll see in the next section before creating your assemblies.

Location of Assemblies in the Virtual Directory

The .NET Framework can figure out where the different assemblies for your different cultures can be found because it expects you to put these assemblies in very specific locations. The parallel main assembly (the assembly that contains the resources for your default culture) should be placed in the bin directory.

All of your culture-specific assemblies (satellite assemblies) should be placed in subdirectories of the bin directory; these subdirectories should have the same name as the culture name of the assembly. For example, while writing this chapter I created a small application that supports neutral English (en) as the default language, Canadian French (fr-CA), neutral German (de), and Swiss German (de-CH). The following is what the bin directory for that application looks like:

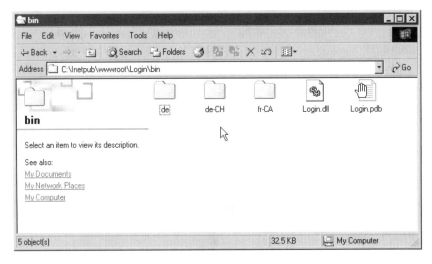

Following this directory structure allows the .NET Framework to find the proper resources. The best part is we don't have to write any code to make this happen; we simply have to follow the rules (no rebels here).

Exam 70-305 will expect you to have a good understanding of the directory structure created by Visual Studio when using satellite assemblies. Although the structure is created for you, it still is important to have this knowledge to test and debug global applications. It also can be very useful if you find yourself in a situation where you're creating your application without the help of Visual Studio (using the .NET Framework SDK or when you only have access to the command prompt).

How the Framework Finds the Right Assembly for the Job

The Framework has very specific rules for finding the right assemblies for the culture requested. Understanding these rules can help us to plan which cultures we might wish to support. The bottom line is we probably will never create an application that tries to support every single culture. But ideally, anyone wishing to view our Web page should be able to do so.

When a user requests a Web page, his or her browser sends as part of the request a list of languages his or her browser supports (in Internet Explorer, click Tools | Internet Options… and you'll notice that at the bottom of the general tab there is a button called "Languages…").

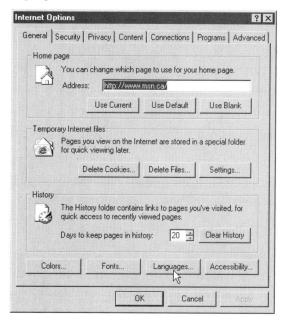

The first place the Framework checks is the Global Assembly Cache, where it searches for the specific resource file for the culture requested. Thanks to shadow copying of our assemblies, if we support this culture, it should be found here. If it finds the appropriate resource file, it searches the resource file for the resource requested (for example, the caption for our OK button). If the specific resource is not found or we do not support this culture (in which case it will not find the resource file), it then searches the bin directory for a subdirectory with the same name as the culture requested (if the culture requested is US English, it looks for a subdirectory called en-US).

Because our assemblies are shadow copied normally, we would not expect the Framework to find our assembly here if it did not find it in the Global Assembly Cache. However, if we have just added support for a new culture, it is possible that it has not yet been copied, in which case it will do so now and will search for the appropriate resource.

If it still can't find the resource or once again we do not support this culture, the next step is to go back to the Global Assembly Cache and search for a parent resource (which most likely is a neutral culture such as neutral English or *en*). It then goes through the previous process again and looks for the specific resource requested. If not found or we do not support the parent culture, it goes back to the bin directory again and looks there.

This process of bouncing back and forth between the Global Assembly Cache and the bin directory continues until there are no further parent cultures to look for, at which time it simply uses the default resource file and returns a response. In the rare situation in which the default resource does not contain the specific resource requested, it will throw an error. This should be avoided at all costs.

To avoid this, you should make sure your default resource file contains all possible resources for your application, which will prevent errors from ever being thrown as a result of a missing resource. This entire process is known as *falling back;* often the default assembly is called the *fallback assembly* because this is the final assembly to which we can fall back. This process can be seen in the following steps:

1. Framework checks the Global Assembly Cache for the culture-specific resource file.
   A. If found, the Framework checks the resource file for the appropriate resource.
   B. If found, it returns it; otherwise, it moves on to Step 2.
2. The Framework searches the bin directory of our application for a subdirectory with the same name as the culture requested.

    A. If found, it checks the satellite assembly contained within for the appropriate resource.

    B. If found, it returns it; otherwise, it moves to Step 3.

3. The Framework moves back to the Global Assembly Cache and checks for the parent culture specific resource file.

    A. If found, the Framework checks the resource file for the appropriate resource.

    B. If found, it returns it; otherwise, it moves on to Step 4.

4. The Framework searches the bin directory of our application for a subdirectory with the same name as the parent culture requested.

    A. If found, it checks the satellite assembly contained within for the appropriate resource.

    B. If found, it returns it; otherwise, it moves to Step 5.

5. The Framework moves back to Step 3 and keeps looking until there are no parent culture resource files left, at which point it moves on to Step 6.

6. The Framework looks for the default culture.

    A. If found, the Framework checks the resource file for the appropriate resource.

    B. If found, it returns it; otherwise, it moves on to Step 7.

7. The Framework throws a run-time error.

One of the most useful ways we can use this process to our advantage is by entering only resources in satellite assemblies that actually differ from their parent assemblies. For example, there is relatively little difference between neutral English and U.S. English, which means we have to add only resources in our U.S. English resource file that differ from neutral English. When the framework searches for a specific resource, it will start by searching U.S. English if the clients' browser is set to U.S. English.

However, if the resource requested does not differ from neutral English, the framework will not find it in the U.S. English resource file and will fall back to the parent resource file, which is neutral English; finding it there, it will return it to the browser. This process can cut down an enormous amount of work preparing resource files, as we have to deal only with the differences between cultures; not simply duplicate every single resource in each resource file. The following is a quick reference that might help you identify some of the problems which may occur as a result of errors in the fallback process.

SCENARIO & SOLUTION

Some of my users are complaining that they get an error when accessing my site that states the system cannot find a resource. I have not implemented a default culture in my parallel main assembly. What should I do?	If you do not have a default culture to fall back to, you either have to support every single culture there is (not reasonable) or simply live with the fact that this will happen. You probably should reconsider your design and add a default culture to your parallel main assembly.
Some of my users are complaining that they get an error message when accessing my site that states the system cannot find a resource. I have a default culture in my parallel main assembly, but it still happens. What should I do?	If this is the case, this error probably is happening quite often. You probably have a resource that has been implemented in your satellite assemblies but has been forgotten in your default assembly. When the system falls back to the default culture the resource is not there. Simply add that specific resource to your default culture resource file and repackage the assembly.
In my application, my default culture is English and I am supporting French. Some of my French users are complaining that only some of the captions on the Web site are in English—not all of them. How can I correct this?	You have localized your application well; however, you have forgotten to add a specific resource to your French language resource file. When the system looks for most of the resources, it finds them; however, when the system looks for the resource you forgot to add, it does not find it and falls back to the default English assembly for that single resource. Simply find the resource you forgot to add to your French language resource file, add it, and repackage your assembly.

Some of you might be thinking that this could have a detrimental effect on the speed at which pages are rendered (and you would be right). However, in most situations you'll find that the bottleneck for rendering a page is not searching for resources; instead, it is most likely database access or some other time-consuming process. This means if you want to make a difference in the speed of your application, your time would be better spent improving data access than it would be improving the speed at which your application finds resources, as this normally would not have a significant effect.

In situations in which every second counts, we can simply ensure that all of our culture-specific resource files contain all of the resources for the application (of course, there are plenty of other areas I would focus on first). The following exercise will demonstrate the fallback capabilities of the Framework and give you some experience implementing a global application.

EXERCISE 4-2

Create a Globalized Application

In this exercise, we will create a globalized application that supports U.S. English as the default language and United Kingdom English using a satellite assembly. We will take advantage of the .NET Framework's fallback capability to avoid entering resources that are not different between the two cultures.

1. Launch Visual Studio.

2. Create a new ASP.NET project called "Rental" (if you're not sure how to do this, please refer back to Chapter 1).

3. Click Project | Add New Item and select Assembly Resource File from the Add New Item dialog box. Name the Assembly Resource File "Rental.resx."

4. Click Open.

5. Add the following resources to your file and click the Save button on the toolbar:

Rental_Greeting	Please enter the address of the apartment you wish to rent with the ZIP code.
Rental_btnOK	OK
Rental_btnCancel	Cancel

6. Create another resource file called "Login.en-GB.resx" by repeating Steps 3–5, this time using the following information:

Rental_Greeting	Please enter the address of the flat you wish to rent with the postal code.

7. Open WebForm1.aspx in design view and add the following controls with the following properties:

TextBox	ID = txtAddress Text = " "
Button	ID = btnOK Text = " "
Button	ID = btnCancel Text = " "

8. Switch to HTML view and enter the following code just after the opening form tag (<FORM...>):

```
<h3><%=rm.GetString("Rental_Greeting")%></h3>
```

9. Click the View Code button in the Solution Explorer window.

10. Add the following lines of code in the code window before the declaration for the rental class:

```
Imports System.Resources
Imports System.Globalization
Imports System.Threading
```

11. Add the following code right after the Inherits System.Web.UI.Page line:

```
Protected rm As ResourceManager
```

12. Add the following code to the Page_Load event:

```
'Set Culture to the language of the user's browser
Thread.CurrentThread.CurrentCulture = _
 CultureInfo.CreateSpecificCulture(Request.UserLanguages(0))
Thread.CurrentThread.CurrentUICulture = _
 New CultureInfo(Request.UserLanguages(0))

'Instantiate the ResourceManager to use our resource file
rm = New ResourceManager("Login.strings",_
 GetType(Login).Assembly)

'Set the OK and Cancel buttons text to the appropriate values
btnOK.Text = rm.GetString("Login_btnOK")
btnCancel.Text = rm.GetString("Login_btnCancel")
```

13. Build your project by clicking Build | Build Login.

14. Right-click the WebForm1.aspx file in the Solution Explorer and select View In Browser.

15. You should see the U.S. English instructions (unless you are from the UK).

16. Open Internet Explorer.

17. Click Tools | Internet Options.

18. Click the Languages button at the bottom of the General tab.

19. Click the Add button and add English (United Kingdom) [en-gb] by selecting it from the list and clicking OK.

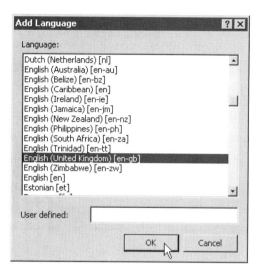

20. Click the English (United Kingdom) [en-gb] from the languages list box and move it up to the top of the list.

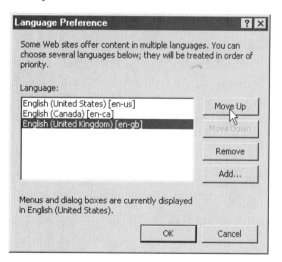

21. In the address bar of Internet Explorer type **http://localhost/Rental/WebForm1.aspx** and hit ENTER (this assumes Visual Studio is using localhost for your web server; if this is not the case, replace localhost with the appropriate domain).

22. You should notice that the OK and Cancel buttons are the same but the instructions have changed to use the words "flat" and "postal code."

CERTIFICATION SUMMARY

In this chapter, we've discussed creating global applications. We've explored the process of creating resource files and packaging them into assemblies. We also have created satellite assemblies (resource-only assemblies) for the specific cultures we wish to support, after which we saw where to put our assemblies and how the Framework searches for specific resources in the assemblies we create.

In a standard project, we would create a parallel main assembly for our default culture and satellite assemblies for each specific culture. It is important to remember that the directory structure of our bin directory must be set up properly for the framework to find the appropriate resources in the appropriate assemblies. It is also important to understand how the framework searches for our resources so that we can properly plan the cultures we will support and the resources we will add to each culture-specific resource file.

The Visual Studio Integrated Development Environment can make the entire process extremely easy. If you have added your default resource file and culture-specific resource files to your project, when you build the project, all of the resource files will be packaged into assemblies, the appropriate subdirectories in the bin directory will be created, and the assemblies will be placed in the appropriate directory.

We also have discussed many of the command-line tools that ship with the .NET Framework SDK, which you can use in situations in which you do not have access to Visual Studio or the Windows GUI is not available. Microsoft has made it extremely easy to implement global applications; therefore, it will be much cheaper and involve much less effort than it has in the past.

TWO-MINUTE DRILL

Create Resource-Only Assemblies

❑ Globalization is the process of separating user interface graphics and text for the programming logic of your application.

❑ Localization is the process of adding support for specific cultures.

❑ Visual Studio uses XML files for resource files.

❑ Resource files can be created using text files, XML files, or .NET Framework–compatible resource files (.resources files).

❑ Text files and XML files must be converted to a .NET Framework–compatible resource file (.resources files) before they can be used by your application or packaged into assemblies.

❑ Text files and XML files can be packaged into assemblies from Visual Studio by building your project (Visual Studio will convert them to .resources files during this process).

❑ Text files and XML files also can be converted to .NET Framework–compatible resource files from the command line by using the ResGen.exe utility.

❑ .NET Framework–compatible resource files can be packaged into assemblies by using the Assembly Generation Utility at the command line.

Create and Implement Satellite Assemblies

❑ In an ASP.NET application, we use a parallel main assembly to store our default resources.

❑ Satellite assemblies are resource-only assemblies that are used to support specific cultures.

❑ For the framework to find your satellite assemblies, they must be placed in specific subdirectories of the bin directory that have the same name as the culture of the assembly.

❑ The parallel main assembly and satellite assemblies are shadow copied into the Global Assembly Cache, which makes editing these assemblies possible without shutting down the Web site.

❑ If the Framework cannot find a specific satellite assembly for the culture requested, it will fall back to that cultures parent assembly and search for the resource there. This fallback will continue until the default assembly is reached.

❑ If the Framework falls back to the default assembly and still the resource cannot be found, it will throw an error.

❑ Using the fallback mechanism to its advantage can save an enormous amount of work when developing applications for different regions that use the same language.

SELF TEST

The following questions will help measure your understanding of the material presented in this chapter. Read all the choices carefully; there might be more than one correct answer. Choose all correct answers for each question.

Create Resource-Only Assemblies

1. The process of creating a global application involves which of the following steps in the following order?

   A. Globalization, deployment, regionalization

   B. Regionalization, globalization, deployment

   C. Globalization, regionalization, deployment

   D. Globalization, localization, deployment

2. Another developer has given you an XML resource file (with the file extension .xml) to use in your application. You have changed the file extension to .resX and are trying to convert it to a .NET-compatible resource file using the ResGen.exe utility. The conversion is not successful. What is the most likely cause?

   A. You have failed to specify the culture using the /c switch.

   B. You should not have changed the file extension.

   C. The XML file does not have a .NET-compatible schema.

   D. You are using the wrong utility. You should be using the Assembly Generation Utility.

3. When creating a text file for a resource file, you can add which of the following elements? (Choose all that apply.)

   A. Key value pairs

   B. Images

   C. Comments

   D. Headers

4. You have converted a .NET-compatible resource file back into a text file using the ResGen.exe utility to add resources to it. When you open the text file, you notice that the images stored in the file are not there; only the name of the image. How can you retrieve the images from the resource file?

   A. Convert the file to an XML file instead of a text file.

   B. Use the /g switch to retrieve the images (graphics).

    C. You can only pull the strings of the resource file.

    D. Use the Assembly Generation Utility (al.exe) with the /u switch.

5. Which of the following resource files can be packaged directly into assemblies?

    A. Text files

    B. Any file with the extension .resources

    C. An XML file

    D. Any file created with the ResGen.exe utility

    E. All of the above

    F. None of the above

6. You've spent an enormous amount of time gathering information and creating resource files for a great number of cultures. One of your junior programmers accidentally deletes all of your source files (resource files in XML format). It is very important—you have to have access to these files, as they are continuously updated, which means sending them out for translation. The same programmer was responsible for performing monthly backups and has failed to do so for the last six months. How can you get this information out of your compiled resource files (.NET-compatible resource files with the extension .resources)? (Choose all that apply.)

    A. Fire the junior programmer.

    B. Write a small program to read the resources in the .NET-compatible resource files using the *ResourceReader* class; then use the *ResourceWriter* class to write this information to XML files.

    C. Use the ResGen.exe utility to convert the .NET-compatible resource files to XML files.

    D. Write a small program to read the resources in the .NET-compatible resource files using the *ResourceReader* class; then use the *ResXResourceWriter* class to write this information to XML files.

7. A .NET Framework–compatible resource file can be created from an XML file in which way(s)? (Choose all that apply.)

    A. By building your project in Visual Studio

    B. With the ResGen.exe command-line utility

    C. With the Assembly Generation Utility (al.exe)

    D. XML files cannot be converted to .NET Framework–compatible resource files

8. You're away on business and do not have access to a computer with .NET on it. You must compile a text file containing resources and package it into an assembly. What options do you have? (Choose the best option.)

A. You'll have to wait until you get back to the office.

B. Buy a copy of Visual Studio and install it on another computer near you.

C. Have your system administrator install terminal server on the Web server so you can run the command-line utilities remotely.

D. Have your system administrator start the telnet service for ten minutes while you log in, compile your resources, and package them into assemblies.

9. What is an assembly that contains only resources known as?

A. Orbital assembly

B. Main assembly

C. Assembly resource file

D. Satellite assembly

10. The translator you're using will perform the translation only in an Excel spreadsheet, as he or she is comfortable with this and does not want to waste valuable time trying to learn a new file format. Because an Excel spreadsheet is not a viable resource format, what can you do? (Choose the best answer.)

A. Copy and paste the information from the Excel spreadsheet into a text file and then prepare it using the proper format.

B. Copy the information by hand into an XML file in Visual Studio.

C. Write a small program that automates Excel, reads the information from Excel, and uses the *ResourceWriter* class to write the information into a .Net-compatible resource file.

D. Find a new translator.

Create and Implement Satellite Assemblies

11. What does shadow copying of an assembly in an ASP.NET application mean?

A. The assembly is copied to your Web server automatically.

B. The assembly is copied to the appropriate culture directory by Visual Studio.

C. The assembly is automatically copied to the global assembly cache.

D. None of the above.

12. You have created a Web application that supports multiple languages. Although everything is working fine, some of your users have commented that they do not recognize some words and others are offensive. What is the most likely problem?

A. You've implemented a neutral culture for these users and should have implemented a specific culture for the country or region they are from.

    B. Someone has hacked your site and you need to tighten security.

    C. The translator who translated your resource file has made some mistakes and you should have the translation checked.

    D. You're using a specific culture for your default culture and probably should have used a neutral culture (with no region-specific language).

13. What is the parent culture of United Kingdom English (en-GB)?

    A. The default culture

    B. Neutral German (de)

    C. When you create the assembly, you'll define the parent culture, which could be anything you want

    D. Neutral English (en)

14. You're editing a resource file for a Web application that has already been deployed. You get a locking error when you try to overwrite the resource file on the Web server. What do you do to fix this problem? (Choose the best answer.)

    A. Shut down the Web site, copy the file, and then start up the Web site again.

    B. Nothing; you cannot edit resource files once they have been deployed.

    C. Shut down the Web site and package your resource files into assemblies so this will not happen again.

    D. The problem is your Web application is not running in its own memory space; therefore, the file is being locked by IIS. Set up the Web application to run in its own memory space so the file will no longer be locked.

15. When searching your assemblies for a specific culture, what will the framework first look in?

    A. The Global Assembly Cache

    B. The resources directory

    C. The bin directory

    D. A subdirectory of the bin directory which matches the target culture

16. You are creating an application that will support United States English, Canadian English, Swiss German, Parisian French, and neutral English as the default culture. Everything in your application seems to work fine for all users; however, one of your German users only sees English. What are the possible causes of this problem? (Choose the best answer.)

    A. You improperly named your assembly resource file in Visual Studio. You forgot to add the culture name before the extension.

   B. You forgot to specify compiled culture information in your project properties.

   C. This user's browser is not set up for Swiss German.

   D. You did not add the Swiss German resource file to your project.

17. If the Framework cannot find a resource for a specific culture, which of the following will it do?

   A. Ignore that resource.

   B. Use English.

   C. Throw an error.

   D. Search for the resource in the parent culture's resource assembly.

18. You have satellite assembly in hand for a culture you now wish to support. Your application has already been deployed and is working fine. What must we do to allow our Web application to take advantage of this new assembly?

   A. Copy the assembly to the bin subdirectory of our virtual directory and use RegSvr32.exe to register the assembly with the registry.

   B. Copy the assembly to the resources subdirectory of your virtual directory.

   C. Create a new Web site based on the old one, adding your new assembly to the new Web site; then remove the old Web site.

   D. Create a new subdirectory of the bin directory with the culture name of this resource assembly. Copy this assembly to this new directory.

19. What should you do to prevent the Framework from throwing an error while searching for resources?

   A. Turn off error handling.

   B. Ensure that you have a default resource file in your parallel main assembly.

   C. Wrap all ResourceManager code in a try block.

   D. Implement resource files for all of the cultures you will support. If the user requests a culture not supported, he or she should get an error stating that you do not support his or her culture.

20. You're working on an application in which the language has been defined as French-Canadian. The problem is you speak only English. None of the users of this application speak anything but French-Canadian (this is not a global application). You're concerned that you will not be able to write the application, as it will be extremely difficult for you to test and debug the application. What steps can you take to become a useful participant in this project? (Choose the best answer.)

   A. Hire a bilingual assistant.

B. Globalize the application by removing all of the user interface text and placing it in resource files. Write the application in English and then have the resource files translated into French. When the application is finished, swap the English resource file for the French resource file.

C. Create the application in English and then have the Web pages translated into French when the application is finished.

D. Hire a bilingual programmer to write the user interface while you still work on the business logic of the application.

LAB QUESTION

You and your programming team have been asked to create a global Web site for a company that sells software. Your specific task for this job is to create a registration page so that users can sign up for a mailing list. This mailing list will be used for direct-mail marketing. The company primarily markets its software in North America; however, they also do a great deal of marketing in Germany, Switzerland, Japan, and France.

   You speak only English, but you have a translation staff available. Your translation staff is not technically competent and has no knowledge of Web development, XML, or any other technical materials you're working with. Explain how you will develop your resource files to make it easy for the translation staff to perform the translation and make it easy for yourself to deal with the results of the translation. You also must create the original resource file in English and in whatever format you choose; it will then be sent off for translation. Please make sure the format you choose is in line with the given situation. The following resources must be included in your original resource file:

Key	Value
FirstName	First Name:
LastName	Last Name:
Address1	Address Line 1:
Address2	Address Line 2:
Apartment	Apartment / Suite Number:
ZIP	ZIP Code:
Phone	Phone Number:
Email	Email Address:

SELF TEST ANSWERS

Create Resource-Only Assemblies

1. ☑ D. Globalization, localization, deployment.
☒ A, B, and C are incorrect, as regionalization is not a standard terminus process.

2. ☑ C. The XML schema must be specific to .NET.
☒ A is incorrect because there is no /c switch with the ResGen.exe Utility. B is incorrect because the file extension is irrelevant if the XML schema is incorrect. D is incorrect because the assembly generation tool does not convert resource files between formats.

3. ☑ A, C, and D. These all are acceptable elements for a text-based resource file.
☒ B is incorrect as you cannot store images and text files.

4. ☑ A. Because XML files can hold images, this is a viable option.
☒ B is incorrect because there is no /g switch. C is a true statement, but it is not an answer to the question. D is incorrect as the assembly generation tool is not the right tool for the job.

5. ☑ F. None of the above is correct.
☒ A is incorrect because text files cannot be packaged into assemblies as resource files. B is incorrect because the content of the file is what is important. Simply changing the file extension of a text file to .resources file does not change the file contents. C is incorrect because an XML file must be converted to a .NET-compatible resource file before being packaged into an assembly. D is incorrect because text files and XML files can be created with the ResGen.exe utility.

6. ☑ C and D. The ResGen.exe utility can convert a .NET-compatible resource file back to an XML file, or you can write a simple utility using the *ResourceReader* class and the *ResXResourceWriter* class.
☒ A is not a bad idea—but hey…everyone deserves a second chance. B is incorrect because the ResourceWriter class will not write information to XML file but only a .NET-compatible resource file.

7. ☑ A and B. XML files can be converted to .NET-compatible resource files by building them in Visual Studio (in which case they are only temporary for package into an assembly) or by using theResGen.exe utility.
☒ C is incorrect because the Assembly Generation Utility does not convert XML files into .NET-compatible resource files. D is incorrect because XML files can indeed be converted to .NET-compatible resource files.

8. ☑ **D.** Although telnet is not considered secure, your system administrator can create a temporary account for you to log in with during your brief access (and can give you the information over the phone). The administrator can disable the account after you are finished.

   ☒ **A** is incorrect because we obviously have other options. **B** is a possible option but is far too expensive to be considered reasonable. **C** is incorrect unless a terminal server is already installed under the Web server. Going through the hassle of installing a terminal server would involve rebooting the system, which would bring your Web site down (not something you want to do).

9. ☑ **D.** Satellite assemblies contain only resources.

   ☒ **A** is incorrect because there's no such thing as orbital assembly (maybe in rocket science). **B** is incorrect as the main assembly contains code and is dynamically created when the Web application is run. **C** is incorrect because an assembly resource file is not an assembly.

10. ☑ **C.** It is not difficult to automate Excel, which makes a tool of this type very easy to create in Visual Basic .NET.

    ☒ **A** and **B** are simply too time consuming and unnecessary for this task. **D** is just mean.

Create and Implement Satellite Assemblies

11. ☑ **C.** Assemblies are copied to the Global Assembly Cache when used. This means you can edit them without locking problems.

    ☒ Although **A** and **B** are factual, they do not define shadow copying.

12. ☑ **D.** If you are using a specific culture for your default culture, some users from other cultures (using the same language) will not recognize slang terms and might even be offended (do you know what they call cigarettes in England?).

    ☒ **A** is incorrect because neutral cultures should not have any language elements that are not common to all cultures using that language. **B** could be true, but what we have stated here would be much more noticeable. **C** also could be true, but it is doubtful that a professional translator would make a simple mistake such as this.

13. ☑ **D.** Neutral cultures are languages without country or region codes.

    ☒ **A** could be the parent culture of en-GB, depending on how you have set up your resources; however, the best answer is D—and you should always remember to choose the best answer (the answer that is correct without any conditions). Cultures have defined parents; they are not defined by the programmer.

14. ☑ **C.** By packaging your resources into assemblies you allow the Framework to shadow copy them into the Global Assembly Cache, thus releasing the lock on the assembly in the virtual directory. This will make it much easier to maintain them.

☒   A is a viable option that will work; however, it does not fix the problem for future maintenance. B is simply not true. D—regardless of whether your Web application is running in its own memory space—has nothing to do with file locking.

15.   ☑   A. The Framework first looks in the Global Assembly Cache.

    ☒   B is incorrect because the resource directory is used only when you're accessing loose resources, in which case you have full control over which files are searched. B is incorrect because the bin directory is searched only when the framework cannot find any specific resources matching the target culture, at which point it looks in the bin directory for the default culture. D is incorrect because the Framework searches the culture directories only after it has checked the Global Assembly Cache.

16.   ☑   C. This is the most likely cause of the problem as other Swiss German users have not made the same complaint.

    ☒   A is incorrect because all Swiss German users would have had the same problem if this were the case. B is incorrect because this option is not available in the project properties. D is also incorrect as all of your Swiss German users would have made the same complaint.

17.   ☑   D. If the framework cannot find a resource for a specific culture, it will fall back to the parent culture.

    ☒   A is incorrect because the framework will never ignore resource. B makes no sense as you might not even wish to support English. C is incorrect because an error is thrown only if the framework falls back to the default assembly and still cannot find the resource.

18.   ☑   D. To support a new culture, all we need to do is create a new satellite assembly, create a new subdirectory of the bin directory with the culture's name, and copy the assembly there. Everything else is taken care of by the Framework.

    ☒   A is incorrect because there is no requirement for assemblies to be registered (you're thinking of COM). B is incorrect because the resources directory is used only for loose resources (and this is not required; it's just suggested). C would work, but it is an enormous waste of time when you consider that D will work as well.

19.   ☑   B. By ensuring that you have a default resource file in your parallel main assembly, you're also ensuring that there is a valid resource in all circumstances (even if it's not the desired resource).

    ☒   A is incorrect because you cannot turn off error handling in the Framework. C is a good idea, but it will not help you with this problem. D is not desirable as this means a user whose culture you do not support will have no chance at all to view your information.

20. ☑ B. Globalizing an application can be very useful, even in situations in which you're not writing a global application.

☒ A is incorrect because it is unnecessary and overly expensive. C is an alternative; however, it is not as simple as B. D also is an alternative; however, once again it is overly expensive and complicated.

LAB ANSWER

In this situation, you probably should use a text file as your format for your resource file. Text files are very easy to manipulate and because your translation staff is not technically competent, it will be easy for them to edit these files directly with very little instruction. This also will allow you to work directly with the results from the translation department instead of converting them into another format (which most often involves either copying by hand or writing a utility to transform the information for you).

Once you have received the text files back from the translation department, you can simply use the ResGen.exe utility to convert them to XML files for inclusion into your Visual Studio project. The following text file would be appropriate for this purpose:

```
; US English Resource File (strings.txt)
; This is the default resource file for Project X
; Translators: please translate the text on the right side of the
; equal sign only. No other text is to be translated in this document.
; Thank You.

[strings]
FirstName = First Name:
LastName = Last Name:
Address1 = Address Line 1:
Address2 = Address Line 2:
Apartment = Apartment / Suite Number:
ZIP = ZIP Code:
Phone = Phone Number:
Email = Email Address:

; End of resource file
```

5

Create Controls

One of the most important characteristics of any modern computer programming language is the capability to reuse code in a simple and efficient way. This is a major selling point of object-oriented languages such as C++. The bottom line is this: The more code you can reuse, the less code you have to write and the more money you save.

There are many different ways to reuse code, of which the least favorite is cut and paste. The problem with cut and paste is that the code you are reusing is not nicely packaged and a developer who reuses code in this way will have to gain intimate knowledge of how that code is constructed. Knowledge of the code is necessary because you will integrate it directly with your own code; therefore, you need to know how it will affect the code that currently exists. On another note, if you copy and paste some code multiple times and then determine you need to make a change, you will need to change every occurrence of that code that was pasted.

We can see the ideal solution in the object-oriented programming model. In a typical scenario, a developer will create a fully encapsulated object (which functions perfectly, of course) for other developers to use. Because developers need to understand only the interface to this object (the details are encapsulated or hidden), it becomes very simple to reuse code without the necessity of gaining an intimate understanding of how that code works.

The Visual Basic language itself is a perfect example of this. Ask yourself this question: How do you display a text box on the screen? If you're a Visual Basic programmer, you simply drag a TextBox on to a form, set its text property, and run your program. If you want to do the same thing using C++, you are now looking at approximately 20–50 lines of code, depending on how you set up your application (the Microsoft Foundation Classes [MFC] for Visual C++ makes this much simpler).

So the question is this: Why is Visual Basic so easy to write code with when compared to C++? Creating a form with a text box on it is actually quite difficult if you use C/C++ and execute system calls (Win32 API calls). With Visual Basic, it is very easy because you can simply use the Form object and TextBox object, and these objects do the system calls for you (guess what language the Form and TextBox objects were written in?). We can use a TextBox over and over again and never have to worry about the complexity of the underlying code. By using objects such as the TextBox, Visual Basic has become a language which is very quick and easy to develop with.

In this chapter, we will learn how to support the reuse of generic pieces of code in our Web applications by using controls. If you have been creating Web applications for long, you probably have written more than a dozen login pages for the secure area of a Web site. Because this is a fairly standard item, we can put it into a control and reuse it on every project for which we need this functionality, saving ourselves the hassle (and boredom) of creating this portion of code over and over again. Throughout this chapter, we will look at a login control as an example (along with some others).

Create Custom Controls and User Controls

There are two major ways to create controls for our Web pages, both of which are covered under one exam objective. The first method—and the most complicated—is to create custom controls. This method offers the most flexibility and power, and often is used to enhance performance instead of just for reusability. The second method is to create user controls, which basically means creating a mini-Web page to use in other Web pages. This is by far the simplest method; however, it is the least flexible and is most often used within a single project. It simply does not lend itself well to long-term reuse.

Create Custom Controls

A custom control basically is a Web server control you create yourself. When your typical text box or label simply won't do the job, you can always do it yourself (after all, if you want it done right, do it yourself). Custom controls are compiled components that are packaged into assemblies and run on the server. Unlike ActiveX controls, which are run on the client, with custom controls, there is no need to ensure that the client's Web browser supports the control, or to install anything on the client's system.

Custom controls also have rich support for the Visual Studio development environment. You can add a control to the toolbox, access its properties through the Properties window, and even customize the way it is displayed at design time. Once added to the toolbox, you can reuse your control over and over again by simply dragging it onto your Web pages, just like you do with standard Web server controls.

e x a m

Ⓦⓐⓣ⓬ⓗ

It is important to understand the difference between a Web custom control and an ActiveX control. An ActiveX control is a compiled COM component that must be installed on the client's machine and runs on the client. A custom control is a .NET component that runs on the server and expresses itself on the client as HTML. A client's browser must support ActiveX controls to use them; however, a custom control needs no specific support in the client's browser.

There are three basic ways to create a custom control. The first method is called *direct rendering,* which is a complicated way of saying "do it all from scratch." We can do this by deriving a class (which represents our control) from a *base control class* (which gives us the functionality common to all controls, but no more).

The second method enables us to reuse most of the functionality of an existing control and simply add specific functionality on top of it. We can do this by deriving a class from an existing Web server control class such as a TextBox or Button. The final way is to create a control that consists of other, preexisting controls. This is called a *composite control* and essentially is the same thing as creating a control in Visual Basic 6 (although the way to do this is quite different).

All three methods share a great deal in common. For this reason, the majority of our discussion on custom controls will center on composite controls. Once learned, creating controls derived from existing Web server controls and using the direct rendering method should be quite easy.

Create Composite Controls

Creating a composite control essentially is creating a control out of other controls. Our first step is to create a class that represents our control. To this class we add child controls, which will implement the user interface of our control. You should note that there is a performance overhead associated with this method (when compared with the direct rendering method) as our class will have to create the child controls. However, when compared with user controls (which we will discuss later in the section "Create User Controls"), the performance gains can be significant.

o n   t h e

Ⓙⓞⓑ

You will find that composite controls are the quickest and easiest way to create robust, reusable components for your Web applications. Although user controls, which we will discuss later, are easier to create, they are not highly reusable.

Like standard Web server controls, custom controls can expose properties, methods, and events. In the case of composite controls, these properties, methods, and events can either be custom members that we create ourselves or can originate in the child controls. The basic process to creating a composite control is as follows:

1. Create a Web control library project.

2. Set up the custom control class appropriately.

3. Override the create child controls method to populate your control with its constituent controls.

4. Create any properties you wish to expose.

5. Create any methods you wish to expose.

6. Create any events you wish to expose.

7. Individualize the control by adding the toolbox icon, a custom TagPrefix, or a control designer.

Throughout this section, we will create our own login control and move through this process.

Create a Web Control Library Project   Our first step is to create the project. From Visual Studio, we can do this using the Web Control Library template.

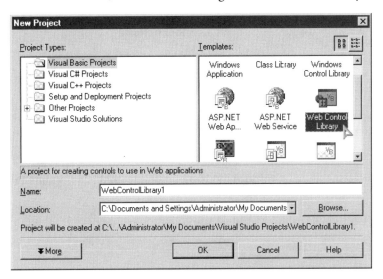

Once the project is created, you will notice that it has the following files:

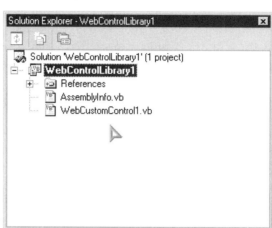

The references folder is common to all of our projects and contains any references to external components. The AssemblyInfo.vb file contains information about our control as a whole (we will look at this later for defining a custom TagPrefix). The last file, named WebCustomControl1.vb, contains the class that will become your control. This is where you will be doing most of your work. The Application Wizard puts the following code in WebCustomControl1.vb:

```
Imports System.ComponentModel
Imports System.Web.UI

<DefaultProperty("Text"), ToolboxData("<{0}:WebCustomControl1 _
runat=server></{0}:WebCustomControl1>")> _
Public Class WebCustomControl1
    Inherits System.Web.UI.WebControls.WebControl

    Dim _text As String

    <Bindable(True), Category("Appearance"), DefaultValue("")> _
    Property [Text]() As String
        Get
```

```
            Return _text
        End Get
        Set(ByVal Value As String)
            _text = Value
        End Set
    End Property

    Protected Overrides Sub Render(ByVal output As _
        System.Web.UI.HtmlTextWriter)
        output.Write([Text])
    End Sub
End Class
```

Set Up the Custom Control Class By default, Visual Studio creates a class
derived from *System.Web.UI.WebControls.WebControl,* which also is the class from
which the Web server controls derive. It calls this class *WebCustomControl,* which
is the same name as the file. Our first and most obvious step is to rename the file
and the class. If you rename the class, you have to remember to change any references
to this class in the class attributes (the stuff in angled brackets before the class
declaration). It also is a good idea at this time to add the following imports because
we will be using objects within these namespaces:

```
Imports System
Imports System.Web.UI.WebControls
```

The WebControl class, from which we are deriving our control, derives from a
simpler class called *System.Web.UI.Control. WebControl* has extra methods and
properties for defining how your control will look on a Web page. Because our control
will consist of other controls (which already have these methods and properties),
we will change the *inherits* clause to inherit from control.

exam
ⓦatch
*The **Control** class is the base class for all controls and has very basic support
for the needs of any control. The **WebControl** class derives from control
and adds support for issues specific to Web controls such as **Font, Backcolor,
Forecolor,** and so forth. The primary difference is that WebControl is designed
for user interface controls.*

Our next step is to implement the *System.Web.UI.INamingContainer* interface. This interface is a marker interface, which means it has no methods or properties. By implementing it, we enable the framework to determine that our control has child controls. This interface ensures that our child controls are put in their own namespace; thus, will have unique names on the page where our control is used.

It is possible for the page developer to insert nested controls between the beginning and end tags of your custom control (you saw how to reference a custom control from a Web page in Chapter 3). When the page developer nests controls within our control, the nested controls actually become children of our control, even though we did not put them there. This obviously could lead to serious naming conflicts, which is why implementing the INamingContainer interface is so important. The following is what our class declaration should look like after we have made these changes:

```
<ToolboxData("<{0}:LoginTest runat=sever></{0}:LoginTest>")>
Public Class LoginTest
    Inherits Control
    Implements INamingContainer
...
End Class
```

You will notice that the class attributes contain only the ToolboxData tag (the default property tag was removed as we don't need it for this control). The ToolboxData data tag specifies what HTML to place on a Web page when your control is dragged onto that Web page from the toolbox in Visual Studio.

Our next step is to clean up the guts of our class. You'll notice that, by default, a text property is created and the *Render* method of the base class is overridden. We will look at the *Render* method later when we create controls that do their own rendering, but for now, we can delete all of this. At this point, we have properly set up our class and it is ready for development. The code should look like this:

```
Imports System.ComponentModel
Imports System
Imports System.Web.UI
Imports System.Web.UI.WebControls

<ToolboxData("<{0}:Login runat=server></{0}:Login>")>  _
Public Class Login
```

```
Inherits System.Web.UI.Control

End Class
```

We now have a control called login that inherits from the base class *Control* and does nothing.

Create the Child Controls   Most of the functionality for our control will come from its constituent controls. You cannot add constituent controls with design-time tools, which means no drag-and-drop. The reason for this is simply that there's nothing to drop the controls onto. We are creating a control that will dynamically display itself to a Web page at run time, which means at design time there's nothing to work with but code.

To add the constituent controls, we first need to choose the controls we will use to create our control. For our login example, we will use one *LiteralControl,* two TextBoxes, and two Buttons. *LiteralControl* is the server-side representation of pure HTML. For example, if we want to make sure our constituent controls are stacked vertically on the client page, we have to insert line breaks between them (<br>). This line break would be a *LiteralControl* from our server's perspective. As we will be using several Web server controls, at this point it would be a good idea to import the *System. Web. UI. WebControls* namespace into our class.

Once we know which controls we will be using, we must override the *CreateChildControls* method of the base class. This method is called by the Framework when our control is created and allows us to populate our control with constituent controls. To override this method, select it from the class name and method name drop-down list boxes in the code editor.

Within the method we create instances of the controls we will use, set any properties we wish, and add the constituent controls to the controls collection of our base class (remember the base class is the *Control* class). The *Controls* collection is what stores all of our constituent controls. Earlier I mentioned that page developer could insert nested controls within our custom controls' HTML tag (which is why we needed to implement the *INamingContainer* interface). If the page designer does this, these nested controls also will be added to the *Controls* collection we're discussing here. Controls are added to the *Controls* collection using the *Add* method. The following is an example of what the *CreateChildControls* method of our control should look like for our login control.

```
Protected Overrides Sub CreateChildControls()
    'Add caption
    Controls.Add(New LiteralControl("<h3>Enter your Username" & _
        and Password.</h3>"))

    'Add UserName Textbox
    Dim txtUserName As New TextBox()
    txtUserName.Text = ""
    Controls.Add(txtUserName)

    'Insert a line break
    Controls.Add(New LiteralControl("<br>"))

    'Add Password Textbox
    Dim txtPassword As New TextBox()
    txtPassword.Text = ""
    Controls.Add(txtPassword)

    'Insert a line break
    Controls.Add(New LiteralControl("<br>"))

    'Add Submit Button
    Dim btnSubmit As New Button()
    btnSubmit.Text = "Submit"
    Controls.Add(btnSubmit)

    'Add Cancel Button
    Dim btnClear As New Button()
    btnClear.Text = "Clear"
    Controls.Add(btnClear)
End Sub
```

Now that we have something to work with, we should test our control to make sure we haven't made any mistakes. To test the control, we will add a test project to our solution. Our test project will be a standard ASP.NET Web application which can be added to our current solution by choosing File | Add Project | New Project. You'll notice you now have two projects open at the same time within the same solution.

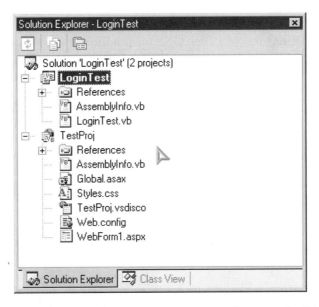

Before we can use the control in our test project, we first must build it. Select Build | Build Solution to build the solution. Now that we have compiled the control, we can add it to the toolbox in Visual Studio. Choose Tools | Customize Toolbox to add the control to the toolbox. Once the Customize Toolbox dialog box appears, click the .NET Framework Components tab and click Browse.

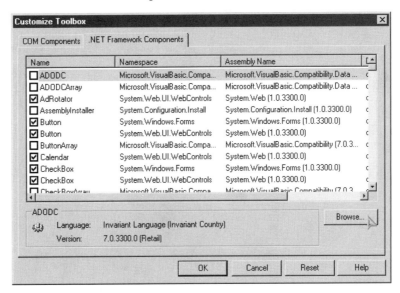

Find the assembly containing your control (it's in the bin directory of your project directory) and click OK. You'll notice your control has been added to the toolbox under the Toolbox tab you currently have expanded (if you cannot find it, check the other tabs in the toolbox, as you'll often find it under the General tab).

You now can drag your control onto the Web page in your test project and test it by viewing the page in the browser. You'll notice that in Visual Studio you cannot see any of your constituent controls, only a marker that contains the name of your control.

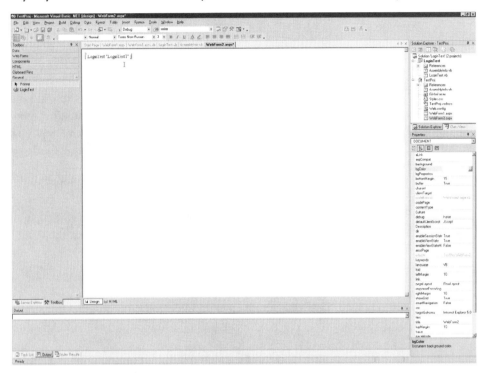

We will discuss later how to create a design-time view of your control. If everything works, you will be able to see your login control when viewed in the browser. However, if you get an error message, the most common place to look for a mistake is in the declaration of your class (specifically, you might have forgotten to change the class attributes when changing the name of your class).

Expose a Constituent Control   Now that we have created the user interface for our composite control, we can develop the programmatic interface to the control. The programmatic interface consists of the methods, properties, and events with which the user of the control will manipulate and interact. If you simply wish to expose most of the functionality of a constituent control to the user (page developer), you can expose the constituent control itself as a property of your control. You can do this by creating a read-only property procedure whose get method returns a reference to the constituent control.

It is important to understand that the user of your control will have full access to all of the methods and properties of the constituent control that is being exposed in this manner. In general, this is not a good idea. You really have to question why you're creating a control in the first place if you're simply exposing the underlying constituent control to a user. A well thought-out control follows object-oriented principles, of which encapsulation is one of the most important. Encapsulation refers to the idea that the internal workings of an object should be hidden to users of the object.

exam

ⓦatch

The better encapsulated a control is, the easier it is to develop with. By paying strict attention to the tenets of object orientation, you will be able to create controls that other programmers will come to love. The true test of success is when developers beg you to upgrade a control you wrote years ago.

A constituent control definitely is part of the internal workings of your object. Imagine if your VCR exposed its motor outside the box. Aside from voiding your warranty, it would be an obvious problem when people started to play with it. That said, the following code shows how to expose a constituent control from your composite control:

```
Public ReadOnly Property Username() As TextBox
    Get
        Return txtUserName
    End Get
End Property
```

A user of this control can now access any method or property of the username TextBox through the Username property. Assuming the user gave your control an ID of login1 on the Web page, he or she can access the text property of the username TextBox as follows:

```
login1.Username.Text = "Ted"
```

You'll notice that if you add this code to our example application as is, it will not work because we have declared the variables that hold our constituent controls local to the *CreateChildControls* procedure. To make this example work, move the variable declarations for the constituent controls from the CreateChildControls procedure to the class itself (making them instance variables). The only other way to access the controls is through the *Controls* collection directly, which involves using an index.

As mentioned before, page developers can insert nested controls into the tag for our control, which has the effect of adding their nested controls to our *Controls* collection. This forms a huge problem when considering indexes in the *Controls* collection. For this reason you should not count on your controls having consistent indexes; therefore, it is preferable to use instance variables to hold references to your constituent controls.

on the
job

*You should not encourage users of your composite controls to access child controls through the **Controls** collection of your composite controls. The **Controls** collection has been declared as public in the **Control** class; therefore, there is not much you can do to prevent them from doing this. However, you should make it clear that your control might not behave as expected if the users of your control take this approach.*

Expose Properties of Constituent Control   A much more prudent way to give users access to information within one of your constituent controls is to expose only a property of a constituent control to the user. This also is done with a property procedure. The benefit of this method is that users will have access only to the specific properties and methods important to your control. For example, in our login control, we might wish to expose the text property of the username and password textboxes to the user. By doing this through a property procedure, we can control access to these *Text* properties.

The following code is an example of a property procedure used to expose the *Text* property of the username *TextBox*. You will notice that it is a read-only property because the page developer really should not be setting the user name; the user of the application should do this. This is a small example of some of the control we impose on access to our underlying constituent controls:

```
Public ReadOnly Property Username() As String
    Get
        Return txtUserName.Text
    End Get
End Property
```

A user of this control now can access only the *Text* property of the username *TextBox* through the Username property. Assuming the user gave your control an

ID of login1 on his or her Web page, he or she can access the *Text* property of the username *TextBox* as follows:

```
login1.Username = "Ted"
```

This also is much more straightforward for the page developer, as it does not expose the underlying implementation of your control (the fact that you are using a *TextBox* with a *Text* property).

Expose Methods from Constituent Controls   Once you've learned how to expose properties of constituent controls, it is extremely easy to expose methods. You can do this by creating a method of your control that calls the method of the constituent control you wish to expose. For example, to expose the *ToString* method of the username *TextBox* we would do the following:

```
Public Function UserNameString() as String
    Return txtUserName.ToString()
End Function
```

A user of this control now can access the *ToString* method of the username *TextBox* through the *UserNameString* method of our control. Assuming the user gave your control an ID of login1 on his or her Web page, he or she can access the *ToString* method of the username *TextBox* as follows:

```
Dim someString As String = login1.UserNameString()
```

In case you are curious, the *ToString* method will return the name of the *TextBox*, not what is in it.

Custom Properties and Methods   There will come a time when the properties and methods of your constituent controls are not enough to give your control the functionality you desire. We now will create custom properties and methods for our control. It is often useful to think of properties and methods as having two parts. The first part is the declaration, which declares that the method or property exists. We often think of this as the "what" part—in other words, this is what the object can do.

The second part is the implementation, which we often refer to as the "how" part. Meaning this is how the object performs what it can do. When creating properties and methods for your control, be sure the names of your properties and methods properly communicate the "what" to the user of the control. For our login control, we will start by adding a method that checks for an empty user name and password. The following is an example of this method:

```
Public Function IsEmpty() As Boolean
    If txtUserName.Text = "" And txtPassword.Text = "" Then
        Return True
    Else
        Return False
    End If
End Function
```

FROM THE CLASSROOM

Public vs. Private Inheritance

Creating a composite control from a single Web server control is not usually recommended. In this case, you should use inheritance instead of composition. One exception to this rule is when a pre-existing Web server control does everything you want it to but exposes too much functionality.

For example, we could create a list box that works like a queue. In other words, you can add items only to the end of the list box and you can remove items only from the top of the list box. The standard list box will allow you to add and remove items anywhere within the list box, and even sort them. This functionality obviously is not what we want developers, who are using our special queue list box, to have.

If we derive our new list box from the existing list box, users of this new control could do anything they could have done with the original. This is because Visual Basic .NET supports only *public inheritance*. With public

inheritance, any public members in the base class are public in the derived class. What we need is *private inheritance*, which Visual Basic does not support.

By using composition, we can simulate private inheritance and get the same result. We can make the standard list box a child control of our control and expose only properties that do not violate the concept of a queue. When we expose the method to add an item to the list we can ensure that items are added only to the end of the list. With the method to remove an item, we also can ensure that only items at the top of the list are removed.

Private inheritance typically is used in situations in which we are implementing something as something else. In this case, we are implementing a queue list box as a standard list box. Think about this the next time you are considering inheritance and do not want all of the functionality of the base class.

—Wayne Cassidy, Bsc, MCSD, MCT

You should note that this has been implemented as a public function and returns a *Boolean* to inform us whether the user name and password are empty. There really is no difference between creating a custom method and exposing a method of a constituent control. In the case of a custom method, you are supplying the implementation; in the case of exposing a method from constituent control, the constituent control provides the implementation. However, in both cases we are supplying the declaration (by declaring the function, we are saying that our control can perform this task).

When creating a custom property, the implementation primarily consists of where we will store the information and any business logic associated with the information. When exposing a property from a constituent control, we are using the constituent control to store the information; therefore, we are using the constituent control's implementation.

When we create a custom property, we have many options such as instance variables, a database, a flat file, the controls *ViewState* (which we will see later in this chapter, in the section "Save State"), and anything else you can think of. For our login control, we will be tracking the number of attempts to log in that the user makes. Later on, we will restrict the user to three attempts, at which point we will no longer allow them to log in. We will use instance variables to store this number, as seen in the following code:

```
Private Shared nAttempts As Integer

Public Property Attempts() As Integer
    Get
        Return nAttempts
    End Get
    Set(ByVal Value As Integer)
        nAttempts = Value
    End Set
End Property
```

You'll notice that we are using a private shared variable to store the number of attempts made to log in. We will discuss the lifecycle of control later in this chapter. For now, it is important to understand that the *nAttempts* variable will always be zero unless we make it a shared variable (can you figure out why?). We will come back to this when discussing control state.

Handle Events from Constituent Controls   Handling an event from constituent controls is no different from handling an event in a Windows Forms project or using code-behind in an ASP.NET application; the only real difference is convenience. Because we're designing our control using only code, you can't simply double-click a button or other control to add the event handler to your code. The good news is we still don't have to write the event handler from scratch unless we want to.

There are two basic ways to handle events from our constituent controls. If you are using instance variables to hold references to your constituent controls, you can simply add the *WithEvents* keyword to the declaration of the control whose events you wish to handle, as shown here:

```
Private WithEvents btnClear As New Button()
```

By doing this, you'll notice that the *btnClear* variable now appears in the Class Name drop-down list box at the top of the code editor. If you select *btnClear* from the Class Name drop-down list box, the Method Name drop-down list box now will contain a list of all of the events you can handle for this control. By selecting one of the events, the event handling procedure is added to your code and the event is wired. The following procedure was added for the *btnClear* button in our login control (I also have listed the *ClearControl* procedure, which is a private procedure I created for simplicity):

```
Private Sub ClearControl()
    txtUserName.Text = ""
    txtPassword.Text = ""
End Sub

Private Sub btnClear_Click(ByVal sender As Object, _
        ByVal e As System.EventArgs) Handles btnClear.Click
    ClearControl()
End Sub
```

The important thing to understand is the use of the *Handles* expression. This expression specifies that this procedure is responsible for handling all click events for the *btnClear* control. You should be aware that you cannot use the *Handles* keyword without first declaring your constituent control variable using the *WithEvents* keyword.

Our next option for handling events from constituent controls does not require the *WithEvents* keyword. This is a form of dynamic event handling in which we will (at run time) dynamically link our event handler to the control whose events we wish to handle. This is useful because at run time we can link and unlink an event handler as needed.

e x a m

ⓦ a t c h

Using the WithEvents keyword is a form of early binding. Early binding means the event is bound to the function that handles it by the compiler. Dynamic event handling is a form of late binding, which means the binding of the event to the function that handles the event is done when the control is run; not when it is compiled. In general, early binding tends to be faster; late binding tends to be more flexible.

Our first task to perform, when using this method, is to create a function to handle the event. The arguments to this function must be the same as the arguments passed from the event. For our login control, we will use dynamic event handling to trap the click event from our Submit button. The procedure to handle this event is as follows:

```
Private Sub SubmitClicked(ByVal sender As Object, ByVal e As EventArgs)
    nAttempts += 1

    If Attempts >= 3 Then
        ClearControl()
    End If
End Sub
```

The *SubmitClick* method accepts the proper arguments and performs the proper task; however, there is no link between the *btnSubmit.Click* event and this method. As mentioned earlier, we will create this link at run time and this will be done in the *CreateChildControls* procedure using the *AddHandler* method as follows:

```
AddHandler btnSubmit.Click, AddressOf Me.SubmitClicked
```

The *AddHandler* method takes two arguments. The first argument is the event you wish to trap; the second argument is the address of the function you will call when the event is triggered. Using the *AddressOf* function, we can easily get the address of the procedure we have just created for this purpose. Our procedure now is linked to the *btnSubmit.Click* event, and everything will work fine.

If at a later time we wish to unlink our procedure from this event, we could use the *RemoveHandler* method which takes the same arguments. Now would be a good time to test your control and ensure that all the properties and methods we've added are working properly. If you're having problems, you'll find a complete code listing for our control later in this chapter.

Raise Events   When creating a custom control, you'll often have the need to communicate with the page developer (this does not mean using the telephone). For example, in our login control, it would be nice to be able to inform our client that there have been too many attempts to log in. In this way, the page developer can either ignore our message or perform some other action such as deleting the user's account (let's hope I never get a job writing online banking applications).

It is important to understand where the events are triggered and where they are trapped. We should always remember that our control is running only on the server. This is not an ActiveX control, which would be transferred to the client, registered, and run on the client computer. Our custom control runs on the server and sends an HTML version of itself to the client. For any of our code in our control to run (for example, when you click the Clear button), the client's browser must post back the page he or she is viewing, at which point our control can run its code and possibly submit a new version of itself back to the client. This can become very confusing when dealing with events triggered from a custom control.

For an event to be triggered from a custom control, obviously the control must be running; therefore, the page would be running on the server. When an event is triggered, it is not sent back to the client; instead, it is sent to the code-behind, which also is running on the server. The page developer then can respond appropriately to the event and resubmit the page (or possibly another page) back to the client browser.

To raise an event, we will need the following five elements (which you've already seen in Chapter 3 and which are stated here only for review):

- **A class to hold our event data**   This class should have properties that the page developer can access to get this information. If you are creating an event that does not send data, you can use the class *System.EventArgs,* which contains no data and saves us the hassle of creating a class to be used with our event.

- **An event delegate**   An event delegate is a class used to connect our event to anyone wishing to subscribe to it (the client).

- **An event member**   This actually is the event delegate being declared in our class.

- **A method that invokes the delegate**   This is a method in your class with the name *OnEventName,* which should be declared as *Protected Overrideable* so that anyone who inherits your control for further use does not have to implement this method again unless they choose to. This is the method in which the *RaiseEvent* method is called.

- **A place to trigger the event**   The event is triggered by calling the method that invokes the delegate. You can do this anywhere you want under the conditions you choose.

For our login control, we will raise an event when a user tries to log in too many times unsuccessfully; we will call it *TooManyAttempts.* Because we're not sending any data with this event, we will use the class *System.EventArgs* to hold the data for this event (which of course is nothing). Also we can use *EventHandler* as our delegate class because we're not passing any data. The following code shows what needs to be added to our class to implement this event:

```
Public Event TooManyAttempts As EventHandler

Protected Overridable Sub OnTooManyAttempts(ByVal e As EventArgs)
    RaiseEvent TooManyAttempts(Me, e)
End Sub

Private Sub SubmitClicked(ByVal sender As Object, ByVal e As EventArgs)
    Attempts += 1

    If Attempts >= 3 Then
        ClearControl()
        OnTooManyAttempts(EventArgs.Empty())
    End If
End Sub
```

The event member is called *TooManyAttempts* and is an instance of the delegate *EventHandler.* The method that invokes the delegate is called *OnTooManyAttempts;* in it, the event is raised. Our event is triggered in the *SubmitClick* method, which is an event handler for our Submit button. The only thing left to do to test our event is to write event-handling code in our test page (this was covered in Chapter 3).

Save State   We now have a fairly sophisticated control. Our login control has custom methods and properties, and even fires and events. That said, our control will have a serious problem if two users try to interact with it at the same time. You will notice that the variable declaration of the *nAttempts* variable has been declared as being a *shared* variable (this is equivalent to a *static* variable in C++ or Java). This means all instances of this class will share the same variable.

It also means when the class containing this variable is destroyed, the variable retains its value and the next time the class is instantiated the value is the same. This was used to overcome a problem we would have encountered because of the lifecycle of our control, as we explained earlier. To review, our control is instantiated and run when the page containing our control is originally requested. Our custom control then sends to the browser an HTML version of itself; it's then destroyed.

When the user of the Web application interacts with our control, causing code within our control to run, the browser performs a postback request, which basically means it requests the page again from the server but this time specifies that a specific method of our control should be run. The key to understanding this is that, in reality, every time the user interacts with our control (assuming it causes a postback), our control is created and destroyed. However, the user perceives that he or she is using the same instance of our control.

This obviously causes a huge problem when it comes to instance variables and constituent controls. If our control is being destroyed every time the user clicks a button, how does our control remember what changes the user has made to it? Using a shared variable solves this problem because the value of that variable was not destroyed when the object was destroyed; however, because all instances of this class will be sharing this variable, all users of this class also will be sharing this variable. If one user makes three attempts to log in, all users after that will be unable to log in. Needless to say, shared variables are not the real solution to this problem.

on the

Job

Beware of using shared variables. Shared variables cause side effects in software, which is one of the largest causes of bugs in released software. This occurs when one portion of a program expects a variable to have a certain value and it does not because another portion of a program has changed the value unexpectedly. These problems can be very hard to track down.

Let's take a look at a specific scenario. The user requests the page containing our login control. Our control is created and renders a version of itself (in HTML) to the browser, after which our control is destroyed on the server. The user of the application now sees a Web page in his or her browser. On that Web page, our control—with the username box, password box, and Submit and Clear buttons—is visible.

However, remember that the user is looking at only a visual representation of our control, not the control itself. The user then types in a user name and password, and clicks the Submit button to submit the user name and password. In our example, clicking the Submit button does not actually submit anything; it simply increments the *nAttempts* variable and checks to see whether the user has made too many attempts. In our example, this means the user should see the same page after he or she has clicked the button, and should still see the user name and password he or she has entered (in a real application, we probably would fire an event to tell the page using our control that the user has submitted their information).

Clicking the Submit button causes our *SubmitClicked* method in our custom control to run. Because the control is not on the client's computer, the only way this method can be run is to post back a request to the server; this is where the problem occurs. If we are posting back a new request to the server, it has to instantiate our object again. This means the TextBoxes and the *nAttempts* variable would be brand new and have nothing in them. This is obviously a problem, as our *nAttempts* variable would have a value of 0. This means that no matter how often the person submits his or her user name and password, the *nAttempts* variable will always have a value of 0 because it is being re-initialized repeatedly every time the user clicks the Submit button.

The obvious solution would be to create an instance of the control on the server and keep it alive while the user interacts with the page. The problem with doing this is we have no way of knowing whether the user is still using our page. He or she could have decided not to bother logging in and surfed off to another site. This would create a large overhead on our server, with a bunch of objects sitting around doing absolutely nothing.

Web servers can handle thousands of users because they do not keep connections to users running. When the user requests a Web page, the server forms a connection with the client's browser, sends the requested page, and then closes the connection. If the user requests another page from the same server, the process is completed again. This process of creating and destroying connections for every single request is very efficient because the bottom line is that when users interact with your Web site, they spend 99 percent of their time looking at your content, not interacting directly with the Web server. This means that when users are reading your Web page, they are not tying up connections on the Web server.

If Microsoft had implemented custom controls such that the connection stayed alive, this would certainly solve the problem of having to create and destroy a control object as the user interacts with it. However, this would drastically reduce the scalability of the Web server. True to form, Microsoft has created a way to keep the scalability of the Web server intact and still allow us to simulate a constant connection to the custom control.

When a user performs an action on your control that causes the control to run some code, a postback occurs. In this postback request is the method on the control that needs to be run as well as a string containing the state of your control. This means the values of the *TextBoxes* in our login control are sent back with the request. When the server instantiates our control, it then will use this information to give the text properties of our *TextBoxes* the proper value. From our perspective, as the control developers, it seems like our control was never destroyed as it is in the same state as the user left it.

This is done automatically by the Framework, using a property of the base class *(Control)* called *ViewState*. The *ViewState* property is a dictionary object that is of type *System.Web.UI.StateBag* and contains name value pairs. These name value pairs correspond to the constituent controls in your custom control and allow the constituent controls to be initialized with their proper values, making the entire process seamless.

The value of this *ViewState* property is stringified and passed back and forth between the client and server as the user interacts with your control, thus keeping the state intact even though the control does not stay intact. Although this works with constituent control properties automatically, the Framework has no way to know whether you have added instance variables to your control; thus, you'll have to write some code to support this yourself.

exam
ⓦatch

The StateBag object is very similar, in form and function, to the PropertyBag object in Visual Basic 6 (although they are certainly not identical).

Although our discussion of control state was quite lengthy, keeping the state of your instance variables intact is quite easy. We simply store the values of these variables in the *ViewState* property instead of instance variables. The following code is an example of how to save the state of your object in the *ViewState* property instead of instance variables. We will now store the number of attempts in the *ViewState* property, as shown here:

```
Public Property Attempts() As Integer
    Get
        Return CType(ViewState("Attempts"), Integer)
    End Get
    Set(ByVal Value As Integer)
        ViewState("Attempts") = Value
    End Set
End Property
```

Notice the similarity between storing information in the *ViewState*, and storing information in the *Application* or *Session* objects. Also, because we are no longer storing the number of attempts in an instance variable, you can remove the declaration for that variable. The value for the number of attempts will now be passed back and forth between the server in the client browser, and the state will stay intact. We no longer have to worry about what will happen when users are using our control at the same time. Because information is being passed back and forth between the client and server, the *ViewState* property has a significant run-time overhead. You should use this property wisely to avoid slowing down interaction with your control.

The base class of our control has an *EnableViewState* property, which is exposed to users of our object. You should be aware that a user of your object can set the *EnableViewState* property to *False,* which means the *ViewState* will not be passed back and forth from client and server while the users of the application interacts with your control. If your control relies on the *ViewState* property for its functionality, this should be noted in the documentation.

Because we're no longer using instance variables to store information, we will have to use the *OnInit* event of your control class to initialize these values. In our login example, the code is as follows:

```
Protected Overrides Sub OnInit(ByVal e As System.EventArgs)
    ViewState("Attempts") = 0
End Sub
```

The following is a complete code listing of our control class. You'll notice that it uses all of the techniques we have discussed to this point—and has a few extras thrown in. You should ensure that you understand the following code well before moving on:

```
Imports System.ComponentModel
Imports System
Imports System.Web.UI
Imports System.Web.UI.WebControls

<ControlBuilderAttribute(GetType(LoginTestControlBuilder)), _
ToolboxData("<{0}:LoginTest runat=server></{0}:LoginTest>")> _
Public Class LoginTest
    Inherits Control
    Implements INamingContainer

    ' Variable and event declaration
    Private txtUserName As New TextBox()
    Private txtPassword As New TextBox()
    Private btnSubmit As New Button()
    Private WithEvents btnClear As New Button()

    Public Event TooManyAttempts As EventHandler

    '----Private functions (helper functions)----
```

```
Private Property Allowed() As Boolean
    Get
        Return CType(ViewState("Allowed"), Boolean)
    End Get
    Set(ByVal Value As Boolean)
        ViewState("Allowed") = Value
    End Set
End Property

Private Sub ClearControl()
    txtUserName.Text = ""
    txtPassword.Text = ""
End Sub

Private Sub SubmitClicked(ByVal sender As Object, _
                          ByVal e As EventArgs)
    Attempts += 1

    If Allowed Then
        If Attempts >= 3 Then
            Allowed = False
        End If
    Else
        ClearControl()
        OnTooManyAttempts(New EventArgs())
    End If
End Sub

Private Sub btnClear_Click(ByVal sender As Object, _
                           ByVal e As System.EventArgs) _
                           Handles btnClear.Click
    ClearControl()
End Sub

'----Protected functions (helper functions)----
Protected Overrides Sub CreateChildControls()
    'Add caption
    Controls.Add(New LiteralControl("<h3>Enter your Username " & _
                " and Password.</h3>"))

    'Add UserName Textbox
    txtUserName.Text = ""
    Controls.Add(txtUserName)

    'Insert a line break
    Controls.Add(New LiteralControl("<br>"))
```

```
    'Add Password Textbox
    txtPassword.Text = ""
    Controls.Add(txtPassword)

    'Insert a line break
    Controls.Add(New LiteralControl("<br>"))

    'Add Submit Button
    btnSubmit.Text = "Submit"
    Controls.Add(btnSubmit)
    AddHandler btnSubmit.Click, AddressOf Me.SubmitClicked

    'Add Cancel Button
    btnClear.Text = "Clear"
    Controls.Add(btnClear)
End Sub

Protected Overridable Sub OnTooManyAttempts(ByVal e As EventArgs)
    RaiseEvent TooManyAttempts(Me, e)
End Sub

Protected Overrides Sub OnInit(ByVal e As System.EventArgs)
    ViewState("Attempts") = 0
    ViewState("Allowed") = True
End Sub

'----Public member functions----
Public ReadOnly Property Username() As String
    Get
        Return txtUserName.Text
    End Get
End Property

'Expose a Method of a Constituent Control
Public Function GetString() As String
    Return txtUserName.ToString()
End Function

Public Property Attempts() As Integer
    Get
        Return CType(ViewState("Attempts"), Integer)
    End Get
    Set(ByVal Value As Integer)
        ViewState("Attempts") = Value
    End Set
End Property
```

```
    Public Function IsEmpty() As Boolean
        If txtUserName.Text = "" And txtPassword.Text = "" Then
            Return True
        Else
            Return False
        End If
    End Function
End Class
```

Control Parsing   Earlier, it was mentioned that the page developer using a custom control can insert nested controls within the tag of the custom control on the Web page. The following is an example of this:

```
<cc1:Login id="Login" runat="server">
    <P>Hello World!</P>
</ccs:Login>
```

In this case, the paragraph tag containing the text "hello world" would be added as a child control of type *LiteralControl* of our custom login control. This is done by calling the *AddParsedSubObject* method of the base class for our custom control. We also call these nested controls the *inner content* of our control. This can be useful in situations in which you want the page developer to add user interface elements to your control (similar to the *DataRepeater* control); however, in general it causes problems.

The first thing we will determine is whether someone has added nested controls to your custom control in this manner. You can do this by using the methods and properties of the *Controls* collection, which is where these controls will be added. In our login example, you'll notice seven controls have been added as child controls in the *CreateChildControls* method. If this number increases, it is obvious that the page developer has nested controls within our custom control's tag.

Using the *Count* property of the *Controls* collection is a simple way to determine whether this has happened. For example, we could create a method of our custom control called *HasNestedControls,* which would return true if this count was greater than seven.

```
    Public Function HasNestedControls() As Boolean
        If Controls.Count > 7 Then
            Return True
        Else
            Return False
        End If
    End Function
```

By default, any control or text inserted between our custom control's tag will be added to our *Controls* collection. To change this behavior, we simply need to override the *AddParsedSubObject* method from our base class, as shown here:

```
Protected Overrides Sub AddParsedSubObject(ByVal obj As Object)
    If (TypeOf Obj Is TextBox)
        Controls.Add(Obj)
    End If
End Sub
```

Overriding this method in this way will allow only *TextBoxes* to be nested as child controls. An easy way to prevent anything from being added as a nested control is to simply override this method and write no code in the body of the method.

Another option for dictating control parsing behavior is to use the *ParsedChildrenAttribute* class attribute. By setting the *ChildrenAsProperties* property of this attribute to true nested controls, it becomes a property of your custom control instead of being added to the *Controls* collection.

```
<ParseChildrenAttribute(ChildrenAsProperties = true)> Public Class Login
```

If we want even more control over the way nested controls are added to our custom control, we can create a custom control builder (this can be combined with the *ParseChildrenAttribute* class attribute). This is a class that we define, and that must be derived from the *ControlBuilder* class. Until now, we have been using the default control builder which, as mentioned before, adds nested controls to the *Controls* collection of our custom control. By overriding the functions *GetChildControlType* and *AppendLiteralString*, we can determine whether nested controls are added to our *Controls* collection.

The *GetChildControlType* takes a tag name and attributes as arguments and returns a class type (the class type of the control to be added). We can determine whether to add a control by evaluating the tag name parameter, after which we can specify the type of control to be added through the return type. The *AppendLiteralString* method is used for literal text and enables us to determine whether a literal string should be added as a *LiteralControl*. The following is an example of a custom control builder class that does not allow literal strings to be added as *LiteralControls*. Instead, it allows only Web Server Button controls to be added to our custom control's *Controls* collection:

```
Public Class LoginControlBuilder
    Inherits ControlBuilder

    Public Overrides Sub AppendLiteralString(ByVal s As String)
```

```
      End Sub

      Public Overrides Function GetChildControlType _
                    (ByVal tagName As String, _
                     ByVal attribs As
System.Collections.IDictionary) _
                    As System.Type

        If tagName = "asp:button" Then
            Return GetType(Button)
        Else
            Return Nothing
        End If
      End Function
End Class
```

To associate our custom control builder class with our custom control, we must use the *ControlBuilderAttribute* class attribute on our custom control class as follows:

```
<ControlBuilderAttribute(GetType(LoginControlBuilder)), _
ToolboxData("<{0}:Login runat=server></{0}:Login>")> _
Public Class Login
...
End Class
```

Notice that the constructor for this class attribute takes the type of your custom control builder class as an argument. From now on, whenever the page developer nests controls within our custom controls tag on the Web page, it will consult our custom control builder class instead of the default control builder. The custom control builder is used to determine the type of object to add to the *Controls* collection; therefore, by returning nothing from this function you can ensure that no control is added.

We have now covered most of what there is to know about creating custom controls and have done so using a composite control as our example. We will now take a look at the details of creating controls which inherit from other controls, and creating controls using direct rendering.

Derive from an Existing Control

Often a Web server control does almost all you want it to do except for a specific behavior you wish you could add. If you have been involved in Web development for long, you've probably wished there were a *TextBox* that accepted only numbers, or a *TextBox* that would put the "http://" in front of a Web address when a user neglects to do so. In these situations, the standard *TextBox* gives us 99.9 percent of the functionality we are looking for, so why re-create it entirely?

In situations such as this in which your control will not be a composite of more than one control, we can derive our custom control class from a pre-existing Web server control. This is where we can see the value that the addition of inheritance to Visual Basic has added.

exam
ⓦatch

Exam 70-305 will expect you to understand the nuances of inheritance well. If you have programmed with only Visual Basic, you should make sure you understand this concept, as previous versions of Visual Basic did not support inheritance.

By deriving our custom control class from a Web server control, we get all of the functionality of the Web server control free, and need only override members we wish to change and/or add members to give it new functionality. For example, we will create a textbox that puts http:// at the front of anything entered into it if the user should forget. The following code is an example of this control class:

```
Imports System.ComponentModel
Imports System.Web.UI

<DefaultProperty("Text"), _
ToolboxData("<{0}:AddHttp runat=server></{0}:AddHttp>")> _
Public Class AddHttp
  Inherits System.Web.UI.WebControls.TextBox

  Protected Overrides Sub OnTextChanged(ByVal e As System.EventArgs)
    If String.Compare(Microsoft.VisualBasic.Left(Text, 7), _
                      "http://", True) <> 0 Then
      Text = "http://" + Text
    End If
  End Sub
End Class
```

You'll notice that our custom control class is now derived from *TextBox* instead of *Control*. The only real change we've made is to override the *OnTextChanged* event in which we add the http:// if the user neglects to do so. If you test this control, you'll notice that it expresses this behavior only when run in the browser, not at design time. Just like our last example, we have not yet discussed how to define the design time behavior of our controls (don't worry—we will get to this soon).

As you can see, when most of the behavior you desire already exists within a pre-existing control it can be a very simple process to create a custom control with unique behavior. All of the principles we discussed with composite controls, except for adding child controls, are applicable here. We can add custom methods, properties, and events to this control—and the best part is that because we have derived our class from the *TextBox*, there is no need to expose methods, properties, or events from the base class as they are already exposed.

If you're not familiar with object-oriented programming and inheritance, you should review how members of a base class are exposed in a derived class. Essentially, all public members of the base class are public members of the derived class. This is much different from using a constituent control, which in object-orientation terminology is called *aggregation*. With aggregation, our controls are members of our class, and not necessarily exposed through the interface.

When deciding on which method to use (deriving from an existing control or creating a composite control), the most straightforward, decision-making factor is whether you're using one or more pre-existing controls to create your custom control. You cannot use inheritance alone to create a custom control based on two or more pre-existing controls; therefore, you should create a composite control. You also should not use composition when you are using only one pre-existing control, as inheritance will be more efficient.

Create a Custom Control Using Direct Rendering

In situations in which the control we wish to create is very unique, often we are forced to create the control from scratch. In this situation, we will have to create almost all of the methods, properties, and events for the control, and then define the run-time look of the control. Until now, we have been borrowing a great deal of functionality from pre-existing controls, which has made our lives quite simple. Although not terribly complicated, in Visual Basic .NET, creating a custom control from scratch is a much more time-consuming process.

Our first step in creating a direct rendered control is to decide on the base class. We can use *Control*, like we did with our composite control, or *WebControl* if we would like to get some of the standard properties associated with Web controls without writing them ourselves. If your control does not provide a run-time user interface, you should derive your control class from *Control*. However, if you're planning to create a user interface for your control (which most controls have), *WebControl* is a much better choice. The *WebControl* class adds the following properties to your custom control:

- Forecolor
- Backcolor
- Font
- Borderstyle
- Height
- Width

Our next step is to define the behavior of the control, which really is not something we can discuss here. What your controls do for you is your own business and I probably don't want to hear about it anyway. You already know how to create properties, methods, and events; this is essentially where the functionality of your control will come from. The only thing left for us to deal with is rendering the control or

SCENARIO & SOLUTION

How do I create a control that records statistics for a Web site (uses logged in, hit counts, and so forth)?	Because this control does not have a visual appearance (assuming it does not display the statistics as well), you should derive your custom control from *Control*. The extra members of *WebControl* will be of no use to you.
How do I create a specialized *TextBox* that accepts SSN numbers and checks to see if they are in the appropriate format?	Derive your class from *WebControl*. This is a very generic control that could be used in many different Web applications. *WebControl* will expose properties that will enable the page developers using your control to customize the look of your control to fit nicely with their own Web applications.
How do I develop a control that is specific for my company, will always be displayed using my corporate colors, and must look the same on every page on which it is displayed?	Derive your control from *Control* as the extra members of *WebControl* will be of little use to you.

providing a user interface to it. You can do this by overriding the *Render* method of the base class.

The render method takes as an argument a *System.Web.UI.HtmlTextWriter* object. This object represents a stream that will be written to the client's browser. If you are a C++ programmer, you'll be quite used to the *STDIN* stream *cin* and *STOUT* stream *cout*.

On the other hand, Visual Basic programmers have not had the same exposure to streams. Think of a stream as a stream of water coming from a garden hose. The only real difference is that the stream we're talking about contains text. When you put things into a stream they come out of the stream in the order in which they were entered. To further advance upon this analogy, imagine a garden hose attached from your custom control to the clients' browser. We put things into the stream and they appear in the clients' browser. The *HtmlTextWriter* object has the following important methods which we will used to manipulate the stream (see the MSDN library for a full listing of its properties and methods):

- **Write** adds data to the stream (this is a pretty simple one).

- **WriteLine** adds data to the stream and adds a line terminator at the end.

- **WriteBeginTag** adds an HTML begin tag to the stream without the closing > character.

- **WriteFullBeginTag** adds an HTML begin tag to the stream with the closing > character.

- **WriteEndTag** adds an HTML end tag to the stream.

- **WriteAttribute** adds an HTML attribute and its value to the stream. These attributes are found within a begin tag.

- **WriteStyleAttribute** adds an HTML style attribute and its value to the stream. Style attributes also are found within a begin tag.

This is by no means a full description of the capabilities of the *HtmlTextWriter* object; however, these are the methods you'll use most of the time to render your control. The following is an example of a direct rendered control. Take special note of the *Render* method and the *HtmlTextWriter* object. This control has a text property that is rendered as a hyperlink:

```
Imports System.ComponentModel
Imports System.Web.UI
```

```
<ToolboxData("<{0}:MyControl runat=server></{0}:MyControl>")> _
Public Class MyControl
    Inherits System.Web.UI.WebControls.WebControl

    Private _text As String

    Public Property Text() As String
        Get
            Return _text
        End Get
        Set(ByVal Value As String)
                _text = Value
            End If
        End Set
    End Property

    Protected Overrides Sub Render(ByVal output As _
                                    System.Web.UI.HtmlTextWriter)
        output.WriteBeginTag("a")
        output.WriteAttribute("HREF", "http://www.Microsoft.com")
        output.Write(HtmlTextWriter.TagRightChar)

        output.Write(_text)

        output.WriteEndTag("a")
    End Sub
End Class
```

If you know HTML well, the sky is the limit as far as how you render your control. You can create HTML controls and tables, and even write client-side script if you like. I'm sure you'll agree that this gives you an enormous amount of control over how your custom control appears to the user.

The *IPostBackDataHandler* Interface We must remember that our custom controls will most likely be running on pages with other controls and elements, which means a postback could occur that was not triggered by interaction with our custom control. If this happens, we might need to evaluate the postback data to see whether the data for our control has been changed.

Throughout this discussion, we have to remember that there are two major components to our custom control: the server-side control object and the representation of our object on the client (which typically consists of HTML controls). Just like with our discussion of the *ViewState* property, the goal here is to keep the data in our server-side control consistent with the data in our client-side representation of our control. To accomplish this, we need a way to instruct the Framework to inform our control whenever a postback has occurred. You can do this by implementing the *IPostBackDataHandler* interface in our custom control. This is exactly what the *TextBox* does, which is the reason we never have to worry about the contents of a *TextBox* during a postback.

For this system to work, the HTML element, which forms the client-side representation of your control, must have a unique ID so the Framework will associate it with the server-side instance of your control. To ensure that it has a unique ID, we can use a method of the base class called unique ID when rendering our elements, as shown here:

```
Protected Overrides Sub Render(output As HtmlTextWriter)
    output.Write(("<INPUT type= text name = " & Me.UniqueID & _
        " value = " & _text & " >"))
End Sub
```

In this example, the control in question simply renders a textbox in the client's browser. You will notice that the name property is set to *Me.UniqueID,* which is a method of the base class (in this case *WebControl,* but actually it is a member of *Control,* from which *WebControl* is derived) that returns the unique ID. This ensures that your client-side control has an ID that can be matched to the server-side object.

The *IPostbackDataHandler* interface has two methods we can override to ensure that the state of our control is kept consistent. The *LoadPostData* method is called by the Framework upon postback and allows you to update your control with any changes the user might have made. The *RaisePostDataChangedEvent* event is called by the Framework after the *LoadPostData* method has finished and only if the *LoadPostData* method returns true. This event usually is used to perform processing such as raising an event from your control to inform any clients, that your control state has changed. (Remember that when we say clients we mean other objects on the server that trap these events and not the browser.)

For example, if our special *TextBox* control was placed on a page that also contained a button, we would want to make sure that if the user clicks that button, causing a postback to occur, we can update the state of our server-side object with any changes the user had made to our client-side *TextBox.* When the postback occurs, the Framework looks for any controls on the page that have implemented the *IPostbackDataHandler* interface and calls their *LoadPostData* methods.

In our control, we will use this method to update the *Text* property of our control on the server side to match the value of the *TextBox* on the client side. If indeed the state of our object has changed, we can return true to signify this; however, if the state of our object has remained the same we can return false. The Framework then will call the *RaisePostDataChangedEvent* event, which will give us a chance to inform any of our server-side clients that our information has changed. The following is a full example of our *TextBox:*

```
Imports System
Imports System.Web
Imports System.Web.UI
Imports System.Collections.Specialized

Public Class CustomTextBox
    Inherits WebControl
    Implements IPostBackDataHandler

    Public Property Text() As String
        Get
            Return CType(ViewState("Text"), String)
        End Get
        Set
            ViewState("Text") = value
        End Set
    End Property

    Public Event TextChanged As EventHandler

    Public Overridable Function LoadPostData(postDataKey As String, _
                    values As NameValueCollection) _
                    As Boolean _
                    Implements IPostBackDataHandler.LoadPostData

        Dim current As String = Text
        Dim postbackData As String = values(postDataKey)
        If Not presentValue.Equals(postedValue) Then
            Text = postedValue
            Return True
        Else
            Return False
        End If
    End Function

    Public Overridable Sub RaisePostDataChangedEvent() _
            Implements IPostBackDataHandler.RaisePostDataChangedEvent
        OnTextChanged(EventArgs.Empty)
    End Sub
```

```
      Protected Overridable Sub OnTextChanged(e As EventArgs)
          RaiseEvent TextChanged(Me, e)
      End Sub

      Protected Overrides Sub Render(output As HtmlTextWriter)
          output.Write(("<INPUT type= text name = " & Me.UniqueID & _
                        " value = " & Text & " >"))
      End Sub
   End Class
```

You should notice that the *LoadPostData* method takes as arguments a collection of name value pairs, which contains the state of the client's Web page and a key that you can use to retrieve your control's specific state from the collection. In this method, we simply check to see whether the state of our object has changed; if so, we update the value in our object. If indeed the state has changed, we return true, which causes the Framework to call the *RaisePostDataChangedEvent* event, enabling us to fire our own *TextChanged* event, and inform our clients on the server that our value has changed.

Some of you might be wondering what the difference is between using the *IPostbackDataHandler* interface to keep the state of our object consistent and using the *ViewState* property. The *ViewState* property specifically works when a user of the Web application is interacting with our control. It does not send its information back and forth when a postback is triggered as a result of the user interacting with some other control. To keep the state of your server-side object consistent with the view on the client side, you should implement both of these.

The *IPostBackEventHandler* Interface

The *IPostBackDataHandler* interface enables us to keep our data consistent between our server-side object and our client-side representation of that object. However, if you are interested in being informed only when a postback occurs, you can implement the *IPostBackEventHandler* interface instead.

A *TextBox* uses the *IPostBackDataHandler* to ensure that the data within the text box is kept consistent. A button uses the *IPostBackEventHandler* to fire off click events on the server whenever a postback occurs. This is a very subtle difference: One is concerned with keeping data consistent, and the other is concerned with being informed when postbacks occur.

When a postback occurs, the Framework will look for any server-side control that implements the *IPostBackEventHandler* interface and has an ID that corresponds to a posted name. If it finds one, it will fire the *RaisePostBackEvent* event within that control. The next code gives an example of a custom button control that responds to postback events.

```
Imports System
Imports System.Web.UI

Public Class CustomButton
    Inherits Control
    Implements IPostBackEventHandler

    Public Event Click As EventHandler

    Protected Overridable Sub OnClick(e As EventArgs)
        RaiseEvent Click(Me, e)
    End Sub

    Public Sub RaisePostBackEvent(eventArgument As String) _
            Implements IPostBackEventHandler.RaisePostBackEvent
        OnClick(EventArgs.Empty)
    End Sub

    Protected Overrides Sub Render(output As HtmlTextWriter)
        output.Write("<INPUT TYPE = submit name = " & Me.UniqueID & _
                    " Value = 'Trigger Postback/>")
    End Sub
End Class
```

You should note that the type of HTML control that is being rendered is a Submit button. Since only buttons and images can trigger a postback, we will have to render our control with one of these types (later we will discuss how to generate client-side JavaScript to enable other control types to trigger a postback). In this example, when we received the *RaisePostBackEvent* event, we simply trigger our own click event.

As mentioned, if we want our custom control to instigate a postback, we must render it in the client as a button or image. If we want to render our control using any other control (for example, an anchor tag), we will need to generate some JavaScript on the client in order to support this. This is actually much easier than it sounds. We can use the *GetPostBackEventReference* method of the *Page* object to emit client-side script that initiates a postback and also creates a reference to the server control that initiates the postback. The following code is an example of the *Render* method of a control that renders itself as an anchor tag in the client and is able to initiate a postback:

```
Protected Overrides Sub Render(output As HtmlTextWriter)
    output.Write("<A id = '" & Me.UniqueID & "' " & _
```

```
                    "href = 'javascript:" & _
                    Page.GetPostBackEventReference(Me) & "'>" & _
                    "Click Me</A>")
    End Sub
```

If you use this code as the *Render* method for your control, you will now have a custom anchor control that can cause a postback (a form to be submitted).

Create a Template Control

Template controls enable us to separate the user interface from our control logic. By doing this, we can leave the user interface up to the page developer and create only the logic in our control. The page developer then can implement the user interface as parameters between template tags in the Web page.

For example, we could create a custom control that stores some text and allows the page developer to determine how that text will be displayed. To support templates in our custom control, first we must inherit from the *INamingContainer* interface (do you know why?). We also must set the *ParseChildrenAttribute* class attribute to true. If you're using *WebControl* as the base class for your custom control, this already has been done for you.

To use the template the page developer will supply, we must create a property of type *System.Web.UI.ITemplate,* which will be used to store the template provided. There's only one method in the *ITemplate* interface, called *InstantiateIn.* We do not have to implement it, just use it. In our *CreateChildControls* method, we will check to see whether the template has been supplied. If so, we will call the *InstantiateIn* method to create a child control using the template.

If the template has not been supplied, we can simply use some default rendering to ensure that our control is rendered in some way. The following is our example of a template control that stores some text and allows the page developer to determine how it will be displayed:

```
Imports System
Imports System.Web
Imports System.Web.UI

Public Class TextItem
    Inherits Control
    Implements INamingContainer

    Private _text As String
```

```vb
    Public Sub New(text As String)
        _text = text
    End Sub
    Public Property Text As String
        Get
            Return _text
        End Get
        Set
            _text = Value
        End Set
End Class

<ParseChildren(true)> Public Class TemplateText
    Inherits Control
    Implements INamingContainer

    Private _textTemplate As ITemplate
    Private _text As String

    Public Property Text As String
        Get
            Return _text
        End Get
        Set
            _text = Value
        End Set
    End Property

    <TemplateContainer(GetType(TemplateItem))> _
    Public Property TextTemplate As ITemplate
        Get
            Return _textTemplate
        End Get
        Set
            _textTemplate = Value
        End Set
    End Property

    Protected Overrides Sub CreateChildControls()
        'If a template has been specified, use it.
        'Otherwise render the control in a default way.
        If Not (TextTemplate Is Nothing)
            Controls.Clear()

            Dim I As New TextItem(Me.Text)
            TextTemplate.InstantiateIn(I)
```

```
              Controls.Add(I)
          Else
              Me.Controls.Add(New LiteralControl(Me.Text))
          End If
      End Sub
  End Class
```

There are a few interesting things to know about this template class—the first is we have created another class called *TextItem* to use with the template. The *InstantiateIn* method will accept only a class that implements the *INnamingContainer* interface. For this reason, we have created our extra class, which will be rendered with the template supplied.

We also have created a property called *TextTemplate* that stores an object of type *ITemplate*. This is the property the page developer will use (indirectly) to supply us with the template. In the *CreateChildControls* method, we check to see whether a template has been provided. If so, we use the *InstantiateIn* method to create our *TextItem* object and give it the string that our custom control class was given. If no template has been provided, we don't need to create the *TextItem* object, and can simply render the text as a *LiteralControl*.

A page developer would supply us with the template using template tags. The following is an example of a template being provided to our control from a Web page:

```
<cc1:TemplateText Text="Hello World!" runat=server>
    <MessageTemplate>
        <h1><b><i><font color="red">
            <%# Container.Text%>
        </font></b></h1>
    </MessageTemplate>
</cc1:TemplateText>
```

Our control now uses this template, which is supplied within the *MessageTemplate* tags, to render our control.

How to Use Styles

Cascading Style Sheets (CSS) have made it very easy for page developers to define a standard look and feel to their Web pages. Cascading Style Sheets enable the page developer to define what certain page elements should look like and then apply this style to any page they wish. This has the benefit of saving the developer a great deal of time defining styles (backcolor, forecolor, font, and so forth) for every element on the page.

on the
!
Job   *Cascading Style Sheets can make a page developer's life much easier.*
If you are not familiar with them or have ignored them in the past, I strongly
recommend you start working with them.

However, if a developer wishes to override a Cascading Style Sheet or not use one at all, he or she can specify styles for individual elements on the page by using the style attribute which is a semicolon-delimited list of styles. The following is an example of setting a style for an HTML textbox:

```
<INPUT type=text style="COLOR: white; BACKGROUND-COLOR: blue;
TEXT-DECORATION: underline">
```

The .NET Framework also supports styles for your custom controls. The first way it can do this is through the use of the *WebControl* class. If your custom control is derived from *WebControl*, certain *strongly typed* style properties are exposed. When we say "strongly typed" we mean these properties are not all grouped together in one style property but are individual properties that take specific data types. The following is a list of the strongly typed styles exposed from *WebControl:*

- BackColor
- BorderColor
- BorderStyle
- BorderWidth
- Font
- ForeColor
- Height
- Width

These properties can be overridden, allowing the control developer to render the control using styles supplied by the page developer. This also enables the page developer to specify individual styles when using the custom control as follows:

```
<cc1:MyControl runat="server" BackColor="Blue"
ForeColor="White">
</cc1:MyControl>
```

To support the use of Cascading Style Sheets, the *WebControl* class also exposes the *CssClass* property, which can be used to specify a Cascading Style Sheet class as a style instead of setting individual style properties. Observe the following CSS classes in a Web page:

```
<style>
    .MyStyle
    {
        font:12pt verdana;
        color:red;
    }
    .YourStyle
    {
        font:15pt times;
        color:blue;

    }
</style>
```

A developer wishing to apply the *MyStyle* class to your custom control would write the following:

```
<cc1:MyControl id="someID" CssClass="MyStyle" Text="Hello
World!" runat="server"></cc1:MyControl>
```

The control developer then can access the elements of this style through the *ControlStyle* property of *WebControl*.

There is one other way *WebControl* can enable a page developer to set the style of your control: through the *ApplyStyle* method. If a page developer wishes to programmatically create a style and assign it to your control, he or she can use this method:

```
<script language="VB" runat="server">
    Sub Page_Load(Src As Object, E As EventArgs)
        Dim SomeStyle As New Style
        SomeStyle.BackgroundColor = Color.Blue
        MyStyle.BorderStyle = BorderStyle.Solid

        Login.ApplyStyle(SomeStyle)
        MyControl.ApplyStyle(SomeStyle)
    End Sub
</script>
```

Using styles on custom control is quite easy and enables the page developer to customize the look and feel of your control to match the look and feel of his or her Web page. The quickest way to discourage page developers from using your control is to not support styles. Nothing is worse than throwing a custom control on your page that looks completely different than the rest of the page.

Custom Control Designers

Up to this point, you will have noticed that some of the controls we have created do not look the same in the designer as they look on a running Web page. In previous versions of Visual Studio, the development environment was responsible for determining the design-time representation of your control; in Visual Studio .NET, it is up to the control itself to define how it looks in the design environment.

We now will create a custom control designer to specify the design-time look of your controls. A custom control designer is a class we must create that is responsible for rendering your control in the design environment only (not on a running Web page). To create a custom control designer, we must add a reference in our control project to the *system.design.dll* by choosing Project | Add Reference and selecting this assembly from the .NET tab.

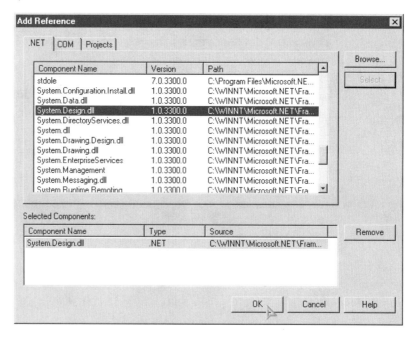

This gives us access to the *System.Web.UI.Design.ControlDesigner* class from which we will derive our custom control designer class. Once we have created this new class, we can override the *GetDesignTimeHtml* method that is called by the designer to retrieve the design-time representation of your control. The following is an example of a custom label using a custom control designer:

```
Imports System
Imports System.IO
Imports System.Web
Imports System.Web.UI
Imports System.Web.UI.WebControls
Imports System.Web.UI.Design

Public Class SampleDesigner
    Inherits System.Web.UI.Design.ControlDesigner

    Public Overrides Function GetDesignTimeHtml() As String
        'Component is the control instance, defined in the base designer
        Dim ctl As WebCustomControl1 = CType(Me.Component, _
                                    WebCustomControl1)

        If (ctl.Text <> "") Then
            Dim sw As New StringWriter()
            Dim tw As New HtmlTextWriter(sw)
            Dim placeholderlink As New HyperLink()

            'Put control text into the link's text
            placeholderlink.Text = ctl.Text
            placeholderlink.NavigateUrl = ctl.Text
            placeholderlink.RenderControl(tw)

            Return sw.ToString()
        Else
            Return Me.GetEmptyDesignTimeHtml()
        End If
    End Function
End Class

<Designer("CustomLabel.SampleDesigner, HttpLabel"), _
DefaultProperty("Text"), _
ToolboxData("<{0}:HttpLabel runat=server></{0}:HttpLabel>")> _
Public Class HttpLabel
    Inherits System.Web.UI.WebControls.WebControl

    Dim _text As String

    Public Property Text() As String
        Get
```

```
            Return _text
        End Get
        Set(ByVal Value As String)
            If String.Compare(Microsoft.VisualBasic.Left(Value, 7), _
                            "http://", True) <> 0 Then
                _text = "http://" + Value
            Else
                _text = Value
            End If
        End Set
    End Property

    Protected Overrides Sub Render(ByVal output As _
                                System.Web.UI.HtmlTextWriter)
        output.Write([Text])
    End Sub
End Class
```

The custom control designer is called *SampleDesigner*. In its *GetDesignTimeHtml* method, it renders the control in the designer as a hyperlink control. This designer class is linked to our control class by using a class attribute. Surprisingly, this attribute is called *Designer* and takes two arguments: the name of the designer and the name of your control. From now on, whenever the designer wishes to display an image of your control in the development environment, it will use your custom control designer to do so.

In general, we try to make the control look the same way in the designer as it will look on a running Web page. However, in specific circumstances, it might be valuable to do otherwise; this method will certainly allow you to do that.

Individualize a Control

If you look in the toolbox at all the controls you have added during this chapter, you will notice that they all use the same icon (a little gear). You'll also notice that when you add your control to a page, it always uses the same tag prefix (cc1). Individualizing a control is giving the control its own tag prefix (this can enable you to organize your controls more logically) and its own icon for quick identification.

To give a custom control its own tag prefix, we must edit the AssemblyInfo.vb file. The first thing we must do is import to the *System.Web.UI* namespace, after which we can add an *Assembly:TagPrefix* attribute. The following are the changes you must make to the AssemblyInfo.vb file:

```
Imports System.Web.UI
<Assembly: TagPrefix("CustomLabel", "xxx")>
```

The first argument to this attribute is the namespace in which your control is found and the second argument is the tag prefix you wish to use (xxx is not a recommendation; just an example). From now on, when you drag your control on to a Web page, it will use the tag prefix you've specified here, instead of cc1.

Creating a custom icon for your control is just as easy. Add a new bitmap to your project by choosing Project | Add Item and selecting the bitmap file template. You must rename the bitmap file so that it has the same name as your control file. This step is very important because this is how your assembly will associate the bitmap to the specific control. The bitmap file now will be open in the editor; however, before you start editing it, be sure to change its size to 16×16 in the Properties browser. Now you can draw whatever you feel like drawing (if you're like me, you might want to have somebody else do the drawing for you; otherwise, they will all come out looking like blobs).

The last step is to set the *BuildAction* property of your bitmap to *Embedded Resource,* which ensures that the bitmap is stored in the assembly. That's all you have to do (it's about time something in this chapter was easy)! The following exercise will give you some experience creating a custom control and individualizing it.

EXERCISE 5-1

Create a Custom Control Using Composition

In this exercise, we will create a control that accepts a user's personal information (name, address, and so forth). It then will expose this information through a single property in the form of a semicolon-delimited string. You will gain experience creating a composite control, adding public members and events, and individualizing the control. Very little code is given in the following exercise.

Before writing Exam 70-305, you should be able to perform this lab without referencing the code examples in the chapter. Read the instructions VERY CAREFULLY and do not skip any steps. The most common reason for failing a Microsoft exam (from my experience with students) is not reading the questions carefully.

1. Launch Visual Studio.
2. Create a new Web Control Library project called UserInfo.
3. Rename the WebCustomControl1.vb file to be UserInfo.vb.
4. Change all references to *WebCustomControl1* in the UserInfo.vb file to *UserInfo.*

5. Inherit from *Control* instead of *WebControl* and implement the *INamingContainer* interface.

6. Remove the *DefaultProperty* class attribute.

7. Remove the *Text* property and *Render* method from the *UserInfo* class.

8. Add any imports you feel are necessary (you will have to determine what you need).

9. Override the *CreateChildControls* method.

10. Add the appropriate controls based on the following illustration (this is what your control should look like when displayed in a Web page. Hint: Use LiteralControls to make a table for your child controls). You should use instance variables to hold your controls.

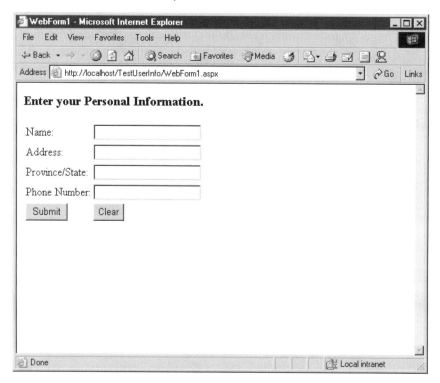

11. Compile (build) your control.

12. Add a test project to your solution called TestUserInfo.

13. Add your control to the toolbox.

14. Drag the *UserInfo* control onto the WebForm1.aspx page in the TestUserInfo project.

15. Save the WebForm1.aspx file.

16. Run the WebForm1.aspx file by right-clicking it and selecting View In Browser.

17. If your page does not look like it does in Figure 5-1, you will have to go back to Step 3 and check to make sure you have preformed each step correctly. The *CreateChildControls* method for your custom control should look similar to the following code:

```
Protected Overrides Sub CreateChildControls()
    Controls.Add(New LiteralControl("<h3>Enter your Personal" & _
                " Information.</h3>"))

    Controls.Add(New
LiteralControl("<TABLE><TR><TD>Name:</TD><TD>"))
    txtName.Text = ""
    Controls.Add(txtName)

    Controls.Add(New
LiteralControl("</TD></TR><TR><TD>Address:</TD><TD>"))
    txtAddress.Text = ""
    Controls.Add(txtAddress)

    Controls.Add(New LiteralControl("</TD></TR><TR><TD>" & _
                "Province/State:</TD><TD>"))
    txtProvince.Text = ""
    Controls.Add(txtProvince)

    Controls.Add(New LiteralControl("</TD></TR><TR><TD>Phone" & _
                " Number:</TD><TD>"))
    txtProvince.Text = ""
    Controls.Add(txtPhoneNumber)

    Controls.Add(New LiteralControl("</TD></TR><TR><TD>"))
    btnSubmit.Text = "Submit"
    Controls.Add(btnSubmit)
    Controls.Add(New LiteralControl("</TD><TD>"))
    btnClear.Text = "Clear"
    Controls.Add(btnClear)
    Controls.Add(New LiteralControl("</TD></TR></TABLE>"))
End Sub
```

18. Create a public property of type string called *Information*. This property will store our user's information in a semicolon-delimited string. Be sure to store the information in the *ViewState* property, not in an instance variable.

19. Trap the click event for the Clear button. Clear the *TextBoxes* and set the Information property to an empty string.

20. Trap the click event for the Submit button. In this method, you will concatenate the user information together, using a semicolon as a delimiter. You then will store this information in your Information property similar to the following code:

```
Information = txtName.Text & ";" & txtAddress.Text & ";" & _
              txtProvince.Text & ";" & txtPhoneNumber.Text
```

21. Declare and wire an event called *UserInfoSubmitted*. This event will be fired when the user clicks the Submit button in your control and will pass no arguments (this one is a little tricky, so don't feel bad if you have to look back at the examples to get it right).

22. Your control is now finished so you can build your solution.

23. Add some code in the WebForm1.aspx page of your test project to trap the event and display the *Information* property (we won't bother parsing it). Your test code should be placed in the code behind the Web page that runs on the server and should look similar to the following:

```
Private Sub UserInfo1_UserInfoSubmitted(ByVal sender As Object, _
        ByVal e As System.EventArgs) Handles UserInfo1.UserInfoSubmitted
    Response.Write(UserInfo1.Information)

End Sub
```

24. Run your Web page. If it looks similar to the above code, you can move on. Otherwise, you should move through the steps again and make sure you have remembered to implement everything.

25. Customize the tag prefix for your control to be xxx (Hint: Edit the AssemblyInfo.vb file).

26. Create your own toolbox bitmap by adding a bitmap file to your control project, drawing a picture (of course), and naming the file UserInfo.bmp (don't forget to set the *BuildAction* property of the bitmap properly).

27. To test these changes, you will have to perform the following steps:

   - Remove your control from the Web page.
   - Delete your control from the toolbox.
   - Rebuild the solution.
   - Add your control to the toolbox again (the new icon should be used now).
   - Add your control to the test page again.
   - Switch to HTML view and check the tag prefix.

Create User Controls

We have finally arrived at the point where we can create user controls for your Web pages. As you will see, creating user controls is extraordinarily simple when compared with creating custom controls. User controls use the same programming paradigm as Web Forms (they are just like writing Web pages). They are not compiled like custom controls and can be developed very quickly.

You might be asking yourself, "if they are so easy to create, why bother creating custom controls all?" User controls are specifically designed to enable you to reuse portions of a Web page throughout your Web application. They are not designed for long-term reuse (you'll typically reuse them in only one application). A good example of this type of control is a menu on a Web page. We often add the same or similar menus on every page in our site and it would be convenient to treat this menu as an object instead of cutting and pasting the code for it onto every Web page.

User controls have a file extension of .ascx to distinguish them from standard .NET Web pages. This is done to prevent them from accidentally being used as stand-alone Web pages (which obviously they are not). They do not have <HTML>, <BODY>, and <FORM> elements; therefore, they would not display in most browsers anyway.

To create a user control, we do not create a separate project like we do with custom controls. Instead, we must have a standard ASP.NET application project open, at which point we can select Project | Add Web User Control to add a new user control to the Web application.

Creating the control is as easy as creating a standard Web page. We can add HTML or Web server control elements, and write code-behind for these elements if we so choose. The following is an example our login custom control written as a Web user control:

```
<%@ Control Language="vb" AutoEventWireup="false" Codebehind="login.ascx.vb"
Inherits="UserControlWeb.login"
TargetSchema="http://schemas.microsoft.com/intellisense/ie5" %>
<P>
    <asp:Label id="Label1" runat="server">Please enter your username and
    password.</asp:Label><br>
    <asp:TextBox id="txtUsername" runat="server"></asp:TextBox><br>
    <asp:TextBox id="txtPassword" runat="server"></asp:TextBox><br>
    <asp:Button id="btnSubmit" runat="server" Text="Submit"></asp:Button>
    <asp:Button id="btnClear" runat="server" Text="Clear"></asp:Button>
</P>
```

You should notice that the only real difference between this and a standard Web page is the removal of the <HTML>, <BODY>, and <FORM> tags. Everything else has been done in the same way as when creating the main Web pages. The code-behind for this user control is as follows:

```
Public MustInherit Class login
    Inherits System.Web.UI.UserControl
    Protected WithEvents Label1 As
System.Web.UI.WebControls.Label
    Protected WithEvents txtUsername As _
        System.Web.UI.WebControls.TextBox
    Protected WithEvents txtPassword As _
        System.Web.UI.WebControls.TextBox
    Protected WithEvents btnSubmit As
System.Web.UI.WebControls.Button
    Protected WithEvents btnClear As
System.Web.UI.WebControls.Button

'Web Form Designer Generated Code

    Public Event UserSubmit As EventHandler

    Protected Overridable Sub OnUserSubmit(ByVal e As EventArgs)
        RaiseEvent UserSubmit(Me, e)
    End Sub
```

```
Public ReadOnly Property Username() As String
    Get
        Return txtUsername.Text
    End Get
End Property

Public ReadOnly Property Password() As String
    Get
        Return txtPassword.Text
    End Get
End Property

Private Sub Page_Load(ByVal sender As System.Object, _
        ByVal e As System.EventArgs) Handles MyBase.Load
    'Put user code to initialize the page here
End Sub

Private Sub btnClear_Click(ByVal sender As System.Object, _
        ByVal e As System.EventArgs) Handles btnClear.Click
    txtUsername.Text = ""
    txtPassword.Text = ""
End Sub

Private Sub btnSubmit_Click(ByVal sender As System.Object, _
        ByVal e As System.EventArgs) Handles btnSubmit.Click
    OnUserSubmit(EventArgs.Empty)
End Sub
End Class
```

This class has a user name and password property, and triggers an event when the user clicks the Submit button. This event can be trapped in the page on which this user control is used. As far as the code is concerned, you'll notice that it works essentially the same way as the code with custom control. The main difference is that the user interface elements do not have to be rendered, as this class is in a code-behind page, which does that for us.

exam

⍵atch

Web user controls are the same basic idea as page objects in Visual Basic 6, with the added bonus that they actually work well.

To use this Web user control on another page, we, unfortunately, cannot add it to the toolbox and drag it from there. Instead, we must drag the file from the Project Explorer window onto the Web page where we would like to use it, and the appropriate

SCENARIO & SOLUTION

How do I make a TextBox that accepts only numbers.?	Derive your control from the *TextBox* Web server control and add the functionality. This control already does 99 percent of what you want it to do.
How do I make a hyperlink in my Web application that will appear on every page and, when clicked, will take the user to a page specific to them?	Create a user control. It is doubtful that you will be able to port this functionality over to other applications without changing it.
I am constantly writing Web applications that expect users to register with my site. I am tired of creating pages that take the users personal information (Name, Address, and so forth). How do I fix this?	Create a composite control with the appropriate pre-existing user controls.
I want to make a control that displays differently depending on the language of the user's browser. The differences are not just in the language of the text but also in what elements are displayed. How do I do this?	Create a direct rendered control. From your control, you can determine the user's language preference, and in your render method display the control based on this setting.

tags are added by Visual Studio for us. We still have a great deal of capability with them, specifically in that we can create custom methods and properties in the same way as we can with composite controls.

However, they are simply not well suited to reusability across applications. As you can see, creating a Web user control is much more simplistic than creating a custom Web control; however, it also is much less robust and powerful.

CERTIFICATION SUMMARY

In this chapter, we have created custom controls by using composition, inheritance, and direct rendering. We've learned how to add properties, methods, and events to our controls, and have explored some of the intricacies of having custom controls work well in a highly generic way. We also have looked at using user controls within a single Web application to simplify the creation of common portions of Web pages (such as a menu).

Custom controls typically are used in situations in which the functionality is highly generic and can be applied to many different Web applications. By using composition, we can create a custom control based on multiple Web server controls. By using inheritance, we can extend the capabilities of a single Web server control. By using direct rendering, we can define both the functionality and the visual interface for the control. User controls are used primarily in situations in which the control can be reused within a Web application. However, this is not generic enough to be used in multiple Web applications.

TWO-MINUTE DRILL

Create Custom Controls and User Controls

❑ Custom controls run on the server, unlike ActiveX controls that run on the client.

❑ Custom controls are precompiled components, whereas user controls are not.

❑ Composite controls consist of pre-existing Web server controls.

❑ A custom control can use *Control, WebControl,* or a specific Web server control as its base class.

❑ The *INamingContainer* interface is a marker interface that ensures that the server expression of your control can be linked with the server implementation.

❑ Events fired from a custom control are raised on the server and trapped on the server.

❑ An event delegate links the control raising the event to clients subscribing to the event.

❑ Custom controls are destroyed immediately after being rendered on the client.

❑ The *ViewState* property of the *Control* class can be used to make the property values of a custom control persist between round trips to the server.

❑ Page developers can nest their own controls inside the tag for our custom controls, thus adding them to the controls collection of our custom control.

❑ The *IPostBackDataHandler* allows our control to examine postback data when the client performs a postback (submits a form).

❑ The *IPostBackEventHandler* allows our control to trap postback events.

❑ Template controls allow us to separate the user interface of our control from the control logic.

❑ Custom control designers can be used to create a custom design-time look to your control.

❑ Web user controls use the same programming paradigm as ASP.NET Web pages.

SELF TEST

The following questions will help you measure your understanding of the material presented in this chapter. Read all the choices carefully as there might be more than one correct answer. Choose all correct answers for each question.

Create Custom Controls and User Controls

1. What does a custom control runs on?

    A. The server.

    B. The client.

    C. There is a server-side component that is linked to a client-side component.

2. You want to make a special list box that works like a stack (you can add only to the end and remove only from the end). What should you implement this stack list box as?

    A. Direct rendered control

    B. Composite control

    C. User control

    D. Control derived from a pre-existing Web server control

3. The method used to add your child controls to a composite control is which of the following?

    A. MakeCompositeControls

    B. CreateCompositeControls

    C. MakeChildControls

    D. CreateChildControls

4. You have implemented a property of your control using the ViewState property of the Control base class so it will persist between calls to the client. The problem is that it is not working. Which of the following is the most likely problem?

    A. You forgot to import the System.Web.UI namespace.

    B. You forgot to implement the *INamingContainer* interface.

    C. You should derive your control from WebControl, not Control.

    D. This is a known bug.

5. Constituent controls are added to the _____ property of the Control class.

   A. ViewState

   B. Collection

   C. StateBag

   D. Controls

6. You are creating a custom control that has a button in it that is supposed to do very different things depending on how certain properties are set for the control. How would you handle the event for this button?

   A. Declare the button within your control using the WithEvents keyword, which is early binding.

   B. Create a custom delegate.

   C. Use dynamic event handling, which is late binding.

   D. Use pointers to functions.

7. Which of the following elements are needed in order to create a custom event? (Choose all that apply.)

   A. An event delegate

   B. The method that invokes the delegate

   C. The WithEvents keyword

   D. A class to hold event data

8. You have created a control and it seems to work fine, but one of the page developers using it has reported that on occasion your control does not behave as expected. You have tracked the problem to the insertion of nested controls by that page developer. How can you prevent page developers from adding nested controls to your control? (Choose all that apply.)

   A. Threaten them with violence and serious injury.

   B. Override the AddParsedSubObject method of your control object and leave the body empty.

   C. Create a custom control builder.

   D. Override the AddChildSubObject method of your control object and leave the body empty.

9. To use a custom control builder, you must do which of the following? (Choose all that apply.)

   A. Create a class that is derived from ControlBuilder.

   B. Edit the AssemblyInfo.vb file.

   C. Override the AddParsedSubObject method.

   D. Add the ControlBuilder class attribute to your Control class.

10. You've been asked to create a control that displays a customized calendar using specific graphics. How should you implement this control? (Choose the best two answers.)

    A. Create a composite control using buttons for the days.

    B. Create a direct rendered custom control.

    C. Create a user control.

    D. Use the calendar control that ships with Visual Studio.

11. The WebControl class has which of the following members not found in the Control class? (Choose all that apply.)

    A. Text

    B. Controls

    C. Font

    D. Width

12. The *IPostBackEventHandler* interface allows a custom control to do what?

    A. Trap postback events.

    B. Examine postback data.

    C. Trigger a postback event from the server.

    D. None of the above.

13. You're creating a custom control that is to trap postback events and implement the *IPostBackEventHandler* correctly. Your control is still not being notified when the postback event occurs. What is the most likely problem?

    A. Your control does not contain a Submit button.

    B. You have not assigned unique IDs to the HTML controls that you are rendering from your custom control.

    C. You have not generated the appropriate client-side JavaScript.

    D. You should have implemented the *IPostBackDataHandler* interface.

14. A Cascading Style Sheet class can be used by your control through which property?

    A. ViewState

    B. Font

    C. CssStyle

    D. CssClass

15. You're creating a control. You would like the page developers to be able to quickly and easily see some of the more important properties of your control in the design environment (without forcing them to look through the properties browser). How can we do this?

    A. Create an ActiveX control.

    B. Use a custom control designer class.

    C. Change the tag prefix.

    D. Create a template control.

16. Which of the following things must you do to change the toolbox bitmap associated with your custom control? (Choose all that apply.)

    A. Add a bitmap file to your project.

    B. Edit the AssemblyInfo.vb file.

    C. Change the size to 16×16.

    D. Set the build action property to embedded resource.

17. A Web user control can have which of the following HTML tags within it? (Choose all that apply.)

    A. <HTML>

    B. <P>

    C. <INPUT>

    D. <FORM>

18. What is the primary benefit of using a Web user control? (Choose all that apply.)

    A. Rapid development of reusable Web-based components.

    B. Speed of execution

    C. Reduced memory requirements

    D. An easy-to-understand programming model

19. You have a Web page that you have been using in other Web pages by cutting and pasting the code. You now wish to create a control based on the functionality of this Web page. Which type of control would be the easiest and quickest to create based on this Web page?

    A. Composite control

    B. Direct-rendered control

    C. User control

    D. ActiveX control

20. What is the file extension of a Web user control?

A. asx

B. aspx

C. ctl

D. ascx

LAB QUESTION

Create a table listing the pros and cons of using a composite control and a user control. In the left side of the table, first list the positive aspects of using a composite control, then the negative aspects. For each row you have created for composite controls, you list the opposite aspects of using a user control in the right-hand column. Remember that some pros and cons are relative to your perspective. What one person considers a pro might be a con to someone else. Don't fret over these as long as you can back up your decision with some logic. Your table should look something like this:

Composite Control	User Control
Pro	Con
Pro	Con
Con	Pro
Con	Pro

If you run into a situation in which there's a pro for one control that also is a pro for the other control (or vice versa) then just leave them at the bottom of the table. Use all the knowledge you've gained in this chapter as well as any experience you have with these types of controls.

SELF TEST ANSWERS

Create Custom Controls and User Controls

1. ☑ A. The server.
   ☒ B would be correct for an ActiveX control but not a Web custom control. C is incorrect as there is no client-side component, only a client-side representation of the custom control.

2. ☑ B. By using composition, we can use most of the functionality of the list box and restrict functionality we don't want available to the page developer.
   ☒ A would be too much work, considering that all the functionality already exists in the ListBox. C is incorrect because user controls do not lend themselves well to long-term reuse. D is incorrect because users would have the capability to add and remove items at any point in the list, which violates the requirements of our control.

3. ☑ D. This is the method of the control class used to add child controls.
   ☒ A, B, and D are simply incorrect.

4. ☑ B. If you have not implemented the *INamingContainer* interface, the framework cannot associate your control properties with the representation of your control on the client.
   ☒ A is incorrect because, although the *INamingContainer* interface exists in the System.Web.UI namespace, our control would not have compiled if we had forgotten to import it. C is incorrect because WebControl is derived from Control; therefore, this would make no difference. D is incorrect because this is not a known bug.

5. ☑ D. The controls property is a collection of the constituent controls.
   ☒ A is incorrect because the ViewState property stores the state of the object and not the constituent controls. B is incorrect because the collection is a type of object, not a specific property in the Control class. C is incorrect because a StateBag is what the ViewState property contains and is not where constituent controls are stored.

6. ☑ C. By using dynamic event handling, we can change the function that responds to the event at run time.
   ☒ A is incorrect because we would not be able to change the function that responds to the event at run time and would be forced to use a large condition statement instead. This would create a very large function that does many different things, and would become hard to debug and test. B is incorrect because the handler of the event does not create the delegate; it is the component that raises the event. D is a viable solution in C++ but not in Visual Basic (although in reality, this is how dynamic event handling works).

7. ☑ A, B, and D. You must have a method that invokes the delegate and passes the delegate of the class that holds the event data. The delegate then takes care of sending the event to the client.
☒ C is incorrect because the WithEvents keyword is used to handle events, not raise them.

8. ☑ B and C. Both of these methods are correct. Although if you're only purpose is to prevent page developers from nesting controls within your control, the easiest way is to override the AddParsedSubObject method.
☒ A is just not nice. D is incorrect because this method does not exist.

9. ☑ A and D. You must create a class that is derived from ControlBuilder, override its methods to define its behavior, and link to your Control class by using the ControlBuilder class attribute.
☒ B is incorrect because the AssemblyInfo.vb file has nothing to do with ControlBuilder classes. C is incorrect because the AddParsedSubObject method is not a method of the control builder class, which was the question.

10. ☑ B and C. Creating a direct-rendered custom control will give you the power and flexibility to do this, and reuse it in the future; however, if the graphics for this control are very specific to the application you're working on, you might wish to implement it as a user control.
☒ A is incorrect because this is an enormous waste of system resources and D is incorrect because it uses specific graphics.

11. ☑ C and D. Font and width both are properties that the WebControl class adds to the Control class.
☒ A is incorrect because neither WebControl nor Control have a text property. B is incorrect because the control class has the Control property.

12. ☑ A. The *IPostBackEventHandler* interface allows a control to trap postback events.
☒ B is incorrect because this is the responsibility of the *IPostBackDataHandler* interface. C is incorrect because postback events are triggered from the client, not the server. D is not correct because A is correct.

13. ☑ B. Without unique ID, there's no way for the framework to associate your client-side HTML controls with your server-side control.
☒ A is incorrect because it is irrelevant whether your control contains a Submit button. C is incorrect because client-side JavaScript does not have to be generated for your control to trap postback events. D is incorrect as the *IPostBackEventHandler* interface is the correct interface to use.

14. ☑ D. The CssClass property enables the page developer to assign a Cascading Style Sheet class to your control.

☒   A is incorrect because the ViewState property is for keeping the state of your object, not the look. B is a strongly typed style, not a class. C is incorrect because the property is CssClass, not CssStyle.

15. ☑   B. A custom control designer is specifically used for creating design-time representations of your control. The example given for this question is a perfect use for this class.
☒   A is incorrect because this is a book on Visual Basic .NET; however, it is also incorrect because you could not create a custom designer using Visual Basic and ActiveX controls. C is incorrect because the tag prefix does not affect the design-time display of the control. D is incorrect because template controls do not alter the design-time view of a control (template controls often use custom control designers because typically they have no user interface until a page developer gives them one with the template).

16. ☑   A, C, and D are the proper way to change the toolbox bitmap, assuming you also named the file the same name as your control.
☒   B is incorrect because it is not necessary to edit the AssemblyInfol.vb file to change the toolbox bitmap.

17. ☑   B and C. The paragraph tag and input tag both are valid HTML tags for the Web user control.
☒   A and D both are invalid tags for a Web user control (so is the <body> tag).

18. ☑   A and D. Web user controls enable you to create reusable, Web-based components very quickly and allow you to use a programming model familiar to a Web developer.
☒   B and C are incorrect because Web user controls are not precompiled.

19. ☑   C. It is extremely easy to convert a Web page into a user control.
☒   A, B, and D are incorrect because none of these controls have an HTML element to them, which means whatever was in the original Web page would have to be translated to pure Visual Basic.

20. ☑   D. ascx is the file extension for Web user control.
☒   A is incorrect because it represents nothing that I know of (although I'm sure someone uses it for something). D is a .NET Active Server Page file. C is a control file from Visual Basic 6.

LAB ANSWER

You were asked to create a pro and con table for composite controls and user controls. Check your table against the following table. If you've left any of these out, this is a good time to add them to your own table, as we tend to remember things better when we write them down. If you have something you don't see in this table, make sure you can support its inclusion with logic and fact. If so, give yourself some bonus marks (I suggest 20 or 30, but you can go as high as 700 if you like).

I have listed only the most obvious here (the kind of points that may be asked on an exam). However, I encourage you to come up with your own additional pros and cons, as this is an invaluable exercise to perform when evaluating new products.

Composite Controls	User Controls
Compiled.	Not compiled.
Stored as an assembly.	Stored as a text file.
Useful for generic redistributable controls that may be used in many Web applications.	Useful for application-specific functionality (reuse within a single application).
Can be added to the Toolbox (can be integrated with a design host).	Cannot be added to the Toolbox (cannot be integrated with a design host).
Created using an object-oriented programming paradigm (authored like a Visual Basic .NET program).	Created using an ASP.NET programming paradigm (authored like a Web page).
Authored almost entirely by writing code (no design-time support).	Extensive design-time support for authoring with visual editing, drag-and-drop, and so forth.
Can greatly improve development time.	Also can improve development time but not to the same degree.

MCAD/MCSD

MICROSOFT® CERTIFIED APPLICATION DEVELOPER
& MICROSOFT® CERTIFIED SOLUTION DEVELOPER

Part III

Consume and Manipulate Data

CHAPTERS

6

Data Access
with SQL Server

Themost important component of a business application is its data. If you think about it, almost every Visual Basic application you have ever written probably has revolved around capturing, manipulating, and analyzing data. This data often is stored in different formats such as relational databases, XML files, and flat files; and when we consider the number of different formats for relational databases alone, we can see the need for some kind of standardization.

ADO.NET is designed to provide this standardization and enables us to access many different types of data, stored in many different formats, in relatively the same way. This idea of accessing data using the same methods regardless of its format is not new to Visual Basic (ADO.NET is based on ADO, which was designed just for this purpose). However, ADO.NET has now optimized data access for the Internet environment by standardizing the way data is transferred.

In this chapter, we will learn to access data from a Microsoft SQL Server database. We will focus on the use of ADO.NET in a Web-based environment and execute stored procedures, which can improve both efficiency and security in our Web applications. For the examples in this chapter, we are using the Northwind database, which ships with SQL Server 7.0 and 2000 (as well as other Microsoft products such as Microsoft Access). I strongly suggest you have SQL Server installed with the Northwind database while you work through this chapter. If you do not have access to SQL Server, you can use the Microsoft Desktop Engine, which is a free desktop version of SQL Server.

CERTIFICATION OBJECTIVE 6.01

Access and Manipulate Data from a Microsoft SQL Server Database

Microsoft SQL Server is a highly functional and efficient relational database management system (RDBMS). Since version 7, SQL Server has been a major player in the realm of high-end server-based databases. Databases of this magnitude (Oracle being another example) often are used as the central data store for many small, medium, and even large companies, and usually are necessary to reliably store enormous amounts of data and allow access to that data quickly and efficiently.

Microsoft SQL Server 2000 certainly has succeeded in this area. We will focus on accessing a SQL Server database; however, note that most of the information contained in this chapter is equally applicable to other databases with very little change. In the next chapter, we will access other relational databases, and use XML files and flat files as a data store. I strongly recommend you use this chapter as a reference while reading the next chapter.

Overview of Data Access

The one common thread among all business applications is the data they must work with. It doesn't matter whether the application is an online e-commerce application, a company's enterprise software, or a small business' accounting application; they all must store, retrieve, and manipulate data in a fast, efficient, and reliable way.

A daunting problem has been that often this data has been stored in very different formats, which has required developers to learn many different ways to do the exact same thing. Microsoft identified this problem very early on and over the years has made concerted efforts to standardize the way in which we access data. One of the first major developments came when Microsoft, IBM, and other database vendors teamed up to develop a standard API that would enable developers to use one method to access all of their databases. The result was *Open Database Connectivity (ODBC).*

The major drawback of ODBC is that it is a low-level API written in C. This makes it very difficult for programming languages, such as Visual Basic, to use it easily. The solution was to create the *Data Access Objects (DAO)* and *Remote Data Objects (RDO).* DAO is an object model that provides access to Microsoft's *JET engine (Joint Engine Technology)* and enabled developers to access most *ISAM (Indexed Sequential Access Method)* databases such as Microsoft Access, FoxPro, and Paradox (these are primarily file-based databases).

The DAO object model also provided access to ODBC-compliant databases such as Microsoft SQL Server and Oracle; however, this access was not very efficient and required enormous amounts of memory. For this reason, RDO was designed to be a small and efficient wrapper around ODBC. At this point, Visual Basic developers could use two basic object models to access databases: DAO for ISAM databases, and RDO for ODBC-compliant databases. Although this greatly simplified database access, it did not enable us to access any data store in a consistent manner. For example, we still had two different ways to access relational databases, and if our data was stored in a flat file on a mainframe we had to use a completely different method of data access.

Universal Data Access

In 1996, Microsoft developed the OLEDB technology, which was built on the Component Object Model (COM) and essentially allowed developers to access any type of data in the exact same way. This was Microsoft's idea of what they called *Universal Data Access (UDA)*. A developer could use OLEDB to access an Access database, SQL Server database, text file, Excel file, and even a flat file on a mainframe; the best part is they could write basically the same code for all sources of data. OLEDB is very small and very fast, but it also is a C++ template technology and, if used directly, requires the developer to take care of a lot of the data management issues (such as cursors). It also is inaccessible from languages such as Visual Basic.

exam
ⓦatch

A cursor is not just a little pointy thing you use to click stuff. In database programming, a cursor is the tabular data retrieved from the database. It is called a cursor because there is always a current record which is tracked by a pointer or cursor. The cursor points at the current record and can move from one record to the next. You will find that when someone mentions a cursor in the database context, most often they mean the tabular data structure; however, they also might mean the little pointer that points to the current record. To make things even more confusing, this pointer also is called an iterator by some people.

The ActiveX Data Objects (ADO) is the object model that gave Visual Basic 6 access to this OLEDB technology. Interestingly, even C++ developers, who had direct access to OLEDB, still typically preferred the ADO object model, as it took care of many of the data management issues; it finally allowed Visual Basic developers to access any data store using the same methodologies. ADO had become the Visual Basic developer's gateway to universal data access. Over the next few years, ADO fulfilled its requirements well, and many of us thought that the days of learning a new data access object model every couple of years were gone. Thanks to the Internet, we were wrong!

ADO.NET

ADO.NET is the .NET version of the ActiveX Data Objects. When I first heard of ADO.NET, I assumed that based on the success of ADO, this was simply ADO using the .NET framework instead of COM. The truth of the matter is that although ADO.NET is based on ADO, it is not a replacement for ADO.

ADO.NET was designed specifically for the Internet environment and other network environments in which a constant connection to a database is not desirable.

The Internet lends itself well to *disconnected data,* which involves connecting to a database, retrieving records, and then disconnecting the link to that database. Users then can manipulate those records without a connection to the database, after which they can reconnect to the database to update the underlying data with any changes they have made. This process works well on the Internet because it does not require constant connection to the database; therefore, the database itself does not need to be exposed to the Internet (which obviously is a security risk) and there is no need to tie up a connection to the database.

Using this scenario let's the user of your Web site request a page that supplies him or her with some data from a database. The Web server would contact an internal database (internal to your network) and request the data on behalf of the user. Once the data is retrieved, the connection to the database is dropped and this disconnected data can be sent back to the client's browser.

As you can see, the client does not need any direct connection to our database, which also means we do not have to open our database to random attacks on the Internet. When the user finishes manipulating the data, he or she can send it back to our server, which will reconnect to our database on behalf of the user and update the underlying data with any changes the user has made. ADO.NET is specifically designed for this type of data access and has made it much easier to write Web applications for the Internet. It should be noted that ADO is not being replaced by ADO.NET; ADO is still available for unmanaged code, backward compatibility, and data access for cases in which it is better to keep alive connections to the database.

One of the biggest problems with creating a disconnected data environment is the data format used to transfer data around the network. In a Web environment, we often have no control over the platform and browser of the client. In the past, this meant that to write a truly portable Web application, developers had to keep database records on the server and return them in a browser-independent way (typically in the HTML format all current browsers support). This often meant writing a large amount of server-side code to retrieve records, convert them to HTML, send them to the browser, retrieve changes from the browser (in HTML again), put these changes back into a database format (Recordset), and update the database. Just reading that sentence is a little overwhelming, let alone writing the code!

We can see the same problem when passing data from a database to other programs or processes on the network. Every application would expect the data to arrive in a specific proprietary format—typically not the same format used by the information provider. ADO.NET now uses XML as a standard format to transmit data, which is fast becoming the data format standard for Internet and non-Internet uses (there is even discussion of using XML as the transfer format for TCP/IP).

By taking advantage of this well-accepted industry standard, Microsoft has made it very easy for developers to send information from a database around a network in a standardized format. This in itself should take a great deal of the complexity out of writing datacentric Web applications and truly supports the idea of Visual Basic as a *rapid application development system (RAD)*.

Visual Studio

In keeping with the Visual Studio .NET concept of visual programming, the Visual Studio development environment gives us access to many visual tools that make data access almost as simple as drag-and-drop or point and click. By using the Server Explorer window, we have access to any SQL Server database installed on our system and can even create links to any other type of data store. This primarily enables us to view the structure and contents of a database, and manipulate the database by doing such things as creating new tables, database objects, and even database diagrams.

Probably the most interesting use of the System Explorer is the capability to drag a table (for example) onto a Web page, and automatically create the ADO.NET objects necessary to connect to that database and retrieve data from a table. Once we have access to this data, we can place controls on our Web page that are bound to this source of data, which allows us to create a data access Web page with very little coding.

The basic idea of the Visual Studio design tools is to enable us to quickly and easily put together a data access Web page, then allow us to manually change the code created to give our Web page its specific functionality. We will discuss the Visual Studio tools in more detail in the next chapter. In this chapter, we'll focus on understanding the underlying code.

Structured Query Language: A Review

The first real standard in database programming came with the advent of the *Structured Query Language (SQL)*. This standard language is used to query databases for information and has gained wide acceptance in the industry. You will be hard-pressed to find any commercial database that does not support SQL queries.

There are two primary ways in which to retrieve and manipulate data from a SQL Server database: *ad hoc queries* and *stored procedures.* Ad hoc queries are SQL statements that are passed to the database. The database can read these SQL queries and perform the appropriate action, which can involve returning records or performing actions on the data in the database. You can think of stored procedures as SQL statements that have already been prepared and stored in the database (although in the case of SQL Server, they are much more advanced than that, and often contain programming logic). From our Web application, we can call stored procedures and have them perform their tasks. This saves us from having to build SQL statements from within our applications and can be much more efficient, as stored procedures are pre-parsed and pre-optimized.

Internally, SQL Server uses a SQL-based language called *Transact-SQL.* This language is an extension of the entry-level ANSI SQL-92 ISO standard, and supports programming constructs and simple query statements. In this section, we will review core SQL based on the entry-level ANSI SQL-92 ISO standard.

If you do a lot of work with Microsoft SQL Server, it will be very valuable for you to learn Transact-SQL and how to use it to create stored procedures. However, Exam 70-305 will not require you to have in-depth knowledge of SQL, so our review will be very basic; it is designed only to refresh your memory on the types of SQL statements you might see on the exam. You also should understand the structure of relational databases, which we will not discuss here. If you are an experienced database programmer, you should already have an in-depth understanding of the SQL language, so you might wish to skip this section.

There are three main categories of statements in the SQL language:

- **Data Definition Language (DDL)**   A set of statements allowing the creation and destruction of database objects such as tables, views, and stored procedures.

- **Data Control Language (DCL)**   A set of statements allowing the definition of security parameters on the data and objects within a database.

- **Data Manipulation Language (DML)**   A set of statements allowing us to query and modify data.

For our review, we will focus on the Data Manipulation Language (DML). This set of SQL statements allows us to query databases for information and modify that information by adding, deleting, and updating records. We typically would not use DDL and DCL in a Web application (although it certainly is possible).

The SELECT Statement

Probably the most common action to request of a database is the retrieval of records, known as a *query*. It is one thing to have data, and a completely different thing to have access to that data. The select statement allows us to select the data we wish to retrieve in a very efficient manner. The basic form of the select statement is as follows:

SELECT *<Field List>* FROM *<TableName>*

The field list contains the columns in the database table you wish to retrieve. The FROM clause specifies the table that contains the records you wish to retrieve. For example, if we wish to retrieve the FirstName and LastName fields from the Employees table, we could write the following:

```
SELECT FirstName, LastName FROM Employees
```

This SELECT statement would retrieve the FirstName and LastName for all of the records in this table. In situations in which you wish to retrieve all of the fields from a table, we can simplify the syntax by using the wild card. By replacing the field list with an asterisk (*), we are requesting all of the fields, like so:

```
SELECT * FROM Employees
```

This SELECT statement retrieves all of the fields and all of the records from the Employees table, which essentially means it will retrieve the entire Employees table.

In most cases, retrieving entire tables is not very efficient. Most often we are concerned with only certain records in a table; in this situation, we would use a WHERE clause to restrict the number of records retrieved. A WHERE clause contains a *Boolean* expression, which is evaluated against all of the records in the database and used to decide which records will be retrieved and which records will not. For example, we could retrieve the first name and last name of all employees in our employees table whose salaries are greater than $100,000 a year, like so:

```
SELECT FirstName, LastName FROM Employee WHERE Salary > 100000
```

To group together multiple WHERE clauses, we can use the logical operators AND, OR, and NOT. This allows us to search based on more than one criterion. For example, if we want to retrieve all of the employees in our Employees table whose salaries are greater than $100,000 a year and who work in London, we can use the following:

```
SELECT * FROM Employees WHERE Salary > 100000 AND City = 'London'
```

For ranges of data, we have the BETWEEN clause. To retrieve all of the employees from our Employees table whose salaries are greater than $50,000 and less than $100,000, we have two options, which are equivalent:

```
SELECT * FROM Employees WHERE Salary >= 50000 AND Salary <= 100000
SELECT * FROM Employees WHERE Salary BETWEEN 50000 AND 100000
```

The last option we will discuss for a WHERE clause involves pattern matching. When searching for patterns, we use the LIKE clause. The LIKE clause uses one of three wild cards and is used to match patterns in strings. The wild cards are as follows:

- % is used to represent any number of characters of any value.
- _ is used to represent a single character of any value.
- [] is used to represent a single character listed within the brackets.

For example, to retrieve all of the employees whose last names start with C or S, we would use the following:

```
SELECT * FROM Employees WHERE LastName LIKE '[CS]%'
```

When retrieving records, we often need to sort them for convenience. The ORDER BY clause is used to sort records based on one or more fields. For example, to retrieve all of the records from the employees table and sort them based on their LastName first and their FirstName second, we would use the following:

```
SELECT * FROM Employees ORDER BY LastName, FirstName
```

Our last note on the SELECT statement involves joining tables. Tables are joined to retrieve records from multiple tables that are related. For example, if our database contains a Products table (which stores a list of our products), and Categories table (which stores a list of different types of products) these tables would be related. For each record in the Categories table there would be associated records in the Products table. If we wish to retrieve all of the products in our database that belong to the Produce category, and the primary key for the Produce category in the Categories table is 7, we would use the following JOIN clause in our SQL statement:

```
SELECT * FROM Products INNER JOIN Categories ON Products.CategoryID =
Categories.CategoryID WHERE Categories.CategoryID = 7
```

Note that the JOIN clause specifies the other table to incorporate into our query and the ON clause specifies the relationship between the two tables (in this case, the categoryID field). We also have used a WHERE clause to specify that the only category we are interested in is the Produce category. Using the INNER keyword simply specifies that we want only records from each table that have an associate record in the other table.

Although we will not discuss this further (as it should not be necessary for the exam) you also should be aware that there are other types of JOINs called OUTER JOINs and CROSS JOINs. These behave a little differently, and you should research them on your own.

The INSERT Statement

The INSERT statement is used to add new records to a table. When executing an INSERT statement, it is very important to understand the underlying structure of the database table into which you are inserting records because there might be constraints on the fields within the database that you have to respect. For example, some fields might be required, which means you must give them a value to add a new record to the table; other fields might not be required, so you can leave them out.

The basic structure of an INSERT statement is to specify the table into which to insert a record, the fields to which you wish to give values, and the values you wish to give them. For example, to insert a new record into the Friends table, we could do the following:

```
INSERT INTO Friends (FirstName, LastName) VALUES ('John', 'Suatac')
```

The UPDATE Statement

The UPDATE statement is used to change the values of fields within a record that already exists. The UPDATE statement can be very efficient, as it can change multiple records with one execution. The basic structure of an UPDATE statement is to specify the table name that contains the records you wish to change, the field you wish to change, the new value, and possibly a WHERE clause to restrict which records get updated. For example, to give everyone in our company a 10 percent raise, we can execute the following UPDATE statement:

```
UPDATE Employees SET Salary = (Salary * 1.10)
```

Now, aren't we generous! Of course, if we weren't that generous, we would do the following:

```
UPDATE Employees SET Salary = (Salary * 1.10) WHERE FirstName = 'Your First
Name' AND LastName = 'Your Last Name'
```

The DELETE Statement

Surprisingly, the DELETE statement is used to delete records from the database. You must be very careful with the DELETE statement because with it you can delete all of the records in a table with one execution. For this reason, almost all DELETE statements have a WHERE clause to restrict which records are deleted. For example, to delete all of the employees in our company who make more than $100,000 a year we would do the following:

```
DELETE FROM Employees WHERE Salary > 100000
```

This is in no way the full description of the SQL language. As a matter of fact, we have probably covered less than five percent of what's available. The goal here is to simply give those of you who rely heavily on database developers and stored procedures a small refresher in SQL. Hopefully this will help you through the exam and give you enough knowledge of SQL to work with the ADO.NET objects we will be using. That said, I strongly recommend that any developer gain an in-depth knowledge of the SQL language, as you most likely will use it for the rest of your career.

Access SQL Server with ADO.NET

Although, as mentioned earlier, ADO.NET is based on ADO, the object model has changed significantly. With ADO there was no significant distinction between the data and the provider of that data. With the new object model, we now have a provider-independent view of the data we're manipulating, and provider-specific objects that we use to communicate with different data sources.

The *DataSet* Object

The data portion of this object model revolves around the *DataSet* object. This object is not specific to any provider and is used to store data retrieved from relational databases, flat files, and XML files. It can even be used as an in-memory database you create yourself. The key to this implementation is that the *DataSet* object has no knowledge of its data source and is totally disconnected.

If you are used to the ADO object model, the *DataSet* object is analogous to the *Recordset* object and stores the records retrieved from the data source. The primary difference is that a *Recordset* object represented a single table or group of records retrieved from a single SQL statement; however, the *DataSet* object can contain one or more tables and the tables can even come from different databases.

DataSet objects also can create constraints on the tables they store and relationships between those tables. This essentially means the *DataSet* object is itself a virtual database and makes a *DataSet* object completely autonomous, allowing it to be the data currency for a system. We can retrieve data from a database (or other data source), and transfer and manipulate this data completely independent of the underlying data source.

If we wish to propagate the changes made to our *DataSet* back to the underlying data source, it can be reconnected at a later time, allowing the changes to become permanent. The *DataSet* object also contains methods that allow the data contained therein to be written and read as XML. This allows us to temporarily store our data in an XML file and retrieve it at a later date, or use an XML file as our permanent data source.

on the
Job

If you wish to create an application that downloads records from a database onto a laptop, the capability of the DataSet to write its data as XML can be invaluable. Laptops are often disconnected from the network and shut down before they are reconnected. The DataSet can write its data to an XML file to persist the data until it can be reconnected to the network at a later time. This is a great solution when you need to take records on the road. Although not specific to Web development, this can be a very useful technique for many business applications.

The *DataSet* object itself contains its own object model, which represents the structure of the data within the *DataSet*. These child objects represent tables, rows, columns, relations, and constraints, and enable us to manipulate the data within the *DataSet* and the structure of the *DataSet* itself. The following key objects make up the *DataSet* object model:

■ **DataTable**   Represents a single table within a *DataSet*, where the *DataSet* can contain more than one table.

■ **DataColumn**   Represents a column or field in the *DataTable*.

■ **DataRow**   Represents each record in a table; think of it as an array of *DataColumn* objects.

■ **DataRelation**   Represents a relationship between two tables in the *DataSet* and is equivalent to a primary key/foreign key relationship in a relational database.

■ **DataConstraint**   Represents a rule that must be enforced on a particular column in a table.

If you are an experienced database developer, you will immediately see that these objects alone enable us to create a fairly robust and advanced database. The most important thing to note is that the *DataSet* in this case is free from any data source. This means it is extremely easy to create a database without needing an actual database product. Because the *DataSet* object can read and write its internal structure and data to an XML file, this can be an extremely useful solution to storing small amounts of read-only relational data in a Web application where cost and overhead of an RDBMS system simply is not necessary.

Please note that without the concurrency control of an RDBMS (record locking) this would not be a reasonable solution for data that is to be written to by multiple users. Even so, it could even be argued that Microsoft Access might have found some competition in this very simple object.

The *DataSet* stores the internal structure of its data in an XML schema. This allows it to be totally disconnected from any notion of a database. At this point, the important thing to understand is that when using a SQL Server database as the underlying source of your data, SQL Server will provide the XML schema.

The SQL Server Data Provider

The portion of the ADO.NET object model specific to different data sources is called the *Managed Data Provider*. Data providers consist of groups of objects that can be used to communicate with specific databases. Presently, only two data providers ship with Visual Studio .NET: One is for SQL Server; the other is a generic OLEDB provider. Although this might not seem like much, you should note that the OLEDB provider can access any OLEDB-compliant data source, which includes many relational databases (even SQL Server) as well as a number of nonrelational sources of data, such as flat files.

The primary difference between the SQL Server provider and the OLEDB provider is that the SQL Server provider is optimized for SQL Server and contains a

SQL Server–specific implementation. On the other hand, the OLEDB provider is not optimized for any specific data source and does not contain any extra functionality that can be found in any specific database. It is expected that in the near future other vendors of data stores will add to this collection of data providers and offer data providers targeted for their products.

The SQL Server data provider consists of six objects:

■ **SqlConnection** This object represents a connection to the underlying database and is similar to the *Connection* object found in ADO. It contains all of the information necessary to form the connection with the database (such as host, database, user name, password, and so forth) and enables us to send commands to the database.

■ **SqlCommand** This object represents a single SQL statement that is to be executed against the database. This object enables us to perform actions on the database and retrieve records.

■ **SqlParameter** This object represents a parameter that is used in a stored procedure or SQL statement, and is used in conjunction with the *SqlCommand* object to execute these queries.

■ **SqlDataReader** This object is very similar to a forward-only, read-only *Recordset* in ADO. The *SqlDataReader* object contains a cursor of data retrieved from the database and is primarily used to quickly and efficiently read data from the database. However, it is not used to add or change information in a database.

■ **SqlDataAdapter** This object was designed to connect the provider-independent world of the *DataSet* object to the provider-specific world of SQL Server. It is our connection between a *SqlConnection* and the *DataSet,* and allows us to retrieve records from a database and update the database with changes made in the *DataSet.* The *SqlDataAdapter* contains *DataCommand* objects, which can be used to specify how the data is selected, inserted, updated, and deleted from the underlying database.

■ **SqlTransaction** This object represents an *atomic transaction* and is controlled by the *SqlConnection* object. An atomic transaction is a group of data actions that must be performed successfully as a group. If one of the data actions fails, all of the actions should fail.

These six objects enable us to contact and manipulate a SQL Server database. In the following sections, we will look at these objects from a more practical viewpoint.

We will specifically look at creating connections to a SQL Server database, retrieving records from the database, and manipulating those records.

Security Settings

Before using ADO.NET to access a SQL Server database, we must talk about some of the security considerations that are unique to Web applications. When a user contacts your Web application and requests information stored in a database, your server-side code will have to create a connection to that database (which we will discuss in the next section). If you plan to use Windows authentication to access SQL Server (as you should for Web applications), we will have to set up a few things.

The first issue is that when Visual Studio .NET is installed, it adds a Windows account to your system called ASPNET; your Web application runs under this account. This also means you will have to give this Windows account access to any databases in SQL Server to which you wish to have access.

The next issue is that ADO.NET will not allow a Web application to access a database that allows anonymous access; you'll have to disable anonymous access in the Internet Services Manager. You can do this by right-clicking your Web application in the Internet Services Manager and selecting properties. When the Connection Properties dialog box appears, you can click the Directory Security tab and click the Edit button in the Anonymous Access and Security Control frame, as shown in Figure 6-1.

This opens another dialog, which allows you to select which security modes you'll support. Now you can uncheck the Anonymous Access check box and click OK, as shown in Figure 6-2.

Once you have disabled anonymous authentication, you must set the identity property in your web.config file for your project. You can do this by adding the <identity> tag to your web.config file, making sure to place it within the <system.web> tag, as shown here:

```
<?xml version="1.0" encoding="utf-8" ?>
<configuration>
  <system.web>
    ...
    <identity impersonate="true"></identity>
  </system.web>
</configuration>
```

This tag instructs your Web application to make itself look like the user logged into IIS instead of the IIS account when accessing other services. Once you have completed this step, your Web application will be able to access SQL Server.

The Directory
Security tab

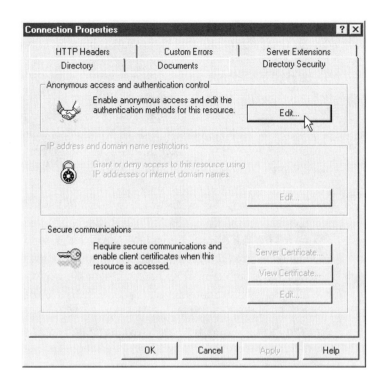

You can select
which security
modes to support

Make a Connection to a Database

Before we can begin our discussion of accessing and manipulating data from a SQL Server database, we must get access to the objects that will do this work for us. All of the data-related objects, such as the *DataSet* object and the Managed Data Provider objects, are contained in the System.Data.dll. Normally, we would have to create a reference to this .dll in our project; however, when you create an ASP.NET application in Visual Studio .NET, the reference to this component is automatically added to your project.

If you look under the references folder for your project in the Solution Explorer, you will see that the reference already exists. If this reference ever disappears (not likely unless you remove it yourself), you can right-click the references and select Add Reference to add it. This brings up the Add Reference dialog box, which you can use to add a reference to the System.Data.dll component.

Assuming you have a reference to the System.Data.dll component, you still need to import the namespace where these objects live. The non-provider-specific objects exist in the *System.Data* namespace and for SQL Server; the provider-specific objects exist in the *System.Data.SqlClient* namespace. If you need access to SQL Server data types, you can find them in the *System.Data.SqlTypes* enumeration. If accessing the database from the code-behind, you simply need to add the following *Imports* statements before the declaration of your class:

```
Imports System.Data
Imports System.Data.SqlClient
Imports System.Data.SqlTypes 'Only needed if you need access to SQL Types
```

To communicate with a SQL Server database, we must have some way to pass queries to the database and retrieve responses. You can do this by creating a *Connection* object. Think of the *Connection* object as a telephone line to your database. With our connection, we can pass commands to the database and the information we have requested (if any) can be sent back on this telephone line.

The SQL Server data provider provides us with a version of the *Connection* object specific to SQL Server, which is optimized for SQL Server and contains some extra functionality specific to SQL Server. This object is called the *SqlConnection* object and contains functions common to all ADO.NET *Connection* objects. Note that all data providers are required to provide specific interfaces for each of their component objects (which the SQL Server provider does); however, providers are free to add functionality by exposing extra methods.

In the case of the *SqlConnection* object, you will find members, such as *Open* and *ConnectionString,* that are common to all other data provider *Connection* objects (for example, the *OleDbConnection* object). However, the SQL Server *Connection* object also exposes specific members such as *PacketSize,* which are seen only in the *SqlConnection* object. This is far different from the ADO object model in which there was one group of objects used for all providers and the provider-specific implementation of these objects was hidden from us.

The *SqlConnection* object contains two constructors that can be used to instantiate the object. The first constructor allows us to specify the *ConnectionString,* which is a string that contains all of the information necessary to connect to the database server. The second constructor takes no arguments and, if used, the programmer must supply the *ConnectionString* at a later time through the *SqlConnection's ConnectionString* property. Before we look at these two constructors and how to use them to instantiate a *SqlConnection* object, we must create connection strings. *ConnectionStrings* have multiple attributes that are separated by a semicolon. Some of the most common attributes are shown in Table 6-1.

It is important to note that not all of these attributes are necessary and some can be left out. Following are some examples of connection strings. This connection string uses Integrated Security (Windows Authentication) and connects to the Northwind database on the local SQL Server (the SQL Server on the same machine on which the code is running).

```
"Data Source=(local); Initial Catalog=Northwind; Integrated Security=true"
```

This connection string uses SQL Server security and connects to the pubs database on the host XYZ using the ABC instance of SQL Server.

```
"Data Source=XYZ\ABC; Initial Catalog=pubs; User ID=sa; Password=xxx"
```

As you can see, a connection string is not a difficult thing to understand; however, it is often hard to write them from memory.

exam
Watch

Do not waste your time memorizing connection strings. You should simply be able to recognize them and identify the proper format.

| TABLE 6-1 | Common *ConnectionString* Attributes |

Attribute	Usage
Data Source	The instance of SQL Server to which you are trying to connect. This involves the host the server is running on and the name of the instance of SQL Server (which can be left off if you wish to connect to the default instance).
Initial Catalog	The database you want to access in the SQL Server database (for example, the Northwind database).
User ID	The SQL Server user name used to authenticate your connection to the database. This is not necessary if you are using Integrated Security.
Password	The SQL Server password used to authenticate your connection to the database. This is not necessary if you are using Integrated Security.
Integrated Security	This can be set to true or false; if set to true, your login user name and password will be used to authenticate you in the database. If set to false, you will need to supply a SQL Server user name and password.
Persist Security Info	If set to false, the user name and password information is released after the connection to the database is made. This means to reopen a connection that has been closed, you will have to re-enter the user name and password. You can set this to true on secure networks to avoid having to re-enter this information every time you reopen the connection. On an unsecured network, this is a serious security risk so this attribute should be set to false.
Connection Timeout	The amount of time to try to make the connection. If the connection cannot be made during this time, it will fail.
Provider	This is not used for the *SqlConnection* object as the provider is known (SQL Server). With the *OleDbConnection* object, this attribute is used to specify the specific provider of the data (for example, Oracle).

Now that we have learned to build connection strings, we can create and open a connection to a SQL Server database. Once you have the connection string the rest actually is extremely simple. Depending on the constructor we use, this can involve two or three lines of code. If you use the default constructor (the constructor that takes no arguments), we will have to instantiate the SQL connection object, set its *ConnectionString* property explicitly, and open the connection as follows:

```
Dim cn As New SqlConnection()
cn.ConnectionString = "Data Source=(local); Initial Catalog=Northwind; " & _
                      "Integrated Security=true"
cn.Open()
```

You should note that if you are using a *SqlDataAdapter* object to transfer information to a *DataSet*, it is unnecessary to open the *SqlConnection* explicitly. The *SqlDataAdapter* object will open and close the connection for you (we will see an example of this later in this chapter). However, if you're creating a connection to be used with a *SqlCommand* object, you will have to explicitly open and close the connection yourself.

The other option for instantiating a *SqlConnection* object is to use the constructor that takes as an argument a connection string. There really is no difference between this method and the previous one except for the number of lines of code it involves and the number of function calls necessary. The following is an example of using the second constructor:

```
Dim cn As New SqlConnection("Data Source=(local); " & _
                            "Initial Catalog=Northwind; " & _
                            "Integrated Security=true")
cn.Open()
```

Once we have created the *SqlConnection* object (and it is open), we have a line of communication to the database. Our next step is to use this line of communication to execute queries on the database, execute stored procedures in the database, and retrieve records.

Retrieve Records from a Database

When retrieving records from a database, we will need a place to store them. As mentioned earlier, two objects are available to store records: one is provider independent (the *DataSet*); another is provider dependent (the *DataReader*). The first object we will look at is the *DataReader* object.

exam
ⓦatch

*Make sure you understand the difference between the **DataReader** object and the **DataSet** object. Focus on the concepts and the conditions under which you would use each of these objects. If you are unclear on this point after reading this chapter, read the appropriate sections of this chapter again.*

Use the *DataReader* Object to Store Retrieved Records   The *DataReader* object is used when you want to read data from a database in a quick and efficient way and not make changes to the data (read only). The *DataReader* object is highly efficient and uses far fewer system resources than the *DataSet* object because it does not retrieve the entire set of records from the database all at once. It contains a forward-only scrolling cursor, which means it must store only one record at a time.

The specific version of this object used for SQL Server is called the *SqlDataReader*. The *SqlDataReader* object itself cannot retrieve records from the database. To do this, we need to execute a command on the database, which means we need a *Command* object. The *SqlCommand* object is the version of the *Command* object provided with the SQL Server data provider. This object has many useful members, as shown in Table 6-2, which can be used to set up a command to be executed on the database and retrieve information.

The members listed in Table 6-2 are the members most often used when executing commands on a database; however, these are not all of the members exposed from a *Command* object (for a full listing, see the MSDN library).

The *Command* object also has two constructors you can use to create the object. One constructor is the default constructor; the other constructor takes two arguments, of which the first one sets the *CommandText* property and the second one sets the

TABLE 6-2   Common Members of the Command Object

Member	Usage
CommandType	You can set this property to *CommandType.StoredProcedure* if you want the *Command* to execute a stored procedure, *CommandType.TableDirect* if you want to retrieve all of the records from one table, and *CommandType.Text* if you want to execute an ad hoc SQL statement.
CommandText	This is the name of the stored procedure to execute, the name of the table you want to retrieve, or the SQL statement you want to execute. What is entered into the *CommandText* property must match the *CommandType* property.
Connection	This is the *SqlConnection* object to use to communicate with the database.
CommandTimeout	This is the amount of time to try to execute the command. If this time elapses without the command finishing, the execution fails.
ExecuteNonQuery	This method executes queries that do not return records.
ExecuteReader	This method executes a query that returns records and retrieves those records as a *SqlDataReader* object.
ExecuteScalar	This method executes a query that returns a single scalar value as a result.
CreateParameter	This method creates a *SqlParameter* to be used with a stored procedure or parameterized query.
Parameters	This property is a collection of *SqlParameters* used by the command.

Connection property. In the following example, we will use a *SqlCommand* object to retrieve records from the Northwind database in the form of a *DataReader* object:

```
Dim cn As New SqlConnection("Data Source=(local); " & _
                            "Initial Catalog=Northwind; " & _
                            "Integrated Security=true")
cn.Open()
Dim com As New SqlCommand("SELECT * FROM Employees", cn)
Dim dr As SqlDataReader = com.ExecuteReader()

' Use the DataReader object

dr.Close()
cn.Close()
```

In this example, we use a SQL statement to retrieve records from the database. You'll often need to execute a SQL statement against a database that uses a WHERE clause. The problem is that the value of the field you are using as the condition expression of the WHERE clause might not be known at design time and can be known only at run time (for instance, if the WHERE clause restricted all retrieved records to those wherein the employee's salary was greater than a value that the user would enter at runtime).

Traditionally, we would simply build a SQL statement as a string at run time to retrieve the value to use in the condition. For example, to retrieve all employees from the database whose salaries are greater than a user-entered value, we could build a SQL statement at run time with the following code:

```
Dim SQL As String = "SELECT * FROM Employees WHERE Salary > " & txtSal.Text
```

Although this has worked well in the past, now we can create a parameterized query that allows us to create a command whose query is a SQL statement with variable values in its WHERE clause. For example, the preceding SQL statement could be entered into a *Command* object in the following way:

```
Dim com As New SqlCommand
com.CommandText = "SELECT * FROM Employees WHERE Salary > @Salary"
```

You'll notice that instead of placing a value in the WHERE clause, we have placed a parameter named "@Salary." The use of the @ sign informs the *Command* object that this is a parameter and will be given a value before the command is executed.

The value to this approach as opposed to creating SQL statements at run time is that we can change the value of these parameters as many times as we like after creating the *Command.* With the other method, we would have to create a new SQL statement every time we wanted to execute the SQL statement with a new parameter.

As mentioned, to use parameterized queries with the command object, we must give the parameters a value before we execute the *Command.* To do this, we must create *SqlParameter* objects that represent the parameters in our queries. You can create the *SqlParameter* objects using the *CreateParameter* method of the *SqlCommand* object. Once you've created a *SqlParameter* object, you must specify its name, type, and value; then add it to the *Parameters* collection of the *SqlCommand* object. This example follows our previous example and adds a *SqlParameter* object to satisfy the parameter in our query:

```
Dim par As New SqlParameter()
par.ParameterName = "@Salary"
par.DbType = DbType.Currency
par.Value = CType(txtSal.Text, Decimal)
com.Parameters.Add(par)
```

You'll notice that we first created a new instance of our parameter, after which we set the *ParameterName, DbType,* and *Value* of the *SqlParameter.* Once the *SqlParameter* was ready, we added it to the *Parameters* collection of our *SqlCommand* object. If you're looking to save yourself a little bit of code, we can take advantage of the fact that the *Add* function for the *Parameters* collection is overloaded. One version of this function will accept the name and value as arguments, and create the *SqlParameter* for you and add it to the collection. The same method returns the newly created *SqlParameter* to you in case you wish to set any other properties. You could write the last example in the following form:

```
Dim par As SqlParameter()
Par = com.Parameters.Add("@Salary", CType(txtSal.Text, Decimal)
```

You might be wondering why we went to the hassle of doing all of this the long way when there is a much shorter method available. The fact is the *Add* method of the *Parameters* collection actually has six overrides available (which I will leave up to you to investigate). This essentially means we have six different ways to add *SqlParameter* objects to our *Parameters* collection; each way will be more useful in one circumstance than another. This is quite common; object-oriented programming allows us to write code that fits our situation and gives us a little more freedom.

Use the *DataSet* Object to Store Retrieved Records   Now we can retrieve records from a database using a SQL query or SQL parameterized query, and store them in a *SqlDataReader* object. Later, we will discuss how to use a *SqlCommand* object to execute stored procedures; for now, we will look at the other place to store these retrieved records: the *DataSet* object.

The *DataSet* object is the provider-independent storage location for retrieved records. This object stores its information in an XML-compatible format, which means it can store data from any provider without using techniques that are dependent on the type of provider used. As stated earlier, it can do this because the structure of the data (for example, the structure of the table in the database) also transfers to the *DataSet* object in the form of an XML schema.

The fact that the *DataSet* object has no knowledge of any data provider should raise the question: How does the *DataSet* object get its data if it doesn't know how to communicate with a database? The *SqlDataAdapter* object, which is part of the data provider, takes the job of transferring data source–specific information (data and table structure) into XML and filling up the *DataSet* object with the information. This essentially means we must use the *SqlDataAdapter* object to fill the *DataSet* object with records from the database. The *SqlDataAdapter* object will use *SqlCommands* and *SqlConnections* to communicate with the database. By now, you should have a basic picture of how these objects "dance" with each other.

One of the most important things to learn is how these objects interact. If you spend your time memorizing methods and properties of objects you are getting only half the picture. You also must understand how they interact with each other and what each object is responsible for. I find it useful to think of all of these objects as people who must perform a certain job.

To retrieve records from a SQL Server database and store them in a *DataSet* object, we first need to create a *SqlConnection* object and a *SqlDataAdapter* object. We created a *SqlConnection* in the last section, so we need only to create a *SqlDataAdapter* object and use it to fill up a *DataSet* with records.

The *SqlDataAdapter* object has four overloaded constructors, which can be used in different circumstances. The first constructor is the default constructor; it is used when you want to set the properties of the *SqlDataAdapter* manually. The second constructor takes a *SqlCommand* object (which must already be associated with an open *SqlConnection*). The third constructor takes a SQL statement as a string and a *ConnectionString*, which allows this constructor to create a *SqlConnection* to the database on the fly. The last constructor is the one we will use and takes a SQL statement as a string and a *SqlConnection* object, which can be open or closed.

The *SqlDataAdapter* object will take care of opening and closing the connection for us, which is useful when trying to minimize the use of database connections; however, you might wish to open and close the connection explicitly if you are using the *SqlDataAdapter* to fill multiple tables in multiple steps. To transfer the records to the *DataSet*, we will use the *Fill* method of the *SqlDataAdapter*. The following code retrieves the Employees from the Employees table and stores them in a *DataSet* through a *SqlDataAdapter:*

```
Dim cn As New SqlConnection("Data Source=(local); " & _
                            "Initial Catalog=Northwind; " & _
                            "Integrated Security=true")
Dim da As New SqlDataAdapter("SELECT * FROM Employees", cn)
Dim ds As New DataSet()
da.Fill(ds)

' Use the DataReader object
```

When we create the *SqlDataAdapter*, we pass it a SQL statement to use when retrieving records and a *SqlConnection* object to use when doing so. You will notice that at no time do we open or close the connection like we did earlier with the *SqlDataReader* object because the *SqlDataAdapter* manages the *SqlConnection* for us. If you pass it an open *SqlConnection* object, it will not manage the connection for us, as it assumes that if we opened it, we want to close it ourselves. For this reason, you should not explicitly open a connection that a *SqlDataAdapter* will use unless you are willing to take over the management of the connection yourself.

You should note that the SQL statement passed to the *SqlDataAdapter* object is used to create an internal *SqlCommand* object, which is executed on the database. The *Fill* method uses this *SqlCommand* object to get the records from the database, after which the *SqlDataAdapter* translates it into XML and fills the *DataSet* object with this XML data.

As mentioned earlier, the *DataSet* object can contain more than one table. Each table can come from different data sources or the same data source. When loading data into multiple tables, we need to use multiple *SqlDataAdapter* objects. Each *SqlDataAdapter* is responsible for filling one table in our *DataSet* object. For example, if we wanted to retrieve the Products and Categories table from the Northwind database and store them in a single *DataSet*, we would have to create two separate *SqlDataAdapter* objects. One would be used to fill the *DataSet* with the records from the Products table, and the other would be used to fill the *DataSet* with the records from the Categories table. Even if these two tables came from different databases, or even different providers, this is possible. In the case where both tables came from different providers, we would use the appropriate *DataAdapter* for each provider. If one table came from a SQL Server database, and the other came from an Oracle database, we would create one *DataSet* to store the records, one *SqlDataAdapter* to retrieve the records from the SQL Server database, and one *OleDbDataAdapter* to retrieve the records from the Oracle database (we will look at the OLEDB data provider in the next chapter). As you can see, the *SqlDataAdapter* allows us to connect the provider-dependent world (in this case SQL Server) to the provider-independent world of the *DataSet*.

Manipulate Records from a Database

Now that we have seen how to retrieve records from a database, we will look at how to read and make changes to them. This will involve different methods depending on what object you are storing the records in, and what changes you wish to make to the database. Because we first looked at retrieving records and storing them in a *SqlDataReader*, we will look at how to read records from this object first.

Read Records from a *DataReader*   Before we begin you should remember that the *SqlDataReader* object is a forward-scrolling, read-only object that allows us to read retrieved records quickly and efficiently. Reading the records in a *SqlDataReader* object revolves around a method called (surprise, surprise) *Read*. The *Read* method advances the cursor to point to the next record, and returns true if there is a next record, and false if there is not. Note that when a *SqlDataReader* is created, the cursor is pointing to the record *before* the first record (in ADO we called this BOF—Beginning of File).

We use the *Read* method to scroll the cursor, not to actually read the records. To do this, we use one of the many *Get* methods (accessor functions) available. There are *Get* methods for all of the SQL Server data types. These methods take a zero-based ordinal (in English that means an index) that represents the column and returns the data found in that field for the record to which the cursor is pointing. The following is an incomplete list of some of the *Get* methods we have available in the *SqlDataReader* object (please see the MSDN library for a complete listing):

GetBoolean	GetByte	GetDecimal	GetDouble	GetFloat
GetSqlDateTime	GetSqlDecimal	GetSqlString	GetSqlMoney	GetSqlSingle

You'll notice that there are different types of *Get* functions for different types of data; however, the good news is there also is a *Get* function called *GetValue*, which will retrieve any type of data in the form of the generic *Object* data type. Because all objects have a *ToString* method, this means it is pretty simple to print out all of your data on a page without getting too deep into the *Get* methods. You also can retrieve values by using a field name lookup. We will look at both methods for contrast in the following example. Before we actually look at the code, there are a few other methods you might find useful:

- **Close**   A method that shuts down the *SqlDataReader* and releases its resources (although it does not destroy the *SqlDataReader* object).
- **FieldCount**   A property that specifies the number of fields in the table.
- **GetOrdinal**   A method that takes a field name as an argument and returns the ordinal for it.
- **IsDBNull**   A method that specifies whether a field contains a null value.

Remember, there are many more methods that can be valuable to you in specific situations. The following is an example of retrieving the Employees table from the Northwind database using a *SqlDataReader*. The FirstName and LastName fields will be printed to a Web page for each record in the table.

```
'Create and open the connection
Dim cn As New SqlConnection("Data Source=(local); " & _
                            "Initial Catalog=Northwind; " & _
                            "Integrated Security=true")
cn.Open()

'Create the command and retrieve the records
Dim com As New SqlCommand("SELECT * FROM Employees", cn)
Dim dr As SqlDataReader = com.ExecuteReader()

'Print out the FirstName and LastName fields if they are not null
While dr.Read()
  If Not dr.IsDBNull(1) And Not dr.IsDBNull(2) Then
    Response.Write(dr("FirstName") & " " & dr.GetString(1) & "<br>")
  End If
End While

'Close the DataReader and Connection
dr.Close()
cn.Close()
```

Notice that we have used both a field name lookup and the *GetString* method to retrieve values in the *SqlDataReader* object's records. Remember that if you wish to change the records in the database, the *SqlDataReader* object will not do the job; this object is only for reading records.

Read Records from a *DataSet*   The second object we were using to store data retrieved from a SQL Server database was the *DataSet* object. As mentioned earlier, this object is used when we need read/write access to a database or when we wish to use a disconnected set of records. Reading records from the *DataSet* object is a little different from reading records from the *SqlDataReader* object. The major difference is that the *DataSet* object does not contain a cursor and therefore does not have a current record. For this reason, those of you who are familiar with ADO and the *Recordset* object might find this a little strange.

The first thing we need to understand is the structure of the data within the *DataSet* object. The *DataSet* object contains its own object model. Because the *DataSet* object can contain multiple tables, it has a *Tables* collection, which stores each *Table* object. Each *Table* object contains a *DataRowCollection* and a *DataColumnCollection*, which store *Row* objects and *Column* objects, respectively. The *DataRowCollection* is called *Rows* and the *DataColumnCollection* is called *Columns;* it is through the Rows property that we get access to individual fields for individual records within these tables. Each *Row* object in the *DataRowCollection* contains an *Item* method that takes as an argument the index or name of the field you wish to retrieve for that row.

The following is an example of retrieving the Employees table from the Northwind database using a *DataSet*. The FirstName and LastName fields will be printed to a Web page for each record in the table. Note the difference between the code in this example and the one we used for the *SqlDataReader* object:

```
'Create the connection to the database and open it
Dim cn As New SqlConnection("Data Source=(local); " & _
                            "Initial Catalog=Northwind; " & _
                            "Integrated Security=true")
cn.Open()

'Create a DataAdapter and DataSet object
Dim da As New SqlDataAdapter("SELECT * FROM Employees", cn)
Dim ds As New DataSet()

'Fill the DataSet object with the DataAdapter
da.Fill(ds)
```

```
'Print the FirstName and LastName to the page
Dim i As Integer
For i = 0 To ds.Tables(0).Rows.Count - 1
  Response.Write(ds.Tables(0).Rows(i).Item("FirstName") & " " & _
                 ds.Tables(0).Rows(i).Item("LastName") & "<br>")
Next i
```

As you can see, this is pretty straightforward, although there certainly are a lot of dot operators (nested members). It is important to note that at no point did we have to open or close the *SqlConnection*. As mentioned earlier, because we're using a *SqlDataAdapter* object, we don't need to open and close the *SqlConnection* explicitly, as the *SqlDataAdapter* object will manage this connection for us.

Insert, Update, and Delete Records from a *DataSet*   Making changes to data held within a *DataSet* is similar to making changes to an ADO *Recordset* object. The biggest difference is that changes made to a *DataSet* object do not affect the data in the database until we explicitly update the database; you can do this only by using the *SqlDataAdapter* that was used to retrieve the records in the first place. Because the *DataSet* object is totally disconnected, it stands to reason that the only object capable of doing this is the *SqlDataAdapter*. We can now look at how to insert, update, and delete records from the *DataSet* object. After these changes have been made, we can make them permanent in the underlying data source.

To insert a record into a *DataSet* object that contains records (or possibly just the table schema) from a SQL Server database, we must add a new row to one of the tables our *DataSet* object contains. Each table in the *DataSet* object is represented by a *DataTable* object, and each row in each *DataTable* object is represented by a *DataRow* object.

The *DataTable* contains a method called *NewRow*, which can be used to create a new *DataRow*. Once we have created our new *DataRow* object, we can give its fields values using the *Item* method (which takes and index or field name), after which we must add the new *DataRow* to the *Rows* collection with the *Add* method. The following is an example of adding a new record to the Employees table in the Northwind database:

```
'Create connection, DataAdapter and use it to Fill and DataSet
Dim cn As New SqlConnection("Data Source=(local); " & _
                            "Initial Catalog=Northwind; " & _
                            "Integrated Security=true")
Dim da As New SqlDataAdapter("SELECT * FROM Employees", cn)
Dim ds As New DataSet()
da.Fill(ds)
```

```
'Create a new DataRow object
Dim row As DataRow = ds.Tables(0).NewRow()

'Give the fields of the new DataRow some values
row.Item("FirstName") = "Bartholomew"
row.Item("LastName") = "Cromwell"

'Add the new DataRow to the table
ds.Tables(0).Rows.Add(row)
```

Making changes to a record in a *DataSet* is even easier. In this situation, all we have to do is change the field value using the *Item* method of the *DataRow* object. We did this in the last example when we added a row; however, if we are not adding a row, we can just skip the creation of a *DataRow* object and skip the line in which we added it to the *DataTableCollection*.

It is important to remember that the changes you make to records in the tables you have retrieved must be appropriate for the constraints on the table. In the case of the Northwind Employees table, only the EmployeeID, FirstName, and LastName fields were required and we didn't need to add the EmployeeID field because it is an *Identity column*. An Identity column is automatically given a unique value whenever a record is added to the database.

Because the table schema is stored in the *DataSet*, the constraints also are stored, which means we will get immediate errors when we violate constraints on the *DataSet*. This prevents us from allowing changes to be made, only to find when we update the original data source that a constraint has been violated. The following is an example of changing the FirstName of the first record in the Employees table of the Northwind database (Nancy Davolio is the first record):

```
'Make a connection and return the Employees table
Dim cn As New SqlConnection("Data Source=(local); " & _
                            "Initial Catalog=Northwind; " & _
                            "Integrated Security=true")
Dim da As New SqlDataAdapter("SELECT * FROM Employees", cn)
Dim ds As New DataSet()
da.Fill(ds)

'Change the first Record
ds.Tables(0).Rows(0).Item("FirstName") = "Bartholomew"
ds.Tables(0).Rows(0).Item("LastName") = "Cromwell"
```

The last change we need to make in the *DataSet* is removing or deleting records. If you are experienced with collections, you might be tempted to execute the remove method of the *DataRowCollection* to remove the row you wish to delete. Although this will remove the row from the *DataSet*, it will not help us to remove the row from the underlying data source once we reconcile our *DataSet* with the database.

We must remember that the *DataSet* is totally disconnected from the data source; therefore, any changes made to it must be tracked. When we add or change a record, the tracking is obvious. If we add a row, there is a row that was not there before. If we change a row its values are not the same as before. If we remove a row, how does the system know that it has been removed?

You might think the system can simply determine this because there is a record in the database with no corresponding record in the *DataSet*. However, this will not work, as the record might not have been transferred to the *DataSet* because it did not satisfy the WHERE clause in the original SQL statement. For this reason, we need a better way to track the changes made to records instead of just trying to figure it out based on the current state of the database and the *DataSet*. The *RowState* property of every *DataRow* object does this for us. This property is set to the following states depending on what has been done to the row:

- DataRowState.Added

- DataRowState.Deleted

- DataRowState.Detached

- DataRowState.Modified

- DataRowState.Unchanged

The *RowState* property is modified whenever the corresponding changes are made to that row. When adding or updating a record, this property is set based on our actions in the examples we have seen previously. However, if we remove a *DataRow* object from the *DataRowCollection*, there is no *DataRow* object to contain the *RowState* property.

Instead, we can execute the *Delete* method of the *DataRow* object we want to remove, which does not actually remove the row but instead simply changes the *RowState* property to *DataRowState.Deleted*. The record still exists and still has the same index but we can no longer read it. Because the record still contains the same index, this can make it difficult to print out records from a *DataSet's* table when one or more records have been deleted. If you try to read one of the deleted records you will get a run-time error.

To prevent this, we should always make sure when reading records from a *DataSet* that the record has not been flagged for deletion. The following example removes the first record from the Employees table and prints out the records properly after it has done so:

```
'Make a connection and return the Employees table
Dim cn As New SqlConnection("Data Source=(local); " & _
                            "Initial Catalog=Northwind; " & _
                            "Integrated Security=true")
Dim da As New SqlDataAdapter("SELECT * FROM Employees", cn)
Dim ds As New DataSet()
da.Fill(ds)

'Delete the first Record
ds.Tables(0).Rows(0).Delete()

'Print the records in the DataSet
Dim i As Integer
For i = 0 To ds.Tables(0).Rows.Count - 1
  'Make sure the row has not been deleted before we read it
  If Not ds.Tables(0).Rows(i).RowState = DataRowState.Deleted Then
    Response.Write(ds.Tables(0).Rows(i).Item(0) & " " & _
                   ds.Tables(0).Rows(i).Item(1) & " " & _
                   ds.Tables(0).Rows(i).Item(2) & "<br>")
  End If
Next i
```

You should note that if it were not for the *If* statement within the *For* loop that checks to make sure the record had not been deleted, this code would have triggered a run-time error when we tried to read the deleted record. The primary practical difference between this and the ADO *Recordset* object is that, although both ADO and ADO.NET simply mark records for deletion and do not actually remove them, ADO would remove the record from the index, which means the indexes were adjusted only to encompass valid records. As you have seen, ADO.NET does not remove the row from the index and, therefore, we still have access to the deleted record.

Update the Database from a *DataSet* Using a *DataAdapter*   We now know how to manipulate data from a SQL Server database using a *DataSet* object;

however, at this point, it is wise to investigate the capabilities of the *SqlDataAdapter* object in a little more detail. The *SqlDataAdapter* object probably is the most complicated object in the ADO.NET object model. This is because it has a great deal of responsibility. When you retrieve records from the database, it is responsible for executing the appropriate command, retrieving the data, converting it to XML, and transferring the XML to the *DataSet*. When changes are made to the data in the *DataSet* the *SqlDataAdapter* also is responsible for executing the appropriate Insert, Update, and Delete commands to make the changes permanent in the underlying database.

The *SqlDataAdapter* enables us to define how communication with the database occurs. The *SqlDataAdapter* has the following four properties, which can be used to store *SqlCommand* objects that represent the appropriate commands to Select, Insert, Update, and Delete records in the underlying database:

SelectCommand	InsertCommand
UpdateCommand	DeleteCommand

This enables the developer to specify just how he or she wants these commands to be performed. For example, if we want to use stored procedures instead of SQL statements to manipulate the database, we could use *SqlCommand* objects that represent stored procedures. The main idea is that the *SqlDataAdapter* puts the control and responsibility of data access back into the hands of the developer.

In an earlier example in the section titled "Use the *DataSet* Object to Store Retrieved Records," we retrieved records from a SQL Server database with a *SqlDataAdapter* and stored them in a *DataSet*. When we did this, you will remember that we passed a SQL statement into the constructor of the *SqlDataAdapter* when we instantiated it. What this actually did was automatically create a *SqlCommand* object for us and stored it in the *SelectCommand* property of the *SqlDataAdapter* object. As you can see, we have already specified how our *SqlDataAdapter* should communicate with the database when retrieving records.

Of course, this in itself is not necessarily that special because we did that with ADO as well; however, when you inserted, updated, or deleted a record using an ADO *Recordset*, the commands to communicate this to the database were automatically created for you (as a matter of fact, most developers didn't even know a SQL command was used to make this happen). Now that we are using a *DataSet* and *SqlDataAdapter*, we will have to specify the commands to use when these kinds of changes must be propagated back to the database. This involves creating four *SqlCommand* objects that will contain instructions on how to perform these actions.

Before we move on, we should make sure we have a good understanding of the steps preformed and players involved in this process. We have already discussed the *SqlDataAdapter's* role in transferring records to the *DataSet.* When we make changes to the *DataSet,* like we did previously, no actual change is made in the database; this, of course, is because the *DataSet* is disconnected.

The changes made can be propagated back to the database by executing the *SqlDataAdapter's Update* method and passing it the *DataSet* with the changed data. The *SqlDataAdapter* looks through the *DataSet* and finds the table within that *DataSet,* which it originally filled with data. Once it finds this table, it looks through the table for any rows that have been changed, (remember the *RowState* property?). For each row that has been changed it executes the appropriate *Command* object that corresponds to the change that was made.

For example, if a row has a *RowState* of *DataRowState.Modified,* it will execute the *SqlCommand* object found in the *UpdateCommand* property. Our job as developers is to create the *SqlCommand* in the *UpdateCommand* property so the *SqlDataAdapter* knows how we want the update to occur. In the upcoming example, we will be using SQL statements; however, we also could use stored procedures, which often are preferred on large-scale, secure databases. The following is a full example of retrieving data from the Employees table of the Northwind database using a *DataSet,* manipulating the data, and finally propagating the changes back to the database:

```
'Create the connection to the database and open it
Dim cn As New SqlConnection("Data Source=(local); " & _
                        "Initial Catalog=Northwind; " & _
                        "Integrated Security=true")

'Create a new DataAdapter object
Dim da As New SqlDataAdapter()

'Create the Select Command
Dim comSelect As New SqlCommand("SELECT EmployeeID, FirstName, " & _
            "LastName FROM Employees ORDER BY EmployeeID DESC", cn)

'Create the Insert Command
Dim comInsert As New SqlCommand("INSERT INTO Employees (FirstName," & _
                    " LastName) VALUES (@FirstName, @LastName)", cn)
```

```
'Add the Insert Command's Parameters
comInsert.Parameters.Add(New SqlParameter("@FirstName", _
                      SqlDbType.NVarChar, 10, _
                      ParameterDirection.Input, _
                      False, CType(0, Byte), CType(0, Byte), _
                      "FirstName", DataRowVersion.Current, Nothing))
comInsert.Parameters.Add(New SqlParameter("@LastName", _
                      SqlDbType.NVarChar, 20, _
                      ParameterDirection.Input, _
                      False, CType(0, Byte), CType(0, Byte), _
                      "LastName", DataRowVersion.Current, Nothing))

'Create the Update Command
Dim comUpdate As New SqlCommand("UPDATE Employees SET FirstName = " & _
 "@FirstName, LastName = @LastName WHERE EmployeeID = @EmployeeID", cn)

'Add the Update Commands Parameters
comUpdate.Parameters.Add(New SqlParameter("@FirstName", _
                      SqlDbType.NVarChar, 10, _
                      ParameterDirection.Input, _
                      False, CType(0, Byte), CType(0, Byte), _
                      "FirstName", DataRowVersion.Current, Nothing))
comUpdate.Parameters.Add(New SqlParameter("@LastName", _
                      SqlDbType.NVarChar, 20, _
                      ParameterDirection.Input, _
                      False, CType(0, Byte), CType(0, Byte), _
                      "LastName", DataRowVersion.Current, Nothing))
comUpdate.Parameters.Add(New SqlParameter("@EmployeeID", _
                      SqlDbType.Int, 4, _
                      ParameterDirection.Input, _
                      False, CType(0, Byte), CType(0, Byte), _
                      "EmployeeID", DataRowVersion.Current, nothing))

'Create the Delete Command
Dim comDelete As New SqlCommand("DELETE FROM Employees WHERE " & _
                      "EmployeeID = @EmployeeID", cn)

'Add the Delete Commands Parameters
comDelete.Parameters.Add(New SqlParameter("@EmployeeID", _
                      SqlDbType.Int, 4, _
                      ParameterDirection.Input, _
                      False, CType(0, Byte), CType(0, Byte), _
                      "EmployeeID", DataRowVersion.Current, Nothing))
```

```
'Add the Commands to the DataAdapter
da.SelectCommand = comSelect
da.InsertCommand = comInsert
da.UpdateCommand = comUpdate
da.DeleteCommand = comDelete

'Create a new DataSet
Dim ds As New DataSet()

'Get the records
da.Fill(ds, "Employees")

'Add a new record
Dim row As DataRow = ds.Tables(0).NewRow()
row.Item("FirstName") = "Heidi"
row.Item("LastName") = "Hagen"
ds.Tables(0).Rows.Add(row)

'Change a record
ds.Tables(0).Rows(1).Item("FirstName") = "Max"
ds.Tables(0).Rows(1).Item("LastName") = "The Cat"

'Delete a record
ds.Tables(0).Rows(0).Delete()

'Make the changes permanent
Dim count As Integer = da.Update(ds, "Employees")
Response.Write(count & " Records Affected...")
```

There are some very important things to notice about this code listing. If you are using the copy of Northwind that came with SQL Server to test this, you will have to add a new record to the database to test the delete functionality. This is because the records in the Employees table are related to other records in other tables; therefore, they cannot be deleted without first deleting the related records.

exam
Watch

To fully understand data access, you also must understand database design. How database objects are related is very important, as it dictates what kinds of actions you can perform on them and in what order these actions must be performed. If you have never created a relational database before, I strongly recommend you design and implement a few before tackling Exam 70-305. Remember, these exams are designed for developers with a great deal of experience; you will be expected to have a wide knowledge base.

All you need to do is add a record. I have added an ORDER BY DESC clause to the SELECT statement so the record you add will be at the beginning of your *DataSet* table (position 0) and it will be easy to delete. Now, regarding the code, you will notice the use of the default constructor when instantiating the *SqlDataAdapter* object. Because we are creating the *SqlCommand* objects ourselves, we don't need to use the constructor that creates the *SelectCommand* for us. Probably the biggest difference you have noticed is the use of a gigantic constructor for creating *SqlParameter* objects. This constructor has the following arguments:

- **ParameterName**   This is the name you gave the parameter in your SQL statement.

- **DataType**   This is the SQL data type used in the database.

- **Size**   This is the size in bytes of the SQL data type used in the database (very important for varchars and nvarchars).

- **Direction**   Specifies whether this is an Input, Output, InputOutput, or ReturnValue parameter. Because we are passing these parameters into the database, they are Input parameters.

- **IsNullable**   Specifies whether this field allows null values.

- **Precision**   Total number of digits allowed (only useful for floating point values).

- **Scale**   Number of decimal places allowed (only useful for floating point values).

- **ColumnName**   This field is very important as it maps this parameter to the column in the *DataSet* from which this parameter's value will come.

- **RowVersion**   We should set this to *Current* so the current value is passed to the database instead of the original value before it is changed.

- **Value**   This is not necessary (hence the nothing) because the value will come from the field in the *DataSet*.

The last thing to point out is the use of a table name when we fill the *DataSet*. The *Fill* method of the *DataAdapter* is overloaded and can take two arguments: the *DataSet* object to fill, and a name to give the table created in the *DataSet*. We have named the table this time so that when we execute the *Update* method, we can specify which table we want to update. Without giving the table a name in the first place, this would be impossible.

You might be thinking that this is a lot of work just to get the same functionality the ADO *Recordset* gave us without any of this hassle. Well, what can I say? You're right! You do have to remember that with power comes pain—and we definitely have a great deal of power here (ouch!).

That said, there is some good news: When the power just isn't needed, we can use something called a *CommandBuilder* to take a great deal of the legwork out of creating these *SqlCommands*. You should note that we definitely will lose some of the flexibility, but in many situations, the *CommandBuilder* will do the job just fine. The *CommandBuilder* is an object that is part of the *SqlDataAdapter* which, when asked, will examine the SELECT statement you provide to retrieve the records and create appropriate INSERT, UPDATE, and DELETE commands based on the SELECT statement. This can take a lot of the grunt work out of setting up a *SqlDataAdapter*. The following example is equivalent to the last example but uses a *CommandBuilder* instead:

```
'Create the connection to the database and open it
Dim cn As New SqlConnection("Data Source=(local); " & _
                            "Initial Catalog=Northwind; " & _
                            "Integrated Security=true")

'Create a new DataAdapter object
Dim da As New SqlDataAdapter("SELECT EmployeeID, FirstName, " & _
            "LastName FROM Employees ORDER BY EmployeeID DESC", cn)

'Create a CommandBuilder and have it set up the DataAdapter
Dim cb As New SqlCommandBuilder(da)

'Create a new DataSet
Dim ds As New DataSet()

'Get the records
da.Fill(ds, "Employees")

'Add a new record
Dim row As DataRow = ds.Tables(0).NewRow()
row.Item("FirstName") = "Heidi"
row.Item("LastName") = "Hagen"
ds.Tables(0).Rows.Add(row)

'Change a record
ds.Tables(0).Rows(1).Item("FirstName") = "Max"
ds.Tables(0).Rows(1).Item("LastName") = "The Cat"
```

```
'Delete a record
ds.Tables(0).Rows(0).Delete()

'Make the changes permanent
Dim count As Integer = da.Update(ds, "Employees")
ds.AcceptChanges()
Response.Write(count & " Records Affected...")
```

When deciding which method to use to set up a *SqlDataAdapter*, there are a few factors to consider. If you need fine control over the SQL statements used to update the database, you should manually configure them, as the *CommandBuilder* will create very simple commands. If you are using a JOIN, you cannot use the *CommandBuilder*; it simply isn't able to figure them out. If you want to use stored procedures to update your data, again you will have to avoid the *CommandBuilder*. Finally, if you require speed, the *CommandBuilder* is slow, has a much higher overhead, and should be avoided. The good news is that in a Web application usually it is a viable option.

on the
job

*Watch out when using the **CommandBuilder**. It is very tempting to use it for everything, as using it means we don't have to write as much code. There is a significant overhead associated with its use and we lose flexibility. It is quite common to use methods such as this for the obvious convenience and then spend excessive amounts of time trying to overcome their restrictions. You should remember to evaluate the strengths and weaknesses of both methods before you start writing any code.*

SCENARIO & SOLUTION

How do I use stored procedures to manipulate the data in the database?	Set up your *SqlDataAdapter* manually, as a *CommandBuilder* cannot help you with stored procedures.
I want to retrieve a single table from the database, make some simple changes to it, and then update the database. How do I accomplish this?	Use a *CommandBuilder* and save yourself some development time.
The data I need in the database exists in multiple tables. How do I access it?	Manually set up your *SqlDataAdapter*. The *CommandBuilder* cannot handle JOINs.
I am creating a component for other developers that directly exposes a DataSet with data from your database. I want to prevent them from adding new records, but they can update and delete records. What is the best method?	Manually set up your *SqlDataAdapter* and do not add a *SqlCommand* object to the *InsertCommand* property.

The last thing we will discuss regarding updating changes will be the *GetChanges* method of the *DataSet*. If you are writing an application that sends a *DataSet* to another process that then updates the data (common with disconnected data), you must realize that you are passing the other process all of the data that was changed. This is good because you now want to update the database with these changes. You also are passing on all of the data that was not changed (which is bad because the other process does not need this if it is only updating changes).

To reduce network traffic, we can use the *GetChanges* method of the *DataSet* object to create a new *DataSet* object, based on the first one, which contains only records that have changed. We then can pass this new, smaller *DataSet* across the wire and save some bandwidth. And now for the code (just one line this time):

```
Dim dsChanges As DataSet = ds.GetChanges()
```

The following exercise will give you some experience using the *DataSet* object to retrieve and manipulate records in a SQL Server database.

EXERCISE 6-1

Access and Manipulate Data from a SQL Server Database

In this exercise, we will return the beverages from the Products table of the Northwind sample database that ships with SQL Server. We will use a *DataSet* object to store and manipulate the records. When we are finished, we will update the underlying data source with the *SqlDataAdapter*. Ensure that as you move through the exercise, you understand everything that ensues. If you are unclear about any code you see, look back to the appropriate section in this chapter.

1. Launch Visual Studio.

2. Create a new ASP.NET application.

3. Open the code-behind of the Webform1.aspx file.

4. Add the imports for the ADO.NET and the SQL Server Data Provider.
   ```
   Imports System.Data
   Imports System.Data.SqlClient
   Imports System.Data.SqlTypes
   ```

5. Create a *SqlConnection* object using the constructor that takes a connection string. Make sure your connection string is appropriate for your database.

6. Create a new *SqlDataAdapter* object using the default constructor.

7. Create a *SqlCommand* object using the following SQL statement. This *SqlCommand* will be used as the *SelectCommand:*

```
SELECT ProductID, ProductName FROM Products WHERE CategoryID = 1
```

8. Create a *SqlCommand* object using the following SQL statement. This *SqlCommand* will be used as the *InsertCommand:*

```
INSERT INTO Products (ProductName) VALUES (@ProductName)
```

9. Create appropriate *SqlParameter* objects for the *InsertCommand* you have just created and store them in the *Parameters* collection.

10. Create a *SqlCommand* object using the following SQL statement. This *SqlCommand* will be used as the *UpdateCommand:*

```
UPDATE Products SET ProductName = @ProductName WHERE ProductID = @ProductID
```

11. Create appropriate *SqlParameter* objects for the *UpdateCommand* you have just created and store them in the *Parameters* collection.

12. Create a *SqlCommand* object using the following SQL statement. This *SqlCommand* will be used as the *DeleteCommand:*

```
DELETE FROM Products WHERE ProductID = @ProductID
```

13. Create appropriate *SqlParameter* objects for the *DeleteCommand* you have just created and store them in the *Parameters* collection.

14. Add the four *SqlCommands* you have just created to the *SqlDataAdapter.* Use the appropriate command properties.

15. Create a new *DataSet,* fill it, and print out the ProductName field for all of the records to the Web page using the *Response* object.

16. Add a new product to the *DataSet* (remember the ProductID is an Identity column and its value will be set by the database so you need to set only the ProductName). Call the product "Go Juice."

17. Change the first records ProductName to "Good Tea."

18. We won't delete any records because it would violate referential integrity.

19. Update the database with the changes you have made and write to the page the number of rows affected.

20. Write the ProductName field for the records to the page one more time.

21. Compile and test your code.

22. Your code should look similar to this:

```
'Create the connection to the database and open it
Dim cn As New SqlConnection("Data Source=(local); " & _
                            "Initial Catalog=Northwind; " & _
                            "Integrated Security=true")

'Create a new DataAdapter object
Dim da As New SqlDataAdapter()

'Create the Select Command
Dim comSelect As New SqlCommand("SELECT ProductID, ProductName " & _
                       "FROM Products WHERE CategoryID = 1", cn)

'Create the Insert Command
Dim comInsert As New SqlCommand("INSERT INTO Products "& _
                       "(ProductName) VALUES (@ProductName)", cn)

'Add the Insert Command's Parameters
comInsert.Parameters.Add(New SqlParameter("@ProductName", _
                 SqlDbType.NVarChar, 40, _
                 ParameterDirection.Input, _
                 False, CType(0, Byte), CType(0, Byte), _
                 "ProductName", DataRowVersion.Current, Nothing))

'Create the Update Command
Dim comUpdate As New SqlCommand("UPDATE Products SET ProductName " & _
                 "= @ProductName WHERE ProductID = @ProductID", cn)

'Add the Update Commands Parameters
comUpdate.Parameters.Add(New SqlParameter("@ProductName", _
                 SqlDbType.NVarChar, 40, _
                 ParameterDirection.Input, _
                 False, CType(0, Byte), CType(0, Byte), _
                 "ProductName", DataRowVersion.Current, Nothing))
```

```vb
comUpdate.Parameters.Add(New SqlParameter("@ProductID", _
                         SqlDbType.Int, 4, _
                         ParameterDirection.Input, _
                         False, CType(0, Byte), CType(0, Byte), _
                         "ProductID", DataRowVersion.Current, Nothing))

'Create the Delete Command
Dim comDelete As New SqlCommand("DELETE FROM Products WHERE " & _
                         "ProductID = @ProductID", cn)

'Add the Delete Commands Parameters
comDelete.Parameters.Add(New SqlParameter("@ProductID", _
                         SqlDbType.Int, 4, _
                         ParameterDirection.Input, _
                         False, CType(0, Byte), CType(0, Byte), _
                         "ProductID", DataRowVersion.Current, Nothing))

'Add the Commands to the DataAdapter
da.SelectCommand = comSelect
da.InsertCommand = comInsert
da.UpdateCommand = comUpdate
da.DeleteCommand = comDelete

'Create a new DataSet
Dim ds As New DataSet()

'Get the records
da.Fill(ds, "Products")

'Write the records to the page
Dim i As Integer
For i = 0 To ds.Tables(0).Rows.Count - 1
  Response.Write(ds.Tables(0).Rows(i).Item(1) & "<br>")
Next i

'Add a new record
Dim row As DataRow = ds.Tables(0).NewRow()
row.Item("ProductName") = "Go Juice"
ds.Tables(0).Rows.Add(row)

'Change a record
ds.Tables(0).Rows(0).Item("ProductName") = "Good Tea"
```

```
'Make the changes permanent
Dim count As Integer = da.Update(ds, "Products")
ds.AcceptChanges()
Response.Write("<P>" & count & " Records Affected...</P>")

'Write the records to the page again
For i = 0 To ds.Tables(0).Rows.Count - 1
  Response.Write(ds.Tables(0).Rows(i).Item(1) & "<br>")
Next i
```

Use Ad Hoc SQL Statements with the Command Object   Often you will want to make a change in the database but have no need to retrieve any records. For example, you might have a client registration page in which a prospective client can add his or her name, address, phone number, e-mail, and so forth. You don't need to show this client any data from the database, you just want to store his or her information in your ProspectiveClients table. In these situations, it is a large waste of resources and bandwidth to load the ProspectiveClients table into a *DataSet* just to add one record.

In the past, I have seen some interesting solutions to this problem; for example, let's assume the maximum ProspectiveClientID is one hundred. I have seen solutions in which the developer used the following query to retrieve the table schema without the data:

```
SELECT * FROM ProspectiveClients WHERE ProspectiveClientID > 100
```

This would load a table with no records; however, this still is a waste of time because you are creating an object (of course, in ADO.NET that would be the *DataSet*), and transferring the table schema to it. A better alternative is to execute a query directly on the database. Those queries that perform an action such as adding a record, but don't return any records, are called *action queries*. The following quick reference will help you decide whether to use a *DataSet* object, a *SqlDataReader* object, or an action query though a *SqlCommand* object.

When you want to execute an action query on the database, you use a *SqlCommand* object instead of messing around with *DataSet* objects. If you refer back to Table 6-2, you will notice a method called *ExecuteNonQuery* that is designed to execute action

SCENARIO & SOLUTION

How do I create a page that allows a user to see orders from a database and make changes to those orders?	Use a *DataSet* object.
How do I create a page that displays the order history of different clients?	Use a *SqlDataReader* object by executing a SELECT statement through a *SqlCommand* object.
How do I create a Web page that allows traveling consultants to submit expense claims remotely?	Use action queries, as they are not requesting any information, just submitting it.
How do I create a Web application to allow online scheduling of my employees?	Use a *DataSet*, as this will involve viewing current bookings, adding new bookings, and changing current bookings.

queries. The return value of this method is an integer that represents the number of rows that were affected by the query. The following example changes the FirstName of the first record in the Employees table (Nancy Davolio):

```
'Create the connection to the database and open it
Dim cn As New SqlConnection("Data Source=(local); " & _
                            "Initial Catalog=Northwind; " & _
                            "Integrated Security=true")
cn.Open()

'Create a new Command object
Dim com As New SqlCommand("UPDATE Employees SET FirstName = 'Heidi' " & _
                          "WHERE EmployeeID = 1", cn)

'Execute the query
Dim count As Integer = com.ExecuteNonQuery()
Response.Write(count & " Records Affected...")

'Close the Connection
cn.Close()
```

Probably the most important thing to notice here is that unlike changes to a *DataSet*, the changes made by executing a SQL statement directly on the database are immediate and it is not necessary to update these changes like we did with the *DataSet*.

FROM THE CLASSROOM

The Efficiency of SQL Statements

SQL statements are a very powerful tool for developers and should not be overlooked. I have often seen data access software in which the only SQL statements you will see are SELECT statements used to retrieve information. In these programs, adding, updating, and deleting records is done using the data access object methods (*Recordset* in ADO or *DataSet* in ADO.NET).

Although this certainly works, it is not always the most efficient way of doing things. When you change *n* records in a DataSet, *n* UPDATE statements are executed on the database when the records are updated. If we add 10 percent to the Salary field of every record in a *DataSet* table with 100 records, when the records are updated, 100 UPDATE statements will be executed on the database.

We could do the same thing with one UPDATE statement (UPATE Employees SET Salary = Salary * 1.10). When this single SQL statement is executed on a SQL Server database, the database can plan out an optimum method for executing the update and changing all of the records. This might

involve much less processing than executing 100 separate UPDATE statements (one for each record).

For this reason, you often will find that executing SQL statements on the database directly is much more efficient than making changes to a *DataSet* and updating the database through the *DataAdapter,* even if you do want to retrieve records. In other words, if you benchmark your application, you might find a performance improvement returning records in a *DataReader* (read-only) or *DataSet* (you will have to make read-only) for viewing and making changes to the database with SQL action queries through a *SqlCommand* object.

This is counterintuitive, as we would think that using a *DataSet* alone relieves a lot of the complexity; however, the performance improvement of letting SQL Server handle complex queries often outweighs the added complexity of avoiding the simple *DataSet* methods. One important thing to note here is that results will vary and you should always benchmark your application to see whether an improvement can be seen.

—*Wayne Cassidy, Bsc, MCSD, MCT*

There is one more method of the *SqlCommand* object that can help us when executing a SQL query that contains an *aggregate* function. An aggregate function is part of the SQL language and gives us statistical information about the data in the table; for example, we can count the number of records in a table with the COUNT aggregate function.

Other examples of aggregate functions are MIN, MAX, SUM, AGV, and STDEV (standard deviation). These functions return single values (such as the number of records) and therefore it does not make much sense to return a table to represent this one piece of information; one variable would be fine. For these types of SQL statements, we have a method of the *SqlCommand* object called *ExecuteScalar* that does just this. The following example prints to a Web page the number of records in the Employees table:

```
'Create the connection to the database and open it
Dim cn As New SqlConnection("Data Source=(local); " & _
                            "Initial Catalog=Northwind; " & _
                            "Integrated Security=true")
cn.Open()

'Create a new Command object
Dim com As New SqlCommand("SELECT COUNT(*) FROM Employees", cn)

'Execute the query
Dim count As Integer = com.ExecuteScalar()
Response.Write("The Employees table contains " & count & " records.")

'Close the Connection
cn.Close()
```

Transactions When working with data from a database, we quite often perform actions or changes on that data that rely on one another. For example, if you want to transfer money from your savings account to your checking account, this would involve two separate actions, both of which rely on each other. The first step could be to withdraw the money from your savings account and the second step could be to deposit the money in your checking account.

A problem with performing actions such as these occurs when one of the steps fails. If you withdraw $100.00 from your savings account and the deposit to your checking account fails, you have just lost $100.00 (which I'm sure would not put a smile on your face). These atomic transactions form a single unit that must succeed or fail as a unit.

To support this concept, ADO.NET allows us to create a transaction space around multiple actions. The *SqlConnection* object is where the transaction space is created. This is a two-step process that involves executing the *BeginTransaction* method of the *SqlConnection* object, which creates an active *SqlTransaction* object and returns a reference to it. This alone does not start the transaction, as you still must assign this new *SqlTransaction* object to the *Transaction* property of the *SqlConnection* objects that will perform the queries. From this point on, you have a transaction space in your *SqlConnection* object, which means all actions you perform through this connection will succeed, or none of them will succeed.

It is important to note that using a *SqlConnection* with a *SqlTransaction* is a little different than using a *SqlConnection* object without a *SqlTransaction*. We no longer associate our *SqlCommand* objects with the *SqlConnection* directly. Instead, we associate it indirectly by using the *SqlTransaction* object we got a reference to when we started the transaction. To make the changes permanent, we execute the *Commit* method of the *SqlTransaction* object, and if an error occurs, we can execute the *Rollback* method of the *SqlTransaction* object. The following is an example of how we would perform our funds transfer transaction using a transaction space:

```
Dim cn As New SqlConnection("Data Source=(local); " & _
                            "Initial Catalog=Northwind; " & _
                            "Integrated Security=true")
cn.Open()

'Start a transaction.
Dim trans As SqlTransaction = cn.BeginTransaction()

'Create a command which uses the transaction
Dim com As SqlCommand = New SqlCommand()
com.Transaction = trans

'Perform the transfer of funds
Try
  com.CommandText = "UPDATE Savings SET Balance = Balance - 100 " & _
                    "WHERE AccountID = 1"
  com.ExecuteNonQuery()
  com.CommandText = "UPDATE Checking SET Balance = Balance + 100 " & _
                    "WHERE AccountID = 2"
  com.ExecuteNonQuery()
  trans.Commit()
  Response.Write("<P>Transfer Successful</P>")
Catch e As Exception
  trans.Rollback()
```

```
Response.Write("An error occurred while processing your " & _
            "transfer:<br>" & e.ToString())
Finally
  cn.Close()
End Try
```

You will notice that we must commit the transaction if everything went fine. If an error occurred (for example, the savings account did not have sufficient funds, which violated a table constraint), we can catch the error and roll back the transaction

Use Stored Procedures

Stored procedures are very advanced SQL statements stored in the database. SQL Server uses a form of the SQL language called *Transact-SQL,* which also contains support for programming constructs such as conditional statements and looping structures. This means some of the datacentric programming logic for our applications can be stored in the database instead of in our code—an extremely useful characteristic of SQL Server, as it allows us to offload some of the processing to the database where the data is.

This actually can speed up your application if you are performing complex transactions that must perform multiple reads and writes to the data within the database. It is much quicker for a stored procedure that "lives" with your data to access it than it is for your application to access it from outside SQL Server.

Another benefit of stored procedures is security. If users have access to the actual table data within your database, they can (if they know how) write their own little programs, which can damage this data. The only way to prevent this is to avoid giving them write access to the database; however, if through their normal work with your application they must make changes to the table data, you will find yourself in a little dilemma. To grant or not to grant…that is the question.

An easy solution to this is through *stored procedures,* in which users are not granted access to the tables they need to work with; they are given access only to stored procedures that do the reads and writes on their behalf. Because a stored procedure is like a small function, we can programmatically control access to the underlying data. This means that a less-than-honorable user who wishes to sidestep your application and create his or her own application to attack your database can execute only the stored procedures that they could have used anyway through your application. In other words, the only damage they can do is damage they could have done through your application; you have not created a new security risk. The only risk is your application, which leaves one less thing to worry about.

on the job

It is possible to overuse stored procedures. If you are creating stored procedures that do a great deal of processor-intensive tasks (as opposed to data-intensive tasks) you will slow down your application instead of speeding it up. Transact-SQL is very good at accessing data but falls short when it comes to processor-intensive tasks. Always remember to use the right tool for the job.

Executing stored procedures is extremely simple if you already know how to execute a parameterized SQL statement though a *SqlCommand* object (which we looked at previously). The *CommandText* property of the *SqlCommand* object is simply set to the name of the stored procedure in the database instead of a SQL statement. We then can create *SqlParameters* for our *SqlCommand* object that represent the parameters for the stored procedure (if any).

The following example executes the CustOrderHist (customer order history) stored procedure in the Northwind database, and stores the data returned in a *SqlDataReader*. This information then is printed to the Web page:

```
'Create the connection to the database and open it
Dim cn As New SqlConnection("Data Source=(local); " & _
                            "Initial Catalog=Northwind; " & _
                            "Integrated Security=true")
cn.Open()

'Create a Command object
Dim com As New SqlCommand()
com.Connection = cn
com.CommandText = "CustOrderHist"
com.CommandType = CommandType.StoredProcedure
com.Parameters.Add(New SqlParameter("@CustomerID", "ALFKI"))

'Create the DataReader and execute the Command
Dim dr As SqlDataReader = com.ExecuteReader()

'Start a table
Response.Write("<TABLE cellspacing=10><tr><td><b>Product " & _
               "Name</b></td><td><b>Total
```

```
Quantity</b></td></tr>")

'Write the results to the Web page
While dr.Read()
  Response.Write("<tr><td>" & dr.GetString(0) & "</td><td>" & _
                 dr.GetInt32(1) & "</td></tr>")
End While

'End the table
Response.Write("</TABLE>")

'Close the connection
cn.Close()
```

CERTIFICATION SUMMARY

In this chapter, we have accessed a SQL Server database from a Web application using ADO.NET. We have primarily looked at writing all of the code ourselves and it should be noted that Visual Studio .NET will handle a great deal of this for us if we wish. In the next chapter, we will look at some of these tools.

The SQL Server data provider enabled us to retrieve records in the form of a read-only *SqlDataReader,* and the provider-independent *DataSet* enabled us to retrieve and manipulate records. The *SqlDataAdapter* allowed us to transfer information to and from our database, and through its *SqlCommand* properties it grants control over how these transfers are made back to the developer. We also have explored an alternative to using the *SqlDataAdapter* and *DataSet* to manipulate data that is executing ad hoc queries on the database directly. Finally, we used stored procedures to retrieve information and execute changes on the database.

In this chapter, you have found various ways to do the same thing—which can be quite overwhelming. The most important thing you can learn is the concepts. Anyone can look up the signature of a function or the properties of an object in a book, but to truly understand something, you have to be able use these tools appropriately; this can be done only if you understand the concepts behind the objects. When studying for this exam, make sure you understand the concepts first and then move on to the details. Microsoft exams are famous for expecting you to understand how to use something and not just what methods and properties something has, which, in my opinion, makes a great deal of sense.

TWO-MINUTE DRILL

Access and Manipulate Data from a Microsoft SQL Server Database

❑ ADO.NET can be used to access almost any type of data.

❑ The *DataSet* object stores relational data in an XML-compatible format.

❑ The *DataSet* is totally disconnected and independent from its source of data.

❑ The SQL Server data provider contains objects that are used to communicate with a SQL Server 7.0 or later database.

❑ The *SqlConnection* object forms a connection with the database and allows other objects to communicate with the database.

❑ The *SqlCommand* object represents a command to be executed on the database.

❑ The *SqlParameter* object represents a parameter for a SQL statement or stored procedure, and is associated with a *SqlCommand* object.

❑ The *SqlDataReader* object is a forward-scrolling, read-only container for tabular data retrieved from a database.

❑ The *SqlDataAdapter* object is used to transfer data from the database to a *DataSet* and back again.

❑ The *SqlTransaction* object is used to create an atomic transaction consisting of multiple queries, all of which must succeed or fail.

❑ Ad hoc queries can be executed directly on the database by using a *SqlCommand* object.

❑ The *SqlDataAdapter* must be set up with the appropriate insert, update, and delete commands to update the database with changes made to the *DataSet*.

❑ The *CommandBuilder* object can set up a *SqlDataAdapter* with very little coding.

❑ You can execute stored procedures by using the *SqlCommand* object.

❑ Stored procedures can improve both efficiency and security.

SELF TEST

The following questions will measure your understanding of the material presented in this chapter. Read all the choices carefully as there might be more than one correct answer. Choose all correct answers for each question.

Access and Manipulate Data from a Microsoft SQL Server Database

1. What is the Data Manipulation Language (DML) responsible for?

   A. Creating database objects.

   B. Querying and modifying data.

   C. Defining security on data.

2. You are creating a Web page that displays sales reports. What is the most efficient object you should use to retrieve this data?

   A. DataReader object

   B. DataAdapter object

   C. RecordSet

   D. DataSet

3. What is a JOIN clause in SQL used for?

   A. Allows us to execute two SQL statements with one command.

   B. Merges two fields together to save space.

   C. Retrieves related records from multiple tables in a database.

   D. Takes two tables in the database and makes them into one table in the database.

4. You wish to retrieve data from tables in two different databases. Which of the following solutions best describes the appropriate method? (Choose the best answer.)

   A. Create two different *DataSets*: one for each table.

   B. Create one *DataSet* and fill it using two different *DataAdapters*, one for each table.

   C. You cannot do this with ADO.NET.

   D. Create one *DataSet* and fill it with one table. Transfer the contents of this *DataSet* to an XML file and retrieve the next table.

5. How does the *DataSet* object store the table structure of its data? (Choose the best answer.)

   A. HTML

   B. XML

   C. HTTP

   D. XML schema

6. You have been asked to write a Web application that retrieves a simple schedule from a SQL Server database and allows users to view and edit it. The business logic is simple and there are no complex rules. All of the data is stored in one table. What would be the best way to set up the DataAdapter used to retrieve the *DataSet?*

   A. Set it up manually by creating select, insert, update, and delete commands for it.

   B. Use an *AdapterBuilder.*

   C. Set its *AutoSetup* property to true.

   D. Use a *CommandBuilder.*

7. Which of the following objects are part of the SQL Server data provider? (Choose all that apply.)

   A. *SqlDataSet*

   B. *SqlDataAdapter*

   C. *SqlCommand*

   D. *SqlDataBuilder*

8. You are creating an application that will access a certain table in the database. You need to update an unrelated table (for example, a log table) whenever you add a record to the table you are working with. Which of the following methods would be acceptable to do that? (Choose all that apply.)

   A. Use an update trigger in the database.

   B. Use referential integrity and a cascade update.

   C. Use a custom insert command with the *SqlDataAdapter* used to access the table and have it call a stored procedure that does all of this for you.

   D. Call a stored procedure in the database that does this for you.

9. What is the preferred method of SQL Server authentication?

   A. Mixed-mode authentication.

   B. Windows-only authentication.

C. Strict authentication.

D. There is no need to authenticate with the server because IIS does this for you.

10. Your Web application must perform multiple changes to each record and you are having problems because the constraints on the table are preventing you from making the changes. You know that if you could just update all of the values in a record at the same time, the constraints would be satisfied; however, since you are using a *DataSet* object, you must change each field one at a time. How can you solve your problem?

A. Use an UPDATE statement directly on the database with a *SqlCommand* object.

B. Remove the constraints from the database.

C. Hunt down the person who designed the database and do very bad things to him or her.

D. Use the *BeginEdit* method of the *DataRow* object to suspend constraint checking and then use *EndEdit* when you are finished to run the row through the constraint check.

11. What is the namespace that contains the SQL Server data provider?

A. *System.Data.SqlTypes*

B. *System.Data.SqlServer*

C. *System.Data.SqlProvider*

D. *System.Data.SqlClient*

12. How can you execute a SQL statement on a database that returns a single value and avoid the overhead of creating a *DataSet* or *SqlDataReader?*

A. Use a stored procedure.

B. Use the *ExecuteScalar* method of the *SqlCommand* object.

C. This cannot be done without a *DataSet* or *DataReader*.

D. None of the above.

13. Which method of the *SqlCommand* object is used to create a *SqlDataReader?*

A. *Fill*

B. *ExecuteQuery*

C. *ExecuteReader*

D. *ExecuteSqlData*

14. You are creating a Web application for an online e-commerce site. This site will display products to clients and allow them to purchase products they see. Choose the different options you think would work well with this application. (Choose all that apply.)

    A. Use a *DataReader* to retrieve products to display.

    B. Use a *DataSet* to retrieve products to display.

    C. Execute a stored procedure through a *SqlCommand* object to make purchases.

    D. Make purchases by adding records to a *DataSet*.

15. True or false: When using a *SqlDataAdapter* to fill a *DataSet*, you have to manage the connection manually (open and close it).

    A. True

    B. False

16. You have created a Web application; however, you cannot get it to open a connection. Which of the following are likely candidates for causing the problem? (Choose all that apply.)

    A. You have an invalid connection string.

    B. Your Web site allows anonymous access.

    C. The SQL statement used by the *SqlDataAdapter* is incorrect.

    D. You have an invalid <identity> tag in your web.config file.

17. When deleting a record from a *DataSet*, which of the following recommendations apply?

    A. Execute the *Delete* method of the *DataTable* object.

    B. Execute the *Remove* method of the *DataRowCollection*.

    C. Execute the *DeleteRow* method of the *DataRowCollection*.

    D. Execute the *Delete* method of the *DataRow* object.

18. Your Web application works fine but you get an error when trying to read records from a *DataSet* periodically. You have been able to replicate it and it only happens when you have just deleted a record in your *DataSet*. What is the problem?

    A. There are no records left in the *DataSet*.

    B. You need to update the database after deleting the record.

    C. You should check the *RowState* property to see whether a row has been deleted before trying to read it or you will get a run-time error.

    D. None of the above.

19. The property of the *DataRow* object that tracks changes made to the row and whether it is a new row or not is called the _____ property.

    A. *RowChange*

    B. *State*

    C. *IsChanged*

    D. *RowState*

20. The *CommandType* property of the *SqlCommand* object supports which of the following types? (Choose all that apply.)

    A. StoredProcedure

    B. Table

    C. Text

    D. TableDirect

LAB QUESTION

You are writing a Web application that must retrieve data from a database, display it to users, and allow them to edit this data. You have decided to use a *DataSet* to store the records and a *SqlDataAdapter* to retrieve the records. The following is the Clients table in a database called Financial. This is the database you will write your code against:

ClientID (*int*)	CompanyName (*nvarchar(50)*)	BillingAddress (*nvarchar(80)*)
1	Money Inc.	1 Main St.
2	BuyThisNow Ltd.	25 MyStreet Ave.
3	Lemons Used Cars	234 Mechanics Rd.
4	Crazy Eddies Back Ally Stereos	State Penn

The ClientID field has been declared in the database as an *int*. It is also an Identity column. The CompanyName and BillingAddress fields are both *nvarchars* which means they are Unicode.

You will not have access to the table directly but have been give the following four stored procedures with which to access and manipulate the data:

- GetClientInfo with no parameters

- AddClient with the following parameters:
  - @CompanyName
  - @BillingAddress
- ChangeClient with the following parameters:
  - @ClientID
  - @CompanyName
  - @BillingAddress
- RemoveClient with the following parameters:
  - @ClientID

In this exercise, you will set up the *SqlDataAdapter* manually using the above information and test it to make sure your *SqlDataAdapter* works. You will do the following things to see whether you have set up your *SqlDataAdapter* correctly:

1. Fill a *DataSet* and print out the contents.
2. Add a client.
3. Change a client.
4. Remove a client.
5. Update the database with these changes.
6. Print the contents of the *DataSet* again.

SELF TEST ANSWERS

Access and Manipulate Data from a Microsoft SQL Server Database

1. ☑ B. Querying and modifying data is done with the Data Manipulation Language (DML).
☒ A is the purpose of the Data Definition Language (DDL). C is the purpose of the Data Control Language (DCL).

2. ☑ A. The *SqlDataReader* object would be the most efficient for this task because it uses very little system resources, and in this situation, you do not need to change the data.
☒ B is incorrect because the *SqlDataAdapter* does not store records. C is incorrect because the *Recordset* is from ADO and this exam will be testing you on your knowledge of ADO.NET. D is incorrect because the *DataSet* object has a much higher overhead, as it must store all of the records retrieved, whereas the *SqlDataReader* object needs to store only one record at a time.

3. ☑ C. A JOIN allows us to retrieve records from multiple tables in the database when those tables are related.
☒ A, B, and D are simply incorrect.

4. ☑ B. One *DataSet* can contain multiple tables, and those tables can come from different databases.
☒ A would work, but is unnecessary and cumbersome. C: Yes, you can. Like A, D is unnecessary and cumbersome even though it would work.

5. ☑ D. The *DataSet* object stores the table structure of its data as an XML schema.
☒ A is incorrect. HTML was not designed to store data; therefore, it is not used by the *DataSet* object. B is also incorrect. The data in the *DataSet* is stored in an XML-compatible format and you could argue that an XML schema is part of XML; however, you must remember to choose the best answer and D clearly is a more specific answer. C is an application protocol for transferring information around the Web and not a storage format.

6. ☑ D. The *CommandBuilder* is a good choice in this situation and will save you some complexity.
☒ A is incorrect because setting up the *SqlDataAdapter* in this situation is not necessary. B is incorrect because there is no such thing as an *AdapterBuilder*. C is incorrect because there is no *AutoSetup* property.

7. ☑ B and C. The *SqlDataAdapter* and *SqlCommand* both are members of the SQL Server data provider.
☒ A and D are incorrect because they do not exist.

8. ☑ A, C, and D. All of these are appropriate for the task; however, some methods would be more appropriate in different circumstances. For example, if you were retrieving records into a *DataSet* C would be very useful because you would have to have a SqlDataAdapter to get the records and would not just be creating it to update the database. If you were not retrieving records, this would be a waste of time, so D would be very useful because it is very efficient to execute a stored procedure through a *SqlCommand* object.
   ☒ B is incorrect because a cascade update only occurs when you edit related fields in two tables, and in this case, the tables are not related.

9. ☑ B. The preferred method of SQL Server authentication is Windows-Only authentication.
   ☒ A is another method of SQL Server authentication, but it is not the preferred method. C is not a form of SQL Server authentication. D is incorrect because IIS does not authenticate you with the SQL Server.

10. ☑ D. *BeginEdit* and *EndEdit* allow you to suspend constraint checking until you finish updating the row. The check will still be performed, which can allow you to make changes that would not be allowed due to an intermediate violation.
   ☒ A would work, but the requirement in the question was that we were using a *DataSet* and it is assumed that we are doing this for a reason. B also would work but is a lazy idea. Constraints help enforce the integrity of your data which means they help keep it accurate. Never remove a constraint unless you have a logical reason to do so—and this is not a logical reason to do so. C is tempting at times, but it's not his or her fault for doing the job well.

11. ☑ D. The namespace that contains the SQL Server data provider is *System.Data.SqlClient*.
   ☒ A is a SQL Server namespace, but contains data types and not the provider. B and D are incorrect, as these namespaces do not exist.

12. ☑ B. The *ExecuteScalar* method of the *DataAdapter* will allow you to execute a SQL statement that returns a single value and will return it as an object.
   ☒ A is incorrect because the question was how do we execute a SQL statement. C is incorrect because it can be done. D is not correct because A is correct.

13. ☑ C. The *ExecuteReader* method of the *SqlCommand* object will fill and return a *SqlDataReader*.
   ☒ A is the method of the *SqlDataAdapter* that fills a *DataSet* not a *SqlDataReader*. B and D are not methods of the *SqlCommand* object.

14. ☑ A. Because users will not be editing product records, this would be a good choice. And also C. Using a stored procedure for purchases would be efficient and would allow you to do things such as checking the client's account and so forth in the database, which could improve performance.

☒   Because users will not be editing product records, B would be unnecessary. D would be a large waste of resources because we are not retrieving purchasing information from the database; we are adding it.

15. ☑   B. You do not have to manage the *SqlConnection* manually when using a *SqlDataAdapter*, as it will manage it for you; however, you may manage it yourself if you wish.
☒   A is incorrect.

16. ☑   A, B, and D are all possible problems that would prevent you from opening a connection with the database from a Web application.
☒   C is incorrect. If your connection won't open, there is nothing the *SqlDataAdapter* could do to affect that.

17. ☑   D. Execute the *Delete* method of the *DataRow* object to properly delete a record in a *DataSet*.
☒   A and C are not valid methods. B is a valid method, but if you use this method, the record will not be deleted in the database when the *DataSet* is updated.

18. ☑   C. You cannot read a record that has been marked for deletion.
☒   If A were the case, we just wouldn't have tried to print any records (the For loop wouldn't have run). B would not cause our problem. D is incorrect because C is correct.

19. ☑   D. The *RowState* property of the *DataRow* object tracks changes made to a row and signifies whether the *DataRow* has been added.
☒   A, B, and C are not properties of the *DataRow* object.

20. ☑   A, C, and D. The *CommandType* property specifies what type of command is to be found in the *CommandText* and can be set to StoredProcedure, Text (SQL statement), and TableDirect (a table name).
☒   B is not a valid value for the *CommandType* property.

LAB ANSWER

You were asked to set up a *SqlDataAdapter* to use stored procedures to access and manipulate data in a Clients table of a database called Financial. Note that to truly test your code, you will have to create a small database with the table and field names given and fill it with some sample data. To check your code, compare it to the following:

```
'Create the connection to the database and open it
Dim cn As New SqlConnection("Data Source=(local); " & _
                            "Initial Catalog=Financial; " & _
```

```vbnet
                              ,          "Integrated Security=true")

'Create a new DataAdapter object
Dim da As New SqlDataAdapter()

'Create the Select Command
Dim comSelect As New SqlCommand("GetClientInfo", cn)
comSelect.CommandType = CommandType.StoredProcedure

'Create the Insert Command
Dim comInsert As New SqlCommand("AddClient", cn)
comSelect.CommandType = CommandType.StoredProcedure

'Add the Insert Command's Parameters
comInsert.Parameters.Add(New SqlParameter("@CompanyName", _
                    SqlDbType.NVarChar, 50, _
                    ParameterDirection.Input, _
                    False, CType(0, Byte), CType(0, Byte), _
                    "CompanyName", DataRowVersion.Current, Nothing))
comInsert.Parameters.Add(New SqlParameter("@BillingAddress", _
                    SqlDbType.NVarChar, 80, _
                    ParameterDirection.Input, _
                    False, CType(0, Byte), CType(0, Byte), _
                    "BillingAddress", DataRowVersion.Current, Nothing))

'Create the Update Command
Dim comUpdate As New SqlCommand("ChangeClient", cn)
comUpdate.CommandType = CommandType.StoredProcedure

'Add the Update Commands Parameters
comUpdate.Parameters.Add(New SqlParameter("@CompanyName", _
                    SqlDbType.NVarChar, 50, _
                    ParameterDirection.Input, _
                    False, CType(0, Byte), CType(0, Byte), _
                    "CompanyName", DataRowVersion.Current, Nothing))
comUpdate.Parameters.Add(New SqlParameter("@BillingAddress", _
                    SqlDbType.NVarChar, 80, _
                    ParameterDirection.Input, _
                    False, CType(0, Byte), CType(0, Byte), _
                    "BillingAddress", DataRowVersion.Current, Nothing))
comUpdate.Parameters.Add(New SqlParameter("@ClientID", _
                    SqlDbType.Int, 4, _
                    ParameterDirection.Input, _
```

```
                            False, CType(0, Byte), CType(0, Byte), _
                            "ClientID", DataRowVersion.Current, Nothing))

'Create the Delete Command
Dim comDelete As New SqlCommand("RemoveClient", cn)

'Add the Delete Commands Parameters
comDelete.Parameters.Add(New SqlParameter("@ClientID", _
                            SqlDbType.Int, 4, _
                            ParameterDirection.Input, _
                            False, CType(0, Byte), CType(0, Byte), _
                            "ClientID", DataRowVersion.Current, Nothing))

'Add the Commands to the DataAdapter
da.SelectCommand = comSelect
da.InsertCommand = comInsert
da.UpdateCommand = comUpdate
da.DeleteCommand = comDelete

'Create a new DataSet
Dim ds As New DataSet()

'Get the records
da.Fill(ds, "Clients")

'Write the records to the page
Dim i As Integer
For i = 0 To ds.Tables(0).Rows.Count - 1
  Response.Write(ds.Tables(0).Rows(i).Item(0) & " " & _
                ds.Tables(0).Rows(i).Item(1) & "<br>")
Next i

'Add a new record
Dim row As DataRow = ds.Tables(0).NewRow()
row.Item("CompanyName") = "My Corp"
row.Item("BillingAddress") = "111 1st st."
ds.Tables(0).Rows.Add(row)

'Change a record
ds.Tables(0).Rows(5).Item("CompanyName") = "Your Corp"

'Delete a record
ds.Tables(0).Rows(2).Delete()
```

```
'Make the changes permanent
Dim count As Integer = da.Update(ds, "Clients")
Response.Write("<P>" & count & " Records Affected...</P>")

'Write the records to the page again
For i = 0 To ds.Tables(0).Rows.Count - 1
  If Not ds.Tables(0).Rows(i).RowState = DataRowState.Deleted Then
    Response.Write(ds.Tables(0).Rows(i).Item(0) & " " & _
                   ds.Tables(0).Rows(i).Item(1) & "<br>")
  End If
Next i
```

MICROSOFT® CERTIFIED APPLICATION DEVELOPER
& MICROSOFT® CERTIFIED SOLUTION DEVELOPER

7

Data Access from a Data Store

CERTIFICATION OBJECTIVES

I n the last chapter, we discussed accessing a SQL Server database using ADO.NET. SQL
Server is not the only source of data ADO.NET can manipulate. With ADO.NET, we can
access many different forms of relational database systems and XML files, flat files, and
other nonrelational sources of data. In this chapter, we will look at a more generic approach to
database access using the OLE DB data provider. We then will explore how Visual Studio .NET
can help us create some of this complicated and tedious code by using visual design tools. At
the end of this chapter, we also will look at one very important aspect to all data access
applications: handling database errors.

CERTIFICATION OBJECTIVE 7.01

Access and Manipulate Data from a Data Store

Data can be stored in many different ways and there are many different forms of
data used by our applications. Presently, one of the most common places to store
data is a *Relational Database Management System (RDBMS)*. Relational databases are
most often used to store large amounts of important data because they do more than
just store this data; they allow us to define the relationships between data. This helps
us ensure its accuracy and consistency, and resolves some of the issues that occur
when multiple users try to access the same data at the same time *(concurrency)*. Also
through normalization techniques, they can reduce storage requirements and allow
us to optimize the amount of space used to store data.

Given its enormous appeal, many developers never consider that there are several
alternatives to an RDBMS. XML is fast becoming one of the most common forms
of data storage available and is typically used to store very small amounts of structured
data that must be portable. XML can be used specifically for storage (as an alternative
to a text file) but it is more often used as a standardized format for transferring data
from one place to another. Other data management software can use XML for this
purpose (for example, SQL Server can use XML to transfer data to an application).

Flat files (straight text or binary files that store data in a nonrelational format) are
one of the oldest forms of data storage and are still commonly used today. We often
think of flat files as archaic technology that we are forced to work with due to the
expense of upgrading a system to use an RDBMS; however, flat files are commonly
used when the speed of reading or accessing data is extremely important.

It is a common misconception that flat files are not practical for large-scale data storage where the data is not read-only. This idea has become common because many developers have experience with only mid-size databases that are not real time, where a flat file is far too cumbersome when compared to an RDBMS. Flat files actually are extremely common for storage of very large amounts of data where its access and manipulation must be done in a real-time environment. In these cases, developers often are left with the daunting tasks of managing data integrity, concurrency, and transaction processing, which usually are done by an RDBMS such as SQL Server and Oracle.

Using a flat file almost always involves a drastic increase in development time and cost but in cases where speed of access is more important than speed of development and cost, often this is the only solution. The most important thing to understand here is that we have different ways to store data for different requirements; therefore, no single storage format is better than another in every situation. For this reason, Exam 70-305 will not just test your knowledge of accessing the SQL Server, it also will test your capability to access data from other relational databases, XML files, and flat files.

Access Data from a Relational Database

Relational Database Management Systems have become extremely popular as storehouses for application data because of their capability to store data in a structured and reliable manner. One of the problems in the industry today (although you could argue that this is a benefit) is the overwhelming number of different database systems; traditionally, this has meant that developers had to learn many different ways to access data. We have systems such as SQL Server, Oracle, Sybase, Informix, DB2, and the list goes on and on.

As mentioned in Chapter 6, ADO.NET enables us to access data from many different data sources using very similar techniques, which means we no longer have to reinvent the wheel every time we want to access a different data store. In Chapter 6, we investigated accessing a SQL Server database. Thanks to the capabilities of ADO.NET, accessing another data store is almost identical. In this section, we will not go through all of the details of accessing other relational databases, as the techniques we learned in Chapter 6 are equally applicable to other database systems. Instead, we will look at the small differences you will find.

FROM THE CLASSROOM

Data Storage Techniques

Storing data has been quite a significant challenge over the years. We are consistently trying to find a balance between speedy access and decreasing space requirements. One of the oldest of the modern approaches to this was to store all of the data in one big file (a flat file). This would be similar to storing all of your data in one Excel spreadsheet. The problem with this method is that often data will be duplicated unnecessarily. For example, if we store our friends' names, addresses, and phone numbers in a spreadsheet, in which each row would represent one friend, we would have some duplicated data. If two of our friends have the same address and phone number (they live together), this information would be repeated on two different rows. This, of course, is what we prevent by structuring or normalizing our data in a relational database.

However, you should be aware that normalizing data, while decreasing the amount of space it occupies, significantly increases the amount of time it takes to analyze and read

that data. This is because the data must now be taken from multiple tables instead of one. We often organize data within a database in a de-normalized format, which trades space for speed. Databases that respond well to this de-normalization technique are databases used for *Online Analytical Processing (OLAP),* which is just a fancy way of saying a database that is designed specifically for reading and evaluating data such as a database full of marketing surveys. Online Transaction Processing (OLTP) systems tend to respond better to normalized data.

The point of this discussion is that there are different kinds of database structures, each of which is designed for different uses. In this chapter and the last, we have primarily discussed using relational databases that were well normalized. You should not forget that a flat file (the ultimate in de-normalized data) can be a very powerful tool when used as an OLAP database.

—Wayne Cassidy, Bsc, MCSD, MCT

The OLEDB Data Provider

To access data from many different data stores, we use the OLEDB data provider. The OLEDB data provider contains drivers for many different data stores, including SQL Server, Oracle, Microsoft Jet (for ISAM databases), the Simple Provider for nonrelational data stores such as flat files, and many more. You might remember OLEDB from ADO in Visual Basic 6. One thing missing from the ADO.NET OLEDB data provider that was found with the ADO OLEDB data provider is support for ODBC. This is because Microsoft has created an ADO.NET provider specific for ODBC, which also means it is separate from the OLEDB provider.

If you check your installation of the .NET Framework, you will notice that this provider is most likely nonexistent. This is because it does not ship with the .NET Framework or Visual Studio .NET and is available separately as a download from Microsoft (at the time of this writing, you could download it from http://msdn. microsoft.com/downloads). If you wish to use SQL Server, you should use the ADO.NET SQL Server provider, if you wish to use ODBC, you should download and install the ADO.NET ODBC provider, and if you wish to access a database available through OLEDB, you can use the ADO.NET OLEDB provider.

Because of the huge industry buy-in for OLEDB and ODBC, this essentially means that through ADO.NET, we have access to a huge variety of data stores even if right now the only ADO.NET provider tuned to a specific database is the SQL Server provider (this will most likely have changed by the time you read this, so check the download site for an Oracle provider or any other RDBMS provider you are interested in). The following quick reference will help you decide which provider to use when accessing a data store.

SCENARIO & SOLUTION

I need to access a Microsoft Access 2000 database. Which provider should I use?	Use the Microsoft.Jet.4.0.OLEDB provider through the ADO.NET OLEDB provider.
I need to access a Microsoft SQL Server 7.0 or later database. Which provider should I use?	Use the .ADO.NET SQL Server provider.
I need to access a Fox Pro 6.0 database. Which provider should I use?	Use the Microsoft.Jet.3.51.OLEDB provider through the ADO.NET provider.
I need to access an Access 97 database. Which provider should I use?	Use the Microsoft.Jet.3.51.OLEDB provider through the ADO.NET OLEDB provider.
I need to access an Informix database. Which provider should I use?	Use the Informix driver (which you will have to download) through the ADO.NET ODBC provider.

on the Job

Don't let the fact that there are only three data providers fool you. Through the OLEDB and ODBC data providers, we have access to almost any data store there is. When the SQL Server provider won't do the trick, try the OLEDB provider. If there is no OLEDB driver for the data source you are working with, download the ODBC provider. If the ODBC provider does not contain a driver for the data source you are working with, you must be using something extremely rare (although you very well may be able to download an ODBC driver for that database from the manufacturer). It also should be noted that some of the data stores that were supported with ADO are no longer supported with the OLEDB provider in ADO.NET. This includes the provider for IIS and MSMQ.

To access the objects provided by the OLEDB data provider, you should import the following namespaces and enumerations:

```
Imports System.Data
Imports System.Data.OleDb
Imports System.Data.OleDb.OleDbType
```

You should note that the *System.Data* namespace is not specifically for the OLEDB provider; however, it gives us access to provider nonspecific objects such as the *DataSet,* whereas the *System.Data.OleDb* namespace gives us access to OLEDB provider–specific objects such as the *OleDbConnection* object. As with the SQL Server provider, the OLEDB provider has an enumeration of data types which are found in the *System.Data.OleDb.OleDbType* enumeration.

In Chapter 6, we looked at a group of objects available through the SQL Server provider. It is important to understand that ADO.NET requires that all providers implement what is called the *base provider.* This base provider defines the functionality that all providers must implement. This base functionality is provided by base objects, which you will find in all providers; these base objects will have a group of methods (an interface) common to all providers.

The objects we looked at in the last chapter were SQL Server's implementation of the base provider. This means the same objects are found in the OLEDB provider, although they will be implemented much differently. The good news is that because of encapsulation, we don't need to know anything about how these objects were implemented; we need to understand only the interfaces they expose. Providers are free to add to the base interfaces (you would see this as new methods for the objects); however, they must always expose the methods of the base interfaces.

Practically speaking, this means the OLEDB provider has the same objects, which have the same methods as those in the SQL Server provider. For that reason, if you read the last chapter, you already know how to use the OLEDB provider because it is essentially the same thing as the SQL Server provider; the main difference is the names of the objects. The following table shows the SQL Server provider object names and the equivalent OLEDB provider object names:

SQL Server Provider	OLEDB Provider
SqlConnection	OleDbConnection
SqlCommand	OleDbCommand
SqlParameter	OleDbParameter
SqlDataReader	OleDbDataReader
SqlDataAdapter	OleDbDataAdapter
SqlTransaction	OleDbTransaction

As you can see, this change is not terribly hard to remember. Just replace the Sql with OleDb. There are very few differences aside from the names.

The next difference you will find is in the connection string used to create a connection. Microsoft has made an effort to make the ADO.NET OLEDB provider connection strings the same as the SQL Server provider; however, because OLEDB itself supports many other providers, they had to add a new attribute. We now must use the *Provider* attribute to specify which OLEDB provider we are using (for example, Oracle provider for OLEDB). The following creates a connection to the Northwind data base from Microsoft Access:

```
Dim cn As New OleDbConnection("Provider=Microsoft.Jet.OLEDB.4.0;" & _
        "User ID=Admin;" & _
        "Data Source=C:\Inetpub\wwwroot\Connection\bin\Norwind.mdb")
cn.Open()
```

You should notice the addition of the Provider attribute to the connection string. This is needed whenever using an OLEDB provider, and represents the specific OLEDB provider to use. The other thing to notice is that we are using attributes different from those used with the SQL Server provider. We did not use Integrated Security = true because Microsoft Access does not have Windows authentication; therefore, you must specify a user ID and password (the password attribute for this connection string was left out because the password is blank).

The last thing to notice is that for Microsoft Access, the Data Source must be set to the file name and path of the database. The most important thing you can take away with you is that although connection strings have common attributes, which attributes you will use and what the values should be set to will depend on the specific provider you are using.

The next difference you will see between the SQL Server provider and the OLEDB provider is with the data types they use. In the last chapter, we looked at setting up a *SqlDataAdapter* in which we set the *SelectCommand, InsertCommand, UpdateCommand,* and *DeleteCommand* properties to *SqlCommands,* which used *SqlParameters.* The following code is shows our setup for the *InsertCommand* property:

```
'Create the Insert Command
Dim comInsert As New SqlCommand("INSERT INTO Employees (FirstName," & _
                      " LastName) VALUES (@FirstName, @LastName)", cn)

'Add the Insert Command's Parameters
comInsert.Parameters.Add(New SqlParameter("@FirstName", _
                      SqlDbType.NVarChar, 10, _
                      ParameterDirection.Input, _
                      False, CType(0, Byte), CType(0, Byte), _
                      "FirstName", DataRowVersion.Current, Nothing))
comInsert.Parameters.Add(New SqlParameter("@LastName", _
                      SqlDbType.NVarChar, 20, _
                      ParameterDirection.Input, _
                      False, CType(0, Byte), CType(0, Byte), _
                      "LastName", DataRowVersion.Current, Nothing))
```

You will notice that the two parameters are of type *SqlDbType.NVarChar.* We must use the OLEDB provider's own data types. For our Microsoft Access database, we would use an *OleDbType.VarWChar* for the same parameters. The following code uses the OLEDB provider:

```
'Add the Insert Command's Parameters
comInsert.Parameters.Add(New OleDbParameter("@FirstName", _
                      OleDbType.VarWChar, 10, _
                      ParameterDirection.Input, _
                      False, CType(0, Byte), CType(0, Byte), _
                      "FirstName", DataRowVersion.Current, Nothing))
comInsert.Parameters.Add(New OleDbParameter("@LastName", _
                      OleDbType.VarWChar, 20, _
                      ParameterDirection.Input, _
                      False, CType(0, Byte), CType(0, Byte), _
                      "LastName", DataRowVersion.Current, Nothing))
```

Not really a big difference; however, the difficult thing about using the OLEDB types is that your database most likely will not be using them directly. When we access a SQL Server database with the SQL Server provider, the types in the database have corresponding types in the *SqlTypes* enumeration. When we use the OLEDB provider, which supports many different types of data stores, we will have to translate them to the native types for the database.

For example, a *Text* data type in Microsoft Access is a *VarWChar* OLEDB data type. The following is an example from the last chapter, in which we used a *DataAdapter* to retrieve the Employees table from the Northwind database and make some changes to the data—only this time we are using the Microsoft Access version of this database:

```
'Create the connection to the database and open it
Dim cn As New OleDbConnection("Provider=Microsoft.Jet.OLEDB.4.0;" & _
          "User ID=Admin;" & _
          "Data Source=C:\Inetpub\wwwroot\Connection\bin\Norwind.mdb")

'Create a new DataAdapter object
Dim da As New OleDbDataAdapter()

'Create the Select Command
Dim comSelect As New OleDbCommand("SELECT EmployeeID, FirstName, " & _
              "LastName FROM Employees ORDER BY EmployeeID DESC", cn)

'Create the Insert Command
Dim comInsert As New OleDbCommand("INSERT INTO Employees " & _
                      "(FirstName, LastName) VALUES " &_
                      "(@FirstName, @LastName)", cn)

'Add the Insert Command's Parameters
comInsert.Parameters.Add(New OleDbParameter("@FirstName", _
                    VarWChar, 10, _
                    ParameterDirection.Input, _
                    False, CType(0, Byte), CType(0, Byte), _
                    "FirstName", DataRowVersion.Current, Nothing))
comInsert.Parameters.Add(New OleDbParameter("@LastName", _
                    VarWChar, 20, _
                    ParameterDirection.Input, _
                    False, CType(0, Byte), CType(0, Byte), _
                    "LastName", DataRowVersion.Current, Nothing))

'Create the Update Command
Dim comUpdate As New OleDbCommand("UPDATE Employees SET " & _
                    "FirstName = @FirstName, LastName = " & _
                    "@LastName WHERE EmployeeID = @EmployeeID", cn)
'Add the Update Commands Parameters
comUpdate.Parameters.Add(New OleDbParameter("@FirstName", _
```

```
                                    VarWChar, 10, _
                                    ParameterDirection.Input, _
                                    False, CType(0, Byte), CType(0, Byte), _
                                    "FirstName", DataRowVersion.Current, Nothing))
comUpdate.Parameters.Add(New OleDbParameter("@LastName", _
                                    VarWChar, 20, _
                                    ParameterDirection.Input, _
                                    False, CType(0, Byte), CType(0, Byte), _
                                    "LastName", DataRowVersion.Current, Nothing))
comUpdate.Parameters.Add(New OleDbParameter("@EmployeeID", _
                                    UnsignedInt, 4, _
                                    ParameterDirection.Input, _
                                    False, CType(0, Byte), CType(0, Byte), _
                                    "EmployeeID", DataRowVersion.Current, Nothing))

'Create the Delete Command
Dim comDelete As New OleDbCommand("DELETE FROM Employees WHERE " & _
                                    "EmployeeID = @EmployeeID", cn)

'Add the Delete Commands Parameters
comDelete.Parameters.Add(New OleDbParameter("@EmployeeID", _
                                    UnsignedInt, 4, _
                                    ParameterDirection.Input, _
                                    False, CType(0, Byte), CType(0, Byte), _
                                    "EmployeeID", DataRowVersion.Current, Nothing))

'Add the Commands to the DataAdapter
da.SelectCommand = comSelect
da.InsertCommand = comInsert
da.UpdateCommand = comUpdate
da.DeleteCommand = comDelete

'Create a new DataSet
Dim ds As New DataSet()

'Get the records
da.Fill(ds, "Employees")

'Add a new record
Dim row As DataRow = ds.Tables(0).NewRow()
row.Item("FirstName") = "Heidi"
row.Item("LastName") = "Hagen"
ds.Tables(0).Rows.Add(row)

'Change a record
ds.Tables(0).Rows(1).Item("FirstName") = "Max"
ds.Tables(0).Rows(1).Item("LastName") = "The Cat"

'Delete a record
```

```
ds.Tables(0).Rows(0).Delete()

'Make the changes permanent
Dim count As Integer = da.Update(ds, "Employees")
ds.AcceptChanges()
Response.Write("<p>" & count & " Records Affected...</p>")

'Write the records to the page again
Dim i As Integer
For i = 0 To ds.Tables(0).Rows.Count - 1
  If Not ds.Tables(0).Rows(i).RowState = DataRowState.Deleted Then
    Response.Write(ds.Tables(0).Rows(i).Item(1) & " " & _
                   ds.Tables(0).Rows(i).Item(2) & "<br>")
  End If
Next i
```

If you look closely through this code you will notice that there are very few differences between the OLEDB provider and the SQL Server provider. This makes it extremely easy to write data-centric Web applications using disparate data sources.

The last difference we will discuss is in stored procedures. In SQL Server, a stored procedure has parameters just like a normal Visual Basic procedure. These parameters are given names similar to the way we name parameters in Visual Basic. In other words, in VB we name parameters with the name of the variable for that parameter.

```
Public Sub SomeRoutine(paramName as ParamType)
```

The following is an example of a SQL Server stored procedure. Notice that the parameters are declared quite similarly, but the names all start with the @ sign:

```
CREATE PROCEDURE GetLocalExpensiveEmployees
        @City    nvarchar(15),
        @Salary money
AS
    SELECT FirstName, LastName FROM Employees
    WHERE City = @City
    AND Salary > @Salary
GO
```

@City and @Salary are the names of the parameters and nvarchar(15) and money are their types respectively. When we use stored procedures from SQL Server (as we saw in the last chapter), we use a command object. To give a parameter a value, we create a *SqlParameter* object and give it a value. We do this by using the parameter name and value in the constructor for the *Parameter* object, as shown here:

```
Dim com As New SqlCommand()
com.CommandText = "GetLocalExpensiveEmployees"
com.CommandType = CommandType.StoredProcedure
com.Parameters.Add(New SqlParameter("@Salary", 50000.0))
com.Parameters.Add(New SqlParameter("@City", "London"))
```

It is important to note that with the SQL Server provider, the order in which we add parameters to the *Parameters* collection of the *Command* object is irrelevant. In the above example, the @City parameter is the first in the stored procedure, but we added the @Salary parameter to the *Command* object first. This is because the provider will figure out which *Command* parameter is which based on the names.

The OLEDB provider does not have this capability because not all databases supported by the OLEDB provider use named parameters for stored procedures. For example, Microsoft Access supports a form of stored procedure called a *stored query* that is a very simple form of stored procedure but does not support named parameters (as well as a lot of other things).

You can name your parameter within Microsoft Access; however, they have no meaning when called from an external process. For this reason, the order in which you add your *Parameter* objects to the *Parameters* collection of the *Command* object becomes extremely important. For example, the following is a stored query I added to the Northwind database for Microsoft Access (I also added a Salary field to the Employees table):

```
PARAMETERS sal Currency, cit Text (255);
SELECT Employees.FirstName, Employees.LastName
FROM Employees
WHERE (((Employees.City)=[cit]) AND ((Employees.Salary)>[sal]));
```

This stored query was saved and called GetLocalExpensiveEmployees. If we set up a *OleDbCommand* object for the stored query with the following code, it will not raise a run-time error—but it also will not work (look at the order in which the *OleDbParameters* were added to the *Parameters* collection):

```
'Create a Command objct
Dim com As New OleDbCommand()
com.Connection = cn
com.CommandType = CommandType.StoredProcedure
```

```
com.CommandText = "GetExpensiveLocalEmployees"

'Add the Parameters
com.Parameters.Add(New OleDbParameter("", 70000.0))
com.Parameters.Add(New OleDbParameter("", "London"))
```

If we switch the order in which we add the *OleDbParameter* objects to the *Parameters* collection, everything will work fine.

```
'Add the Parameters
com.Parameters.Add(New OleDbParameter("", "London"))
com.Parameters.Add(New OleDbParameter("", 70000.0))
```

You should notice that the parameter names have been left blank (empty string). You could and probably should add a name to the parameter for the sake of code clarity; however, these names are ignored by the OLEDB provider. The following is the full code for calling our Microsoft Access stored query (note that I have added parameter names for code clarity):

```
'Create the connection to the database and open it
Dim cn As New
OleDbConnection("Provider=Microsoft.Jet.OLEDB.4.0;" & _
          "User ID=Admin;" & _
          "Data
Source=C:\Inetpub\wwwroot\Connection\bin\Norwind.mdb")
cn.Open()

'Create a Command objct
Dim com As New OleDbCommand()
com.Connection = cn
com.CommandType = CommandType.StoredProcedure
com.CommandText = "GetExpensiveLocalEmployees"

'Add the Parameters
com.Parameters.Add(New OleDbParameter("Salary", 30000.0))
com.Parameters.Add(New OleDbParameter("City", "London"))

'Create a new DataSet
Dim dr As OleDbDataReader

'Get the records
dr = com.ExecuteReader()

'Write the records to the page again
```

```
While dr.Read()
  Response.Write(dr.GetString(0) & " " & _
                 dr.GetString(1) & "<br>")
End While

'Close the connection
cn.Close()
```

As you can see, accessing any relational database is very easy if you already know how to access SQL Server. The differences lie mainly in the names of the objects, the data types, and the ordering of parameters when calling stored procedures. Don't forget that if the underlying data source does not support stored procedures, you cannot use them.

Using Visual Studio .NET to Access Data

It's now time to sit back and relax. I have some good news for you: Everything we have done in the last chapter and up to this point can be done by pointing here and clicking there. That's right: Visual Studio .NET has design-time support for most of the actions we have performed and you will have to write only a few lines of code. This does not mean that you do not need to understand all of this code. If you don't understand it, you can't debug it and, of course, you won't pass the exam. Nonetheless, our lives will be much easier during this section.

The Server Explorer   The first visual tool we will look at from Visual Studio .NET is the Server Explorer. The Server Explorer allows us to manage our server from within Visual Studio. You can do everything from managing services to creating stored procedures in a database. This can be extremely convenient, as this means we don't need to move from one program to another (and possibly another computer) when creating a Web application.

One important thing to remember is that the Server Explorer can only enable you to manage a server—and you still must have the permissions to do so. If, for example, you do not have Administrator privileges in SQL Server, you will not be able to administer SQL Server even if the Server Explorer can allow you to do this. The following is a list of some of the common administrative tasks you can perform with the Server Explorer (note that this is not a complete list and only contains common administrative tasks you might perform while developing a Web application).

■ View and manipulate the contents of an OLEDB-compliant database

■ View your server's event logs

- Administer Message Queues
- Start and Stop services
- View and manipulate the contents of a SQL Server database

Of course, we will only be discussing the data access functionality of the Server Explorer. The first thing the Server Explorer can do for us in this respect is view and manipulate the contents of a database. This can be done in one of two ways. If the database server is a SQL Server, the connection will already be made. The Server Explorer exposes connections to servers that are running SQL Server 7.0 or later. You will notice that it looks very similar to the SQL Server Enterprise Manager, as seen in Figure 7-1.

FIGURE 7-1

The Visual Studio .NET Server Explorer

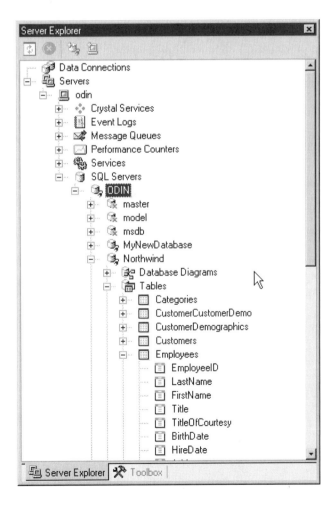

You can view the contents of a table or stored procedure by simply double-clicking the corresponding object in the Server Explorer. In the case of tables, this also allows you to edit the data within the table. In the case of stored procedures, this allows you to edit the procedure and even groups the different blocks of a stored procedure visually (see Figure 7-2).

This is my favorite thing about the Server Explorer. Not only can you edit your stored procedures from within Visual Studio, you can debug them (even in conjunction with the application that calls them).

FIGURE 7-2   Editing Stored Procedures through the Server Explorer

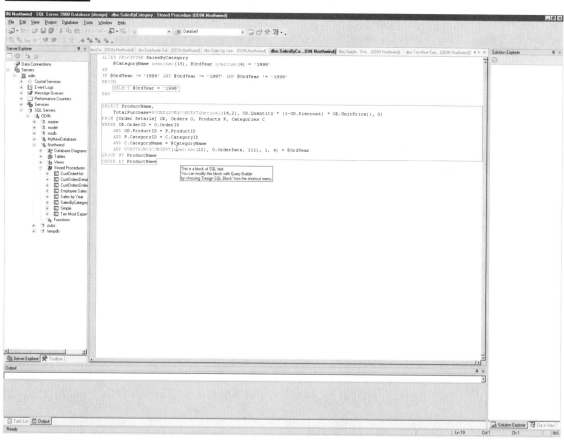

The key to using the Server Explorer is the context menu. Right-click absolutely everything you see! For example, to create a new database diagram in a SQL Server database, right-click Database Diagrams node under the database in question and select New Diagram. To add a table to the database, right-click the Tables node under the database in question and select New Table. Are you getting the hang of it? This basically means we can do almost all of the important development tasks from Visual Studio instead of switching back and forth between Visual Studio and SQL Server Enterprise Manager.

Microsoft exams tend to focus on the underlying technology and code, not on visual tools used to automate these processes for us. That said, often it is quite common for an exam to expect you to know all of the different ways of performing a task (such as how to write the code, whether there are any visual tools, or whether there are any wizards to perform the task).

If you want to access a database other than SQL Server, you will have to make a connection to it manually. One of the useful things of making these connections in the Solution Explorer is that they are set for Visual Studio, not for your application. In other words, they will stick around until you remove them and they are not saved with your project, which means you will have to manually set them up on any computer on which you are editing your project. To make a connection to a database, right-click the Data Connections node in the Server Explorer and select Add Connection. This brings up the Data Link Properties page, which you might remember from Visual Basic 6, as shown in Figure 7-3.

The Data Link Properties page starts up with the Connection tab visible and assumes that you want to add a connection to SQL Server, which usually means you need to switch to the Provider tab to choose the appropriate provider (see Figure 7-4).

Once you have selected the appropriate provider, you can click the next button, which sends you back to the Connection tab. The Connection tab will look different depending on the provider you are using; however, it is pretty straightforward to work through the different entries. Once you have finished entering your connection data, you can click OK (or possibly the Test Connection button to make sure your entries are valid); you now have a new connection. This puts a new node under the Data Connections node in the Server Explorer and, just like SQL Server, will allow you to manage your database.

FIGURE 7-3

The Data Link
Properties page

FIGURE 7-4

Specifying a data
provider

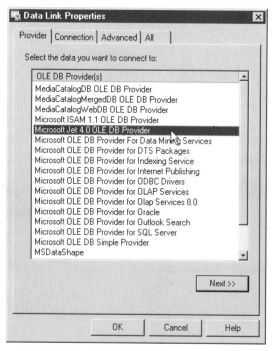

Although the Server Explorer is quite capable of enabling you to manage a database, in most professional situations you will find that you do not have the appropriate permissions on the database to use this tool thoroughly. Remember that the Server Explorer can let you do only what you are allowed to do—no more. You will almost never have any permissions on a production database and unless you are the sole developer, you will usually have limited permissions on a development database. That said, the Server Explorer is a convenient way to do whatever you have permission to do.

Managing a database with the Server Explorer is very convenient, but the most useful of its capabilities is that it can add fully configured *Connection* objects and *DataAdapter* objects to your application. If you want access to a table or view in a database, all you need to do is drag that table or view onto a Web page; it will write all of the code necessary to set up a *Connection* and a *DataAdapter,* which has its *SelectCommand, InsertCommand, UpdateCommand,* and *DeleteCommand* manually set up (not using a *CommandBuilder*). There are icons for these objects located at the bottom of your page, which allow you to set their properties visually, as shown in Figure 7-5.

With the *Connection* object, you can set its properties in the Properties window, which in most cases would be unnecessary (aside from changing its name) unless you want to tweak the connection string. Important to note is that the code for these objects actually is written in the code-behind for the Web page to which the control was added; this means you also can go directly to that code and edit it manually if you like (aren't you glad we discussed how to write the code yourself?). The *Connection* object really does not have much to it aside from the connection string, so there is not much else in the way of design-time support for it.

*Using the Server Explorer to create the **Connection** and **DataAdapter** code for you can be a useful way to learn the code-behind for these objects. Try using the Server Explorer to create links to different types of databases (such as SQL Server, Oracle, Access, and so forth) and then take a look at the code created. This can help show you how the code fits together and is especially useful for understanding how a connection string is built.*

The *DataAdapter* is much more complex than the *Connection* object. For this reason, there also is a wizard that can help you set it up the way you want, although the wizard was designed to be used when you drag an empty *DataAdapter* from the Toolbox. When you have a previously configured *DataAdapter,* such as the one you

FIGURE 7-5 Adding a connection and *DataAdapter* from the Server Explorer

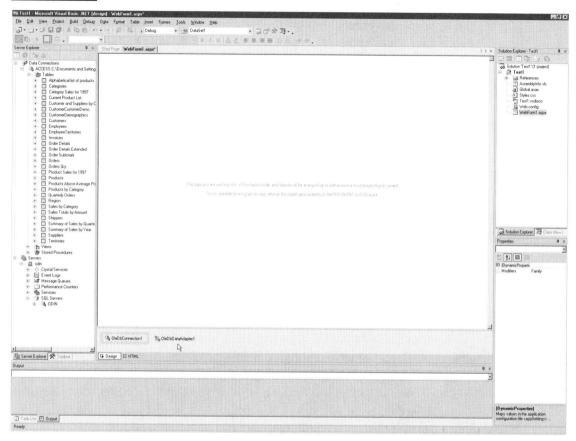

will have after dragging a table from the Solution Explorer, the wizard can be a little hard to manipulate. When you drag a table or view onto a page, the *DataAdapter* is set up to retrieve the entire table. The *InsertCommand, UpdateCommand,* and *DeleteCommand* also are set up and will use SQL statements.

If you want to tweak the SQL statements behind these *Command* objects, you have three options, although only two are reasonable. The first thing you can do (and my personal choice) is to look in the code behind the form and edit everything directly. All of the code can be found in the *InitializeComponent* event. If you prefer a more visual approach, you can edit the *Command* properties in the Properties window. If you click the *DataAdapter* object on your Web page, you will notice that the *SelectCommand, InsertCommand,* and so forth have a plus sign next to them which, when clicked, allow you to edit the properties of the associated command (see Figure 7-6).

FIGURE 7-6

Editing commands in the Properties window

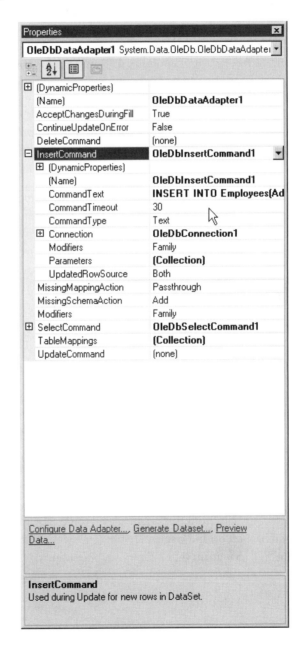

The last option (not really a good one) is to use the wizard by right-clicking the *DataAdapter* and selecting Configure Data Adapter. This is not a good option because your *DataAdapter* object is associated with the *Connection* object that was placed on your Web page when you dragged the table onto your page. The wizard is designed to be used when you add the *DataAdapter* from the Toolbox, not from the Server Explorer. When you add it from the Toolbox, it is not configured, and the wizard can help you configure it from scratch; however, because in this case, it was added from the Server Explorer, the wizard is not really the best option.

e x a m
ⓦa t c h

Avoid wizards when studying for an exam. It is often tempting to use a wizard to write the code for you—but you are cheating yourself. Use a wizard to get a good idea of how the code should be created. After that, always write the code yourself. We learn by repetition.

Now let's backtrack and talk about configuring the *DataAdapter* by using the Properties window. You will have to edit two main properties for each *Command* object. The first is the *CommandText* property, which stores the SQL statement for the command. If you wish to change it to a stored procedure or alter the statement, you can edit the property directly or use the Query Builder. The Query Builder allows us to build SQL queries in a visual way. To open the Query Builder, click the ellipse button next to the *CommandText* property; the Query Builder window will appear, as shown in Figure 7-7.

The Query Builder consists of four panes. The first, the *Diagram* pane, contains the table you are working with. This is where you can add the tables you want to work with and choose the fields you want to use. The second pane is called the *Grid* and is where you will see the fields you have chosen. It also allows you to do things such as setting constraints, filters, sorting order, and so forth. The third pane is the SQL pane, which shows you the results of the decisions you have made in the previous two panes. You can edit the SQL directly in this pane and the results of your changes will be seen in the Diagram pane and Grid.

The final pane is called the Results pane. If you right-click anywhere within the Query Builder, you will notice a Run menu item on the context menu that pops up. Selecting Run from this menu allows you to test your query and see the results. Once you have set up and tested the SQL statement you have created, you can click OK to save the SQL statement in the *CommandText* property of the *Command* you were editing.

FIGURE 7-7. The Query Builder

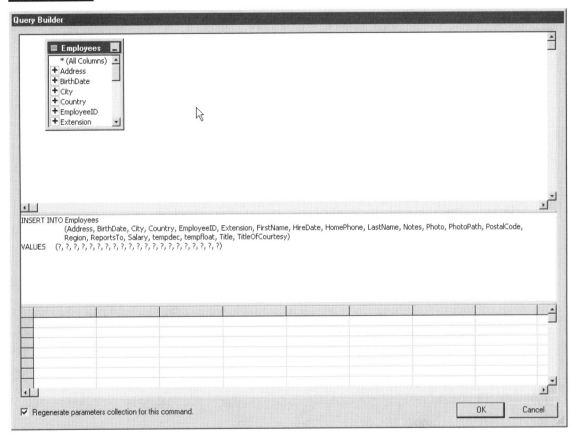

To change the parameters used for a specific command, you can click the ellipse button next to the *Parameters* property. This opens the Parameter Collection Editor (see Figure 7-8).

This editor is fairly straightforward and allows you to add and remove parameters and edit their properties.

Once you have your *Connection* and *DataAdapter* set up the way you want them, you will need to create a *DataSet* to hold the records. You should have noticed by now that a *DataSet* was not added to your page when you dragged the table over, which

FIGURE 7-8

The Parameter
Collection Editor

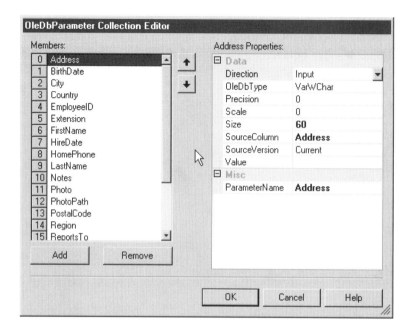

means you will have to add it yourself. If you look in the Data tab of the Toolbox, you will find components related to data access, which should look familiar by now. To add a *DataSet* to a page, you can simply drag one from the Toolbox or you can have the *DataAdapter* generate one for you. If you drag a DataSet from the Toolbox, the Add Dataset dialog box will appear, as shown in Figure 7-9.

This dialog box allows you to choose between an existing *Typed DataSet* and a new *Untyped DataSet*. In the previous chapter, we created untyped *DataSet* objects. Untyped *DataSet* objects are objects of type *DataSet* (I'm sure that shocked you). With these types of *DataSet* objects, the *DataAdapter* will create the table schema when it fills the *DataSet* and the tables, columns, and rows must be accessed through collections. This has worked fine for us up to this point; however, this can add unnecessary overhead to your application, as every time the *DataSet* is filled, the *DataAdapter* must infer the table schema from the data and add it to the *DataSet*. The other alternative is to create a typed *DataSet*.

A typed *DataSet* is a *DataSet* that has its table schema defined at design time by the developer or by Visual Studio. A typed *DataSet* is not of type *DataSet;* instead, it is based on a class that is derived from *DataSet*. This wrapper class exposes tables and columns as properties instead of collections, which can make it easier to read and

The Add Dataset
dialog box

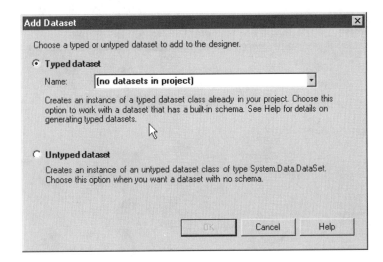

write code. To create a typed *DataSet*, do not drag a *DataSet* object from the Toolbox.
Right-click the *DataAdapter* object you added to your project and select Generate
DataSet. This opens the Generate DataSet dialog box, which allows you to specify
whether you want to create a new *DataSet* or regenerate an existing *DataSet*.

You also can choose the *DataAdapter* to use as the source of the data (it will
default to the *DataAdapter* you used to execute Generate DataSet) and give your
DataSet class a name. This little wizard will create a new class based on the *DataSet*
object and will generate an XML schema file (file extension .xsd) with the same
name. This XML schema file contains the table schema and, therefore, the table
schema is hard-coded instead of having the *DataAdapter* infer its schema every time
the *DataSet* is filled, which can save on overhead. The .xsd file is added to your
project and can be opened in the designer, as shown in Figure 7-10.

A typed *DataSet* exposes its tables and columns as properties instead of
collections, which adds even more efficiency. For example, the following code from
the last chapter shows how we would set the value of the FirstName field of a record
in our *DataSet;* this *DataSet* is untyped:

```
ds.Tables("Employees").Rows(0).Item("FirstName") = "Ted"
```

The following does the same thing; however, it uses a *DataSet* object called
Employees1 (which is an instance of a typed *DataSet* class called *Employees*):

```
Employees1.Employees(0).FirstName = "Ted"
```

FIGURE 7-10 The XML Schema file for a typed *DataSet*

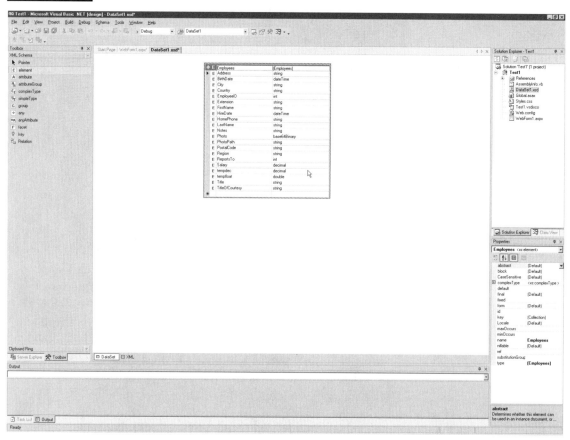

As you can see, typed *DataSet* objects are not just more efficient, they are easier to work with. If you are looking for the declaration of the typed *DataSet* class (which is called Employee in the previous example), you will not find it in the Solution Explorer. A file called *TypedDataSetClassName.vb* is placed in your virtual directory but is not added to the Solution Explorer, which means you will have to open it yourself if you are interested in taking a peek at it.

exam
ⓦatch

I strongly recommend that you take a look at the file containing the typed DataSet. If you can read through this file and make sense of it, you are well on your way to understanding the new concepts in Visual Basic .NET, and well on your way to passing the exam.

Now that we have a *Connection, DataAdapter,* and *DataSet,* we need to do something with them. The first thing we need to do is fill the *DataSet.* Typically, we would use the *Fill* method of the *DataAdapter* in the *Page_Load* event but you can do this in any reasonable place. Now that the *DataSet* has some data, we will need to access it. Using the techniques from the previous chapter, we can programmatically do anything we want; however, you also can bind the *DataSet* to a control on your Web page. The *DataGrid* control is a good candidate for this and will allow us to display the entire table in a grid. The *DataGrid* control is a Web Form Control and contains the following members which allow us to attach it to a *DataSet* object:

■ **DataSource** specifies where the *DataGrid* will get its records. In this case, we will use the *DataSet* object.

■ **DataMember** specifies which table within a *DataSet* will supply the records. If you do not set this property, the default table of the *DataSet* will be used.

Once you have set the members appropriately, you can execute the *DataGrid* objects *DataBind* method, which loads the *DataGrid* with the data from the *DataSet.,* When your page is viewed, the data will magically appear. When using bound controls and the Solution Explorer, the entire process becomes so simple you really have only to write two lines of code. The following are the two lines of code you will have to write yourself to set up a *DataGrid* using Visual Studio and its visual tools. This code was placed in the *Page_Load* event:

```
SqlDataAdapter1.Fill(Employees1, "Employees")
DataGrid1.DataBind()
```

We now have seen the visual method for setting up data access. It should be noted that we have not explored every avenue as visual programming tends to be very intuitive and simple. You should investigate, on your own, binding to other types of controls and using the Data Adapter Wizard. If you drag a *DataAdapter* from the Toolbox, the Data Adapter Wizard will display and walk you through the steps of setting up the *DataAdapter,* and will allow you to set up a new connection if necessary.

One of my favorite attributes of the Data Adapter Wizard is its versatility in setting up the four commands for us. It will even allow you to use stored procedures if you like. If you can follow simple instructions, you can use this wizard. We have already discussed the underlying concepts, which means you should understand the results.

Access Data from XML Documents

XML is fast becoming the information format for the internet. The XML standard, developed by *W3C (World Wide Web Consortium)* is a simple and efficient format for representing structured data in a consistent way. Due to its wide industry acceptance, the use of XML by the .NET Framework will have very positive consequences. Through the use of XML, Web applications written with .NET will be free to transfer data, and thus communicate, with processes and systems of disparate origin.

The one common characteristic of the Internet is the multitude of different technologies that are all linked together, which makes the use of a standard data format a very useful idea. In this section, we will look at the support Visual Studio has for creating and editing XML files, and how to read and write to these files programmatically.

Visual Studio .NET Support for XML

The first thing we will look at is Visual Studio .NET's support for XML. Visual Studio .NET contains an editor for XML and an editor for XSD (XML Schema Definition). This allows us to easily create XML and XML schema files either directly, by writing the code, or using a visual editor. This is equivalent to editing an HTML file in Visual Studio in that you can use a visual designer (the Design tab) or edit the HTML directly (the HTML tab). To add an XML file to Visual Studio, choose the XML File template from the Add New Item dialog box (see Figure 7-11).

You will notice that this adds a blank XML file which contains only an XML directive. Note that you cannot use the visual designer until you have formed the basic structure of your XML file or have created a schema for this file (this XML file can use a schema file for its structure; just set the Target Schema property in the Property Explorer to a valid XSD file). For example, we could use the following XML structure (without the actual data) to represent an Employee:

```
<?xml version="1.0" encoding="utf-8" ?>
<NewDataSet>
  <Employee id="">
    <FirstName></FirstName>
    <LastName ></LastName>
  </Employee>
</NewDataSet>
```

FIGURE 7-11

Adding an XML
file to a project

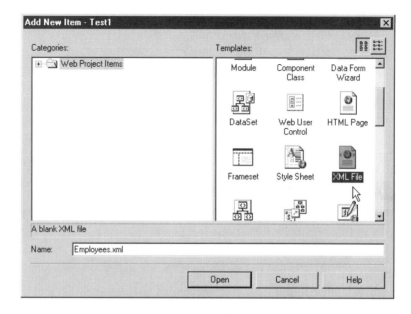

This gives the visual editor enough information to allow you to add records to
your XML file using a tabular format similar to Excel. You will notice that we have
combined attributes (the id) and tags (the FirstName and LastName) to represent
our data. XML is a very flexible language that allows you to represent data in different
ways to suit your specific needs. You also should notice that there is no data entered.
We have only added the basic structure so we can use the Visual Editor (click the
Data button at the bottom of the form), which would look like Figure 7-12.

As you can see, it is now very easy (and quick) to enter some employees into our
XML file. If you look back at the XML created from the preceding additions in the
Visual Editor, you would find the following code written for you:

```
<?xml version="1.0" encoding="utf-8" ?>
<NewDataSet>
  <Employee id="1">
    <FirstName>Max</FirstName>
    <LastName>TheCat</LastName>
  </Employee>
  <Employee id="2">
    <FirstName>John</FirstName>
    <LastName>Smith</LastName>
```

```
    </Employee>
    <Employee id="3">
      <FirstName>Iman</FirstName>
      <LastName>Animal</LastName>
    </Employee>
  </NewDataSet>
```

To create an XML schema file, we can choose an XML Schema File from the Add New Item dialog box (see Figure 7-13).

FIGURE 7-12   The Data tab of the XML designer

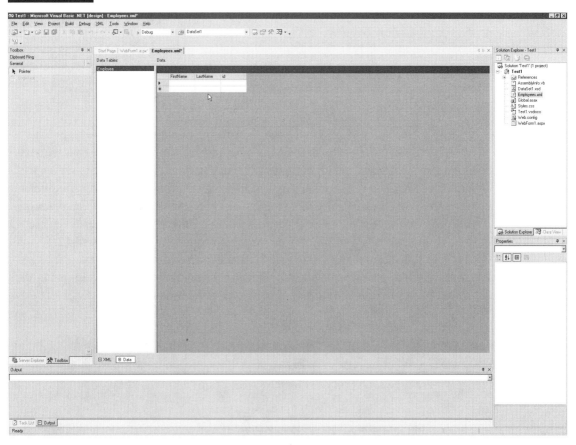

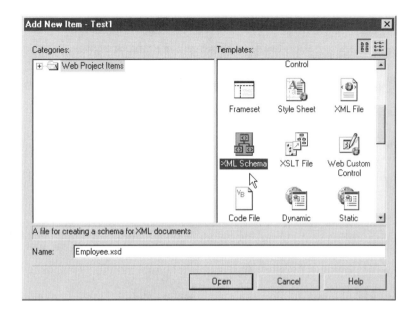

FIGURE 7-13

Adding an XML Schema file to a project

Once you have added an XML Schema file, the Toolbox changes to offer you objects specific to XML Schema files. Figure 7-14 is an illustration showing the state of Visual Studio while editing an XML Schema file.

Once you have designed your schema structure, you can use the schema file as the structure of an XML file, or you can use it to create a strongly typed *DataSet* object.

XMLReader and XMLWriter

One of the simplest and most straightforward ways to read and write to an XML file programmatically is to use the *XmlReader* and *XmlWriter* objects. These objects are fine when you wish to read or write XML using a stream; however, if you want to manipulate the XML in a hierarchical or relational way, you should use the *XmlDocument* or *DataSet,* respectively.

The *XmlReader* and *XmlWriter* classes can be found in the *System.Xml* namespace, but these classes are abstract and cannot be used directly. Both of these classes serve as base classes for a subset of classes used to manipulate XML. You can use the *XmlTextReader* class to read an XML file using a text stream in a forward-only, read-only manner. The constructor is heavily overloaded and one of the overloads takes a *TextStream* object as an argument.

FIGURE 7-14   Editing an XML Schema file

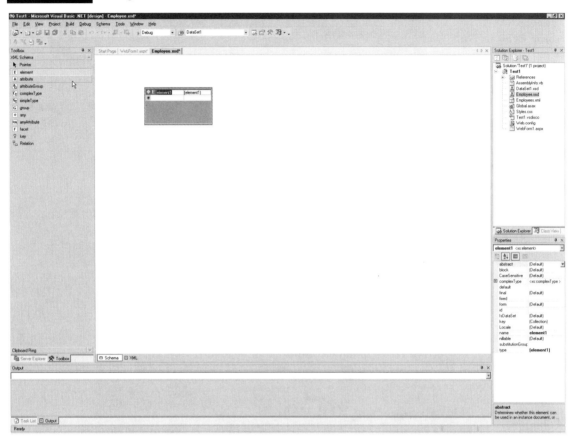

Reading the elements from an *XmlTextReader* is similar to reading records from a *DataReader*. The *Read* method of the *XmlTextReader* method scrolls to the next element and returns true if there is a next element, false if there is not. The following is an example of reading records from an XML file containing employee records similar to the Employees table we have been working with throughout this chapter:

```
'Create a StreamReader to access the XML file
Dim sr As New StreamReader(Server.MapPath("Employees.xml"))

'Create an XMLReader to access the XML
Dim xin As New XmlTextReader(sr)
```

```
'Print all of the elements to the page
Dim i As Integer = 1
While xin.Read()
  If xin.NodeType = XmlNodeType.Text Then
    i += 1
    If i Mod 2 = 0 Then Response.Write("<br>")
      Response.Write(xin.Value & " ")
    End If
End While

'Close the file
xin.Close()
```

The first thing to notice is that we have created a stream to the file using the *StreamReader* object, which then is used by the *XmlTextReader* object to read each XML node from file. We then loop through all of the nodes in the file and print any node that is of type *XmlNodeType.Text,* which is an element with a value in it (our FirstName and LastName fields). Once we are finished, we close the file.

Writing XML to a file using a stream is almost as easy. For this we will use an *XmlTextWriter* object. The *XmlTextWriter* object has different methods to write different XML tags to a file. The following code writes one record to a new XML file:

```
'Create an XMLReader to access the XML
Dim xout As New XmlTextWriter(Server.MapPath("") & "\new.xml", Nothing)

'Write the XML to the file
xout.WriteStartDocument(True)
xout.WriteStartElement("Employee")
xout.WriteAttributeString("id", "1")
xout.WriteElementString("FirstName", "Max")
xout.WriteElementString("LastName", "TheCat")
xout.WriteEndElement()
xout.WriteEndDocument()

'Close the stream
xout.Close()
```

In this case, we used a constructor that takes a file name as an argument. If the file exists, it will be overwritten; otherwise, it will create the file. By using the appropriate write methods, we can create elements, attributes, and more. The most important thing to notice is the *WriteStartDocument* method, which is used to place the opening directive in the XML file. The following is the file created from the preceding code:

```
<?xml version="1.0" standalone="yes" ?>
<Employee id="1">
```

```
    <FirstName>Max</FirstName>
    <LastName>TheCat</LastName>
</Employee>
```

As you can see, reading and writing to an XML file is quite easy with the *XmlReader* and *XmlWriter* objects. However, these objects are not very versatile and do not follow the standard format of the Document Object Model (DOM). For this functionality, we will have to take a different approach.

on the job *You will find that the* **XmlReader** *and* **XmlWriter** *classes are extremely useful when combined with the* **DataSet** *object. They give us a very quick way to put XML from a file into a* **DataSet** *object and write it back to a file again. The value here is that we have more control over the stream of XML when using an* **XmlReader** *and* **XmlWriter** *class. We will see more detail on this in the next section.*

The Document Object Model (DOM) and the *DataSet*

Where it is valuable to manipulate XML, in a hierarchical manner, it is preferable to use the *Document Object Model (DOM),* which treats an XML document as the root node for a structure of child nodes. The child nodes represent the XML data within the document, which is very similar to the structure of a file system. This is done through the *XmlDocument* object, which exposes the child nodes in a collection called, interestingly enough, *ChildNodes.*

The data within the *XmlDocument* is cached (not directly linked to the file) and fully editable (you can change it). However, you will have to use a *TextReader* or similar object to retrieve the data to the file and a *TextWriter* or similar object to write the data back to the file. The following code loads the Employees.xml file into an *XmlDocument* object and prints out the Employees file:

```
'Create an XMLDocument from a file
Dim dom As New XmlDocument()

'Open the file and read it as a string
Dim sin As New StreamReader(Server.MapPath("Employees.xml"))
Dim sXML As String = sin.ReadToEnd()
sin.Close()

'Load the XML from a file
dom.LoadXml(sXML)
```

```
'Write out each node
Dim node As XmlNode
For Each node In dom.ChildNodes(1).ChildNodes
  Response.Write(node.ChildNodes(0).InnerText & " " & _
                 node.ChildNodes(1).InnerText)
  Response.Write("<br>")
Next
```

The most noticeable thing about this code is that we must navigate the nodes to find the information we are looking for. You can make changes to the nodes within the *XmlDocument,* which can later be rewritten to the file from which we originally read. This can be done with the *Save* method. A full discussion of the Document Object Model is beyond the scope of this text, but because it is a standardized method for accessing XML data, it is recommended that you investigate it further.

exam
Ⓦatch
The XML DOM is very popular in Web-based development. It is very tempting, when given choices, to latch on to the first option you come across and work with it exclusively. In this case, many readers might be tempted to use the **DataSet** *object for all of their needs but DOM should not be overlooked—not only for your own purposes but for the sake of the exam. That said, DOM was designed to access data and the editing capabilities are not very robust. We certainly would not use it to retrieve data from a database and make changes to that data like we would with the* **DataSet** *object.*

The next object we will look at is the *DataSet* object. As noted previously, the *DataSet* object stores its data in an XML format, which makes it perfectly suited for dealing with XML files. One of the most valuable characteristics of using the *DataSet* object is that we can manipulate the data from an XML file in a relational way using the same techniques we used previously when accessing a database. This gives us a valuable option when compared with the *XmlDocument* object (hierarchical manipulation) and the *XmlReader* object (serial manipulation). XML data access revolves around the following methods:

- **ReadXml**   Loads XML data from an *XmlReader,* stream, *TextReader,* or directly from a file.

- **WriteXml**   Writes XML data to a stream, *TextWriter, XmlWriter,* or directly to a file.

■ **ReadXmlSchema**   Loads an XML schema from an *XmlReader,* stream, *TextReader,* or directly from a file. The file or stream must contain XML schema.

■ **WriteXmlSchema**   Writes XML schema to an *XmlReader,* stream, *TextReader,* or directly to a file. The file or stream must contain XML schema.

■ **InferXmlSchema**   Can infer or generate an XML schema from XML data in a stream or file. Note that this is a best guess at the schema and might not truly represent the schema of the data.

The following example loads our Employees.xml file into a *DataSet* object:

```
'Create a DataSet object
Dim ds As New DataSet()

'Open the file and read it as a string
ds.ReadXml(Server.MapPath("Employees.xml"))

'Write out each node
Dim i As Integer
For i = 0 To ds.Tables(0).Rows.Count - 1
  Response.Write(ds.Tables(0).Rows(i).Item(0) & " " & _
                 ds.Tables(0).Rows(i).Item(1))
  Response.Write("<br>")
Next i
```

You should note that aside from the *ReadXml* method we have used to load the data, everything else works the same way it did when we loaded data from a SQL Server or Microsoft Access database. This is the real value of the *DataSet;* one set of methods to manipulate all types of data. Once any changes are made, we can simply update the underlying XML file using the *WriteXml* method of the *DataSet* object.

One small issue that arises when using the *DataSet* object is how it is synchronized with the underlying XML file. Simply put, it is not. When you read the XML file, only the XML that is recognized is loaded into the *DataSet,* which means comments and tags that do not satisfy the schema being used are not loaded. When the XML is written back to the file, the file is overwritten with the XML from the *DataSet.* This means any comments and any tags that do not satisfy the schema will be lost.

If you desire synchronization, you can use the *XmlDataDocument* object as a source of data instead of the XML file itself. This also enables us to use a *DataSet* style relational view of the XML data and an *XmlDocument* style hierarchical view, which can be synchronized. Any changes made to the *DataSet* then would be visible through the *XmlDataDocument* and vice versa. This essentially works by loading the XML data into the *XmlDataDocument,* which contains a *DataSet* object as a member.

If you wish to use the hierarchical view, you use the *XmlDataDocument;* if you wish to use the relational view, you use the *DataSet* contained within. This way both views of the data are synchronized because there is only one actual copy of the data. The *XmlDataDocument* also loads the entire XML data, does not ignore information that violates schema, and does not ignore comments or whitespace. The following example loads our Employee.xml file using an *XmlDataDocument* and reads the records from the *DataSet* held within:

```
'Create an XmlDataDocument
Dim xdd As New XmlDataDocument()

'Open the file and read it as a string
Dim sin As New StreamReader(Server.MapPath("Employees.xml"))
Dim sXML As String = sin.ReadToEnd()
sin.Close()

'Get the DataSet object and create the schema
Dim ds As DataSet = xdd.DataSet()
ds.InferXmlSchema(Server.MapPath("Employees.xml"), Nothing)

'Load the XML from a file
xdd.LoadXml(sXML)

'Write out each record
Dim i As Integer
For i = 0 To ds.Tables(0).Rows.Count - 1
  Response.Write(ds.Tables(0).Rows(i).Item(0) & " " & _
                 ds.Tables(0).Rows(i).Item(1))
  Response.Write("<br>")
Next
```

The first thing to note is that we must have a schema in the *DataSet* object to access any of the XML data. This schema is used to determine what data to expose, and in our case, we simply inferred the schema from the original data file. We also could have created one or more schema files for our project and used one of those. On another note, you must remember to set the schema before you load the XML data. Once the XML data is loaded, you cannot change the *DataSet* object's schema. After the data is loaded, you can manipulate it in the same way we have done previously and it will stay synchronized with the *XmlDataDocument.*

As you have seen, there are many different types of data available to our Web applications and many different ways to access this data. The *DataSet* object is the glue that ties all of this data together, and enables us to use very standard techniques to access and manipulate this data. By taking advantage of this standardization, you will be able to create robust and reusable data-access Web applications that can manipulate data from disparate data sources.

EXERCISE 7-1

Access and Manipulate Data from a Data Store

In this exercise, we will return the Beverages from the Products table of the Northwind sample database that ships with Microsoft Access. We will be using a *DataSet* object to store and manipulate the records and when we are finished, we will update the underlying data source with the *DataAdapter*. Ensure that as you move through the exercise, you understand everything that ensues. If you are unclear of any code you see, look back to the appropriate section in this chapter.

1. Launch Visual Studio.

2. Create a new ASP.NET application.

3. Open the code-behind for the Webform1.aspx file.

4. Add the imports for the ADO.NET and the OLEDB Data Provider, as shown here:

```
Imports System.Data
Imports System.Data.OleDbClient
Imports System.Data.OleDb.OleDbTypes
```

5. Create an *OleDbConnection* object using the constructor that takes a connection string. Make sure your connection string is appropriate for your database.

6. Create a new *OleDbDataAdapter* object using the default constructor.

7. Create an *OleDbCommand* object using the following SQL statement; this *OleDbCommand* will be used as the *SelectCommand:*

```
SELECT ProductID, ProductName FROM Products WHERE CategoryID = 1
```

8. Create an *OleDbCommand* object using the following SQL statement. This *OleDbCommand* will be used as the *InsertCommand:*

```
INSERT INTO Products (ProductName) VALUES (@ProductName)
```

9. Create appropriate *OleDbParameter* objects for the *InsertCommand* you have just created and store them in the *Parameters* collection.

10. Create an *OleDbCommand* object using the following SQL statement; this *OleDbCommand* will be used as the *UpdateCommand:*

```
UPDATE Products SET ProductName = @ProductName WHERE ProductID =
@ProductID
```

11. Create appropriate *OleDbParameter* objects for the *UpdateCommand* you have just created and store them in the *Parameters* collection.

12. Create an *OleDbCommand* object using the following SQL statement; this *OleDbCommand* will be used as the *DeleteCommand:*

```
DELETE FROM Products WHERE ProductID = @ProductID
```

13. Create appropriate *OleDbParameter* objects for the *DeleteCommand* you have just created and store them in the *Parameters* collection.

14. Add the four *OleDbCommands* you have just created to the *OleDbDataAdapter.* Use the appropriate command properties.

15. Create a new *DataSet,* fill it, and print out the ProductName field for all of the records to the Web page using the *Response* object.

16. Add a new product to the *DataSet* (remember the ProductID is an Identity column and its value will be set by the database so you only need to set the ProductName). Call the product "Go Juice."

17. Change the first records ProductName to "Good Tea."

18. We won't delete any records because it would violate referential integrity.

19. Update the database with the changes you have made and write to the page the number of rows affected.

20. Write the ProductName field for the records to the page one more time.

21. Compile and test your code.

22. Your code should look similar to this:

```
'Create the connection to the database and open it
Dim cn As New OleDbConnection("Provider=Microsoft.Jet.OLEDB.4.0;" & _
        "User ID=Admin;" & _
        "Data Source=C:\Inetpub\wwwroot\Connection\bin\Norwind.mdb")

'Create a new DataAdapter object
```

```
Dim da As New OleDbDataAdapter()

'Create the Select Command
Dim comSelect As New OleDbCommand("SELECT ProductID, ProductName " & _
                    "FROM Products WHERE CategoryID = 1", cn)

'Create the Insert Command
Dim comInsert As New OleDbCommand("INSERT INTO Products "& _
                    "(ProductName) VALUES (@ProductName)", cn)

'Add the Insert Command's Parameters
comInsert.Parameters.Add(New OleDbParameter("@ProductName", _
                    VarWChar, 40, _
                    ParameterDirection.Input, _
                    False, CType(0, Byte), CType(0, Byte), _
                    "ProductName", DataRowVersion.Current, Nothing))

'Create the Update Command
Dim comUpdate As New OleDbCommand("UPDATE Products SET ProductName " & _
                    "= @ProductName WHERE ProductID = @ProductID", cn)

'Add the Update Command's Parameters
comUpdate.Parameters.Add(New OleDbParameter("@ProductName", _
                    VarWChar, 40, _
                    ParameterDirection.Input, _
                    False, CType(0, Byte), CType(0, Byte), _
                    "ProductName", DataRowVersion.Current, Nothing))
comUpdate.Parameters.Add(New OleDbParameter("@ProductID", _
                    Integer, 4, _
                    ParameterDirection.Input, _
                    False, CType(0, Byte), CType(0, Byte), _
                    "ProductID", DataRowVersion.Current, Nothing))

'Create the Delete Command
Dim comDelete As New OleDbCommand("DELETE FROM Products WHERE " & _
                    "ProductID = @ProductID", cn)

'Add the Delete Command's Parameters
comDelete.Parameters.Add(New OleDbParameter("@ProductID", _
                    Integer, 4, _
                    ParameterDirection.Input, _
                    False, CType(0, Byte), CType(0, Byte), _
                    "ProductID", DataRowVersion.Current, Nothing))

'Add the Commands to the DataAdapter
da.SelectCommand = comSelect
da.InsertCommand = comInsert
da.UpdateCommand = comUpdate
da.DeleteCommand = comDelete
```

```
'Create a new DataSet
Dim ds As New DataSet()

'Get the records
da.Fill(ds, "Products")

'Write the records to the page
Dim i As Integer
For i = 0 To ds.Tables(0).Rows.Count - 1
  Response.Write(ds.Tables(0).Rows(i).Item(1) & "<br>")
Next i

'Add a new record
Dim row As DataRow = ds.Tables(0).NewRow()
row.Item("ProductName") = "Go Juice"
ds.Tables(0).Rows.Add(row)

'Change a record
ds.Tables(0).Rows(0).Item("ProductName") = "Good Tea"

'Make the changes permanent
Dim count As Integer = da.Update(ds, "Products")
Response.Write("<P>" & count & " Records Affected...</P>")

'Write the records to the page again
For i = 0 To ds.Tables(0).Rows.Count - 1
  Response.Write(ds.Tables(0).Rows(i).Item(1) & "<br>")
Next i
```

CERTIFICATION OBJECTIVE 7.02

Handle Data Errors

One of the most common things you will encounter when accessing a database are errors. Error handling when accessing a database is a special case. With normal error handling, one line of code can cause one error. If an error occurs, no further processing can occur until the error is dealt with. In the case of data access error handling, one SQL statement can cause multiple errors, which means we need a more flexible method of passing those errors to an error handler. For example, if we want to log all of the errors thrown as a result of an UPDATE statement, we would need a way to read and then store all of the errors thrown, not just the first one (assuming your *DataAdapter* has not been set up to fail after the first error is encountered).

To begin this discussion we will look at errors thrown when opening a connection to a database. This is one area where you can expect errors to be thrown on a regular basis. Many different problems can occur when opening a connection, such as

- Invalid user name and password
- The database server is down and not taking requests
- Invalid catalog within the database server (wrong database)
- Invalid server name
- Network connectivity problems

Different errors will be more or less common in different kinds of database applications. For example, if the server name is hard-coded (assuming that it is appropriate to do so), you should not get an invalid server name error unless a network administrator is playing games with the server name (something that should never happen). However, if the user must enter the server name to which he or she is connecting, this will be a common error for you to deal with, as users can make typing mistakes or forget the name of the server. You can catch these types of errors using the *SqlException* or *OleDbException* object. The *SqlException* object has the following common properties (for a full listing of its properties, see the MSDN Library):

- **Number** identifies the error number associated with the error.
- **Message** is the description of the error.
- **Class** is the severity level of the error.
- **Errors** is a collection of *SqlError* or *OleDbError* objects. This gives us access to all of the errors thrown.
- **Source** identifies the data provider that threw the error.
- **ToString** is a method that allows us to print the error to a stream.

You should note that the *SqlException* or *OleDbException* objects are set to the last error thrown. We will see soon how the *Errors* collection can be used to find all of the errors thrown as a result of accessing data from a database. The next code shows a typical exception handling structure used to open a connection:

```
Try
  'Make a connection and return the Employees table
  Dim cn As New SqlConnection("Data Source=(local); " & _
                              "Initial Catalog=Northwind; " & _
                              "Integrated Security=true")
  Dim da As New SqlDataAdapter("SELECT * FROM Employees", cn)
  Dim ds As New DataSet()
  da.Fill(ds)
Catch ex1 As System.Data.SqlClient.SqlException
  Select Case ex1.Number
    Case 18452
      Response.Write("Invalid UserName")
    Case 18456
      Response.Write("Invalid Password")
    Case 17
      Response.Write("Invalid Server Name")
    Case 4060
      Response.Write("Invalid Database")
  End Select
Catch ex2 As System.Exception
  Response.Write("Unknown Exception")
End Try
```

exam
ⓦatch

*It is not necessary to memorize all of the common error numbers. It is highly doubtful that Exam 70-305 would ever expect you to recognize a specific error number from a database. Make sure you do understand the difference between the **SqlException**, **OleDbException**, and **System.Exception**.*

When accessing data from a database, we often run into the previously mentioned problem of multiple errors for a single SQL statement. For situations such as these, we need to use the *Errors* collection to gain access to all of the errors. The *Errors* collection contains *SqlError* or *OleDbError* objects. These objects contain the following properties used to identify the error that has occurred:

- **Number** identifies the error number associated with the error.
- **Message** is the description of the error.
- **Class** is the severity level of the error.
- **LineNumber** is the line number in the batch SQL statement or stored procedure that caused the error.
- **Procedure** is the name of the stored procedure that caused the error.

- **Source** identifies the data provider that threw the error.

- **ToString** returns a string containing the error information.

The following example executes a SQL statement through a *SqlCommand* object and lists all of the errors (if any) thrown on a Web page:

```
Try
  Dim cn As New SqlConnection("Data Source=(local); " & _
                              "Initial Catalog=Northwind; " & _
                              "Integrated Security=true")
  cn.Open()
  Dim com As New SqlCommand("UPDATE Employees SET Salary = " & _
                            "Salary * 1.10", cn)
  com.ExecuteNonQuery()
  cn.Close()
Catch ex1 As System.Data.SqlClient.SqlException
  Dim i As Integer
  For i = 0 To ex1.Errors.Count - 1
    Response.Write("Error number " & i & "<br>")
    Response.Write("Number: " & ex1.Errors(i).Number & "<br>")
    Response.Write("Description: " & ex1.Errors(i).Message & _
                   "<br><br>")
  Next i
End Try
```

In this example, we are increasing the salary of all employees in the Employees table of our database by ten percent. If we had a constraint placed on the Salary field that specified that the maximum salary was $100,000.00, this would cause an error for any employee whose salary was equal to or greater than approximately $90,910.00. This could cause any number of errors, to which we would have access through the *Errors* collection.

CERTIFICATION SUMMARY

In this chapter, we have accessed disparate data sources by using the OLEDB data provider for ADO.NET. This data provider gives us access to many different types of data stores, including Microsoft Access, Oracle, Flat Files, and many more. We also have seen how Visual Studio .NET provides design-time access to visual tools that can greatly simplify the process of accessing these storehouses of data. We did this primarily using the Server Explorer window, which allows us to link to a database, and drag tables and stored procedures onto our Web pages, thus writing the code necessary to access them.

The XML file format is fast becoming the data currency of the Internet, and as such, we have examined the different ways to manipulate such data. We used the *XmlReader* and *XmlWriter* objects to read and write XML data as a stream. When looking for a more structured approach to manipulating XML, we can use the *DataSet* object for a relational approach and the *XmlDocument* object for a hierarchical approach. We also have seen how the *XmlDataDocument* can give us access to an internal *DataSet* object and thus give us access to both approaches.

In the final section of this chapter, we used Structured Exception Handling to deal with errors that commonly occur while accessing a data store. These errors could be single errors such as the result of passing an incorrect connection string or multiple errors such as the result of an UPDATE statement that violates a constraint on a field in the database. This unique form of error handling was addressed using the *SqlException* and *OleDbException* objects.

TWO-MINUTE DRILL

Access and Manipulate Data from a Data Store

❑ ADO.NET can be used to access almost any type of data.

❑ The OLEDB data provider gives us access to disparate data sources.

❑ When using the OLEDB data provider to execute a stored procedure we must add parameters to the *Parameters* collection of the *OleDbCommand* object in the order they appear in the stored procedure. This is not necessary with the SQL Server data provider.

❑ Visual Studio .NET contains visual tools for generating data access code.

❑ The Server Explorer window can be used to administrate services on a server from Visual Studio .NET.

❑ You can generate *Connection* and *DataAdapter* objects by dragging a table from a database in the Server Explorer onto a Web page.

❑ A strongly typed *DataSet* is a class that is derived from the *DataSet* object, and makes programming with a *DataSet* easier and less error prone.

❑ Web server controls can be bound to a *DataSet* object.

❑ You can use the *XmlReader* and *XmlWriter* objects to read and write XML data from and to a stream.

❑ The Document Object Model (DOM) is a hierarchical object model that allows us to programmatically manipulate XML data.

❑ The *XmlDocument* object contains a representation of XML data consistent with the Document Object Model.

❑ The *XmlDataDocument* object contains a representation of XML data consistent with the Document Object Model as well as a *DataSet* property that gives us a relational view of the same data.

Handle Data Errors

❑ One SQL statement can trigger multiple errors at the same time.

❑ The *SqlException* and *OleDbException* objects are thrown by the SQL Server and OLEDB data providers respectively when data access errors occur.

❑ The *SqlException* and *OleDbException* object both have an *Errors* collection, which allows us to see all of the errors which occurred as the result of a data transaction.

SELF TEST

The following questions will help you measure your understanding of the material presented in this chapter. Read all the choices carefully as there might be more than one correct answer. Choose all correct answers for each question.

Access and Manipulate Data from a Data Store

1. With ADO.NET, we can access which of the following data sources? (Choose all that apply.)

   A. Microsoft Access

   B. Oracle

   C. Microsoft SQL Server

   D. DB2

2. You are working on an application that retrieves its data from a flat file. Which data provider would you use? (Choose the best answer.)

   A. SQL Server provider.

   B. OLEDB provider.

   C. ODBC provider.

   D. You cannot access a flat file with a data provider.

3. Which class, provided by the OLEDB data provider, stores records returned from a data source?

   A. *DataSet*

   B. *OleDbDataSet*

   C. *OleDbDataReader*

   D. *DataReaderOleDb*

4. You have transferred your Access database to a SQL Server database and now must change your application to use the new database. What will you have to change in your application for this to work? (Choose all that apply.)

   A. Change the database library you are using and rewrite all of the data access code.

   B. Change the name of all provider objects from OleDb<Object> to Sql<Object> (such as OleDbConnection to SqlConnection, OleDbCommand to SqlCommand, and so forth).

   C. Change the connection string used by the Connection object to point to the new database.

   D. Create a Data Source Name (DSN) that points to the new SQL Server database.

5. You are executing a parameterized stored procedure on a database using a *Command* object. Which provider does not expect the parameters to be added to the *Command* object in the same order they appear in the stored procedure?

   A. SQL Server Provider

   B. ODBC Provider

   C. OLEDB Provider

   D. None of the above

6. How can you create a strongly typed *DataSet* in Visual Studio?

   A. Right-click a DataAdapter object and select Generate DataSet.

   B. Use the DataSet Wizard.

   C. Use the DataSet generation tool.

   D. Set the DataSet object's Type property to Typed.

7. The Server Explorer in Visual Studio .NET can do which of the following? (Choose all that apply.)

   A. View a server's event logs.

   B. Add and remove programs on a server.

   C. Add a table to a SQL Server database.

   D. Administer Message Queues.

8. You are loading an XML file into a *DataSet* object. When you save the changes made to the *DataSet* object back to the XML file, you notice that the original comments in the XML file have disappeared. Which of the following is a viable solution to this problem?

   A. Use an *XmlDocument* object instead of a *DataSet* object and change the code you are using to access the information.

   B. This is a known problem with the *DataSet* object and there is no solution.

   C. Use an *XmlDocument* object to create your *DataSet* object. This way the *DataSet* object will stay synchronized with the underlying XML file.

   D. Use an *XmlDataDocument* object to create your *DataSet* object. This way the *DataSet* object will stay synchronized with the underlying XML file.

9. The *DataMember* property of the *DataGrid* control should be set to _____ when the *DataSource* property has been set to a *DataSet* object. (Choose the best answer.)

   A. A column in the *DataSet*.

   B. A table in the *DataSet*.

    C. Nothing; it is not needed when using a *DataSet* as a source of data.

    D. This is a trick question. The *DataMember* property should be set to the *DataSet* object and the *DataSource* property should be set to a column in the *DataSet*.

10. You wish to read and write XML to and from a file using an *XmlReader* and *XmlWriter* class. These two classes are abstract classes, meaning you cannot create an instance of them directly, but instead can create only an instance of classes that are derived from them. Which classes are derived from *XmlReader* and *XmlWriter* that allow you to read and write XML to a text file? (Choose all that apply.)

    A. *XmlDataReader*

    B. *XmlTextReader*

    C. *XmlDataWriter*

    D. *XmlTextWriter*

11. Which of the following developed the XML standard?

    A. Microsoft

    B. Sun Microsystems

    C. The Object Management Group (OMG)

    D. The World Wide Web Consortium (W3C)

12. You are using an *XmlDataDocument* and a *DataSet* object to view some XML data. Before loading the XML into the *XmlDataDocument,* you must get a reference to its *DataSet* object through its *DataSet* method. Once you have this reference, what must you do to the *DataSet* object before you load the XML into the *XmlDataDocument* to be able to view the data through the *DataSet* object?

    A. Set its synchronize property to true.

    B. You must create a table within the *DataSet* to hold the XML data.

    C. Nothing.

    D. Load an XML schema that indicates which data you wish to view.

13. The *XmlWriter* object treats XML data as which of the following?

    A. A stream of XML

    B. A hierarchical object model of XML

    C. A relational object model of XML

    D. None of the above

14. You have created a Web application that uses stored procedures. Which of the following properties of the *SqlError* or *OleDbError* objects can help you figure out which stored procedure is causing the error and where in the stored procedure the error is being thrown? (Choose all that apply.)

A. *ErrorStatement*

B. *LineNumber*

C. *Procedure*

D. *ProcedureName*

15. The *DataSet* object can make a best guess at the schema of the XML data with which of the following methods?

A. *WriteXMLSchema*

B. *WriteXML*

C. *DetermineXMLSchema*

D. *InferXMLSchema*

Handle Data Errors

16. You have created a Web application that uses a SQL Server database but you cannot get it to open a connection. Which of the following errors would be a good candidate to catch? (Choose all that apply.)

A. 18452—Invalid user name

B. 17—Invalid server name

C. 2812—Stored procedure not found

D. 4060—Invalid database

17. XML data from a file can be synchronized with XML data within a *DataSet* object by using which of the following objects?

A. *XmlReader*

B. *XmlDataDocument*

C. *XmlDocument*

D. None of the above

18. Which of the following activities can you perform on a SQL Server database through the Server Explorer in Visual Studio .NET?

    A. Create a new database.

    B. Create a database diagram.

    C. Add or remove a table in a database.

    D. Create and edit a stored procedure.

    E. All of the above.

19. The Class property of the *SqlError* object is used to specify which of the following?

    A. The type of error that occurred.

    B. The severity level of the error.

    C. The type of provider throwing the error.

    D. This property is for future use and is not employed presently.

20. To access the FirstName field of the first record in a strongly typed *DataSet* (called dsEmployees) that contains an Employees table (holding the fields EmployeeID, FirstName, and LastName in that order) we would use which of the following code? (Choose the best answer.)

    A. dsEmployees.Tables("Employees").Rows(0).Item("FirstName")

    B. dsEmployees.Employees(0).FirstName

    C. dsEmployees.Tables(0).Rows(0).Item(1)

    D. dsEmployees.Fields!FirstName

LAB QUESTION

You are writing a Web application that must retrieve data from an XML document and display it to users. You have decided to use a *DataSet* to store the records. The XML file contains the following: The XML file is called "Bank.xml."

This file contains data that represents a person's bank accounts and the root node is called "Accounts" with child Account nodes that have the following members:

- AccountID (an attribute that is an integer representing the Account Number)

- Description (a string representing the type of account, such as Chequing)

- Balance (a floating point number representing the current balance)

You can use the following XML file (which you should create in Visual Studio .NET using the XML Editor; don't use Notepad):

```
<?xml version="1.0" encoding="utf-8" ?>
<Accounts>
        <Account AccountID="1">
                <Description>Savings</Description>
                <Balance>500.00</Balance>
        </Account>
        <Account AccountID="2">
                <Description>Chequing</Description>
                <Balance>1200.00</Balance>
        </Account>
        <Account AccountID="3">
                <Description>Line of Credit</Description>
                <Balance>-250.00</Balance>
        </Account>
        <Account AccountID="4">
                <Description>Stock Portfolio</Description>
                <Balance>13500.00</Balance>
        </Account>
</Accounts>
```

In this exercise, you will load the XML file into a *DataSet* object in any manner you choose (there is more than one way to skin this cat). Once the data has been loaded, you should print the account information for the user to a table .

SELF TEST ANSWERS

Access and Manipulate Data from a Data Store

1. ☑   A, B, C, and D. ADO.NET can access multiple data sources.

2. ☑   B. The ADO.NET OLEDB provider contains a Simple provider for accessing flat files.
    ☒   A is incorrect because the SQL Server provider is used to access a SQL Server database. C is incorrect because ODBC was designed to access relational databases and does not have robust access to flat files. D is incorrect because you can access a flat file with the OLEDB data provider.

3. ☑   C. The *OleDbDataReader* class is provided by the OLEDB data provider to store records returned from a data source.
    ☒   A, which is the *DataSet,* can store records returned from a data source but it is not provided by the OLEDB provider. B and D are not classes in ADO.NET.

4. ☑   B and C. Assuming the data and its structure have not changed, all you will need to do is switch over to the SQL Server provider and change the connection string.
    ☒   A is incorrect because ADO.NET does not require the use of a specific proprietary database library, which means changing the provider is sufficient, and no further changes to your code are necessary. In D, if you are using a DSN, this would be required, but it is not necessary to use a DSN with ADO.NET.

5. ☑   A. The SQL Server provider allows you to add parameters in any order as long as the name of the parameter matches the name found in the stored procedure.
    ☒   B, C, and D are incorrect. When using the ODBC and OLEDB providers, you must add parameters to the *Command* object in the same order they appear in the stored procedure.

6. ☑   A is one way to create a strongly typed *DataSet* in Visual Studio .NET.
    ☒   B, C, and D are incorrect and do not exist.

7. ☑   A, C, and D. You can view a server's event logs, add a table or other database object to a SQL Server database, administer message queues, and much more through the Server Explorer in Visual Studio .NET.
    ☒   B is incorrect because you cannot install software through the Server Explorer.

8. ☑   D. You can get the *XmlDataDocument* to load the XML file and create a *DataSet* object for you, which then will be synchronized with your XML file. This means you will not lose any information in the underlying XML file when you write it back to disk.
    ☒   A is a possible solution; however, it should not be necessary to change your data access code. B is incorrect because D is the solution. C is incorrect because the *XmlDocument* object cannot create a *DataSet* object for you.

9. ☑   B. The *DataMember* property of the *DataGrid* control should be set to a table within the *DataSet*.

    ☒   A is incorrect and we should remember that a *DataGrid* control is designed to display a table, not a single column (although it is possible). C is not completely incorrect, but if you set the *DataMember* property to nothing, it will default to the default view of the *DataSet*. D is incorrect because this is not a trick question.

10. ☑   B and D. *XmlTextReader* and *XmlTextWriter* are derived from *XmlReader* and *XmlWriter* and allow you to read and write XML to a text file.

    ☒   A and C are incorrect because they are not classes.

11. ☑   D. The XML standard was developed by the World Wide Web Consortium (W3C).

    ☒   A is incorrect, as Microsoft did not develop it but it certainly recognized its value. B also is wrong; Sun Microsystems developed the Java standard but not the XML standard. In C, the Object Management Group developed the CORBA standard, which is similar to COM.

12. ☑   D. You must load XML schema (which can be obtained directly from an XSD file or inferred from the XML file) into the *DataSet* to view any of the data.

    ☒   A is incorrect because there is no synchronize property. B isn't quite right because although you can manually create a table in a *DataSet* object, this will not help us here. C is not correct because D is correct.

13. ☑   A. The *XmlWriter* object treats XML data as a stream.

    ☒   In B, the *XmlDocument* object treats XML data as a hierarchical object model. C is wrong because the *DataSet* object treats XML data as a relational object model. D is incorrect because A is correct.

14. ☑   B and C. The LineNumber and Procedure properties specify the line number in the stored procedure where the error was raised and the procedure that caused the error.

    ☒   A and D are incorrect because they are not properties of the *SqlError* or *OleDbError* objects.

15. ☑   D. *InferXMLSchema* will make a best guess at the schema of XML data from the data itself.

    ☒   A is wrong because *WriteXMLSchema* writes the schema to a stream. B is incorrect because *WriteXML* writes the data to a stream. C is not a method of the *DataSet* object.

Handle Data Errors

16. ☑   A, B, and D all are possible problems, which would prevent you from opening a connection with the database from a Web application; therefore, they should be caught.

    ☒   C is incorrect because if the connection cannot be opened, we would not have a chance to try and execute a stored procedure.

17. ☑ B. The *XmlDataDocument* allows us to synchronize an XML file with the data within a *DataSet* object.

☒ A is incorrect because the *XmlReader* object is used only to transfer XML data from a file to a *DataSet* and does not keep it synchronized. C is incorrect because the *XmlDocument* does not work in conjunction with the *DataSet* object. D is incorrect because B is correct.

18. ☑ E. You can do all of this from the Server Explorer.

19. ☑ B. The Class property represents the severity level of the error that has been thrown.

☒ A is incorrect because the type of error thrown is determined with the Number and Message properties. C is incorrect because the type of provider is the SQL Server provider which can be determined by the fact that the object in question is the *SqlError* object. D is incorrect because this property is being used for the severity level.

20. ☑ B. This is the appropriate way to use a strongly typed *DataSet*.

☒ A is incorrect because this is the appropriate way to use an untyped *DataSet*. C is incorrect because this is another way to use an untyped *DataSet*. D is incorrect because this would only be appropriate for a *Recordset* object in ADO, not a *DataSet* in ADO.NET.

LAB ANSWER

You were asked to set up a *DataSet* to load an XML file containing bank account information. The code in your *Page_Load* event should look as follows:

```
'Create a DataSet object
Dim ds As New DataSet()

'Open the file and read it as a string
ds.ReadXml(Server.MapPath("Bank.xml"))

'Create the table header
Response.Write("<TABLE><TH><TD>Account ID</TD><TD>Description</TD>")
Response.Write("<TD>Balance</TD></TH>")

'Write out each node
Dim i As Integer
For i = 0 To ds.Tables(0).Rows.Count - 1
  Response.Write("<TR><TD>" & ds.Tables(0).Rows(i).Item(0) & _
                 "</TD><TD>" & ds.Tables(0).Rows(i).Item(1) & _
                 "</TD><TD>" & ds.Tables(0).Rows(i).Item(2) & _
                 "</TD></TR>")
Next i
Response.Write("</TABLE>")
```

MCAD/MCSD

MICROSOFT® CERTIFIED APPLICATION DEVELOPER
& MICROSOFT® CERTIFIED SOLUTION DEVELOPER

8

Test and Debug an ASP.NET Application

One of the most daunting problems with software development is the human factor: No matter how much of an expert you are, you will make mistakes. You can catch most of these mistakes while creating your software, or during unit testing. A few will be caught during formal system testing. Users will catch some. And a few (hopefully very few) might never be caught. We simply have to come to grips with the fact that there will be mistakes.

We also need to understand that the amount of time between when a mistake is made and a when a mistake is caught is directly proportional to the financial cost of the mistake. For this reason, the focus on errors and omissions in software should be to catch errors as quickly as possible after they are made. You can accomplish this by using many different strategies, such as code inspections, unit testing, system testing, and too many others to mention here.

In this chapter, we will focus on strategies developers can perform, of which the primary focus is on unit testing and debugging. Unit testing involves testing small units of code such as functions, objects, and pages (in the case of Web development). The theory is that it is much easier to test small bits of code then larger ones. If we test the bits before we put them together, any mistakes will be much less costly because we have caught them early on (right after we have created the bits).

It also is easier to test the bits after they are put together, as we can be fairly confident that any mistakes are caused by the integration of our units and not by the units themselves (although this should never be ruled out completely). It is important to remember that we are talking about formal testing; not just running some code to see if it works, which unfortunately is how many developers perform unit testing.

Formal testing involves creating test plans that can help us determine how our code will work in different situations and when it will fail. Often, these tests are performed by the developer of the unit but it is not uncommon in larger, highly structured development settings for there to be a separate testing section that performs unit testing. In most corporate environments, higher levels of testing, such as integration testing and system testing, usually are performed by separate testing sections (although your experience may vary based on the standards of your company).

In this chapter, we will look at the basics of unit testing and discuss some important concepts in creating unit test plans. We also will discuss some tools that Visual Studio .NET provides for us to help us test and debug our code. This includes tracing, which allows us to monitor our code while it is running, and the debugging environment, which can allow us to run code one line at a time, monitor the state of our data, and change the state to test different scenarios.

CERTIFICATION OBJECTIVE 8.01

Create a Unit Test Plan

Unit testing involves breaking down a program into logical units that perform tasks integral to the requirements of the software. These units often are functions, objects, or Web pages that have specific responsibilities and perform specific tasks. By formally testing these units before they are integrated into the application, we give ourselves an opportunity to catch any mistakes that were made very early in development.

When our units have been tested and the errors fixed, they can be integrated with other tested units to form the application. As units are put together, we can test the interaction of these units, which is called *integration testing*. This approach to testing is called the *Evolutionary* approach, which revolves around the fact that as you create and test units, you add them to the application. Every time you add a unit to the application, you add functionality to it and the application evolves.

It is important to understand the difference between testing and debugging. Testing is a formal process in which tests are planned and designed to inform us when a mistake is made, and to help us define the limitations of our application. Debugging is the process of determining the exact cause of a mistake so that we can fix it. It also is important to understand that testing is not the only way to find mistakes in software.

The following is a list of common techniques for finding defects in software and their approximate mean (average) defect detection rates. Note that these are approximate averages and the variation in detection rates is high. If you read through the common literature on defect detection, you will find widely varying reports, although when you look at the detection rates for different kinds of detection techniques, you will find that, regardless of the absolute rate reported, they are relatively stable in relation to each other.

Detection Technique	Description	Mean Detection Rate
Design Reviews	Formal review of a design.	50%
Code Inspections	Formal code walk-through by a development team.	60%
Prototyping	Building a small example of the full application to determine whether it will fulfill the requirements.	60%

Detection Technique	Description	Mean Detection Rate
Unit Testing	Testing of small units of code.	25%
Integration Testing	Testing as the system is built and when it is finished.	45%
User Testing	Testing in a work environment, also known as *live* testing.	50%
Combined Testing	Testing using all of the preceding techniques combined.	90%

You should note that the most effective method of testing is not unit testing. So why do we continue to use unit testing? Each type of defect detection technique finds different types of errors. For example, prototyping will not typically help you find errors in code, but it is excellent at finding errors in requirements (the requirements of the software were incorrectly determined). You also should notice that using all of the techniques listed gives us a detection rate of approximately 90 percent, which is not the sum of the rates for each individual technique. This is because many of the techniques will find some of the same errors.

The moral of this story is that any decent defect detection strategy should use a combination of techniques, not just a few. Once again, it is important to note that we will focus on unit testing. This discussion has been added so that we can grasp the role of unit testing in the overall defect detection process.

When planning unit tests, the main idea is to come up with enough unique tests so that you can find all of the defects in your code without performing many redundant tests. For example, suppose we have a Web page that will allow a user to enter his or her name for registration purposes. In planning our testing strategy, we could try 100 names from the phone book to see whether our application responded as expected.

The problem with this method is that it is not well thought out. We must consider that many of the names we would obtain from a phone book do not differ significantly enough to find different errors. For example, if we enter the name "Ted," we can determine whether our application could handle a three-letter string consisting of alphabetic characters. If we then enter the name "Ned," we would not learn anything new about our application. We might be able to safely assume that if the application works with "Ted," it will work with "Ned." This extra test would be redundant and therefore unnecessary.

It is therefore very important to know your data, know your code, and then determine the tests you will perform based on that understanding. For example, we know that if the name we are taking from this Web page is being stored in a database, there is most likely a maximum size for this string based on the requirements for the system; therefore, it would be useful to test a name that is just long enough to fit into the database (if the field size in the database is 20 characters, test a name with 20 characters). In this way, we can determine whether we have made a mistake defining the field in the database or in the code that transfers this information to the database.

This test definitely will tell us something the "Ned" test did not: whether our unit can process names of 20 characters as the requirements state. We then could test the application with a 21-character name, which we would expect to fail. If it does not fail, once again we have found a mistake, as the requirements clearly state that the maximum size of the name was 20 characters. If it does fail, we are testing our error-handling code to determine whether this error is handled correctly.

This is a very basic example and the tests mentioned certainly would not fully test the unit; however, the important point to understand is that the goal of unit testing is to learn about the behavior of the unit in all possible situations that produce unique behavior. This means using tests that differ enough so that they will shed light on different possible defects, not just planning tests and picking test data randomly.

One type of test is *exhaustive testing*, which involves trying every possible combination of data and ensuring that every line of code written has been exercised. This might seem logical, but in practice it is inefficient. As stated before, many of the tests would not help us to discover different defects, and therefore would be redundant. Even worse, it could take years to test the number of combinations of data that would have to be tested, even if the number of inputs is quite small (think about the number of possible combinations of data in a form that takes a name and address—it would be enormous).

For this reason, exhaustive testing is not a good approach to unit testing. Instead, we use many techniques for planning unit tests, which tend to shed light on different types of errors in an application. In the following sections, we will discuss these techniques. It is important to understand that these techniques are not mutually exclusive and are used together in an attempt to determine test cases that fully exercise our code while minimizing redundancy.

Structured Basis Test

The primary goal of *structured basis testing* is to exercise every line of code with a minimal number of tests. We do not focus on data, only the flow of our code, which also means structured basis testing tends to show us errors in the structure of our code and not with the values of data. The best way to approach this is to determine

FIGURE 8-1 A Web page that performs simple calculations

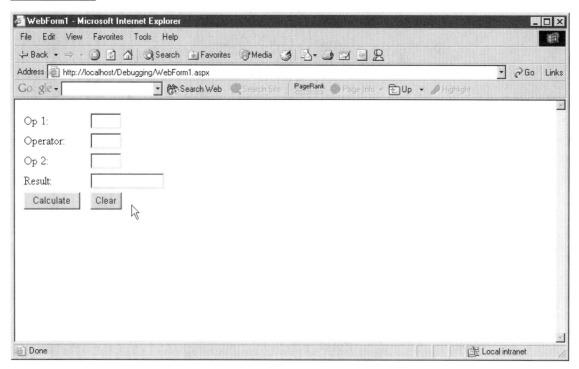

the number of tests needed to exercise every line of code and pick your test data based on this idea. You can use the following rules to determine the minimum number of tests to conduct to cover all of your bases:

- Add one test for the nominal path (or straight-through path) through your code.

- Add one test for each If statement, ElseIf statement, While loop, Do loop, And keyword, Or keyword, and Catch block in your unit.

- Add one test for each Case in a Select Case statement and add one more if the Case does not have a Case Else.

The next code example is taken from a page that performs simple calculations. The Web page looks like Figure 8-1.

The click event for the Calculate button looks like this:

```
'Initialize variables
Dim op1 As Double = CType(txtOp1.Text, Double)
```

```
Dim op2 As Double = CType(txtOp2.Text, Double)
Dim operator As String = txtOperator.Text
Dim result As Double

'Perform calculation
Select Case operator
  Case "+"
    result = op1 + op2
  Case "-"
    result = op1 - op2
  Case "*"
    result = op1 * op2
  Case "/"
    result = op1 / op2
  Case Else
    txtResult.Text = "Operation not supported"
    Exit Sub
End Select

'Set the result
txtResult.Text = result
```

If we use the preceding formula, we determine that we will need five tests to cover all of our bases. We need one test for the nominal path and four tests for the Select Case (one for each Case). Now that we know how many tests we need, we must define the state of the data for these tests. The following are the tests we will perform. You will notice that only variables that affect the flow of code are varied. The variables that do not alter the flow of code will be kept static. In this case, we will keep the op1 and op2 variables to a value of 5 each since they do not affect the flow of code.

1. The straight-through path in this case will represent the Case Else of the Select Case and, therefore, we will set the txtOperator text box to X, which will in turn set the operator variable to X.

2. For Case + we will set the txtOperator textbox to +.

3. For Case - we will set the txtOperator textbox to -.

4. For Case * we will set the txtOperator textbox to *.

5. For Case / we will set the txtOperator textbox to /.

Notice that the nominal path does not need to represent a normal condition. Also notice that our test cases will indeed exercise every line of code. You might be thinking that the preceding test cases would not be sufficient to fully test this unit and you would be correct. Structured basis testing tends to find errors in code structure (such as If statements that can never run because of a condition that can never be satisfied).

The test cases we have mentioned would not find an obvious defect in our code, which is the case when op2 = 0 and operator = / (a divide by zero for which we have no catch handler to handle it). The important thing to understand is that structured basis testing is only one tool we will use to plan our test cases and ensures that every line of code gets some exercise. It does not ensure that our code is fully tested but it does provide a good starting point.

Data-Flow Testing

Data-flow testing can be thought of as the opposite of structured basis testing in that we are now focusing on the data instead of the flow of our code. Data can exist in one of three states. Data can be *defined,* which means it has been initialized and contains a value; however, this data has not been used for anything yet. Data can be *used* in a calculation or as an argument to a function, which essentially means it has been read somehow. Finally, data can be *killed,* which means it is no longer accessible; this often happens when a variable goes out of scope or a file/database has been closed.

The first step in data-flow testing is to visually test for anomalous state sequences. A state sequence is the state of some data combined with a descriptor describing whether we have just *Entered* the unit or *Exited* the unit. For example, we would expect Entered-Defined to be a normal state sequence. The routine was entered and then the data was defined. However, we would not expect to see Entered-Used unless the data in question was not local to the unit. In other words, a local variable should be defined before it is used. You should check the state sequences for each chunk of data to make sure they make sense. The following are some examples of abnormal state sequences:

- **Defined-Defined** You should not need to initialize a variable twice to use it; this often appears when you have forgotten to use the variable before it was redefined.

- **Defined-Killed** If you aren't using some data, why create it?

- **Defined-Exited** If this is a global variable, it might make sense to enter a routine, initialize the global variable, and then exit; however, this is clearly an anomaly to a local variable.

- **Entered-Killed**   Once again, this could make sense with a global resource such as a file (a routine that closes a file); however, if this was a local variable, this would be a syntax error in VB.

- **Entered-Used**   Not a problem if this is a global resource, but with a local variable, this is a problem. You have forgotten to define the variable first.

- **Killed-Killed**   This is a clear problem and you probably should stop picking on this poor data (it's not nice to kick something when it's down).

- **Killed-Used**   This situation is much more common in languages such as C++ but it can still happen in VB. For example, if you set an object variable to nothing (which is the equivalent of killing it) and later try to use the variable, you will have a Killed-Used state.

- **Used-Defined**   This can happen in normal situations in which you redefine a variable (give it a value twice). You would see this as a Defined-Used-Defined state; however, if you do not see the first Defined, there is a problem.

For example, if you see a Defined-Killed sequence (the data was initialized and immediately killed), you most likely would find a bug. In other words, you have forgotten to do something with the data. The normal sequence of states should be Defined-Used-Killed (although at times other state sequences can make sense as well).

Once you have ruled out any problems with anomalous sequences, you can develop your data-flow test case. This is simply determining test cases that satisfy all Defined-Used sequences. In the following code, you will notice that there are two Defined-Used sequences for the variable *y:*

```
Dim X As Integer
Dim y As Integer

y = 0                  'y is defined
X = 500

If (y < 10) Then
  X *= y               'First Defined-Used Sequence
Else
  X += y               'Second Defined-Used sequence
End If

'Do something with X
```

You probably will find that many of your data-flow test cases are the same as your structured basis test cases, which is normal. The unique test cases derived from this method will be added to your list of test cases. You will notice in the preceding example that there would be no new test cases defined by data-flow testing.

Equivalence Partition

Equivalence partitioning is the idea that different test cases should flush out different errors. If you have two test cases that would discover the exact same errors, they are redundant and one of them can be removed from your list of test cases. This method does not tend to help you find new test cases that you have found with structured basis testing and data-flow, but instead helps to minimize the number of test cases needed to fully test your unit. However, this method is very useful when looking at a unit from the outside. It enables us to plan tests related to the interface of the unit (the arguments to a function, for example).

Error Guess

Error guessing is simply the idea that our experience shows us that some mistakes are common and we are more likely to catch these mistakes with certain specific tests. This is one argument for keeping error logs on coding mistakes. The most common types of errors can be caught using different kinds of analysis on your data. Error guessing is very datacentric.

Boundary Analysis

Boundary analysis revolves around the idea that most errors occur on the boundaries of data. For example, an off by one error—which probably will be the most common mistake you make in programming—often is a type of boundary error. This occurs when a value is one more or one less than the value it should have or that you expect it to have. You often see these when using the counter variable from a *For* loop after the loop has finished.

Boundary errors also are very common when using the value 0. 0 is a boundary between negative numbers and positive numbers and therefore is prone to errors. Often you will find this in a divide by zero error. Other types of boundary errors occur when we use comparisons. It is quite common to use the wrong operators (such as using >= instead of >), which cause you to think a value is on one side of a logical boundary when it really is on the other.

FROM THE CLASSROOM

Store Your Errors in a Database

Tracking detailed error information might seem like a large work project. To be truly useful, you really need to store this information in an easy-to-search format such as a database, which can involve a lot of development overhead in itself. It can also, on the other hand, be one of the most useful assets a development team can have. By understanding the most common mistakes, we can ensure that, during testing, we give special attention to these possible defects and ensure that we catch them. This is very useful because about 80 percent of your mistakes, are the same mistakes made over and over again. By testing for these common mistakes we can reduce the error pool by 80 percent right off the bat, which often can drastically reduce the time spent determining a suite of test cases.

When you set up a database of errors, store lots of information on the errors. What type of application it was, what type of variable caused the problem, whether it was a structural error, what the symptom was, and so forth. With all of this information, you can generate lists of common errors for each type of software you create. When you work on a new project, you can generate a list of common errors for that type of project and then move through the process of developing test cases based on the techniques we are looking at in this chapter. You will most likely find that with a list of common errors, you have to add very few test cases to the list to fully exercise your code. You also will find that the number of errors that gets through testing will decrease steadily as long as you keep the error database up to date.

—*Wayne Cassidy, Bsc, MCSD, MCT*

The most important point about boundary analysis is that you must know your data. By understanding your data, you will understand the boundaries of that data, which is where you will find most of the mistakes. Once you have defined your boundaries, you can test the boundary by supplying test data to test the valid side of the boundary, the boundary itself, and the invalid side of the boundary. For example, to test the boundary seen in the following *If* statement, we need three values for the test data *Y*:

```
Dim Y as Integer
Dim X as Integer
Y = 10
If(Y >= 10) Then
```

```
   X = 5
Else
   X = 10
End If
```

The test cases we would need to fully test the boundary of the If statement would be as follows:

1. The true side of the boundary with the value Y = 9.

2. The boundary itself with Y = 10 (this is where you would discover that you instead meant to write Y > 10—that is, if you got an unexpected outcome with the preceding code).

3. The false side of the boundary with the value Y = 11.

Bad Data

Bad data is one of the most common areas in which to find defects. Giving a unit some bad data should not cause the unit to crash; this obviously is not desirable to users. Can you imagine a login dialog box that causes your computer to crash when someone forgets to enter their user name? This is an overexaggerated example, but it proves a certain point: If you do not handle situations in which bad data is given to a unit (you can do this with structured exception handling or preemptive error checking), your applications will not be robust and fault tolerant, which can make the difference in user acceptance (would you use a system that crashed every time you forgot to enter your user name?).

One common problem with testing is that we often tend to ignore bad data and test thoroughly with good data. If we don't test with bad data, we won't know how our application responds to it. Will it handle it well and continue, or will it fail? Bad data can be categorized into different classes:

■ **Too Little Data**   It is very common to provide a unit with too little data. If you pass too few arguments to a function, your code will not compile; therefore, we rarely need to test for this. However, when passing arrays of information it can be very common to pass too few data. For example, will your unit (which we will assume takes an array as an argument) handle the case in which it is passed a valid array that contains no valid elements (a zero length array)? Does the unit respond with correct behavior (throw an error, return an appropriate value for this condition, and so forth) or does it respond inappropriately (try to read beyond the bounds of the array).

- **Too Much Data**   It also is common to have too much data. For example, if we have a unit that sorted an array, what is too much data? Exactly how many data elements can an array contain? One limit on this is the length property. The length property is an Integer, which means it wouldn't make much sense to have an array with greater than 2,147,483,647 elements. Of course, if this was an array of integers, you would need a system with 7.9GB of free memory for this allocation to work (very doubtful). That doesn't even take into consideration working memory to perform the sort. We need to determine how much data is too much data and how our application responds to too much data.

- **Wrong Kind of Data**   In many circumstances, a program will not compile if a unit within the program is called with the wrong kind of data. For example, a unit expects an Integer as an argument and receives a String instead. In other situations, such as when a user enters information on a Web page, the wrong kind of data can be entered without a compiler catching it (entering a number into a textbox that expects a name). The question is this: How will your unit respond to the wrong kind of data? One important thing to remember is that you should not look at kinds of data from a programmer's perspective but instead from the logical perspective of the problem domain. In other words, the types of data we are dealing with are things such as addresses, names, test scores, and so forth. You should test your units to see how they react to bad types of data even if they do not challenge the type-checking system (if we pass a unit the number 300 when it expects the number of tires a vehicle has, will it respond appropriately?).

- **Uninitialized Data**   In Visual Basic, if you do not explicitly initialize a variable, it will be initialized to a null value (0, empty string, nothing, and so forth) for you. For this reason, it is often hard to see how data can be uninitialized. In this situation, we must simply consider the situation in which we pass null values to a unit and do not need to worry about truly uninitialized data as we would in C++. If a unit expects to use an object through a variable and that variable has not explicitly been initialized to reference a valid object, how will the unit react? These kinds of tests are very important as it will often catch null pointer exceptions. This is the case in which you try to execute a method on a null pointer (an object reference in Visual Basic that does not reference a valid object but instead has been set to nothing).

Analyzing bad data is especially good for finding omissions on error handling. We basically are looking at how our unit responds to mistakes, which is a very effective way to determine whether you have missed a catch block or have not checked the input data well enough. For this reason, it is very important to focus heavily on analyzing bad data to create units that are tolerant to inappropriate data and can respond with little inconvenience to the user.

One other purpose for analyzing bad data is that it is an effective way to determine the limitations of a unit. This is necessary to prevent unexpected errors. You need to know and document the situations in which a unit will fail and what will happen when it fails (whether errors are handled properly).

Good Data

Interestingly, we often focus so much on areas that are known to cause many problems (such as boundaries) that we forget to test appropriate data properly. This involves testing nominal data, maximum and minimum values of good data (which most often is covered in a boundary analysis), and old data if this is not the first iteration of this unit.

■ **Nominal Data**   Data we expect to be used with our application. Some knowledge of statistics can be extremely valuable in analyzing nominal data. We must understand the distribution of nominal data (how the data is distributed across reasonable values for the data). This can be tricky because nominal data can become strange data when you take the distribution into consideration. For example, if we create an application that processes test scores, we expect the distribution to be fairly wide and to center around 66 percent. What happens if we supply the unit with 100 test scores in which everyone gets a score of 70 percent on the test? This is nominal data because a score of 70 percent with 100 scores is within normal parameters; however, the distribution is abnormal and if your unit is calculating a *Z-score* (a simple calculation to determine how far away from the average a person's score is), you would wind up with a divide by zero error. This is because the standard deviation of 100 scores of 70 percent would be zero and part of the Z-score calculation is to divide by the standard deviation. In this situation, the data is normal, but because of a quirk in the calculation it causes a problem. You should always include an allowance in your test cases for nominal data, abnormal combinations, or distributions of data.

- **Maximum Data**   Most likely, maximum data is taken care of by a boundary analysis. When looking at maximums for good data, we most often just check to make sure the boundary analysis covers all the possibilities. One situation that is commonly missed is when the maximum for one piece of data depends on the value for another piece of data. This often is missed in a boundary analysis and therefore should be checked here.

- **Minimum Data**   Most likely minimum data is taken care of by a boundary analysis. When looking at minimums for good data, we most often just check to make sure the boundary analysis covered all the possibilities. One situation that is commonly missed is when the minimum for one piece of data depends on the value for another piece of data. This often is missed in a boundary analysis and therefore should be checked here (sound familiar?).

- **Old Data**   Often the unit you are working on is a newer version of an older unit. Therefore, it can be very useful to try all of the test cases for the earlier versions of the unit to see whether the new unit will still work with older data. This is a form of *regression testing.*

Test Data

The last thing we must discuss when developing test plans is using the test data. By using the methods listed in the preceding sections, we can create a detailed set of test data that fully exercises our unit, and discover most of the defects in our code. We must fully document these data sets of test data so that we can come back to them later and understand what they were trying to discover, and how they were performed.

It is very important to use data that is easy to test. You undoubtedly will have to perform some kind of hand or visual calculation to ensure your tests succeed (or not). Using a number such as 5673421 is much more cumbersome (and more likely to create a mistake in a hand calculation) than the number 5,000,000, which will probably discover the exact same errors.

Use data that is easy to verify by hand calculations. This is very important because you are just as likely to make a mistake during testing as you are during coding. For this reason, it also is important to stay away from writing overly complicated testing code as well. Low tech usually is the best approach to testing.

CERTIFICATION OBJECTIVE 8.02

Implement Tracing

One of the tools we can use to aid in testing and debugging is *tracing*. Tracing involves printing out information regarding the state of your application as it runs. For example, we might wish to print the value of a variable at a given time to ensure that its value is within defined parameters. You could do this by using standard methods to print to a Web page such as a *Response.Write;* however, the problem with this is that there is no simple way to shut off this functionality.

When we release our application or simply want to see how it will look to a user, we must remember to remove or comment out all of the statements related to tracing. For this reason, a few other options are available to view the state of our application as it runs. We can use the Visual Studio debugger, the *Debug* object, and the *Trace* object.

- **The Visual Studio debugger** allows us to step through our code and look at the state of our application as it progresses. The debugger is very advanced and allows us to see many aspects of an application, such as the state of variables, the call stack, and so forth.

- **The *Debug* object** allows us to print messages to the output window in the Visual Studio environment. This allows us to print the value of variables or any other message we wish to print, which can help us figure out what is happening within our application as it runs.

- **The *Trace* object** allows us to print information regarding the state of our application to the Web pages themselves and does not require the presence of the Visual Studio environment. This can be useful when we wish to see how an application is running in a production environment that normally would not have Visual Studio installed on it.

In the following sections, we will investigate the *Trace* object, *Debug* object, and Visual Studio debugger and see how and when we should use them to test and debug our applications.

Trace and *Debug* Objects

The *Trace* and *Debug* objects are used when you want to add debugging code to your applications. This is code that is part of your application, but is designed to give developers information about how the application is running. This is in contrast to the Visual Studio debugger which does not add code to your application; instead, it is a container within which we can run an application and control how that application is run.

With the *Trace* and *Debug* objects, we can output the state of our application; however, we also can output any message we desire and have the message output only in certain circumstances. The primary idea is that because these objects are part of our code, we have the power of the programming language behind us, which allows us to do many things.

exam
Watch

*It might seem that the **Trace** and **Debug** objects do basically the same thing—and they do. The biggest difference is that the **Trace** object does not require symbolic debug information; the **Debug** object does. Therefore, the **Trace** object is useful when you need to trace information printed from a Web application that is running without a debugger and the **Debug** object is useful only when running the application in the debugger. It also should be noted that if you are compiling your programs from the command line compiler, you will have to compile them with the tracing enabled. You do not have to worry about this if you are using Visual Studio, as it is done automatically; however, if you are compiling from the command line, you should add the following switch: /d:TRACE=TRUE.*

The *Trace* Object

The *Trace* object in ASP.NET contains methods we can use to write messages to a Web page or to memory while it is running. The big difference between using the *Trace* object and writing trace information using a *Response.Write* is that you can switch all tracing on and off very easily with a setting in the web.config file if you use application-level tracing (which we will look at later, in the section "Application-Level Trace").

This is a significant contrast to *Response.Write* statements, which must be commented out or removed to stop outputting the trace information. This functionality enables us to write trace statements throughout our code that can print the value of variables, assertions (these print whether a condition has been met), and the execution path of the application (track the flow of your code). It also allows us to print this information only when we need it by giving us a simple way to switch it on and off.

One of the benefits of using the *Trace* object instead of the *Debug* object for tracking the state of an application is that the *Trace* object will do its job even if we are not running the application in the Visual Studio debugger. This can be very useful when testing, as a proper test environment would contain only the software that would be expected to be installed in the production environment.

It is not uncommon for an application to work well when Visual Studio is installed and completely break down on a system without it. This usually is caused by a missing component and the only way to determine whether this will happen is to install the Web application as we would in the production environment. The capability to continue tracing even without the debugger can be invaluable in this situation.

The *Trace* object actually is a very simple object that contains methods and properties specifically designed to organize the information you output. You can send the output to the page you are viewing, or to memory (we will look at how to view the output later). The following are some of the more common members of the *Trace* object:

Member	Description
IsEnabled	A Boolean property that most often is used to figure out whether tracing is enabled. You also can use it to dynamically turn tracing on or off.
Write	A method used to write messages for tracing.
Warn	A method used to write messages for tracing but in an ASP.NET.

The methods *Write* and *Warn* are your tools for writing trace information. *Write* and *Warn* do essentially the same thing, but *Warn* will write information in red and is designed to be used when you have a problem with the state of your application (for example, a variable is not within its normal parameters).

exam
ⓦatch

Note that the Trace object in the System.Web namespace is not the same as the Trace object in the System.Diagnostics namespace. The Write and Warn methods belong to the Web version of the Trace object and are not present in the application version. The application version also has methods such as Assert that do not exist in the Web version. Don't let this get you on the exam. The Web version actually is an instance of a class which is System.Web.TraceContext. The Application version is a static class called Trace, which means its methods are shared methods. We will look further at the System.Diagnostics version of Trace next.

The following example gets some information from a textbox, performs a calculation on it, and uses trace output to display what is happening:

```
Trace.Write("Test Button", "Starting btnTest_Click")

'Do a calculation on the data
Dim ans = CType(txtValue.Text, Integer) * 100

If (ans > 1000) Then
  Trace.Warn("Test Button", "Answer is outside the acceptable " & _
             "range of 0-1000")
End If

Response.Write("The answer is " & ans)

Trace.Write("Test Button", "Ending btnTest_Click")
```

This example normally prints when the procedure starts and when the procedure ends using *Trace.Write*. When the procedure is run and the calculation results in a value outside the normal values we are expecting it to use, *Test.Warn* is used to print the information.

If you have some experience tracing in Visual Basic .NET Windows applications, you might have noticed that the *Trace* object has different methods and properties from the *Trace* object we are discussing here; this is because they are different objects. The *Trace* object used in ASP.NET is the *System.Web.Trace* object. It sends its output to Web pages or memory and is fairly limited in its functionality.

The *Trace* object used in Windows applications is the *System.Diagnostics.Trace* object and is almost identical to the *Debug* object, which we will discuss later. This version of the *Trace* object does not output its information to Web pages; instead, it will output information to a debugger or message box, depending on which methods are called on it. You can even customize it to output information to almost anywhere you desire by adding something called a *TraceListener* to it (something you cannot do with the ASP.NET *Trace* object). This can cause problems when you are trying to trace into components that you will use in the *System.Diagnostics.Trace* object.

If you are using custom controls or components on your Web page, you might wish to output trace information to your Web page, which means we need a way to use the appropriate *Trace* object. By default, components will not send their trace information to a Web page, as they are not necessarily running on a Web page.

To enable the component to send its trace output to the page it is running on, we first must import the *System.Web* namespace in our component like this:

```
Imports System.Web
```

Once this is done, we must enable tracing to the Web page by using the *HttpContext.Current* object. This object represents the current http request associated with the page in which our component is running. The following code would be placed in the constructor for the control to enable tracing to the Web page:

```
HttpContext.Current.Trace.IsEnabled = True
'You can also use
Me.Trace
Page.Trace
```

The final step we must take is to use the *HttpContext.Current.Trace* object to write our trace output, which gives us our link between the component and the Web page. This *Trace* object is the ASP.NET *Trace* object (*System.Web.Trace*) that we have been discussing; we use the same methods and properties to output our trace information, which we can see in the following code:

```
HttpContext.Current.Trace.Warn("MyComponent", "Something Bad Happened")
```

Page-Level Trace   To use the trace output we have created previously, we must turn on tracing. We can do this at the page level or the application level. To turn on tracing at the page level, we use the page directive as follows:

```
<%@ Page Language="vb" trace="true" %>
```

This causes trace information to be printed on the Web page when it is loaded. Note that if you are using a grid layout for the page, the trace information will be printed behind the controls on the page so it is a good idea to use the flow layout for pages that might display trace information. Compare the following two examples of trace output. Figure 8-2 shows trace output to a page that is using a grid layout; Figure 8-3 shows trace output to a page that is using a flow layout.

Notice that there is a great deal of information listed about the page, along with the trace output. This information can be invaluable in tracking down problems within a Web application; however, we will be focusing on the trace output. You should make sure you can see the *Trace.Write* output and *Trace.Warn* output, from the above example, both of which use the category "Test Button."

FIGURE 8-2   A grid layout

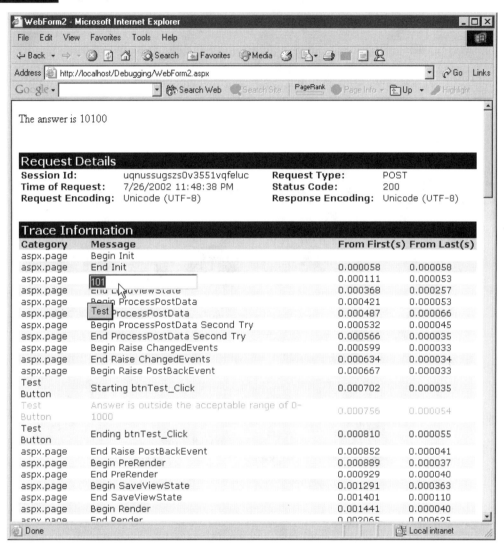

Application-Level Trace   With application-level tracing, it is unnecessary to turn on tracing for each page. Any page that does not specify in its page directive that tracing is on will automatically have tracing turned on at the application level (by default, it is off).

FIGURE 8-3   A flow layout

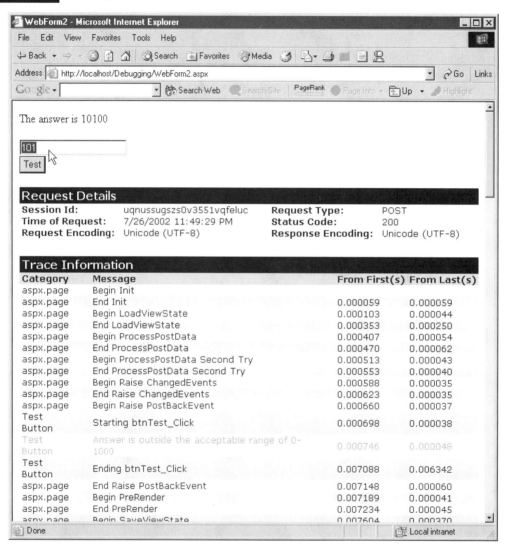

If tracing is explicitly turned off in the page directive, tracing will be turned off regardless of the application-level setting. The next table shows the different combinations of page-level and application-level tracing states along with the result of these settings for a single page:

Page-Level Setting	Application-Level Setting	Result
On	On	Trace information displayed.
On	Off	Trace information displayed.
Off	On	No trace information displayed.
Off	Off	No trace information displayed.
Not Set	On	Trace information displayed.

From this table, we can see that the setting at the page level takes precedence over the setting at the application level. If the page level setting is not set, the application-level setting is respected.

The question I'm sure you probably are asking is "so how do I turn on application-level tracing?" The answer to that question is found in the web.config file. The web.config file has a trace tag within it, which will look similar to this:

```
<?xml version="1.0" encoding="utf-8" ?>
<configuration>
  <system.web>
    ...
    <trace enabled="true" pageOutput="true" localOnly="true"/>
    ...
  </system.web>
</configuration>
```

The three attributes in the preceding code determine the following (for a full listing of the attributes for the trace tag, see the MSDN library):

- **enabled** turns on application-level tracing if set to true, and turns it off if set to false.

- **pageOutput** determines where the trace output goes. If set to true, the trace output is sent to the page; if false, the trace output is placed in memory.

- **localOnly** ensures that trace output can be viewed only on the system hosting the Web server. This is useful for viewing trace information on a production system where we would not want users to accidentally be presented with some trace output (that can be an embarrassing support call).

We mentioned previously that trace output could be printed to the page or to memory. This is allowed for application-level tracing and is determined by the setting of the pageOutput attribute of the trace tag in the web.config file. If pageOutput is set to true, the results are essentially the same as if we used page-level tracing. In other words, the trace output is printed to the page.

If the pageOutput attribute is set to false, the trace output is placed in memory. In this situation, we can view the trace output by navigating to the trace viewer, a page called trace.axd page, which can be found by navigating to *http://servername/projectname/ trace.axd*. On this page, all of the requests are accessible. If you click a request you will see the exact same output as that appended to the bottom of a page when pageOutput is set to true; however, it does not clutter your pages when it's cached to memory. Figure 8-4 is our example viewed from the trace viewer in Internet Explorer.

If you want to remove the trace viewer from your Web server, you can do so in the machine.config file. In the httpHandlers section, you will find the following tag:

```
<httpHandlers>
  <add verb="*" path="trace.axd"
type="System.Web.Handlers.TraceHandler"/>
</httpHandlers>
```

You can set the path attribute to an empty string (" ") to disable the trace viewer for the Web server. Note that you cannot disable the trace viewer for an individual Web application, only for the server.

The *Debug* Object

The next object we can use to output trace information in a Web application is the *Debug* object. The *Debug* object does not write its output to the Web page, instead it writes its output to the output window (as with *TraceListeners,* it is connected similarly to the *System.Diagnostics.Trace* object) in the Visual Studio development environment. To use the *Debug* object, we must first include the *System.Diagnostics* namespace. Once this is done, we will have access to the members of the *Debug* object, which you will notice gives us more options for tracing an application than the *Trace* object methods do. The following are the most common members of the *Debug* object (please note that the *System.Diagnostics.Trace* object discussed earlier has the same members):

- **Assert** Takes a condition and a message as arguments, and prints out the message if the condition is false. It is used to assert that a condition must be true and warns us if it is not.

FIGURE 8-4   Internet Explorer's trace viewer

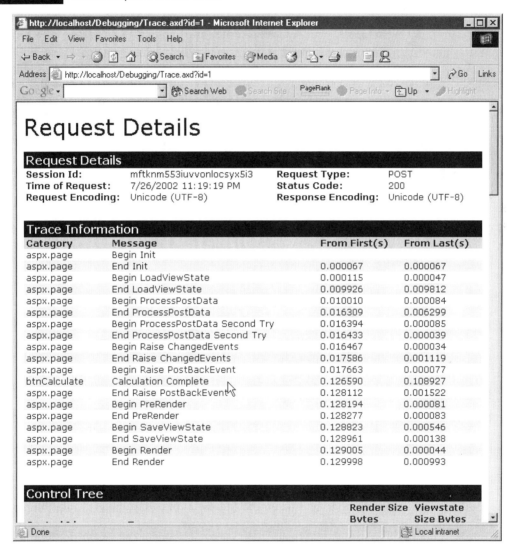

- ■ **Fail**   Used to print out error messages.
- ■ **Write**   Writes a message to the output window.
- ■ **WriteIf**   Writes a message if a condition is true and can be thought of as the opposite of the Assert method.

- **WriteLine**   Writes a message to the output window like the Write method does, but it also adds a line terminator to the message.

- **WriteLineIf**   Similar to the WriteIf method but it also adds a line terminator to the message printed.

The following example is equivalent to the example presented earlier using the *System.Web.Trace* object; however, this time we will use the debug object to do the equivalent:

```
Debug.WriteLine("Starting btnTest_Click", "Test Button")

'Do a calculation on the data
Dim ans = CType(txtValue.Text, Integer) * 100

Debug.Assert((ans <= 1000), "Answer is outside the acceptable " & _
             "range of 0-1000")

Response.Write("The answer is " & ans)

Debug.WriteLine("Ending btnTest_Click", "Test Button")
```

Notice the *Assert* method was used to ensure that the *ans* variable was less than or equal to 1000, our acceptable value. A message will print to the output window if the variable is greater than 1000. It is important to note that the debug statements will run only if you run the application in the Visual Studio debugger. This means if you use the View In Browser command in Visual Studio, you will not see anything in the output window. To see the output from the *Debug* object, you must start the page in the debugger. You can do this by using the following steps:

1. Right-click the project in the Solution Explorer and select Set As StartUp Project.

2. Right-click the page you wish to run and select Set As Start Page.

3. Select Debug | Start from the Menu Bar or the equivalent from the Toolbar, or press F5 to start debugging your page.

As your page runs, any debug statements will be printed to the output window. The result of the preceding code example, as seen in the output window, is shown in Figure 8-5.

You can watch the output window as the page runs or use it like a log. When the page is stopped the output window does not clean itself out, which means you can

FIGURE 8-5   The code output window

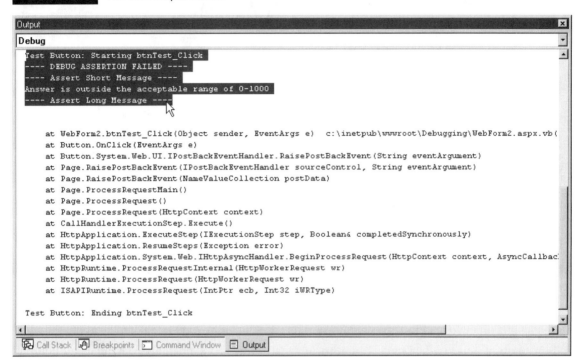

run the page and when you're finished go back to the output window to see what happened. You should be aware that the data in the output window will be cleared the next time you run the debugger. If there is anything you wish to keep from the output window, you can right-click the output window and select Copy to copy the entire output window or, if you don't want the entire window, select the text you wish to copy before you select Copy.

When deciding which object to use (*Trace* or *Debug*) to output trace information, the decision should primarily be made based on when trace output must be available.

Add Trace Listeners and Trace Switches to an Application

Earlier, we mentioned that the *Trace* object we have been discussing for tracing through Web pages (*System.Web.Trace*) is not the same as the *Trace* object you would be using in a component (*System.Diagnostics.Trace*). The *System.Web.Trace*

SCENARIO & SOLUTION	
I want to enable tracing on the production server that will not have Visual Studio installed on it. How do I do this?	Use the *Trace* object.
How do I track down a bug that has been found and fix it?	Use the *Debug* object, as you should do this on your development system. Once your bug is fixed, you will have no use for the trace information.
How do I track down an error that only occurs in optimized code (release version)?	Use the *Trace* object, as the *Debug* object will not work with optimized code.
I want to have the last error encountered placed in a file so that support staff do not have to rely on users to get error information in a production web application. How do I do this?	Use the *Trace* object.
I want to log the usage of my application. This logging will be used as historical data for the life of the application so I would like to store it in a database. How do I do this?	Create a custom trace listener that outputs trace information to the database (see the next section on trace listeners).

object is fairly light and its primary attribute is the capability to write its output to Web pages. The *System.Diagnostics.Trace* object is much more advanced and contains support for directing its output to various *TraceListeners,* which also is something the *Debug* object can do.

TraceListeners

A *TraceListener* is an object that accepts trace output from the *Trace* and *Debug* objects and directs it somewhere. The *TraceListener,* which is used by default, is the *DefaultTraceListener* (I'm sure that one surprised you). This listener sends output from *Write, WriteLine, WriteIf,* and *WriteLineIf* statements to *Debugger.Log,* which is how an attached debugger displays the trace output.

This listener also displays a message box in response to *Assert* methods. There are two other listeners we can attach to the *Trace* and *Debug* objects: the *TextWriterTraceListener* and *EventLogTraceListener.* The *TextWriterTraceListener* allows us to output trace information to a stream or file. The *EventLogTraceListener* allows us to output trace information to the Windows event log. If the *DefaultTraceListener,*

TextWriterTraceListener, or *EventLogTraceListener* are not what you are looking for, you can even create your own. All you need to do in this case is derive your own listener class from the base class for all listeners: *TraceListener.* By overriding its members, you can define any behavior you like for your listener.

To add a new listener to the *Trace* and *Debug* objects, we use their *Listeners* collections. In the following example, we have created a new *TextWriterTraceListener,* which will output its information to a file, and attach it to the *Listeners* collection of the *Trace* object:

```
'Create a text file for the trace listener to use
Dim logFile As New System.IO.FileStream("C:\TraceLog.txt", _
                                    IO.FileMode.OpenOrCreate)

'Create the new trace listener
Dim fileListener As New TextWriterTraceListener(logFile)

'Add the new listener to the Listeners collection
Trace.Listeners.Add(logFile)

'Set AutoFlush to true so that trace output is written to the file right
after we execute a trace statement. This prevents lost messages.
Trace.AutoFlush = True
```

The *Trace* and *Debug* objects share a *Listeners* collection; therefore, if you add a listener to the *Trace* objects *Listeners* collection, that listener also is added to the *Listeners* collection of the *Debug* object. When any of the *Trace* or *Debug* objects methods are executed (the methods that output trace information), the output will be sent to all of the listeners in the *Listeners* collection.

Two of the methods of the *TraceListener* objects warrant detailed discussion. The *Flush* method takes all buffered output from a *TraceListener* and sends it wherever it is supposed to go (a text file in our example). This can be useful when you are monitoring the output at run time and you want to ensure it gets to where it is going before you take a look at it.

The second method is the *Close* method, which essentially turns off the listener. For example, if we are using a *TextWriterTraceListener,* as we did in the previous example, to monitor a specific portion of our program and we now want to shut it down, we could do this:

```
fileListener.Flush()
fileListener.Close()
logFile.Close()
Trace.Listeners.Remove(fileListener)
```

First, we flush the listener to ensure that any output it contains is sent to the file. Also note that we could have used the *Flush* method of the *Trace* object, which in turn calls the *Flush* method of each listener in the *Listeners* collection. We then close the listener and the file. Once the listener is closed it will no longer accept output; however, to be tidy, we also remove it from the *Listeners* collection of the *Trace* object.

It is possible to use a *TraceListener* without adding it to the *Listeners* collection. In this case, we would not use the methods of the *Trace* object to output our trace information; instead we can use the methods of the *TraceListener* object, which will contain some of the methods of the *Trace* object. For example, the *TextWriterTraceListener* object contains *Write* and *WriteLine* methods but does not contain the *Assert* method. In this situation, we must remember to execute the *Flush* method when we want the trace information printed to the file, as it will not do so otherwise. With the *Trace* object, we use the *Flush* method only for convenience.

On a final note for *TraceListeners*, if you are using an Application Configuration File for your component, you can place some XML in that file that will initialize a *TraceListener* and add it to the *Listeners* collection when your component runs. The following is an example of adding the listener we added in code previously, but this time we will add it in the configuration file. The following XML code would be placed in the configuration file:

```
<configuration>
  <system.diagnostics>
    <trace autoflush="true" indentsize="0">
      <listeners>
        <add name="fileListener"
             type="System.Diagnostics.TextWriterTraceListener,System"
             initializeData="TraceLog.txt"/>
      </listeners>
    </trace>
  </system.diagnostics>
</configuration>
```

The *add* element, you will notice, has three attributes. The *name* attribute is fairly obvious; however, the *type* attribute contains two arguments. The first argument is the actual listener type and the second argument is the assembly this type is found within (the *System* after the comma). The last attribute is *initializeData* which is passed to the constructor for this type and in this case is the filename for the file you wish to use.

Trace Switches

Trace switches allow us to enable tracing, disable tracing, and filter tracing. Essentially a trace switch turns tracing on and off in a very low-tech but flexible way. There are three basic switches you can use: a *BooleanSwitch,* a *TraceSwitch,* and a developer-defined switch. The *BooleanSwitch* allows us to enable or disable all tracing. This is very useful in production environments, as it gives us a very simple way to turn off tracing until we need it. With a *TraceSwitch,* we can filter tracing or turn tracing on for only specific types of messages. To use a switch, we must first create it. The following two statements create a *BooleanSwitch* and a *TraceSwitch:*

```
Dim bSwitch As New BooleanSwitch("gSwitch", _
                              "Global application switch")
Dim tSwitch As New TraceSwitch("filtered", _
                              "Switch for filtering output")
```

You will notice that the constructor for both types of switches takes two arguments. The first argument is the name of the switch; the second argument is a description for the switch. The *BooleanSwitch* has an *Enabled* property that can be set to true or false. The *TraceSwitch* has a *Level* property that can be set to one of the following constants, which are part of the *TraceLevel* enumeration. They are designed to represent different types of trace information; however, it is up to the developer to respect these levels and they are not enforced in any way.

Integer Value	Enumeration Constant	Type of Trace Message
0	Off	None
1	Error	Error messages
2	Warning	Warning messages
3	Info	Information messages
4	Verbose	Messages with a detailed description

You can set the *Level* property of the *TraceSwitch* object to one of the preceding constants to define the types of messages you want to output. The levels are cumulative, which means if you set the level to *Error,* you will get only error messages; however, if you set the level to *Warning,* you will get both warning and error messages. The following example disables our *BooleanSwitch* and sets our *TraceSwitch* to the *Info* level:

```
bSwitch.Enabled = False
tSwitch.Level = TraceLevel.Info
```

You might be wondering how you attach these switches to the *Trace* object so it will respect the settings of the switches. This actually is very simple and almost anticlimactic: You don't! You simply check the state of your switch before you try to use the *Trace* object. For the *BooleanSwitch* object, you can simply check its *Enabled* property. For the *TraceSwitch* object, there are four properties we can use to determine at which state we are (alternatively, we could use the *Level* property directly).

Property	Description
TraceError	Returns true if the level is set to Error.
TraceWarning	Returns true if the level is set to Warning.
TraceInfo	Returns true if the level is set to Info.
TraceVerbose	Returns true if the level is set to Verbose.

The following example outputs a warning message only if our *TraceSwitch's* level is set to *Verbose, Info, or Warning:*

```
If (tSwitch.TraceWarning) Then
  Trace.WriteLine("Don't eat yellow snow!")
End If
```

A more elegant approach to this would use the *WriteLineIf* method of the *Trace* object like this:

```
Trace.WriteLineIf(tSwitch.TraceWarning, "Don't eat yellow snow!")
```

As you can see, you must remember to use the switches you create; there is nothing automatic about their usage.

One of the problems with creating and setting switches in this way is that to change their states (such as disabling a *BooleanSwitch* or changing the level of a *TraceSwitch*) we must change our code. This means once a component is deployed, the switches become inflexible. Because the whole purpose of the *Trace* object is flexibility (after all, we could just use message boxes or write to the console) this is undesirable. It would be better if we could flexibly initialize them, which does not involve changing code.

Instead of setting their states (*Enabled* for a *BooleanSwitch* and *Level* for a *TraceSwitch*) in code, we can use an Application Configuration file as was mentioned previously with *TraceListeners*. When your program creates a switch, it checks the configuration file for settings matching the switch that is made; if it finds any settings it uses them. The following example initializes our two switches, but this time it is done in the configuration file (which you should remember contains XML):

```
<system.diagnostics>
  <switches>
    <add name="bSwitch" value="0" />
    <add name="tSwitch" value="2" />
  </switches>
</system.diagnostics>
```

The *name* attribute of the *Add* element must match the name you used when creating your switch in your code (see the previous discussion of creating switches if you do not remember this). You should notice that we cannot use the constants here to set the level. Because of this, you probably should place some comments in the configuration file that explain what appropriate values are for the attributes so an administrator or user can change the configuration file at a later date.

CERTIFICATION OBJECTIVE 8.03

Debug, Rework, and Resolve Defects in Code

Trace output is very useful in discovering mistakes you might have placed in your code. Once you discover your mistakes and get an idea of where they are, you will need to track down the exact problem, determine the cause, and fix them. Undoubtedly, the most useful tool available to help you with this is the Visual Studio debugger.

The debugger is integrated with the Common Language Runtime, which will allow you to debug all of the files within your solution, regardless of the language they were written in. This can be invaluable when using multiple languages, which often happens when creating components for a Web application. On another note, if you do a lot of programming in different Visual Studio languages, you will have to learn how to use only one debugger, which is a nice little bonus.

Configure the Debugging Environment

The first thing we need to discuss is how to set up your application for debugging. For a debugger to work, your compiled code needs symbolic debug information added to it. The framework runs compiled code that is different from your source code. For the debugger to show you which source code lines are running at any given moment, it must have information that associates source code statements with compiled code statements. It also must have information that matches the names of your objects, functions, and variables with the names found in the compiled code, which are not the same as they are in the source code.

Note that this extra symbolic debug information will make your compiled files much larger, so we should remove the symbolic debug information when we deploy an application to a production environment. To tell the compiler to add symbolic debug information, we must add or modify the compilation element in the web.config file. By default this element is set to add symbolic debug information; therefore, we don't actually have to do anything to have debug info added to our compiled code. However, if we want to have our code compiled without the debug information, we will have to change this element like this:

```
<compilation defaultLanguage="vb" debug="false" />
```

By setting the debug attribute to false, you can remove the symbolic debug information from the complied code.

exam
ⓦatch

Removing symbolic debug information from release code is very important as it will reduce the scalability of a Web application. When your code gets bigger, your system loses memory, and on a Web server, memory is extremely important to handle more users.

When compiling your Web application, you also can choose whether to compile it in debug or release mode. This should not be confused with adding symbolic debug information, as it is a separate option. When you compile your application in release mode, certain compiler options are enabled that alter your code to run as efficiently as possible.

These optimizations are not compatible with the debugger, so you cannot run release versions of an application in the Visual Studio debugger, regardless of whether there was any debug information in the compiled files. For this reason, we also can compile our applications in debug mode, which forces the compiler to produce code that does not contain any optimizations and therefore is compatible with the Visual Studio debugger.

on the
job

Compiler optimizations can greatly increase the speed of code by reorganizing it. For example, if you assign 5 to x on line 3 of your function and then assign 6 to x on line 4, the compiler will remove line 3, as the variable is not used after x is assigned to 5 (the value is not used). The problem with using optimizations while debugging is that your code has been reorganized, which makes it much harder to track down errors and determine whether they were a result of the optimizations. The best solution is to test your program fully with the debug version and then test it with the release version (optimized version). In this way, we can determine that any failed tests were a result of the optimizations, and specifically look at how to fix them in that context.

To set the mode for the compilation you desire (release or debug), you can choose the appropriate mode from the *Solutions Configurations* drop-down list box in the tool bar, as shown in Figure 8-6.

FIGURE 8-6   The Solutions Configurations drop-down list

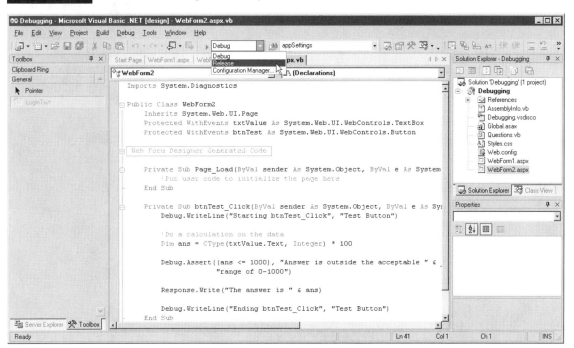

You also can choose the appropriate mode by selecting Build | Configuration Manager from the menu bar, which opens the *Configuration Manager* dialog box. Simply choose your desired build configuration from the *Active Solution Configuration* drop-down list box and click the Close button, as shown in Figure 8-7.

Once you have chosen the appropriate build configuration, you can build your application in the standard way, and the output will be based on the configuration you have chosen.

If you are trying to run the application in the debugger (which is the point of this chapter), you will have to ensure that the compilation element in the *web.config* file has its debug attribute set to true and that you are compiling in debug mode. Assuming this is true, you still can choose whether to run your application in the debugger. If you do not want to run your application in the debugger, you have a few options:

■ Right-click the page you wish to run in the Solution Explorer and select View In Browser (this also works on an open page in the designer).

■ Select a Start Page (which we will see later) and select Debug | Start Without Debugging.

■ Select a Start Page (which we will see later) and press CTRL-F5.

■ Select a Start Page, select Release mode from the *Solutions Configurations* drop-down list box in the toolbar, and click the Start button in the toolbar.

FIGURE 8-7

The
Configuration
Manager
dialog box

Project	Configuration	Platform	Build
Debugging	Debug	.NET	✓

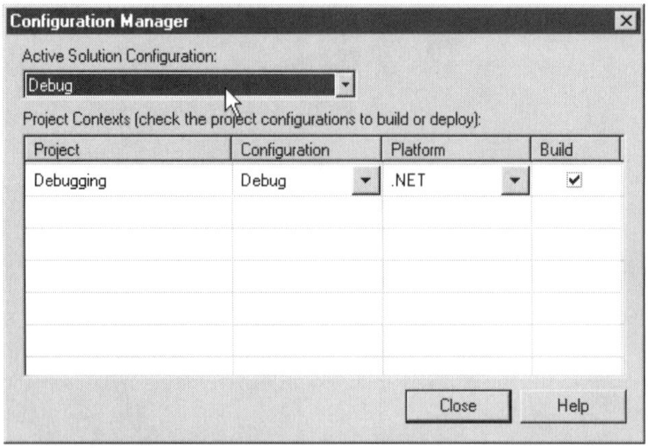

If you want to run your application in the debugger, you must have the active build configuration set to debug, after which you have the following options:

- Select a Start Page and then click the Start button in the toolbar.
- Select a Start Page and then choose Debug | Start from the menu bar.
- Select a Start Page and press F5.

To set your Start Page, you first must set your startup project if you have multiple projects in your solution; do this by right-clicking the project you wish to debug and selecting Set as StartUp Project. Once you have done this, or if you have only one project in your solution, you can right-click the page you wish to run and select Set As Start Page.

Using the Debugger

All debuggers essentially allow us to do three major things. They allow us to run the program at a speed more acceptable for us mere mortals; in other words, it allows us to step through our code one line at a time. Second, they allow us to view the state of an application while it is running. This includes viewing the values of variables and objects, and low-level structures such as the *call stack*. Finally, they allow us to edit the run time state of our application and execute portions of it through nonstandard means. For example, we can execute a function without having the application itself flow into the function. With these three capabilities, we can test the application and therein discover the causes of errors.

Add and Manage Breakpoints

When you have discovered approximately where in your code a problem exists, you will need to step through that area to see how it operates. We can do this by adding a breakpoint to a line of code within that area. A breakpoint is attached to an executable line of code, and when running your code in the debugger, the debugger will pause execution of your program when it reaches a breakpoint. The fact that it pauses and does not stop the execution of your code means the state of your application is intact and available for your viewing pleasure.

There are many different ways to add a breakpoint to your code and many ways you can set them up. By far, the easiest way is to simply click the margin in the code editor window next to the line where you want to put the breakpoint. As you can see in Figure 8-8, the line turns red and a red dot appears in the margin next to that line:

To remove the breakpoint, just click it again. You must remember that the purpose of a breakpoint is to tag a line of code which, when hit at run time, will cause the program to pause, which means breakpoints can be placed only on executable lines of code. For example, the following line of code (a variable declaration) is not executable:

```
Dim x As Integer
```

whereas the following line of code is

```
x = 5
```

FIGURE 8-8   Add a breakpoint to your code, like this

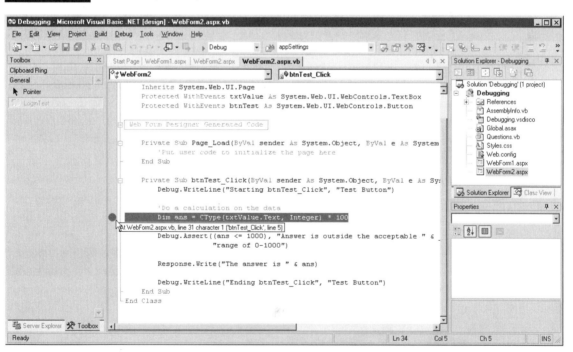

Another method of adding a breakpoint to our code is much more advanced and we can even create breakpoints that pause our code only when certain conditions arise or when they have been hit a certain number of times. If you select Debug | New Breakpoint in the menu bar, the New Breakpoint dialog box appears, as shown in Figure 8-9.

From the Function tab of this dialog box, you can specify the function to place the breakpoint, the line and character to stop on, and the language in which the function is written. The purpose of the function tab is to specify a breakpoint relative to a function. The File tab allows you to specify a breakpoint relative to a file, and the Address tab allows you to specify a memory address where you would like to break.

The final tab is the Data tab, which allows you to set a breakpoint on a variable. The debugger will break when the value of that variable changes. You will notice that below the tabs in the dialog box, there are two buttons: Condition and Hit Count. Clicking the Condition button opens the Breakpoint Condition dialog box, as shown in Figure 8-10.

FIGURE 8-9

The New
Breakpoint
dialog box

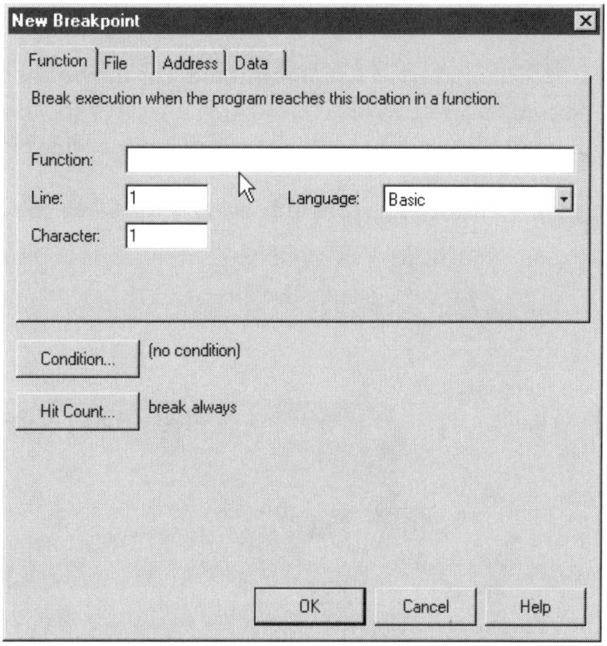

FIGURE 8-10

The Breakpoint
Condition
dialog box

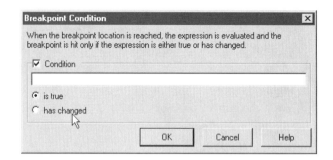

This allows you to attach a condition to a breakpoint (such as *x* > 5). When the condition is true, the debugger will break execution. You can add a condition (or remove an existing condition by unchecking the check box) and specify whether the debugger should break when the condition is true or when the condition changes.

If you are a Visual Basic 6 developer and are looking for conditional watches (a watch that breaks when a condition is true), this functionality has been transferred to breakpoints. A breakpoint with a condition attached in VB.NET is equivalent to a conditional watch in VB6.

Clicking the Hit Count button opens the Breakpoint Hit Count dialog box, as shown in Figure 8-11.

This allows you to specify the following options:

- The debugger should always break when this breakpoint is encountered.
- The debugger should break when the hit count (number of times the break point has been reached) is equal to a number you enter.

FIGURE 8-11

The Breakpoint
Hit Count
dialog box

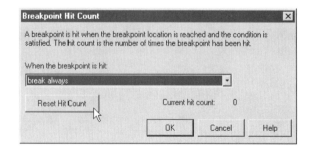

■ The debugger should break when the hit count is a multiple of a number you enter.

■ The debugger should break when the hit count is greater than or equal to a number you enter.

You also can reset the counter from here, which is useful only if you are editing a breakpoint while running your code in the debugger, which brings us to our next discussion regarding breakpoints: the breakpoint window (see Figure 8-12).

When your code is running in the debugger and it hits a breakpoint, it pauses, as shown in Figure 8-12. You will notice that the line of code on which the debugger

FIGURE 8-12   Edit a breakpoint while running the debugger

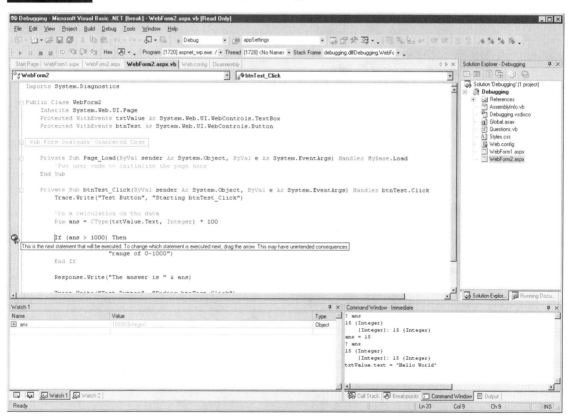

paused is highlighted in yellow. This is the next line marker and marks the next line of code to be executed. You also will notice that at the bottom of Visual Studio there are two windows. The window on the right is the window with the Call Stack, Breakpoints, Command Window, and Output tabs. If you click the Breakpoints tab, you will see a list of any breakpoints you have added to your code, as shown in Figure 8-13.

From this window, you can manage your breakpoints by adding a new breakpoint, editing existing breakpoints, or deleting breakpoints. You can even view the assembly code for the function you are in (which is something very new to Visual Basic). The little toolbar above this window is your gateway to this functionality.

If you want to disable a breakpoint without removing it, you can simply uncheck the check box next to it. If you want to edit a breakpoint, you can right-click it and select Properties, or just click the properties icon on the toolbar. This is a very intuitive tool; thus, we will leave the discussion at this. I would suggest fooling around with it for a minute to get the hang of it.

Step Through Code

Now that we have paused our code, we can look at stepping through it. Stepping through code involves running your program one line at a time with you in control. While in the debugger, you will notice the presence of the Debug toolbar (if it's not there, you can add it by right-clicking the toolbar and selecting Debug).

FIGURE 8-13   You can see which breakpoints you have added

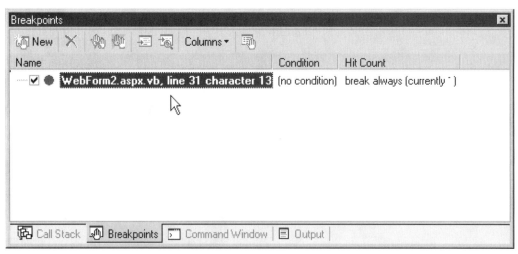

On the toolbar, there are three buttons that control stepping (use the tool tips to find them). The first button is the Step Into button. Step Into runs the next line of code and pauses after it finishes. If the next line of code contains a call to a function, it steps into that function and allows you to keep stepping through code in that function.

If you do not want to step into a function (perhaps you are confident that it is not the problem), you can click Step Over. The Step Over button executes the function at full speed and pauses when it returns. This allows us to treat a function call like a single line of code.

The final button, Step Out, is very useful when you get yourself into an area where you don't want to be. If you have stepped into and wish you hadn't, you can click Step Out, which runs the rest of the function at full speed and pauses when the function ends.

Two other useful tools for stepping through code are not found in the Debug toolbar. If you are paused in the debugger, you can right-click a line of code and select either Set Next Statement or Run To Cursor. Set Next Statement lets you specify the next statement to be executed. This can be useful if you want to skip some code or possibly back up and run some code again. Run to Cursor lets you run some code at full speed and pause again once you get to the cursor. Run to Cursor is very useful for running loops without having to step through them.

Monitor State

One of the reasons we need the capability to pause and step through code is so that we can view the state of our application as we execute each line of code. The state of our application is mainly the value of variables, the state of objects, and the call stack (which lists which functions have been called and in which order).

Along with monitoring state comes the capability to change state. This can be very useful to unit testing and means the debugger can be quite a useful testing tool. The tools available to monitor and change state are the Autos window, Locals window, Watch window and Call Stack window.

The Autos Window   The Autos window shows us the value of variables on the current statement, and three statements before and after the current statement (see Figure 8-14).

This is useful when you want to view the variables that are relevant to the current statement. You also can change the value of variables by double-clicking them and editing their values. By default, numeric values are displayed in decimal format, but

FIGURE 8-14   The Autos window

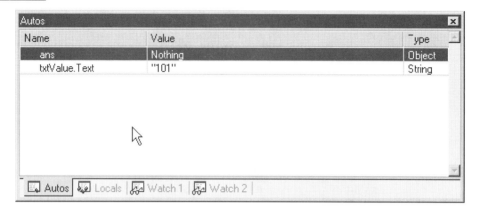

if you want to view integers in hexadecimal format, you can click the Hex button in the Debug toolbar to toggle the view between decimal and hexadecimal. If you are using the hexadecimal view and wish to edit the value, you can still enter a new value in decimal format; it will automatically convert it for you.

The Locals Window   The Locals window shows us the variables local to the current context (see Figure 8-15).

FIGURE 8-15   The Locals window

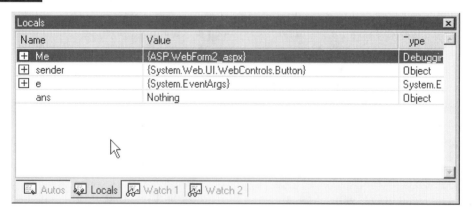

This context is the function you are in. You can change this context from the Debug Location toolbar (see Figure 8-16).

The toolbar has three drop-down list boxes used to select the context. These allow you to choose the program (if your solution has more than one), the thread, and the stack frame (the function).

The Watch Window   The watch window works like the Autos window and the Locals window. In other words, it allows us to view and edit variables within our code and does so in the same way as the Locals and Autos windows. The big difference is that it shows you only the value of variables you choose to see.

FIGURE 8-16   You can see the context in this window

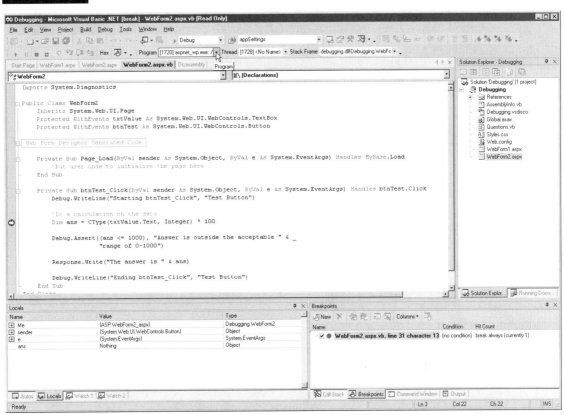

While in debug mode, you will notice that the Watch window (there are four from which to choose, so you can organize your watches) contains nothing until you add a variable to it. To add a variable, you can do one of the following:

- Double-click an empty line in the Watch window and type in the expression you wish to watch.
- Drag an expression from the code editor to the Watch window.
- Add a watch from the QuickWatch dialog box.

Once a watch is added, your Watch window should look like Figure 8-17.

As mentioned, you also can add a watch through the QuickWatch dialog box, which is used to quickly view the value of a variable. The QuickWatch dialog box is a little redundant, as putting the mouse cursor over a variable in the code window will show you its value in a tool tip; however, it is still useful if you want to look at a complex expression (for example, you could watch the expression x > 5, which would evaluate to true or false) and then add it as a permanent watch. You can display the QuickWatch dialog box by choosing Debug | Quick Watch. The dialog, as shown in Figure 8-18, allows you to add a variable or expression, view and change its contents, and add the watch permanently by choosing Add Watch.

The Call Stack Window   The Call Stack window is one of the most useful and, in my experience, most underused tools in the Visual Studio debugger. I once saw a student (who had considerable experience with VB) writing down the chain of function calls in his program on a piece of paper so he could figure out how his code arrived at a certain function. This is the job of the Call Stack window.

FIGURE 8-17

The Watch window

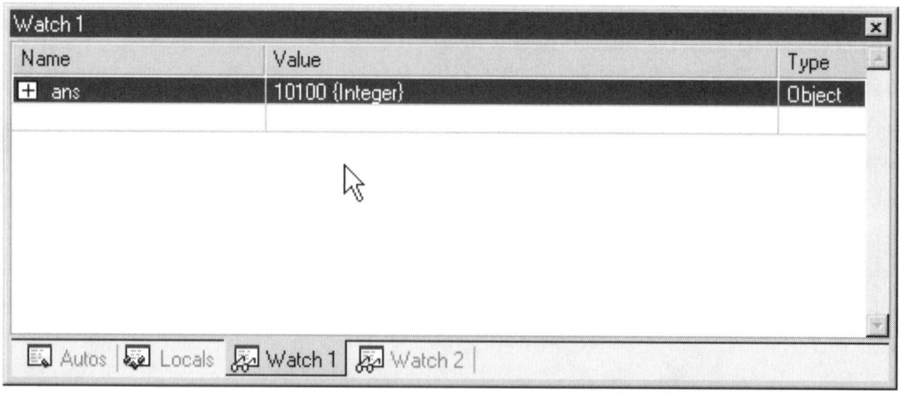

FIGURE 8-18

The QuickWatch
dialog box

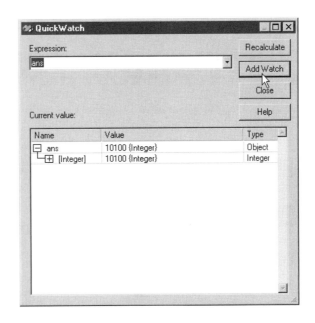

When you call a function, the variables local to it are placed on a structure called the *call stack*. If that function calls another function, the called function is placed on top of the calling function in the call stack. This is how a program remembers which function called which function and keeps local variables local. This stack works like a stack of dishes. You can add dishes only to the top of the stack and remove dishes only from the top. If you take the bottom dish off, the stack would fall over and "crash" (hint, hint).

The Call Stack window shows us the state of this call stack and allows us to see how we arrived at a certain point in our code. This can be very useful when an error in a function is caused by the function that called it. This would normally happen if the calling function passed invalid data to the called function or perhaps, through a side effect, altered a global variable on which the calling function relies (this is the reason we try to avoid using global variables). The Call Stack window looks like Figure 8-19; you should notice that there are many system functions in it at any given moment.

The function on the top is the most recent function called; the function at the bottom is the first function called. If you double-click one of the functions in the Call Stack window, you can view that function without changing the execution pointer (next line to execute). You also can right-click a function in the call stack

FIGURE 8-19 What the Call Stack window looks like

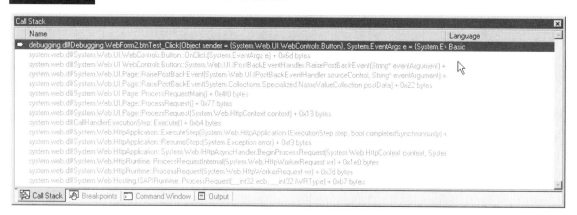

and select Run To Cursor, which runs everything at full speed until you get back to the function you have selected. This is analogous to clicking Step Out several times until you arrive back at that function.

on the

job

Using breakpoints, the Watch window, Run To Cursor, and the Set Next statement allows us to use the debugger as a simple testing engine for small units. You can use the breakpoint to stop at the beginning of a unit, the Watch window (or Locals or Autos) to set the value of data for the test, and run to cursor to run the unit of code to the end and pause. You can use the Watch window again to view results of the test, then use set next statement to move back to the top of the unit to run another test. This is very useful for small units such as functions, which might have few tests; however, it becomes cumbersome for larger units.

Execute Commands

The final tool we will discuss is the Command Window. This window used to be called the Immediate Window in Visual Basic 6. In this window, you can execute single line commands as if you were adding code to your program (which of course you are not). This gives us an easy way to do light unit testing. We can execute a function in the same way we would execute it from within our code and view the results. This in no way affects the execution pointer; however, if your actions change the state of your application, these changes are real. Figure 8-20 shows a few commands that have been executed through the Command Window.

The Command
Window

```
Command Window - Immediate                                              ×
? ans
15 {Integer}
     [Integer]: 15 {Integer}
ans = 15
? ans
15 {Integer}
     [Integer]: 15 {Integer}
txtValue.text = "Hello World"




◄                                                                     ►
🔲 Call Stack  🕹 Breakpoints  🖅 Command Window  ▤ Output
```

Notice the use of the "?" This is a shortcut for print (taken from early Basic) and
often is used in the Command Window to print the value of variables or the return
value of a function to the Command Window. You can do almost anything from the
command window as long as you can fit it on a single line as it will execute a line
after you press ENTER, which prevents us from using multiline statements. The
debugger would try to execute a multiline statement after you type the first line,
which would cause a syntax error.

There is a simple workaround for this: You can use a colon to put multiple lines
on one line. What you cannot do is anything that would cause the creation of a
memory structure on the stack or static storage. (This basically means you cannot
declare variables.)

on the
job

*You might have noticed that you cannot edit your code in the debugger as
you could with Visual Basic 6. Visual Studio .NET does not support edit-and-
continue for Visual Basic. You will have to stop your program, make changes,
recompile, and rerun the program in the debugger.*

Execute Tests

When it is time to execute the tests we have planned, we will need to do it without
too much trouble. The most common way is to use the application as a user would;

however, this normally takes far too much time and often cannot be done because we are testing units and the full application might not exist in an executable state.

A more efficient way to test your software is to use other software. There are many software packages on the market specifically designed to help you test your software (which we won't discuss further, as they are not directly related to the exam). It also is quite common to write bits of code to do the testing for you. If you have a function you wish to test, you could write another function (which is not part of your application) that calls your function with the proper test data. This type of function is called a *driver* because it drives the unit.

Where a procedure is designed to run another piece of code that has not yet been created (procedure A is the unit we are testing; its job is to call procedure B, which is not available), we can create a prototype version of the called procedure (procedure B) to test our unit. This type of procedure is called a *stub*.

The use of drivers and stubs is very common and useful. An important note is that you are as likely to make a mistake writing a driver or stub as you are to make a mistake writing any other code. For this reason, you should be extremely careful when writing drivers and stubs, and it is highly useful to perform code inspections on them before they are put into use (a code inspection is a formal walkthrough with other developers to ensure that the code is accurate).

We have seen how to use tracing to place the results of a test on a Web page or file. This can be extremely useful to prevent one of the most frustrating mistakes made during testing: errors in hand calculations and hand checking. To prevent errors in hand calculations, we should simply be smart about things. Use a spreadsheet and check your calculations multiple times. To prevent errors in hand checking, don't check things by hand. If you output your results to a file, you can use a file comparison tool to check your results against what was expected. This is where tracing can be extremely useful, as it allows us to output our results to a page or a file.

Resolve Errors and Rework Code

Once we have tested a unit and discovered its defects, it is time to fix them. Reworking code is essentially just fixing your mistakes. However, there are some important points to make about how we should rework our code.

One of the most important notes to make is that you should never remove code that is incorrect. Instead, comment it out, because the fix might be worse than the original solution. This way it's nice to have the original code around to work with.

This also helps document the history of the code, which can be useful if a fix does not work. By seeing the other solutions to the problem, we can avoid trying to fix some code with a solution we have already tried.

On another note, never try to hack a mistake. Hacking is simply trying a fix blindly. Have you ever added the number one to an answer variable just because you noticed all of your answers were exactly one off? In this situation, the symptoms of the mistake are removed (the answer is now correct), but the problem has not been fixed (what caused the answer to be wrong in the first place?). That is not the correct approach to producing reliable, robust software.

Hacking also is one of the reasons that upgrading software often uncovers many new problems. Hacks tend to work for one release but break down during upgrades because the fix is not in the same area of your code as the problem. This means that during an upgrade, the fix can become decoupled from the problem, thus reintroducing the problem.

The last thing we will mention about reworking code is that all of your tests should be performed again after the code has been reworked, not just the tests that failed. This is because fixing one bug often can uncover another. If all of the planned tests succeed, you can be confident that the fix worked without affecting other code.

CERTIFICATION SUMMARY

In this chapter, we have looked at planning unit testing. We discussed how formal unit testing is an extremely effective way for developers to contribute to the overall testing strategy for the software. We determined appropriate tests for a software unit using structured basis testing, data-flow testing, equivalence partitioning, and error guessing.

We also looked at the *Trace* and *Debug* objects for outputting trace information, which can help us evaluate the state of an application during testing. The *Trace* object outputs its trace information to the Web page or memory. The *Debug* object outputs its trace information to the output window in the Visual Studio development environment.

Finally, we used the Visual Studio debugger to help us resolve and rework errors in our code. We used breakpoints to pause our code in the debugger, step commands to step through our code, and a multitude of windows to view and change the state of our application (autos, locals, watch, call stack, output, and command windows). By using these tools, we can determine the exact cause of a code defect and repair it.

TWO-MINUTE DRILL

Create a Unit Test Plan

❑ Unit testing is the testing of small units of code such as functions and objects.

❑ Unit testing is a formal testing method that uses scientific theory to find defects in code and provide evidence to suggest the effectiveness of a unit.

❑ Methods for determining tests to be performed during unit testing include structured basis testing, data-flow testing, equivalence partitioning, and error guessing.

Implement Tracing

❑ Tracing is a useful method to output information regarding the state of an application at run time.

❑ Trace output can be written using the *Trace* object or *Debug* object.

❑ Tracing with the *Trace* object can be enabled at the page level or the application level.

❑ Statements using the *Debug* object are not compiled into release versions of an application.

❑ To switch tracing on and off, we can use the page directive at the page level and the web.config file at the application level.

❑ You can direct trace output to the page or to memory.

❑ You can set up trace listeners to redirect trace output to nonstandard places.

❑ You can set up trace switches to enable and disable tracing.

Debug, Rework, and Resolve Defects in Code

❑ The Visual Studio debugger is integrated with the Visual Studio development environment and contains tools that can help us find and fix mistakes.

❑ Breakpoints allow us to define lines of code where the debugger should pause.

❑ You can view the state of an application in the debugger by using the autos, locals, watch, and call stack windows.

❑ The Command Window allows us to execute commands (lines of code) on our applications while an application is in the debugger.

SELF TEST

The following questions will help you measure your understanding of the material presented in this chapter. Read all the choices carefully as there might be more than one correct answer. Choose all correct answers for each question.

Create a Unit Test Plan

1. What is a unit of code in the context of unit testing? (Choose all that apply.)

    A. A function

    B. An object

    C. A subsystem

    D. A library

2. What is the best technique for testing?

    A. Code Inspections

    B. Unit Testing

    C. Combined Testing

    D. Prototyping

3. Structured basis testing is a technique used to derive test cases. What does this technique ensure?

    A. The boundary of data values is tested thoroughly.

    B. Every line of code is exercised.

    C. Odd distributions of data do not cause problems.

    D. You have not forgotten to catch any exceptions.

4. Which of the following data-flow state sequences would be appropriate for a local variable in a procedure?

    A. Entered-Used

    B. Entered-Defined

    C. Used-Killed

    D. Defined-Used

5. Every time you develop test cases for a unit, you notice that, once the tests are complete, you have many test cases that show the exact same errors. What technique for developing test cases can you use to reduce redundancy in your test cases?

   A. Error guessing

   B. Data-flow testing

   C. Structured basis testing

   D. Equivalence partitioning

Implement Tracing

6. Trace information can be output from a Web application using which of the following objects and methods? (Choose all that apply.)

   A. Response.Write

   B. System.out.PrintTrace

   C. Debug.WriteLine

   D. Trace.Warn

7. You are creating a Web application and wish to have tracing turned on and off dynamically at run time. How can you do this?

   A. Use the IsEnabled property of the *Trace* object, which can be set to true or false to turn tracing on and off, respectively.

   B. Edit the web.config file and set the enabled attribute of the trace tag to false.

   C. Edit the Web page you are viewing and set the trace attribute to true or false in the page directive.

   D. This cannot be done. Tracing must be enabled or disabled before the application is run.

8. You have created a Web application and have not set the trace attribute of the page directive of any Web pages. In the web.config file, you have set the enabled attribute of the trace tag to true, and the pageOutput attribute to false. Given these settings, which of the following correctly describes the output (if any) from any *Trace* object statements in your application?

   A. No trace output will be displayed.

   B. Trace output will be seen on the page containing the trace statement.

   C. Trace output will be stored in memory.

   D. Trace output will be sent to the output window in the Visual Studio debugger.

9. How can we read trace output from the *Trace* object that has been stored in memory instead of displayed on a Web page?

   A. Use the trace viewer page (http://servername/projectname/trace.axd).

   B. Use the Visual Studio debugger.

   C. Use the trace viewer page (http://servername/projectname/traceviewer.axd).

   D. Use the trace viewer program (c:\inetpub\wwwroot\traceview.exe).

10. You are publishing a finished Web application to a production server. You have decided to leave tracing on in the application while it is stabilized. You are using application-level tracing to memory for all of your trace output. How can you prevent outside users from viewing your trace output by using the trace viewer while still having the trace output accessible?

   A. Set the localTrace attribute of the trace tag in the web.config file to true.

   B. Edit the machine.config file and set the path attribute of the add tag of the httpHandlers element to " ".

   C. Set the localOnly attribute of the trace tag in the web.config file to true.

   D. None of the above.

11. You want to add some trace output to an application that will print a message for you only when the variable x is not within normal parameters. In other words, you want to make sure that x is less than 100. Which of the following statements is the most direct way to do this?

   A. Debug.Write("X is greater than 100 and is " & x)

   B. Debug.WriteIf(x > 100, "X is greater than 100 and is " & x)

   C. Debug.Assert(x <= 100, "X is greater than 100 and is " & x)

   D. Debug.Warn("X is greater than 100 and is " & x)

12. You are running your Web application in Visual Studio but your trace output from the *Debug* object is not being printed to the output window of the debugger. What is/are the most likely problem(s)? (Choose all that apply.)

   A. You are not running the application in the debugger (you have used View In Browser instead of Debug | Start).

   B. You are running the Release build of your application instead of the debug build.

   C. You haven't compiled your application with symbolic debug information.

   D. All of the preceding.

13. You have created a *TextWriterTraceListener* for your custom control so that any trace information can be output to a file. Your custom control is being used in the Web application you are creating. Which of the following errors (caused by the *TextWriterTraceListener*) would be very likely to occur for the multiuser Web environment in which the control is running? (Choose the best answer.)

    A. A null pointer exception caused when one user has a reference to the *Trace* object and another user tries to create an instance of it.

    B. An access violation caused when one user is using the *TextWriterTraceListener* object and another user tries to access it.

    C. The errors we will get are logic errors caused by the fact that the *TextWriterTraceListener* object is not thread safe, which will cause concurrency problems when multiple users try to access it on multiple threads.

    D. File locking errors with the text file to which the trace output is going.

14. A *BooleanSwitch* is used for _____ and a *TraceSwitch* is used for _____.

    A. Turning tracing on and off; setting tracing to accept differing levels of tracing.

    B. There is no such thing as a *BooleanSwitch*; turning tracing on and off.

    C. Turning tracing and debugging on and off; turning tracing on and off.

    D. Switching from one tracing level to another; turning tracing on and off.

15. Which of the following are valid tracing levels? (Choose all that apply.)

    A. Error

    B. Info

    C. Critical

    D. Verbose

Debug, Rework, and Resolve Defects in Code

16. You have created a Web application that has a memory footprint much larger than you expected. Your application also runs slower than expected. What debugging issues should you check that would make your application large and slow? (Choose all that apply.)

A. Make sure you have created a Release build.

B. Make sure you have removed all of the *Debug* object statements.

C. Ensure that you are not compiling symbolic debug information into your application.

D. Remove all of your breakpoints.

17. To prevent the compiler from adding symbolic debug information to your application, we must:

A. Choose Debug | Start Without Debugging to compile the application.

B. Select Release Build from the Solution Configuration list box on the Standard toolbar.

C. Choose Project | Properties and uncheck the Debug Info check box.

D. Assign the debug attribute of the compilation element in the web.config file to false.

18. You want your application (running in the debugger) to pause when the variable x is greater than 20 so you can see what went wrong. What tool within the Visual Studio debugger can you use to do this?

A. Conditional watches

B. Conditional breakpoints

C. CTRL-Break

D. None of the above

19. The autos window shows you which variables in a procedure?

A. All of them

B. Only the variables on the current line

C. All variables on the three lines preceding and following the current line, as well as the current line

D. The variables on the current line and the previous two lines

20. What can you not do in the Command Window? (Choose all that apply.)

A. Execute a procedure.

B. Change the value of a variable.

C. Declare a variable.

D. Print the value of a variable.

LAB QUESTION

You are creating a custom control and are required to create a *TraceListener* that writes its output to the Windows event log. Create a *BooleanSwitch* to govern the activity of the trace statements. Write the code to do the following things:

- Create the *TraceListener*.
- Attach the listener to the *Trace* object.
- Create the *BooleanSwitch*.
- Set up the *BooleanSwitch*'s state in the application.config file.
- Write trace output respecting the *BooleanSwitch*'s state.

SELF TEST ANSWERS

Create a Unit Test Plan

1. ☑ A and B. Both functions and objects can be considered units of code.
   ☒ C and D. Both subsystems and libraries are created by integrating units of code; however, in the context of unit testing, neither a subsystem nor a library could be considered a unit of code.

2. ☑ C. A combined technique is the preferred method for testing.
   ☒ A, B, and D are incorrect because no single technique testing is as effective as a combined technique.

3. ☑ B. Structured basis testing ensures that your suite of test cases will exercise every line of code.
   ☒ A is incorrect because boundary analysis (which is a form of error guessing) provides us with test cases that thoroughly test the boundary of data. C is incorrect because odd distributions of data cannot be caught by structured basis testing and usually are dealt with when testing good data. D is incorrect because testing with bad data will determine whether you have caught all appropriate exceptions.

4. ☑ B, C, and D are all valid data-flow state sequences for a local variable. The overall sequence would be Entered-Defined-Used-Killed-Exited.
   ☒ A would not work for a local variable because you cannot use a variable (or should not) before you define it.

5. ☑ D. Equivalence partitioning is based on the idea that different kinds of test data will discover different errors. By partitioning your test cases based on the errors, they will discover you can minimize the test cases you use by removing test cases that do not discover anything new.
   ☒ A is incorrect because error guessing is very useful for increasing the number of test cases you have, but does not tend to reduce them. B is incorrect because data-flow testing tends to add tests that have been discovered using other methods such as structured basis testing and error guessing. C is incorrect because structured basis testing usually is a starting point for discovering test cases and therefore will tend to add test cases, not narrow them.

Implement Tracing

6. ☑ A, C, and D. The preferred method is to use the *Trace* or *Debug* objects; however, you can still use a *Response.Write* if you wish.
   ☒ B is incorrect because I made it up (sorry).

7. ☑ A. By setting the IsEnabled property of the *Trace* object to false, the *Trace* object will simply ignore any Write or Warn requests.
   ☒ B and C are incorrect because the web.config file and the page directive cannot be changed at run time. D is incorrect because A is correct.

8. ☑ C. The output from *Trace* object methods will be stored in memory.
   ☒ A is incorrect because trace output is being stored in memory. B is incorrect because the pageOuput attribute would have to be set to true. In D, trace output is not sent to the output window because it must work outside the debugger.

9. ☑ A. The trace viewer page located at http://servername/projectname/trace.axd is where you can view trace information stored in memory.
   ☒ B is incorrect because the Visual Studio debugger does not display trace output (from the *Trace* object) stored in memory. C is incorrect because the trace viewer is not http://servername/projectname/traceviewer.axd. D is incorrect because the trace viewer is not an executable file.

10. ☑ C. Setting the localOnly attribute of the trace tag in the web.config file to true will prevent anyone from accessing the trace output using the trace viewer except users of the local system (the Web server).
    ☒ A is incorrect because the attribute is not called localTrace. B is incorrect, as this would completely disable the trace viewer for the entire Web server. D is incorrect because A is correct.

11. ☑ C. The Debug.Assert method is designed to assert that a condition is true and therefore is exactly what we are looking for.
    ☒ A is incorrect because the Debug.Write method will execute every time it is encountered; not just when x > 100. B would be acceptable, but we are trying to assert that *x* is less than 100; therefore, the Assert method is a little more direct. Note that this answer would be acceptable if the question had not stated "the most direct way." D is incorrect because the *Debug* object does not have a Warn method.

12. ☑ D. To enable the *Debug* object to print trace output to the output window of the debugger, your application must be compiled with symbolic debug information, you must be running the Debug build, and you must start the application in the debugger (Debug | Start from the menu bar).

13. ☑ D. You will most likely get file locking problems. When the first user accesses a page with your control, the file will be accessed. When the next user accesses a page with your control, the file the *TextWriterTraceListener* must access will be locked. Even if the first user has closed

his or her browser, the garbage collector will most likely not have released the file yet. For this reason, you need to watch out when accessing a log file from a web application.

☒   A is incorrect because it is complete garbage. This would never cause a null pointer exception. B also is incorrect as an Access violation occurs when an application tries to access memory it does not own which is clearly not the case here. D is incorrect because although the *TextWriterTraceListener* object's instance methods are not thread safe, we wouldn't even get to this point due to the file locking problem mentioned in the preceding.

14. ☑   A. A *BooleanSwitch* allows us to turn tracing on or off, and a *TraceSwitch* allows us to set tracing to accept differing levels of tracing.

     ☒   B is incorrect because there is a *BooleanSwitch*. C is incorrect because a *BooleanSwitch* does not turn debugging on and off. D is incorrect because a *BooleanSwitch* does not allow you to switch from one tracing level to another.

15. ☑   A, B, and D are valid tracing levels.

     ☒   C is not a valid tracing level (it would be equivalent to Error).

Debug, Rework, and Resolve Defects in Code

16. ☑   A and C both are correct. Make sure you are compiling the Release build of your application. This will speed it up due to compiler optimizations and ensure that you are not compiling symbolic debug information into your application, which will make your application larger than it needs to be.

     ☒   B and D are incorrect because breakpoints and Debug object statements are not compiled into the Release build of an application (and in the case of breakpoints, they aren't compiled into the Debug build, either).

17. ☑   D. To remove symbolic debug information from your application, set the debug attribute of the compilation element in the web.config file.

     ☒   A is incorrect because this will simply run your program without the debugger and has no effect on how it is compiled. B is incorrect because this will prevent the compiler from optimizing your code and won't actually remove the symbolic debug info. C is incorrect because there is no Debug Info box in the project properties.

18. ☑   B. Visual Studio .NET uses conditional breakpoints to break when a condition is true.

     ☒   A is what Visual Basic 6 used to do. C and D are just plain wrong (not to mention a little silly).

19. ☑   C. All variables on the three lines preceding and following the current line as well as the current line.

    ☒   A and B are incorrect. D is true for C++ but not Visual Basic.

20. ☑   In C, you cannot declare a variable from the Command Window.

    ☒   A, B, and D are all things you can do from the Command Window.

LAB ANSWER

You were asked to set up an *EventLogTraceListener* and a *BooleanSwitch* to use with a custom control. The following is what your code should look like for each section:

■ Create the *TraceListener*:

```
Dim logListener As New EventLogTraceListener("mylog")
```

■ Attach the listener to the *Trace* object:

```
Trace.Listeners.Add(logListener)
```

■ Create the *BooleanSwitch*:

```
Dim bSwitch As New BooleanSwitch("gSwitch", _
                                "Global application switch")
```

■ Set up the *BooleanSwitch*'s state in the application.config file:

```
<system.diagnostics>
  <switches>
    <add name="bSwitch" value="0" />
  </switches>
</system.diagnostics>
```

■ Write trace output respecting the *BooleanSwitch*'s state:

```
Trace.WriteLineIf(bSwitch.Enabled, "Some Message")
```

Part IV

Deploy a Web Application

MCAD/MCSD

MICROSOFT® CERTIFIED APPLICATION DEVELOPER
& MICROSOFT® CERTIFIED SOLUTION DEVELOPER

9

Plan and Deploy a Web Application

CERTIFICATION OBJECTIVES

T his chapter examines the deployment of ASP.NET Web applications. We will discuss different deployment scenarios, including using removable media, Web-based deployment, and deploying to Web farms. We will use Visual Studio's Web Setup projects to create Windows installers that allow the application to be customized and uninstalled. We also will discuss the requirements and steps involved in using XCOPY and Copy Project to deploy Web applications.

CERTIFICATION OBJECTIVE 9.01

Plan the Deployment of a Web Application

Deployment is the process of identifying and packaging all the components and files that make up an application and moving them to the target machine for installation. The architecture of the .NET Framework simplifies the deployment of Web applications when compared to ASP. Depending on the complexity of the Web application, it can be as simple as copying the files to the target Web server or, for more complex applications and deployment scenarios, you can build deployment projects in Visual Studio .NET.

ASP.NET's machine.config and web.config files allow for a simpler and more portable configuration model than ASP. Assemblies allow application resources to be easily shared in a global cache or placed in a local assembly for use by individual applications.

From a deployment perspective, the main benefits of ASP.NET are that it is no longer necessary to be "hands on" with the server to configure the Web application or register components. web.config files and assemblies also can be updated or replaced on the fly without having to shut down the server, and can be replaced remotely. Another benefit is that .NET assemblies allow multiple versions, thus avoiding the inherent versioning problems of COM components, which resulted in the aptly named "DLL Hell," in which newer versions of components could "break" existing applications.

Planning the deployment of a Web application requires identifying the production server configuration, whether it is a single IIS server or a multiple-server environment such as a cluster or Web farm. There must be access to the production server either through the network or the Internet, and the appropriate permissions must be granted to write files to the server and configure the virtual directories in Internet Information Server (IIS).

If the application is deployed using the simple copy method, it needs to be prepared for the deployment by identifying the required files. If the deployment is handled using removable media or Web-based deployment, or requires a setup program to install and allow for uninstall, you will use a Visual Studio deployment project to create the deployment package.

Requirements for Deployment

ASP.NET applications can be deployed in three ways:

- Through installers created from Setup Projects in Visual Studio.
- Using Copy Project in Visual Studio.
- Using the XCOPY command over the network.

Using the Visual Studio tools for deployment is preferable for all but the most simple, direct deployment scenarios. The resulting Windows Installer (msi) files will configure IIS settings, verify the location of assemblies, identify and copy only the required files, and handle registration of application components. They also can be configured to test the server for the availability of required services and components such as IIS and data access components before the install process begins.

Application Requirements

Whatever the deployment method, a Web application must be built (compiled) before it can be deployed. This creates the DLLs that contain the code. The next step is to remove all unnecessary files from the Web directory, as there is no point in copying the source files to the production server, where they serve no purpose and possibly increase security risks by exposing the source code. When using XCOPY deployment, you will need to do this manually before deployment.

If you use Visual Studio to deploy the application, whether using Copy Project or Setup Project, it will automatically identify and copy only the required files to the server. The files in a Visual Studio ASP.NET application that should be removed are

- All Visual Studio solution files (vbproj, csproj, and so forth)
- All code-behind pages and any resource files

The files required for deployment are

- All Web Form, user control, and Web service files
- Configuration files such as web.config, Global.asax, and so forth
- The \bin directory and its contents (DLL files)
- Any support files in the directory such as graphic files and XML files

All Web Forms, XML Web services, and user control files are copied "as is" to the server, where they will be processed by the CLR on request by the user. All code-behind pages and .NET components are compiled during the build, and the resulting DLLs copied to the production server, not the .vb or .cs source files or the like. This means the interface elements of the application such as the Web Forms, .aspx files, and others can be modified directly on the server without rebuilding or redeploying the application, or alternately on the development server and then copied to the production server.

Any changes to the application logic contained in the code-behind pages and components must be recompiled—most likely on the development server—and then redeployed to the production server. When you conduct maintenance on the application, it is not necessary to deploy the entire application again—only those files that have been modified.

If the application uses COM components, they must be installed and registered on the server. This can be accomplished using COM+ for COM+ components and REGSVR32.EXE for non COM+ COM DLLs. Visual Studio .NET also provides a CAB Project that can be used to package ActiveX components that need to be downloaded from the Web server to the client browser. This is required if the Web pages use ActiveX controls. The CAB Project will produce the CAB files to be deployed to the server for any ActiveX controls that the pages use. The client browser then can access the CAB files to install and register the ActiveX component on the client machine as needed.

Production Server Requirements

To run ASP.NET Web applications, the production Web server must have the Common Language Runtime installed on the server. The server will therefore need the .NET Framework installed and obviously Internet Information Server (IIS). To successfully deploy a Web application, you must have the necessary security permissions to access the server, which vary with the deployment method used but will require at minimum the ability to write files.

To deploy a Web application using the Visual Studio deployment tools, you must be on the same network (on the same domain) as the production server and, as Visual Studio deployment configures IIS virtual directories for the application, you must have administrative rights to the computer hosting the Web server. You also probably will need access rights to configure any other resources the Web application uses such as database servers, MSMQ, and so forth, as you might require permissions to add stored procedures to the database to support the Web application.

To deploy using the Copy Project method from Visual Studio, FrontPage Server Extensions must be installed on the target server. This method uses HTTP to copy to the production server and requires the necessary privileges on the server to write files to it. Copy Project does not enable you to directly configure IIS, so administrative privileges are not directly required for the actual deployment. However, IIS virtual directories will still need to be configured, and if the person deploying the application is doing this, he or she will need administration access and hands-on access to the server to create the virtual directories.

EXERCISE 9-1

Prepare and Deploy a Web Application Using XCOPY

In this exercise, we will build a simple Web application in Visual Studio and prepare it for deployment using the XCOPY method.

1. Create a new ASP.NET application in Visual Studio and name it "Chapter9."

2. Rename WebForm1.aspx "Home.aspx."

3. From the menu choose Project | Add Web Form. Name the new page "Page1.aspx" and click Open.

4. Switch to Home.aspx in Design view and add a label at the top of the page. Set the text property for the label to Chapter Nine Home Page and set the font size to X-Large.

5. Add two labels to the page and set the text to User Name and Password, respectively.

6. Add two textboxes beside the labels. Set the ID of the first one to txtUserName and the second one's ID to txtPassword. Change the TextMode property of txtPassword to Password.

7. Add two RequiredFieldValidator controls beside the textboxes and set the ControlToValidate properties of each control to the appropriate textbox.

8. Add text to the ErrorMessage properties of each of the validation controls to display an error message if there is no input in the textboxes.

9. Add a Button Web control to the page; set its ID to btnLogon and its text property to Log On.

10. The resulting page should look like this:

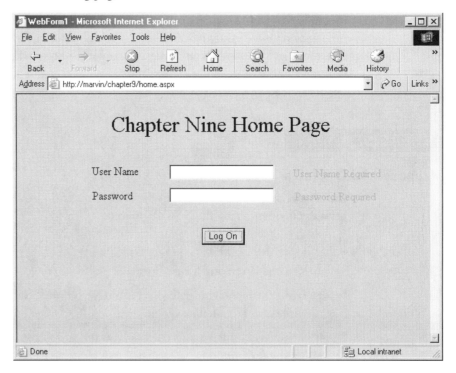

11. Double-click the Log On button in design mode to open the code-behind page.

12. Add the following code to the btnLogOn_Click event:

```
Response.Redirect("Page1.aspx")
```

13. Save the files and build the project. Test the application in the browser. As long as there is text entered in both of the controls, it should validate and redirect to Page1 when you click the Log On button.

14. Open Windows Explorer and navigate to the project directory. This should be \documents and settings*yourloginname*\My documents\Visual Studio Projects\Chapter9 *or* \Inetpub\wwwRoot\Chapter9. To retain the original project files for further use and modification, copy the Chapter9 directory, and contents, including subdirectories to another location. In the copied directory, change the directory name to "Chapter9DeployXCOPY."

15. Remove the following files from the \Chapter9DeployXCOPY directory:

    ■ AssemblyInfo.vb

    ■ Chapter9.sln

    ■ Chapter9.vbproj

    ■ Chapter9.vbproj.webinfo

    ■ Chapter9.vsdisco

    ■ Global.asax.vb

    ■ Global.asax.resx

    ■ Home.aspx.vb

    ■ Home.aspx.resx

    ■ Page1.aspx.vb

    ■ Page1.aspx.resx

    The remaining files should be Global.asax, Home.aspx, Page1.aspx, Styles, web.config, and the \bin directory and contents.

16. If you have a separate target server to deploy to, use XCOPY from the command prompt to copy the files to a \Chapter9DeployXCOPY directory on the server. If you are working on the same server (localhost) for the purposes of this exercise, you can copy to another directory on localhost and change the name of the target directory.

17. You now will need to create a virtual directory in IIS for the deployed Web application. Open Internet Information Services Manager. In Windows 2000, click Start | Settings | Control Panel; then choose Administrative Tools and then Internet Services Manager.

18. Click the "+" beside your server name, right-click Default Web Site, and choose New | Virtual Directory from the pop-up menu, shown here:

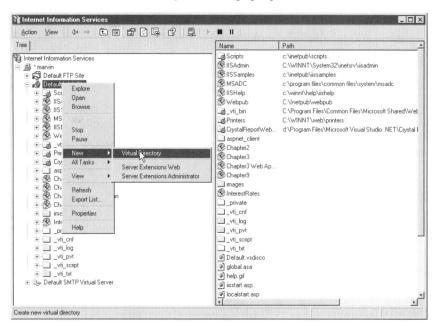

19. If you are using IIS on Windows 2000, a New Virtual Directory Wizard will open. Next, click the opening window, enter the alias **Chapter9DeployXCOPY**, shown next, and click the Next button. Browse to the directory containing the deployed files (\Chapter9DeployXCOPY\) and click OK, shown next.

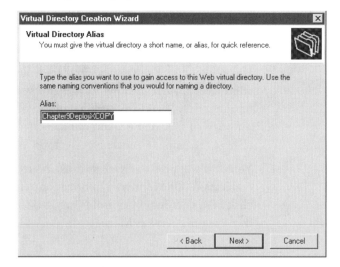

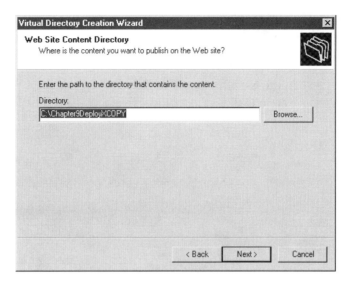

20. On the Access Permission pages, make sure only read and run scripts are chosen, click the Next button, and then click Finish.

21. Notice that your Chapter9DeployXCOPY site has been created under the default Web site in IIS.

22. Test the application in the browser by using http://*yourservername*/Chapter9DeployXCOPY/Home.aspx.

The XCOPY deployment method is relatively uncomplicated but requires a number of steps to be performed, such as removing unwanted files from the application before copying. The Copy Project method from Visual Studio is a simple way to move the application files to the target Web server. Like the XCOPY method, it does not configure the IIS directory settings or handle any registration issues, but it will automatically copy only the files required to run the application. For simple deployments from Visual Studio, it is an easier method of deployment. The following exercise will use the Copy Project to deploy the same application we built in the previous exercise.

Deploy a Web Application Using Copy Project

In this exercise, we will deploy the Chapter9 Web application from Exercise 3-1 using Visual Studio's Copy Project.

1. Open the Chapter9 project in Visual Studio .NET.

2. From the menu, choose Project | Copy Project.

3. Accept the defaults on the Copy Project dialog, as shown here:

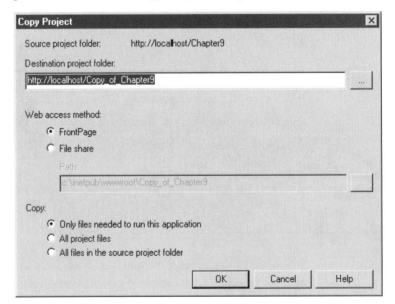

4. Click OK.

5. The application files will be copied to \Inetpub\wwwroot\Copy_of_Chapter9\. Open the directory in Windows Explorer and view the contents. Notice that only the required files have been copied.

6. Open Internet Services Manager and notice that the Virtual Directory has been created for you. This has occurred only because you have Administrative privileges on the server.

7. Test the application in the browser.

Copy Project requires that Front Page Server Extensions be installed on the target Web server. As you saw in the preceding exercise you can specify the destination folder on the server, and copy just the required files or all files in the application.

Another method of deployment is to use Web Setup projects in Visual Studio. When deploying a complex application that requires IIS configuration or registration of components, this is by far the best method. Web Setup projects produce a setup application and allow specific deployment conditions to be managed. We will explore Web Setup projects to plan deployments using removable media and Web-based deployment.

CERTIFICATION OBJECTIVE 9.01

Plan a Deployment that Uses Removable Media

To deploy using removable media, you need to create a deployment project in Visual Studio for the Web application. To do this, you add a new Web Setup Project to the existing Web project, and add the output of the Web application project to the deployment project. When built, this process will create Windows Installer (.msi) files that can be copied to other media including floppy disks, CD-ROMs, or a network server directory for installation.

Planning for deployment that uses removable media is similar to planning using any other method of deployment, except you will have no direct knowledge of the server on which the application eventually will be deployed. Without this knowledge, it is important that the deployment package include all required resources to ensure the application runs successfully.

Deployment planning consists primarily of ensuring that all required components are included with the deployment package and that the application will be configured correctly on the target server. When building and testing a Web application on the development server, this is a relatively simple and logical task. When deploying to a known production server, it is relatively simple to ensure that the server is configured correctly and the required resources are installed and available. The developer also can directly test and debug the application after deployment to the production server.

However, when deployment will be handled using removable media, this is not the case, as the target server is unknown and therefore you must plan for all possibilities.

It is necessary to identify the requirements for successful deployment, including the required operating systems and services, and where possible, either include the required components or notify the user that a requirement is missing on the server, such as IIS.

The most obvious requirements for a successful deployment of an ASP.NET Web application is that the target server has both the .NET Framework and IIS installed. Without either, a successful installation is impossible and should be aborted. Other components also might be required. For example, if the application references the System.Data namespace for data access, the Microsoft Data Access Components version 2.6 (MDAC) will need to be installed on the server or the application will fail.

The Visual Studio deployment tools will not detect the requirement for MDAC in the application. To ensure that these types of errors do not occur with the installation, you can add launch conditions to a Web Setup project. These will test for the existence of the components and display specific error messages to the user performing the install if there is a problem. The required components then can be installed before deploying the Web application.

EXERCISE 9-3

Create a Web Setup Project to Deploy with Removable Media

In this exercise, we will build a Web Setup Project that will create an installer that can be copied to a directory on a server, or to a floppy disk or CD-ROM. Because this is specifically for a removable media deployment, we also will view the default Launch conditions that verify that the target server has the .NET Framework and at least IIS 4, and set a condition to ensure that MDAC 2.6 is installed.

1. Open the original Chapter9 exercise used in the last exercise.

2. From the File menu, choose Add Project and then New Project.

3. In the Add New Project dialog box, choose Setup and Deployment Projects and Web Setup Project. Enter the name **Chapter9Setup** in the Name box. Click OK.

4. The Setup Project will be added to the Solution and the File System Editor will open.

5. Select the Web Application folder in the File System Editor and choose Action | Add | Project Output.

6. In the Add Project Output Group dialog box, choose Chapter9Setup from the Project list box.

7. Set both the Primary Output and Content Files from the list and click OK. Use CTRL-click to select both items.

8. Select the Web Application folder and in the Properties window check that the Virtual Directory is set to Chapter9Setup.

9. Set the Default Document property to Home.aspx.

10. To set Launch Conditions, select View | Editor | Launch Conditions from the menu.

11. Expand the Search Target Machine node and click the Search for IIS entry. This is a default search condition for IIS set in a Web Setup Project. Notice the property settings in the Properties window. Regkey is set to *SYSTEM\ CurrentControlSet\Services\W3SVC\Parameters,* which sets the registry key to search for, and Root is set to *vsdrrHKLM*, which specifies the HKEY_ LOCAL_MACHINE hive in the Registry. Click the root property to see the drop-down menu and notice the available settings.

12. Under Launch Conditions, click IIS Condition and view the properties in the Properties Window. By default, the Condition property is set to IISVERSION >= "#4". The Message property is set to a standard localized message. If you wish, you can enter your own message string but it will not be localized.

13. There also is a default launch condition named MsiNetAssemblySupport. This will test for the existence of the .NET Framework on the target server. Like the IIS condition, it has a standard localized message. If any launch condition is not met, the message will display and the setup will terminate.

14. We now will set up a launch condition for MDAC 2.6. Select the Requirements on Target Machine node and from the menu choose Action | Add Registry Launch Condition.

15. Select the Search for RegistryEntry1 node. Enter **Software\Microsoft\ DataAccess** in the RegKey property in the Properties window.

16. In the Root property, set the value to vsdrrHKLM. This should be the default.

17. In the Value property, enter **FullInstallVer.**

18. Set the Property property to MDACSEARCH.

19. Select the Condition1 node and set the Condition property to MDACSEARCH>="2.6".

20. Enter a message to the Message property—for example, **MDAC version 2.6 is required for this application and must be installed prior to setup.**

21. On the menu, choose Build | Build Chapter9Setup.

22. In Windows Explorer, navigate to the project directory to find the installer. It should be in \documents and settings*yourloginname*\My Documents\Visual Studio Projects\Chapter9Setup\Debug\Chapter9Setup.msi or in \Inetpub\wwwroot\Chapter9\Chapter9Setup\Debug\Chapter9Setup.msi.

23. Copy the Chapter9Setup.msi file and all files and subdirectories to the desired media or server directory. To install, double-click the Setup.exe file.

24. To properly test this exercise, you will need a computer that does not have IIS or MDAC 2.6 installed.

---

exam
Watch

Our application does not have any need for MDAC 2.6, as we do not use data access; however, it is included here to show you the capability of searching for a condition based on a Registry entry.

In addition to the launch conditions we have seen in the preceding exercise, there are other conditions that can be evaluated. A file launch condition will allow you to search for a specific file, such as an .exe file on the target server, and then evaluate the result of the search. If the search is not successful, a message is displayed to the user and the installation is aborted. You also can add a launch condition in the Launch Conditions Editor to test values exposed by the Windows Installer. We will revisit the Launch Conditions Editor in more detail along with the other deployment editors when discussing Web-based deployment.

exam
Watch

At first glance, deployment in ASP.NET seems to be a simple procedure; in fact, most ASP.NET books and even the Microsoft courses pay it little attention beyond the XCOPY method. From the discussion in this chapter and the number of 70-305 Exam Objectives based on deployment, it should be clear that this is an aspect of ASP.NET you should be familiar with before attempting the exam.

CERTIFICATION OBJECTIVE 9.02

Plan a Web-Based Deployment

Initially Web-based deployment seems like an oxymoron. The whole point of ASP.NET deployment is to deploy to a production Web server from a development Web server. As we have already seen, deployment can be carried out over a network using XCOPY, Copy Project from Visual Studio, or a Windows Installer setup on removable media or a network folder.

Using Copy Project from Visual Studio allows a Web application to be copied to the target server across the Web using FrontPage server extensions. Although it isn't deployment in the strict sense, as it does not automatically configure the IIS directory settings, it does allow the application files to be moved to the target server.

We used Copy Project in Exercise 9-2 to simply copy the Web application to localhost. When using Copy Project, the Destination Project Folder can be any Web server on which you have the privileges to create, write, and run code. The Web Access method of Copy Project can be set to either *Front Page* or *File Share*.

Using File Share access requires you to be on the same domain as the target Web server, whereas FrontPage access allows access with HTTP. This means you can copy across the Internet, including across firewalls, as long as the firewall will pass HTTP requests. As mentioned previously, the target server must have FrontPage Server Extensions installed; once the files are on the server, the IIS directory settings will require configuring by an IIS Administrator. Refer to Figure 9-5 for the Copy Project options.

Web applications also can be deployed over the Web using installers. As we saw in Exercise 9-3 a Web Setup Project will build an installer for our application, which can be copied to the target server and executed. The advantage of this method is that it is a true deployment in the sense that the application is automatically configured on the target server based on settings and conditions built into the installer. However, the installer package still needs to be physically placed on the server, which requires either a direct network connection or copying from a CD-ROM.

Another method of deploying an application is to download the Windows Installer (msi) file from a Web server. To enable this, you need to copy the installer to a Web server and configure a virtual directory for the installer directory. You then set the Virtual Directory Execute Permissions to Scripts and Executables, and set the security for the directory to restrict access to administrators or another defined group that would be responsible for installing the application. You then can navigate to the virtual directory on the Web server using a browser, and download and install the application.

The capability to deploy an application for download from a Web server is a very useful feature for regular Windows- or Forms-based .NET applications, but it is highly unlikely that a Web application would require this approach. .NET applications can easily be packaged in Web Setup Projects to provide the capability for the users to install from a Web server on the intranet or from the Internet.

Use Deployment Editors

In Exercise 9-3, we used the Launch Conditions Editor to search and respond to specific launch conditions required for successful deployment of the application. The Visual Studio .NET Web Setup Project provides six editors that can be used to configure the installer:

- File System
- Registry
- File Types
- User Interface
- Custom Actions
- Launch Conditions

The editors are accessed from the deployment project menu under View | Editors. Let's take a closer look at each of the editors.

The File System Editor

The File System Editor enables you to add folders, files, and project output to the deployment project. For a simple Web application, this might not be required, as the file system that will be deployed will match the application file structure of the development Web application. However, for more complex applications, including sites that consist of multiple Web applications, the File System Editor allows you to build a single deployment project, which can include multiple project outputs, components, and so forth. You also might want to include custom folders containing files that are specific to the deployed application such as readme text files or HTML help files.

Add Folders   The File System Editor automatically displays a set of folders for the target server that represents the folder structure for the deployment. You can add standard folders called *special folders* to the top level, as well as custom folders and subfolders.

To add a special folder:

1. Select the File System on Target Machine node in the File System Editor.

2. Choose Action | Add Special Folder from the menu.

3. Choose the folder required from the resulting drop-down menu. See Figure 9-6 for details.

To add a custom folder:

1. Select the File System on Target Machine node in the File System Editor.

2. Choose Action | Add Special Folder, then Custom Folder or Web Custom Folder from the menu.

3. The new folder is inserted and highlighted in the left pane of the File System Editor.

4. Enter a name for the folder.

To add a subfolder:

1. Select the parent folder in the File System Editor.

2. Choose Action | Add | Folder.

3. The new subfolder will be added to the folder list beneath the parent folder. If it is in the wrong place, you can simply drag it to a new location.

4. Type in a name for the new folder.

Removing Folders   To remove a folder, simply highlight it and press DELETE or choose Edit | Delete from the menu. The Web Application folder cannot be deleted, nor can any folders containing files or outputs without deleting the contents of the folder first (see Figure 9-1).

Add Project Outputs from the File System Editor When you have one or more projects in your solution, you can add the project outputs to target folders for deployment. In a Web application, these will be added to a Web custom folder. You also can add project outputs from the Solution Explorer but this will add the output to the application folder rather than a target folder.

To add project output to a target folder:

1. Select the Target Folder.

2. From the Action menu, choose Add | Project Output.

FIGURE 9-1 Adding folders in the File System Editor

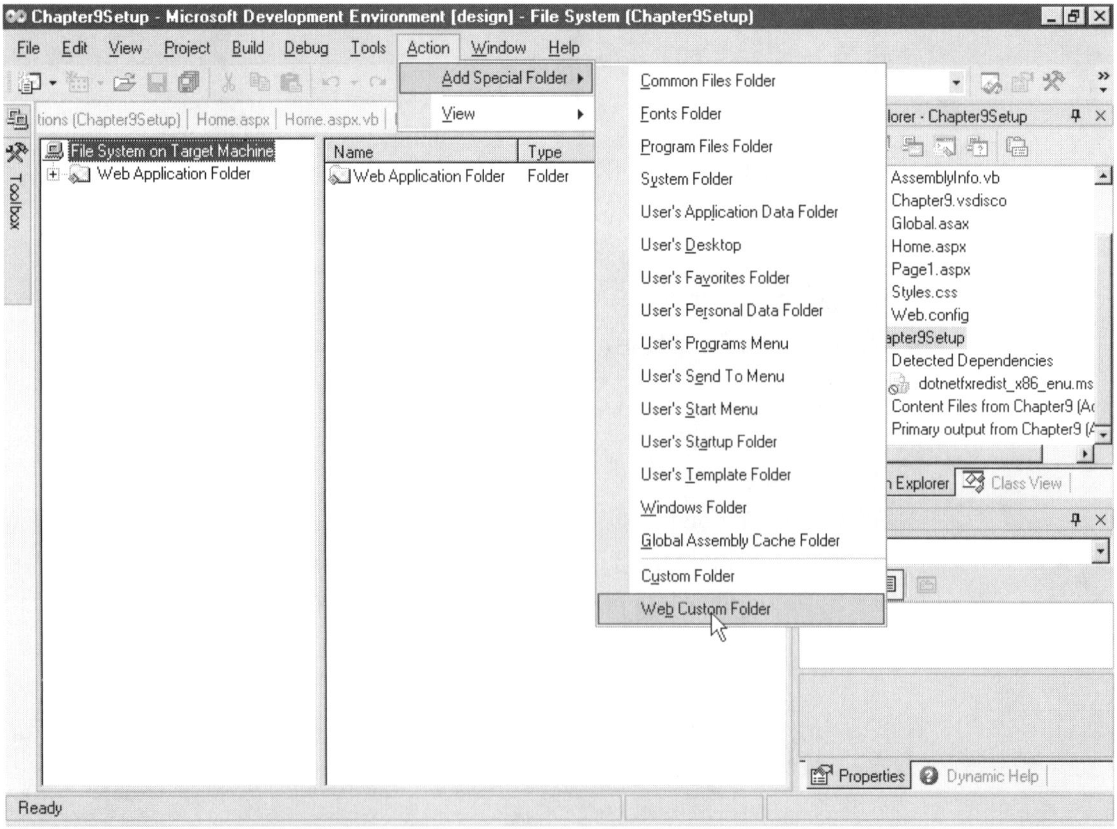

3. In the Select Project Output Group dialog box, choose the project and output types, and click OK.

To remove a project output, select it in the File System Editor and press DELETE.

Add Files from the File System Editor   To add a file to a target folder:

1. Select the Target Folder.

2. From the Action menu, choose Add | File.

3. In the Add Files dialog box, browse for the file and click Open.

You can add files from the Project menu but this will add the file to the Application folder. You must use the File System Editor to add files to a specific folder.

To delete a file, highlight it and delete it, either from the keyboard or the menu.

The Registry Editor

The application you are deploying might need to modify or add registry keys and values to the target server's registry. The Registry Editor allows you to define these keys as part of the installer. By default, the Registry Editor displays a standard set of keys: HKEY_CLASSES_ROOT, HKEY_CURRENT_USER, HKEY_LOCAL_ MACHINE, HKEY_USERS, and User/Machine Hive. You can add your own keys under these keys or any subkey. Figure 9-2 depicts the Registry Editor.

Add and Delete Registry Keys from the Registry Editor   Registry keys can be added beneath any top-level key; if it does not exist on the target computer, it will be added during installation.

To add a registry key:

1. Choose View | Editor | Registry from the menu to open the Registry Editor.

2. Select a top-level key and choose Action | New Key.

3. Type in a name for the new key.

To add a subkey:

1. Select a key in the Registry Editor.

2. From the menu, choose Action | New | Key.

3. Type in a name for the new key.

FIGURE 9-2   The Registry Editor

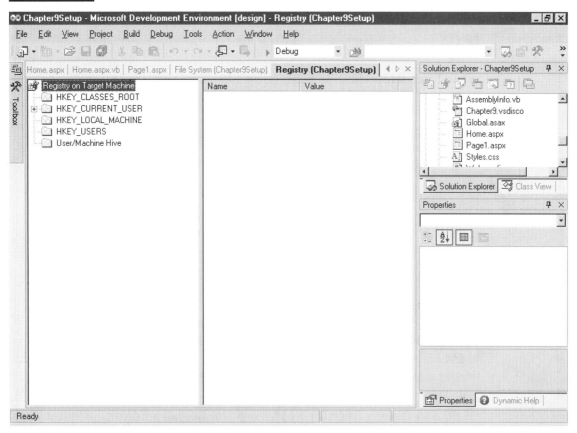

Registry keys can be deleted in the editor by pressing DELETE on the keyboard or choosing the same from the Edit menu. When you delete a key, it will delete the key value and all subkeys.

Add and Delete Registry Values from the Registry Editor   Registry values can be added for new or existing registry keys on the target computer but not to the top-level nodes. Any existing values will be overwritten by the values you specify on installation. The values can be string, binary, or DWORD data types.

To add a registry value:

1.   Select the key node and choose Action | New from the menu, and then selecting the data type of the value.

2. Enter a name for the new value.

3. From the Properties window, select the Value property and enter the value.

Registry values can be deleted or moved between keys by dragging and dropping, or using Cut and Paste.

Import Registry Files in the Registry Editor　To save time and work, you can import an entire section of a registry into the Visual Studio Registry Editor. The existing registry can be exported to a registry file (.reg) from the Registry menu in the Registry Editor in Windows (Regedit.exe), as shown in Figure 9-3.

The section of the registry exported will depend on which key is selected at the time. To export the complete registry, select My Computer; for a subset, choose the key—for example, HKEY_LOCAL_MACHINE \Software\myProgram, and so forth. It is not likely that you would choose such a high-level key. The idea is to take the registry settings on the development machine that are specific to the application, and bring them into the Web Setup Project as a block. Then they can be individually modified using the Registry Editor in Visual Studio if required.

FIGURE 9-3	
Exporting the registry from the Windows Registry Editor	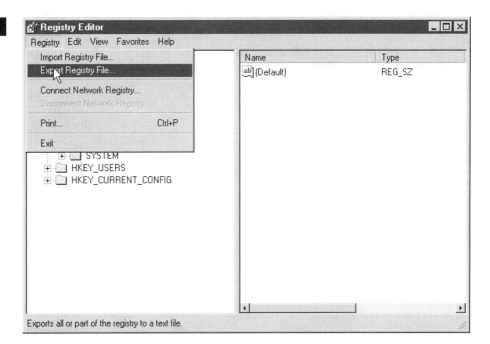

To import a registry file:

1. After exporting the section of the existing registry from the Windows Registry Editor, select the Registry on Target Machine node in the Visual Studio Registry Editor.

2. Choose Action | Import from the menu.

3. In the Import Registry File dialog box, browse to the registry file (.reg) exported previously and click Open.

Each registry key has a set of properties that can be set in the Registry Editor. Table 9-1 lists the properties and their descriptions.

exam
ⓦatch

Microsoft has been busy changing the nature of exams over the last couple of years. Some of the newer "innovations" in its testing format include "Select and Place" and "Simulations." Up to this point, none of the programming exams have included these features except for the 70-100 Analyzing Requirements and Defining Solution Architectures; however, it is likely they will appear in the new exams. Before you attempt the exam, make sure you are familiar with this exam style by visiting http://microsoft.com/traincert/mcpexams/policies/innovations.asp.

The File Types Editor

The File Types Editor allows you to associate file extensions with the application on the target server.

| TABLE 9-1 | Registry Keys and Their Properties |

Property	Description
AlwaysCreate	Specifies whether to create the selected registry key as part of every installation, even if the registry key is empty.
Condition	Specifies a Windows Installer condition that must be true for the registry key/value to be installed.
DeleteAtUninstall	Specifies whether the selected registry key and any subkeys will be deleted when the product is uninstalled.
FullPath	Contains the full registry path for the selected registry key. Read-only.
Transitive	Determines whether the installer will reevaluate the Condition property for the selected item when installing or reinstalling on a target computer.

Add and Delete Associated File Types   To add and delete associations, you need to add a document type to the setup project and associate the document type to a file extension or executable file. To add a document type:

1. Choose View | Editor | File Types from the menu.

2. Select the File Types on Target Machine node in the File Types Editor.

3. From the menu, choose Action | Add File Type.

4. Enter a name for the new document type.

To add a file extension:

1. Select the Document Type node.

2. Select the Extensions property in the Properties window for the document and type in the file extension without the leading period (dat, not .dat). Multiple extension types can be separated by a semicolon—for example, dat;var.

Figure 9-4 shows the File Types Editor with a document type of Dat File and the Extension property set to *dat*.

To associate an executable file with the document type, do the following:

1. Select the Document Type.

2. Click the ellipsis button in the Command property for the document.

3. Choose the executable file to associate.

The User Interface Editor

The Windows Installer predefines a set of dialog boxes used in the Installation Wizard. There are two sections of dialog boxes set out in a tree control: Install and Administrative Install. Each section contains dialog boxes that will be included in the install program separated into three nodes: Start, Progress, and End. The Start node contains a Welcome box, an Installation Address box, and a Confirm Installation box. The Progress node contains a Progress box which includes a progress bar to display the progress of the installation to the user. The End node contains a Finished

FIGURE 9-4 The File Types Editor

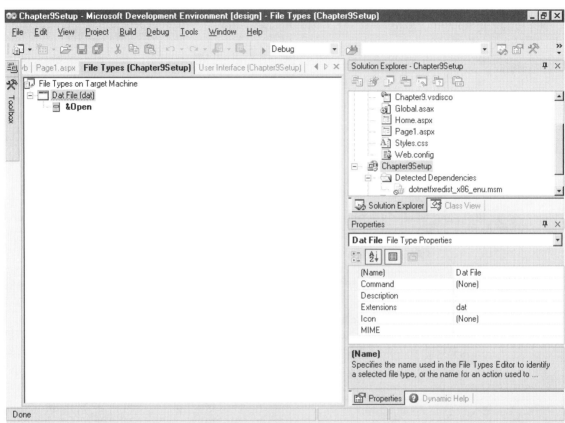

dialog, which will display when the installation is complete. Figure 9-5 shows the default set of dialog boxes for a Web Setup Project.

A predefined set of user interface dialog boxes are available to add to the installation. If you don't see a need for any dialogs, you can remove the defaults from the project in the editor. Table 9-2 lists the dialog boxes supplied by the Web Setup Project. Note that the dialog boxes are limited to the number available in the editor and can be used only once, which is the reason there are multiples of some boxes such as the check-box dialogs.

FIGURE 9-5   Default dialog boxes in the User Interface Editor

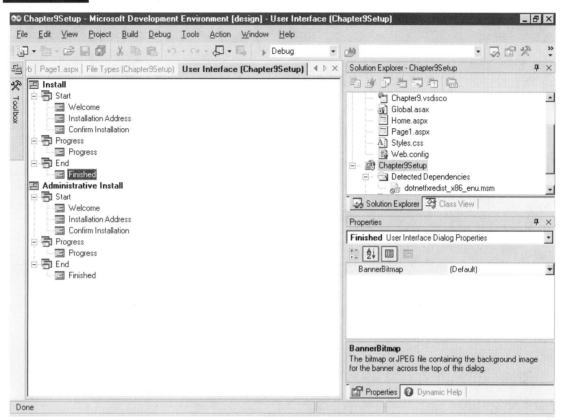

TABLE 9-2   User Interface Dialog Boxes

Dialog Box	Purpose
Check Boxes A, B, or C	Presents as many as four choices using check boxes.
Confirm Installation	Allows the user to confirm settings such as installation location before beginning the installation.
Customer Information	Prompts the user for information, including name, company, and serial number.
Finished	Notifies the user when the installation is complete.
Installation Address	Allows the user to choose the Web location where application files will be installed.
Installation Folder	Allows the user to choose the folder where application files will be installed.

| TABLE 9-2 | User Interface Dialog Boxes *(continued)* |

Dialog Box	Purpose
License Agreement	Presents a license agreement for the user to read and acknowledge.
Progress	Updates the user on the progress of the installation.
RadioButtons (two buttons)	Presents a choice between two mutually exclusive options using option (radio) buttons.
RadioButtons (three buttons)	Presents a choice among three mutually exclusive options using option (radio) buttons.
RadioButtons (four buttons)	Presents a choice among four mutually exclusive options using option (radio) buttons.
Read Me	Allows the user to view a ReadMe message in rich text.
Register User	Allows the user to submit registration information.
Splash	Presents a bitmap to the user to display a logo or branding information.
Textboxes A, B, or C	Prompts the user for custom information using one to three textboxes.
Welcome	Presents introductory text and copyright information to the user.

Add Installation Dialog Boxes   To add dialog boxes to the install:

1. Choose View | Editor | User Interface from the menu.
2. Select Start, Progress, or Finish node in the left pane of the editor.
3. Choose Add Dialog from the Action menu.
4. Choose the dialog you wish to add from the resulting Add Dialog box.
5. Set the properties for the Dialog box in the Properties window.

You can re-order the dialog boxes by using the Move Up or Move Down options from the Action menu. To move boxes among categories, you can use drag-and-drop or cut and paste. To delete a dialog, highlight it and press DELETE or use the Edit menu.

The Custom Actions Editor

Custom actions are additional actions that are run at the end of the installation process in the form of program logic. Custom actions must be contained in the project solution as outputs of a project such as DLL or EXE files, or as compiled components or files added to the deployment project using the File System Editor. There are four stages to an installation: Install, Commit, Rollback, and Uninstall. Each stage is represented in the editor by separate folders. A deployment project can contain multiple custom actions and the actions can be dependent on conditions specified in the Condition property.

A common use of a custom action is to run a program to create a database on the target server for the application. The action that executes the program to create the database would be placed in the Install folder and might be conditional on the type of database server available on the target server. The database also could be removed from the server when the application is uninstalled by another program that would be executed by a Custom Action placed in the Uninstall folder.

To add a custom action:

1. Select View | Editor | Custom Actions from the menu.

2. Select a folder in the editor.

3. Choose Add Custom Action from the Action menu.

4. In the resulting Select Item In Project dialog, navigate to the file that contains the program or output for the action. If the item has not been added to the project, you can click Add File, Add Output, or Add Assembly to add the item, which also will add it to the project.

Custom Actions can be reordered by using Move Up and Move Down from the Action menu or by dragging. They can also be deleted.

The Launch Conditions Editor

Earlier in this chapter, we used the Launch Conditions Editor in Exercise 9-3 to specify conditions for a deployment targeted to removable media. In that instance, we wanted to set conditions to test for the .NET Framework, IIS, and MDAC 2.6 or later. You can use launch conditions to search the target computer to determine whether a particular file, registry key, or Windows Installer component exists, or to specify conditions required for a successful installation.

The Launch Conditions Editor provides a number of conditions that can be evaluated prior to installation. Predefined Launch Conditions add both a search and a condition in a single step. If the search is not successful, an error message will be displayed and the installation terminated.

Add a File Launch Condition   A *file launch condition* will determine whether a file exists on the target machine and roll back the installation if it is not found. To add a file launch condition:

1. In the Launch Conditions Editor, select the requirements on Target Machine node.

2. On the Action menu, choose Add File Launch Condition.

3. Select the Search for File node. In the Properties window, select the FileName property and enter the name of the file to search for.

4. Select the Folder property and type the name of the folder where the search will start. This can be either the bracketed name for a Windows Installer special folder provided in the list, or the full path to any folder that you specify.

5. If required, you can set the depth (subsequent levels of folders to search), date, size, and version properties.

6. Select the Condition node. In the Properties window, select the Message property and type an error message to be displayed if the file is not found.

Add a .NET Framework Launch Condition   A .NET Framework Launch condition will determine whether the .NET run-time files exist on the target machine and roll back the installation if it is not found. To add a .NET Framework Launch condition:

1. In the Launch Conditions Editor, select the Requirements on Target Machine node.

2. From the menu, choose Action | Add .NET Framework Launch Condition.

3. Select the Condition node. In the Properties window, the Message property contains a property specifying the standard localized error message that will be displayed.

Add a Registry Launch Condition   A Registry Launch Condition will test whether a registry entry exists on the target machine, and if not, roll back the installation. To add a Registry Launch condition:

1. In the Launch Conditions Editor, select the Requirements on Target Machine node.

2. On the menu, choose Action | Add Registry Launch Condition.

3. Select the Search for RegistryEntry node. In the Properties window, select the Root property and select the registry root to be searched from the list.

4. Select the RegKey property and enter the name of the registry key to search for, including the full path to the registry key, excluding the root; or set the Value property to search for a specific value in the registry key.

5. Select the Condition node. In the Properties window, select the Message property and enter the error message to be displayed if the registry entry is not found.

Add an Internet Information Services Launch Condition   An IIS Launch Condition will test whether IIS exists on the target machine, and if not, roll back the installation. To add an IIS Launch condition:

1. In the Launch Conditions Editor, select the Requirements on Target Machine node.

2. On the Action menu, choose Add Internet Information Services Launch Condition.

3. Select the Condition node. By default, the Condition property is set to REGISTRYVALUEn >= "#4", which specifies that the value contained in the registry key must be greater than or equal to 4 for IIS 4.0. If you wish to search for a different version, replace the 4 with the major version number you want to find.

Add a Launch Condition in the Launch Conditions Editor   The Launch Condition can be used to test a condition on the installer, such as an operating system version, or to evaluate the Property property from other elements in the installer such as a file search. To add a launch condition:

1. Select the Launch Conditions node in the Launch Conditions Editor.

2. On the Action menu, choose Add Launch Condition.

The new condition is highlighted in the conditions list.

1. Type a name for the condition.

2. In the Properties window, select the Condition property and enter a valid condition. For example, the installer has properties set to identify the

operating system version. Setting the Condition property to *VersionNT>=4* will specify that the operating system must be NT 4 or greater, or the install will terminate. Table 9-3 describes some of the more common Windows Installer properties you can use.

3. Select the Message property and type the text for the error message that will be displayed if the condition evaluates to false.

We now will look at some typical installer scenarios and their solutions using the Deployment Editors.

exam
ⓦatch

Expect the exam to include a number of questions concerning setup projects—especially regarding editors. The questions probably will be in the select-and-place and simulation styles, as opposed to the typical multiple-choice questions.

TABLE 9-3   Common Launch Condition Properties

Windows Installer Property	Description
Version9X	Version number for the Windows operating system.
VersionNT	Version number for the Windows NT/Windows 2000 operating system.
ServicePackLevel	The version number of the operating system service pack.
WindowsBuild	Build number of the operating system.
SystemLanguageID	Default language identifier for the system.
ComputerName	Computer name of the current system.
LogonUser	User name for the user currently logged on.
AdminUser	Set on Windows NT/Windows 2000 if the user has administrator privileges.
PhysicalMemory	Size of the installed RAM in megabytes.
Intel	Numeric processor level if running on an Intel processor.
COMPANYNAME	Company name of user performing the installation. Corresponds to the organization entered in the Customer Information installation dialog box.
USERNAME	User performing the installation. Corresponds to the name entered in the Customer Information installation dialog box.

SCENARIO & SOLUTION

I have built a Windows Installer to deploy my Web application but I don't require the Setup Wizard. Can I remove it from the installer?	Yes. Open the User Interface Editor in the Web Setup Project and delete all dialog boxes in the Start, Progress, and Finished nodes.
I need to include multiple new Registry keys and values in the setup. Do I need to add each one separately in the Registry Editor?	No. Use Regedit.exe from Windows to export the required keys and values to a .reg file from the development server. You then can import the file into the Registry Editor.
My Web application requires a specific program to be installed on the Production server for a successful install. How should I test for this?	Add a File Launch Condition in the Launch Conditions Editor, and in the Search for File node, set the FileName property to the program executable file.
I want to automatically display a ReadMe file to the user at the end of the installation. What is the best way to do this?	Add a Read Me dialog box to the End node in the User Interface Editor. You can place this either before or after the Finish dialog. Set the ReadmeFile property to point to the ReadMe file.

CERTIFICATION OBJECTIVE 9.03

Plan the Deployment of an Application to a Web Garden, a Web Farm, or a Cluster

Throughout this chapter, our discussion on deployment has assumed that the Web application is to be deployed to a single target server. However, depending on the size and criticality of the application, it could need to be installed to a server *cluster*.

A cluster is a group of physically connected servers that present an application or service to the client as a single image. Clusters are used to provide scalability and high availability of the application. The application or service is installed on all servers in the cluster; cluster software provides the logic to programmatically handle the application as if it were on a single server, and provide load balancing and failover.

Load balancing is the process of distributing the load across multiple servers to prevent one server from becoming overworked. *Failover* provides the capability of automatically transferring to another server in case of server failure, which guarantees availability of the application in case of hardware failure or other disaster.

Network Load Balancing (NLB) provides scalability and high availability for TCP/IP-based applications and services such as Web servers. A Web server is a common use for Network Load Balancing and requires each host in the cluster to run separate copies of the Web program. A Web application running on multiple cluster servers is generally referred to as a *Web farm*. An application running in multiple processes but on one server is referred to as a *Web garden*.

A Web farm requires the Web application to be deployed to each server in the farm. Network Load Balancing enables all the servers in the cluster to maintain their own IP addresses but be addressed by the same set of cluster IP addresses. Incoming requests then are distributed across the host servers in the cluster.

Network administrators probably will handle the design and installation of clusters and Network Load Balancing, as well as the installation of the Web applications. The developer's task is to produce an application and a deployment model that will work effectively in such a scenario. This undoubtedly will require working with the administrators to determine the requirements for the application deployment.

You can handle the deployment to the servers in the cluster in a number of ways. The application can be installed on one server and deployed on the other servers in the cluster by replicating an image. As long as the server hardware meets the requirements, you can do this using Microsoft Application Center 2000. If the servers are of differing hardware configurations and manufacturers, it might require a separate install for each server.

Network Load Balancing is installed using Windows 2000 Server or Advanced Server, and can include Commerce Server components. Microsoft Application Center 2000 provides software load balancing where multiple computers are clustered together. Separating the business logic from the database tier in the cluster configuration is another thing that should be planned for as the Web servers and database servers probably will be separate computers or clusters.

Thus, when planning for deployment it could be important for the Web install package to not automatically create the databases on the Web server by using a custom action. A separate install package might be required to create databases, set up message queues, produce event logs, and so forth.

Another consideration when deploying a Web application to a Web farm or load-balanced environment is application state. Application data will be available only to the process in which it is running, which means it will not be visible in the true sense to the application as a whole in a clustered environment. Remember that the application is now distributed over multiple computers and therefore consists of multiple processes. To overcome this problem the application should store data in an external data store such as a database that is available to all process instances.

CERTIFICATION OBJECTIVE 9.04

Create a Setup Program that Installs a Web Application and Allows It to Be Uninstalled

When you create a Windows Installer for the Web application using a Web Setup Project as we did in Exercise 9-3, the installer (.msi) file includes the output from the Web application to be installed, the launch conditions for the install, and logic for the setup application itself (Setup.exe). The Windows Installer also automatically builds in the uninstall capability for the application. All applications installed with the installer can be uninstalled from Add/Remove Programs in the Windows Control Panel. This is an automatic process as a result of building the installer.

EXERCISE 9-4

Uninstall the Chapter9Setup Web Application

In this exercise, we will uninstall the Chapter9Setup application we installed in Exercise 9-3. If you did not install the application, you will have to do so to complete this exercise.

1. Choose Start | Settings | Control Panel.

2. Select Add/Remove Programs.

3. Choose Chapter9Setup and then click the Change/Remove button.

4. The application will be uninstalled.

As you can see, the capability to uninstall the application is automatic when using Windows Installer to deploy a Web application. There are two optional properties of the deployment project that relate to the uninstall process. The *AddRemoveProgramsIcon* will allow you to add a custom icon to the project, which will appear in the Add/ Remove Programs window. The *RemovePreviousVersions* property is set to False by default, but if set to True, will automatically remove any previous versions of the application when reinstalling.

FROM THE CLASSROOM

Windows Installers and ASP.NET

Since the inception of the World Wide Web, Web sites have evolved into increasingly more complex applications. In the beginning, a Web site consisted of only static pages and links to other pages and sites. This evolved into dynamic sites that processed requests on the Web server and returned content based on that process using scripting languages on the server. As browser capabilities evolved, client-side scripting, ActiveX controls, Java applets, and DHTML were added to the mix. As a result, the Web gained the capability to provide complex interactive applications hosted by Web servers.

As Web applications became more complex, so did the deployment of those applications. A simple static Web site basically just needs HTML and supporting media files to be both copied to the Web server and configured as a virtual directory. Dynamic Web applications, such as IIS applications using ASP, also can be deployed in this manner but generally require hands-on maintenance of the server to configure the IIS directories, install and register components, and so forth.

The .NET Framework—specifically ASP.NET—alleviates most of the deployment headaches by introducing Web Setup Projects that produce Windows Installers. The installers can be configured to test conditions on the server before install, write registry entries, automatically execute programs on completion, and provide a customized setup wizard. In other words, the capability of providing an interactive setup application that automatically handles setup issues now is available for Web applications as it has been for standard program installation.

—David Shapton, MCSD, MCT, CTT+

CERTIFICATION OBJECTIVE 9.05

Add Assemblies to the Global Assembly Cache

In Chapter 4, we discussed creating and implementing satellite and resource-only assemblies. Assemblies are the basic method of sharing and reuse in the Common Language Runtime (CLR) and generally are a single DLL file, but can consist of multiple files. Because .NET DLL files are not registered, they are not easily shared between multiple ASP.NET applications.

Assemblies are placed in a local cache by the CLR where it is locked so other applications cannot access it. The default cache is the \bin subdirectory in the application root, which is deployed to the target server and configured to deny access to client requests. Each computer with the CLR installed also has a machine-wide cache called the Global Assembly Cache (GAC), which contains the assemblies that are to be shared by multiple Web applications on the server.

The GAC is installed in the \WINNT\Assembly directory. To share assemblies between Web applications, they must be placed in the Global Assembly Cache. The GAC supports side-by-side versioning, which means you can have multiple copies of the same assembly but with different version information in the GAC.

There are three ways to deploy an assembly into the Global Assembly Cache:

- Use Windows Explorer to drag and drop the assembly into the GAC on the target server. By default, this is located in \WINNT\Assembly.

- Use the Global Assembly Cache tool (*Gacutil.exe*) provided with the .NET Framework.

- Use a Visual Studio Web Setup project to build an Installer to deploy the assembly to the Global Assembly Cache folder.

For deployment to a production server, you should use the Installer, as it will provide reference counting for the assembly, which keeps track of the clients using the assembly and allows an automatic uninstall of the assembly if it is no longer required. The Gacutil.exe or Windows Explorer deployment methods should be used only to deploy development servers.

In the following exercise, we will walk through the tasks required to add an assembly to the GAC in a Web Setup Project. To avoid having to build our assembly, we will use an existing assembly from the .NET Framework.

EXERCISE 9-5

Using a Web Setup Project to Add an Assembly to the Global Assembly Cache

This exercise will add an existing assembly to the Chapter9Setup Web Setup Project.

1. Open the Chapter9Setup project and view the File System Editor.

2. Select the File System on Target Machine node in the left pane of the editor.

3. Choose Action | Add Special Folder | Global Assembly Cache Folder from the menu. Add the Global Assembly Cache folder beneath the File System on Target Machine node.

4. With the Global Assembly Cache folder selected, choose Action | Add | Assembly from the menu.

5. Choose an existing component from the list. At this point, you also could click the Browse button to add a compiled assembly of your choosing. If you had a project in your solution for an assembly, you could choose Action | Add | Project Output from the menu, which would add the assembly when you build the solution.

6. Click the Select button to add the assembly to the Selected Components list. At this point, you could add more assemblies to the list if required.

7. Click OK.

8. On the menu, choose Build | Build Chapter9Setup to build the installer.

9. The Chapter9Setup.msi file is now built and ready for deployment including the assembly in the GAC.

The Global Cache utility also can be used to add assemblies to the GAC, but as mentioned, it is not recommended when deploying to a production server. It can also be used to list the contents of the Global Assembly Cache and uninstall an assembly from the GAC.

Use the gacutil.exe from the command prompt; the syntax is as follows:

```
Gacutil <option> [<parameters>]
```

To install an assembly, use the –i option, including the name of the assembly as a parameter:

```
Gacutil -i myAssembly.dll
```

To uninstall, use the –u option with the assembly name as a parameter:

```
Gacutil -u myAssembly.dll
```

Gacutil –l will list the contents of the Global Assembly Cache and Gacutil -? displays a help screen.

When building and testing Web applications on a development server, it is likely much easier to simply drag and drop the assemblies into the server GAC. You probably will have direct network access to the server and will not want to go through the time-consuming process of using the gacutil.exe tool or building a Setup Project. However, remember that this is not recommended for a production server.

CERTIFICATION OBJECTIVE 9.06

Deploy a Web Application

Throughout this chapter, we have examined the various deployment options in ASP.NET and have deployed the applications as we have progressed. As we have seen, planning and preparation are the main parts of deployment. Deploying in ASP.NET is a much simpler process than classic ASP deployment. In reality, all we need to do is copy the required files to the target production server; there is no longer a need to register components or fine-tune the server settings.

The actual deployment method we choose is dependent on our own, or our server administrator's, requirements. Our choices are as follows:

- Simply copy the required files to the production server using XCOPY or Windows Explorer.
- Use Copy Project from Visual Studio.
- Create a Windows Installer file to provide a setup application that can be deployed to a network directory, a virtual directory on a Web server for Internet download, or removable media such as a CD-ROM.

As we have seen, the last method provides many advantages for ease of deployment including automatic configuration of IIS, launch conditions to evaluate the target server environment before install, an uninstall program, the capability to include assemblies in the Global Assembly Cache, and more. Let's look at some general deployment scenarios and possible solutions.

SCENARIO & SOLUTION

My Web application is required to keep track of statistics concerning requests from users, hit counters, and so on. The application will be deployed to a Web farm. How should I handle this?	Obviously you can't use application state; there will be a different process running on each server in the farm. The best approach is to use a database to store and update the values.
I am both the developer and administrator for the Web site. What would be the best deployment method to use?	For a first-time deployment, it would be easiest to use Copy Project and specify required files only. If you use the XCOPY method, you will need to delete the unneeded files before copying. If you are updating individual files after an initial install, you can just copy the files to the server.
I have updated a local assembly for my application. Do I need to shut down my application to deploy it?	No. Shadowed copies of assemblies are used by ASP.NET, which means the assemblies can be replaced at any time without a restart. ASP.NET will detect when the assembly changes, and produce a new shadow copy for future use.

CERTIFICATION SUMMARY

In this chapter, we learned how to plan and deploy a Web application in ASP.NET. We discussed the requirements for deployment and the three methods of deploying Web applications in ASP.NET.

We planned a general deployment—specifically, deployment using removable media, Web-based deployment, and clustered environments. We deployed applications using XCOPY and Copy Project, and created Windows Installer files from Web Setup Projects in Visual Studio using the editors to customize the install. Finally, we learned how and why to add assemblies to the Global Assembly Cache, and reviewed the actual process of deployment.

✓ TWO-MINUTE DRILL

Plan the Deployment of a Web Application

❏ Deployment is the process of identifying and packaging all the components and files that make up an application for installation, and then moving them to the target machine.

❏ To deploy a Web application, you must have access to the production server, and have the appropriate permissions to write files to the server and configure the virtual directories in Internet Information Server.

Plan a Deployment that Uses Removable Media

❏ ASP.NET applications can be deployed using installers created from Setup Projects in Visual Studio, Using *Copy Project* in Visual Studio, or using the XCOPY command over the network.

Plan the Deployment of an Application to a Web Garden, a Web Farm, or a Cluster

❏ Only the required files need to be copied to the production server. Source code, project, and solution files and the like should not be deployed.

❏ To run ASP.NET Web applications the production Web server must have the Common Runtime and IIS installed on the server.

Create a Setup Program that Installs a Web Application and Allows It to Be Uninstalled

❏ To deploy using the Copy Project method from Visual Studio, Front Page Server Extensions must be installed on the target server.

❏ A Web Setup Project in Visual Studio can be used to build a Windows Installer file for deployment, which automatically includes the capability to uninstall the application.

❏ The Web Setup Project includes editors that enable you to modify the install. The editors are the File System Editor, Registry, File Types, User Interface, Custom Actions, and Launch Conditions.

Add Assemblies to the Global Assembly Cache

❑ You can add assemblies to the Global Assembly Cache when the assembly is shared by multiple applications on the server.

❑ Multiple assemblies of the same name can be placed in the GAC as long as they have different versioning information.

SELF TEST

The following self test questions will measure your understanding of the material presented in this chapter. Read all the choices carefully as there might be more than one correct answer. Choose all correct answers for each question.

Plan the Deployment of a Web Application

1. Which of the following files should be removed from the Web application before deploying using XCOPY? (Choose all that apply.)

   A. Code-behind files

   B. Project files

   C. Styles

   D. web.config

2. Using Copy Project as a deployment method has advantages over using the XCOPY method. Which of the following statements are true about Copy Project? (Choose all that apply.)

   A. Copy Project can be set to deploy only the required files to run the application.

   B. You can transfer the files through HTTP to the target server.

   C. Copy Project will automatically configure the IIS virtual directories.

   D. You can transfer the files directly through a file share.

Plan a Deployment that Uses Removable Media

3. You have some additional files that require adding to the deployment project in a new subfolder. How would you accomplish this?

   A. Use the File System Editor and add a Web custom folder. Add the files to the new folder.

   B. Use Add Files in the Project menu to add files to the application.

   C. Use the File System Editor and add a custom folder. Add the files to the new folder.

   D. Use the File System Editor and add the files to the Web application folder.

Plan the Deployment of an Application to a Web Garden, a Web Farm, or a Cluster

4. You are building a Web application that requires an uninstall capability. Which deployment method would you use to enable this?

A. Copy Project

B. XCOPY

C. Web Setup Project

D. This feature is not available in Web applications.

5. Which statement is true about Web applications running in a Web farm?

A. There is a single process instance of the Web application shared by each server.

B. There are multiple process instances of the application on one server.

C. Each Web server in the farm runs a separate process instance of the application.

D. None of the above.

Create a Setup Program that Installs a Web Application and Allows It to Be Uninstalled

6. What are the accepted data types for registry values?

A. String only

B. DWORD only

C. String and Binary only

D. String, Binary, and DWORD

7. You have created registry keys and subkeys for the application deployment using the Registry Editor in the Web Setup Project. What will happen to the keys when the application is uninstalled?

A. They will be deleted.

B. They will not be deleted.

C. They will be deleted if there is no value in the key.

D. The DeleteAtUninstall property value will specify what action to take.

8. When you add registry values for existing keys on the target computer from a Web Setup Project, what happens if the registry key already contains a value when the installation is performed?

A. An error message will display and the installation will abort.

B. The current value of the key is retained.

C. The value is overwritten with the value specified in the setup.

D. The current value of the key is retained but a warning message is displayed.

9. You need to associate a particular file extension with a program on the target server. Which editor in the Web Setup Project would you use to do this?

   A. Launch Conditions Editor

   B. File Types Editor

   C. Registry Editor

   D. Custom Actions Editor

10. At a minimum, which launch conditions should be evaluated prior to installing an ASP.NET Web application? (Choose all that apply.)

    A. .NET Framework

    B. Internet Information Server

    C. Windows 2000 Advanced Server

    D. Microsoft Transaction Server

Plan a Web-Based Deployment

11. The User Interface Editor in a Web Setup Project provides a way to customize the Setup Wizard. What are the stages of installation represented in the editor?

    A. Start and end

    B. Install and finish

    C. Begin, progress, and end

    D. Start, progress, and end

12. Which statements about the Registry Editor are false? (Choose all that apply.)

    A. Any registry key or value can be modified on installation.

    B. Registry files can be imported into the Registry Editor.

    C. Existing registry key values will be overwritten by those specified in the install.

    D. The Registry Editor can be used to search for registry entries.

13. What is a custom action?

    A. A property in the Launch Conditions Editor

    B. A program that is executed as part of the install

    C. A property on an install dialog box

    D. A setup wizard dialog box

14. You are deploying using a Windows Installer and want to remove the Setup Wizard from the deployment. How can you do this?

    A. Delete the Install and Administrative Install nodes in the User Interface Editor.

    B. Delete the Start, Progress, and End nodes in the User Interface Editor for the Install category.

    C. Delete the Start, Progress, and End nodes in the User Interface Editor for the Administrative Install category.

    D. Delete all dialog boxes from all nodes in the User Interface Editor.

15. When you set a launch condition in the installer, such as a test for a specific operating system, and it evaluates to false when installing, what is the result?

    A. An error message is displayed and the install continues.

    B. The install aborts and displays a standard error message.

    C. The install aborts without displaying a message.

    D. The message specified in the message property is displayed and the install aborts.

16. Which of the following are valid Windows Installer properties? (Choose all that apply.)

    A. SystemLanguageID

    B. VersionNT

    C. ComputerName

    D. AssemblyVersion

Add Assemblies to the Global Assembly Cache

17. What are the advantages of placing assemblies in the Global Assembly Cache? (Choose all that apply.)

    A. File security

    B. Side-by-side versioning

    C. File sharing

    D. Ease of deployment

18. How can you add assemblies to the Global Assembly Cache on the target server? (Choose all that apply.)

    A. Use Windows Explorer to copy the assembly to the \WINNT\Assembly directory on the server.

    B. Build an installer to deploy the assembly to the Global Assembly Cache folder.

C. Use the Global Assembly Cache tool.

D. Copy the assembly to the application root directory.

Deploy a Web Application

19. After testing and debugging an application on a development server, you fix some bugs in a local assembly and recompile the DLL. What is required to redeploy the application to continue testing?

A. You must redeploy the whole application to the server.

B. You can redeploy just the updated assembly but first must shut down the application.

C. You can copy the updated assembly to the application's local assembly cache on the production server without shutting down the application.

D. You must redeploy and reregister the assembly on the target server.

20. What steps are required to update files on the production Web server?

A. Shut down the Web application, shut down IIS, deploy the files, and then restart IIS and the application.

B. Shut down the Web application and deploy the files.

C. Shut down the Web application, deploy the files, and then restart the Web application.

D. Deploy the files.

LAB QUESTION

Your company has developed an ASP.NET Web application to conduct surveys on the Web. The application will be sold to multiple clients to be installed on their Web servers. The application will enable clients to generate their own survey questions, and provides textual and graphical reports based on the analysis of the survey data. It can use either SQL Server or Microsoft Access as the database. Plan the deployment for the application, including the deployment method, deployment requirements, and how they will be met.

SELF TEST ANSWERS

Plan the Deployment of a Web Application

1. ☑ A and B. Source code files and Visual Studio Project files should be removed before deployment.

☒ C and D. Styles and the web.config file are required for the application to run.

2. ☑ A, B, and D all are correct.

☒ C is incorrect. Copy Project will copy only the files to the server. It won't automatically configure IIS.

Plan a Deployment that Uses Removable Media

3. ☑ C is correct. You need to create the new folder first and then add the files.

☒ A is incorrect because the Web custom folder is used for project outputs for multiple projects in the solution. B and D are incorrect as the files will be added to the Web application folder, not to a subfolder.

Plan the Deployment of an Application to a Web Garden, a Web Farm, or a Cluster

4. ☑ C is correct. A Web Setup Project will build a Windows Installer that will automatically include an uninstall.

☒ Both A and B are just methods of moving the files to the production server. D is wrong.

5. ☑ C is correct. Each server in the farm will have a separate instance of the application running on it. The clustering software will manage the redirection of requests to the individual servers.

☒ A, B, and D are incorrect.

Create a Setup Program that Installs a Web Application and Allows It to Be Uninstalled

6. ☑ D is correct.

☒ A, B, and C are incorrect.

7. ☑ D is correct. The DeleteAtUninstall property determines whether they will be removed or not.

☒ A, B, and C all are incorrect.

8. ☑ C is correct. The key value will be overwritten.
  ☒ A, B, and D are incorrect.

9. ☑ B is correct. The File Type Editor allows you to associate file types.
  ☒ A, C, and D are incorrect.

10. ☑ A and B are correct. ASP.NET requires the .NET Framework and IIS.
  ☒ C is wrong, as .NET can run on NT 4. D is incorrect.

Plan a Web-Based Deployment

11. ☑ D is correct.
  ☒ A, B, and C are incorrect.

12. ☑ A and D are false. A because you cannot modify or add a top-level key; D because the Registry Editor does not search for registry entries. You can do this using the Launch Conditions Editor.
  ☒ Both B and C are true.

13. ☑ B is correct. A custom action is a program that is run when the install process is completed. It can be set to execute on Install, Commit, Rollback, or Uninstall.
  ☒ A, C, and D are wrong.

14. ☑ D is correct. These are defaults and can be removed.
  ☒ A, B, and C are all incorrect. None of the nodes in the User Interface Editor can be deleted, only the dialog boxes.

15. ☑ D is correct. The message property is displayed and the install aborts.
  ☒ A, B, and C are all incorrect.

16. ☑ A, B, and C are all valid installer properties.
  ☒ D is incorrect.

Add Assemblies to the Global Assembly Cache

17. ☑ A, B, and C are correct. The GAC is in the \WINNT directory, which typically has access restrictions. Multiple versions of the same assembly arc allowed in the GAC, and the assemblies are all shared by .NET applications on that machine.
  ☒ D is incorrect. Local assemblies are easy to deploy, as they need only to be placed in the \bin directory under the application root.

18. ☑ A, B, and C are correct, although it is recommended that you use an installer.
  ☒ D is incorrect.

Deploy a Web Application

19. ☑ C is correct. You can simply copy the assembly to the application's \bin directory without having to shut down the application.
☒ A, B, and C are incorrect.

20. ☑ D is correct. There is no need to shut down IIS or the application in ASP.NET.
☒ A, B, and C are incorrect.

LAB ANSWER

This type of application is somewhat unusual for a Web application in that it will be installed on multiple servers for multiple clients. The first thing to determine is the deployment method we will use. As we will not have direct access to the production Web servers, neither the XCOPY nor Copy Project method will work. We will need to build a Windows Installer package and either copy it to a CD-ROM for the clients to install, provide a Web deployment that can be downloaded from our company Web site, or both.

You will need to create a number of launch conditions to test that the following exist on the target server:

- The .NET run time
- Internet Information Server
- MDAC 2.x (probably 2.6 or later) for data access
- SQL Server, if that is their preferred database for the application

We will need to add a dialog box from the User Interface Editor to ask which database he or she will be using. This can be done with a two-button RadioButtons dialog box under the Start node. Based on the choice from the dialog, it will need a launch condition to check for the existence of SQL Server if that was the chosen option. Also, based on the database choice will be a custom action that will run a program to either create the SQL Server or Access database and build the connection.

Other features might be required or nice to include. For example, you might want to include License Agreement, Register User, or Customer Information dialog boxes in the install.

Part V

Maintain and Support a Web Application

CHAPTER

MCAD/MCSD

MICROSOFT® CERTIFIED APPLICATION DEVELOPER
& MICROSOFT® CERTIFIED SOLUTION DEVELOPER

10

Support Web Applications

CERTIFICATION OBJECTIVES

10.01	Optimize the Performance of a Web Application
10.02	Diagnose and Resolve Errors and Issues
✓	Two-Minute Drill
Q&A	Self Test

I n this chapter, we discuss optimization and testing of ASP.NET Web applications. We will examine the use of ASP.NET's capabilities for page, fragment, and data caching, and discuss when and how to implement each caching method to optimize application performance. We also will use the Performance Monitor and Application Center Test to monitor the application and server performance, and to stress test the Web application on the development server for potential performance problems.

Optimize the Performance of a Web Application

Performance optimization should be in the forefront throughout the design and implementation phases of application development. A bad design or inefficient coding will adversely affect the performance of any application; however, due to their nature Web applications offer additional performance challenges.

The variables that can affect the speed of a Web site include aspects that the developer has no direct control over such as the connection speed from the client or the amount of traffic on the site at any given time. An optimized site will guarantee that the response times will be the fastest possible, whatever the connection or server load.

ASP.NET offers performance advantages over classic ASP simply by compiling the Web pages. Compiled code executes faster than interpreted script, which means ASP.NET pages already have a built-in performance advantage. Another major performance advantage in ASP.NET is the capability to implement and control caching.

ASP.NET Caching

Caching was first introduced with Internet Information Server (IIS) to speed access to a Web site's pages. Classic ASP has no built-in caching capability and simply uses the page caching provided with IIS. Now ASP.NET provides a native caching capability using three different caching methods: *page* caching, *fragment* caching, and *data* caching. Each of these caching methods provides a new way of optimizing the performance of an ASP.NET Web application.

What Is Caching?

Caching is a technique in which frequently used data or output is temporarily stored in memory or on a hard drive for repeated retrieval. Caching is used in many programs in which the data can be reused within a limited time span, such as the results of a database query. In a Web application, caching increases performance by retaining data across multiple requests, avoiding the need to recreate the page or process the data.

Web caching can be either client side or server side. Client-side caching is a feature of the user's browser that stores pages accessed from the Web in temporary files on the client, either in memory or on the hard drive. The cached files are used when the user requests the same page again rather than accessing the page from the Web site. The client-side cache is available only to each individual user on his or her local machine; therefore, it cannot be shared among multiple users.

Server-side caching can service multiple users by fulfilling the requests from page output placed in the cache on the server. This avoids the need to execute the same code for each request, thereby increasing performance, as the output cache is shared among all clients but is useful only when the output for each request is the same.

ASP.NET provides three levels of caching. The first is page output caching, in which the page is compiled and executed on the initial request, and the page output is placed in the output cache where it is available for subsequent requests. This type of caching is very efficient, but useful only if the content of the page does not change between requests. The cached paged is removed from the cache either when the page source is changed or a prespecified cache timeout is reached.

Fragment caching allows the portions of the Web page to be cached, as opposed to the whole page. This is very useful when a page has a mixture of content wherein some output changes frequently and other parts of the page are static. Fragment caching is not as efficient as page caching, but it does enable you at least to partially cache pages that otherwise would not be candidates for caching.

Data caching enables you to cache individual objects. This approach is very similar to adding items to a dictionary object and serves as temporary storage for data that can be accessed from multiple pages. Unlike page and fragment caching, which are declarative, data caching is programmatic and requires additional code to implement.

The caching methods used will be dependent upon the output of the page in question but also can be impacted by the server resources. Caching incurs a cost in memory resources on the server, which might negatively impact the performance gains realized from the caching itself. For this reason, it is important that the caching strategy be fully tested to obtain optimal performance. Testing should be done on the production server and can be accomplished using the Microsoft Application Center Test tool available with Visual Studio .NET Enterprise, which is discussed later in this chapter, in the section "Microsoft Application Center Test (ACT)."

Page Output Caching

Page output caching enables you to cache the entire page response into server memory. On the first request, the page code is executed and the response is cached; subsequent requests for the page are retrieved directly from the cache. The page is updated in the cache when a change occurs in the page, or the cache expires. This method of caching is best suited to relatively static pages and should be used for the most frequently accessed pages on the site.

To cause a page to be cached, set the @ OutputCache directive at the beginning of the page. When the page is executed, ASP.NET translates the parameters of the directive into HttpCachePolicy class methods. Another method of accessing the HttpCachePolicy is through the HttpResponse.Cache property, which is a lower-level API that gives you a finer degree of control over the caching policy.

The @ OutputCache Directive   The @ OutputCache directive has two required attributes: Duration, which specifies the duration in seconds that the page will be cached, and VaryByParam, which allows the caching of the page to be based on a GET query string or POST parameter. The page then will be added to the ASP.NET application cache and subsequent requests will access the cached page, rather than re-executing the page. If no parameters are required, the VaryByParam must still be included and set to a value of None.

For example, to cache a page for one minute with no parameters, you would use the following OutputCache directive:

```
<%@ OutputCache Duration="60" VaryByParam = "None"
```

To see this at work, we will build a new Web application and use the OutputCache directive on the main page.

EXERCISE 10-1

Using the OutputCache Directive

This exercise will demonstrate page caching in ASP.NET.

1. Open a new Web application in Visual Studio .NET and name it "Chapter 10."

2. Rename the default WebForm1.aspx to "PageCache.aspx."

3. Add a label Web Form control to the page and change its ID to "lblTime."

4. Double-click the page to open the PageCache.aspx.vb code-behind page.

5. Add the following code to the Page_Load event to initialize the lblTime label each time the page is loaded:

```
lblTime.Text = DateTime.Now.ToString()
```

6. Save the file and build the project.

7. Test the page in a browser. Click the refresh button on the browser to see that the page re-executes and displays the current time.

8. Open the PageCache.aspx in HTML view and add the following directive:

```
<%@ OutputCache Duration=10 VaryByParam="None" %>
```

9. Save the file and refresh it two or three times in the browser. Notice that the time does not change. Wait ten seconds and refresh again; the time will change.

In Chapter 1, we discussed the ASP.NET execution model and how ASP.NET pages are processed on the server. If you recall, we discussed how ASP.NET parses the requested page and generates a page class, then compiles the page class into a .NET assembly, which is cached on the server. An instance of the page class then is created and the response is returned to the user. In subsequent requests for the same page, an instance of the class is created from the cached page class and then sent back to the client browser.

The efficiency of this model is based on the fact that the pages are compiled on the first request, and then retained for future requests. Each subsequent request will execute the page from the cached version of the page class. Output caching takes this one step further by caching the output generated from the initial request and returning that as the response. It does not re-execute the page for each request, but returns a previously executed, cached version of the page. Setting the duration attribute in the OutputCache directive specifies the lifetime of the cached page; when this time is exceeded, the page output is removed from the cache. The next request will execute the page class and that output will be placed in the cache.

There obviously is quite a performance advantage to be gained by not having to re-execute the page for each request, but this is useful only if the response output is the same over multiple requests. For this reason, the OutputCache directive provides attributes that allow us to control caching of multiple page outputs.

The VaryByParam attribute is a list of semicolon-separated strings that vary the output based upon on a query string value sent by a GET or a parameter from a POST method. Each request received with different parameters will result in a different cached version of the page.

EXERCISE 10-2

Create Multiple Cached Pages Using the VaryByParam Attribute

In this exercise, we will add some input controls to the form and use the VaryByParam attribute to cache multiple versions of the page based on the values in the form.

1. Modify PageCache.aspx to include a textbox for the user to enter his or her name and a button to submit the form. Name the textbox "txtName" and button "btnSubmit," and set the text property of the button to Submit. The page should look like the following:

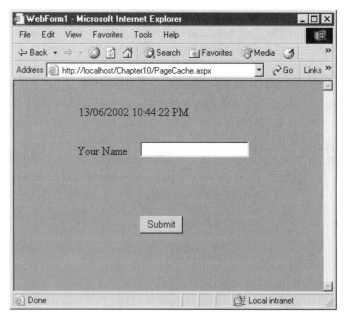

2. Modify the @ OutputCache directive on the page to change the duration to two minutes and set the VaryByParam attribute to txtName:

```
<%@ OutputCache Duration=120 VaryByParam="txtName" %>
```

3. Save the file and view it in the browser. Enter your name and click the submit button. Notice the time displayed.

4. Enter another name and submit. Notice the time; then enter your name again and submit. The page response is cached for your name and the resulting page displayed has the same time as the original response.

5. Add another textbox on the form called "txtCity."

6. Modify the VaryByParam attribute to include the txtCity parameter:

```
<%@ OutputCache Duration=120 VaryByParam="txtName;txtCity" %>
```

7. Save the file and test. You will find that each combination of name and city values will result in a different cached page. You might want to increase the duration to give you time to test the different combinations.

The VaryByParam attribute also can be set to *, which will result in a different cached page for all possible combinations of values on the form. This is not generally recommended, especially on a form with many input values, as it will result in multiple cached pages for all possible combinations of values on the form.

The VaryByHeader attribute enables you to control the caching based upon the HTTP request header values. There are multiple header variables; one of the most useful for caching purposes is Accept-Language. Setting the attribute to Accept-Language results in multiple cached versions of the page based on the accepted language of the requestor. For example, we can set the VaryByHeader attribute with the following code:

```
<%@ OutPutCache Duration=60 VaryByParam="None"
    VaryByHeader="Accept-Language" %>
```

Each request with a different Accept-Language header will result in a cached version of the page for that language.

You can use the VaryByCustom attribute to cache the page output based on the type of browser accessing the application. The following code will cache for each major version number of the browser:

```
<%@ OutPutCache Duration=60 VaryByParam="None"
    VaryByCustom="browser" %>
```

This will result in a separate cached page for Internet Explorer 6, Opera 5, Netscape Navigator 4, and so on.

You can use the Location attribute to specify the location of the cache, also known as its *cacheability*. The default value for the location is Any, which means the cache can be located on the browser, proxy server, or Web server. To limit the cache to a specific location, use one of the following settings:

Value	Description
Any	The output cache can be located on the browser, on a proxy server participating in the request, or on the server where the request was processed.
Client	The output cache is located on the browser only.
Downstream	The output cache can be stored in any HTTP 1.1 cache-capable device other than the origin server. This includes proxy servers and the browser that made the request.
None	The output cache is disabled for the requested page.
Server	The output cache is located on the Web server where the request was processed.

When setting the cacheability declaratively using the Location attribute in the @ OutputCache directive you also must include the two required attributes Duration and VaryByParam. The Duration must be set to a value greater than 0. If you do not want to cache the page based on parameters set VaryByParam to None. The following declaration will force the cache to be located only on the Web server:

```
<%@ OutPutCache Duration=60 VaryByParam="None"
    Location="Server" %>
```

The HttpCachePolicy Class   Rather than controlling the cache declaratively with the @ OutputCache directive, you can set the HttpCachePolicy Class programmatically by using HttpResponse.Cache. This gives you control at a lower level than using the @ OutputCache directive. For example, the duration attribute in the directive sets the expiry on the page cache to a finite period. The page cache will expire after one minute if set to 60, even if the cached page has been accessed since that time.

By using the Response.Cache.SetSlidingExpiration method, you can set the expiration policy so that the cache duration is extended each time the cached page is requested. The following code sets the expiry on the cache to 60 seconds after the last request from the cache:

```
Response.Cache.SetExpires(DateTime.Now.AddSeconds(60))
Response.Cache.SetSlidingExpiration(true)
```

The SetExpires method can be used to specify an absolute expiration time, which can be useful with pages that change infrequently. For example, you might have a page that changes only on a daily basis. You can use the following code to set the expiry to 12:00 A.M.:

```
Response.Cache.SetExpires(DateTime.Parse ("12:00:00 AM"))
```

The Response.Cache can be used exclusively to control the cache but it is best to use it only when requiring the low-level control it offers. Use @ OutputCache directive for the higher-level settings as this centralizes the settings and makes the code more manageable.

on the **job**

Setting the output cache should be the last task accomplished in the development of a Web application. Including it earlier in the cycle might cause problems when debugging, as you might be testing with pages that are stored in the output cache. The output cache will be cleared after a recompile of a page; however, the application should be fully tested and debugged before implementing caching.

Fragment Caching

The entire HTML output of the page is cached by default when you use the @ OutputCache directive on the page. However, in some situations, you might want to cache only parts of the page and have other parts generated dynamically for each request. You can accomplish this by using *fragment caching.*

Fragment caching is accomplished by separating the output of a page into user controls. Each user control can have its caching behavior controlled separately with individual @ OutputCache directives in the control page. When the user control is instantiated in the container page, it inherits the page's cache settings and applies its own settings.

A typical situation might be a page that needs to be dynamically generated on each request that contains the results of a database query. To optimize the performance, you want to cache the results of the query, thereby cutting down on the data server's workload. To implement this, you would place the code for generating the query in a user control and use the control in the main page. The control would be cached but not the page.

Fragment Caching

This exercise uses a simple example to demonstrate the use of fragment caching.

1. Add a new Web Form to the Chapter 10 project and call it "FragmentCache."

2. Add a Web user control to the project and name it "Fragment1."

3. Add two labels to the control. Set the text property of the first label to display the name of the control (Fragment1). Set the ID of the second label to lblTime.

4. Add the following directive to the control to enable caching for two minutes:

```
<%@ OutputCache Duration=120 VaryByParam="None"  %>
```

5. Add the following code to the Page_Load event to display the current time in lblTime:

```
lblTime.Text = DateTime.Now.ToString()
```

6. Save the control.

7. Add two label controls to FragmentCache.aspx. Set the text of the first label to FragmentCache Page and the ID of the second label to lblTime.

8. Place the Fragment1 control on the page by adding the following code to the top of the page:

```
<%@ Register TagPrefix="CacheCtl" TagName="Control1"
  Src="Fragment1.ascx" %>
```

9. Add the following code to the Page_Load event to display the current time in lblTime:

```
lblTime.Text = DateTime.Now.ToString()
```

10. Save all the files and build the solution.

11. Open the FragmentCache page in the browser. The time will be identical for both the page and the control. Refresh the page and notice that the page time has been updated but the control time is the same. Your results should be similar to Figure 10-1. Wait for two minutes and refresh the page again. Both the page and control now display the same time, as the cache for the control has expired.

FIGURE 10-1

Fragment cache
results from
Exercise 3

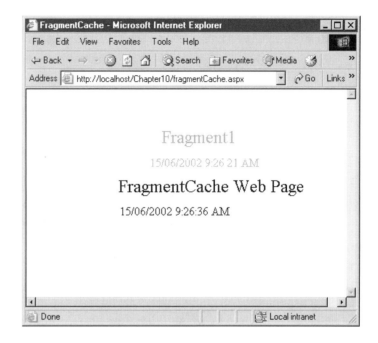

Implementing caching on User Controls is handled through either the @ OutputCache directive or the HttpCachePolicy class. User control caching differs from page caching in that it does not support the VaryByHeader, VaryByCustom, or Location attributes. The VaryByParam attribute works in the same way on a user control as it does with page output caching.

The user control has an additional attribute, VaryByControl, which has a similar function to the VaryByParam in page output caching. VaryByControl varies the output cache based on properties of the user control and is required unless you have a VaryByParam attribute.

Fragment caching offers two optimization benefits. The prime benefit is the capability to cache only portions of the page while the remainder is dynamically generated. Although this is not as efficient as caching the entire page, it does allow some caching to take place that would otherwise be impossible. A second benefit is that if you have several pages that use a common user control, the control is cached on its first request and the cached data is used for subsequent requests from any page. This means you can optimize server resources by caching controls used on multiple pages.

Data Caching

So far, we have seen page output caching, which caches the entire page, and fragment caching, which enables the caching of parts of the page. The third caching method is known as *data caching*, which provides an even finer degree of control over the cached data.

To build high-performance Web applications, you will face situations in which it is advantageous to place individual items in the cache, and access them directly from the cache for later requests. ASP.NET's caching engine provides the capability to do this using the *Cache* object. The *Cache* object is a member of the System.Web.Caching namespace; each *Cache* object is private to the application. Items placed in the *Cache* object are stored in server memory and are available to any page in the application.

Using the *Cache* object is very simple: It uses key/value pairs to add and retrieve objects to the cache in exactly the same way items are added to a dictionary. The syntax for adding data in the cache is as follows:

cache("*keyname*")=*value*

You can retrieve items from the cache with the following syntax:

Value=cache("*keyname*")

The *Cache* object provides methods of tracking dependencies on the cached data and setting expiration policies for the cached items. It implements automatic locking, so it is safe to access the cached values concurrently from more than one page in the application. The *Cache* object can be used to store information that would otherwise be stored in application variables and provides a number of advantages:

- **Internal locking**   Items in the cache are automatically locked.
- **Automatic management of cache resource**   Items in the cache are automatically removed on a regular schedule.
- **Callback functions**   Code that runs when an item is removed from the cache.
- **Removable based on dependencies**   If an item is dependent on another cached item or a file, it can be removed based on actions to the dependency.

The main disadvantage to using the *Cache* object is that it cannot be used in Web farms. The cached items are stored in memory on the server and cannot be accessed by other servers on the farm.

In the following exercise, we use the dictionary-style method to store and retrieve a simple data item to the cache.

EXERCISE 10-4

Using the Cache Method

In this exercise, we will use the cache method to add an item to the cache and retrieve it on a subsequent request for the page.

1. Add a new Web form to the Chapter 10 project called "DataCache1.aspx."

2. Add two labels to the page. Set the text property of the first label to DataCache1.

3. Set the ID property of the second label to lblOutput.

4. In the Page_Load event for the page, add the following code:

```
Dim strDataItem As String = "First Data Item"
If Cache("DataItem") <> Nothing Then
    lblOutput.Text = CStr(Cache("DataItem")) & _
         " Data retrieved from cache"
Else
    lblOutput.Text = strDataItem
    Cache("DataItem") = strDataItem
End If
```

The code declares a string variable to hold the data and assigns the string "First Data Item" to the variable. It then checks for the existence of the DataItem cache object, and if it exists, displays the cached value in the output label along with a message to let us know the data came from the cache. If the object does not exist, it creates the item in the cache and displays the string value in the label.

5. Save the file and rebuild the project.

6. Open the page in the browser. It will display First Data Item in the label. Refresh the page and it will display data retrieved from cache.

One advantage we mentioned concerning the *Cache* object is automatic cache management. A cached item has a lifetime equal to the lifetime of the application, which means it should be available until the application is shut down or restarted. This is not quite true, however, as ASP.NET will automatically remove items from the cache when the server becomes low on memory.

In order to control the lifetime of the items in the cache, we need to use either the Cache.add or Cache.insert methods. These methods are very similar and support the same options; however, the cache.add method will fail if you attempt to add a key that already exists in the cache. The cache.insert will overwrite any existing key of the same name in the cache. Both methods have the capability of either expiring the cached item based on a dependency on another cache object or file, or expiring it on a specified time interval. They also provide options to control the cached object's cache priority and to obtain notification when an object is removed from the cache. The syntax for the cache.insert and cache.add methods is the following:

Cache.insert ("*keyname,*" *value, dependencies, absoluteExpiration, slidingExpiration, priority, onRemoveCallback*).

Using the Dependency Option   When you define a dependency for a cached object ASP.NET will monitor the dependency and expire the object when the dependency changes. Dependencies can be other cached objects or files. For example, the cached object could be dependant upon an XML file that provides data for the page. If the XML file is updated, you want the cached object to expire and be re-created with the new data. It is possible to have another cached object that is dependant upon the first object, in which case the second object would also be removed from the cache.

EXERCISE 10-5

Cache Data Dependent on an XML File

In this exercise, you will learn to create a file dependency. We will use a data grid to display output from a course catalog in an XML file and define the caching dependency on the file.

1. Add a new Web Form to the Chapter 10 project and call it "DependencyCache."

2. Add a heading to the page, a label control, and a DataGrid control.

3. Set the heading to Web Training Courses Available.

4. Set the ID of the label to lblMessage.

5. Set the ID of the DataGrid to CourseDataGrid.

6. Arrange the controls and change colors for visual effect. Your HTML should be similar to the following:

```
<body bgColor="#cccc99" MS_POSITIONING="GridLayout">
<h3>Web Training Courses Available</h3>
<br>
<form id="Form1" method="post" runat="server">
<asp:datagrid id="CourseDataGrid" style="Z-INDEX: 101; LEFT: 18px;
 POSITION: absolute; TOP: 93px" runat="server" BackColor="Cornsilk">
<HeaderStyle BackColor="Tan"></HeaderStyle>
 </asp:datagrid>
<asp:label id="lblMessage" style="Z-INDEX: 102; LEFT:
  17px; POSITION: absolute; TOP: 49px" runat="server"
  Width="242px">Label</asp:label>
</form>
</body>
```

7. Create a short XML file called Courses.xml and save it in the application root directory \inetpub\wwwroot\Chapter10\. The code for Courses.xml is as follows:

```
<catalog>
    <course>
        <id>1</id>
        <name>Introduction to HTML</name>
        <duration>1 day</duration>
    </course>
    <course>
        <id>2</id>
        <name>Introduction to XML</name>
        <duration>2 days</duration>
    </course>
    <course>
        <id>3</id>
        <name>Introduction to ASP</name>
        <duration>2 days</duration>
    </course>
</catalog>
```

8. Open the code-behind file for DependencyCache.aspx and add the following code:

```
'Import the namespaces required for File 10, data binding and caching
Imports System.Data
Imports System.10
```

```
Imports System.Web.Caching

Public Class DependencyCache
    Inherits System.Web.UI.Page
    Protected WithEvents CourseDataGrid _
     As System.Web.UI.WebControls.DataGrid
    Protected WithEvents lblMessage As System.Web.UI.WebControls.Label

Private Sub Page_Load(ByVal sender As System.Object, _
                    ByVal e As System.EventArgs) Handles MyBase.Load
    Dim srcFile As DataView
    'Set the sourcefile for the DataGrid to the cached item
    srcFile = Cache("CourseCatalog")

    'If the item does not exist read the data from the Courses.xml file
    If srcFile Is Nothing Then
        Dim ds As DataSet
        Dim fs As FileStream
        Dim sr As StreamReader
        Dim DependantStr As String
        ds = New DataSet()
        fs = New FileStream(Server.MapPath("courses.xml"), _
                            FileMode.Open, FileAccess.Read)
        sr = New StreamReader(fs)
        ds.ReadXml(sr)
        fs.Close()
        srcFile = New DataView(ds.Tables(0))

        'insert the source file into the cache with a dependency on
        'courses.xml. Any changes to the source xml file will result in the
        'cache being expired.
        DependantStr = Server.MapPath("courses.xml")
        Cache.Insert("CourseCatalog", srcFile, _
                    New CacheDependency(dependantStr))
        'Display message in the label
        lblMessage.Text = "Generated data from XML "
    Else
        lblMessage.Text = "Data from cache"
    End If
    CourseDataGrid.DataSource = srcFile
    CourseDataGrid.DataBind()
End Sub
End Class
```

The code is commented to explain its function.

9. Save all the files and build the solution.

10. Open DependencyCache.aspx in the browser. The results are shown next. As this is the first request, the data has been generated from the XML file.

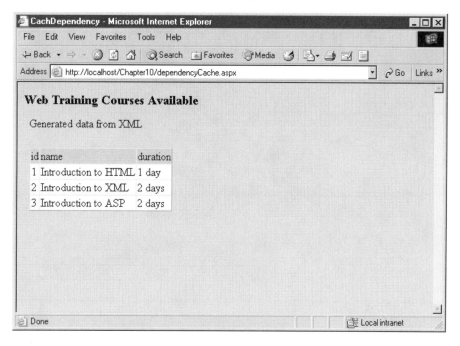

11. Refresh the page. Notice how much faster the load is and that the data is refreshed from the cache.

12. Open the Courses.xml file in an editor and modify the file by deleting or adding a record. Refresh the page in the browser and notice that the data has been generated from the XML file; the result is shown next. As soon as you

modified Courses.xml, the cache expired based on the dependency and the data was regenerated from the XML file.

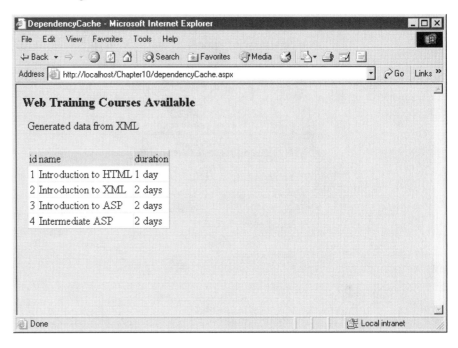

Using the Expiration Options   The second option allows you to set the expiration policy on the cached object. As with the page cache, the data cache has two policies for setting the expiration of the cache. The first is to specify an absolute expiration time, which can be a specific time or a time relative to the current time. The second is a sliding time, in which the expiration time is set to a period after the last request for the cached object. The following code inserts a *Cache* object that expires after five minutes:

```
Cache.Insert("key", value, Nothing, _
             DateTime.Now.AddMinutes(5),TimeSpan.Zero)
```

When using Cache.Insert or Cache.Add, you must specify the dependency option either as a valid dependency object or as "Nothing." Both the expiration and sliding expiration options must be included, although you can use only one option. TimeSpan.Zero or DataTime.MaxValue are passed to the option not being set.

In the preceding code, the expiration is set to five minutes and therefore the sliding expiration is set to TimeSpan.Zero. The following code sets the cache to expire 30 seconds after the last request for the cached object:

```
Cache.Insert("key", value, Nothing, _
            DateTime.MaxValue,TimeSpan.FromSeconds(30))
```

This time, the expiration option is DateTime.MaxValue, which sets it to the maximum value possible, effectively disabling it.

Using the Priority Options   Whatever method you use to set the cache options to control the duration of an object in the cache, they are overridden by ASP.NET's automatic cache management. When the server memory resources get too low, ASP.NET will clear out the cache until the available memory returns to a useful level. To ensure any critical cached data is not automatically purged, you can set the CacheItemPriority option.

The CacheItemPriority option enables you to set priorities on the cached objects when ASP.NET manages the cache. You can set the priority to *NotRemovable*, which should be used sparingly as it will exempt the object from being removed from the class. If this is used on many objects, it can interfere with ASP.NET's memory management and negatively affect the performance of the application. The other values range from low to high, where low indicates the object should be the first to be purged and high should be the last; normal is the default setting.

The CacheItemRemovedCallback option allows the application to be notified when an item is removed from the cache. CacheItemRemovedCallback is a delegate that defines a signature to use when writing event handlers to respond when an item is removed from the cache. The steps required to implement this are as follows:

1. Create a local variable of type CacheItemRemovedCallback to raise the event for the delegate. For example:

```
Private Shared OnRemove as CacheItemRemovedCallback = Nothing
```

2. Create an event handler to respond when an item is removed from the cache. For example:

```
Public Sub RemovedCallback(key As String, value As Object, _
                           reason As CacheItemRemovedReason)
     'Implementation code to respond to the cache object being purged
End Sub
```

3. Create an instance of the delegate that calls the event handler. For example:

```
onRemove = New CacheItemRemovedCallback(AddressOf me.RemovedCallback)
```

4. Add the item to the cache specifying the local variable created in Step 1 as the option value. For example:

```
Cache.Insert("MyData1", Source, null, DateTime.Now.AddMinutes(2), _
             NoSlidingExpiration, CacheItemPriority.High, _
             CacheItemPriorityDecay.Slow, onRemove)
```

When the MyData1 item is removed from the cache, the RemovedCallBack event handler is fired. This can contain code to notify the application or handle the situation in any way that makes sense. The RemovedCallBack event handler has three parameters: key, value, and CacheItemRemovedReason. CacheItemRemovedReason identifies the reason the cache was removed. It can be one of the following values:

Reason	Definition
DependencyChanged	Occurs when files, directories, or keys that are specified as dependencies are changed.
Expired	Occurs when a cached object expires because the absolute expiration time has been met.
Removed	Occurs when a cached object is explicitly removed or replaced due to using the same key.
Underused	Occurs when the cached object is removed by ASP.NET due to low system resources or because it is under utilized.

SCENARIO & SOLUTION

The page generally stays the same, but some of the data displayed in tables changes regularly. Which caching method should I use?	Use fragment caching. Use output caching for the page, and place the table data in a user control. Have the user controls dynamically generate the output or set them to short duration.
Some of the page contents change on a daily basis based on new data that is made available every evening. How should I handle the caching?	Use page output caching and set the duration to an explicit time that matches the time the new data is available.
Some of the objects used on the page are relatively static but the page changes frequently. Can I use caching?	Yes. Generate the page dynamically for each request but use data caching for the static objects.

You can remove any cached object programmatically from the cache using the Cache.Remove method. You might need this to give the user an updated or non-cached version of the data or simply to clean up resources manually. The syntax is

```
Cache.Remove("Key")
```

exam
ⓦatch
The new caching features are central to the optimization of an ASP.NET application. Be sure to understand the different caching methods on a theoretical and implementation level.

CERTIFICATION OBJECTIVE 10.02

Diagnose and Resolve Errors and Issues

After an application has been tested, debugged, and deployed to a production server, there are still issues that arise concerning performance and errors. Although the application might have been extensively tested, you still might discover some stray bugs in the logic after deployment, and errors might be triggered in the application due to resource problems on the server. General performance issues also will arise, especially in peak usage periods.

Run-time errors and bugs will have to be handled as they would in development or testing. The errors will need to be identified and a solution implemented. Notification and resolution of these types of problems have been covered elsewhere in the book, specifically in Chapter 8 and Chapter 2. Implementing an error-handling strategy that writes errors to a log file, or notifies an administrator of errors through e-mail, for example, will ensure that errors and issues are identified and handled in a timely fashion.

Testing an application for performance issues is the other side of the equation. To fully understand the potential performance issues, you will need to monitor the performance of the application and stress test it to its limits. Once this has been done, you can confidently address the issues that were uncovered and respond with solutions. Depending upon the issues uncovered, the solutions could include implementing or fine-tuning caching, increasing server resources, or clustering Web and data servers.

Monitor Application Performance

The main tools for monitoring application performance are the Performance Monitor and the Microsoft Application Center Test. The Performance Monitor enables you to monitor performance on the server by selecting specific counters from a list of performance objects on the server. The Microsoft Application Center Test (ACT) is a tool provided with Visual Studio .NET Enterprise Edition that enables stress testing of Web servers by simulating large numbers of users sending requests to the server. We will begin by discussing the Performance Monitor and identifying some of the counters we can use to measure the performance and efficiency of ASP.NET applications, and then use the Application Center Test to simulate multiple users on the application.

The Performance Monitor

The Performance Monitor consists of two parts: the System Monitor and Performance Logs and Alerts. The System Monitor gives you the ability to collect data in real time concerning memory, disk, processor, and application activity on the server, and then view that data as a report, graph, or histogram. The Performance Logs and

Alerts allow you to configure logs to record performance data and produce alerts that notify when a counter exceeds a specific range of values.

The Performance Monitor can be used to monitor the production Web application and identify any issues or problems that arise. It is located in Administrative Tools in the Control Panel on Windows 2000. On NT 4.0, you can access it by choosing Start | Programs | Administrative tools. The Windows 2000 System Monitor is shown in Figure 10-2.

The System Monitor   To use the System Monitor, you need to set counters for the data you wish to monitor. You do this by using the Add counter toolbar in the monitor and specifying the performance objects and counters you wish to monitor. Two of the performance objects of interest will be the ASP.NET and ASP.NET Application objects. ASP.NET provides global counters for all running ASP.NET applications that are useful to monitor the general load on the Web server; the available ASP.NET counters are described in Table 10-1.

FIGURE 10-2

The System
Monitor

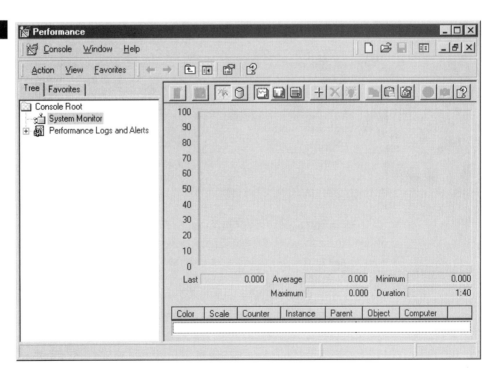

TABLE 10-1	Counter	Description
ASP.NET Object Performance Counters	Application Restarts	The number of times an application has been restarted during the Web server's lifetime.
	Application Running	The number of applications running on the server computer.
	Requests Disconnected	The number of requests disconnected because of a communication failure.
	Requests Rejected	Total requests not executed because of insufficient server resources to process them.
	Request Wait Time	The time in milliseconds that the most recent request waited for processing in the queue.
	State Server Sessions Abandoned	The number of explicitly abandoned user sessions. These are sessions ended by specific user actions, such as closing the browser or navigating to another site.
	State Server Sessions Active	The number of currently active user sessions.
	State Server Sessions Timed Out	The number of user sessions that have become inactive through user inaction.
	State Server Sessions Total	The number of sessions created during the lifetime of the process. This is the cumulative value of State Server Sessions Active, State Server Sessions Abandoned, and State Server Sessions Timed Out.
	Worker Process Restarts	The number of times a worker process has been restarted on the server computer.
	Worker Process Running	The number of worker processes running on the server computer.

To monitor a specific application, use the ASP.NET Application performance object, and choose the specific application you are monitoring and the counters you wish to monitor. The counters are grouped into various categories including Anonymous Requests, Cache Totals, Cache API, Errors, Output Cache, Requests, Sessions, Transactions, Compilation, and Debugging. Table 10-2 describes some of the more useful counters for determining application performance and errors. For a complete list of counters, refer to the .NET Framework SDK documentation under Performance Counters for ASP.NET.

TABLE 10-2	**Counter**	**Description**
ASP.NET Application Object Counters	Cache Total Entries	The total number of entries in the cache.
	Cache Total Hits	The total number of hits from the cache.
	Cache Total Misses	The number of failed cache requests per application.
	Cache Total Hit Ratio	The ratio of hits to misses for the cache.
	Cache Total Turnover Rate	The number of additions and removals to the total cache per second. If the turnover is large, the cache is not being used efficiently.
	Cache API Entries	The total number of entries in the application cache.
	Cache API Turnover Rate	The number of additions and removals to the cache per second through the external APIs, excluding internal use by the ASP.NET page framework. If the turnover is large, the cache is not being used effectively.
	Errors During Execution	The total number of errors that occur during the execution of an HTTP request. Excludes parser and compilation errors.
	Output Cache Entries	The total number of entries in the output cache.
	Output Cache Hits	The total number of requests serviced from the output cache.
	Output Cache Misses	The number of failed output-cache requests per application.
	Output Cache Hit Ratio	The percentage of total requests serviced from the output cache.
	Output Cache Turnover Rate	The number of additions and removals to the output cache per second. If the turnover is large, the cache is not being used effectively.
	Requests Executing	The number of requests currently executing.

Figure 10-3 shows the Add Counters dialog box with the Chapter 10 application selected. To select counters for all ASP.NET applications, choose the _Total item in the list. You can add and delete counters; and view data as a chart, histogram, or report. Figures 10-4, 10-5, and 10-6 show the same output data in each of the three formats.

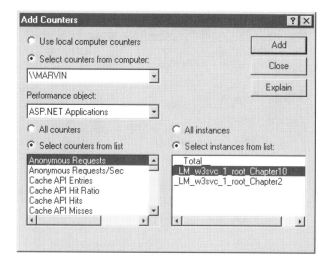

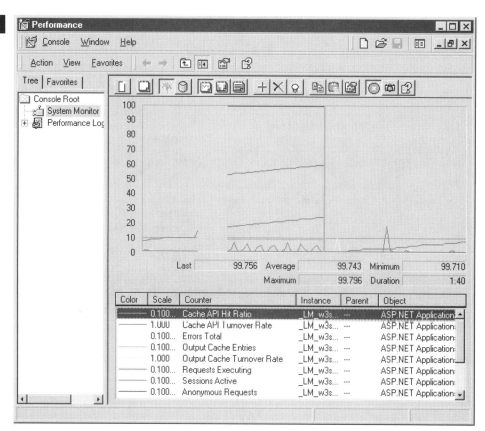

System Monitor
histogram output

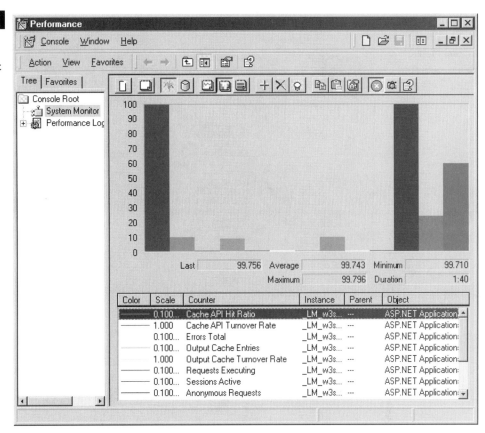

Performance Logs and Alerts   The main purposes of performance logs and alerts are to trace and notify the system administrator of specific conditions that arise on the server. By setting counters and specifying conditions on those counters, you can trigger an alert that can add an entry to the application event log, send a network message, or run a specified program. For example, you might want to be alerted when the system memory drops below a certain threshold and correlate this with other counters such as the number of requests occurring on the Web server or a specific ASP.NET application. You can write this information into the application event log for analysis.

FIGURE 10-6

System Monitor
report output

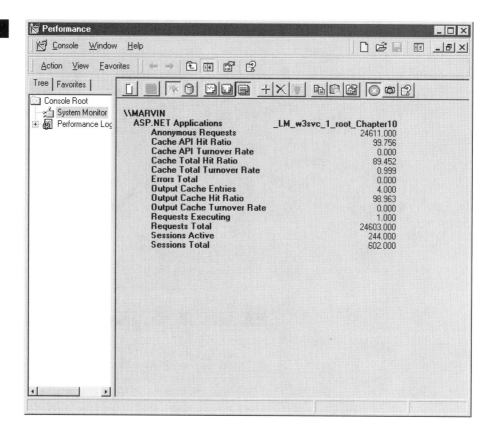

To add an alert:

1. Right-click the Alerts node in the Performance Monitor.

2. Choose New Alert Setting... from the menu and type in a name for the alert.

3. On the General tab of the resulting Properties dialog box, click the Add button and select a counter.

4. Set a condition for the alert and specify when the data should be sampled. For example, the following image displays the required settings to trigger an alert when the system memory falls below 30 MB with the data sampled every five seconds:

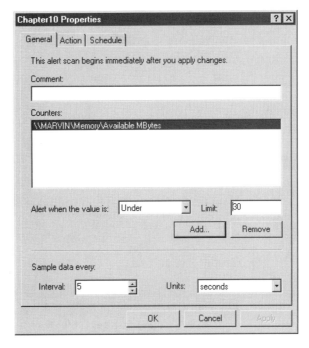

5. On the Action tab, choose the action to occur when the alert is triggered.

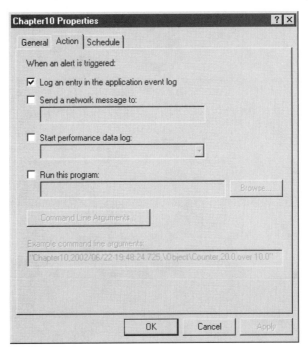

In addition to alerts, you can set counter and trace logs in the Performance Monitor, and specify start and stop times for the data to be written to the logs. The counter logs can be useful for monitoring resources versus activity for specific time periods. For example, you can create a counter log to monitor available memory and activity counters such as user requests on the Web server. Adding a counter log is similar to adding an alert. To add a counter log:

1. From the Counter Log node in the Performance Monitor, right-click and choose New Log Settings... from the menu.

2. From the General tab, add the required counters.

3. From the Log Files tab, specify a location and file name for the log file, and a log file type. The file types are comma-separated-value (CSV), tab-separated-value (TSV), binary, and Perfmon format. CSV files can be viewed in Microsoft Excel.

4. On the Schedule tab, specify when to start and stop the logging.

5. Once the log is created, you may open the log file and review the results. The following image shows the results of a counter log using MB of available memory and server request totals as displayed in Microsoft Excel:

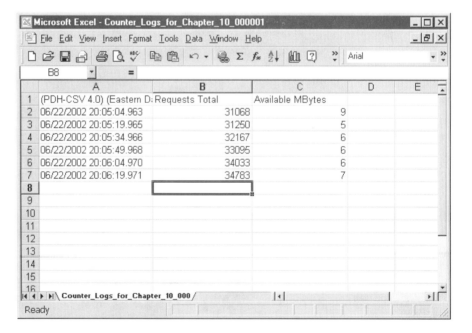

Although the Performance Monitor is a useful tool for identifying potential server and application resource issues while the application is in production, it also can be used in conjunction with the Application Center Test to monitor application counters in development stress testing before deployment.

The Microsoft Application Center Test (ACT)

The Application Center Test (ACT) is supplied with Visual Studio .NET and is part of Application Center 2000. It analyzes the performance of Web applications and identifies potential scalability problems by simulating heavy traffic on the application and server by opening multiple connections and rapidly sending HTTP requests. The version that ships with Visual Studio .NET is based on the same technology as the stand-alone version, but allows the developer to create and run tests and view the results from within the Visual Studio Integrated Development Environment (IDE).

Using ACT from Visual Studio .NET   You can add ACT projects to existing Visual Studio .NET solutions, providing a number of advantages over the stand-alone version of ACT:

- The Web application you are testing and its ACT tests can be managed from the same location.

- The ACT tests can be created and modified from the source code editor in Visual Studio.

- The test runs are started and the results displayed within the Visual Studio IDE.

- When tests are run from within Visual Studio, the test results are optimized for a smaller number of pages than the stand-alone version, and the reports show only the most important data required for optimizing the application.

- ACT projects, tests, and results created in the Visual Studio .NET IDE are fully compatible with the stand-alone version of ACT.

To create a new ACT project from the Visual Studio IDE:

1. Choose File | New | Project from the Visual Studio menu.

2. From the resulting New Project dialog, under the Other Projects node choose Application Center Test Projects and then the ACT Project template.

3. Specify a path and name for the project. To add the ACT project to an existing solution, specify the existing solution path and name, and choose the Add To Solution option.

Visual Studio solutions can contain only one ACT project and an ACT project can be open in only one application at a time. If you decide to run or modify the ACT project in the stand-alone version of ACT, you have to close the Visual Studio solution containing the project.

Application Center Tests are written in either JScript or VBScript using the ACT Test Object Model. Test scripts can be written directly by the developer or generated by recording browser activity. Recording browser activity obviously is the easier approach, and the test scripts created in this method can be modified to further enhance the test.

Remember that even though you are using the Visual Studio Code Editor to build the tests, you are not using a .NET language. The ACT tests are written in unmanaged code using VBScript or JScript and the Application Center Test objects. To create a test from the VS .NET IDE:

1. Right-click the ACT project in Solution Explorer and choose Add | Add New Item from the resulting menu.

2. Choose one of the templates. The Test(.js) and Test(.vbs) will create a blank test that will require the source code to be added manually. The browser-recorded test (.vbs) will generate source code from an IE browser session.

3. Enter a name for the test and click Open. If it is a browser-recorded test, a Browser Record dialog will open for you to start the recording process.

Once the test is created, you can set the test properties in the properties window. The following test properties can be set:

Property	Description
Iterations	Specifies the number of times the test iterates during the test run. Setting this value will automatically clear the RunTime property value.
RunTime	Specifies the test duration by setting the amount of time the test run lasts. Specifying a RunTime value will automatically clear the Iterations property value.
WarmupTime	Sets warm-up time in seconds. Requests are sent at the beginning of a test run, but request and response data is not recorded until the warmup time expires. This property is available only when the test duration is specified using the run time rather than iterations.
Connections	Specifies the amount of load to create by setting the number of simultaneous browser connections ACT simulates during the test run.

Right-click the test in the Solution Explorer and choose Start Test to run a test. The Output Window will display the data from the test run, including any error messages, the status as it runs, and a summary of the final results when the run finishes. When running the ACT test from within Visual Studio, the results are limited to the common data requirements for analyzing Web application performance. The descriptions of the result data returned are described in Table 10-3.

To view more detailed information not displayed in Visual Studio, the ACT project and report will need to be opened in the stand-alone ACT program. Using the ACT program to view the results also will allow you to view the test data in a graphical format.

You can compare and sort the results from multiple test runs by right-clicking the ACT test in Solution Explorer and choosing View Results. The resulting window will display the results for all tests in a columnar format. To sort on a specific column, choose the column and click the column heading.

TABLE 10-3	Result	Description
ACT Test Result Data	Requests per Second	The rate at which the Web server is responding to HTTP requests from ACT.
	Iterations	Indicates the number of times the test has looped since the start of the test run. This is displayed for all tests, regardless of whether the test duration was specified using iterations or a run time.
	HTTP errors	Indicates response codes in the 400–499 and 500–599 ranges that are being received. These errors can be caused by various problems with either the requests or the Web application.
	DNS errors	Indicates errors that occurred resolving the server's address. These can be caused by requests that use an invalid server name, or they could be due to network configuration problems.
	Socket errors	Indicates the Web server is unable to maintain some or all connections. The Web server usually will begin rejecting connections after its maximum capacity is exceeded.
	Average Time to first byte (TTFB)	Measures the time between sending the request and receiving the first part of the Web server's response stream.
	Average Time to last byte (TTLB)	Measures the time between sending the request and receiving the end of the Web server's response stream.

exam
ⓦatch

The Application Center Test project is an important tool for testing the Web application. To fully understand its capabilities, get some hands-on experience using it to test Web applications before attempting the exam.

Now that we have discussed the Performance Monitor and the Application Test Center, we will work through an exercise using the Chapter10 Web application to test and monitor its performance.

EXERCISE 10-6

Monitor and Performance Test an ASP.NET Application

In this exercise, we will add navigation and a home page to the Chapter 10 application and use the Application Center Test to simulate multiple users using the application. We also will set counters in the Performance Monitor to display performance data concerning the caching and general performance of the application while testing with the ACT test.

1. Open the Chapter 10 project in Visual Studio and add a new Home.aspx page to the project.

2. Create a simple interface on all the Web Forms in the application with navigational links to each of the other pages. A simple home page for the exercise is shown here:

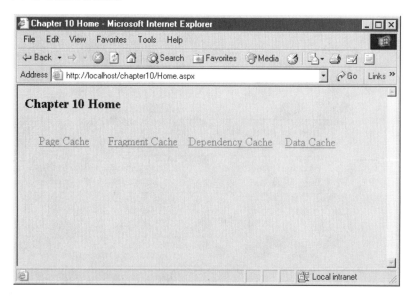

3. Save, build, and test the project to ensure all the links and pages work properly.

4. Close the solution and then open a new project. Choose an ACT Project from the Application Center Test Projects node under Other Projects.

5. Name the project "Chapter 10 ACT Project" and accept the default location. Click OK.

6. Right-click the Chapter 10 ACT Project in the Solution Explorer and choose Add | Add New Item from the pop-up menu.

7. Choose the browser-recorded test (.vbs) template in the dialog box, enter the name as **ACT-VBSTestChapter10.vbs**, and click Open.

8. Click the Start button on the Browser Record dialog box. Internet Explorer will open automatically. Browse to the Chapter10 home.aspx page. The ACT test now is recording from the browser.

9. Fully navigate through all of the pages in the application. Fill in the form on the page cache a few times and submit the data. Refresh each of the other pages to observe the caching behavior. When finished, click the Stop button on the Browser Record and click OK.

10. A VBScript test file will be added to the project. Look through the code that has been generated.

11. Right-click the test in Solution Explorer and choose Start Test. The default is set for 300 seconds. You might not want to wait five minutes for the test to complete; if not, right-click the test and choose Stop Test.

12. Scroll to the bottom of the Output window and look at the Final Results. Right-click the test and choose View Results. Review the results shown in the results window.

13. In the Property window for the test, change the Runtime property to 30 and the Connections to 10. Run the test again and view the results to compare the tests. Notice the difference in the Avg Time to First Byte (msecs) and Avg Time to Last Byte (msecs) values; the extra connections have impacted the performance.

14. Start the Performance Monitor from Administrative Tools.

15. Select the System Monitor in the left-hand pane and click the Add button from the toolbar. In the Add Counters dialog box, choose ASP.NET Applications in the Performance object drop-down list box, and the

Chapter10 application from the instances list box on the right (refer to the next image). Select the following counters:

■ Cache API Entries

■ Cache API Turnover Rate

■ Cache Total Entries

■ Cache Total Turnover Rate

■ Errors Total

■ Output Cache Entries

■ Output Cache Turnover Rate

■ Requests Total

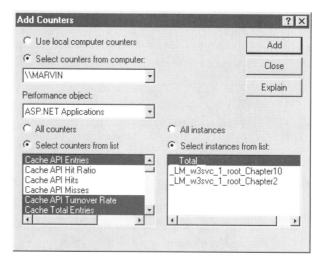

16. The counters now are showing in the default chart, but because there is no activity in the application, the values are flat. Switch to Visual Studio and run the ACT test for Chapter 10. Switch back to the Performance Monitor and view the chart. When the chart shows activity, click the View Histogram and then View Report buttons on the toolbar. You might want to increase the run time in the test to a longer time limit to view the counters.

17. Now we will add a counter log for the Web application. Right-click the Counter Logs node in the left pane of the Performance Monitor. Choose

New Log Settings from the pop-up menu and enter **Chapter 10 Counter Logs** in the name box. On the General tab of the resulting dialog box, click the Add button and select the same counters used in the system monitor earlier.

18. On the Log Files tab, specify a location and file name and set the Log file type to Text File – CSV.

19. Start the ACT test for Chapter 10 in Visual Studio and then double-click the Counter Logs node in the Performance Monitor. Right-click the counter log file you just created in the right-hand pane of the Performance Monitor and select Start. When the test ends, stop the counter log.

20. In Windows Explorer, find the counter log file. By default, it should be in C:\PerfLogs. Double-click the file to open it in Microsoft Excel and view the results. The output should be similar to this:

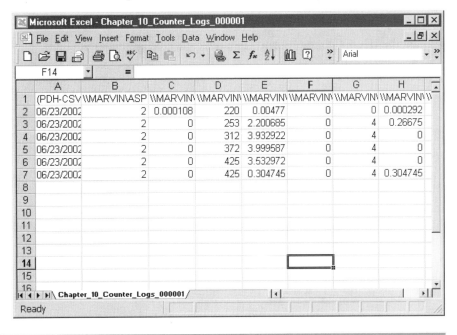

The Performance Monitor allows you to monitor just about any aspect of the Web application and server resources necessary to identify problems or issues concerning the performance of the application. ACT tests can be applied to the application before deployment to identify potential issues with the finished product.

Let's look at some typical questions concerning performance monitoring and testing.

SCENARIO & SOLUTION

Should I use the Application Center Test on production servers?	No. ACT should be used only on development or test Web servers with no other network or Web traffic. This will give you accurate results for your test.
Should I test my Web application using proxy servers?	No. The point of a stress test is to bring the load up to the point that the Web server or Web application becomes the bottleneck. Accurate measurements will be impossible if other components on the system can cause a bottleneck.
The Web application receives high load levels at predicable time periods. Can I automatically get performance data for these periods?	Yes. Use the Performance Monitor and set up counter logs. Schedule the counter logs for the specific time periods you want to monitor by setting the Start log and Stop log options. You can view the log files after the monitoring period is finished.

FROM THE CLASSROOM

Web Application Performance and ASP.NET Caching

Optimizing the performance of Web applications is a difficult task due to the inherent nature of the Web itself. Feature- and content-rich Web sites result in large amounts of data that must be processed and communicated to the user. Connection speeds vary and are beyond the control of the developer. To overcome this problem, the developer must strive to keep the size of the response as small as possible. Complex Web applications require dynamic processing on the server side to query and update databases, produce the response content, and so forth. The server resources must be capable of handling the load and need to be monitored to ensure that they are not reaching capacity. Scalable applications enable server resources to be increased without requiring modifications to the application itself. The technologies available for optimizing processing also can contribute greatly to application performance.

ASP.NET includes a number improvements over Classic ASP designed to increase the performance of Web applications. The use of compiled code as opposed to interpreted script is the first and probably most obvious, but the extended caching capabilities also are important. ASP.NET caching, when properly implemented, can result in impressive performance gains without negatively impacting the quality or accuracy of the data returned to the user. Page, Fragment, and Data caching allows the developer to specifically tailor the caching to the task at hand without the risk of returning stale data.

—*David Shapton, MCSD, MCT, CTT+*

CERTIFICATION SUMMARY

In this chapter, we optimized Web applications using ASP.NET's caching capabilities. We discussed the implementation and uses of page Output caching, Fragment caching, and Data caching. We then examined the Performance Monitor to gather data on various performance counters to identify potential issues with application and server performance. Finally, we looked at the Application Center Test and used it to simulate multiple requests to stress test the Web application and server.

TWO-MINUTE DRILL

Optimize the Performance of a Web Application

❑ ASP.NET now provides a native caching capability using three different caching methods: page caching, fragment caching, and data caching.

❑ Page output caching is the process of compiling and executing a page on the initial request, and placing the output in a cache where it is available for subsequent requests.

❑ Fragment caching entails separating the page into user controls and caching each control individually. This enables portions of the page to be cached and others to be dynamic.

❑ Data caching enables you to cache individual objects that can be shared among all pages in the application.

❑ Pages and user controls can be cached using the @ OutputCache directive, or the Response.Cache property for lower-level control over the caching policy.

❑ Multiple cached outputs can be specified for page and user controls based on input parameters by using the VaryByParam attribute, HTTP header values using the VaryByHeader attribute, and by browser type or other custom value using the VaryByCustom attribute.

❑ Cached output can be located on the browser, proxy server, or Web server.

❑ Caches can be set to expire at a specific time, at a specific time interval after the initial request, or at a specific time interval after the last request from the cache.

❑ Cached output can be set to expire dependent on the expiry of other cached items or changes to files such as XML data files.

Diagnose and Resolve Errors and Issues

❑ ASP.NET automatically manages cached items to preserve server resources such as memory. Cached items can be set to different priority levels to determine in what order ASP.NET will purge the items.

❑ The Performance Monitor's System Monitor gives you the capability to monitor performance on the server by selecting specific counters from a list of performance objects on the server.

❑ Performance counters can be logged to files and scheduled for specific periods using the counter logs in the Performance Monitor.

❑ The Application Center Test (ACT) is a testing tool designed to stress test Web servers, simulating a large number of users on the application by opening multiple connections to the server and rapidly sending HTTP requests.

❑ ACT can be run from within the Visual Studio .NET IDE or from the stand-alone program.

SELF TEST

The following self test questions will help you measure your understanding of the material presented in this chapter. Read all the choices carefully as there might be more than one correct answer. Choose all correct answers for each question.

Optimize the Performance of a Web Application

1. Which directive will cache the page for one minute and not be dependent on any values on the form?

    A. `<%@ OutputCache Duration="60" VaryByParam = "None"`

    B. `<%@ OutputCache Duration="1" VaryByParam = "None"`

    C. `<%@ OutputCache Duration="1"`

    D. `<%@ OutputCache Duration="60" VaryByParam = "*"`

2. How would you set the page cache to expire two minutes after the last request from the cache?

    A. `<%@ OutputCache Duration="2",SetSlidingExpiration=true.`

    B. `Response.Cache.SetExpires _`
        `(DateTime.Now.AddSeconds(120))`
        `Response.Cache.SetSlidingExpiration(true)`

    C. `<%@ OutputCache Duration="2",VaryByParm = "None" _`
        `SetSlidingExpiration=true.`

    D. `Response.Cache.SetExpires _`
        `(DateTime.Now.AddSeconds(120))`

3. Which of the following values are valid for the Location attribute in the @ OutputCache directive?

    A. Downstream

    B. All

    C. Server

    D. None

4. You have a page that includes the results of a database query. You would like to reduce the workload on the data server while maintaining dynamic output for other elements on the page. What would be the most efficient caching strategy?

   A. There is none. Dynamically generate the complete page, including the query, for each request.

   B. Use data caching. Cache the data from the database query in cache objects.

   C. Use page OutputCaching. Cache the entire page output but specify a short expiry time limit.

   D. Use fragment caching. Use a user control to query the database and cache the output. Leave the page to generate dynamically or set the page to cache for a short time.

5. Which attributes are required in the @ OutputCache directive for a user control?

   A. Duration and VaryByControl

   B. Duration and VaryByParam

   C. Duration and either VaryByParam or VaryByControl

   D. Duration

6. Which of the following statements about the cache object are true?

   A. Items in the cache are automatically locked.

   B. Cached items are removed if they are dependent on another cached item or file.

   C. Cached items are removed if the source code for the item is changed.

   D. Cache objects can be used in Web farms.

7. Which option of the Cache.Insert or Cache.Add methods allows the developer to set the priority level on how a cached object should be purged from the cache by ASP.NET when system resources run low on the server?

   A. CacheItemPriority

   B. slidingExpiration

   C. onRemoveCallback

   D. CacheItemPriorityDecay

8. When using the Cache.Insert method to cache an object and set its expiry to a set time interval, which arguments are required?

   A. Key, Value, and Expiration

   B. Key, Value, Expiration, and slidingExpiration

   C. Key, Value, Dependency, and Expiration

   D. Key, Value, Dependency, Expiration, and slidingExpiration

9. A Web page displays data based on the location requested, identified by City and State in the request. The data itself is relatively static and a good candidate for caching. Which caching approach would be the most efficient for this page?

    A. Use fragment caching. Cache the page but dynamically generate the page data for each location requested.

    B. Use Output caching for the page varied by the parameters for city and state.

    C. Use data caching to cache the data for each city.

    D. Use fragment caching to cache the data for each city and dynamically generate the rest of the page.

10. Setting the CacheItemPriority of a cached object to High has what result?

    A. The item will be one of the first items removed from the cache.

    B. The item will never be removed from the cache.

    C. The item will be one of the last items removed from the cache.

    D. The item will be one of the last items removed from the cache if it has been used recently.

11. What is the result of the following code on an ASP.NET page?

```
<%@ OutputCache Duration=180 VaryByParam="*" %>
```

    A. It will create multiple page caches for each input value specified in the GET or POST.

    B. It will create one cached page based on all input values specified in the GET or POST.

    C. It will create one cached page with an expiry of three minutes from the last request.

    D. It will create one cached page with an expiry of three minutes from the last request from the cache.

Diagnose and Resolve Errors and Issues

12. Which performance object in the Performance Monitor will allow you to set counters to monitor performance for all running ASP.NET applications?

    A. ASP.NET Applications

    B. ASP.NET

    C. Browser

    D. Active Server Pages

13. Which ASP.NET Application object counter will indicate whether the Output cache is being used effectively?

   A. Output Cache Misses

   B. Output Cache Hit Ratio

   C. Output Cache Turnover Rate

   D. Output Cache Entries

14. Which actions can be specified as the result of an alert in the Performance Monitor? (Choose all that apply.)

   A. Send a network message.

   B. Run a program.

   C. Log an entry in the application event log.

   D. Send an e-mail.

15. Which statements are true about using the Application Center Test in the Visual Studio .NET IDE? (Choose all that apply.)

   A. ACT tests can be created in the Visual Studio source code editor.

   B. ACT tests can be written in the VB.NET language.

   C. ACT projects created in Visual Studio cannot be used in the stand-alone Application Center Test program.

   D. Visual Studio solutions can contain multiple ACT projects.

16. Which ACT project test property will affect the duration of the test run? (Choose all that apply.)

   A. RunTime

   B. WarmupTime

   C. Connections

   D. Iterations

17. Which of the ACT test results best measures the server responsiveness?

   A. Requests per second

   B. HTTP errors

   C. DNS errors

   D. Average time to first byte

18. What is the purpose of the Application Center Test?

   A. To analyze performance data on live Web applications.

   B. To increase the load on production Web servers by simulating an increased number of users to determine potential issues.

   C. To stress test Web applications before development, or test servers before deployment to identify potential performance issues.

   D. To stress test Web applications on production servers.

19. Which is not true of the Performance Monitor Counter Logs?

   A. They can be saved to binary and text data files.

   B. They can be limited to a maximum size.

   C. They will overwrite earlier logs.

   D. They can be scheduled for specific time periods.

20. Which statement is incorrect concerning counter and trace logs?

   A. Trace logs record data in response to an activity.

   B. An alert can be set on a trace log.

   C. Counter logs can record data on local or remote computers.

   D. An alert can be set on a counter log.

LAB QUESTION

You have developed an ASP.NET Web application that displays and updates employee schedules. The schedules can be updated either by the employee or by the employee's supervisor(s). Other employees in the company can view the schedules but not modify them. To view an employee's schedule, the employee name can be chosen from an employee list generated by a database query. Outline a caching strategy that would optimize this application.

SELF TEST ANSWERS

Optimize the Performance of a Web Application

1. ☑ A is correct. The duration is in seconds and the VaryByParam attribute must be included, but set to None if no parameter is to be specified.

   ☒ B is incorrect as the duration is set to one second. C is incorrect because the duration is set to one second and the VaryByParam is missing. D is incorrect because the VaryByParam is set to include all values on the form.

2. ☑ B is correct. The Response.Cache allows you to set the expiration time as well as a sliding expiration from the time the page was last requested from the cache.

   ☒ A is incorrect because the @ OutputCache directive does not have a SetSlidingExpiration attribute. C is incorrect for the same reason as A. D is incorrect because it does not include SetSlidingExpiration.

3. ☑ A, C, and D are all correct.

   ☒ B is incorrect. All is not a valid location attribute value. The correct value is Any.

4. ☑ D is correct. By using fragment caching, you can cache the page and user control in different fragments.

   ☒ A is incorrect, as the page will not be cached and will result in the query being run for each page request. B is incorrect because the data cache will require multiple items to cache the query. C is incorrect because the whole page will be cached.

5. ☑ C is correct. A user control requires either a VaryByParam or a VaryByControl attribute in the @ OutputCache directive.

   ☒ A, B, and D are incorrect.

6. ☑ A, B, and C are all true.

   ☒ D is false. Cache objects cannot be used in Web farms.

7. ☑ A is correct. CacheItemPriority sets the priority level of when a cache object should be purged by ASP.NET.

   ☒ B is wrong because it specifies an expiration based on its last request from the cache. C is incorrect because it does not set the priority. D is incorrect because it does not exist.

8. ☑ D is correct. The key and value attributes are always required. If setting an expiration, both the expiration and slidingExpiration attributes must be set.

   ☒ A, B, and C are all incorrect.

9. ☑ B is the correct answer. This will create multiple cached pages for each city, which is the most efficient.
    ☒ A is incorrect as it does the opposite of what is intended by not caching the data. C and D are incorrect as they would result in less efficient caching than A.

10. ☑ C is correct; it will be one of the last items removed from the cache.
    ☒ A, B, and D are incorrect.

11. ☑ A is correct. The VaryByParam = "*" will result in multiple cached pages for all combinations of values in the GET or POST.
    ☒ B, C, and D are incorrect as multiple pages will be cached.

Diagnose and Resolve Errors and Issues

12. ☑ B is correct. ASP.NET provides counters for all ASP.NET Web applications.
    ☒ A is wrong as it only provides counters for specific applications. C is wrong as it only provides counters for the browser. D is wrong because it only handles ASP counters.

13. ☑ C is correct. Output Cache Turnover Rate will indicate the effective use of the cache. If the value is high, it means that there are a lot of additions and removals to the cache, which is inefficient.
    ☒ A, B, and D are not indicative of the cache efficiency but provide data on cache usage.

14. ☑ A, B, and C are all correct.
    ☒ D is wrong. You cannot directly send an e-mail in response to an alert.

15. ☑ A is correct.
    ☒ B is wrong. ACT tests cannot be written in VB.NET. C is incorrect as ACT projects can be used in both environments, but only in one at a time. D is wrong as a Visual Studio solution can contain only one ACT project.

16. ☑ Both A and D are correct.
    ☒ B is wrong as warmup time does not affect the duration of the run; it specifies a time interval before starting to record the results. C is wrong as it specifies only the number of connections, not the duration of the test.

17. ☑ D is correct. Average time to first byte measures the time from the request to the first byte of the response. With an increased load on the server, this time will increase.
    ☒ A is incorrect because it does not measure server responsiveness, only the number of requests received per second. B is wrong, as it measures only HTTP errors which might have nothing to do with the server but could be due to incorrectly entered URLs. C is wrong, as it reflects errors in resolving URLs to DNS entries, not server responsiveness.

18. ☑   C is correct. ACT is used to stress test Web applications before deployment by simulating multiple users.
    ☒   A is incorrect. This is a function of the Performance Monitor. B and D both are wrong. ACT is used to test applications prior to deployment to a production server.

19. ☑   C is untrue. The logs will increment file names and add a new file for each log.
    ☒   A, B, and C are all true statements.

20. ☑   B is incorrect. An alert cannot be set on a trace log.
    ☒   A, C, and D are all correct statements.

LAB ANSWER

You can cache the page that displays the employee list using a page output cache. It is unlikely that the employee list will be updated frequently and so can be set to a relatively long expiration time.

The page that displays the employee schedule can use a page cache with a VaryByParam set to the employee name or ID. This will cache the page for each employee. If the requests for this information and the changes to the employee schedule are frequent, it might be useful to create a cache object dependent on the schedule data so the cached schedule will be purged and regenerated when the schedule changes. The page used to update the schedule probably should not be cached.

Part VI

Configure and Secure a Web Application

MCAD/MCSD

MICROSOFT® CERTIFIED APPLICATION DEVELOPER
& MICROSOFT® CERTIFIED SOLUTION DEVELOPER

11

Configure a
Web Application

CERTIFICATION OBJECTIVES

I n previous chapters we have explored configuration files for our Web applications in the context of very specific functionality. For example, in Chapter 8 we enabled application-level tracing by altering the trace tag in the web.config file. In this chapter, we will look at the configuration of Web applications in general.

One common theme in .NET Framework configuration is using configuration files, which give us a centralized location in which to change the machine configuration and the configuration for individual Web applications. By using configuration files, we can easily change the way a Web application works after it is deployed without recompiling and redeploying the application.

Additionally, we will discuss *session state,* which is extremely important to a Web application. While a user interacts with a Web application, we need a way to track that user's actions and any information specific to the user (such as a list of products in a shopping cart). This information is *session specific,* which means it is needed only while the user is interacting with your Web application; once the user is finished, it can be discarded.

To end the chapter, we will install and configure Internet Information Server and look at managing FrontPage Server Extensions. We will not look at this from a system administrator's point of view, but from that of a developer.

CERTIFICATION OBJECTIVE 11.01

Configure a Web Application

We configure a Web application in the .NET Framework by editing configuration files, of which there are two main types. The first, the *machine.config* file contains configuration information for all of the Web applications running on the server. There also is at least one web.config file for each .NET Web application that contains configuration information for the individual application. Both of these configuration files contain well-formed XML and are case sensitive (all well-formed XML is case sensitive).

The XML within these files contains a nested hierarchy of XML elements that correspond to different application settings. The elements use XML attributes to define the values of different configuration elements. Element names and attribute names in the configuration files are in *camelCase,* meaning the first character of a tag or attribute is lowercase and the first character of subsequent concatenated words are in uppercase. Remember that case is important; thus, you must respect the case expected by the .NET Framework when editing configuration files.

Attribute values are in *PascalCase,* which means the first character is uppercase, as are the first characters of subsequent concatenated words. All of the configuration elements are enclosed within the root element of the XML document, which is the <configuration></configuration> element. Without the root element, a run-time error will occur when the framework tries to read the configuration from the file.

exam ☑ atch

Well-formed XML documents have exactly one root element, which is the parent for all other elements within the XML document. The configuration files we are discussing are well-formed XML documents, which is why we must have one root element (the <configuration> element) that contains all of our other configuration elements.

The configuration tags in the machine.config and web.config files are essentially the same. The system works using an inheritance paradigm in which all Web applications inherit the configuration settings from machine.config and the settings found in an applications web.config file override the settings found in the machine.config file.

As mentioned previously, subdirectories of a Web application's virtual directory also can have their own web.config files. In this situation, the settings in the machine.config file are read first to build a preliminary list of settings for the application. After the machine.config file is processed, the web.config file for the application (found in the root directory for the application) is processed and any settings found override the settings found in the machine.config file. This forms the final list of settings for the application. If there is a web.config file in a subdirectory of the application, the settings found override the settings for the application; however, they only override the application settings for the pages in the subdirectory in which the web.config file was found. This makes for a very flexible system and means we only have to add settings to the application's web.config file or a subdirectory web.config file when the settings should differ from the parent configuration file. In the case of a subdirectory web.config file, the parent configuration file is the application's web.config file, and in the case of the application's web.config file, the parent configuration file is the machine.config file.

If you have application settings common to all of the applications you are creating (or hosting), you would put these settings in the machine.config file. Any settings specific to a particular application would be placed in the web.config found in the root directory of the application (the application's web.config file). If you have any groups of pages within the application that have their own special settings, you can place them in their own subdirectory and give them their own web.config file.

Application Settings in the web.config File

Each Web application has at least one web.config file that contains application-specific configuration settings. You can find this file in the root directory of your Web application's virtual directory. A Web application also can have web.config files for any subdirectories of your Web application's virtual directory.

FROM THE CLASSROOM

Change Application Settings on a Live Application

When changing application settings in classic ASP, it was necessary to use the *MMC (Microsoft Management Console)*. This involved the administrator changing the settings for the Web application, stopping the application, and then restarting it. With ASP.NET, we can avoid starting and stopping a Web application to change its settings. The Framework is capable of detecting when a configuration file has been changed (either the machine.config file or an application-specific web.config file). When it detects a change to a configuration file, it will reload the settings for the application.

One possible issue is when the server is in the middle of fulfilling requests for one or more users. In this case, it would be detrimental for the system to change the configuration settings halfway through fulfilling a request, as the results could be unpredictable. Imagine

processing half the request with tracing enabled and the other half with tracing disabled. This obviously would create a very strange result.

For this reason, any requests that are being processed when new settings are loaded will follow the old settings until the request has been processed. Any new requests made will follow the new settings. This ensures that all requests are processed under consistent settings even if the settings are a little out of date.

You should be aware of this and, on a high capacity Web site, it is sometimes desirable to manually stop the server, change the settings, and restart the server. This gives you a natural break between setting changes. Note that this would very rarely be required and you should, in most cases, take advantage of the fact that settings can be changed while a Web site is running.

—*Wayne Cassidy, Bsc, MCSD, MCT*

The following is the web.config file that is placed in the root directory of a Web application's virtual directory when you create a new ASP.NET Web application through Visual Studio .NET:

```
<?xml version="1.0" encoding="utf-8" ?>
<configuration>
  <system.web>
    <!-- DYNAMIC DEBUG COMPILATION
         Set compilation debug="true" to insert debugging symbols
         (.pdb information) into the compiled page. Because this
         creates a larger file that executes more slowly, you should
         set this value to true only when debugging and to
         false at all other times. For more information, refer to the
         documentation about debugging ASP.NET files.
    -->
    <compilation defaultLanguage="vb" debug="true" />

    <!-- CUSTOM ERROR MESSAGES
         Set customErrors mode="On" or "RemoteOnly" to enable custom
         error messages, "Off" to disable. Add <error> tags for each
         of the errors you want to handle.
    -->
    <customErrors mode="RemoteOnly" />

    <!-- AUTHENTICATION
         This section sets the authentication policies of the
         application. Possible modes are "Windows", "Forms",
         "Passport" and "None"
    -->
    <authentication mode="Windows" />

    <!-- AUTHORIZATION
         This section sets the authorization policies of the
         application. You can allow or deny access to application
         resources by user or role. Wildcards: "*" mean everyone, "?"
         means anonymous (unauthenticated) users.
    -->
    <authorization>
        <allow users="*" /> <!-- Allow all users -->

            <!-- <allow    users="[comma separated list of users]"
                           roles="[comma separated list of roles]"/>
                 <deny     users="[comma separated list of users]"
                           roles="[comma separated list of roles]"/>
            -->
    </authorization>

    <!-- APPLICATION-LEVEL TRACE LOGGING
```

```
     Application-level tracing enables trace log output for every
     page within an application. Set trace enabled="true" to
     enable application trace logging.  If pageOutput="true", the
     trace information will be displayed at the bottom of each
     page. Otherwise, you can view the application trace log by
     browsing the "trace.axd" page from your web application root.
-->
<trace enabled="false" requestLimit="10" pageOutput="false"
       traceMode="SortByTime" localOnly="true" />

<!-- SESSION STATE SETTINGS
     By default ASP.NET uses cookies to identify which requests
     belong to a particular session. If cookies are not available,
     a session can be tracked by adding a session identifier to
     the URL. To disable cookies, set sessionState
     cookieless="true".
-->
<sessionState
       mode="InProc"
       stateConnectionString="tcpip=127.0.0.1:42424"
       sqlConnectionString="data source=127.0.0.1;
                            user id=sa;password="
       cookieless="false"
       timeout="20"
/>

<!-- GLOBALIZATION
     This section sets the globalization settings of the
     application.
-->
<globalization requestEncoding="utf-8" responseEncoding="utf-8" />
</system.web>
</configuration>
```

You should notice the comments placed in the web.config file, which are very useful when you can't quite remember how to use a configuration element. We also can learn by example and remember to add detailed comments to any configuration elements we might add later. Remember that the purpose of placing the configuration for a Web application in an easy-to-access XML file is that a Webmaster or network administrator can easily change the configuration after release. Detailed comments in your configuration files can be invaluable in ensuring that your network admin pals don't mess up your applications, and they can greatly reduce the need for support calls. When you think about it, some detailed commenting can save a great deal of time and money by helping to prevent common configuration mistakes.

The root element of the web.config file is the <configuration> element. You should notice that all other elements are within the begin and end tags for this element. Any element placed outside these tags will cause problems for the XML parser that must read this file and you will receive a run-time error when you try to run the Web application.

The <configuration> element of the web.config file has two main areas. The first section is the *configuration section handler declaration area* (try saying that five times without taking a breath—it's hours of fun); the second section is called the *configuration section settings area.* The configuration section handler declaration area allows us to define our own configuration sections and extend the standard configuration settings; the configuration section settings area is where you put the configuration settings (the <system.web> tag is placed here).

If you look at the web.config file created by Visual Studio .NET, you will notice that the element that follows the <configuration> opening tag is the <system.web> element. This is the configuration section defined for ASP.NET. The purpose of the configuration section handler declaration area is to allow us to create our own sections to use for our own configuration purposes. The following is an example of how to declare a new configuration section:

```
<configSections>
  <sectionGroup name="corporateInfo">
    <section name="supportInfo"
            type="System.Configuration.NameValueSectionHandler,
                  System, Version=1.0.3300.0, Culture=neutral,
                  PublicKeyToken=9b35aa32c18d4fb1" />
  </sectionGroup>
</configSections>
```

The configuration section handler declaration section is found within the <configSections> and </configSections> tags. Within these tags, you can organize any configuration sections you choose to add in groups; these groups also can be nested. In the preceding example, a section called *supportInfo* was declared and is found within the *corporateInfo* group. The <sectionGroup> element defines the group and the <section> element defines the section.

The <section> element has two primary attributes, which define the section and the handler that will parse the configuration information found in this section. The first attribute is *name* and defines the name of the section. The second attribute, *type,* defines the handler that will be used to read and parse the configuration. This handler must be a .NET Framework class that implements the IConfigurationSectionHandler interface. The handlers' job is to read the configuration information for the section with which it is associated and return a configuration object containing the information.

In the preceding example, you will note that the configuration handler is called System.Configuration.NameValueSectionHandler, which is the same handler that is used to process the <appSettings> section of the web.config file (we will look at the <appSettings> element shortly). Because this handler is part of the .NET Framework we do not need to create our own. Once we have declared a new section and handler, we can add configuration information to our new section as follows:

```
<corporateInfo>
  <supportInfo>
    <add key="PhoneNumber" value="555-1234" />
  </supportInfo>
</corporateInfo>
```

It is important to remember that this is a new section; therefore, it would be placed directly within the <configuration> element and not in the <system.web> element. In this scenario, we are storing the phone number for tech support because it changes quite often. To retrieve this information from within a Web page covered by this configuration, we would do the following:

```
Dim config As NameValueCollection
Dim phone As String

config =
ConfigurationSettings.GetConfig("corporateInfo/supportInfo")
phone = config("PhoneNumber")
Response.Write("<H5>Call support at: " & phone & "</H5>")
```

Using the *ConfigurationSettings* object we can execute the *GetConfig* method to retrieve a *NameValueCollection* object. The *GetConfig* method takes as an argument the group and section names that contain the configuration information we are looking for. Using the *NameValueCollection* object, we can obtain any key value pairs we have added to the web.config file by name.

If you wish to add application settings with very little hassle, a section and handler have already been declared specifically for this purpose. In the preceding example, we added our own section; however, if you do not need the convenience of a separate section, you can use the <appSettings> section. This means we don't have to create a new handler; however, if you have many settings that can benefit from a custom handler or can benefit from categorization, a custom handler is preferred. If we use the <appSettings> section for the preceding example, it would look as follows:

```
<appSettings>
  <add key="phoneNumber" value="555-1234" />
</appSettings>
```

To read these settings from your application, we would do as follows:

```
Dim phone As String

phone = ConfigurationSettings.AppSettings("PhoneNumber")
Response.Write("<H5>Call support at: " & phone & "</H5>")
```

You will notice that in this example we did not need to declare a new section, nor did we need to retrieve a *NameValueCollection* object as the *AppSettings* property is the *NameValueCollection* object for the <appSettings> section. The following quick reference can help you decide whether to use the <appSettings> section to store application settings or declare your own section using the <configSections> element.

SCENARIO & SOLUTION

I am creating a Web application that stores information in a log file. For convenience, the path to this file should be left up to the system administrator and not hard-coded. How should I store this setting?	Use the <appSettings> section as this is one simple setting for your application and will not benefit from complex organization or a custom XML tag.
I am creating a Web application that will be sold as a retail product. I have many settings that control the behavior of the Web application and I need to ensure that users of the product can manage these settings appropriately. How should I store these settings?	Create your own XML tags using the <configSettings> element. This way you can organize your settings in different sections and create custom XML tags, which will make it much easier for users to set up the application properly.
I am creating a Web application that will have a large number of disparate Boolean settings. How should I store these settings?	Use the <appSettings> section as there is no real connection between the settings, and each setting is a simple Boolean. Creating your own sections would just add unnecessary complexity, and creating your own tags would not significantly simplify anything.
I have a large number of related settings that are related in a hierarchical manner. How should I store these settings?	Create your own XML tags using the <configSettings> element. This way you can organize your settings in a hierarchy of XML tags that more closely matches the structure of the settings. This will make it much easier for users to set up the application properly.

If you look back at the web.config file added to your project by default, you will notice that the only section it contains is the <system.web> section. All of the other configuration elements are within this section. The <system.web> element is a child of the <configuration> element and contains all of the configuration information relevant to ASP.NET applications. The following is a full list of the configuration sections recognized by the .NET Framework (as stated previously you can add your own custom sections):

Element	Responsibility
<configSections>	Used for custom configuration settings.
<mscorlib>	Used for cryptography.
<runtime>	Used to define some of the behavior of the common language run time such as how it handles garbage collection.
<startup>	Used to specify the version of the common language run time to use.
<system.diagnostics>	Used to set up trace listeners and switches (see Chapter 8).
<system.net>	Used to specify how the .NET Framework connects to the Internet.
<system.runtime.remoting>	Used to configure client and server applications that implement remoting.
<system.web>	Controls how ASP.NET applications behave.

We have already discussed the <configSections> section and will discuss the <system.web> section in detail. You can consult the MSDN library for a detailed discussion of the other sections. The <system.web> section contains configuration settings specific to Web applications and each setting is expressed by the appropriate XML element. In the following sections, we will discuss each of these elements and settings in detail.

The <compilation> Element

The <compilation> element defines the settings used by the compiler when you compile your application. We briefly looked at this element in Chapter 8. The basic structure of the <compilation> element is as follows:

```
<compilation debug="true/false"
             batch="true/false"
             batchTimeout="seconds"
             defaultLanguage="language"
```

```
            explicit="true/false"
            maxBatchSize="number of pages"
            maxBatchGeneratedFileSize="kilobytes"
            numRecompilesBeforeAppRestart="number"
            strict="true/false"
            tempDirectory="path" >
    <compilers>
        <compiler language="language"
                extension="file extension"
                type=".NET Type"
                warningLevel="number"
                compilerOptions="options" />
    </compilers>

    <assemblies>
        <add assembly="assembly" />
        <remove assembly="assembly" />
        <clear />
    </assemblies>
</compilation>
```

The <compilation> element has attributes and child elements. Table 11-1 describes the attributes for the <compilation> element.

TABLE 11-1   <compilation> Attributes

Attribute	Value Type	Description
debug	Boolean	Determines whether symbolic debug information is added to your program.
batch	Boolean	Determines whether batching is supported.
batchTimeout	Number	Determines the number of seconds the compiler will attempt to compile a batch. If the compiler cannot compile the batch in this time, it will revert to a single compile.
defaultLanguage	Text	Determines the programming language to use by default.
explicit	Boolean	Used to set the Visual Basic explicit compile option.
maxBatchSize	Number	Specifies the maximum number of pages for a batch compilation.
maxBatchGenerated FileSize	Number	Specifies the maximum size in KB of the generated source file per batch compilation.
numRecompiles BeforeAppRestart	Number	Specifies the number of dynamic recompiles of resources before the application is restarted.

TABLE 11-1		<compilation> Attributes *(continued)*

Attribute	Value Type	Description
strict	Boolean	Used to set the Visual Basic strict compile option.
tempDirectory	Text	The path to a temporary directory to be used during compilation.

The two attributes used in a web.config files <compilation> element by default are the language and debug attributes. There also are two child elements that can be used with the <compilation> element. The first element is the <compilers> element, which is used to set up the compilers for different languages you may be using. The second element is the <assembly> element, which is used to specify which assemblies need to be added during compilation.

The <customErrors> Element

The <customErrors> element is used to specify how your application will deal with errors it encounters. The basic structure of the <customErrors> element is as follows:

```
<customErrors defaultRedirect="url"
              mode="On|Off|RemoteOnly">
  <error statusCode="statuscode"
         redirect="url"/>
</customErrors>
```

The <customErrors> element has attributes as well as child elements. The following table describes the attributes for the <customErrors> element:

Attribute	Value Type	Description
defaultRedirect	Text	Specifies the URL to which to direct the browser if an error occurs. If this is not specified, a generic error message is displayed instead.
mode	Enumeration	Specifies whether custom errors are enabled, disabled, or shown only to remote clients. If set to RemoteOnly, local users are given ASP.NET errors and remote users are given custom error messages.

In a web.config file the <customError> element is added by default and the mode is set to RemoteOnly. The child element that can be used with the <customError> element is the <error> element, which is used to define custom errors.

The <authentication> Element

The <authentication> element is used to specify how your application will authenticate users. The basic structure of the <authentication> element is as follows.

```
<authentication mode="Windows|Forms|Passport|None">
    <forms name="name"
            loginUrl="url"
            protection="All|None|Encryption|Validation"
            timeout="30" path="/" >
        <credentials passwordFormat="Clear|SHA1|MD5">
            <user name="username" password="password" />
        </credentials>
    </forms>
    <passport redirectUrl="internal"/>
</authentication>
```

The <authentication> element has attributes as well as child elements. The following table describes the attributes for the <authentication> element:

Attribute	Value Type	Description
mode	Enumeration	Specifies the authentication mode to use. Windows is used for windows authentication. Forms is used for ASP.NET Forms-based authentication. Passport is used for Microsoft Passport authentication. None is used for anonymous access only.

In a web.config file, the <authentication> element is added by default and the mode is set to Windows. The child elements that can be used with the <authentication> element are the <forms> and <passport> elements. The <forms> element is used to configure an application for custom Forms-based authentication. The <passport> element is used to configure an application for Microsoft Passport authentication.

The <authorization> Element

The <authorization> element is used to specify who can gain access to the resources of your Web application. The basic structure of the <authorization> element is as follows:

```
<authorization>
    <allow users="comma-separated list of users"
            roles="comma-separated list of roles"
            verbs="comma-separated list of verbs" />
    <deny users="comma-separated list of users"
```

```
              roles="comma-separated list of roles"
              verbs="comma-separated list of verbs" />
</authorization>
```

The <authorization> element has only child elements and no attributes. The <allow> and <deny> child elements are used to allow or deny access to the Web application. You can allow or deny individual users, groups, or verbs (HTTP transmission methods). By default, the <authorization> element is added to your web.config file with the users' attribute of the <allow> sub tag set to *, which means allow all users.

When a user tries to access a resource in the Web application the system searches through the access rules to find a rule that matches the user's credentials. The first rule it finds is the rule it uses, which means if you have a user account listed in both the <allow> and <deny> subtags, the order of the subtags in the config file will determine whether the user is allowed or denied access.

If the <allow> subtag comes first, the user will be allowed access, and if the <deny> sub tag comes first, he or she is denied access. For this reason, watch out when using wild cards (such as *), because if the wild card is placed in the <allow> subtag (which by default comes before the <deny> tag), none of the users listed in the <deny> sub tag will be denied access.

on the job

The <authorization> element is a very useful place to quickly block access to a Web application. If you find out that someone is using your application in a suspicious way or causing problems, you can block him or her from your application by adding their account to the <deny> tag and making sure the <deny> tag comes before the <allow> tag (to prevent the problem with wild cards just mentioned). You do not need to disable the user's Windows account (although this might be desirable if the user's intent is malicious) and do not need to change his or her NTFS permissions.

The <trace> Element

The <trace> element is used to set up tracing an ASP.NET application as we saw in Chapter 8. The basic structure of the <trace> element is as follows:

```
<trace enabled="true|false"
       localOnly="true|false"
       pageOutput="true|false"
       requestLimit="integer"
       traceMode="SortByTime|sortByCategory" />
```

The <trace> element has only attributes and no child elements. The following table describes the attributes for the <trace> element:

Attribute	Value Type	Description
enabled	Boolean	Specifies whether tracing is on or off.
localOnly	Boolean	Specifies whether tracing is seen by only local users or both local and remote users.
pageOutput	Boolean	Specifies whether trace information should be displayed to the page or stored in memory.
requestLimit	Number	Specifies the number of trace requests to store on the server. The default is 10.
traceMode	Enumeration	Specifies the order to display the trace output. If set to SortByTime, the trace output is sorted in the order in which it is processed. If set to SortByCategory, the trace output is sorted by user-defined category in alphabetical order.

In a web.config file, the <trace> element is added by default and the enabled attribute is set to false, requestLimit is set to 10, pageOutput is set to false, traceMode is set to SortByTime, and localOnly is set to true.

The <sessionState> Element

The <sessionState> element is used to configure the session state settings for the Web application. The basic structure of the <sessionState> element is as follows:

```
<sessionState mode="Off|Inproc|StateServer|SQLServer"
              cookieless="true|false"
              timeout="number of minutes"
              stateConnectionString="tcpip=server:port"
              sqlConnectionString="sql connection string" />
```

The <sessionState> element has only attributes; no child elements. The following table describes the attributes for the <sessionState> element:

Attribute	Value Type	Description
mode	Enumeration	Specifies where to store the session state. Off is used to indicate that session state is not enabled. Inproc is used to indicate that session state is stored locally (in process). StateServer is used to indicate that session state is stored on a remote server. SQLServer is used to specify that session state is stored on a SQL Server.

Attribute	Value Type	Description
cookieless	Boolean	Specifies whether cookies should be used to track a session.
timeout	Number	Specifies the number of minutes a session can be idle before it is dropped.
stateConnectionString	Text	Specifies the server name and port of the remote server where session state is stored. This is used in conjunction with mode="StateServer".
sqlConnectionString	Text	Specifies the SQL Server connection string that points to the SQL Server where session state is stored. This is used in conjunction with mode="SQLServer".

In a web.config file, the <sessionState> element is added by default and the mode is set to InProc, the stateConnectionString attribute is set to the loopback address (127.0.0.1) and port 42424, the sqlConnectionString is set to the loopback address, the cookieless attribute set to false, and the timeout set to 20.

The <globalization> Element

The <globalization> element is used to specify the default culture for your application as well as other related globalization settings. The basic structure of the <globalization> element is as follows:

```
<globalization requestEncoding="any valid encoding string"
               responseEncoding="any valid encoding string"
               fileEncoding="any valid encoding string"
               culture="any valid culture string"
               uiCulture="any valid culture string" />
```

The <globalization> element has only attributes; no child elements. The following table describes the attributes for the <globalization> element:

Attribute	Value Type	Description
requestEncoding	Text	Specifies the assumed encoding for incoming requests
responseEncoding	Text	Specifies the encoding to use for outgoing responses.
fileEncoding	Text	Specifies the default encoding for .aspx, .asmx, and .asax file parsing.
culture	Text	Specifies the default culture for incoming requests.
uiCulture	Text	Specifies the default culture for processing locale-dependent resource searches.

In a web.config file, the <globalization> element is added by default with the requestEncoding attribute is set to utf-8 and the responseEncoding set to utf-8. For a more detailed look at globalization, see Chapter 4.

The <browserCap> Element

The <browserCap> element defines the settings used by the browser capabilities component. The browser capabilities component can determine the capabilities of the user's browser when he or she makes a request. The header of an http request contains information that specifies the browser being used to make the request. The <browserCap> element contains a listing of capabilities for each browser, such as whether it supports frames. You then can use the browser capabilities component to determine what the user's browser can handle, which allows you to avoid sending content it cannot handle to the client's browser. The basic structure of the <browserCap> element is as follows:

```
<browserCaps>
    <result type="class" />
    <use var="HTTP_USER_AGENT" />
        browser=Unknown
        version=0.0
        majorver=0
        minorver=0
        frames=false
        tables=false
    <filter>
        <case match="Windows 98|Win98">
            platform=Win98
        </case>
    <case match="Windows NT|WinNT">
        platform=WinNT
    </case>
    </filter>
</browserCaps>
```

The <browseCaps> element has no attributes and three child elements. The <use> element specifies the server variables used while evaluating <filter>, <case>, and assignments in the section. The <filter> element evaluates the first child <case> element that matches. The <result> element specifies the *HttpCapabilitiesBase*-derived class used to hold the resulting key/value string pairs from parsing this section.

By default, the <browseCaps> element is not added to a web.config file. The settings found in the machine.config file are used by default.

The <httpModules> Element

The <httpModules> element configures the http modules in an application. The basic structure of the <httpModules> element is as follows:

```
<httpModules>
    <add type="classname,assemblyname" name="modulename" />
    <remove name="modulename" />
    <clear />
</httpModules>
```

The <httpModules> element has no attributes and three child elements. The <add> element adds an http module to an application. The <remove> element removes an http module from an application, and the <clear> element removes all http modules from an application. By default, the <httpModules> element is not added to a web.config file.

The <httpHandlers> Element

The <httpHandlers> element maps incoming requests to the appropriate *IHttpHandler* or *IHttpHandlerFactory* class, according to the URL and HTTP verb specified in the request. The basic structure of the <httpHandlers> element is as follows:

```
<httpHandlers>
    <add verb="verbs"
        path="path/wildcard"
        type="type,assemblyname"
        validate="" />
    <remove verb="verb list"
            path="path/wildcard" />
    <clear />
</httpHandlers>
```

The <httpHandlers> element has no attributes and three child elements. The <add> element adds an http handler to an application. The <remove> element removes an http handler from an application, and the <clear> element removes all http handlers from an application. By default, the <httpHandlers> element is not added to a web.config file.

The <processModel> Element

The <processModel> element is used to configure the process model settings for Internet Information Server (IIS). This element is processed by the *aspnet_isapi.dll* unmanaged DLL and not by the .NET Framework configuration system. Because of this fact, changes to these settings are not updated until IIS is restarted. This is in direct contrast to all of the other settings discussed thus far and is the exception to the rule. The basic structure of the <processModel> element is as follows:

```
<processModel enable="true|false"
              timeout="minutes"
              idleTimeout="minutes"
              shutdownTimeout="hrs:mins:secs"
              requestLimit="number"
              requestQueueLimit="Infinite|number"
              memoryLimit="percentage"
              cpuMask="number"
              webGarden="true|false"
              userName="username"
              password="password"
              logLevel="All|None|Errors"
              clientConnectedCheck="HH:MM:SS"
              comAuthenticationLevel="Default|None|Connect|Call|

Pkt|PktIntegrity|PktPrivacy"
              comImpersonationLevel="Default|Anonymous|Identify|
                                      Impersonate|Delegate"
              maxWorkerThreads="number"
              maxIoThreads="number" />
```

The <processModel> element has attributes but no child elements. Table 11-2 describes the attributes for the <processModel> element.

TABLE 11-2   <processModel> Attributes

Attribute	Value Type	Description
enable	Boolean	Specifies whether the process model is enabled.
timeout	Number	Specifies the number of minutes until ASP.NET spawns a new worker process to take the place of the current one.
idleTimeout	Number	Specifies the number of hours:minutes:seconds of inactivity after which ASP.NET automatically ends a worker process.

TABLE 11-2	<processModel> Attributes *(continued)*

Attribute	Value Type	Description
shutdownTimeout	Time	Specifies the number of minutes allowed for the worker process to shut itself down before ASP.NET forces a shutdown.
requestLimit	Number	Specifies the number of requests that can be handled before ASP.NET spawns a new worker process to take the place of the current one.
requestQueueLimit	Number	Specifies the maximum number of requests that can be queued before ASP.NET returns a server-too-busy error (503). By default, this is set to 5000.
memoryLimit	Percent	Specifies the maximum percentage of total system memory the worker process can consume before ASP.NET launches a new process and reassigns existing requests. The default is 40 percent.
cpuMask	Number	Specifies which processors on a multiprocessor server are eligible to run ASP.NET processes.
webGarden	Boolean	Specifies whether this is a Web garden (a Web garden is a multi-CPU Web application).
username	Text	The user name under which the worker process should run. If not set, it will run under the system account.
password	Text	The password for the preceding user name.
logLevel	Enumeration	Specifies which process events should be logged to the event log. If set to None, nothing will be logged. If set to All, everything will be logged. If set to Errors, only error events will be logged.
clientConnectedCheck	Time	Specifies how long a request is left in the queue before ASP.NET does a client-connected check.
comAuthenticationLevel	Enumeration	Specifies the level of security to use for DCOM authentication. If set to Default, it will use the normal authentication algorithm. If set to None, it will not use authentication. If set to Connect, a client will be authenticated when a connection is made. If set to Call, a client will be authenticated every time a remote procedure call is made to the server. If set to Pkt, all packets are authenticated. If set to PktIntegrity, a check will be made to ensure that all packets arrive unmodified from the client. If set to PktPrivacy, DCOM will authenticate all previous levels and will encrypt arguments to remote procedure calls.

| TABLE 11-2 | <processModel> Attributes *(continued)* |

Attribute	Value Type	Description
comImpersonationLevel	Enumeration	Specifies how impersonation is dealt with for DCOM. If set to Default, it will use the normal authentication algorithm. If set to Anonymous, the client is anonymous to the server (not supported in this release). If set to Identify, the server can impersonate the client for Access Control List (ACL) checking but it cannot access system objects as the client. If set to Impersonate, the server can impersonate the client for local requests but not across machine boundaries. If set to Delegate, the server can impersonate the client across machine boundaries.
maxWorkerThreads	Number	Specifies the maximum number of worker threads per CPU.
maxIoThreads	Number	Specifies the maximum number of Input/Output threads per CPU.

The <processModel> element is not added to a web.config file by default.

exam
☮atch

Don't forget that changes to the process model are not active until the Web site is restarted. This is much different from the other configuration elements we have discussed and is a perfect trick question for an exam.

The <identity> Element

The <identity> element defines the user account under which the Web application runs. We briefly looked at this element in Chapter 6. The basic structure of the <identity> element is as follows:

```
<identity impersonate="true|false"
          userName="username"
          password="password"/>
```

The <identity> element has attributes only and no child elements. The following table describes the attributes for the <identity> element:

Attribute	Value Type	Description
Impersonate	Boolean	Specifies whether impersonation is used or not.
userName	Text	Specifies the account to use for impersonation.
password	Text	Specifies the password for the account used for impersonation.

The <identity> element is not added to a web.config file by default.

Machine-Level Settings in the machine.config File

The machine.config file contains the configuration settings for the Web server. Due to the inheritance paradigm mentioned earlier, this is the top-level file for all configuration settings in all Web applications on your Web server. Any configuration settings found in the machine.config file that are not overridden in a web.config file will be respected for any ASP.NET Web application that runs. This is a convenient location for configuration settings common to many of the Web applications you are working with. If a setting is inappropriate for a specific application, the setting can be easily overridden in the web.config file for that application.

There is only one machine.config file per server. This file can be found at C:\ *WindowsDirectory*\Microsoft.NET\Framework\version\CONFIG\machine.config. The machine.config file has the same format as the web.config files we discussed previously and accepts the same configuration information. Essentially, the machine.config file is just a web.config file that is used for all Web applications; not a single application or directory.

If you look at your machine.config file, the most obvious thing you will see is the declaration of all of the standard sections such as <system.net> and <system.web>. These sections are declared in the machine.config file, which is the reason we do not see a declaration for them in the web.config file. The following quick reference will help you decide whether you should put configuration settings in the machine.config file or your application's web.config file.

SCENARIO & SOLUTION

I have a setting common to all of my Web applications. Where should it be placed?	Use the machine.config file and you will not have to replicate this setting in all of your web.config files.
I have a setting that is used by only one application. Where should it be placed?	Use the web.config file because you won't be sharing the setting. Also, it will be much easier for administrators to find.
I have a setting that is used by many different applications; however, the settings have different values for many different applications. Where should the settings be placed?	It might be tempting to put each setting in the web.config file; however, you are hurting yourself if you do not also add the setting to the machine.config file. Figure out the most common value for the setting and add it to the machine.config file. Override it when necessary in the web.config files that have unique values for this setting. This will give you a reasonable default and simplify administration.

EXERCISE 11-1

Configure a Web Application

In this exercise, we will configure a Web application with defined settings. After the instructions for this exercise is a listing of the web.config file with the settings. I would suggest you use this listing to check your work (in other words, don't just copy it). The following is a list of settings we will use:

- Do not compile your application with symbolic debug information.

- Redirect the user to a custom error page called MyErrors.aspx whenever any error is received.

- Set up authorization for anonymous access only.

- Enable tracing so that trace output is stored in memory and is accessible through the trace.axd page.

- Enable impersonation with the user account MyAccount and the password meep.

1. Launch Visual Studio.

2. Open any existing ASP.NET application or create a new one (your choice).

3. Open the web.config file in the editor.

4. Add the appropriate configuration information for the preceding settings. When you are finished, it should look as follows (comments were removed for space reasons, but you should always use comments in your config files):

```xml
<?xml version="1.0" encoding="utf-8" ?>
<configuration>
  <system.web>
    <compilation defaultLanguage="vb" debug="false" />
    <customErrors defaultRedirect="MyErrors.aspx" mode="RemoteOnly" />
    <authentication mode="None" />
    <authorization>
        <allow users="*" /> <!-- Allow all users -->
    </authorization>
    <trace enabled="true" requestLimit="10" pageOutput="false"
          traceMode="SortByTime" localOnly="true" />
    <sessionState
          mode="InProc"
          stateConnectionString="tcpip=127.0.0.1:42424"
          sqlConnectionString="data source=127.0.0.1;
                            user id=sa;password="
          cookieless="false"
```

```
                    timeout="20"
        />
        <globalization requestEncoding="utf-8" responseEncoding="utf-8" />
        <identity impersonate="true" userName="MyAccount" password="meep"
    />
      </system.web>
    </configuration>
```

CERTIFICATION OBJECTIVE 11.02

Configure and Implement Session State

Http is a stateless protocol, which means when a server gets a request it does not know whether this is the first request from a client, or the client is interacting with a page and this is a subsequent request. When users are using interactive Web pages in ASP.NET, pages can be reposted to the server several times while the user interacts with them; every time the page is posted back to the server, the Web page is re-created. This essentially means that the state of the page is destroyed every time the page is posted.

ASP.NET has several methods of tracking session state. In Chapter 5, we looked at the ViewState object, which was used to track the visual state of a Web page and used the client to store this information. In this section, we will look at storing session state on the server.

There are three primary options available to store state on the server. We can store state within the process we are running, which essentially means storing state in the memory used by our Web application. We can store state using the Session State Service, which uses a separate process to store session state. Finally, we can use SQL Server to store state for our sessions. Using session state is the same, regardless of the method used to store it.

exam
ⓦatch

Do not confuse session state with the ViewState object. The ViewState object has nothing to do with session state and is considered a client-side entity. View state is sent to the server, but it is not processed on the server and therefore is a client-side method of storing state. Finally, view state is specific to an individual page whereas session state is specific to the session, which usually involves viewing several pages.

Before we continue, it is important to understand how state is tracked considering that http will not track it for us. State is tracked using a 120-bit string called a *SessionID,* which is generated by an algorithm that guarantees uniqueness and randomness. This string is given to users when they make their first requests to a Web application. Upon subsequent requests, the string is returned to the server, which then can associate the request with a specific session and its state.

The way in which the *SessionID* is transferred back and forth to the client differs depending on whether the Web application or the user's browser supports cookies. If the Web application is using cookies, the *SessionID* will be sent back and forth to the client through a cookie. If the Web application is cookieless, the *SessionID* will be sent back and forth to the client by embedding the *SessionID* into a modified URL. The method used depends on the configuration settings for the Web application. As we have seen earlier, the *cookieless* attribute of the <sessionState> element in the web.config file controls whether cookies will be used.

Session state is accessible through the *Session* object. The *Session* object is instantiated from the *SessionStateModule* class, which is derived from *IHttpModule.* This http module is added to all Web applications because it is declared by default in the machine.config file. To use the *Session* object for session state is very easy; classic ASP developers will be pleased to know it works the same way the *Session* object did in classic ASP. The *Session* object exposes the state it contains using a dictionary model. The following example stores some information in the *Session* object and retrieves it:

```
Session("Advice") = "Don't eat yellow snow eh!"
Response.Write("<h2>" & Session("Advice") & </h2>")
```

Store Session State Within a Process

By default, session state is stored *in process,* which means it is stored in the same memory as that used by your Web application. The benefits of this method are its simplicity and speed. It is fast because your application has direct access to its state and does not need to make a Remote Procedure Call (RPC) to access its state in another process.

The downside to this is fault tolerance. If your Web application goes down or is restarted by the administrator, all of the session state stored is lost. In many applications, this probably is not a big deal; if the application goes down, it might make sense to throw out any session state that was stored. If you wish to support recovery, this method of storing session state would not be appropriate.

The method of storing session state is defined in the web.config file. For example, to configure the state management system to store session state in process, we would need to ensure that the <sessionState> element in the web.config file has its mode attribute set to *InProc* as follows:

```
<sessionState
    mode="InProc"
    cookieless="false"
    timeout="20"
/>
```

on the job

Session state in classic ASP was stored in process. We did not have the capability to store it in a separate process or database unless we developed our own methods for session state (in other words, we would not use the Session object for session state). If you are upgrading a classic ASP application, you do not have to worry about the difference because, regardless of where you store session state, you access it the same way.

Store Session State with the Session State Service

If the default of storing session state in process is not adequate for your application, you can use the Session State Service instead. The Session State Service is an out-of-process server that stores session state, which means if your application goes down, the session state associated with any current sessions stays intact. It is possible to restart a Web application while users are connected to it without the users knowing about it. Imagine spending 20 minutes filling in an online order—then your information is dropped just before the final submission! With the Session State Server, we can prevent this.

To use the Session State Service you must ensure that the Session State Server is running. You can start the Session State Server from the Services snap-in or by executing `net start aspnet_state` from the command line. Figure 11-1 shows the Session State Service being started from the Services snap-in.

Once the server is running, we must inform our Web application that it is to use the Session State Server. You can do this by setting the *mode* and *stateConnectionString* attributes of the <sessionState> element in the web.config file as follows:

```
<sessionState
    mode="StateServer"
    stateConnectionString="tcpip=127.0.0.1:42424"
    cookieless="false"
    timeout="20"
/>
```

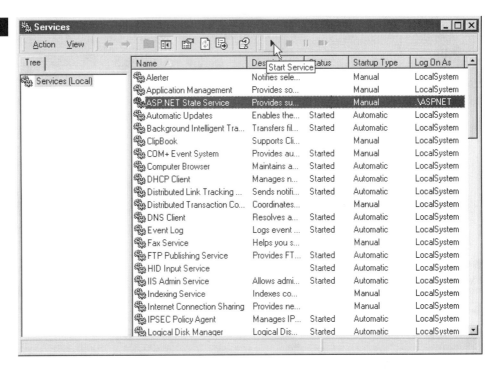

FIGURE 11-1

Starting the
Session State
Service

The stateConnectionString attribute is set to the server and port on which the Session State Server is running. If you are using the Session State Server for a Web farm (multiserver) it is important to note that only one instance of the Session State Server can be running for the Web farm.

Store Session State with SQL Server

If you are considering using the Session State Server to store session state and security is a prime concern, you might wish to consider using a SQL Server database. SQL Server can be used in place of the Session State Server, which gives us access to a mature, robust, and secure system for storing session state. To use SQL Server for storing session state, we need to install the database that will hold our session state. A SQL script ships with the .NET Framework that must be run on the database when you use SQL server to store session state. The script can be found at C:\WINNT\ Microsoft.NET\Framework\ *<version>*\ and is called InstallSQLState.sql.

This script creates a database called ASPState, and adds the ASPStateTempApplications and ASPStateTempSessions tables to the TempDB database. Once you have set up

SQL Server to handle session state, you must instruct your application to use SQL Server. This is done by setting the mode attribute of the <sessionState> element of the web.config file to SQLServer and setting the SqlConnectionString as follows:

```
<sessionState
      mode="SQLServer"
      sqlConnectionString="data source=127.0.0.1;user
                           id=sa;password=nonblankpassword"
      cookieless="false"
      timeout="20"
/>
```

The sqlConnectionString attribute should be set to a valid SQL Server connection string.

EXERCISE 11-2

Configure and Implement Session State

In this exercise, we will configure a Web application to use the Session State Service to store session state.

1. Launch Visual Studio.

2. Open any existing ASP.NET application or create a new one (your choice).

3. Open the web.config file in the editor.

4. Change the web.config files <sessionState> element to use the Session State Service. It should look as follows:

```
<sessionState
      mode="StateServer"
      stateConnectionString="tcpip=127.0.0.1:42424"
      cookieless="false"
      timeout="20"
/>
```

5. Start the Session State Service from the Services applet in the Control Panel.

6. Test the application by using the Session object to store something and retrieve it. The following code is what I used (you will need to add a button to your Web page):

```
Private Sub btnClear_Click(ByVal sender As System.Object, _
                           ByVal e As System.EventArgs) _
                           Handles btnClear.Click
    Session("Variable") = "Hello World!"
    Response.Write(Session("Variable"))
End Sub
```

Install and Configure Server Services

Although you might never install or configure Internet Information Server (IIS) on a production server, eventually you will need to install and configure IIS for a development system. In this section, we will discuss installing and configuring, IIS and Microsoft FrontPage server extensions from a developer's point of view. IIS is the Microsoft Web server we have been using throughout this book to run our Web applications. Its role includes handling requests from users, implementing Web server security, interpreting and running server-side code, and much more.

FrontPage server extensions are essentially scripts that can be installed on a Web application, thus allowing developers to remotely access and manipulate the contents of a Web application without the need to log on to the local system. They are extremely valuable when updating a Web application across the Internet (when you are not logged onto the network local to the Web server).

Both of these services are of primary importance to the Web developer, as their presence and configuration directly affect how a Web application will run and how we can work with it. This section could be a book unto itself, thus we will discuss only issues that are directly related to developers and Exam 70-305.

Install and Configure a Web Server

Installing Internet Information Server is a very uneventful activity. If you can follow simple directions, you can install IIS. The only important thing to mention involves the .NET Framework. IIS 5.0 does not ship with support for the .NET Framework. When you install the .NET Framework (which most likely was installed when you installed Visual Studio .NET), you also are setting up IIS to support .NET applications. If you are installing IIS after you have installed the .NET Framework (or reinstalling IIS), you will have to reinstall the .NET Framework or none of your .NET Web applications will function.

on the
job

On more than one occasion I have known IIS to spontaneously stop processing .NET application code (although it would still display an .aspx file). At the time of this writing, this is not a documented bug and I have been unable to determine the reason for this; however, reinstalling the .NET Framework fixed it every time.

On a final note, IIS is not installed by default and you will have to go to the Add Remove Programs applet in the Control Panel to install it. Aside from that, everything is relatively straightforward. Make sure you have installed IIS and the .NET Framework (which you probably have already done if you've been using any of the code in this book) before you write the exam. The experience will help you with any questions that arise.

When comparing installing IIS to configuring IIS, we can see where the focus should be in this discussion. Configuring IIS is much more difficult than installing it (don't worry—it's actually still pretty easy). Depending on which operating system you are using, you might have a different version of IIS.

For example, if you are running Windows 2000 Server or Advanced Server, you will have the full production version of IIS 5.0, but if you are running Windows 2000 Professional, you will have the desktop version of IIS. From a developer's perspective, there really is no difference between the two; both versions of IIS support Active Server Pages and both versions can run .NET Web applications if you have installed the .NET Framework.

However, the differences are of primary interest to an administrator. For example, the version of IIS that comes with Windows 2000 Professional can host only one Web site and will support only ten current connections. This, of course, does not mean you can develop only one Web site at a time with Windows 2000 Professional. You simply use separate virtual directories for each Web application. If you are using Visual Studio .NET as your development environment, you will notice that Visual Studio takes care of setting up your Web applications appropriately.

To configure Web applications running on IIS, typically we use the Microsoft Management Console (MMC) snap-in called the Internet Services Manager. You can find this in the Administrative Tools directory in the Control Panel, as shown in Figure 11-2.

FIGURE 11-2 The Administrative Tools directory

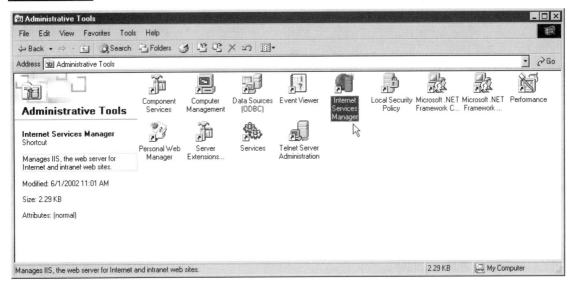

When opened, you will notice that this snap-in will allow you to administer IIS, Simple Mail Transfer Protocol (SMTP) Server, and File Transfer Protocol (FTP) Server. IIS is accessible by clicking the Default Web Site node (it might not be called Default Web Site on your computer if you have changed the description), as shown in Figure 11-3.

When this node is expanded, you will see a list of the virtual directories running under IIS. First notice the different icons; some look like little boxes and some like directories. This is the distinction between a Web application and a simple directory. A directory you see under the Default Web Site node is just a subdirectory with some content.

A Web application is much more advanced. The little box signifies that this is the starting point (or root) of a Web application. Anything within the directory representing the root is part of the application; anything not within the root is not part of the application. If you choose one of the Web applications you have been working with, right-click and select properties on the node that corresponds to it and you will see the Resource Properties dialog box. This dialog box contains everything you will need to properly configure your Web application.

FIGURE 11-3

Click the Default
Web Site node

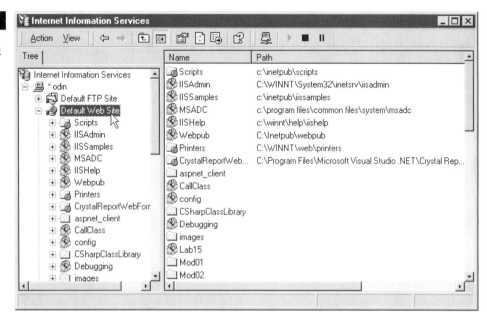

The first tab displayed is the Directory tab (see Figure 11-4). On this tab we can set up the directory that holds the contents of the Web application. You can set the permissions for the Web application and set its application settings.

There are four check boxes that define the standard permissions of the Web application. If you check the Script Source Access check box, you will allow users to view the source code behind a script. This obviously is not desirable in a production environment (unless of course you're trying to share script code) and is not checked off by default.

The Read and Write check boxes are fairly self explanatory and, as expected, the Write check box is not checked by default. To be specific, if you allow write access to the Web application, a user who is able to access the site can post content and change the current content. Checking the Directory Browsing check box allows users to view a list of the contents of this directory. You should note that this will happen only if the directory does not contain a start page (default.htm, index.html, and so forth).

One setting of further importance is the Execute permissions. With this drop-down list box, you can allow users to execute scripts only on the server, execute scripts and executable files on the server, or not allow the execution of server-side code at all. The default is to allow scripts only, which is sufficient for most Web applications and should be mandatory for a Web application on the Internet.

The Directory
tab, which sets up
the Web
application
contents

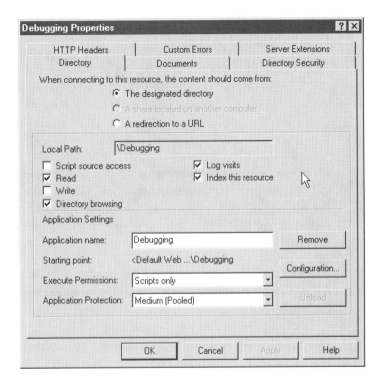

If you want to turn a directory into a Web application or turn a Web application
back into a directory, you can use the Create/Remove button. If you are looking at
the properties of a Web application, the button will be labeled Remove. If, on the
other hand, you are looking at the properties of a directory, the button will be labeled
Create. Note that a .NET Web application must be set up as an IIS application to
run, which is done for you if you create the application through Visual Studio .NET.

The Application protection drop-down list box has been advanced from IIS 4.0.
In IIS 4.0, you could specify that a Web application should run its code within the
same process space as IIS or in a separate process space. We now have three options:

- ■ **Low (IIS Process)** Runs the Web application in the same process as IIS.
  This increases the performance of the Web application; however, if the Web
  application crashes, it also brings down the Web server.

- ■ **Medium (pooled)** Runs the Web application in a separate process from IIS.
  However, this process is shared by other Web applications that run under
  medium protection. This setting is a very nice middle ground. If your Web

application crashes, the Web server keeps running; however, any other Web applications set to medium protection also would go down.

■ **High (isolated)**   Runs the Web application in its own process space. This is valuable for complex Web applications, especially if they are a little buggy (if you are stabilizing a Web application after it's gone live). In this situation, the Web application can harm no other applications (at least not by crashing), but the overall scalability of the Web server will degrade.

on the job   *I strongly recommend that you do not run more than ten Web applications in isolation (in their own process space). This number is an average (from the IIS help files) so you should remember that the more you spend on a server (more processors, memory, and so forth), the higher this number can reasonably become.*

If you click the Configuration button on in this tab, you are presented with the Application Configuration dialog box. In this dialog box, there are three tabs. The first tab is the App Mappings tab. This is where you can associate different resources to different programs that will process these resources. For example, when a resource with the file extension .asp is requested, the Web server knows that asp.dll should process this page because the two are associated here.

As a .NET developer you will rarely—if ever—need to set any application mappings; however, if you are using CGI scripting (for example PERL), this is the place you would inform IIS that all .pl files should be processed by perl.exe. The App Options and App Debugging tabs are specific to classic ASP pages; therefore, we will not discuss them further (take a look at them anyway because you probably will have to set up debugging for a classic ASP application someday).

The next tab in the Resource Properties dialog box is the Documents tab. In this tab, you can specify which (if any) file will be your default Web page for this directory. As shown in Figure 11-5, there are four files entered by default: Default.htm, Default.asp, iisstart.asp, and Default.aspx (Default.aspx will be in this list only if you have installed the .NET Framework).

When a user requests access to a virtual directory but does not specify which resource he or she would like, the defaults are used in the order in which they appear in the list box. If you want to use a page that is not listed in the list box, you can click the Add button (for example, if you want your start page to be home.aspx).

FIGURE 11-5

The four
default files

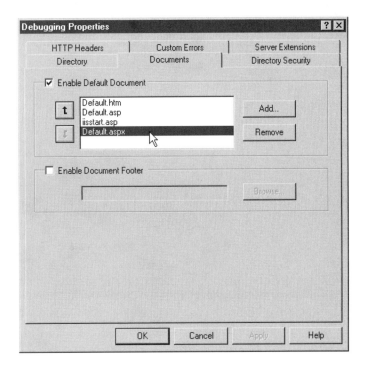

The Directory Security tab contains a group of settings a developer will need to understand because it directly affects how you will write a Web application. Figure 11-6 shows that there are three frames within this tab.

The IP addresses and domain name restrictions frame allows us to block users from our Web application based on IP address or domain. The Secure communications frame allows us to set up certificates and requires secure communication for this resource. You will most often visit the Anonymous access and authentication control frame. There is only one button in this frame (the Edit button); pressing it brings up the Authentication Methods dialog box, as shown in Figure 11-7.

From here we can allow or deny the following forms of authentication:

- **Anonymous access** means users do not need to log on to the server running IIS (or its domain). If the user does not log on to the server, he or she will be logged on using the IUSR_*ComputerName* account. This account is a member of the Guests group and allows the user to retrieve content from the Web server without giving the user access to the rest of the system (unless of course you are a silly person and give the IUSR_*ComputerName* account access to the rest of the system).

FIGURE 11-6

The three frames
in the Directory
Security tab

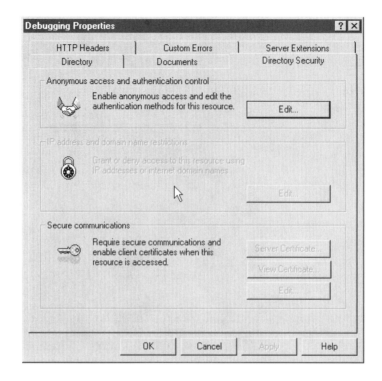

FIGURE 11-7

The
Authentication
Methods
dialog box

- **Basic authentication** requires that the user logs in to the system with a valid account; however, user names and passwords are sent in clear text (unencrypted). This would be suicide on the Internet, as anyone with intermediate knowledge of networking and a packet sniffer could read your user name and password. If you have ever surfed a Web site and been presented with a login dialog box, you have used Basic authentication.

- **Digest authentication** is similar to Basic authentication but user names and passwords are put through a hashing algorithm before they are sent to the server. The server sends the browser some extra information that is to be included with the user name and password, after which the browser puts the combined information through the hashing algorithm and sends it to the server. Once the server receives the hashed user name and password, it can compare the hash value to the equivalent hashed versions of user names and passwords on its domain. If everything checks out, the user is authenticated. This is not as secure as Windows authentication but it is much more secure than Basic authentication. Digest authentication also will work across proxy servers and firewalls, which means it is viable on the Internet. It should be noted that only a Windows 2000 domain controller with a plain text copy of the user accounts and passwords can use Digest authentication. If digest authentication is grayed out, this means your system is not a Windows 2000 domain controller.

- **Integrated Windows authentication** is the most secure form of authentication. It uses encryption to send credentials across the network. It also is convenient for users because they do not have to enter their user names and passwords when logging on to a Web site. The credentials sent are the credentials you have logged on to your own system with. If these credentials do not check out, you then will be presented with a logon dialog box. Note that Windows authentication will not work across a proxy server or firewall and therefore was never intended to be used on the Internet. However, it is the preferred method of authentication on an intranet.

At this point, you should note that all of the authentication and authorization techniques we have talked about are through IIS and are related to the virtual directory. If you wish to have finer control over the authorization of resources, you also should use NTFS permissions, which allow you to assign permissions on individual files.

Install and Configure Microsoft FrontPage Server Extensions

FrontPage Server Extensions originally were designed to allow authors the capability to post and edit content to a Web server remotely using Microsoft FrontPage. They now are capable of allowing administrators to view and manage a site and no longer are used only for FrontPage. They also give other applications such as Visual Studio access to a Web site for authoring purposes.

exam
Ⓦatch

If you do not use Copy Project in Visual Studio, you do not need FrontPage Server extensions on your Web site. In my personal work, I never use Copy Project to post a Web application as my Web applications are usually integrated with CORBA (a technology similar to DCOM that works on many different platforms including Windows, Unix, Linux, and so forth) and require a more "personal" touch to install. In this situation, I usually remove the FrontPage Server extensions for security reasons.

FrontPage server extensions are installed by default when you install IIS. If you do not want to install them, you can do so when you install IIS. When installing IIS from the Add Remove Programs Applet in the Control Panel, you can click Details, which will show you the components of IIS that are to be installed (see Figure 11-8).

This brings up the list of IIS components, as shown in Figure 11-9.

You can simply clear the FrontPage 2000 Server extensions check box and they will not be installed. This also works after you have installed IIS to remove them from your system. If you have installed them, by default all of the Web sites you add to your Web server will be installed with FrontPage extensions; however, this does not mean you can't create a Web site that does not contain them.

If you want to add or remove FrontPage server extensions from a Web site, you can right-click the Web site and select All Tasks | Remove Server Extensions to remove them, or All Tasks | Configure Server Extensions to add them. The latter brings up the FrontPage Server Extensions Wizard, which will guide you through the process.

Configuring server extensions is done from the Resource Properties dialog box. When we discussed this dialog box previously, you might have noticed that we did not discuss the Server Extensions tab. This is where we can configure the FrontPage

FIGURE 11-8

Installation
components
for IIS

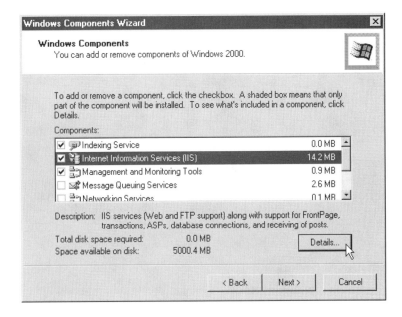

server extensions for our Web application or Web site. Figure 11-10 shows the
Server Extensions tab of the Resource Properties dialog box.

FIGURE 11-9

IIS components

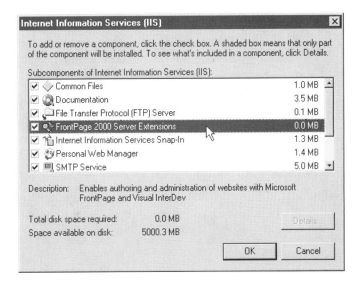

FIGURE 11-10

The Server
Extensions tab

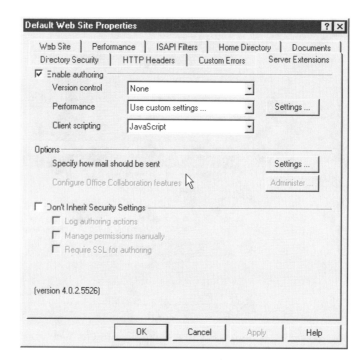

From this tab, we can do the following:

- **Enable Authoring** This option enables authors to use FrontPage to access and modify the Web site. Clearing this check box prevents anyone from accessing and modifying the Web site.

- **Version Control** Version control is essentially source code control. It is designed to prevent one author from damaging the changes another author has made. You can choose either the built-in source control or an external program such as Visual SourceSafe. You should note that Visual SourceSafe is much more advanced source control software than what is found natively with FrontPage extensions.

- **Performance** You should specify the approximate number of pages that are in the Web site or application. This number tells the system how much memory to reserve for caching.

- **Client Scripting** Specify either JScript or VBScript, one of which will be the scripting language generated in pages automatically by the FrontPage Server Extensions.

■ **Specify How Mail Should Be Sent** FrontPage can be used to create e-mail–enabled Web pages; this is where you would define how that mail would be sent (there are much better ways to e-mail enable a Web page than using FrontPage extensions; this is just an easy-to-use option for FrontPage users).

■ **Configure Office Collaboration Features** This option allows you to configure Web pages to work with Microsoft Office. This option is unavailable if the Office Web Server (OWS) is not installed on your computer.

■ **Don't Inherit Security Settings** By default, each Web application inherits the global security settings of the Web server. If you want to override these settings for a Web application, you can clear this check box.

■ **Log Authoring Actions** This enables the system to record the time an author's action was performed, the author's user name, the Web name, the remote host, and per-operation data. This information is stored in a log file in _vti_log/Author.log, in the root Web. Clear this check box if you do not want to log authoring actions.

■ **Manage Permissions Manually** Clear this check box if you want to allow the security settings to be changed by using the FrontPage Server Extensions administrative tools instead of IIS.

■ **Require Secure Sockets Layer (SSL) for Authoring** Check this box if you wish to use SSL to authenticate Web authors.

■ **Allow Authors to Upload Executables** This setting enables authors to upload CGI scripts or active server pages to the selected Web application. This would not be a good idea for a Web application (for obvious reasons) and really is intended for layman Web authors who are creating simple personal Web sites.

EXERCISE 11-3

Install and Configure Server Services

In this exercise, we will remove and replace the FrontPage Server Extensions for a Web site.

1. Launch the IIS MMC snap-in from the Control Panel (in the Administrative Tools folder).

2. Right-click the Default Web Site and select All Tasks | Remove Server Extensions (if this menu option is not available, you do not have server extensions and you will notice another menu option: Configure Server Extensions).

3. When the following message box appears, click OK:

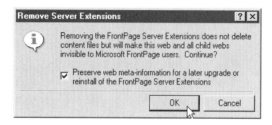

4. Right-click the Default Web site again and this time, choose All Tasks | Configure Server Extensions.

5. Use the wizard to configure your server extensions. The second page of the wizard asks you if you would like to set up the Browsers, Authors, and Administrator groups to be used with FrontPage server extensions. You will have to add user accounts to these groups based on their roles. The following illustration shows the second page of the wizard. Click next to continue, as the defaults are fine.

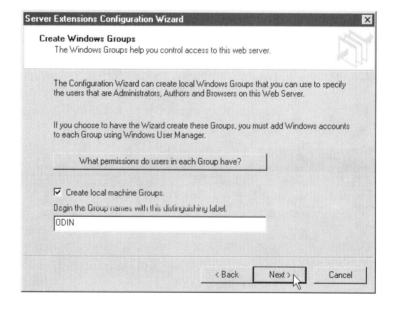

6. On the third page of the wizard, you are asked to specify the user or group that will administer the Web site. The default is the Administrators group, which is fine.

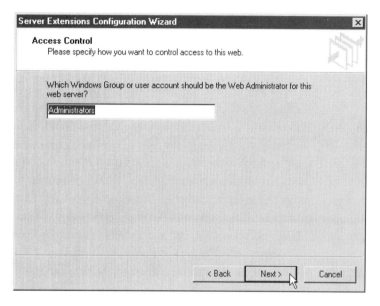

7. The next page asks us to set up e-mail for the site. Choose No, I'll do it later and click Next.

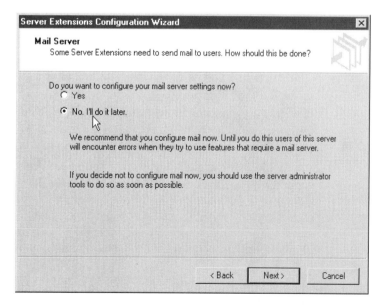

8. The next page is the summary page. You can click Finish and check to see whether the extensions have been installed.

CERTIFICATION SUMMARY

In this chapter, we have looked primarily at configuring Web applications. The machine.config file contains configuration settings for the entire server. The web.config file contains configuration settings for an individual Web application or directory. We also have seen how the .NET framework uses an inheritance paradigm to govern these settings. For example, the settings in a web.config file override the settings in the machine.config file. If a setting is not present in the web.config file, the same setting from the machine.config file will be used. This dramatically simplifies the process of setting up configuration settings for a Web server and its applications.

We also set up the way a Web server manages session state. The default is to store session state in the same process in which the Web application is running. Where fault tolerance is important, we also can store session state in the Session State Service, which is a separate process. This means our Web application can be restarted without losing session state.

It is important to remember that the Session State Server must be started first, which can be done from the Services applet in the Control Panel. For even better security and fault tolerance, you also can use SQL Server to store session state. Once again, SQL Server must be running and you must install the session state database using the script provided with the .NET Framework.

In the last section of this chapter, we looked at installing and configuring a Web server and FrontPage server extensions. Through the MMC snap-in for IIS, we can configure authentication and authorization for a Web application. If you are looking for finer control for authorization, you also can use NTFS permissions, which will allow you to set permissions on individual pages within a Web application. Overall, you should find that installing and configuring a Web server and FrontPage extensions is not terribly complicated. Once you have done this a few times, it will become second nature.

TWO-MINUTE DRILL

Configure a Web Application

❑ Configuration files in ASP.NET are well-formed XML files.

❑ The machine.config file contains configuration information for the server.

❑ Web.config files contain configuration information for individual Web applications or directories.

❑ Configuration files use an inheritance paradigm in which the settings in a web.config file override the settings in the parent directory's web.config file (if any), and the machine.config file.

Configure and Implement Session State

❑ Session state is information we store in relation to a user's session with our Web application.

❑ Session state can be stored in process, in the Session State Server, or in SQL Server.

❑ The Session State Service is a Windows out-of-process server that stores session state for our Web applications.

❑ To use the Session State Service, it must be started.

❑ To use SQL Server to store session state, you must install the ASPState database.

❑ The <sessionState> element in the web.config file is used to specify where session state will be stored.

Install and Configure Server Services

❑ Installing IIS can be done through the Add/Remove Programs applet in the Control Panel.

❑ Configuring IIS is done through the MMC snap-in for IIS.

❑ FrontPage Server Extensions are designed to allow authors to post and edit content for a Web site remotely using Microsoft FrontPage.

❑ FrontPage Server Extensions are needed if you wish to use Copy Project in Visual Studio.

❑ You also can configure FrontPage Server Extensions through the MMC snap-in for IIS.

SELF TEST

The following questions will help you measure your understanding of the material presented in this chapter. Read all the choices carefully as there might be more than one correct answer. Choose all correct answers for each question.

Configure a Web Application

1. Configuration files in ASP.NET are in what form? (Choose the best answer.)

    A. DHTML

    B. Text

    C. XML

    D. Well-formed XML

2. You have a group of settings that are common to all of the Web applications you create. Where should you place these settings?

    A. Place the settings in a text file and read them from the Application_OnStart event in the global.aspx file.

    B. The machine.config file

    C. The web.config file for each application

    D. None of the above.

3. What is the root element of a configuration file in ASP.NET?

    A. <configuration></configuration>

    B. <system></system>

    C. <system.web><system.web>

    D. <?xml version="1.0" encoding="utf-8" ?>

4. You are working with a Web application and you have noticed that a custom setting in the machine.config file is not being respected (in other words, the setting seems like it is being ignored but the application still runs). Which of the following are likely causes of the problem? (Choose all that apply.)

    A. You cannot add custom settings to the machine.config file (this is a trick question).

    B. You need to restart the Web server.

    C. The setting has not been formatted properly.

    D. The setting is being overridden in the applications web.config file.

5. In what case are the attribute names in a configuration file found?

    A. camelCase

    B. Uppercase

    C. Lowercase

    D. PascalCase

6. To create your own configuration sections, you must make a declaration in which of the following?

    A. <system.web> element

    B. <configSections> element

    C. <configDeclarations> element

    D. <system.declarations> element

7. To gain access to configuration settings from a custom section you have defined, which of the following would you do? (Choose the best answer.)

    A. config = CustomConfig.GetConfig("group/section")

    B. config = CustomConfig.GetSettings("group/section")

    C. config = ConfigurationSettings.AppSettings("section")

    D. config = ConfigurationSettings.GetConfig("group/section")

8. You are getting ready to release an application that has finished testing. How can you remove the symbolic debug information and thus decrease the size of the compiled code?

    A. <debugInfo include="false" ... />

    B. <debug symbolicInfo="false" ... />

    C. <compiler debug="false" ... />

    D. <compilation debug="false" ... />

9. You are getting reports that some users of your Web application are unable to access your Web application. Which configuration elements of the web.config file for the application should you check?

    A. <authentication>

    B. <authorization>

    C. <identity>

    D. <login>

10. You have changed to <processModel> settings for your application and have noticed that they have not taken hold. Which of the following actions will most likely fix the problem? (Choose the best answer.)

    A. Just wait; when new users log on, the settings will take hold for them.

    B. Restart IIS.

    C. The <processModel> element must be formatted improperly, so you will have to reformat it.

    D. None of the above.

Configure and Implement Session State

11. Sessions in ASP.NET are tracked in which way? (Choose all that apply.)

    A. With the SessionID object

    B. Cookies

    C. A SessionID embedded in a modified URL

    D. The ViewState object

12. Which of the following configuration elements will set up session state to be stored in the same process as the Web application running?

    A. <sessionState mode="InProc" ... />

    B. <sessionState mode="InProcess" ... />

    C. <sessionState mode="StateServer" ... />

    D. <sessionState location="InProc" ... />

13. You are creating a Web application and are concerned about the scalability of session state. You are storing a great deal of state information and are supporting many users. Which of the following methods of storing session state will improve scalability the most?

    A. In process

    B. Session State Server

    C. SQL Server

    D. None of the above

14. The InstallSQLState.sql script sets up SQL Server for use with session state. Which of the following objects are added to SQL Server? (Choose all that apply.)

    A. The SessionState database

    B. The ASPState database

    C. The ASPStateTempApplications table in the TempDB database

    D. The ASPStateTempSessions table in the TempDB database

    E. All of the above

15. If you set the mode attribute of the <sessionState> element to SQLServer, which other attribute must you supply?

    A. stateConnectionString

    B. sqlConnectionString

    C. connectionString

    D. dbConnectionString

Install and Configure Server Services

16. You are installing a new server to run your ASP.NET application. Once you have finished, you test your application and notice that, although for the most part the pages display properly and the client-side scripts seem to run fine, the server-side code behind your pages is not running at all. You do not receive any errors and it is as if the server-side code does not exist. Which of the following could cause this? (Choose all that apply.)

    A. Your virtual directory has not been configured as a Web application in IIS.

    B. You're losing your marbles.

    C. You need to add the install attribute="true" to the <compilation> element in the web.config file.

    D. You forgot to install the .NET framework after you installed IIS.

    E. None of the above.

17. How many Web sites can you have on the Windows 2000 professional version of IIS?

    A. 1

    B. 5

    C. 10

    D. 100

    E. Unlimited (limited only by the system hardware)

18. You are configuring a Web server that must host many different Web applications. You have one application that is mission critical and want to make sure it keeps running no matter what happens to the other Web applications. Which of the following techniques would support this idea? (Choose all that apply.)

   A. Run two instances of IIS on the server; use one for your mission-critical application and the other for the rest of the applications.

   B. Use Medium (pooled) application protection for all of your applications except the mission-critical application. Use High (isolated) application protection for the mission-critical application.

   C. Use High (isolated) application protection for all of your non-critical applications and Low (IIS Process) application protection for the mission-critical application.

   D. Use Low (IIS Process) application protection for the non-critical applications and High (isolated) application protection for the mission-critical application.

19. To use Digest authentication, you must meet the following requirements. (Choose the best answer.)

   A. Users must have valid accounts on the Web server.

   B. The Server must be a Windows 2000 domain controller.

   C. There must be a clear text copy of the user names and passwords in a text file for the system to read.

   D. All of the above.

20. You are using Visual Studio .NET on your development environment. No one on your team uses FrontPage. Which of the following are valid reasons to install FrontPage Server Extensions? (Choose all that apply.)

   A. If you don't, you will not be able to edit your Web application using Visual Studio.

   B. You want to use Visual Studio's Copy Project to copy the Web application from a development server to a testing server.

   C. FrontPage Server Extensions are needed in order to install the .NET framework.

   D. Without FrontPage Server Extensions, you can use Basic authentication only for your Web site.

LAB QUESTION

You are creating a Web application and want to use SQL Server to store session state. Take all steps necessary to set up your Web application to use SQL Server for storing session state.

SELF TEST ANSWERS

Configure a Web Application

1. ☑ D. Configuration files in ASP.NET are well-formed XML files.
☒ A is incorrect because DHTML is not the format for configuration files. B is true but it is not the best answer because these text files are in an XML format. C also is true but it is not the best answer because the XML must be well formed.

2. ☑ B. Settings common to all of your Web applications should be placed in the machine.config file, which prevents you from copying them to every application you create.
☒ A would actually work fine; however, you would have to stop and start the application every time you wanted to change a setting. C also would work but you would have to copy the settings to every new application you created, which would not be as practical as putting them in the machine.config file. D is incorrect because B is correct.

3. ☑ A. The <configuration> element of a configuration file is the root element.
☒ A is incorrect because system is a namespace and not the root element. B is incorrect because <system.web> is the element that contains Web configuration; however, it is not the root element for the configuration file. D is incorrect because it is the XML declaration for the file and not the root element.

4. ☑ D. The most likely cause of your problem (although not the only possibility) is that the setting is being overridden in the web.config file for the application.
☒ A is incorrect because you can add custom settings to the machine.config file and trick questions are not nice. B is incorrect because, unlike classic ASP, when a setting is changed in a configuration file, you do not need to restart the Web server for the new setting to be respected. C is incorrect because if the setting is formatted improperly, you will get an error and the application would not run.

5. ☑ A. camelCase is used for the names of attribute elements in configuration files.
☒ B is incorrect, as by standard nothing in the configuration files is placed in uppercase. C is incorrect because, by default, nothing is placed in lowercase in the configuration files. D is incorrect because, by default, attribute values are in PascalCase but not the names.

6. ☑ B. The <configSections> element is used to declare new configuration sections.
☒ A is incorrect because the <system.web> element is part of the configuration section settings area, which defines the settings for a section but does not declare new sections. C is incorrect because there is no <configDeclarations> section (unless you want to declare your own). D is incorrect for the same reason that C is incorrect.

7. ☑ D. The GetConfig method of the ConfigurationSettings object gives us access to the configuration settings from a custom section.
☒ A and B are incorrect because there is no CustomConfig object. C is incorrect because the AppSettings method of the ConfigurationSettings object gives us access to custom settings set in the <appSettings> section; not a custom section.

8. ☑ D. To remove the symbolic debug information from your project set the debug attribute of the <compilation> element to False.
☒ A is incorrect because there is no <debugInfo> element. B is incorrect because there is no <debug> element. C is incorrect because the <compiler> element is a child of the <compilation> element that declares a compiler but does not specify whether to include the symbolic debug info.

9. ☑ B. The <authorization> element defines who has access to the resources of the Web application and who does not. Improper settings for this element could cause this problem.
☒ A is incorrect because the <authentication> element defines how users are authenticated; not who is given access. C is incorrect because the <identity> element does not affect whether you can log on or not. D is incorrect because there is no <login> element.

10. ☑ B. Unlike the other settings, when you change the <processModel> settings, you must restart IIS to effect the changes.
☒ A would work for other settings but not the <processModel> settings. C is incorrect because if the <processModel> element is formatted incorrectly, you would receive a run time error (however, it is possible that the <processModel> element is formatted incorrectly and you would not find out until you restart IIS). D is incorrect because B is correct.

Configure and Implement Session State

11. ☑ B and C. Sessions in ASP.NET are tracked with cookies or with an embedded SessionID in a modified URL (if you don't want to count on your users enabling cookies).
☒ A is incorrect because there is no SessionID object. D is incorrect because the ViewState object tracks the state of the visual interface; not the session.

12. ☑ A. <sessionState mode="InProc" ... /> will configure session state to be stored in the same process as the Web application.
☒ B is incorrect because mode cannot be set to InProcess. C is incorrect because if the mode is set to StateServer, session state will be stored in a separate process. D is not correct because there is no location attribute of the <sessionState> element.

13. ☑ C. SQL Server is a very scalable product that supports multiple CPUs, optimized querying, cached execution plans, connection pooling, and much more. SQL Server offers a great deal of scalability when compared with the other methods mentioned.

☒ A is by far the least scalable option and is not recommended for applications that store many session states or many users. B, using the Session State Service, will increase scalability to a certain degree but not to the level that SQL Server would, and is recommended mainly for applications in which session state is considered mission critical. D is incorrect because C is correct.

14. ☑ B, C, and D. The InstallSQLState.sql.

☒ Because users will not be editing product records, A would be unnecessary. E would be a great waste of resources because we are not retrieving purchasing information from the database, but adding it.

15. ☑ B. If you set the mode attribute of the <sessionState> element to SQLServer, you also must set the sqlConnectionString attribute to a valid SQL Server connection string.

☒ A is incorrect because the stateConnectionString is used when you set the mode attribute to StateServer. C and D are incorrect because connectionString and dbConnectionString are not attributes of the <sessionSate> element.

Install and Configure Server Services

16. ☑ D. If you do not install the .NET framework after you install IIS, all of your .aspx pages will be processed as if they were simple html pages. Any server-side code will not run.

☒ A is incorrect because if you do not configure your virtual directory as a Web application, you will wind up with a run-time error when the system tries to read your web.config file. Although it often feels like you're losing your marbles when problems like this occur, I can assure you that B is not correct (I have to say this; otherwise, I would have to admit my marbles left long ago). C is incorrect because there is no install attribute for the <compilation> element. E is incorrect because D is correct.

17. ☑ A. You can have only one Web site on the Windows 2000 Professional version of IIS (don't forget you can still have multiple Web applications in one Web site).

☒ B, C, D, and E are incorrect.

18. ☑ B. If your mission-critical application is using High (isolated) application protection and the others are using Medium (pooled) application protection, any failures in the noncritical applications will not affect the mission-critical application. Also, C is a viable option. If you use Low (IIS Process) application protection for the mission-critical application and High (isolated) for the noncritical applications, once again, any failure in the noncritical applications will not affect the mission-critical application. However, most likely this would be a waste of resources, as there really is no reason to place each of the noncritical apps in their own process space. However, it does solve our problem.

☒ A is incorrect because you cannot run two instances of IIS on the same machine (you can with SQL Server, though). D is incorrect because if the noncritical applications are using Low (IIS Process) application protection and one of them crashes, IIS will crash as well; even if your mission-critical app is in its own process space there will be no Web server to serve it.

19. ☑ D. To use Digest authentication, you must be running IIS on a Windows 2000 domain controller, have a valid user account for users who wish to log on, and have a clear text copy of the user names and passwords in a text file for the system to read.

☒ A, B, and C are all correct; thus, D is the best answer.

20. ☑ B. If you want to use Copy Project in Visual Studio, you will need to install the FrontPage Server Extensions on the Web site.

☒ A is incorrect because you do not need FrontPage extensions to edit your Web application with Visual Studio. Visual Studio requires that you have a Web server on your network to develop a Web application and FrontPage Server Extensions are mainly used to allow remote access to a Web server. C is incorrect because you do not need FrontPage Server Extensions to install the .NET Framework. D is incorrect because the method of authentication you use is not dependent on the presence of FrontPage Server extensions.

LAB ANSWER

You were asked to set up your Web application to use SQL Server for storing session state. The following are the steps necessary to use SQL Server to store session state:

1. Open SQL Query Analyzer from the Start menu.

2. Connect to the instance of SQL Server you wish to use.

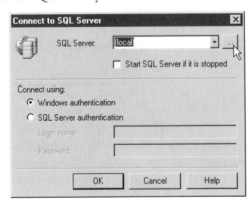

3. Set the active database to Master (this is necessary when creating a new database and actually is done in the script; however, it is a good practice to get into when running a script that creates a new database, just in case the developer of the script forgot to add a *Use Master* clause at the beginning of the script, which will set the active database to the master database programmatically).

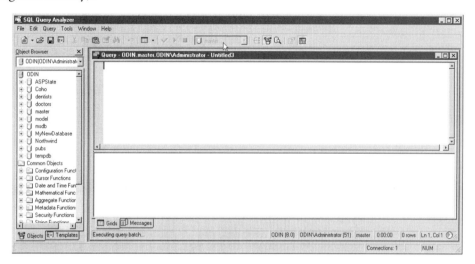

4. Open the script in SQL Query Analyzer by clicking File | Open and selecting the InstallSQLState.sql script, which can be found at C:\WINNT\Microsoft.NET\Framework\ *<version>*\ (substitute the appropriate drive, Windows directory, and version). You now can look through the script to see what it does (notice the Use Master at the top as just mentioned).

5. Click the Execute Query button and watch it run...yeeeeeehaaaa!!!!

6. Close SQL Query Analyzer.

7. Open the project you are developing in Visual Studio .NET.

8. Open the web.config file in the editor.

9. Alter the <sessionState> element.

10. Save your changes and run the application.

12

Configure Security for a Web Application

This chapter examines security in an ASP.NET application. We will begin by discussing security basics and the reasons for securing a Web site. We will see what options ASP.NET provides to secure a Web application, including the different mechanisms to authenticate users using Windows-based, Forms-based, and Passport authentication. We then will learn how to authorize users by using the Access Control Lists in Windows from a custom credential store such as a database, and using settings in the web.config file. We will finish by discussing impersonation in ASP.NET.

CERTIFICATION OBJECTIVE 12.01

Select and Configure Authentication

Web security is a complex and critical topic for Web developers and administrators. By their nature, Web applications allow users access to resources on the Web servers, and by extension, to data. It is therefore critical to understand the security measures that are available to provide a secure environment for Web applications in ASP.NET.

exam
ⓌＡＴＣＨ

This chapter specifically covers the exam objectives for configuring security for an ASP.NET application, and as such does not go into any great detail on network and Web security. Although the exam will specifically test the security aspects of ASP.NET applications, it is paramount that you have an understanding of security concepts in general, and about Web security in particular.

Security Basics

By default, a Web application will allow anonymous access. This means anyone with an Internet connection can access the pages in your site. All requests for pages are processed and responses returned to the client browsers. Although this might be fine for some pages, or in some cases even the complete site, in many cases some form of security is required to limit access only to authorized users. The reasons for this can be numerous and could include any of the following:

- Sensitive information such as financial data on the company or clients that is restricted to certain users.

■ Account or personalized information pertinent to only a specific user.

■ Access to a site or portions thereof, which is restricted to members or others that pay a fee for its services.

■ Web-based administration interface for the site or server that must be restricted to administration personnel.

ASP.NET automatically restricts access to certain files and directories on the server. For example, all configuration files such as the web.config and machine.config files, resource files, the bin directory and assemblies, Global.asax files, and so forth are restricted from Web access. A client attempting to access these areas from the browser is presented with an error page specifying that "This type of page is not served."

Securing a Web application first requires *authentication*, which is the process of identifying the user who is requesting the page. You can accomplish this by requiring the user to supply credentials, which usually consist of a username and password but also can include other methods of identification such as cookies and certificates. If the credentials supplied by the user are valid, the user is given a known identity.

With Windows-based authentication, the ASP.NET application relies on the Windows operating system to authenticate the user in conjunction with IIS. When a user requests a secure page, the request goes through IIS, which authenticates the user's credentials against a Windows user account. If the identity is not verified, the request is rejected. This authorization method is useful when you have an intranet application with a restricted number of users logged on to the company network, but because it requires each user to have a valid Windows user account, it is not generally appropriate for a public Internet application.

With Forms-based authentication, requests for secure pages are redirected to a login page consisting of an HTML form. The user's credentials are input on the form and submitted to the application for authentication. If authenticated, the system issues an authentication cookie, which is returned to the user. Any subsequent requests in the same browser process will contain the cookie in the request headers and the user will be authenticated.

The third authentication method, Microsoft Passport, is a centralized authentication service. Once authenticated, the user can access all sites that use the service. Passport requires the site to pay a subscription fee to use the Microsoft Passport Service.

Once a user is authenticated and given an identity, the system determines which resources he or she has access to. This process is called *authorization*. Each authenticated user is authorized to access certain pages and data in the application based on permissions assigned to that user's identity. The third aspect of security in a Web application is *impersonation,* which consists of ASP.NET assuming the role of an identity passed to it by IIS.

FROM THE CLASSROOM

Compare ASP.NET Authentication Methods

ASP.NET authentication is handled through authentication providers, which are modules that authenticate the requests from Web clients. There are three methods for authenticating users in ASP.NET, each handled by a separate provider: Windows, Forms, and Passport. Each ASP.NET application can use one provider, which is configured in the <authorization> section of the web.config file for the Web application. Each of the providers has inherent advantages and disadvantages; thus, you should choose the authorization method for the application to match the particular situation.

Windows-based authentication uses the existing Windows security infrastructure. It uses Access Control Lists (ACL) and IIS authentication mechanisms to control access to files and resources. This method of authentication is best suited for Intranet applications in which the clients are existing users on the network. Each client requires a Windows account, which is a disadvantage in a public Internet application, as it requires the creation and management of accounts for each user.

Forms-based authentication is a good choice for Internet applications. User credentials can be easily created, stored, and managed programmatically. User credentials can be stored in databases, XML files, or other storage mechanisms and authorization settings are managed in an XML configuration file. However, one disadvantage to this method is that it is based on cookies.

Microsoft Passport authentication provides a single sign-on for users that applies to all Passport sites. It removes the need to maintain a database of user credentials for the application and allows customization of its appearance to match the client site. The main disadvantages of Passport are that it requires a fee for the service and uses cookies.

—*David Shapton, MCSD, MCT, CTT+*

Authentication

In ASP.NET, authentication is controlled through the web.config file by specifying the authentication mode. The mode can be set to use Windows, Forms-based, or Passport authentication; or None. Once specified in the web.config, the authentication method specified must be implemented in the Web application.

Windows Authentication

When a request is made to the Web application, it is handled by Internet Information Server (IIS). IIS can either authenticate the user directly or pass it off to the ASP.NET application for authentication. If handled by IIS authentication, it is done in conjunction with the operating system to validate the user's credentials.

The security system in Windows is based on roles, with each role defining an identity that responds to its role on the computer. For example, an administrator will have an identity that is part of the administrator's role, which enables him or her to manage the computers' resources (including installing and configuring hardware and software, and managing system resources and security for the server). A guest role will be able to use resources on the computer such as applications, but will not have any control over managing the system itself.

Each role on the server can have multiple users, each of which is an individual account within that role. So, for example, you might have a number of people who administrate the computer and each has his or her own user account, but all belong to the administrator's role.

To view the existing users on your Web server (assuming you have administrator privileges) open Users and Passwords from the Control Panel. You will see a dialog box similar to Figure 12-1 that lists the current users on the server. There should be at least one user in the administrators group, and if you scroll down the list, you will see a user name of IUSR_*yourservername,* which belongs to the Guest group. This user is the default anonymous identity created for clients to access the Web server. Because it is an anonymous account, it does not need a password, and as such, has minimal permissions assigned to it. Unless Windows Authentication is enabled, this is the account that all clients of the Web server will use.

FIGURE 12-1

Users and
Passwords in
Windows 2000

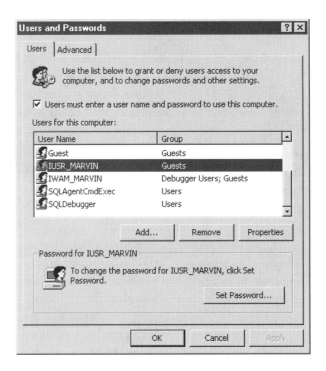

To enable Windows Authentication, we must configure the Web.config file for
the Web application. To do so, we need to set the authentication tag to specify the
Windows mode, as in the following:

```
<configuration>
  <system.web>
    <authentication mode="Windows" />
  </system.web>
</configuration>
```

IIS uses three types of Windows authentication: Basic, Digest, and Integrated
Windows Security. Before you can use Windows authentication, IIS must be
configured to one of these mechanisms.

Basic Authentication   Basic authentication has a low security level but is
supported by most browsers. When a user without credentials requests a page from a
Web application set to Basic, the browser prompts him or her to provide a username
and password. The username and password then are returned to IIS where they are

authenticated and if successful, the user has access to the page. Once authenticated, the user may continue to access pages in the application until the browser is closed.

The username and password are passed to IIS as clear text, which is not very secure as the transmission could be intercepted, and the username and password acquired and used to access the system.

Digest Authentication   Digest Authentication is similar to Basic but it encrypts the username and password sent to the server. The browser sends an encoded hash called a Message Digest to the server that contains the logon information, rather than sending the plain text of the Basic mechanism. This mechanism is more secure, and it will pass through firewalls and proxy servers; however, it requires the browser to be Internet Explorer 5.0 or later and will work only with Active Directory accounts. To enable Digest authentication, your server must be connected to the domain and you must make sure that Anonymous access is not selected.

Integrated Windows Security   If the user requesting the page is already an authenticated user on the network he or she already has credentials that the browser can pass to IIS. Unlike Basic or Digest, the credentials passed to the server do not consist of the username and password but an encrypted token that indicates the user's security status within the network. This type of authentication is useful only on an intranet in which the user is logged on to the network and therefore already authenticated.

Now that we have discussed the three types of Windows authentication, we will examine these mechanisms in an exercise.

EXERCISE 12-1

Configure IIS and Windows Authentication

In this exercise, we will enable Windows authentication to secure a Web application.

1. Create a new Web application in Visual Studio called "Chapter12" with Home.aspx and Page1.aspx Web forms. Add headings to each page to identify the pages, and a hyperlink to the other page.

2. In the web.config file for the application, make sure the authentication is set to Windows. Open the web.config file in the solution and enter the following:

```
<authentication mode="Windows" />
```

3. Open IIS Manager from Administrative Tools and expand the Default Web Site node. Find the Chapter12 Web site, right-click, and choose Properties.

4. In the Chapter12 Properties dialog, choose the Directory Security tab and click the Edit button under Anonymous Access and Authentication Control. Your screen should look like this:

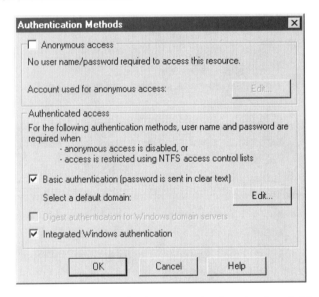

5. Deselect Anonymous Access and select Basic Authentication. Make sure everything else is deselected. Click OK and OK again.

6. Open the browser and navigate to the Chapter12 home page. You will be prompted for a user name and password. Enter your information and you

will be able to access the page. Enter incorrect information and you will be re-prompted up to three times.

7. Use the hyperlink on the page to navigate to Page1.aspx. Close the browser; then reopen it and navigate to Page1.aspx . Notice that you are prompted again for your username and password.

8. Go back to the Directory security for IIS and select Anonymous Access from the Authentication window in addition to Basic Authentication.

9. Open the Chapter12 home page in the browser. Notice you are not prompted for user credentials this time. Even though Basic is still selected, Anonymous access is used, requiring no logon information. If you have multiple mechanisms selected, IIS will use the least secure and only move to a higher mechanism if that fails.

10. Change the security to Integrated Windows, and deselect Anonymous and Basic.

11. Open the page in the browser again and notice you get access without having to provide a username and password. This is because you are already logged on to the server with a Windows user account.

12. Once a user is authenticated, you can read the user information from any page in the Web application by using the User.Identity object. Add three labels to the Home.aspx page and give them IDs of lblUsername, lblAuthType, and lblAuth.

13. Add the following code to the Page_Load event:

```
lblUserName.Text = "User Name: " & User.Identity.Name
lblAuthType.Text = "User Authentication Type: " & _
User.Identity.AuthenticationType
lblAuth.Text = "User Authenticated: " &
User.Identity.IsAuthenticated
```

14. Save and rebuild the solution.

15. Open the Home page in the browser. The labels will display the user identity information. The result should be similar to the following:

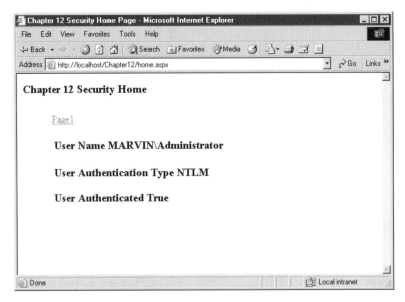

16. From the Control Panel go to User and Passwords, and add a new user called "Chapter12." Give the user a password.

17. From IIS manager, change the authentication back to Basic.

18. Open the home page in the browser and when prompted log in as Chapter12. Notice the user identity information now supplied.

Forms-Based Authentication

Windows authentication really is useful only when the users of the Web application are already logged on to the network and using the Web application through an intranet. Authenticating public users requires a lot of work to create Windows user accounts for each user on the system. Rather than using IIS and Windows, you can use Forms authentication, which uses ASP.NET to authenticate the users and allows you to store credential information in a credential store such as a database, XML file, and so forth instead of through Windows accounts.

Forms-based authentication uses the following process to authenticate user requests:

1. A client requests a secure page in the Web application.

2. IIS has its authentication mode set to Anonymous, which allows the request through to ASP.NET. ASP.NET checks for a valid authentication cookie in the request. If the cookie does not exist, it redirects the user to a login form so the user can enter the credential information. The login form URL is specified in the `loginURL` attribute of the Authentication tag in the web.config file.

3. The credentials are submitted through a form post, and if determined to be valid, ASP.NET creates an authentication cookie on the client.

4. The client then is redirected back to the originally requested page.

5. Once an authorization cookie is created, all subsequent requests will be authorized. The cookie is valid until the user closes the browser or until the session ends.

EXERCISE 12-2

Using Forms-Based Authentication

In this exercise, we will create a login form and use forms-based authentication to access the Web application.

1. Add a new Web form to the Chapter12 solution called login.aspx. It will include two text boxes called txtUsename and txtPassword. It should look like the following:

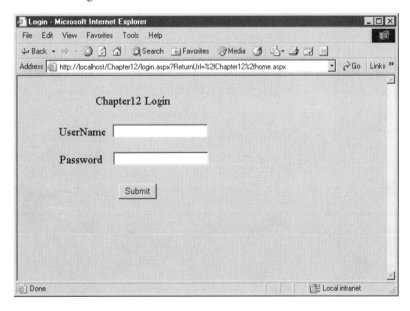

2. Modify the <authentication> tag in web.config to the following:

```
<authentication mode="Forms">
        <forms name="AuthCookie" loginUrl="login.aspx" />
</authentication>
```

This code changes the authentication method to forms, and specifies the name of the cookie to use in authentication and the URL of the login page to use.

3. Modify the <authorization> tag in the web.config to the following:

```
<authorization>
        <deny users="?" />
</authorization>
```

This code secures all pages in the Web application by denying access to anonymous users, which are represented by the "?" The result is that all users are now forced to log on. We will look at authorization in more detail later in the chapter.

4. Add the following code to the Submit button's click event:

```
If txtUserName.Text = "Marvin" And _
    txtPassword.Text = "Depressed" Then
    FormsAuthentication.RedirectFromLoginPage(txtUserName.Text, False)
Else
    lblMessage.Text = "Invalid login,try again"
End If
```

This is a simple hard-coded authentication for a user named Marvin whose password is "Depressed." This would normally be coded to authenticate the credentials against a credential store such as a database. If authenticated, the user is redirected to the originally requested page; if not, a message is displayed in a label named lblMessage.

5. Save all files and rebuild the solution.

6. Open the home page in the browser; the login page will appear. Enter a wrong username and password, and you will be notified that the login was invalid. Enter the right username and password; you will be redirected to the home page and the user identity information will be displayed.

| TABLE 12-1 | FormsAuthentication Methods |

Method	Description
Authenticate	Using the supplied credentials, it attempts to validate the credentials against those contained in a credential store.
GetAuthCookie	Creates an authorization cookie for the user name.
GetRedirectUrl	Returns the URL for the original page requested that caused the redirect to the logon page.
RedirectFromLoginPage	Redirects to the original URL requested after authentication. Also creates the authorization ticket and attaches it to the cookies collection in the response.
SetAuthCookie	Creates authorization ticket for the user name and attaches it to the cookies collection in the outgoing response.
SignOut	Removes the authentication ticket by using SetCookie with an empty value.

You can use the FormsAuthentication object in the authentication process. In the exercise, we used the RedirectFromLoginPage method to redirect the user back to the originally requested page after being successfully authenticated. Table 12-1 lists some of the common methods for this object.

Using the web.config File as a Credential Store   In the previous exercise we used simple logic in the click event of the Submit button to authenticate the user. In a real application, the code would likely query a credential store such as a database to authenticate the supplied credentials. Another method of storing user names and passwords is to specify user tags in the credentials section of the web.config file. The FormsAuthentication.Authenticate method then authenticates the user against the credential store, which in this case is the web.config file.

EXERCISE 12-3

Using the web.config File as a Credential Store

We now will modify our Forms-based authentication to validate the user's credentials against user tags in the web.config file.

1. Open the web.config file for the Chapter12 application and add a credentials section with a password format set to Clear.

2. Add some users within the <credentials> section with user name and password attributes for each. Your authentication section of the web.config file should resemble the following:

```
<authentication mode="Forms">
    <forms name="AuthCookie" loginUrl="login.aspx" >
        <credentials passwordFormat="Clear">
            <user name="Marvin" password="Depressed" />
            <user name="Ford" password="Prefect" />
        </credentials>
    </forms>
</authentication>
```

3. Replace the existing code in the Submit button click event with the following code:

```
If FormsAuthentication.Authenticate(txtUserName.Text, _
    txtPassword.Text) Then
    FormsAuthentication.RedirectFromLoginPage(txtUserName.Text, False)
Else
    lblMessage.Text = "Invalid login,try again"
End If
```

This code calls the authenticate method by passing the user name and password supplied on the form, which attempts to validate the credentials against the users in the web.config file. If successful, it sets the authorization cookie and redirects to the originally requested page; if not, it displays the same error message we used previously. The arguments for the RedirectFromLoginPage are the user name as string to be used as the cookie for authentication purposes, and a Boolean value that specifies whether the cookie should be saved across browser sessions.

4. Save the files and rebuild the solution.

5. Open the home page in the browser, and enter an invalid user name and password combination. Try again with a valid combination.

Hash User Passwords   As you can see from the previous exercise, the web.config file can be used as a credential store for as many users as you wish. You can set the passwordFormat attribute to Clear, which stores the passwords in clear text, or either the MD5 (Message Digest 5) or SHA1 hash digests, which require the stored passwords to be hashed before placing them in the web.config file.

If the passwords are not hashed, they are clearly visible to anyone with access to the web.config file. ASP.NET automatically restricts Web access to the web.config file, but anyone having network access to the server could potentially gain access to the file and therefore the passwords. A hashed password still is visible in the file but it is of no use, as the hashed value cannot be converted back to the original password value.

In the application, a login form submits the user's password using the Authenticate method; ASP.NET then hashes the password and compares it to the hashed value stored in the web.config file. This is obviously a more secure approach but requires that the passwords be hashed before inserting them into the configuration file—and at this time there is no tool available to do the hashing. Fortunately, this can be handled very simply using either the HashPasswordForStoringInConfigFile method of the FormsAuthentication class or the System.Security.Cryptography classes.

EXERCISE 12-4

Create a Hashing Tool for User Passwords

In this exercise, we will create a hashing tool as a Web form using the HashPasswordForStoringInConfigFile method of the FormsAuthentication class, and store and test the hashed values in the web.config file.

1. Create a new Web Form in the Chapter12 application called "HashTool.aspx."

2. Build the page so it looks like the page shown in the next illustration and use the following code as a guide:

```
<%@ Page Language="vb" AutoEventWireup="false" Codebehind="HashTool.aspx.vb"
    inherits="Chapter12.Copy" %>
<!DOCTYPE HTML PUBLIC "-//W3C//DTD HTML 4.0 Transitional//EN">
<HTML>
  <HEAD>
      <title>Hashing Tool</title>
  </HEAD>
      <body bgColor="#d7b27d" MS_POSITIONING="GridLayout">
      <h3>Hashing Tool</h3>
      <form id="Form1" method="post" runat="server">  
        <asp:label id="Label1" runat="server" >Password</asp:label>
        <asp:textbox id="txtPassword" runat="server"> </asp:textbox>
        <asp:label id="Label2" runat="server" >Hashed Password</asp:label>
        <asp:textbox id="txtHashed" runat="server"> </asp:textbox>
```

```
            <asp:radiobutton id="optSHA1" runat="server" Text="SHA1 Hashing"
            GroupName="Hashing"></asp:radiobutton>
            <asp:radiobutton id="optMD5" runat="server" Text="MD5 Hashing"
            GroupName="Hashing"></asp:radiobutton>
            <asp:button id="btnHash" runat="server"
            Text="Hash Password"></asp:button>
        </form>
        </body>
    </HTML>
```

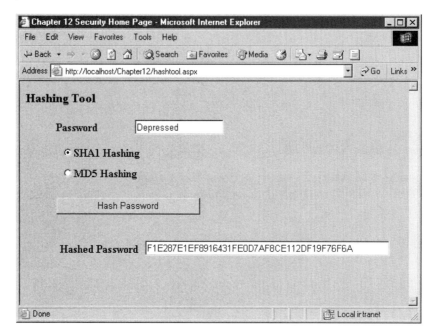

3. In the code-behind page for the page, add a statement to import System.Web.Security.

4. Add the following code to the click event for btnHash:

```
Private Sub btnHash_Click(ByVal sender As Object, ByVal e As _
        System.EventArgs) Handles btnHash.Click
    Dim HashType As String
    If optSHA1.Checked Then
        HashType = "SHA1"
```

```
    Else
        HashType = "MD5"
    End If
    txtHashed.Text = _
    FormsAuthentication.HashPasswordForStoringInConfigFile _
    (txtPassword.Text, HashType)
End Sub
```

This hashes the contents of the txtPassword text box based on the hash type specified with the option button settings. The result is placed in the txtHashed text box.

5. Save the files and rebuild the solution.

6. Open HashTool.aspx in the browser, enter the password **Depressed**, and choose the SHA1 option. Click the Hash Password button.

7. Copy the resulting hashed value over the password for Marvin the web.config file.

8. Repeat the procedure for "Prefect," and copy to the web.config file.

9. Modify the passwordFormat attribute in the <credentials> section to be "SHA1."

10. The authentication section should contain the following:

```
<authentication mode="Forms">
    <forms name="AuthCookie" loginUrl="login.aspx" >
      <credentials passwordFormat="SHA1">
          <user name="Marvin"
          password="F1E287E1EF8916431FE0D7AF8CE112DF19F76F6A"/>
          <user name="Ford"
          password="3DA2499EB36E75BAC2B9CCD2B2BC0F78BDA2686A"/>
  </credentials>
      </forms>
</authentication>
```

11. Test the login by opening the home page in the browser and entering a valid logon.

on the *Job*

The concept of the web.config file in ASP.NET has greatly simplified configuration of Web applications. As an XML file, it provides the usual advantage of containing data that is readily readable by both human and machine. Placing user information in such a file is convenient but also a potential security risk. Hashing the password for storage eliminates some of the risk, but for truly secure applications you should consider some other method of storing credentials.

Microsoft Passport Authentication

Microsoft's .NET Passport authentication is a centralized authentication service that replaces the forms authentication functionality you normally would have to build into your application. To use Passport, you need to become a member by paying a fee, and then download the Passport SDK and configure your application for passport. Users accessing your application will be authenticated by Passport and therefore will have to log in using Passport credentials. There are some advantages to using this service:

- Users can benefit because of the single sign in (SSI) that Passport provides. This means a user can use the same user name and password to sign in to all sites that use Passport authentication, which means there are fewer user names and passwords for users to remember and manage. For example, most of Microsoft's sites now use Passport authentication, which includes services such as Microsoft HotMail, Microsoft MSN, and other restricted access sites for Microsoft partners, Microsoft Certified Professionals, and so forth.

- Site developers do not have to implement their own authentication system, which eliminates the need to build and maintain databases to store registration information.

- Passport provides a unique Passport ID (PUID), which is available to the companies using Passport for their own needs. For example, the PUID can be used as a database key to uniquely identify the user in the company's customer database.

- You can customize the Passport registration and sign-in pages to blend with your site's design.

More information on Passport authentication information can be found at http://www.passport.com/business, including the services fees, developer information, and a sample site. At the time of writing, Passport is still a beta service; therefore, some features are still likely to be enhanced or changed. One possibility is that Microsoft might reposition the service so that third parties can host their own Passport servers, rather than force everyone to use Microsoft's data store.

To implement Passport, you will have to purchase the Passport service and download the Passport SDK. The next step is to configure the Passport service in the web.config file by setting the authentication mode to Passport:

```
<authentication mode="Passport"
</authentication>
```

When a user requests a secure page from a Web application implementing Passport authentication, the following occurs:

1. IIS authenticates the user as anonymous and sends the request to ASP.NET.

2. ASP.NET checks for a valid Passport authentication cookie. If the cookie is not present, the request is rejected and the user is redirected to Passport.com for authentication.

3. The user is presented with a login form from Passport. The form and login information are submitted to the Passport site.

4. Passport authenticates the user against its database and returns a cookie with an authentication ticket to the user.

5. The user is redirected back to the original site, this time providing the cookie with the authentication ticket.

6. IIS authenticates the user as anonymous; then ASP.NET authenticates the user based on the authentication ticket and returns the Web Form to the user.

After a user is authenticated, he or she can access any other site using Passport authentication. This can be advantageous if you have multiple sites or associations with other sites. For example, on Microsoft sites, if you sign in to MSN messenger you also are logged on to Hotmail.

User information can be retrieved in Passport authentication the same way it is accessed in Forms authentication by using the User.Identity object. Passport also supplies other attributes called *core profile attributes,* which include

- **Birthdate** The user's birthdate
- **City** A GeoID that maps to the user's city
- **Country** A country code for the user's country

- **Gender** The user's gender
- **Nickname** A friendly name supplied by the user
- **PreferredEmail** The user's e-mail address
- **PostalCode** The postal code used in the U.S. and other countries

Microsoft Passport has many advantages that are useful to Web developers. As a packaged authentication method, it eliminates the need to develop authentication mechanisms for each site and provides a familiar and unified login for the users, which could be useful for heavily used public sites. There are some downsides to using such a service, however, the most obvious being the cost, although that can be easily rationalized for large projects.

Now that we've discussed the different authentication methods available in ASP.NET, let's look at some authentication scenarios and their solutions.

SCENARIO & SOLUTION

The site will be on the company intranet and all users will be logged on to the network. Which authentication method should I use?	Use Windows authentication and set the IIS authentication to Integrated Windows Security, as the clients will already be logged on to the network.
My web application is private to the employees in my company and to specific external clients that will require access from the Web. Which authentication method would work best?	Use Windows authentication with IIS authentication preferably set to Digest. You will need to create Windows accounts for the external clients. If the external clients are not using a Microsoft browser, you will have to use Basic authentication and possibly SSL to secure the requests.
My site requires a paid membership to access all areas. Users that are not members can access some areas of the site. Which authentication should I implement?	Use Forms-based authentication. You can easily deny access to the parts of the site that require authentication, and the credentials of the paid members could be stored in the same database used to record their membership information.
Our company has a number of related sites, both within our organization and in conjunction with other organizations. We need to authenticate clients that access the sites but don't need to keep separate access information for each site. Which authentication method would be most useful to use?	Consider using Microsoft .NET Passport. Although it is a service that requires paying a fee, it requires little implementation on your part and you can access the passport information. It also will provide a single logon capability for all the sites.

Configure Authorization

Authenticating the clients requesting pages from an application is only the first step in a secure system. Once we know the identity of the user or role the user belongs to, we must specify which resources the user has access to on our system.

When we used forms authentication in Exercise 12-2, we had to let IIS pass unauthenticated users through to ASP.NET by configuring Anonymous access in IIS and allowing only authenticated users access to the pages in our application. We did this by creating an authorization section in the web.config file and denying all anonymous users access with the following code:

```
<authorization>
      <deny users="?" />
</authorization>
```

Because the anonymous user was then denied access to the requested form, the login form to which we redirected the user in the authentication section of the web.config was presented to the user, and the code in the form's Submit button click event authorized the user based on the credentials supplied. This approach works only if we want to authorize specific users for all pages in the application. To fully implement a secure site, we will need to mark specific pages as secure, and authorize specific users or users in specific roles to access those pages.

There are two ways to configure authorization in ASP.NET. One is to use Windows to control the access to individual files on the server based on the user identities and permissions stored in the Access Control Lists on the Windows operating system. This method is known as *file authorization* and requires the application to use Windows-based authentication. The second method is known as *URL authorization,* and requires user identities to be mapped to directories and files in the web.config file. This method can use both Windows-based and Forms-based authentication.

File Authorization

File authorization relies on permissions stored for the folder or file in Access Control Lists (ACL) in Windows NT or Windows 2000. It is a relatively easy method of implementing authorization but can require a lot of management of the ACLs. If you have a site with many directories, each containing a number of files, it can quickly become a headache to manage the permissions.

Configuring a site using file authorization requires the following steps:

1. If required, create accounts for users of the site.

2. Set the permissions for the folders and files in the web application for each identity or role.

3. In IIS, set the Authentication control for the directories and files to something other than Anonymous.

4. In the web.config file in the application root, set the authorization to Windows.

When a client attempts to access a file or page on the site that is restricted to Anonymous users, he or she is authorized by Windows Authorization. Let's reconfigure our Chapter12 application to use file authorization.

EXERCISE 12-5

Using File Authorization

In this exercise, we will configure the Chapter12 Web application to use file authorization and ACLs.

1. Set the authentication mode in the web.config file to Windows:

   ```
   <authentication mode="Windows" />
   ```

2. From Users And Passwords in the Control Panel add a new user name, "Non-Authorized User."

3. From Windows Explorer, right-click the Chapter12 application directory and choose Properties.

4. On the Security tab, choose the Internet Guest Account in the list and deny all permissions for this account. Use the following as a guide:

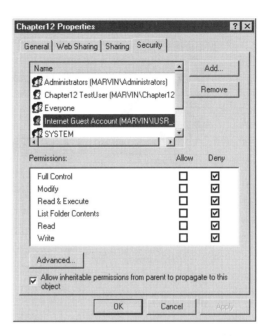

5. Click the Add button; in the resulting Select Users Or Groups dialog, choose the Chapter12 user we created earlier and click the Add button. Chapter12 should be added to the bottom list as in the next image.

6. Choose the Non-Authorized User and add it to the list.

7. Click OK.

8. Deny all permissions for the Non-Authorized User.

9. Click OK.

10. Disable Anonymous access in IIS for the Chapter12 root directory and enable Basic authentication. This will allow you to log in as different users on the site without having to log off and log in again as a different user on the server.

11. Open the browser and navigate to the Chapter12/Home.aspx.

12. Log in as the Non-Authorized User. The Enter Network Password dialog will be redisplayed, as you are not authorized to view the page with this user's

credentials. Try this twice more and you will be presented with an error page notifying you that access is denied.

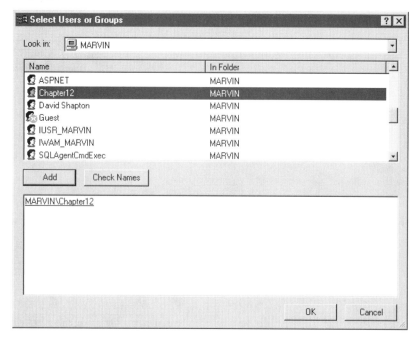

13. Refresh the page and logon with the Chapter12 account. You will now have access to the page. Click the link to Page1 and you will be able to access it. Close the browser.

14. In Windows Explorer, right-click the Page1.aspx file and choose Properties. On the Security tab, choose the Chapter12 account and deny all permissions.

15. Open the browser and log in to the Chapter12 Home page as the Chapter12 user.

16. Click on the Page1 link. You will be presented with the Enter Network Password dialog again. If you attempt to access the page using the Chapter12 account, you will be denied access. If you use another account with permissions for the page, such as an administrator's account, you will be given access. If you do this and then click the home link on Page1, you will notice that now you are using the administrator's identity on the site.

As you can see from the exercise, managing authorization using Access Control Lists is relatively simple, especially if the application is a private Intranet application. In that scenario, users and roles will be defined for the employees of the company and you must assign the security permissions only for the roles or user accounts at the application directory and folder level.

However, if it is a public Internet application, you will have to create and manage accounts for external users in the ACL, which will become a chore. In addition, because you are using Windows authentication you will run into the same disadvantages discussed previously concerning the authentication methods of IIS: Basic authentication will work with any browser but the password is sent in plain text; Digest authentication requires a Microsoft browser.

URL Authorization

Another method of implementing authorization is to configure it in the web.config file. When we used Forms authentication earlier, we denied anonymous users access to all pages in the application by placing `<deny users ="?"/>` in the authorization section of the web.config file for the application. In that case, we had configured IIS to allow anonymous access and set the authentication mode to Forms so that ASP.NET would then authenticate the user by presenting a login form and validating the user credentials.

You can set the authorization section of web.config to secure specific pages in the application, and to specify access to particular users or roles. To mark a specific page as secure, you need to create a <location> section with a <system.web> and <authorization> section for each page. If you want to secure the Page1.aspx page in the Chapter12 application, use the following code:

```
<location path="Page1.aspx">
  <system.web>
      <authorization>
            <deny users="?"/>
      </authorization>
  </system.web>
</location>
```

The "?" specifies anonymous users and therefore means that anyone accessing this page will need to supply credentials. You can use the "*" to specify all users, or specifically allow or deny users by using the following syntax:

```
<authorization>
   <allow users="[comma separated list of users]"
          roles="[comma separated list of roles]"/>
   <deny  users="[comma separated list of users]"
          roles="[comma separated list of roles]"/>
<authorization/>
```

To control access to multiple files, you can either create separate <location> sections in the application's web.config file or create a separate directory containing all the secured files. You then add a web.config file to the directory containing the settings as in the following:

```
<configuration>
  <system.web>
       <authorization>
            <deny users="?"/>
       </authorization>
  </system.web>
</configuration>
```

All files in the directory will now require a specific login. The directory web.config cannot contain an <authentication> section, as all directories in the application must use the same authentication method, which is defined in the web.config file in the application root directory.

To control access for specific users, use the <allow> and <deny> tags. To specifically deny access to Ford and Marvin but allow access for all other users, use the following configuration:

```
<authorization>
      <deny users="Ford,Marvin" />
      <deny users="?" />
</authorization>
```

To explicitly allow access to Ford and Marvin but exclude all other users, even if they are authenticated, you would use the following configuration:

```
<authorization>
      <allow users="Ford,Marvin" />
```

```
                 <deny users="*" />
        </authorization>
```

Be careful how you logically position the <allow> and <deny> tags. ASP.NET reads the list from top to bottom, continues with any web.config file inherited from a parent directory, and ends with the machine.config file. It will stop as soon as it finds a logical rule that precludes it searching further. If you reversed the settings from the preceding example, it would stop on the <deny users="*" /> tag; therefore, Ford and Marvin would not have access.

We now will use URL authentication and Forms authorization to secure the pages in the Chapter12 application.

Using URL Authorization

In this exercise, we will restrict access to Page1 to two users and add a new administrator page that will be restricted to a single new user.

1. Create a new Web Form in the Chapter12 application that is a copy of Home.aspx; call it "Administer.asp." You can copy the file to another temporary directory and change the name before copying it back into the Chapter12 solution explorer. Visual Studio will prompt you to create a class file for the page, which you will need to do. Change the title to read "Secure Chapter12 Administration Page," and add links to Page1.aspx and Home.aspx. Copy the code from the Page_Load event in the Home.aspx.vb file to the Administer.aspx.vb Page_Load event.

2. Replace the code in the Login.aspx Submit_Click event to implement forms authentication from the users specified in the web.config file. This was entered in Exercise 12-3 and consists of the following code:

    ```
    If FormsAuthentication.Authenticate(txtUserName.Text, _
        txtPassword.Text) Then
        FormsAuthentication.RedirectFromLoginPage(txtUserName.Text, False)
    Else
        lblMessage.Text = "Invalid login,try again"
    End If
    ```

3. Add a new user named "Admin" with a password of "Secret" in the authentication section of the web.config file, in addition to the users you

added in Exercise 12-3. Uncomment the existing code if necessary. It should look like this:

```
<authentication mode="Forms">
    <forms name="AuthCookie" loginUrl="login.aspx" >
        <credentials passwordFormat="Clear">
            < user name="Admin" password="Secret" />
            <user name="Marvin" password="Depressed" />
            <user name="Ford" password="Prefect" />
        </credentials>
    </forms>
</authentication>
```

4. Add the following code to the web.config file to secure the three pages, and indicate authorization for specific users on Page1.aspx and Administer.aspx:

```
<configuration>
    <location path="Page1.aspx">
      <system.web>
            <authorization>
                <deny users="?,Ford" />
                <allow users="Admin,Marvin" />
            </authorization>
      </system.web>
    </location>
    <location path="Home.aspx">
      <system.web>
            <authorization>
                <deny users="?" />
            </authorization>
      </system.web>
    </location>
    <location path="Administer.aspx">
      <system.web>
            <authorization>
                <allow users="Admin" />
                <deny users="*" />
            </authorization>
      </system.web>
    </location>
```

This configuration will require a login to the home page by denying anonymous users. It restricts access to the Administer page to only the Admin user, and allows only the users Admin and Marvin to access Page1. Notice the placement of the <location> sections directly below the <configuration> section.

5. Add a link on the Home page to Administer.aspx.

6. Save all files and rebuild the solution.

7. Set the directory security in IIS to Anonymous access for the Chapter12 application.

8. Open Home.aspx in the browser.

9. Log in as Ford.

10. Click the link to Page1. Notice you are required to log in again because Ford is denied access to the page.

11. Log in as Marvin.

12. Click the Home link. Notice you are now logged in as Marvin on the Home page.

13. Click the Admin page link. You are required to log in again because access to the page is restricted to Admin.

14. Log in as Admin.

15. Close the browser.

16. Edit the web.config file for the administer location to reverse the <allow> and <deny> tags. They will be in the following order:

    ```
    <deny users="*" />
    <allow users="Admin" />
    ```

17. Save the file and open the application in the browser. Log in as Admin and then click the Admin page link. Notice you are requested to log in again. Log in as Admin again and it will not give you access to the Admin page. Because the <deny users="*" /> tag is first, ASP.NET is stopping at that line and not reading the <allow users="Admin" />.

18. Switch the lines back again in web.config, save, and try again. This time you will gain access to the page.

---

exam
ⓦatch

URL Authorization is relatively simple on the surface, but as it is a new feature for ASP.NET, it has a lot of potential for both direct and indirect questions in the exam. Be prepared to field questions that are more complex than they first appear.

Implement Impersonation

ASP.NET executes all code using a specific account created for this purpose when the .NET is installed; therefore, by default, the code is executed under an identity that is not the user's identity. This can cause problems with security because the ASP.NET account has more liberal permissions than a guest account, including read-write capabilities to the directories in which Web pages are compiled. Although this is necessary for ASP.NET, as it requires access to these resources to operate correctly, it also means code can be executed to access resources to which the client should not have access.

For example, if you have code in the application that lists or displays the contents of files, you can restrict access to the files by specifying permissions at the file level. If a file is restricted to specific users but the application code is running under the ASP.NET account identity, the client may gain access to the file through the application. To counter this problem, you must take measures such as URL authorization to secure access to the files.

Another way around this is to use *impersonation.* When impersonation is enabled, ASP.NET runs under the user's identity passed to it by IIS. If the user is unauthenticated, it will impersonate the anonymous user; otherwise, it will use the authenticated user's identity. Impersonation works with Windows authentication, as it needs an authenticated Windows account to impersonate.

To enable impersonation, you add an <identity> tag to the web.config file as in the following:

```
<configuration>
     <system.web>
          <identity impersonate="true" />
     </system.web>
</configuration>
```

In this example, ASP.NET will impersonate the identity of the user passed to it by IIS, which is either a Windows authenticated user or the anonymous Internet user account.

You also can specify a specific account to impersonate. In this instance, ASP.NET runs under the supplied identity, not the user's authenticated identity. This can be useful if you want to impersonate the identity of an account that has appropriate permissions set, without having to bother setting permissions to multiple accounts. The following configures impersonation specifically to the Marvin identity:

```
<configuration>
     <system.web>
          <identity impersonate="true" username="Marvin"
          password="Depressed" />
     </system.web>
</configuration>
```

Note that it is not possible to encrypt the password in the <identity> tag as we did with the <user> tag, so this could present a security risk.

Let's look at some scenarios concerning authorization and impersonation in ASP.NET.

SCENARIO & SOLUTION

Which method of authorization should I use in an intranet application that is using Integrated Windows authentication?	You could use either File or URL authorization, but if you are using Windows authentication, you already have configured the Windows user accounts. It probably will be a simpler process to use File authorization to set user and role permissions for the application resources.
I am using Forms-based authentication and URL authorization in an ASP.NET application. Should I set the file permissions in the application web.config file or create directory configuration files?	This depends on how common the permissions are across the files. If you have a number of files requiring the same access permissions, you should place them all in a separate directory and use a directory web.config file to set permissions. If each of the files requires different access permissions, it will be necessary to create separate <location> sections in the application web.config.
My ASP.NET application is configured to use Windows authentication. Many users have individual Windows accounts in varying roles using the application. The permissions on the application resources are identical for all users but require multiple application file permissions to be set for each user account. Is there a simple way to manage the accounts?	One method of handling this problem is to create a user account specifically for the application and impersonate that identity. This way all authenticated users will use the common impersonated identity and any future changes to the application permissions can be handled by modifying the permissions in a single account.

CERTIFICATION SUMMARY

In this chapter, we learned how to secure an ASP.NET application. We began by discussing security basics and defining authentication, authorization, and impersonation. We learned how to use IIS and Windows to restrict access to files and directories in the ASP.NET application and examined the IIS authentication methods. We then discussed Forms-based authentication, and built a login form and implemented it in our application. We also discussed the Microsoft Passport authentication service.

We used the web.config file to implement authorization in conjunction with ASP.NET Forms authentication and discussed the uses of impersonation in ASP.NET.

TWO-MINUTE DRILL

Select and Configure Authentication

- ❏ Securing a Web application first requires *authentication.* Authentication is the process of identifying the user who is requesting the page.

- ❏ ASP.NET supports three types of authentication, Windows, Forms-based, and Microsoft Passport.

- ❏ In Windows-based authentication, the ASP.NET application relies on the Windows operating system to authenticate the user in conjunction with IIS.

- ❏ In Forms-based authentication, requests for secure pages are redirected to a login page consisting of an HTML form. The user's credentials are input on the form and submitted to the application for authentication.

- ❏ IIS uses three types of Windows authentication: Basic, Digest, and Integrated Windows Security. Before you can use Windows authentication, IIS must be configured to one of these mechanisms.

- ❏ Basic authentication prompts the user for a Windows user name and password and sends him or her to the server as plain text.

- ❏ Digest authentication is similar to Basic but it encrypts the user name and password sent to the server. The browser sends an encoded hash called a Message Digest to the server containing the login information.

- ❏ Integrated Windows Security passes an encrypted token to IIS. This is available only if the user is already logged in to the network.

Configure Authorization

- ❏ Forms-based authentication uses ASP.NET to authenticate users, rather than Windows and IIS. Credential information can be stored in a database, XML file, or the web.config file.

- ❏ Forms-based authentication requires IIS to be configured to allow anonymous access.

- ❏ When using the web.config file as a credential store, the passwords can be hashed with MD5 or SHA1 hashing.

❏ Microsoft's .NET Passport authentication is a centralized authentication service that replaces the forms authentication functionality you normally would have to build into your application.

❏ There are two methods to configure authorization in ASP.NET: File authorization and URL authorization.

❏ File authorization requires the application to use Windows-based authentication. URL authorization requires user identities to be mapped to directories and files in the web.config file.

❏ Impersonation allows ASP.NET to assume the identity of a Windows user account while executing on the server.

❏ Setting an <identity> tag in the web.config file enables impersonation.

SELF TEST

The following self test questions will help you measure your understanding of the material presented in this chapter. Read all the choices carefully as there might be more than one correct answer. Choose all correct answers for each question.

Select and Configure Authentication

1. You are building an intranet application in which all users will be logged on to the network. Which Windows authentication should you use?

   A. Basic

   B. Digest

   C. Integrated

   D. None

2. Your Web application is configured for Windows authentication. In IIS you have selected Anonymous, Basic, Digest, and Integrated Windows authentication. Which authentication method will be tried first?

   A. Anonymous

   B. Basic

   C. Digest

   D. Integrated

3. Which of the following are valid properties of the User.Identity object? (Choose all that apply.)

   A. User.Identity.Name

   B. User.Identity.IsAuthenticated

   C. User.Identity.IsAuthorized

   D. User.Identity.AuthorizationType

4. Which of the following must be true to configure an ASP.NET application for Forms-based authentication? (Choose all that apply.)

   A. IIS must have its authentication mode set to Anonymous.

   B. Each user must have a Windows user account.

   C. IIS must be configured for Integrated authentication.

   D. The authentication mode in the web.config file must be set to Forms.

5. Which Forms.Authentication method will create an authorization ticket and attach it to the cookies collection? (Choose all that apply.)

   A. Authenticate

   B. GetAuthCookie

   C. GetRedirectUrl

   D. SetAuthCookie

6. Which of the following are valid passwordFormat values in the <credentials> tag? (Choose all that apply.)

   A. Clear

   B. None

   C. MD5

   D. SHA1

7. When hashed passwords are stored in the web.config <user> tags, how does ASP.NET validate the password?

   A. The password is hashed on the client and then posted to the server from the login form. ASP.NET compares the hashed password directly against the hashed value in the web.config file.

   B. The password is posted to the server from the login form as a string. ASP.NET then hashes the password received and compares it directly to the hashed value in the web.config file.

   C. The client browser sends a token to ASP.NET, which it hashes and compares against the hashed password value in the web.config file.

   D. The password is encrypted by the browser and posted to the Web server. ASP.NET then unencrypts the value and then hashes it to compare it against the hashed value in the web.config file.

8. In the following code, what purpose does the false argument serve?
   ```
   FormsAuthentication.RedirectFromLoginPage(txtUserName.Text_
   ,False)
   ```

   A. It specifies that the user is authenticated but should not redirect to the original requested page.

   B. It specifies that the authorization cookie should be saved over multiple browser sessions.

   C. It specifies that if the user is not authenticated, ASP.NET should not display an error page.

   D. It specifies that the authorization cookie should not be saved over multiple browser sessions.

9. Which method of the Forms.Authentication class is used to hash strings to be stored as passwords in the web.config file?

    A. HashPassword

    B. HashPasswordToConfigFile

    C. EncryptPassword

    D. HashPasswordForStoringInConfigFile

10. Which statement concerning Microsoft Passport is false?

    A. Passport provides a single sign-in for all sites using the Passport service.

    B. Passport provides a unique Passport ID, which is available to users of the service for their own purposes.

    C. Passport provides an authorization mechanism to authorize authenticated users.

    D. You can customize Passport's registration and sign-in pages to blend with the subscriber's site.

Configure Authorization

11. Which <authorization> tag in web.config will deny access to Joe and Jane while allowing access to all other authenticated users?

    A. <deny users="?" />

    B. <deny users="Joe, Jane" />

    C. <deny users="Joe, Jane" />
        <allow users="?" />

    D. <allow users="*" />
        <deny users="Joe, Jane" />

12. A public ASP.NET application contains some pages that are restricted to registered users, while the balance is available to the general public. All authenticated users will have access to the restricted pages. What would be the most efficient strategy to use to implement the required authentication?

    A. Use Windows authorization with IIS configured for Basic authentication. Create user accounts for each registered user and set the file permissions to disallow access by anonymous users for each of the restricted pages.

    B. Use Forms-based authentication. Set IIS to Anonymous authentication and create a separate <location> tag for each restricted page in the web.config file that denies anonymous access. Authenticate the user from the Logon form against the registration database.

C. Use Forms-based authentication. Set IIS to Anonymous authentication and place all restricted pages in a separate directory. Create a web.config file for the directory and set the <authorization> tag in the web.config file to deny anonymous access to the directory. Authenticate the user from the Logon form against the registration database.

D. Use Forms-based authentication. Set IIS to Anonymous authentication and place all restricted pages in a separate directory. Create a web.config file for the directory and set the <authorization> tag in the web.config file to deny anonymous access to the directory. Use <user> settings in the web.config to store user credentials and authenticate from the login form.

13. What is the result if the following web.config file is placed in an application directory?

```
<configuration>
 <system.web>
      <authorization>
            <deny users="?" />
            <deny users="Joe" />
      < authorization />
 <system.web />
 <configuration />
```

A. It restricts access to all users except Joe.

B. It allows access to all authenticated users except Joe.

C. It restricts anonymous access for a specific directory.

D. It allows access to all authenticated users except Joe for the application.

14. What does the following application level web.config file accomplish?

```
<configuration>
        <system.web>
            <identity impersonate="true"
                username ="Admin" password="password" />
            < authorization />
        <system.web />
    <configuration />
```

A. Provides authentication information for the Admin user.

B. Restricts access for all pages to the Admin user.

C. Configures ASP.NET to impersonate the Admin identity.

D. Configures ASP.NET to impersonate the identity passed by IIS unless it is the Admin identity.

15. Which of the following statements are true of impersonation? (Choose all that apply.)

A. ASP.NET automatically impersonates the identity passed to it by IIS.

B. Impersonation is the default in ASP.NET.

C. If impersonation is not enabled, ASP.NET will execute code under the Anonymous Internet User identity.

D. The impersonated identity must be a valid Windows user account.

16. What should you use to set permissions for user accounts in Windows?

A. The Internet Information Server Manager

B. Windows Explorer

C. Users And Passwords in Administrative Tools

D. Computer Management in Administrative Tools

17. What Windows user account is used for Anonymous access in IIS?

A. ASPNET_USER

B. IUSR_*Machinename*

C. IWAM_*Machinename*

D. ASPNET_*Machinname*

18. If impersonation is enabled in the ASP.NET application and the user is not authenticated, under what account is the ASP.NET code executing?

A. ASPNET

B. IUSR_*Machinename*

C. IWAM_*Machinename*

D. ASPNET_*Machinename*

19. Which statements are true concerning URL authorization? (Choose all that apply.)

A. Windows user accounts are required for each user of the application.

B. File or directory permissions must be set from the Windows Explorer interface.

C. Access permissions are specified in the web.config file.

D. Access permissions can be set at the individual file and directory level in the web.config file.

20. Which statements are true concerning directory level web.config files?

A. They can contain an <authorization> section.

B. They can contain an <authentication> section.

C. They inherit configuration settings from web.config files in parent directories.

D. They override configuration settings from web.config files in parent directories.

LAB QUESTION

You are building a public Web application that requires users to be registered with the site to access most of its functionality. Users will be able to register online and the registration process will include gathering information about the user including name, address, phone number, occupation, e-mail and other data. The home page and some of the other pages do not require the user to be registered, but most of the remaining pages do.

Outline the security you would implement on the site, including authentication and authorization methods and explain your reasons.

SELF TEST ANSWERS

Select and Configure Authentication

1. ☑   C is correct. If all the users of the application are logged on to the network, Integrated authentication will automatically pass the identity token to the server without prompting for credentials.
    ☒   A and B are not needed, as the user will already be logged on to the domain. D is wrong because some form of authentication is required.

2. ☑   A is correct. If all are selected Anonymous is tried first. If not successful, it attempts the other mechanisms.
    ☒   B, C, and D are incorrect.

3. ☑   A and B are valid properties.
    ☒   C and D are incorrect. The User.Identity object does not contain any authorization information or capability.

4. ☑   A and D are correct. The authentication mode must be set to Forms and IIS must be configured for Anonymous to enable it to pass through to ASP.NET for authentication.
    ☒   B is incorrect because Forms authentication does not require a Windows user account. C is wrong; it needs to be set to Anonymous.

5. ☑   C and D are correct. GetRedirectUrl creates an authorization ticket in addition to redirecting to the originally requested page, SetAuthCookie creates an authorization ticket.
    ☒   A is wrong, as it only authenticates the user without creating an authorization ticket. B is wrong as it gets the authorization cookie.

6. ☑   A, C, and D are all valid password formats.
    ☒   B does not exist.

7. ☑   B is correct.
    ☒   A , C, and D are wrong. The password on the client is not hashed or encrypted in any way.

8. ☑   D is correct. This argument specifies that the authorization cookie named in the first argument will not be durable.
    ☒   A, B, and C are wrong.

9. ☑   D is correct.
    ☒   A, B, and C do not exist.

10. ☑ C is a false statement. Passport does not authorize users.
    ☒ A, B, and D are true statements.

Configure Authorization

11. ☑ C is correct.
    ☒ A is wrong because it denies only anonymous users. B is wrong because it denies access to Joe and Jane but allows unauthorized users. D is wrong because it allows all users, including Joe and Jane.

12. ☑ C is the most efficient method. It uses Forms authentication, which does not require the management of ACLs. By placing all the restricted pages in a directory, one <authorization> tag in a directory web.config will disallow anonymous users without needing to produce separate <location> sections for each page. Storing user credentials in a database is more efficient than storing them in the web.config file, as it can be automated from the registration page. Also, the database will need to exist to store other information in addition to user names and passwords.
    ☒ A, B, and D are incorrect. See the preceding.

13. ☑ B is correct. It denies anonymous users and Joe, thereby giving access to authenticated users.
    ☒ A, C, and D are incorrect.

14. ☑ C is correct. This sets impersonation to on and specifies the Admin account to impersonate.
    ☒ A, B, and D are all incorrect.

15. ☑ D is a correct statement. An impersonated identity has to exist as a Windows user.
    ☒ A is incorrect. It will do so only if impersonation is enabled without a specific identity. B is wrong. C is incorrect because if impersonation is not enabled, ASP.NET will use the System Account identity.

16. ☑ B is correct. You use Windows Explorer to set permissions on files and directories in Windows.
    ☒ A, C, and D are incorrect.

17. ☑ B is correct. IUSR_*servername* is the anonymous account used by IIS.
    ☒ A, C, and D are incorrect.

18. ☑ B is correct. If impersonation is enabled but the user is not authenticated, then the client is an Anonymous Internet user which is the IUSR_machinename account.
    ☒ A, C, and D are incorrect.

19. ☑ C and D are correct.

☒ A and B are incorrect. URL authorization does not require Windows user accounts, and the access permissions are set in the web.config file.

20. ☑ A, C, and D are correct. Directory-level web.config files can contain <authentication> tags, and they inherit the settings from configuration files higher in the hierarchy and override the settings in those files if set in the lower-level file.

☒ B is incorrect. Authentication settings have to be configured at the application-level web.config file.

LAB ANSWER

The best approach for this application is to use Forms-based authentication. You should set the IIS security to Anonymous authentication to pass the authentication through to ASP.NET. All pages that are accessible to only registered users should be placed in a separate directory and a web.config file created for the directory that denies access to anonymous users.

You will need to create a registration page and login page for the site, along with a database to contain the user credentials. Because you want the users to register online, the registration page will create a record in the database for each new user, and include the user name, password, and any other information such as address, phone number, and so forth that is required.

The authentication mode in the web.config will be set to Forms and will specify the login form name as the loginUrl. When an unauthenticated user attempts to access a page restricted to registered users, the login form will be displayed to the user. If he or she is registered and subsequently authenticated against the credentials in the registration database, you can use the FormsAuthentication. RedirectFromLoginPage to redirect him or her to the originally requested page. If the authentication fails, you can ask the user to try again in case he or she entered the wrong password, or if the user is not registered, redirect him or her to the registration page.

The registration page will accept the user's information, including a user name and password, and if validated, insert it into the registration database. At this point, the user can either be automatically authenticated for immediate access to the site or, depending on the requirements of the application, you could e-mail him or her with the status of the registration after doing some other processing such as credit checks.

Part VII

Appendixes

A

About the CD-ROM

T he CD-ROM included with this book comes complete with MasterExam, MasterSim, the electronic version of the book, and Session #1 of LearnKey's online training. The software is easy to install on any Windows 98/NT/2000/XP computer, and must be installed to access the MasterExam and MasterSim features. You may, however, browse the electronic book directly from the CD-ROM without installation. To register for LearnKey's online training and a second bonus MasterExam, simply click the Online Training link on the Main Page and follow the directions to the free online registration.

System Requirements

The Software requires Windows 98 or later and Internet Explorer 5.0 or later and 20MB of hard disk space for full installation. The electronic book requires Adobe Acrobat Reader. To access the online training from LearnKey, you must have RealPlayer Basic 8 or the Real1 plugin, which will automatically be installed when you launch the online training.

LearnKey Online Training

The LearnKey Online Training link will allow you to access online training from Osborne.OnlineExpert.com. The first session of this course is provided at no charge. Additional sessions for this course and other courses may be purchased directly from www.LearnKey.com or by calling (800) 865-0165.

The first time you run the training, you will be required to register with the online product. Follow the instructions for a first-time user. Please make sure to use a valid e-mail address.

Prior to running the online training, you will need to add the Real1 plugin and the RealCBT plugin to your system. This will automatically be facilitated to your system when you run the training the first time.

Installing and Running MasterExam and MasterSim

If your computer's CD-ROM drive is configured to auto run, the CD-ROM will automatically start up upon inserting the disk. From the opening screen, you may install MasterExam or MasterSim by pressing the MasterExam or MasterSim buttons. This will begin the installation process and create a program group named "LearnKey." To run MasterExam or MasterSim, choose Start | Programs | LearnKey. If the auto run feature did not launch your CD-ROM, browse to the CD-ROM and click the RunInstall icon.

MasterExam

MasterExam provides you with a simulation of the actual exam. The number of questions, type of questions, and the time allowed are intended to be an accurate representation of the exam environment. You have the option to take an open-book exam, including hints, references, and answers; a closed book exam; or the timed MasterExam simulation.

When you launch the MasterExam simulation, a digital clock will appear in the top-center of your screen. The clock will continue to count down to zero unless you choose to end the exam before the time expires.

MasterSim

The MasterSim is a set of interactive labs that will provide you with a wide variety of tasks to allow the user to experience the software environment even if the software is not installed. Once you have installed the MasterSim, you may access it quickly through this CD launch page or you may access it through Start | Programs | LearnKey.

Electronic Book

The entire contents of the Study Guide are provided in PDF format. Adobe's Acrobat Reader has been included on the CD-ROM.

Help

A help file is provided through the help button on the main page in the lower left-hand corner. Individual help features are also available through MasterExam, MasterSim, and LearnKey's Online Training.

Removing Installation(s)

MasterExam and MasterSim are installed to your hard drive. For best results in the removal of programs, use the Start | Programs | LearnKey | Uninstall options to remove MasterExam or MasterSim.

If you want to remove Real Player, use the Add/Remove Programs icon from the Control Panel. You may also remove the LearnKey training program from this location.

Technical Support

For questions regarding the technical content of the electronic book or MasterExam, please visit www.osborne.com or e-mail customer.service@mcgraw-hill.com. For customers outside the United States, the e-mail address is international_cs@ mcgraw-hill.com.

LearnKey Technical Support

For technical problems with the software (installation, operation, removing installations) and for questions regarding LearnKey Online Training and MasterSim content, please visit www.learnkey.com or e-mail techsupport@learnkey.com.

MICROSOFT® CERTIFIED APPLICATION DEVELOPER
& MICROSOFT® CERTIFIED SOLUTION DEVELOPER

B

Exam 70-305:
Certification
Objective
Mapping

Objective	Found in Chapter
Create user services	1
Create ASP.NET pages	1
Add and set directives on ASP.NET pages	1
Separate user interface resources from business logic	1
Add Web server controls, HTML server controls, user controls, and HTML code to ASP.NET pages	1
Set properties on controls	1
Load controls dynamically	1
Apply templates	1, 5
Set styles on ASP.NET pages by using cascading style sheets	1, 5
Instantiate and invoke an ActiveX control	1
Implement navigation for the user interface	1
Manage the view state	1
Manage data during postback events	1
Use session state to manage data across pages	1
Validate user input	2
Validate nonLatin user input	3
Implement error handling in the user interface	2
Configure custom error pages	2
Implement Global.asax, application, page-level, and page event error handling	2
Implement online user assistance	2
Incorporate existing code into ASP.NET pages	2
Display and update data	1, 2, 6
Transform and filter data	2, 6
Bind data to the user interface	2, 6
Use controls to display data	2, 6
Instantiate and invoke Web services or components	3
Instantiate localizability for the user interface	3

Objective	Found in Chapter
Instantiate and invoke a COM or COM+ component	3
Instantiate and invoke a .NET component	3
Call native functions by using platform invoke	3
Implement globalization	3
Implement localizability for the user interface	3
Convert existing encodings	3
Implement right-to-left, and left-to-right mirroring	3
Prepare culture-specific formatting	3
Handle events	1
Create event handlers	1
Raise events	1
Implement accessibility features	3
Retrieve values from the properties of intrinsic objects	3
Set values on the properties of intrinsic objects	3
Use intrinsic objects to perform operations	3
Create and manage components and .NET assemblies	4
Create and modify a .NET assembly	4
Create and implement satellite assemblies	4
Create resource-only assemblies	4
Create Web custom controls and Web user controls	5
Consume and manipulate data	6
Access and manipulate data from a Microsoft SQL Server database by creating and using ad hoc queries and stored procedures	6
Access and manipulate data from a data store. Data stores include relational databases, XML documents, and flat files. Methods include XML techniques and ADO.NET	7
Handle data errors	7
Test and debug	8
Create a unit test plan	8

Objective	Found in Chapter
Implement tracing	8
Add trace listeners and trace switches to an application	8
Display trace output	8
Debug, rework, and resolve defects in code	8
Configure the debugging environment	8
Create and apply debugging code to components, pages, and applications	8
Provide multicultural test data to components, pages, and applications	8
Execute tests	8
Resolve errors and rework code	8
Deploy a Web application	9
Plan the deployment of a Web application	9
Plan a deployment that uses removable media	9
Plan a Web-based deployment	9
Plan the deployment of an application to a Web garden, a Web farm, or a cluster	9
Create a setup program that installs a Web application and allows for the application to be uninstalled	9
Deploy a Web application	9
Add assemblies to the global assembly cache	9
Maintain and support a Web application	10
Optimize the performance of a Web application	10
Diagnose and resolve errors and issues	10
Configure and secure a Web application	11
Configure a Web application	11
Modify the web.config file	11
Modify the machine.config file	11
Add and modify application settings	11
Configure security for a Web application	11

Objective	Found in Chapter
Select and configure authentication type. Authentication types include Windows Authentication, None, Forms-based, Microsoft Passport, Internet Information Services (IIS) authentication, and custom authentication	12
Configure authorization. Authorization methods include file-based methods and URL-based methods	12
Configure role-based authorization	12
Implement impersonation	12
Configure and implement caching. Caching types include output, fragment, and data	10
Use a cache object	10
Use cache directives	10
Configure and implement session state in various topologies such as a Web garden and a Web farm	11
Use session state within a process	11
Use session state with session state service	11
Install and configure server services	11
Install and configure a Web server	11
Install and configure Microsoft FrontPage Server extensions	11

INDEX

I

INTERNATIONAL CONTACT INFORMATION

AUSTRALIA
McGraw-Hill Book Company Australia Pty. Ltd.
TEL +61-2-9415-9899
FAX +61-2-9415-5687
http://www.mcgraw-hill.com.au
books-it_sydney@mcgraw-hill.com

CANADA
McGraw-Hill Ryerson Ltd.
TEL +905-430-5000
FAX +905-430-5020
http://www.mcgrawhill.ca

**GREECE, MIDDLE EAST,
NORTHERN AFRICA**
McGraw-Hill Hellas
TEL +30-1-656-0990-3-4
FAX +30-1-654-5525

MEXICO (Also serving Latin America)
McGraw-Hill Interamericana Editores S.A. de C.V.
TEL +525-117-1583
FAX +525-117-1589
http://www.mcgraw-hill.com.mx
fernando_castellanos@mcgraw-hill.com

SINGAPORE (Serving Asia)
McGraw-Hill Book Company
TEL +65-863-1580
FAX +65-862-3354
http://www.mcgraw-hill.com.sg
mghasia@mcgraw-hill.com

SOUTH AFRICA
McGraw-Hill South Africa
TEL +27-11-622-7512
FAX +27-11-622-9045
robyn_swanepoel@mcgraw-hill.com

**UNITED KINGDOM & EUROPE
(Excluding Southern Europe)**
McGraw-Hill Education Europe
TEL +44-1-628-502500
FAX +44-1-628-770224
http://www.mcgraw-hill.co.uk
computing_neurope@mcgraw-hill.com

ALL OTHER INQUIRIES Contact:
Osborne/McGraw-Hill
TEL +1-510-549-6600
FAX +1-510-883-7600
http://www.osborne.com
omg_international@mcgraw-hill.com